D0051280

Puerto Vallarta & Pacific Mexico

Greg Benchwick

John Hecht

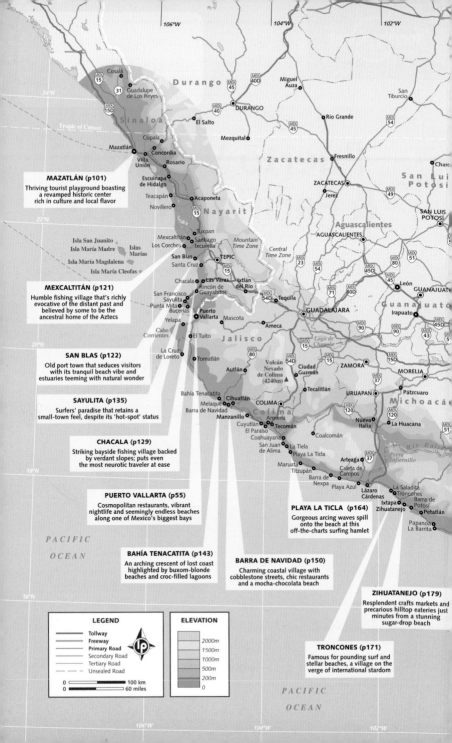

MAZATLÁN (p101)
Thriving tourist playground boasting a revamped historic center rich in culture and local flavor

MEXCALTITÁN (p121)
Humble fishing village that's richly evocative of the distant past and believed by some to be the ancestral home of the Aztecs

SAN BLAS (p122)
Old port town that seduces visitors with its tranquil beach vibe and estuaries teeming with natural wonder

SAYULITA (p135)
Surfers' paradise that retains a small-town feel, despite its 'hot-spot' status

CHACALA (p129)
Striking bayside fishing village backed by verdant slopes; puts even the most neurotic traveler at ease

PUERTO VALLARTA (p55)
Cosmopolitan restaurants, vibrant nightlife and seemingly endless beaches along one of Mexico's biggest bays

BAHÍA TENACATITA (p143)
An arching crescent of lost coast highlighted by buxom-blonde beaches and croc-filled lagoons

BARRA DE NAVIDAD (p150)
Charming coastal village with cobblestone streets, chic restaurants and a mocha-chocolata beach

PLAYA LA TICLA (p164)
Gorgeous arcing waves spill onto the beach at this off-the-charts surfing hamlet

ZIHUATANEJO (p179)
Resplendent crafts markets and precarious hilltop eateries just minutes from a stunning sugar-drop beach

TRONCONES (p171)
Famous for pounding surf and stellar beaches, a village on the verge of international stardom

LEGEND

Tollway
Freeway
Primary Road
Secondary Road
Tertiary Road
Unsealed Road

ELEVATION

2000m
1500m
1000m
500m
200m
0

0 ___ 100 km
0 ___ 60 miles

PACIFIC OCEAN

PACIFIC OCEAN

ACAPULCO (p191)
Death-defying cliff divers and party-all-night discos

PIE DE LA CUESTA (p208)
Welcome escape from the din of nearby Acapulco – perfect for bonfires and birding

LAGUNA DE MANIALTEPEC (p244)
Enchanted phosphorescent waters in a lagoon set afire by abundant bird and plant life

MAZUNTE (p253)
Leave the strictures of modern life for a few days in this off-beat coastal paradise

PUERTO ESCONDIDO (p235)
European-styled mini-resort with big barreling waves and a low-key Riviera chic

OAXACA (p214)
Ancient cosmopolis caught between the tide of tradition and the march of progress

MONTE ALBÁN (p232)
Dramatically situated ruins that once held an amazing treasure trove

On the Road

GREG BENCHWICK Coordinating Author

There ain't anything much better than sharing a cold *corona familiar* with your buddies. After about 2000 miles of coastal travel – and more beaches and sunburns than one man should see in a lifetime – I was more than ready to kick back with my good friends Gautham and Lara in their home in the Oaxaca hills. Every day with this amazing couple proved to be a grand adventure, from cooking *tlayudas* (massive corn tortillas topped with all the fixings) with the ladies down at the neighborhood church to drinking mezcal and *muchas coronas familiares* on hot, sunny afternoons.

JOHN HECHT About 20 minutes before boarding a water taxi to the beach of Yelapa, a crowd had gathered on the beach, pointing at something in the water. A crocodile? Turns out when the rivers swell during the rainy season crocs occasionally swim downstream to the ocean and follow the shoreline to a habitat at Marina Vallarta. Pandemonium ensued when we realized the crocodile was approaching a group of bodyboarders about 200m ahead. Fortunately, a man darted down the beach and warned them just in the nick of time.

For author biographies see p307.

Store# 00966 Term# 003 Trans# 160225
Operator: 245MA   10/29/2009 11:18

SALE

****
LONELY PLANET PUERTO VALLART $24.95G
9781741048063
****

Items: 1

Subtotal:		$24.95
GST:	5.0%	$1.25
Total:		**$26.20**
DEBIT CARD:		**$26.20**

****
You could have saved
$2.50 with irewards.

JOIN TODAY!
****

****

Store# 00966 Term# 003 Trans# 160225
GST Registration # R897152666

0096600301602251

may be exchanged or refunded onto a credit note for the value of the item at the time of purchase. Please note we cannot provide an exchange or refund of magazines or newspapers.

Si vous n'êtes pas entièrement satisfait d'un de vos achats, n'hésitez pas à le retourner pour un remboursement ou un échange dans un délai de 14 jours. Nous exigeons cependant que l'article soit dans le même état qu'au moment de l'achat et que vous présentiez un reçu provenant d'une de nos librairies. Les articles accompagnés d'un reçu-cadeau et retournés en condition de revente peuvent être échangés ou remboursés par une note de crédit pour la valeur de l'article lors de l'achat. Veuillez noter qu'aucun échange ou remboursement ne sera accepté pour les magazines ou les journaux.

If, for any reason, you purchase an item that is not totally satisfactory, please feel free to return it for refund or exchange within 14 days; we simply ask that the item be returned in store-bought condition and be accompanied by a proof of purchase from any of our stores. Items accompanied by a gift receipt and returned in store-bought condition may be exchanged or refunded onto a credit note for the value of the item at the time of purchase. Please note we cannot provide an exchange or refund of magazines or newspapers.

Si vous n'êtes pas entièrement satisfait d'un de vos achats, n'hésitez pas à le retourner pour un remboursement ou un échange dans un délai de 14 jours. Nous exigeons cependant que l'article soit dans le même état qu'au moment de l'achat et que vous présentiez un reçu provenant d'une de nos librairies. Les articles accompagnés d'un reçu-cadeau et retournés en condition de revente peuvent être échangés ou remboursés par une note de crédit pour la valeur de l'article lors de l'achat. Veuillez noter qu'aucun échange ou remboursement ne sera accepté pour les magazines ou les journaux.

If, for any reason, you purchase an item that is not totally satisfactory, please feel free to return it for refund or exchange within 14 days; we simply ask that the item be returned in store-bought condition and be accompanied by a proof of purchase from any of our stores. Items accompanied by a gift receipt and returned in store-bought condition may be exchanged or refunded onto a credit note for the value of the item at the time of purchase. Please note we cannot provide an exchange or refund of magazines or newspapers.

Si vous n'êtes pas entièrement satisfait d'un de vos achats, n'hésitez pas à le retourner pour un remboursement ou un échange dans un délai de 14 jours. Nous exigeons cependant que l'article soit dans le même état qu'au moment de l'achat et que vous présentiez un reçu provenant d'une

Puerto Vallarta & Pacific Mexico Highlights

This is a coast of plenty – a honey-tongued sliver of paradise where colossal holiday destinations such as Mazatlán, Puerto Vallarta, Manzanillo, Ixtapa and Acapulco were born. It's a coast of spirited colonial port cities, glitzy resorts that party till dawn, lost beaches, thunderous waves, tangerine sunsets and broad-smiled locals. From heading out on a whale-watching adventure on the Bahía de Banderas to slipping through the dawn on a birding expedition in one of the coast's many mangrove estuaries, visitors fill their days with more adventures than one person could enjoy in a lifetime. There's big surf, big personalities and big fun. And always, there's the thrill of watching those halcyon days roll by.

DAN GAIR

1 PUERTO VALLARTA

With dining and entertainment options galore, it's no wonder so many visitors gravitate toward Puerto Vallarta's historic center (p55). Waterfront restaurants and bars lie within stumbling distance of raucous discos, making it oh-so-easy for carousing about town. For some, exploring beyond downtown's bustling cobblestone streets is a mere afterthought.

John Hecht, Lonely Planet Author, USA

FINDING YOUR SUN-SCORCHED SLIVER OF PARADISE

This is a land of possibilities. And beyond the pomp and circumstance of the coast's major resort areas, there's a million-and-one lost beaches just waiting to be discovered.

Greg Benchwick, Lonely Planet Author, USA

3

2

ALLOWING THOSE GUILTY LITTLE INDULGENCES

We burned ourselves to a crisp sunning on the mirror-like pool, while hydrating ourselves with fruity, alcoholic beverages served in big, hollowed-out pineapples. Later, after the refrigerated aloe cream and a nap to recover from the sunstroke, we feasted on *ceviche* and nearly went blind gazing at the spectacular sunset that lit up the sky like atomic fireworks. Ixtapa (p174) is the perfect place to indulge oneself, even at the risk of injury.

Clare Kleinedler, Traveler, USA

4

WATER TAXI TO PARADISE

Climb aboard a water taxi (p87) and head southwest of Puerto Vallarta for some fun in the sun at the heavenly beach of your choice. Drop-off points include Quimixto (p98) and Yelapa (p98; pictured) or you can hop off at any of the quieter spots along the way. All of these beaches are only accessible by boat and some have small hotels should you conveniently miss the last departure.

John Hecht, Lonely Planet Author, USA

SPECTACULAR ANCIENT CITY

Monte Albán (p232) is an old Zapotec site and one of the very first cities in the region. The site is vast and spectacular, set in a forested valley, although it feels like you are up in the clouds! You can hire a local guide to show you around (they tend to be real locals, and so don't speak English!). It really adds to the experience.

Phillipa Blitz, Lonely Planet Staff, Australia

LEE FOSTER

6

ANTHONY PLUMMER

5

PERFECT PACIFIC COAST DAY

My perfect day involved taking a bumpy bus ride from Puerto Vallarta to Mismaloya (p95; pictured) early in the morning. We then hopped on a fishing boat with a 14-year-old driver (and his 10-year-old skipper) and rode out to Los Arcos (p65) to snorkel. Afterward, we ate *ceviche* and drank beer on the sand until the sun went down.

Jennye Garibaldi, Lonely Planet Staff, USA

PAUL KENNEDY

7

DROPPING IN OR TUNING OUT

Charging down a double-overhead barrel at world-class surf spots like Puerto Escondido's Mexican Pipeline (p239; pictured), Troncones (p171), or Playa Boca de Pascuales (p162) is enough to get your blood pumping – and stay pumping for a long while. But for those who prefer tranquil sunsets and 'Cheech-meet-Chong' chill, there are desolate and decadent throwback villages like Zipolite (p249) and Mazunte (p253) where clothing is optional and *libertad* (freedom) still reigns.

Greg Benchwick, Lonely Planet Author, USA

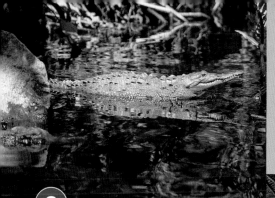

BUMMING IT

Fancy the life of an original beach bum, with a hammock and open *cabaña* for accommodation, campfire for a stove, a murky river for freshwater bathing and a surf board for entertainment? Try heading for Barra de Nexpa (p166), a bumpy ride from Lázaro Cárdenas (p167) on the Guerrero border. Surf's up!

Paul Day, Traveler, UK

9

8 INTO THE WILD

You don't have to be a nature buff to enjoy a San Blas boat tour (p122) that meanders through a precious mangrove estuary rife with exotic birds. The trip ends at a crocodile nursery, where the reptiles are reared in captivity for later release in the wild. Keep your limbs in the boat to avoid becoming croc bait.

John Hecht, Lonely Planet Author, USA

10 LOOKING BACK

Mexico refuses to let go of its past. And while many of the modern resorts on the coast do little to preserve this living patrimony, there's plenty of history here. You just need to look past the boom-boom of rampant development toward the hills that are home to the Mixtec, Zapotec and Nahuatl, and toward the gilded colonial cities of Oaxaca (p214; pictured), Colima (p157) and Taxco (p199), and the coastal ports of Zihuatanejo (p179) and Acapulco (p191).

Greg Benchwick, Lonely Planet Author, USA

Contents

Regional Map Contents

Mazatlán p103

Nayarit p120

Puerto Vallarta & Around p59

Jalisco, Colima & Michoacán Coasts p140

Ixtapa, Zihuatanejo & the Costa Grande p170

Acapulco & the Costa Chica p191

Oaxaca pp214-5

Destination Puerto Vallarta & Pacific Mexico

Mexico's Pacific coast is a fairy-tale land: a place where sky and mountain descend to sea and pitch-perfect honey-sand beaches in delicious harmony. It is beautiful and bountiful and blessed. And it's changing at a rapid-fire pace, each day struggling and adapting to a new cultural scene, a new drug lord, a newly developed beach town just waiting to be explored.

There are new environmental threats to be dealt with and new economic meltdowns to be weathered. And always, there is the sun and the sand and a resilient people with smiles as broad and open as the vast arching horizon that shelters the sun each day.

The major headline of the past 500 years is one of inequality and migration. People are moving en masse to resort towns like Mazatlán, Puerto Vallarta, Acapulco, Manzanillo, Ixtapa and Puerto Escondido in search of the almighty peso, in turn straining infrastructure and the environment. And while it hasn't always been good for the sea turtles, marine fauna or monarch butterflies, it has been relatively good for the pocketbook. People are making more: GDP per person rose from US$8500 in 2000 to US$12,400 in 2008.

The rise in international tourism has also created a renewed interest in protecting fragile ecosystems in places where a sea turtle is now worth three times more alive than dead, and cultural traditions like weaving, ceramics and cooking are now highly prized skills, ensuring the essence of these centuries-old skills passes on to the next generation. But with the worldwide economic crisis brewing, and the peso losing steam to the US dollar – it went down 21% in 2008, and was continuing to lose its grip in the first months of 2009 – the specters of unemployment, inflation and decreased visitation are looming large on the horizon.

There's also the plague of drugs. Nearly 90% of US-bound cocaine passes through Mexico, and coastal cities – especially Puerto Vallarta and Acapulco – have seen spikes in violence as a result, though this violence is rarely targeted at tourists. But this hasn't kept folks from coming here. Mexico is the seventh most popular tourist destination in the world, and many Pacific coast resort towns are undergoing facelifts, as the government invests in infrastructure and other capital improvements to keep these places on top.

Behind this glitzy facade, the ever-looming issue of inequality continues to simmer. But these complications aren't conspicuous when you walk the streets of Oaxaca or stretch out on the sand at a lost Michoacán beach. The region's overarching happiness and hope (and a rather morbid intimacy with death) seem to cut through all the economic hardships and politics, making room for the important things in life: a perfect sunset, a bucket of chilled beer and the makings of one great party.

FAST FACTS

Population: 21 million (Pacific coast states), 106.5 million (national)

Life expectancy: men 74 years, women 79 years

Population growth: 1.142%

Type of government: Federal Republic

Dominant religions: Roman Catholic (76.5%), Protestant (6.3%)

Literacy rate: 91% (US 99%)

GDP per person: US$12,400 (as compared to US$46,000 per person in the US)

Foreign tourists entering Mexico per year: 21 million (3.8 million in Puerto Vallarta)

Monthly remittances from US: US$2.4 billion (October 2008)

Price to prepare a *taco al pastor*: M$2.79 (November 2008)

Getting Started

Traveling in this part of Mexico requires little planning. Just grab your passport, get on a plane or bus or in your car, and go! You'll rarely have trouble finding suitable accommodation on any budget, and travel by road or plane within Mexico is easy. If you have limited time and specific goals, work out a detailed itinerary and reserve accommodations in advance. If this is your first trip to Mexico, be ready for more crowds, noise, bustle and poverty than you might be accustomed to. But don't worry – most Mexicans will be only too happy to help you feel at home in their country. While English is widely spoken here, especially in the larger resort areas, it makes sense to invest a little time before your trip in learning even just a few phrases of Spanish – every word you know will make your trip that little bit easier and more enjoyable.

WHEN TO GO

See climate charts (p270) for more information.

The Tropic of Cancer cuts across Mexico just north of Mazatlán, so this stretch of coast is officially tropical. The driest months, when it may not rain at all, are from November to April. These months are also the coolest, with temperatures averaging a comfortable 79° to 84°F (26° to 29°C).

The hottest months, May to October, are also the wettest, and the hottest and wettest of all are June, July and August, with temperatures in the high 80s F (low 30s C) along much of the coast. Rainfall increases as you move south from Mazatlán toward Acapulco, with Acapulco receiving twice as much rain as Mazatlán. The Oaxaca coast is drier but closer in average rainfall to Acapulco than Mazatlán. May to October is also extremely humid, and it's generally more humid the further south you move. Hurricanes do pass through here, but normally only one or two make land each year. Hurricane season runs from May 15 to November 30, and peaks between July and September.

DON'T LEAVE HOME WITHOUT...

- Your passport or required documentation (p282)
- Sandals or other beach-friendly shoes
- A swimsuit and clothes to cope with Mexico's climatic variations: air-conditioned and non-air-conditioned rooms (and buses)
- Any specific toiletries you require, including contact-lens solutions and contraceptives, as these can be difficult to obtain in Mexico (also consider carrying a copy of prescriptions for any medications you will take with you – this might save you from scrutiny at customs)
- A flashlight for some of those not-so-well-lit streets and stairways – and for power outages
- An inconspicuous container for money and valuables, such as a small, slim wallet or an under-the-clothes pouch or money belt (p271)
- Sun protection: a hat, sunglasses and sunscreen
- A small padlock
- A small Spanish dictionary and/or phrasebook
- A backpack for carrying it all – you can make it reasonably theft-proof with small padlocks; a light daypack, too, is useful

THE PRICE OF A PESO

When this book went to press, the peso had suffered a serious decline against the US dollar, dropping 21% in 2008 and more than 4% in the first two months of 2009. This could mean inflation in Mexico, recession (experts said the economy would shrink by 1.16% in 2009) or cheaper prices for visitors traveling with foreign currency. In an economy that largely uses US dollars for business transactions, and for hotel rates at midrange to top-end hotels, this could also mean that some of the prices in this book may become inaccurate. As always, things change. And it's advisable to call ahead or check online (especially for those higher-end hotels that base their rates on dollars) for the latest prices.

The peak holiday periods are July and August, mid-December to early January, and a week either side of Easter. At these times, resorts attract big tourist crowds, room prices go up, and rooms and public transport are heavily booked, so reservations are recommended. November to April is reliably dry, warm and blissful, and many North Americans and Europeans choose these months to travel the coast.

Happily for beach bums, the water along Mexico's Pacific coast is perfect for swimming all year long. Diving and snorkeling can be good at any time, but visibility is usually highest (except during plankton blooms) in the dry winter months. Fun surf can be reasonably expected year-round, but waves are biggest from May through to November. Deep-sea fishing, also practiced all year, has its own species-specific seasons (see p50). Bird-watchers often prefer winter visits, when birds migrate down to the coastal lagoons from North America. Whale-watching is best from January to March.

COSTS & MONEY

On Mexico's Pacific coast, a frugal budget traveler can pay about M$250 to M$400 a day by camping or staying in budget accommodations and eating two to three meals a day in the cheapest restaurants. Add in other costs (snacks, purified water, entry to archaeological sites, long-distance buses etc), and you'll be up to M$350 to M$500 a day. If you share rooms, costs per person drop considerably.

In the midrange you can live well for M$500 to M$1000 per person per day. In most places two people can easily find a clean, modern room with private bathroom and TV for M$400 to M$600.

At the top of the scale are hotels and resorts charging anywhere from M$1000 to M$3500 and restaurants where you pay M$140 to M$350 per person. You can save money by booking high-end hotels over the internet.

These figures do not take into account expenses such as internal airfares or car rentals – not to mention heavy tequila consumption, disco admissions and shopping, which you should certainly budget for.

While traveler's checks, US dollars and euros are accepted in some of the bigger hotels and by money changers, it makes sense to just use your ATM card (most towns with more than 1000 residents have an ATM machine). ATMs will give you the best exchange rate anyway. For information on exchange rates, see the inside front cover of this book.

HOW MUCH?

Coco frío (fresh coconut) M$10

Internet per hr M$10-20

Corona beer M$10-20

Street taco M$5-10

Local small-car rental per day M$350-600

TRAVELING RESPONSIBLY

Sustainable travel is all about respect. Respect the environment, respect the culture, respect the economy and respect the rules. There are some easy steps you can take to lower your impact, including offsetting your travel (p284), hiring local guides, diving responsibly (p49) and staying the night in small villages rather than just visiting them for the day. This encourages locals to preserve their culture and traditions, and mitigates the rampant urban migration that is affecting the cultural makeup of this diverse region.

There's nothing better than seeing wildlife in its natural environment, and it's best to avoid buying crafts made from endangered species, and visiting animal shows, like those 'dolphinariums' you'll see in most major resorts.

This book also has a handy 'GreenDex' (p319) to get you started.

TRAVEL LITERATURE

Few travel books stick solely to the subject of Pacific Mexico, but several books deal with the country as a whole and make great reading on any trip to Mexico.

Expatriate memoirist Tony Cohan rambles around Mexico to 'see how the puzzle of old and new fit together' in *Mexican Days: Journey into the Heart of Mexico* (2006). In the style of *Mexican Days* (2000), Cohan deftly travels the literary territories of history, contemporary life and old-fashioned journalism.

The Mexico Reader: History, Culture, Politics (2002) is a massive compilation of articles, essays, poetry and photographs providing an encompassing introduction to the history and culture of Mexico.

British writer Isabella Tree takes peyote with the Huichol and meets the matriarch of Juchitán in *Sliced Iguana: Travels in Unknown Mexico* (2001), a warm, perceptive account of Mexico and its indigenous cultures.

The People's Guide to Mexico by Carl Franz (13th edition, 2006) has for more than 30 years been an invaluable, amusing resource for anyone on an extended trip. It doesn't attempt hotel, transport or sightseeing specifics, but does provide a great all-round introduction to Mexico.

Carlos Castaneda's *Don Juan* series, which reached serious cult status in the 1970s, tells of a North American's experiences with a peyote guru in northwestern Mexico.

For information on Mexican literature, see p30.

INTERNET RESOURCES

Lanic (http://lanic.utexas.edu/la/mexico/) Best broad collection of Mexico links, from the University of Texas.

LonelyPlanet.com (www.lonelyplanet.com) Succinct summaries on travel in Mexico, traveler forums and more.

Mexican Adventure & Ecotourism Society (www.amtave.org) Lists some 'green' tourism operators.

Mexican Wave (www.mexicanwave.com) 'Europe's gateway to Mexico,' a treasure trove of travel, culture and food-related material.

Mexico Connect (www.mexconnect.com) Packed with news, message and chat boards, accommodation information, articles and an endless variety of other content and links.

Mexico Tourism Board (www.visitmexico.com) Worth a peek.

Mexiconservación (www.mexiconservacion.org) Has limited info on flora and fauna, and the ecological challenges facing the nation.

Mexperience (www.mexperience.com) Full of valuable information for travel to and within Mexico.

Planeta.com (www.planeta.com) Great articles and listings for anyone interested in Mexico's ecology.

Responsibletravel.com (www.responsibletravel.com) Keeps it green.

Tomzap's Pacific Coast of Mexico (www.tomzap.com) For fun, quirky and extensive information about the coasts of Jalisco, Colima and Oaxaca.

TOP PICKS

ADVENTURES AROUND EVERY CORNER

There are countless options for outdoor enthusiasts, including the following:

- Surfing the big barrels at Puerto Escondido (p239), Mexico's Pipeline
- Volunteering with sea-turtle ecologists in Playa San Francisco (p135)
- Bird-watching on tropical Laguna de Manialtepec (p244)
- Boating through tropical mangroves to La Tovara (p122)
- Mountain biking in the hills overlooking Bahía de Banderas (p67)

- Sharing the seas with whales or dolphins in Bahía de Banderas (p66)
- Scuba diving in the gorgeous waters off Manzanillo (p158)
- Exploring the superb hilltop ruins and tombs of Monte Albán (p232)
- Cloud-forest hiking in the gorgeous Manantlán Biosphere (p161)

PARTYING IT UP! FESTIVALS & EVENTS

You'll really catch the Mexican mood at these events.

- The commemoration of Father José María Mercado livens up San Blas (p122) on January 31 with a parade, a march by the Mexican navy, and fireworks
- Carnaval (Carnival; p109), the week leading up to Ash Wednesday, in late February/early March, is celebrated most vividly in Mazatlán
- Semana Santa (Holy Week), Palm Sunday to Easter Sunday, is particularly colorful in Puerto Vallarta (p69) and Acapulco (p200)
- The Fiesta de San Pedro Apóstol (p121), on June 29, celebrates the patron saint of fishing and brings a beautiful pageant to Mexcaltitán
- Guelaguetza, held in Oaxaca city (p224) on the first two Mondays after July 16, is a brilliant feast of Oaxacan folk dance

- The Sinaloa Arts Festival (p109) brings a series of cultural events to Mazatlán's beautiful Teatro Angela Peralta from late October through mid-November
- The Festival de los Artes, film festival and gourmet festival (p69) dominate the cultural calendar in Puerto Vallarta each year in November
- Día de Muertos (Day of the Dead; p221) is a big event in Oaxaca city, with music and dance at the main cemetery on November 2
- The festival for the Virgen de Guadalupe (p201) is celebrated by all of Mexico on December 11 to 12, but it's particularly vivid in Acapulco

GUILTIEST INDULGENCES

Everything in moderation? Bullshit! This is your vacation, and you earned it! Here are some great spots to feed your inner Bacchus:

- La Casa Que Canta (p185) costs upwards of M$4000 a night, and is worth every penny
- Eat the worm at Oaxaca's venerable drinking hole, La Casa del Mezcal (p228)
- Spend a week of Zen at Troncones' Present Moment Retreat (p173)
- Drink a margarita for breakfast!

- Pamper yourself at the luxurious Grand Velas resort (p76) if your pockets go deep, and we're talking real deep
- Los Osuna Distillery (p118) – devil's water never tasted so good
- Pie in the Sky (p91) – a sweet slice of nirvana

Itineraries
CLASSIC ROUTES

BUMMING AROUND THE
BAHÍA DE BANDERAS
One Week / Puerto Vallarta & Around

You can easily spend three to five days in **Puerto Vallarta** (p55). Stroll on **Isla Río Cuale** (p61) in the morning, along **Playa de los Muertos** (p61) in the afternoon, and along the **malecón** (boardwalk; p67) at dusk, noting the **public sculptures**.

Spend a day **biking** (p67), **horse riding** (p66) or **diving** (p64). Or shop for **Huichol crafts** (p84) and hit the **art galleries** (p84). After sunset, sample the taste-bud-popping **cuisine** (p76), before heading on to a **dance club** (p81).

After you've filled up on PV, head south to **Mismaloya** (p95) for its fine beach and the stellar snorkeling around **Los Arcos** (p65), a marine park and ecological preserve. Amble into Mismaloya village for **tequila tasting** and **demonstrations** (p96), or for lunch in a **jungle restaurant** (p97).

From nearby **Boca de Tomatlán** (p97) catch a water taxi to **Yelapa** (p98), where you can sleep in an elegant hillside hotel. Next morning rent a horse or hike to beaches or waterfalls.

Alternatively, head north to the understated pleasures of **Bucerías** (p87), or get back to basics in the fishing village of **La Cruz de Huanacaxtle** (p92). You might even make it to **Punta de Mita** (p93) for some **surfing action** (p93).

If you've only got a week, there's no reason to leave the sunny embrace of Puerto Vallarta's beautiful Bahía de Banderas; this trip is a mere 74km.

THE BEST OF THE PACIFIC COAST   Three Weeks / Mazatlán to Acapulco

Get your bearings in **Mazatlán** (p101), lingering only long enough to enjoy a romantic evening on Plazuela Machado. Heading south, develop a taste for idleness in the ancient fishing village of **Mexcaltitán** (p121). From **San Blas** (p122) head by boat into gorgeous mangrove wetlands or sharpen your surfing skills on Bahía de Matanchén. Then why not lose a few days on the beautiful cove at **Chacala** (p129) or witness a baby-turtle release in **Playa San Francisco** (p135)?

Empty your wallet of pesos during a spell in **Puerto Vallarta** (p55), enjoying world-class dining, shopping and an all-round good time. Pause for a week of Spanish-language instruction in beautiful **La Manzanilla** (p145) or head to **Barra de Navidad** (p150) to relax with a book or venture into the lagoon. Stop by **Manzanillo** (p154) for some world-class scuba diving or just to enjoy the ambience of the newly gussied-up downtown waterfront.

Continue south into the wilds of Michoacán, stopping first at gorgeous **Playa Maruata** (p165), where black sea turtles come ashore nightly in season. At laid-back **Barra de Nexpa** (p166) or up-and-coming **Troncones** (p171) assume the life of a surfer dude while enjoying world-class waves.

Continue your beach-happy existence in Ixtapa at tiny **Barra de Potosí** (p188), a quiet town with good scuba diving and opportunities for ecotourism. Allow for a visit to the crafts markets of neighboring **Zihuatanejo** (p179). You should be wonderfully well-rested by now, and ready for the bright lights and resort-town decadence of **Acapulco** (p191).

This madcap 1409km long-haul journey appeals to never-say-die road warriors with time to spare and living to do. You'll get your fill of fun, sun and sand while getting up close and personal with the coast's most beguiling towns.

ROADS LESS TRAVELED

WANDERING AROUND OAXACA   Two or Three Weeks / Oaxaca City & Back

Before seeking out roads less traveled, spend a few days rambling through the cobblestone center of **Oaxaca city** (p214), enjoying the cuisine, museums and galleries, and exemplary handicrafts shopping. Take a day trip to the Zapotec capital of **Monte Albán** (p232), one of Mexico's most impressive ancient sites.

Head south on the spectacular, winding Hwy 175, climbing high into mountainous pine forests then dropping precipitously to **Pochutla** (p245), gateway to the beach towns of **Puerto Ángel** (p246), **Mazunte** (p253) and **Zipolite** (p249). All have wonderful beaches and ample accommodation.

> Oaxaca's got it all: a beautiful and artistic capital, pre-Hispanic towns and a spectacular, varied landscape. This 750km expedition gets you deep into the thick of it and out again.

The coastal route of Hwy 200 leads west to **Puerto Escondido** (p235), where the big draws are astounding waves and, naturally, surf action. Nearby, **Lagunas Los Naranjos and Palmazola** (p245) boast abundant birdlife and a local crocodile population. Bird lovers will want to go further, to the **Laguna de Manialtepec** (p244), where roseate spoonbills are common, and to the **Parque Nacional Lagunas de Chacahua** (p234), where mangrove-fringed islands harbor numerous exotics.

Backtrack to **Bahías de Huatulco** (p255), and take your pick of beautiful beaches backed by forest. Surfers will love the right-hand point break at **Barra de la Cruz** (p263). Continue on to the sweaty, low-country **Isthmus of Tehuantepec** (p263), where Zapotec culture is strong and gringos are few. Visit the towns of **Tehuantepec** (p263) and **Juchitán** (p264) and the ancient Zapotec fortress of **Guiengola** (p265). From here, return to Oaxaca city on Hwy 190.

TAILORED TRIPS

TRAVELING WITH THE TOTS

Kids certainly need more than just sandcastle construction – and destruction – to fill their vacation. Begin in **Puerto Vallarta** (p55), where you can head over to an **aquatic park** (p68), check out the flying **Voladores de Papantla** (p69) on weekends, or head out for a **whale-watching trip** (p66). From PV you can take day trips, or quick overnighters, to **San Blas** (p122) for an estuary excursion, or to **Playa San Francisco** (p134), where you'll learn more about sea turtles, and might even witness the hatchlings taking their first steps to the ocean. From there, head south, stopping along the way in the off-beat and family-friendly towns of the **Bahía Tenacatita** (p143), before you hit up **Manzanillo** (p154), a good jumping-off point for day trips to colonial **Colima** (p157) – a great learning experience – and the **El Salto Falls and Manantlán Reserve** (p161). Or head over to an all-inclusive hotel that has a kids' club and enjoy a bit of peace and quiet as a spirited assemblage of counselors keeps your kids busy.

SURFING SAFARI

With powerful waves curling into the coast's sand-rimmed bays, it's no wonder the Pacific coast has attained legendary status among surfers. Novices, boogie boarders and people that just dig the surfing scene are welcome as well, though some of the waves get too big for beginners.

South of San Blas, **Bahía de Matanchén** (p124) receives amazingly long waves in September and October, while mellow but satisfying surfing can also be had at **Playa San Francisco** (p134) and **Sayulita** (p136), a good spot to get started. On the northern tip of Bahía de Banderas, **Playa El Anclote** (p93) offers a potent point break.

Continuing south, **Playa Boca de Pascuales** (p162) is a legendary spot with aggressive barrel swells up to 5m. Deep in Michoacán are more affable – but still challenging – waves at the gorgeous **Playa La Ticla** (p164). A well-established scene in **Barra de Nexpa** (p166) celebrates point-break waves curling in from the left, some allowing rides as long as 150m.

Further south in Ixtapa, the beaches near **Troncones** (p171) feature more than a dozen breaks, and some of the best beginner surf. But the most famous surfing locale on the Pacific coast is **Puerto Escondido** (p239), where you'll find waves to challenge beginners and experts alike. The biggest of these, at Zicatela, offers serious punishment to all but the most experienced surfers. You have been warned!

History

While the history of Pacific Mexico is less dramatic than that of the nation – there's a distinct lack of grand pre-Hispanic civilizations on much of the coast, and major development here didn't really even begin till the 20th century – there are, nevertheless, interesting stories to be told. And like the rest of Mexico, it is a tale of disparity and casual cruelty, of altruism and courage, of development, progress, decline and defeat, and a story of a nation that at times feels like it will live forever in its past.

FIRST AMERICANS

It's widely accepted that, barring a few Vikings in the north and some possible direct trans-Pacific contact with Southeast Asia, the pre-Hispanic inhabitants of the Americas arrived from Siberia. They came in several migrations between perhaps 60,000 BC and 8000 BC, during the last Ice Age, crossing land now submerged beneath the Bering Strait. The earliest human traces in Mexico date from about 20,000 BC. These first Mexicans hunted big animal herds in the grasslands of the highland valleys. When temperatures rose at the end of the Ice Age, the valleys became drier, ceasing to support such animal life and forcing the people to derive more food from plants.

Archaeologists have traced the slow beginnings of agriculture in the Valle Tehuacán in Puebla state, where, soon after 6500 BC, people were planting seeds of chili and a kind of squash. Between 5000 BC and 3500 BC they started to plant mutant forms of tiny wild maize and to grind the maize into meal. After 3500 BC, beans and a much better variety of maize enabled the Valle Tehuacán people to live semipermanently in villages. Pottery appeared around 2500 BC, and some of the oldest finds in Mexico are from sites near Acapulco.

Jürgen Buchenau's travel-sized Mexican Mosaic *(2008) is a handy historic companion for the historically inclined.*

PRECLASSIC PERIOD (1500 BC–AD 250)

This epoch is generally defined by the rise and fall of the Olmec. Perhaps the oldest Mesoamerican culture of dramatic scale, the Olmec lived near the Gulf coast in the humid lowlands of southern Veracruz and neighboring Tabasco from 1200 BC to around 600 BC. Their civilization is famed for the awesome 'Olmec heads,' stone sculptures up to 3m high with grim, pug-nosed faces combining the features of human babies and jaguars.

During the civilization's decline, the two great Olmec centers, San Lorenzo in Veracruz and La Venta in Tabasco, were violently destroyed by marauding invaders from Oaxaca, marking a significant shift of power. By 300 AD, Monte Albán (p232), the hilltop center of the Zapotecs of Oaxaca, had grown into a town of perhaps 10,000. Many carvings here have hieroglyphs or dates

For a few interesting articles on the pre-Hispanic cultures of the Pacific coast, including the Opeño of northwestern Michoacán and the Capacha of Colima, check out www.famsi.org.

TIMELINE

20,000–2500 BC	1200 BC–AD 250	300–700
Humans arrive in Mexico, first hunting and gathering across the highland valleys, then adopting agricultural practices beginning in the Valle Tehuacán of Puebla state. Pottery appears around 2500 BC, with some great finds near Acapulco.	The Olmec civilization in Tabasco and Veracruz is dominant from 1200 BC to 600 BC. On the coast, independent chiefdoms reign, pottery and 'sophisticated' architecture (shaft-tomb construction) begin to take root.	In the southern half of Mexico, the Zapotecs begin to rise, first destroying a few Olmec cities, then building the hilltop center Monte Albán. They also create writing and number systems.

in a dot-and-bar system, which quite possibly means that the elite of Monte Albán invented writing and the written calendar in Mexico.

The early history of the rest of western Mexico remains shrouded in mystery. Until the 1940s the area was all but ignored by archaeologists, probably because it lacked the grand architecture, writing systems and dramatic religious deities that attracted researchers to the rest of Mesoamerica. Archaeological sites went unexcavated and unprotected for decades, and most were looted over the years by non-archaeologists who sold their findings to collectors. When study of the region's ancient past began in earnest, archaeologists faced the challenges of drawing conclusions from sites that no longer existed.

From Sinaloa south to the state of Guerrero, people lived in small, independent villages and chiefdoms. They practiced a religion focused on a cult of the dead, but each village most likely had its own distinct culture and language. Archaeologists and art historians treat western Mexico as a unified region, El Occidente, which is defined by its tradition of shaft or chamber tombs. These underground burial chambers at the base of shafts 2m to 16m deep have been found throughout the area. The oldest of these have been dated as far back as 1900 BC, but the most significant were probably built between 1500 BC and 800 BC. Much of what is known of the cultures of western Mexico is based on the excavation of these tombs and analysis of the clay sculptures and vessels found within, some of which can be viewed at the Museo Regional de Nayarit (p127) in Tepic.

The highly interactive website www .ancientmexico.com offers a terrific breadth of material on the art, culture and history of ancient Mesoamerica.

CLASSIC PERIOD (AD 250–900)

The shaft-tomb tradition that so defined Nayarit, Jalisco and Colima began to die out in the early Classic period, as culture from Teotihuacán, central Mexico's first great civilization, began to influence the character of the area. Teotihuacán grew into a city of an estimated 125,000 people during its apogee between AD 250 and 600, and it controlled what was probably the biggest pre-Hispanic Mexican empire. Teotihuacán had writing and books, the dot-and-bar number system and the 260-day sacred year. The building of a magnificent planned city, located just 50km northeast of the center of modern Mexico City, began around 300 BC and took some 600 years to complete.

Objects from Teotihuacán have been found in Nayarit, Jalisco, Colima and Michoacán, which suggests that Teotihuacán was probably absorbing western Mexican cultures into its sphere. Teotihuacán was probably interested in the area for its precious stones and minerals.

The collapse of Teotihuacán in the 7th century was felt throughout western Mexico – as it was throughout Mesoamerica – but the scattered, independent chiefdoms that characterized the coastal states continued well into the Postclassic period. The fertile coastal ecology provided plentifully for the people who hunted and farmed the coastal plains and upland valleys, and fished the coastal waters.

Mexico: From the Olmecs to the Aztecs by Michael D Coe gives a concise, learned and well-illustrated picture of ancient Mexico's great cultures.

250–900	1100–1200	Around 1325
The Classic Period. Great civilizations are on the rise in central Mexico (Teotihuacán) and the Yucatán Peninsula (Maya) with advances in architecture, astronomy and the arts. Teotihuacán absorbs west-coast shaft-tomb culture.	The Tarasco (Purépecha) culture takes root in parts of Michoacán, Guanajuato and Guerrero, with its center at the site of Tzintzuntzan near Lake Pátzcuaro. Mixtec culture dominates the Zapotec in the south.	Tenochtitlán, site of present-day Mexico City, is founded by the Aztecs who dominate the Pacific and Gulf coasts and central Mexico. The Tarasco and Yopes (present-day Acapulco) resist Aztec expansion, but the Mixtec fall.

By the beginning of the Classic Period, in AD 250, the Maya of the Yucatán Peninsula and the Petén forest of Guatemala were already building stepped temple pyramids. This brilliant civilization would go on to create advanced calendars and a sophisticated writing system.

POSTCLASSIC PERIOD (900-1521)

The Aztecs, who eventually controlled much of central Mexico (with outposts on the Pacific coast as well), are the defining civilization of the Postclassic period. The location of their ancestral homeland is unknown, but some place it on the island of Mexcaltitán in northern Nayarit.

The Aztec capital, Tenochtitlán, was eventually founded on a lake-island in the Valle de México (site of present-day Mexico City) in the first half of the 14th century. At the height of its power, the total population of the empire's 38 provinces may have been about five million. The empire's main concern was extracting resources absent from the heartland – jade, turquoise, cotton, paper, tobacco, rubber, lowland fruits and vegetables, cacao and precious feathers.

But the bellicose Aztecs were unable to stretch their empire into the portions of western Mexico controlled by the Tarascos, known as the Purépecha before the Spanish arrival. The Tarascos were 'a culture as highly evolved as the Aztecs,' according to Eric Van Young, a professor of Mexican history at the University of California, San Diego. They ruled present-day Michoacán – and parts of Jalisco, Guanajuato and Guerrero – from the 12th century until the arrival of the Spanish in 1521.

Meanwhile in the south, after about 1200, the remaining Zapotec settlements of Oaxaca, such as Mitla and Yagul, were increasingly dominated by the Mixtecs, famed metalsmiths and potters from the uplands around the Oaxaca-Puebla border. Mixtec and Zapotec cultures became entangled before much of their territory fell to the Aztecs in the 15th and 16th centuries. Around the same time, the Aztecs were establishing small strategic presences along the Guerrero coast. The Yopes, who lived around the Bahía de Acapulco, were one of the few groups who successfully resisted the expansionist Aztecs.

ENTER THE SPANISH

Almost 3000 years of civilization was shattered in just two short years following the landing by Hernán Cortés near modern-day Veracruz on April 21, 1519.

The Spaniards were well received by the Gulf coast communities that resented Aztec dominion. Cortés thus gained his first indigenous allies. After much vacillation, the Aztec god-king Moctezuma II invited Cortés to meet him, and the Spaniards were lodged in the palace of Axayácatl, Moctezuma's father. After six months in Tenochtitlán, and apparently fearing an attack, the Spaniards struck first and killed about 200 Aztec nobles trapped in a square during a festival.

> For a wealth of information about the Aztecs, including a Nahuatl dictionary and lessons in the language, see www .mexica.net. The site also contains miscellaneous information about Mexico's indigenous peoples and history.

1512	1519–21	1523–31
The Spanish 'discover' the Bay of Acapulco; people had already been living in the area for some 2000 years. The native population will drop from 25 million to one million in less than 100 years.	Hernán Cortés lands near Veracruz and later captures Aztec god-king Moctezuma II, and conquers and destroys Tenochtitlán. The Spaniards found the new capital of Mexico City as the seat of the viceroyalty of Nueva España (New Spain).	The Spanish establish ports along the coast, and begin a road to Mexico City from Acapulco. In 1529 they establish the city of Oaxaca around the existing zócalo of the Aztec settlement of Huaxyácac.

Cortés and his force returned to the Aztec capital only to come under fierce attack. Trapped in Axayácatl's palace, Cortés persuaded Moctezuma to try to pacify his people. According to one version of events, the king went up to the roof to address the crowds but was wounded by missiles and died soon afterward; other versions have it that the Spaniards killed him.

Following this, full-scale war broke out. After only a few major battles, 900 Spaniards and some 100,000 native allies waged a successful attack on Tenochtitlán in May 1521. By August 13, 1521, Aztec resistance had ended.

'The initial conquest of the [Pacific] coast was unusually brutal,' says Van Young. 'A companion of Hernán Cortés, Nuño Guzmán, was at one point in charge of the exploration of the western coastal areas. A bit of a loose cannon, he enslaved a lot of people and left kind of a nasty taste with the indigenous people there.'

> Bernal Díaz del Castillo's *The Conquest of New Spain* narrates a fascinating firsthand account of a Spanish foot soldier who witnessed the fall of the Aztec empire at the hands of conquistador Hernán Cortés.

THE COLONIAL ERA

Great wealth and even greater disparity were created during the colonial era, from the 16th to 19th centuries. Spanish-born colonists were a minuscule part of the population but were considered nobility in Nueva España (New Spain, as Mexico was then called), however humble their status in their home country. By the 18th century, criollos (people born of Spanish parents in Nueva España) had acquired fortunes in mining, commerce, ranching and agriculture, and were seeking political power commensurate with their wealth. Below the criollos were the mestizos, of mixed Spanish and indigenous ancestry, and at the bottom of the pile were the remaining indigenous people and African slaves, who had been imported by the Spaniards as early as the 1520s. (Until 1700, the slave trade brought about 250,000 Africans to the colony.) 'The point is that the indigenous and mestizos had separate courts and rights,' says Jürgen Buchenau, a professor of Mexican history at the University of North Carolina. 'But racial mixture was common, and races were not segregated.'

But the colonial party would not last, and the catalyst for rebellion came in 1808 when Napoleon Bonaparte occupied most of Spain – direct Spanish control over Nueva España (Mexico) suddenly ceased and rivalry between Spanish-born colonists and criollos intensified. On September 16, 1810, Miguel Hidalgo y Costilla, a criollo parish priest, issued his call to rebellion, the Grito de Dolores. In 1821 Spain agreed to Mexican independence.

> In 1524 Spanish conquistador Francisco Cortés de Buenaventura, a nephew of Hernán Cortés, arrived on the Jalisco-Nayarit coast. He was met by an army of 20,000 native warriors armed with bows festooned with colorful cloth banners. The bay where this occurred was thereafter known as the Bay of Flags (Bahía de Banderas).

MEXICAN REPUBLIC

Some 22 years of instability followed independence, during which the presidency changed hands 36 times. In 1845, the US congress voted to annex Texas, leading to the Mexican-American War (1846–48), in which US troops captured Mexico City. Under the Treaty of Guadalupe Hidalgo of 1848, Mexico ceded western Texas, California, Utah, Colorado and most of New Mexico and

1500–1810	1810–1843	1845–1867
The Colonial Period. The Spaniards gain control of most of Mexico, instituting the *encomienda* system. Commerce passes through Pacific ports and a few forts are built to protect from pirate attacks.	The War of Independence begins in 1810, finally coming to a close some 11 years later. This is followed by 22 years of instability, during which the presidency changes hands 36 times.	Mexico battles the US in the Mexican-American War (1846–48), losing much northern territory. Benito Juárez, Mexico's first indigenous president, ends the French Intervention (1862–67).

Arizona to the US. In the late 1840s the Maya rose up against their overlords and almost succeeded in driving them off the Yucatán Peninsula. By 1862 Mexico was heavily in debt to Britain, France and Spain, who ordered a joint debt-collection force to Mexico. In the end, only France followed through with the invasion, after which Napoleon III decided to go one step further and colonize Mexico, sparking another war. In 1864 French occupation troops and their Mexican allies invited the Austrian archduke, Maximilian of Habsburg, to become emperor of Mexico. His reign was ended in 1876 by forces loyal to the country's former president, Benito Juárez, a Zapotec from Oaxaca.

William Henry Prescott's mammoth *History of the Conquest of Mexico* remains a classic, although it was published in 1843 by an author who never visited Mexico.

With the slogan 'order and progress,' dictator Porfirio Díaz (ruled 1876–1911) avoided war and piloted Mexico into the industrial age with strong-handed tactics. Very early in the 20th century a liberal opposition formed, but it was forced into exile in the USA. In 1906 the most important group of exiles issued a new liberal plan for Mexico from St Louis, Missouri. Their actions precipitated strikes throughout Mexico – some violently suppressed – that led, in late 1910, to the Mexican Revolution.

FROM REVOLUTION TO REFORM

During the 10-year Mexican Revolution, successive attempts to create stable governments were undermined by competing ideologies and egos, with leaders such as Emiliano Zapata and Pancho Villa failing to reach consensus.

After the revolution, former revolutionary leader Alvaro Obregón became president (1920–24) and steered the country toward national reconstruction. More than a thousand rural schools were built and some land was redistributed from big landowners to the peasants.

Obregón's successor, Plutarco Elías Calles, built more schools and distributed more land. He also closed monasteries, convents and church schools. 'Following a law that forbade outdoor religious processions and required the registration of priests with the state, the church went on strike on July 31, 1926, and ended religious services,' precipitating the bloody Cristero Rebellion by Catholics, which lasted until 1929. 'This rebellion centered on western and central Mexico, including the states of Jalisco, Michoacán and Guanajuato,' says Buchenau.

The documentary film *Mexico: The Frozen Revolution* provides an interesting snapshot of the Mexican revolution and its legacy.

At the end of Calles' term, in 1928, Obregón was elected president again but was assassinated by a Cristero. Calles reorganized his supporters to found the Partido Nacional Revolucionario (PNR; National Revolutionary Party), precursor of today's PRI (Partido Revolucionario Institucional). Lázaro Cárdenas, former governor of Michoacán, won the presidency in 1934 with the PNR's support and stepped up the land reform program.

Up to this time, Pacific Mexico had been sitting in relative isolation, but with a new road from Mexico City to Acapulco, both national and international tourists started visiting the port city, and to the north, great fishing and hunting lured vacationers to Mazatlán. It was the beginning of a golden era of tourism that would see unprecedented growth along the coast.

1876–1911	**1910–20**	**1930s**
The dictatorship of Porfirio Díaz attracts foreign capital to build railroads and port facilities. Land and wealth become concentrated, and very early in the 20th century a liberal opposition forms, but is forced into exile.	Nearly two million people die and the economy is shattered in the Mexican Revolution, a period of shifting allegiances between a spectrum of leaders. National reconstruction and small-scale land redistribution begin at the war's end.	With a new paved road from Mexico City, tourists start arriving in Acapulco. Mazatlán also gets its start. With the establishment of *ejidos* (peasant landholding cooperatives), nearly one-third of the population receives landholdings.

MODERN MEXICO

The economy expanded after WWII, and by 1952 the country's population had doubled from what it was two decades earlier. On the coast, several resort towns got their starts in the 1960s and '70s, with development in places like Ixtapa and Puerto Vallarta. Overpopulation and lack of sufficient sanitation resulted in environmental problems, and by the '80s some coastal beaches, most notably near Acapulco, were widely contaminated. Meanwhile, the oil boom of the 1970s finally went bust in the early '80s, leading to Mexico's worst recession in decades. Fueled by a climate of economic helplessness and corruption, dissent grew on both the left and the right, and even within the PRI.

The Harvard-educated Carlos Salinas de Gortari took the presidency in 1988 and set about transforming Mexico's state-dominated economy into one of private enterprise and free trade. The apex of his program was NAFTA, the North American Free Trade Agreement, which came into effect on January 1, 1994. The same day a group of 2000 or so indigenous peasant rebels calling themselves Ejército Zapatista de Liberación Nacional (EZLN; Zapatista National Liberation Army) shocked Mexico by taking over San Cristóbal de Las Casas and three other towns in the country's southernmost state, Chiapas. 'Its masked leader, Rafael Guillén, was a light-skinned outsider from the northern state of Tamaulipas,' says Buchenau. 'Better known as Subcomandante Marcos, the leader got international renown for his rejection of globalization.'

After the EZLN uprising, Salinas pushed through electoral reforms against ballot-stuffing and double voting, and the 1994 presidential election was regarded as the cleanest to date. But it was hardly spotless. In March 1994 Luis Donaldo Colosio, Salinas' chosen successor as PRI presidential candidate, was assassinated in Tijuana. Colosio's replacement as PRI candidate, 43-year-old Ernesto Zedillo, won the election with 50% of the vote.

> A contingent of 250,000 Mexican and Mexican-American men fought in WWII. One thousand were killed in action, 1500 received purple hearts and 17 received the congressional Medal of Honor.

Zedillo

Within days of President Zedillo taking office in late 1994, Mexico's currency suddenly collapsed, bringing on a rapid and deep economic recession. It led to, among other things, a big increase in crime, intensified discontent with the PRI, and large-scale Mexican emigration to the USA. Zedillo's policies pulled Mexico gradually out of recession and by the end of his term in 2000, Mexicans' purchasing power was again approaching what it had been in 1994.

Zedillo was an uncharismatic figure, but he was perceived as more honest than his predecessors. He set his sights on democratic reform and set up a new, independent electoral apparatus that in 1997 achieved Mexico's freest and fairest elections since 1911.

> It's not easy being a journalist in Mexico these days. Reporters Without Borders (www.rsf.org) says this is the most dangerous nation in the Americas for reporters.

The Fox Presidency

The independent electoral system set in place by Zedillo ensured that his party, the PRI, lost its 70-year grip on power in the 2000 presidential election.

1960s–70s	1980s	1994
Massive protests against the conservative Díaz Ordaz administration (1964–70) highlight the 1968 Mexico City Olympics. Puerto Vallarta and Ixtapa emerge as tourist destinations, and there's an oil boom in the Gulf.	Deflated petroleum prices lead to recession. The 1985 Mexico City earthquake kills 10,000. With overdevelopment and pollution, tourists stop coming to Acapulco, and the government begins development around Bahías de Huatulco.	NAFTA comes into effect, cheaper imports make it hard for small-scale Mexican farmers to compete, and the left-wing Zapatista uprising in Chiapas begins. The Mexican peso collapses, sending the country into recession once again.

INSIDE THE DRUG GAME

The CIA factbook calls Mexico a 'major drug-producing nation.' And while this assertion may seem a bit over the top, the country has continued to up its illicit drug production in recent years (mainly heroine and marijuana), and is now the number-one stopover point for cocaine passing from South America to the US, with more than 90% of US-bound cocaine passing through Mexico each year.

This rise has not gone unnoticed by either Mexican or US politicians – it's not easy being *numero uno*. Presidents Zedillo (1994–2000), Fox (2000–06) and Calderón (since 2006) each brought the armed forces into the fray, arguing that local police forces were simply too corrupt to battle the powerful gangs. At the beginning of his term in 2006, Calderón mobilized around 24,000 Mexican troops to combat narco-trafficking. This crackdown created an unprecedented surge in violence, with an estimated 5300 drug-related murders in 2008 (an estimated 1500 people died in drug-related violence in 2005). And the coastal resorts did not go unscathed, with numerous gangland-style murders and even beheadings, especially in the towns of Acapulco and Puerto Vallarta.

As of press time, the reports of violence were still coming in, leading us to ask, 'Is it safe to visit Mexico?' The answer is yes. Most of this violence happens in northern cities like Tijuana and Juárez, and the violence in the resort areas is rarely directed at tourists. Though, as always, you should proceed with 'big-city caution.'

The winner was Vicente Fox of the right-of-center Partido Acción Nacional (PAN; National Action Party).

By the end of Fox's term of office in 2006, Mexicans' overall standard of living was only a little higher than when he took power. Peasants and small farmers felt the pinch of NAFTA, as subsidized corn (maize) from the USA was sold more cheaply in Mexico than was Mexican corn. Mexicans did enjoy a certain social liberation, however, after the PRI's grip was prized loose.

Today & Tomorrow

The incisive film *Un Poquito de Tanta Verdad* (A Little Bit of So Much Truth) documents the 2006 Oaxaca protests. You can get a copy at www.corrugate.org.

The summer of 2006 was a long, hot one, marked by massive protests in Oaxaca (p216), a tightly fought presidential election, and continued drug-related violence (above). PAN candidate Felipe Calderón narrowly defeated the left-of-center Andrés Manuel López Obrador in the election. But Obrador and his supporters cried foul, and staged large protests, going as far as to set up an alternative government. But the protesters were unable to find concrete evidence of the fraud, and the protests eventually faded.

And while GDP per capita had grown from US$8500 in 2000 to US$12,400 in 2008, the economic indicators were not good at the close of 2008. There's a saying that 'when the US gets a cold, Mexico get pneumonia,' and all indicators were that Mexico was headed toward a long season of coughing and sneezing. The peso plummeted by nearly 34% in just three months relative to the US dollar, crime was on the rise, emigration to the US was down, and Mexico's all-important oil industry was in need of an overhaul.

2000	**2006**	**2008**
Vicente Fox is elected president, bringing to an end 70 years of power by the PRI. But drug violence and lack of economic reform continue, while on the coast tourist development spreads to smaller villages.	PAN's Felipe Calderón narrowly defeats left-of-center Andrés Manuel López Obrador in the presidential election, triggering huge protests alleging electoral fraud. A teachers' protest in Oaxaca leads to violence and a takeover of Oaxaca's center.	With the worldwide economy in shambles, the peso begins to stutter. A mobilized army brings the fight to drug traffickers and violence spikes, with more than 5300 murders in 2008. Emigration to the US declines.

The Culture Carolina A Miranda

REGIONAL IDENTITY

This region shares many of the national cultural traditions – family first, death second (and ever present in the national psyche), food, fun and fancy last of all – but riffs out with its own unique takes on art, culture and lifestyle. It's a relatively young culture – back in the 1950s this was merely a string of sparsely inhabited fishing villages punctuated by the occasional port – and is still finding its unique voice against the deep baritone of Mexico's national spirit and character.

With the coming of wide-scale tourist development, the feel and identity of the region is slowly transforming. Indigenous hamlets have ceded way to gleaming resorts and retirement communities. The hodgepodge of cultural groups that line this 2000km stretch of coast – from the Huichol in the north to the Zapotecs in the south (see p29) – mix tentatively with other segments of Mexico and the world. The northern end has a decidedly cowboy feel. Hard-working ranchers live a life centered on agriculture and livestock, entertaining themselves with rodeos and bullfights. The people of the south, more indigenous in spirit, stoically pass age-old artistic traditions from one generation to the next. In between lie pockets of settlers from all over: entrepreneurial Mexico City hoteliers who make a buck off booming Pacific coast tourism, former agricultural workers taken in by the growing regional service economy, and waterlogged expats in search of the next good wave.

This is just another layer on the many that already existed. The coast has never had one identity, but it has always been united in its aim, which is to show visitors a good time. This is where Mexico rolls out the welcome mat to the world, where resort towns and fishing villages receive travelers with A-list hospitality and down-home taco stands. It is where the national appreciation of revelry and music are brought to climax in tequila-soaked carnivals. It's the spot where Mexico – and the world – comes together to have a little fun.

Fast-rising Mexican Google search terms at the end of 2008 included Day of the Dead, Mexican Revolution, myths and legends, and Belinda (Peregrín). YouTube, games, hi5, hotmail, translator and music beat them out as the top search terms for the year.

LIFESTYLE

The tourism industry on the coast continues to attract new generations of workers from the countryside and this has put some of the country's richest people next to its poorest. The affluent inhabit lavish summer homes, gated and guarded for security, while working-class city dwellers live in multigenerational units in neighborhoods that offer few parks or open spaces. The poorest are left in hastily constructed shantytowns. In the countryside, there is a more spacious environment, with families occupying traditional houses made of wood or adobe and living on the land they cultivate.

Tourism has brought both benefit and harm. The industry keeps thousands employed along the Pacific coastline. It has brought with it a greater awareness of the need to protect vintage architecture, indigenous tradition and the natural environment. But it has also fed the drug trade and prostitution. Despite these challenges, family ties remain strong and there have been many social improvements. Gender roles, for example, continue to relax among the middle class and jobs are more accessible to women in general, though 'machismo,' masculine bravura, remains a formidable social force, especially in the countryside.

A Mexican woman today will have an average of 2.37 children – in the early '70s, that average was seven. As in many Latin American countries, the overall divorce rate remains low (0.68 per 1000 people) – especially when compared with the US, which has a rate of 3.6 per 1000 people. And while

---

THE MARIACHI TRADITION

Nothing defines Mexican music better than mariachis: the groups of nattily clad itinerant musicians who wander from town to town (or restaurant to restaurant) in search of the next paid gig. Though there is some disagreement about the origins of the word, historians do agree that 'mariachi' came into existence sometime in the middle of the 19th century in the state of Jalisco, just south of Guadalajara. Mariachi bands largely comprised wandering laborers for whom music was a secondary pursuit. By default, mariachis were, for decades, the keepers of Mexican musical folklore: harvesting and archiving local sounds and lyrics as they moved around in search of agricultural work. During the revolution, in the early 20th century, they carried news, along with arsenals of new songs about battle-hardened heroes and the loves they had lost.

In addition to a singer, a traditional mariachi group consists of a couple of violins, a Spanish guitar, a *vihuela* (a small, high-pitched, five-string guitar) and a *guitarrón* (an acoustic bass instrument that is held like a guitar). Modern mariachi bands typically include a trumpet or two as well.

---

the church remains a focal point, especially for the older generations, people are becoming increasingly secular, eschewing the traditions prescribed by the Catholic Church. For gays and lesbians, the big resort towns – particularly Puerto Vallarta (see p81 and p75) – offer a well-developed and welcoming scene, while in the country, things remain more closeted.

ECONOMY

Mexico's economy has always been one of 'haves' and 'have nots.' If you are part of the elite, you enjoy a lifestyle and stability akin to that found in the US or Europe; if you are poor, you live hand to mouth. The country's biggest export is oil, and tourism brings in around US$4 billion a year, and continues to grow. Money sent back from abroad accounts for another large chunk of Mexico's economy, about US$2.4 billion per month from the US alone. Drops in tourism, oil prices and other exports, combined with a 34% freefall of the peso to the dollar, have led economists to predict slow growth of about 2% between 2008 and 2010. GDP growth from 2004 to 2007 averaged 3.8%.

POPULATION

About 75% of Mexico's 110 million people currently lives in cities, and by 2030, UN projections say as much as 83% of the population will live in cities. This represents a major shift for a country with a largely rural history. In the early part of the 20th century, only 10% of the population lived in cities. Much of this growth is due to a high level of migration: one in five Mexicans now lives in a city other than the one they were born in, and one in 10 lives in the US. As a result, heavily agricultural (and poor) states such as Oaxaca, on the southern coast, have seen thousands of young people depart to big cities in search of greater economic opportunities, and some small rural towns have a distinct scarcity of young men. In Michoacán, for example, more than two million migrants have departed, leaving the state with a population of just over four million. The government is trying to discourage these mass migrations by supporting development and job-creation programs locally.

Guadalajara is the largest city in Mexico's west and the second largest in the country, with a population of about five million. New housing is continually built by migrants on rural lands surrounding city centers, while local governments invest their pesos in industrial development. This rapid growth has left a strained urban infrastructure often devoid of necessary public services. But relief seems to be ahead. Though the country's population doubled between 1970 and 2000, the birth rate has slowed from 2.3% in 2000 to 2% in 2008.

Overpopulation is one of Mexico's biggest problems. In 1944 the country had a population of 22 million. Today, there's around 110 million.

On the coast, fertility rates remain well below the national average on the northern end, but swell towards the southern coast.

Mexicans certainly value education. The overall literacy rate is 91% according to Unicef, with 98% of people aged 15 to 24 considered literate. Around 97% of Mexican children attends primary school, with about 94% making it past the fifth grade.

SPORTS

The national sport is *fútbol* (football, aka soccer), which is less a sport than a religion. Mexico has an 18-team national division, with two of these teams based in Guadalajara: the Atlas and Chivas. The latter team has the biggest following and has a new, 45,000-seat stadium slated to be finished sometime in 2009. There are many small local leagues, so you can catch a match year-round. Along the beach there's usually a pick-up game to be had – ask nice and they just might let you play.

Second on the list is bullfighting. A popular adage maintains that Mexicans are punctual for only two things: funerals and bullfights. *Corridas de toro* are a Sunday-afternoon tradition during the October to March bullfighting season. Guadalajara, Puerto Vallarta and Acapulco are good spots to catch a *corrida*. *Charreadas* (rodeos) are also popular, particularly on the northern coast, and take place from February to November.

American football and basketball are popular, as is baseball. There is a northwest Mexican baseball league, **Liga Mexicana del Pacífico** (www.ligadelpacifico .com.mx, in Spanish) and its website has information on games and locations. Increasing in visibility is the *juego de pelota* (ball game), a contemporary variant of an ancient sport; see below.

Get a comprehensive calendar (in English!) of cultural events around Mexico on the handy website www.the realmexico.com. For a slang dictionary, check out www.mexicoguru .com.

MULTICULTURALISM

The most significant ethnic division in Mexico is between assimilated mestizos (mixed-race Mexicans) and more insular full-blooded Indians who often speak native languages. Mestizos make up the majority of the population – between 60% and 90% depending on who's counting. Along the western coast, indigenous peoples are largely represented in one of the following ethnic groups: Zapotecs and Mixtecs in Oaxaca, Guerrero and Puebla; Purépecha in Michoacán; and Huichol in Jalisco and Nayarit. As is happening all over the continent, the younger generations are abandoning traditional lifestyles to go work in cities. As a result, some languages and traditions are disappearing. The tourism industry, however, has had the unexpected effect of preserving some aspects of these cultures. In Teotitlán del Valle in Oaxaca, for example, travel to the region supports a local textile industry that is keeping traditional weaving techniques alive. See p30 for more on the indigenous traditions of Oaxaca.

THE OLD BALL GAME

Perhaps the world's oldest team sport – a ballcourt dating to around 1400 BC was discovered along the Chiapas coast at Paso de la Amada – the Mesoamerican ball game, *juego de pelota*, was played consistently by various cultures in pre-Hispanic times. It took place on a flat court with sloping walls where players scrambled to keep a heavy rubber ball in the air by kicking it around with their hips, thighs, knees or elbows. It was volleyball meets soccer meets human sacrifice. (Some historians claim that players may have been killed after matches as an offering.) The game survives to this day – *sans* sacrifice, of course. In Michoacán it's called *juego de pelota purépecha*, in the Mazatlán area it's known as *ulama* and in Oaxaca it is *pelota mixteca*. As a visitor, it's easiest to see a game in Oaxaca city during Guelaguetza festivities every July when the city hosts a *pelota* competition.

RELIGION

Despite loosing its flock at a rapid pace – and a rocky history highlighted by indigenous subjugation – the Catholic Church (and to a larger degree, the Virgin of Guadalupe) remains the focal point of religious life. But the Church's grip is loosening. In 1970 more than 96% of the country identified as Roman Catholic; by 2000 that figure had slipped to 76.5%. Part of this is due to a growing evangelical movement comprised of, among other groups, Protestants, Seventh-Day Adventists and Mormons. And more and more Mexicans are leaving church life behind all together, with just over 3% of the population claiming no religious affiliation.

Catholicism nonetheless remains a deep-seated national force. Members of the clergy were present during the early days of the Spanish conquest. By the mid-19th century the Church owned more than a quarter of all land in Mexico and controlled most schools, hospitals and charitable institutions. This led the federal government to pass a series of measures intended to clamp down on ecclesiastic power. The constitution of 1917 forbade the Church from owning property, running schools or newspapers and banned clergy from voting. After a series of anticlerical purges in the late 1930s, anti-Church sentiment eased, and in 1950 the constitutional provisions ceased to be enforced. In the early '90s, President Carlos Salinas de Gortari removed them from the constitution entirely.

> The origins of the Day of the Dead celebrations go back 3000 years to Mesoamerican birth and death rituals; the dead are now honored annually on November 1 and 2.

Indigenous Religion

The early missionaries won over indigenous people by grafting Catholic beliefs onto pre-Hispanic ones. Today, indigenous Christianity remains a fusion of traditional Indian and Christian belief. The Huichol of Jalisco, for example, have two Christs, neither of which is as important as Nakawé, the fertility goddess. A crucial source of wisdom comes from the use of the hallucinogenic drug peyote. In Oaxaca a number of carnival celebrations are as much indigenous in content as Catholic: the Guelaguetza festival has its roots in Zapotec maize-god rituals.

Customs such as witchcraft and magic still flourish. When illness strikes, indigenous communities will often seek guidance from the local *brujo* (witch doctor) or *curandero* (curer).

ARTS
Literature

A dive into Mexican literature can easily begin with Nobel Prize–winning poet and cultural critic Octavio Paz (1914–98). His most prominent work,

---

UNRAVELING THE INDIGENOUS TRADITIONS OF OAXACA

With their deep-rooted, pre-Hispanic–influenced traditions in festivals, handicrafts, cuisine and clothing, Oaxaca's 15 indigenous peoples are the driving force behind the state's fine *artesanías* and unique festivities.

The people you will probably have most contact with are the Zapotecs, approximately 500,000 strong, who live mainly in and around the Valles Centrales and on the Isthmus of Tehuantepec. About 500,000 Mixtecs are spread around the mountainous borders of Oaxaca, Guerrero and Puebla states, with more than two-thirds of them in Oaxaca. The state's other large indigenous groups include 160,000 or so Mazatecs in the far north, 100,000 Mixes in the mountains northeast of the Valles Centrales, and 100,000 Chinantecs around Valle Nacional in the north. In Oaxaca city you may well see Triquis, from western Oaxaca; the women wear bright red *huipiles* (sleeveless tunics). The Triquis are only about 15,000 strong and have a long history of violent conflict with mestizos and Mixtecs over land rights.

El laberinto de la soledad (The Labyrinth of Solitude; 1950), is a book-length essay examining the roots of Mexican identity and culture.

The country has been home to no small number of accomplished novelists. Foremost among them is Juan Rulfo (1918–86), who was born near Guadalajara and whose plots often unfold in the coastal state of Jalisco. His most legendary work is *Pedro Páramo,* which takes place in the turbulent period preceding the Mexican Revolution (p23). This complex yet slim novel is often cited as the precursor to magic realism.

Also significant is novelist and political commentator Carlos Fuentes (b 1928). His novel *La muerte de Artemio Cruz* (The Death of Artemio Cruz; 1962) is a metaphor for the birth of post-revolutionary Mexico. Other prominent works include *Terra nostra, Cambio de piel* (A Change of Skin) and *Gringo Viejo* (The Old Gringo), the latter an intriguing tale about an American who joins the army of Mexican revolutionary leader Pancho Villa (c 1877–1923). Other admired works that fictionalize the Mexican Revolution are *Los de abajo* (The Underdogs) by Mariano Azuela (1873–1952) and *Como agua para chocolate* (Like Water for Chocolate) by Laura Esquivel (b 1950).

Mexico has also generated some of the continent's most lauded female writers, beginning with 17th-century Hieronymite nun and poet Sor Juana Inés de la Cruz. English-speakers interested in her work can pick up *A Sor Juana Anthology* by Alan S Trueblood. More contemporary feminist authors include Rosario Castellanos (1925–74), whose best-known novel *Oficio de tinieblas* (The Book of Lamentations) is the tale of an Indian rebellion; and Elena Poniatowska (b 1932), whose work *Tinisima* re-imagines the life of photographer Tina Modotti (p33). Also worth a read is short-story writer Elena Garro (1920–98), author of the novellas *Primer amor* and *Busca mi esquela,* available in the English volume *First Love & Look for My Obituary.*

A new generation of writers is focused on some of the immediate issues facing Mexican society: drug trafficking, corruption and the omnipresent neighbor to the north. Élmer Mendoza (b 1949), Raúl Manriquez (b 1962), Rafa Saavedra (b 1967) and Juan José Rodríguez (b 1970) have all produced works in this vein. Unfortunately, they are yet to be translated.

NON-MEXICAN AUTHORS

Mexico has long been a muse for the voluminous travel lit produced by foreigners. Popular contemporary accounts include Tony Cohan's *On Mexican Time* and Mary Morris's *Nothing to Declare.* Of special interest to coastal travelers is *Western Mexico: A Traveller's Treasury* by Tony Burton, which contains detailed information about the region's history, art and archaeology. Truly worthwhile is *In Search of Captain Zero,* the engaging surf memoir by Allan Weisbacker, much of which unfolds on the Pacific coast.

Vintage accounts from the early 20th century include *Mornings in Mexico* by novelist DH Lawrence and John Steinbeck's *A Log from the Sea of Cortez.* The latter title received a tribute from contemporary American writer Andromeda Romano-Lax in 2002. She retraces the famous author's voyage in *Searching for Steinbeck's Sea of Cortez.* Also of interest are *Survivor in Mexico* by early British feminist Rebecca West and the novel *Under the Volcano* by Malcolm Lowry. A truly classic travelogue on the country is Graham Greene's *The Lawless Roads,* which covers the bitter period following the clerical purges of the '30s and served as the basis for his seminal novel *The Power and the Glory.*

Chilean-born novelist and poet Roberto Bolaño (1953–2003) often lived in Mexico, and several of his novels are set here. Two of his best-known works are *The Savage Detectives* and *2666.*

The Huichol of Jalisco and Nayarit speak a language that bears a very close resemblance to Nahuatl, the language of the ancient Aztecs.

Luis Humberto Crothswaite (b 1962) is one of the few contemporary novelists available in translation. His humorous novella *La luna siempre será un amor difícil* (The Moon Will Forever Be a Distant Love) can be found on book websites such as Amazon.com.

For the seminal view on Frida Kahlo's life and work, read Hayden Herrera's artfully written *Frida: A Biography of Frida Kahlo.*

Cinema & TV

Mexico is enjoying a cinematic renaissance reminiscent of its 'Golden Era of Cinema' in the 1940s and '50s. Back in the day, when stars like María Félix and Mario 'Cantinflas' Moreno graced the silver screen, the industry was churning out up to a hundred feature films a year. Yet as time moved on, government funding dried up and production plummeted.

In recent years, however, newly created tax breaks and filming incentives have jump-started the industry, allowing Mexican cinema to gain wider appeal at home and abroad. Leading the way in the revival are crossover directors Alfonso Cuarón, Guillermo del Toro and Alejandro González Iñárritu.

Cuarón's coming-of-age road movie *Y tu mamá también* (And Your Mother Too, 2001), set against the backdrop of the Pacific coast, reflects on class differences in Mexico as it takes you on a comical journey with two horny teens played by Mexican heartthrobs Gael García Bernal and Diego Luna. Del Toro's Oscar-winning dark fairy tale *Pan's Labyrinth* was such a resounding success that he was chosen to direct two installments of *The Hobbit*. And González Iñárritu's gritty drama *Amores perros* (Love's a Bitch, 2000) garnered a slew of awards on the festival circuit and an Oscar nomination for best foreign film.

Close friends and collaborators, the so-called 'Three Amigos' have inspired a new generation of talented filmmakers, including Carlos Reygadas (*Luz silenciosa*; Silent Light, 2007), Fernando Eimbcke (*Temporada de pato*; Duck Season, 2006) and Francisco Vargas (*El Violín*; The Violin, 2005).

And, of course, a number of films have been made about Mexico's Pacific coast. John Huston's 1964 *The Night of the Iguana* is probably the most famous of these, but *Fun in Acapulco* (1963), starring Elvis Presley, has to come in a close second.

On the TV front, two broadcasters dominate the airwaves: Televisa and TV Azteca. Given the industry's lack of competition, it's often difficult to distinguish between rival networks' programming. Standard fare consists of a steady dose of reality shows, celebrity gossip programs, soccer matches and melodramatic *telenovelas* (soap operas).

Despite a new tendency among Mexican networks to produce US-style series, soaps continue to top the ratings charts in Mexico. Airing in such far-flung places as China, Russia and Nigeria, they also have become one of the nation's leading exports.

Be that as it may, Televisa and TV Azteca rank among the world's leading producers of Spanish-language content.

Fine & Traditional Arts

Mexico offers an artistic feast that dates back more than two millennia. Viewers can gorge themselves on dramatic pre-Hispanic sculpture, colonial-era paintings and even cutting-edge contemporary installations.

Pre-Hispanic works are well represented throughout the country, though the best pieces are generally kept in Mexico City museums. On the Pacific coast it was the ancient Zapotec (AD 300–700) and Mixtec (1200–1600) cultures that predominated artistically. Fine examples of their work are on display in Oaxaca city at the Museo Rufino Tamayo (p219) and the Museo Regional de Oaxaca (p218). Intricate funerary ceramic sculpture, created between 200 BC and AD 800 by the shaft-tomb cultures (p21) of Nayarit, Jalisco and Colima, can be found in Guadalajara at the Museo de Arqueología.

During the colonial period and after independence, Mexican art consisted largely of European-style portraiture and religious painting. The Oaxacan-

---

'Gringo en México,' a Spanish-language travel program airing on Unicable, has become a huge international hit. Nerdy host Robert Alexander, who admits that he cringes when he hears his thick gringo accent, is always good for laughs as he explores Mexican culture.

TV critics complain that Mexican soaps often reinforce stereotypes across racial and socio-economic lines. Lead roles often go to light-skinned actors who play well-heeled characters, whereas thespians with dark indigenous features typically land parts as domestic servants or criminals.

born Miguel Cabrera (1695–1768) was particularly notable. He created a famous portrait of poet Sor Juana Inés de la Cruz (p31), which now resides at the Museo Nacional de Historia in Mexico City.

Out of the ashes of the revolution came the muralists. The celebrated Diego Rivera (1885–1957), David Alfaro Siqueiros (1896–1974) and José Clemente Orozco (1883–1949) were the movement's figureheads. Orozco was born in the state of Jalisco and lived for a while in Guadalajara, where his house is now open to visitors.

Other leading modern painters include Frida Kahlo (1907–54), the surrealist self-portraitist married to Diego Rivera, and Rufino Tamayo (1899–1991), who was born in Oaxaca and is known for his abstract spin on Mixtec and Zapotec art. Visitors can view the objects of Tamayo's inspiration in Oaxaca city, where a pristine collection of his pre-Hispanic figurines lies in the museum (p219) that bears his name.

In a class by herself is photographer Tina Modotti (1896–1942). Though born in Italy, she settled in Mexico in the early 1920s and became an accomplished photographer. A political activist and contemporary of the muralists (she appears in several of Rivera's works), Modotti reached international acclaim for her stark portraits.

A trip along the coast will reveal plenty of contemporary indigenous fine and folk art. In Nayarit and Jalisco, you'll find colorful beaded sculptures and yarn paintings by the Huichol. But it's Oaxaca city that is richest in artistic treasures: dexterously woven textiles, polished black ceramics, elaborate *alebrijes* (wooden figurines), metal sculpture and contemporary fine art. The city's streets are lined with galleries catering to every taste.

> Oaxaca is home to a thriving contemporary art scene. And local artists like Francisco Toledo, Abelardo López, Arnulfo Mendoza and Ariel Mendoza – who got their start with art workshops organized by Tamayo in the 1970s – are beginning to gain national acclaim for their eclectic works.

Architecture

The architecture of the coastline is, to some degree, unremarkable. The bigger cities – Mazatlán, Puerto Vallarta and Acapulco – didn't see real development until the late '60s and construction consisted largely of bland, modernist resorts. Any trip slightly inland, however, will turn up plenty of architectural treasures. The pre-Hispanic city of Monte Albán (p232) in Oaxaca offers present-day visitors a unique glimpse of ancient Zapotec architecture. The countryside in this region is also dotted with 16th- and 17th-century Spanish churches built in the Gothic and baroque styles. Many of these have indigenous decorative elements: wall frescoes and colorful floor tiles. The Basílica de la Soledad (p219) in Oaxaca city is a great example of an immaculate baroque building. In Guadalajara, you can knock out a few architectural styles with a single visit to the cathedral. The design techniques here consist of everything from the Churrigueresque and the baroque to the neoclassical. It's odd but educational.

Many of the older cities, such as Mazatlán, Guadalajara, Puerto Vallarta and Oaxaca city, still retain examples of Spanish colonial architecture in their older corners.

> Get an up-to-date list of the plentiful art galleries and community museums in Oaxaca city at www .oaxacaoaxaca.com /galleries.htm. All listings are in English.

Music

As with the country's art and literature, there is a vast terrain to be explored. Let's start with rock. Mexico is one of the most important hubs for Latin American rock, known universally as *rock en español*. Beginning in the '80s, bands such as El Tri, Los Caifanes and Maná (the latter hailing from Guadalajara) helped make this musical form an inherently Mexican product. One of the most consistently innovative rock bands is Café Tacuba.

More recent acts include the rock-rappers Molotov from Mexico City. The group has gained international acclaim with raunchy lyrics and subversive political statements. Other acts include the jazzier Plastilina Mosh,

> Loads of information on Mexican museums, pre-Hispanic art and historical monuments can be found online in English and Spanish at www .mexicodesconocido .com.mx.

whose 1998 album, *Aquamosh*, was a smash hit, and Tijuana crooner Julieta Venegas, whose tender vocals provide plenty of easy listening. For fans of electronica, the DJs of the Nortec Collective from Tijuana will keep you grooving with a clever synthesis of dance and traditional *norteño* (below) beats. Their album *Tijuana Sessions Vol 1* is a must-have in this genre.

<aside>Born in Tlaxiaco, Oaxaca, Lila Downs fuses traditional Mexican rhythms and sounds with contemporary lyrics to create her uniquely Pan-American sound. Check out her best-of album, released in 2008, or www.liladowns.com.</aside>

MEXICAN REGIONAL MUSIC

Mexican music has its roots in *son* (sound), folk music that dates back to the early part of the 20th century and grew from a fusion of Spanish, African and indigenous sounds. These musical styles have splintered into distinct regional types.

In the dusty north, along the border, it is *norteño* that flourishes, a boot-stomping brand of polka-infused country music accompanied by boisterous accordions and *bajo sextos,* the Mexican 12-string guitar. Its roots lie in the traditional ballads – *corridos* – of the revolution. Long considered fuddy-duddy music for old-timers, the style received a boost in the 1980s when bands began singing *narcocorridos,* ballads about the drug trade. Their popularity is attributed to Chalino Sánchez, a raspy-voiced singer from Sinaloa who took on the drug establishment, crooning about dope deals gone bad and corrupt police officials. In 1992, at the age of 32, Sánchez was found with two bullets in his head on the side of a Sinaloa road. His death (still unresolved by the police) made him a legend and ensured that *narcocorridos* would become a permanent part of the musical pantheon. Some of the biggest, long-running *norteño* bands today include Los Tigres del Norte, Los Rieleros del Norte and Los Tucanes de Tijuana.

<aside>In San Blas listen to Maná's *Sueños Líquidos* album. The melancholy song 'El muelle de San Blas' makes frequent reference to the town's dock.</aside>

Banda also hails from the traditional *corrido,* but substitutes the string section with lots of brass. The sound is all oompah. One of the genre's most renowned groups is Banda El Recodo, whose members come from the port of Mazatlán. The band has been around, in one guise or another, since 1938. The music, to be honest, is an acquired taste, but El Recodo has nonetheless toured internationally. Other genres, such as *grupera,* combine *norteño* with Colombian *cumbia,* a tropical style of folk music from that country's Caribbean coast. Grupo Límite from Monterrey is one of the best-known bands in this arena.

Ranchera is a classical style of Mexican country music cultivated in the hills of Guadalajara. The most legendary of the country's *ranchera* singers is Vicente Fernández, who is known as 'El Rey' (the King) and has taken to the stage in silver-studded regalia for more than three decades. His baritone-voiced son Alejandro is equally talented (in addition to being quite easy on the eyes). Anyone interested in reveling in the sweet agony of an achingly sung *ranchera* should listen to Alejandro's album *Que Seas Muy Feliz* (May You Be Very Happy; 1995). Pick up some tequila, drown your sorrows and let him sing your pain.

<aside>If you're in the mood for vintage *rancheras,* pick up *20 Éxitos* by Lola Beltrán (1931–96). She was known as 'Lola La Grande' for singing her ballads with so much drama and emotion.</aside>

Dance

Mexico is home to hundreds of regional dances, most of which reveal a significant amount of pre-Hispanic influence. One of the most spectacular of these is the Danza de las Plumas (Feather Dance), which tells the story of the Spanish conquest from a Zapotec Indian point of view. A good time to see it is during Guelaguetza (p224) in Oaxaca. In Michoacán, the Danza de los Viejitos (Dance of the Little Old Men) originated as a mockery of the Spanish, whom the local Tarasco Indians thought aged very fast. The dance is generally performed around Christmas time.

Food & Drink James Peyton

In Mexico, food is life. And the cuisine of the Pacific coast (and Mexico as a whole) is far more varied and interesting than you probably imagine, with an intoxicating mix of spices, ingredients, textures and flavors colliding to create one of the world's culinary archetypes. And no matter where you choose to dine – be it a roadside stall choked with smoke and sweating locals or a perfectly climate-controlled cliff-top eatery – exploring the culinary roadmap of this coast will certainly be a highlight of your trip.

When the Spanish arrived in Mexico, they found a cuisine based on corn, beans, squash, chili and, along the coasts, seafood. To this they contributed beef, pork, lamb, chicken, wheat, dairy products and spices like cumin and cinnamon. While these foods combined in ways that created common threads, each area developed its own regional interpretations. To this day, the states along Mexico's Pacific coast – Sinaloa, Nayarit, Colima, Jalisco, Guerrero and Oaxaca – maintain their distinctive culinary traditions. In each of them, talented chefs continue to innovate, developing new flavors, textures, colors, smells and tastes, making this one of the world's most diverse and delicious cuisines. But prepare yourself for some surprises: what you find here will probably bear only a passing resemblance to the items served in most Mexican restaurants outside Mexico.

The Taste of Mexico, a cookbook by famed Mexican chef Patricia Quintana, contains more than 225 regional recipes, including fish and seafood dishes prepared along Mexico's coast.

STAPLES & SPECIALTIES
Seafood
For those who do not live near the coast, this is your chance to sample some truly fresh fish *(pescado)* and shellfish *(mariscos)*. You will find fish cooked either whole *(entero)* or filleted *(filete or fileteado)*. One of the most common ways of preparing both fish and shrimp is *al mojo de ajo* (with garlic sauce). Another favorite way of using seafood is as a filling for tacos. A popular version of seafood tacos in the state of Guerrero is called *pescadillos,* and is made with fish, tomato and olives, flavored with bay leaf and cinnamon. Dried seafood, often shark, is made into a hash called *machaca* that is popular at breakfast. All along the coast you will find seafood served *al diablo*. While there are infinite variations, most versions consist of seafood served with a sauce of tomato and various chilies.

In terms of preparation, fish can be sautéed *(salteado)*, pan-broiled *(a la plancha)*, grilled *(al carbón or a la parrilla)*, breaded *(empanizado)*, steamed *(al vapor)*, smoked *(ahumado)*, or deep fried *(frito)*. You will also find seafood or poultry dishes prepared *en escabeche* (simmered in a broth with mild fruity vinegar, onions, squash, other vegetables and exotic spices, and served at room temperature).

Mexico's Pacific coast has some of the most delicious seafood soups anywhere. They are usually made with a tomato-infused broth and can include everything from fish and squash to a medley of four or five kinds of seafood and several vegetables. Hominy may be added, creating a dish called *pozole,* and sometimes the fish and other seafood is ground and rolled into 'meatballs,' called *albóndigas.*

According to Mexican food authority Amando Farga, ceviche was first called cebiche by Captain Vasco Núñez de Balboa, who was given some by fishermen following his discovery of the Pacific Ocean in 1513. Farga speculates that the name comes from the Spanish verb cebar, one of whose meanings is 'to penetrate or saturate.'

Seafood cocktails, most often of shrimp, but also made with crab, octopus, squid, oysters and scallops, are a special treat. They are often referred to as *campechanas,* named for the port city, Campeche, where they originated. A close cousin to the cocktails is *ceviche,* where raw fish is marinated in lime juice; the acid in the lime 'cooks' the fish, which is then combined with spices, chilies, onions, tomatoes, cilantro (coriander) and sometimes pineapple

---

PESCADO ZARANDEADO – A COASTAL SPECIALTY

A specialty of Sinaloa, Nayarit and Jalisco, *pescado zarandeado* is the signature dish of the Pacific coast. Originally prepared on a wooden grill over coals, it consists of an entire specially filleted fish. The fillets are very thin and marinated with a unique combination of spices and herbs, often including garlic, mild chilies and *achiote* (the powdered seeds of the annato tree). The results are a taste-bud-popping symphony that will leave your head spinning.

---

or orange juice. For these dishes, some caution is advised. While the lime juice makes the fish opaque and firms it up, no heat is applied, so the juice does not cook the fish to the extent that all bacteria is destroyed. Therefore it should be especially fresh – sushi quality.

Meat, Poultry & More

The Food and Life of Oaxaca (Zarela Martinez, 1997) has recipes and stories from the Oaxaca heartland. The regional tamale recipes will leave you salivating.

Those who prefer meat will find a mouthwatering selection. There are many restaurants specializing in *comida norteña* (northern-style cooking) that feature char-broiled meats in various combinations – think fajitas (which are often referred to as *arracheras*). Steak *tampiqueña* (Tampico-style), which includes a thin tenderloin steak served with an enchilada, quesadillas and similar *antojitos* (appetizers), as well as rice and beans, is available in myriad combinations. For poultry fans, Sinaloa has a special dish called *pollo sinaloense*, where chicken is marinated in a perfectly balanced combination of chilies, juices and spices, and broiled over coals.

Coastal areas in Jalisco and Guerrero (especially on Thursdays) serve the *pozoles* for which those states are famous. Usually made with pork, on the coast these hominy soups are often made with seafood. They are traditionally accompanied by small bowls of lime wedges, chilies, cilantro and oregano so that diners can spice up their offerings. In Guerrero you may find a breakfast dish, called *baila con tu mujer* (dance with your woman), of eggs scrambled with tomato, onion, green chilies and bits of corn tortillas. In the market of Zihuatanejo they serve special breakfast *tortas* (sandwiches) made with roast pork, pineapple, raisins, almonds, plantains, onion and potatoes.

Oaxaca is known as the 'Land of Seven Moles,' and many of these rich, complex stews of chilies, fruits, nuts and exotic spices are found on the coast. Particular favorites include *mole negro* (black mole), *coloradito* (red) and *verde* (green), named for the color of the final dish. Oaxaca also produces special tamales that are wrapped in banana leaves and filled with either *mole negro* or seafood.

In addition to many other items, such as corn and turkey, two of the world's most beloved edibles, chocolate and vanilla, originally came from Mexico.

Dessert

For dessert, coastal cooks take full advantage of local tropical fruits, such as *guayaba* (guava), mango, papaya and coconut. They are served fresh, and in puddings, custards, various confections and ice cream. You may also find *tacuarines*, which are doughnut-like pastries. Acapulco cooks make special use of coconut, ginger and pineapple. They appear in both desserts and special confections called *cocadas* and *alfajores*. Jalisco is famous for a flanlike custard dessert called *jericalla*.

DRINKS
Alcoholic

You will find tequila, Mexico's national drink, everywhere, and bartenders prepare margaritas of every hue and flavor. If you wish to go native, try your tequila either neat with a bite of lime and a lick of salt, or with *sangrita* (a chaser of orange juice, grenadine, chili and sometimes tomato juice).

Oaxaca is famous for mezcal (p227), a drink similar to tequila. Rum drinkers will find interesting light and dark varieties that are often served in a cocktail called Cuba libre (with Coca Cola and lime juice). Visitors will also find good selections of both imported and Mexican wines (whites, reds and rosés) and beers.

Nonalcoholic

Mexico has a long tradition of nonalcoholic drinks. The most popular are *tamarindo,* made with tamarind pods; *Jamaica,* made with dried hibiscus leaves; *horchata,* a combination of melon and its seeds and/or rice; and limeade. Be careful, however, in regard to sanitation when sampling these drinks. Look around the restaurant or street stall: if things appear clean, you are far better off. You can also ask if the drink was prepared with purified water: '*¿Está preparada con agua purificada?*'

You will also discover a variety of delicious and healthy smoothies and milkshakes called *licuados,* made with milk, fruits, yogurt and honey. Orange juice, nearly always freshly squeezed, is available everywhere, as are juices of other fruits and vegetables. Many of these items are found in street *puestos* (stalls) and in larger, barlike establishments.

Some of the best coffee in the world is grown in Mexico, and Mexicans have a unique way of making it, called *café de olla.* This 'coffee from the pot' is brewed in a special clay vessel with cinnamon and a raw sugar called *piloncillo. Café con leche* (coffee with milk) is also very popular. For ordinary coffee, with cream on the side, simply ask for *café con crema.* Waiters will often pour both coffee and cream at the table according to your instructions. In Oaxaca, you will find a pre-Hispanic drink called *champurrado* (hot chocolate with ground, dried corn) that is rich and delicious. Bottled water *(agua purificada)* and sparkling water *(agua mineral)* are available everywhere. See p295 for more on drinking the water in Mexico.

> Mexicans add salt, lime, ice and occasionally Clamato or Bloody Mary mix to beer, producing a *chelada* or *michelada.* At most places on the coast, a *chelada* includes only lime, while a *michelada* has Bloody Mary mix. It's always worth asking first.

CELEBRATIONS

Feast days in Mexico are taken seriously, but resort areas are more casual in their observations. For the most part, they do not allow their traditions to interfere with the enjoyment of their visitors. However, be aware that at Christmas, New Year, Holy Week, and during the Day of

---

WE DARE YOU

Intrepid gastronomes will love to challenge their taste buds with some of the region's creepy-crawly specialties. One of the most popular foods is *chapulines* (chop-ooo-lean-ace), which is grasshoppers (purged of digestive matter and dried, you will be happy to hear). They come in large and small sizes, the latter often smoked, and can be sautéed in butter, flamed in brandy or served as filling for tacos. The small, smoked variety are quite tasty and less likely to leave bits of carapace and feelers protruding from your teeth!

Jumiles are beetles, actually a type of stink bug, esteemed in central Mexico when in season in late fall and early winter. They are usually either ground with chilies, tomatoes and tomatillos to make a sauce or used as a taco filling, either toasted or live. Many of these traditional ingredients are now being used by daring chefs to create fantastically presented and prepared dishes that combine traditional regional recipes and ingredients with modern cooking techniques for a culinary fusion known as *la nueva cocina mexicana.*

Other favorites include stewed iguana, which tastes like a cross between chicken and pork, as do armadillos, whose copious, small bones are their most irritating quality. And for dessert, you can always eat the worm at the bottom of your mezcal bottle.

the Dead, celebrated on the first two days of November, nontouristy establishments may be closed. During these times special items are often available, including *pan de muertos* (bread of the dead), made with yeast, flour, eggs, butter, nutmeg and aniseed and topped off with sprinkled or glazed sugar. Vegetarian specialties (below) are popular during Holy Week, and at Christmas and New Year *bacalao* (dried cod) is often served in a mild chili sauce.

Not sure where to dine in Puerto Vallarta? Check out www.vallartarestaurants.com for in-depth reviews and a few informative articles.

WHERE TO EAT & DRINK

Where you eat will depend on your mood and budget, and the number of choices will delight you. *Palapas* are casual, thatched-roof structures found on nearly every popular beach. In urban areas you will find *puestos,* street stalls that usually specialize in a single item – tacos, burritos etc. Slightly more formal are *loncherias, comedores* and *taquerías,* small sit-down eateries often found in private homes in villages and at markets in towns and cities. A step up are cafés that serve Mexican specialties, including corn- and tortilla-based *antojitos* such as tacos and enchiladas and simple but delicious meat and seafood dishes, usually accompanied by homemade soups, steaming rice pilafs, beans and fresh vegetables.

Resorts and large cities offer upscale dining with local atmosphere and a mix of international foods and elegant Mexican creations. Many of their chefs practice Mexico's upscale version of fusion cooking called *la nueva cocina mexicana* (new Mexican cooking), which combines regional Mexican dishes, ingredients and cooking techniques in new, aesthetically pleasing and delicious ways.

For a good list of Mexican food and handicraft markets, check out www.mexicanmercados.com.

To make certain your experience is positive, exercise some caution when picking your spot. Avoid establishments that do not appear to be busy or that seem messy or unclean. Be particularly wary of seafood served from street stalls. Remember that if it smells fishy it isn't fresh! Also, avoid mayonnaise-based sauces (which are made with egg yolks) whenever possible.

VEGETARIANS & VEGANS

Tourist establishments have learned to cater to vegetarian patrons. Visitors will find vegetarian offerings on most menus, certainly by special order.

Most waiters in the larger eateries are knowledgeable about what they serve and anxious to please. However, they are often unaware of the specific requirements of vegetarians, and especially vegans, and may find the concept difficult to understand – most Mexicans do without meat only because they cannot afford it, and many Mexican vegetarians eat what they do purely because they believe vegetables are healthy, rather than for ethical or philosophical reasons. So you must make your requirements very clear. Your server may believe he is bringing you a vegetarian meal when the items have been flavored with beef or chicken broth, or cooked in lard. Many Mexican soups, for instance, are vegetarian, although they are often made with chicken broth or flavored with crushed bouillon. The more upscale the restaurant, the better your chances of being accommodated.

Diana Kennedy is the acknowledged doyenne of Mexican food. Her latest book, *The Art of Mexican Cooking* (2008), offers up 512 pages of recipes, stories and emotive (and mouthwatering) anecdotes.

EATING WITH KIDS

Mexicans adore children and Mexico is a child-friendly place. Most waiters will cheerfully do anything within reason to please your child, and virtually all restaurants have high chairs; just ask for a *silla para niños.* Supermarkets carry a full range of American and international brands of baby food. Stock up if you intend to visit small or remote towns.

SESOS DE SOYA: RETHINKING HOW WE EAT BRAIN

Mmmmm, there's nothing better than a taco dripping with greasy, chewy cow brains (sesos). But it turns out that consuming the brain or spinal material of cattle may put you at risk of contracting Creutzfeldt-Jakob disease (the human equivalent of mad cow disease). And while Mexico has yet to report mad cow, many locals, especially in Oaxaca state, are turning to a healthy cow substitute, soy (soya), for their taco fillings. Beware, just because it's a seso de soya doesn't mean it wasn't prepared in animal grease. But it sure does taste yummy!

HABITS & CUSTOMS

Coastal eating customs are less formal than in other parts of Mexico. Instead of the afternoon *comida* (meal) served in most of Mexico between 1:30pm and 4pm, lunch is usually available no later than noon, and many restaurants do not open until 6pm for dinner. It is customary for entire families to dine together, either at someone's home or at a restaurant, especially for the Sunday-afternoon *comida*. If invited to someone's home for dinner, chocolates or tequila are good choices for a gift. This being Mexico, arriving 10 to 15 minutes late is the cultural norm. It seems odd, but showing up on time might be considered a bit uncouth.

Mexico's attitude toward liquor is usually quite liberal, but be aware that in many communities liquor cannot be sold on election days or when the president is visiting. Also, while alcoholic beverages are usually considered a normal part of life, drinking while driving is a serious no-no!

In better restaurants, tipping is expected. While 10% is considered on the low side, 15% is the norm, and 20% is above average. Most restaurants add on Mexico's value-added tax of 15%, which is noted as IVA.

> Afternoon munchies? Try the fruit in a bag sold on most beaches. It only costs M$6 to M$15. Add some salt, lime or chili powder to make a uniquely Mexican treat.

COOKING COURSES & TOURS

In Oaxaca, **Seasons of My Heart** (☎ 951-508-0469; www.seasonsofmyheart.com) is operated by well-known cookbook author Susana Trilling. She also conducts culinary tours in Oaxaca and other regions of Mexico. For details of other cooking classes, see p219.

For those with particular interest in cooking and food, cookbook author and Mexico culinary expert Marilyn Tausend (www.marilyntausend.com) conducts terrific, reasonably priced culinary tours of Mexico, most of which include market tours and workshops with noted food experts and chefs.

EAT YOUR WORDS

For non-Spanish speakers, travel and dining in Mexico is no problem, as English is understood almost everywhere. However, a few words in Spanish will indicate a respect for Mexicans and their culture, not to mention a willingness to risk embarrassment, and that can make a huge difference.

For further tips on pronunciation, see p296.

> Tacos cost just M$5 to M$10. Interesting fillings include *tripa* (intestine), *uba* (udder), *cabeza* (head meat) or *lengua* (tongue). Of course, the much more palatable and common-place meat choices are *carne asada/res/bistek birria* (varieties of grilled beef) or *chorizo*.

Useful Phrases

Are you open?
  ¿Está abierto?   e·sta a·byer·to
When are you open?
  ¿Cuándo está abierto?   kwan·do e·sta a·byer·to
Are you now serving breakfast/lunch/dinner?
  ¿Ahora, está sirviendo desayuno/   a·o·ra e·sta ser·vyen·do de·sa·yoo·no/
  la comida/la cena?   la ko·mee·da/la se·na
I'd like to see a menu.
  Quisiera ver la carta/el menú.   kee·sye·ra ver la kar·ta/el me·noo

Do you have a menu in English?
   ¿Tienen un menú en inglés?   tye·nen oon me·*noo* en een·*gles*
Can you recommend something?
   ¿Puede recomendar algo?   pwe·de re·ko·men·*dar* al·*go*
I'm a vegetarian.
   Soy vegetariano/a. (m/f)   soy ve·he·te·*rya*·no/a
I can't eat anything with meat or poultry products, including broth.
   No puedo comer nada con carne o aves,   no *pwe*·do ko·*mer* al·*go* de *kar*·ne o *a*·ves
   incluyendo caldo.   een·kloo·*yen*·do *kal*·do
I'd like mineral water/natural bottled water.
   Quiero agua mineral/agua purificada.   *kye*·ro *a*·gwa mee·ne·*ral/a*·gwa poo·ree·fee·*ka*·da
Is it (chili) hot?
   ¿Está picante?   es pee·*kan*·tee
The check, please.
   La cuenta, por favor.   la *kwen*·ta por fa·*vor*

Food Glossary
MENU DECODER

arroz mexicano	a·*ros* me·khee·*ka*·na	pilaf-style rice with a tomato base
chilaquiles	chee·la·*kee*·les	fried tortilla strips cooked with a red or green chili sauce, and sometimes meat and eggs
chile relleno	*chee*·les re·*ye*·no	chili stuffed with meat or cheese, dipped in egg batter and usually fried
empanada	em·pa·*na*·da	pastry turnover filled with meat, cheese or fruits
enchilada	en·chee·*la*·da	corn tortillas dipped in chili sauce, wrapped around meat or poultry and garnished with cheese
ensalada	en·sa·*la*·da	salad
filete al la tampiqueña	fee·*le*·te al la tam·pee·*ke*·nya	steak, Tampico-style – a thin tenderloin, grilled and served with chili strips and onion, a quesadilla and enchilada
huevos fritos	*hwe*·vos *free*·tos	fried eggs
huevos rancheros	*hwe*·vos ran·*che*·ros	fried eggs served on a corn tortilla, topped with a sauce of tomato, chilies and onions
huevos revueltos	*hwe*·vos re·*vwel*·tos	scrambled eggs
nopalitos	no·pa·*lee*·tos	sautéed or grilled sliced cactus paddles
papas fritas	*pa*·pas *free*·tas	french fries, also called *papas a la francesa*
picadillo	pee·ka·*dee*·yo	a ground-beef filling that often includes fruit and nuts
quesadilla	ke·sa·*dee*·ya	cheese and other items folded inside a tortilla and fried or grilled

COOKING METHODS

a la parilla	a la pa·*ree*·ya	grilled
a la plancha	a la *plan*·cha	pan-broiled
adobada	a·do·*ba*·da	marinated with *adobo* (chili sauce)
al carbón	al kar·*bon*	char-broiled
al mojo de ajo	al *mo*·kho de *a*·kho	with garlic sauce
alambre	al·*am*·bre	shish kebab
empanizado	em·pa·nee·*sa*·do	breaded
frito	*free*·to	fried
salteado	sal·te·a·do	sautéed

DAIRY PRODUCTS

crema	*kre*·ma	cream
leche	*le*·che	milk
mantequilla	man·te·*kee*·ya	butter
margarina	mar·ga·*ree*·na	margarine
queso	*ke*·so	cheese

SOUPS

caldo	*kal*·do	broth or soup
pozole	pa·*so*·le	a hearty soup or thin stew of hominy, meat or seafood, vegetables and chilies
sopa	*so*·pa	soup, either 'wet' or 'dry,' as in rice and pasta

FISH & SEAFOOD

calamar	ka·la·*mar*	squid
camarones	ka·ma·*ro*·nes	shrimp
cangrejo/jaiba	kan·*gre*·kho/*khay*·ba	crab
langosta	lan·*gos*·ta	lobster
mariscos	ma·*rees*·kos	shellfish
ostras/ostiones	*os*·tras/os·*tyo*·nes	oysters
pescado	pes·*ka*·do	fish
pulpo	*pool*·po	octopus

MEAT & POULTRY

albóndigas	al·*bon*·dee·gas	meatballs
aves	*a*·ves	poultry
bistec	bis·*tek*	steak
brocheta	bro·*che*·ta	shish kebab
carne	*kar*·ne	meat
carne de puerco	*kar*·ne de *pwer*·ko	pork
carne de res	*kar*·ne de res	beef
carnitas	kar·*nee*·tas	pork simmered in lard
cerdo	*ser*·do	pork
chorizo	cho·*ree*·so	Mexican-style bulk sausage made with chili and vinegar
chuleta	choo·*le*·ta	chop, as in pork chop
costillas de res	kos·*tee*·yas de res	beef ribs
jamón	kha·*mon*	ham
lomo	*lo*·mo	loin
lomo de cerdo	*lo*·mo de *ser*·do	pork loin
pechuga de pollo	pe·*chu*·ga de *po*·yo	chicken breast
pollo	*po*·yo	chicken
tocino	to·*see*·no	bacon

VEGETABLES, LEGUMES & GRAINS

arroz	a·*ros*	rice
calabacita	ka·la·ba·*see*·ta	squash
cebolla	se·*bo*·ya	onion
papas	*pa*·pas	potatoes
verduras	ver·*doo*·ras	vegetables

OTHER FOODS

azúcar	a·*soo*·kar	sugar
pan	pan	bread

pan integral	pan in·te·*gral*	wholemeal bread
pimienta	pi·*myen*·ta	pepper
sal	sal	salt

FRUIT

coco	*ko*·ko	coconut
coctel de frutas	*kok*·tel de *fru*·tas	fruit cocktail
fresa	*fre*·sa	strawberry
naranja	na·*ran*·kha	orange
piña	*pee*·nya	pineapple
platano	*pla*·ta·no	banana or plantain

DESSERTS

cajeta	ka·*khe*·ta	goat's milk and sugar boiled to a paste
helado	e·*la*·do	ice cream
nieve	*nye*·ve	sorbet
pastel	pas·*tel*	cake
postre	*pos*·tre	dessert

DRINKS

agua mineral	*a*·gwa mee·ne·*ral*	sparking mineral water or club soda
agua purificada	*a*·gwa poo·ree·fee·*ka*·da	bottled uncarbonated water
café americano	ka·*fe* a·me·ree·*ka*·no	black coffee
café con crema/leche	ka·*fe* kon *kre*·ma/*le*·che	coffee with cream/milk
café negro	ka·*fe* ne·gro	black coffee
jugo de manzana	*khoo*·go de man·*sa*·na	apple juice
jugo de naranja	*khoo*·go de na·*ran*·kha	orange juice
jugo de piña	*khoo*·go de *pee*·nya	pineapple juice
té de manzanilla	te de man·sa·*nee*·ya	chamomile tea
té negro	te *ne*·gro	black tea

Environment

Rugged, precipitous coastal mountains plunge madly to the ever-blue sea on this diverse and remarkably beautiful coast. It's no wonder so many resorts have popped up on the honey-kissed beaches and near the riotous mangrove lagoons. From palm-shaded shorelines and deciduous tropical-forested headlands all the way up to the cloud forests that crown the highest reaches of the Sierra Madre, this verdant coast is home to amazing biodiversity. And out to sea, where turtles, rays and whales cruise effortlessly through the deep and dark Pacific, this diversity is amplified – an ecological kaleidoscope just waiting to be explored.

Environmental scientists, however, have reason to worry. As in other ecologically precious territories around the globe, the human impact on the environment has been enormous, and the coast has a litany of problems that threaten not only the fauna and flora, but also the people.

THE LAND

It's nearly 2000km by road from Mazatlán, the northernmost destination in this book, to the southeastern resort of Bahías de Huatulco in Oaxaca. Mazatlán sits about midway down a dry coastal plain that stretches south from Mexicali, on the US border, almost to Tepic, in Nayarit state. Inland from the flats stands the rugged, volcanically formed Sierra Madre Occidental, which is crossed by only two main transport routes – the Barranca del Cobre (Copper Canyon) railway, from Chihuahua to Los Mochis, and the dramatic Hwy 40 from Durango to Mazatlán.

South of Cabo Corrientes (the lip of land protruding into the Pacific near Puerto Vallarta), the Pacific lowlands narrow to just a thin strip and the mountains rise dramatically from the sea. The Sierra Madre Occidental widens near Nayarit and finishes in Jalisco, where it meets the Cordillera Neovolcánica, a volcanic range running east–west across the middle of Mexico. Known in English as the Trans-Mexican Volcanic Belt, the Cordillera Neovolcánica includes the active volcanoes Popocatépetl (5452m) and Volcán de Fuego de Colima (3960m), as well as Pico de Orizaba (5610m), the nation's highest peak.

The main mountain range in southern Mexico is the Sierra Madre del Sur, which stretches across the states of Guerrero and Oaxaca, and separates the Oaxacan coast from its capital city. As the crow flies, it's only about 160km from Puerto Ángel, the southernmost town in Oaxaca, north to Oaxaca city, but crossing the crinkled back of the Sierra takes about six hours by car.

The US Sierra Club's prestigious Chico Mendes Prize, for bravery and leadership in environmental protection, was awarded in 2005 to Felipe Arreaga and two other leaders of a peasant organization battling indiscriminate logging in the state of Guerrero. Arreaga was unable to collect the award because he was in jail on what he said was a trumped-up murder charge.

WILDLIFE
Animals
LAND LIFE

Raccoons, armadillos, skunks, rabbits and snakes are common. One critter you'll encounter is the gecko, a harmless, tiny green lizard that loves to crawl across walls and squawk at night. Michoacán and Guerrero are home to more species of scorpions and spiders than anywhere in Mexico.

Both black and green iguanas are common along the entire coast. Both are prized for their meat and have been overhunted, especially in Guerrero and Oaxaca. Boa constrictors are sometimes spotted in lagoons.

Rarer animals – which you'll be extremely lucky to see – include spider monkeys and the beautiful, endangered jaguar, which once inhabited much of the coast.

SEA TURTLES

The Pacific coast is among the world's chief sea-turtle breeding grounds. Of the world's eight sea-turtle species, seven are found in Mexican waters, and six of those in the Pacific. Their nesting sites are scattered along the entire coast. For information about where you have the best chances of encountering sea turtles, see p52.

Female turtles usually lay their eggs on the beaches where they were born, some swimming huge distances to do so. They come ashore at night, scoop a trough in the sand and lay 50 to 200 eggs in it. Then they cover the eggs and go back to the sea. Six to 10 weeks later, the baby turtles hatch, dig their way out and crawl to the sea at night. Only two or three of every 100 make it to adulthood. Turtle nesting seasons vary, but July to September are peak months in many places.

Playa Escobilla, just east of Puerto Escondido, is one of the world's main nesting grounds for the small olive ridley turtle, the only sea-turtle species that is not endangered. Between May and January, about 700,000 olive ridleys come ashore here in about a dozen waves – known as *arribadas* – each lasting two or three nights, often during the waning of the moon. Playa Escobilla's turtles are guarded by armed soldiers, and there is no tourist access to the beach.

The rare leatherback is the largest sea turtle – it grows up to 3m long and can weigh 900kg and live 80 years. One leatherback nesting beach is Oaxaca state's Playa Mermejita, between Punta Cometa and Playa Ventanilla, near Mazunte. Another is Barra de la Cruz, east of Bahías de Huatulco.

The green turtle is a vegetarian that grazes on marine grasses. Most adults are about 1m long. For millennia, the green turtle's meat and eggs have provided protein to humans in the tropics. European exploration of the globe marked the beginning of the turtle's decline. In the 1960s, the Empacadora Baja California in Ensenada, Baja California, was canning as many as 100 tonnes of turtle soup a season.

The loggerhead turtle, weighing up to 100kg, is famous for the vast distances it crosses between its feeding grounds and nesting sites. Loggerheads born in Japan and even, it's thought, Australia, cross the Pacific to feed off Baja California. Females later return to their birthplaces – a year-long journey – to lay their eggs.

The hawksbill turtle nests along both of Mexico's coasts and can live 50 years. The coast's sixth species, the black turtle, sticks to the Pacific.

The smallest and most endangered sea turtle, the Kemp's ridley (parrot turtle), lives only in the Gulf of Mexico.

MARINE LIFE

Dolphins can be seen off the coast, as can gray, humpback and blue whales, especially from November to March, when a whale-watching

Dreaming of 'Blue Turtles?' Check out the websites www.project-tortuga.org, www.turtles.org and www.seaturtlestatus.org for great informative features and a few interactive maps on these amazing creatures.

San Francisco, Nayarit-based Grupo Ecológico de la Costa Verde released about 76,000 turtles to the sea in 2008 and the number of nests has soared tenfold since 1991.

BIRDS OF A FEATHER

The lagoons and wetlands of Pacific Mexico host hundreds of species of native and migratory birds, and any break-of-dawn boat trip will send bird lovers squawking. Birds from as far north as Alaska migrate here each winter – the best season for racking up your species-spotted list. You may see parrots and parakeets, loons, grebes, frigate birds, herons, hawks, falcons, sandpipers, plovers, ibis, swifts and boobies (to name only a handful).

In Oaxaca it's not uncommon to spot ospreys soaring above the ocean cliffs. Of course, the bird you'll see most, wherever you are, is the *zopilote* (vulture). For the best birding locations, see p52.

PROTECTING MEXICO'S TURTLES

Despite international conservation efforts, turtle flesh and eggs continue to be eaten, and some people still believe the eggs to be aphrodisiacs. Turtle skin and shell are used to make clothing and adornments. And the world's fishing boats kill many turtles by trapping and drowning them in nets. In Mexico, hunting and killing sea turtles was officially banned in 1990, but the illicit killing and egg-raiding still goes on – a clutch of eggs can be sold for more than a typical worker makes in a week.

You can visit turtle hatcheries in Cuyutlán (p162) and Mazunte (p253). If you want to get involved in conservation efforts, volunteer opportunities exist at the Grupo Ecológico de la Costa Verde (p134) and through Red de los Humedales de la Costa de Oaxaca (p234) – for more volunteering resources, see p280.

To help the turtles that use Mexican beaches – and most people who have seen these graceful creatures swimming at sea will want to do that – follow these rules if you find yourself at a nesting beach:

■ Try to avoid nesting beaches altogether between sunset and sunrise.

■ Don't approach turtles emerging from the sea, or disturb nesting turtles or hatchlings with noise or lights (lights on or even near the beach can cause hatchlings to lose their sense of direction on their journey to the water).

■ Keep vehicles – even bicycles – off nesting beaches.

■ Don't build sandcastles or stick umbrellas into the sand.

■ Never handle baby turtles or carry them to the sea – their arduous scramble is vital to their development.

■ Boycott shops or stalls selling products made from sea turtles or any other endangered species.

trip is recommended (see p52). Early in the year, even while lying on the beach you'll probably spot whales. Stingrays and the larger Pacific manta rays can often be seen when they burst from the water with wild abandon. Tide pools harbor sea anemones, urchins, octopuses, starfish, sea slugs and an array of crabs. Spend any time *under* water and you'll probably see such beauties as the Cortez angelfish, seahorses, moray eels, rays, puffers and even whale sharks. Jellyfish are abundant at the beginning of the rainy season. See p50 for information on the larger Pacific fish.

Coastal lagoons, especially in the south, once harbored thousands of crocodiles. They've nearly been hunted to extinction, but you will still see them in the lagoons of La Manzanilla, Parque Nacional Lagunas de Chacahua and San Blas.

Marine mammals are best spotted November to March. The Whale and Dolphin Conservation Society (www.wdcs.org) includes information about how to get involved in global efforts to protect them.

Plants

The Sierra Madre Occidental, the Cordillera Neovolcánica and the Sierra Madre del Sur still have some big stretches of pine forest and, at lower elevations, oak forest.

Tropical forest covers much of the lowest western slopes of the Sierra Madre Occidental and the Cordillera Neovolcánica, and can also be found in Oaxaca. These forests lose their leaves during the dry winter but are lush and verdant in the summer rainy season. Pink trumpet, cardinal sage, spider lily, *mata ratón* (literally 'rat killer') and *matapalo* (strangler fig) bloom in these forests during the rainy season. Much of this plant community, however, has disappeared as the land has been taken over by ranches and cropland.

Along the dry Pacific coastal plain, from the southern end of the Desierto Sonorense to Guerrero state, the predominant vegetation in this savanna is thorny bushes and small trees, including morning glory and acacias.

The coastal lagoons that dot the Pacific coast are home to dense mangrove forests that have thick leathery leaves and small seasonal flowers.

PARKS & RESERVES

With all the spectacular beaches and accessible lagoons, you don't have to search for a park to experience the natural elements. Fortunately, federal, state and local governments have created a handful of protected areas to preserve some of the coast's fragile ecosystems. Some are easily accessible with private transport while others require the use of local guides (who will also greatly increase your chances of spotting any wildlife).

The largest national park in this book is the Parque Nacional Volcán Nevado de Colima (21,930 hectares; p157), where you'll find two volcanoes: the extinct Volcán Nevado de Colima and the active Volcán de Fuego. The smallest national park is the 192-hectare Isla Isabel (p122), a volcanically formed island north of San Blas, Nayarit. Parque Nacional Lagunas de Chacahua (p234), in Oaxaca, protects 14,000 hectares, which incorporate two mammoth lagoons, mangroves, fishing communities and more than 13km of coastline.

The ancient Zapotec city of Monte Albán (p232) in Oaxaca is a protected archaeological zone of 2078 hectares.

ENVIRONMENTAL ISSUES

Mexico's environmental crises, including those of the coast, are typical of a poor country with an exploding population struggling to develop. From early in the 20th century, urban industrial growth, intensive chemical-based agriculture, and the destruction of forests for logging and to allow grazing and development were seen as paths to prosperity, and little attention was paid to their environmental effects. And despite the growth in environmental awareness from the 1970s, and the formation of a few national parks along the coast, very little has been achieved in terms of protecting the natural environment.

Forest Depletion

Deforestation has increased considerably on the coast since the passage of NAFTA in 1994, which gave international corporations access to vast *ejido* (communal) landholdings. The developers are not just after the white and sugar pine that is logged in the region, they are also clearing land for cattle ranching and mining. According to an article in *Cambio de Michoacan,* 90% of the tropical forests of Michoacán – near Lázaro Cárdenas, Aquila and Coahuayana – has been destroyed. Deforestation has caused massive erosion and contributed to increased flooding, local climate changes and oversilting of rivers. And less forest means there are fewer places for wild animals to forage and hide, and depleted resources for a culture that remains – at least to a certain degree, especially in the poorer corners – subsistence based. Nationally, around 6 million hectares of primary forest vanished between 1990 and 2005, but encouragingly, since the turn of the century, prime forest deforestation has dropped by 15%.

Wetland Depletion

Mexico's rich coastal lagoons and wetlands have experienced considerable harm in recent years from shrimp farming. Shrimp farms contribute to the destruction of mangroves, the permanent flooding of lagoons, the privatization

The definitive website for Eco Travels in Latin America (www.planeta .com) brims with information and links about Mexican flora and fauna.

Defending the Land of the Jaguar (1995) by Lane Simonian tells the story of Mexico's long, if weak, tradition of conservation.

Joel Simon's *Endangered Mexico: An Environment on the Edge* examines Mexico's varied environmental crises with the benefit of excellent first-hand journalistic research.

of communal fishing waters, and the introduction of massive amounts of fertilizers and chemicals. The industry is booming in Sinaloa, Nayarit and Oaxaca, and receives heavy investment from the Mexican government and the World Bank. The biggest market for Mexican-farmed shrimp is the USA.

Cattle grazing also has a devastating impact on wetlands where they are drained to create pastureland. Laguna de Manialtepec (p244) in Oaxaca was being reduced at an alarming rate until considerable protests from local fishing communities put a stop to it in the late 1990s.

Erosion & Water Contamination

Erosion is mainly the result of deforestation followed by cattle grazing or intensive agriculture on unsuitable terrain. In the Mixteca area of Oaxaca, around 80% of the arable land is gone.

Some rural areas and watercourses have been contaminated by excessive use of chemical pesticides and defoliants. Sewage, and industrial and agricultural wastes contaminate most Mexican rivers, and eventually flow out to the ocean. While efforts have been put in place to stem the flow of contaminants, some of Mexico's coastal waters are still considered unsafe for swimming.

Tourism

In some places in Mexico it's hoped that ecologically sensitive tourism will benefit the environment by providing a less harmful source of income for local people. An example is Mazunte (p253), Oaxaca, a village that lived by slaughtering sea turtles until the practice was banned in 1990. Villagers then turned to slash-and-burn farming, threatening forest survival, before a low-key and successful tourism program was launched. Likewise, the mangrove lagoons of the coast – especially around San Blas (p122), Laguna de Manialtepec (p244) and Barra de Potosí (p188) – have all benefited from the rise in awareness and stewardship that increased tourism has brought. And while increased visitation can have a noisome impact on local ecosystems, it seems that, for now at least, the influx of tourists has left a largely positive footprint on these unique regions.

In other cases, despite official lip service paid to conservation, large-scale tourism developments have destroyed fragile ecosystems. Acapulco grew at such a rate and pumped so much sewage into the Bay of Acapulco in the 1970s and '80s that drastic measures had to be taken to reverse damage to the bay. In the case of now-developing Bahías de Huatulco, the federal government has taken steps to prevent water pollution by resorts, limited construction heights on hotels and even created a national park nearby to preserve fragile ecosystems. But local communities have been displaced, and inland lagoons critical to the local ecosystem have been mysteriously drawn out of park boundaries (where golf courses may be drawn in), according to environmentalists. For more on responsible tourism, see p13. We've also put together a GreenDex (p319) to get you started.

Environmental Movement

Environmental consciousness first grew in the 1970s, initially among the middle class in Mexico City, where nobody could ignore the air pollution. Today nongovernmental action is carried out by a growing number of groups around the country, mainly small organizations working on local issues.

Between 1999 and 2001, Guerrero's Costa Grande made continuous headlines and attracted international criticism after the military arrested and imprisoned antilogging activists Rodolfo Montiel and Teodoro Cabrera. Montiel and Cabrera started a community environmental group in 1997, which fought heavy logging of the Costa Grande. Montiel and Cabrera

Dedicated birders should seek out the Spanish-language *Aves de México* by Roger Tory Peterson and Edward L Chalif. An alternative is *A Guide to the Birds of Mexico & Northern Central America* by Steve NG Howell and Sophie Webb.

Drink responsibly! Around 2.5 million tonnes of plastic is used to bottle water each year. Stay green by asking your hotelier to provide a water cooler or by carrying your own filter.

were imprisoned for 16 months after reportedly being tortured into confessing to trumped-up drug and weapons charges. After intense international pressure, President Fox finally ordered their release; it came a month after their original defense lawyer was assassinated in Mexico City.

Environmental campaigning today is carried out mainly by small organizations working on local issues, though some successful campaigns in recent years have rested on broader-based support, even from outside Mexico. One was the defeat in 2000 of the plan for a giant saltworks at Laguna San Ignacio in Baja California, a gray-whale breeding ground. Another was the annulment in 2001 of a large hotel project at the Caribbean turtle-nesting beach of Xcacel. Ideas for hydroelectric dams on the Río Usumacinta, along Mexico's border with Guatemala, attract broad opposition whenever they resurface, owing to their consequences for the huge watershed of what is Mexico's biggest river and for the area's many Mayan archaeological sites.

Increased global interest in environmentalism may bode well for 'developing' countries like Mexico. For instance, in 2007 the World Bank announced plans to create a carbon-offset scheme in which they would reward 14 developing countries, including Mexico, for protecting their forests.

And a different kind of grassroots environmentalism is popping up on the back of the emerging ecotourism sites in places such as San Blas (p122), Oaxaca's Pueblos Mancomunados (p223) and Barra de Potosí (p188), where tour operators and locals are joining forces to protect the local environment and fight illegal logging and rampant growth in favor of a more sustainable future.

The Mexican government recently announced it will spend M$163 million to protect the exceedingly rare vaquita marina (an endangered porpoise) in the northern Gulf of California. The plan calls for paying fishermen to steer clear of the vaquita's protected habitat.

Puerto Vallarta & Pacific Mexico Outdoors

Staying active along this coast is no problem. There's great surfing, decent snorkeling and diving, and some of the world's best sportfishing. Add mountain biking, hiking, kayaking, wildlife-watching, water-skiing, parasailing and co-ed naked volleyball to the list, and you have a dream destination for the active.

Refer to this book's destination sections for details on equipment rentals and the availability and advisability of guides.

DIVING & SNORKELING

Though it's tough to compete with the azure waters and coral reefs of the Caribbean, there are some outstanding dive sites unique to the Pacific coast – and plenty of dazzling snorkeling spots. Mazatlán (p107), Puerto Vallarta (p64), Barra de Navidad (p150), Manzanillo (p155), Zihuatanejo (p182), Troncones (p172), Faro de Bucerías (p165), Puerto Escondido (p239), Puerto Ángel (p247) and Bahías de Huatulco (p258) all have highly praised dive sites nearby, not to mention first-rate outfitters who will tank you up and take you out. Operators generally charge around M$400/700 for a guided one-tank/two-tank dive, and around M$700 for a night dive.

Most dive shops offer guided snorkeling excursions, or rent snorkel equipment so you can go it alone. On beaches with good snorkeling nearby, restaurants and booths usually rent equipment, though you should check gear carefully for quality and comfort before heading out for the day. There are plenty of places to snorkel without a guide, but with a guide, you're usually taken by boat to better, hard-to-reach spots.

Many diving outfitters are affiliates of the international organizations PADI (www.padi.com) or NAUI (www.naui.org) and post their certifications in plain view. Both organizations' websites allow you to search for their affiliated dive shops in Mexico.

SURFING

Describing all the epic surf spots on Mexico's Pacific coast would be as arduous as paddling out against a double-overhead set at Playa Zicatela – well, almost. From the 'world's longest wave' near San Blas (p124) to the screaming

---

SAFETY GUIDELINES FOR DIVING

Before embarking on a scuba-diving trip, carefully consider the following points to ensure you have a safe and enjoyable experience:

- Obtain a current diving certification card from a recognized scuba-diving instructional agency, either at home or from one of many in Mexico.
- Obtain reliable information about physical and environmental conditions at the dive site (eg from a reputable local dive operation).
- Be aware of local laws, regulations and etiquette about marine life and the environment.
- Make sure that you are comfortable diving and dive only at sites within your realm of experience; if available, hire a competent, professionally trained dive instructor or dive master.
- Be aware that underwater conditions vary significantly from one region, or even site, to another. Seasonal changes can significantly alter site and dive conditions. These differences influence the way divers dress for a dive and what diving techniques they use.
- Ask about the environmental characteristics that can affect your diving and how local, trained divers deal with these considerations.

barrels of Puerto Escondido's 'Mexican Pipeline' (p239), the Pacific coast is bombarded by surf, with good spots for experts and beginners alike. Sayulita (p136), Barra de Navidad (p150), Manzanillo (p154), Playa Boca de Pascuales (p162), Playa La Ticla (p164), Barra de Nexpa (p166), Playa Azul (p167), Playa Troncones (p171), La Saladita (p174), Ixtapa (p176), Playa Revolcadero (p199), Chacahua (p235), Barra de la Cruz (p263) – the list goes on and on.

Most beach breaks receive some sort of surf all year, but wave season is really May to October/November. Spring and fall can see excellent conditions with fewer people, while the biggest months are June, July and August, when waves can get *huge* and the sets roll like clockwork.

Shipping a surfboard to Mexico is not a problem, but most airlines charge anywhere from M$1000 to M$3000, and some will hit you for another fee on your way home. Some airlines don't allow surfboards, period.

A good board bag is advisable, but a better one doesn't necessarily guarantee fewer mishaps on the aircraft. You'll rarely, if ever, need a wetsuit, but a rash guard is highly recommended for protection against the sun. Bring plenty of warm-water wax, as it's tough to find south of the border. Soft racks (or some sort of packable tie-downs) are easy to carry and indispensable if you plan to do any driving or want to secure your board to a taxi. Unless you plan to surf one spot only, renting a car, or driving your own, makes everything much easier.

Surf towns like Troncones and Puerto Escondido have surf shops where you can normally repair dings, and pick up a new or used 'travel board,' which will certainly save you money, as you can sell it back when the trip's over. Used boards are generally cheaper than in the US, costing anywhere from M$800 to M$3000.

For Pacific Mexico surf reports, check out www .magicseaweed.com.

Each year swimmers are killed by undertow, cross-currents, whirlpools and other ocean hazards. Whenever possible seek local advice before entering the water, and keep in mind that swimming conditions can change rapidly.

FISHING

Mexico's Pacific coast has world-famous billfishing (marlin, swordfish, sailfish) and outstanding light-tackle fishing year-round. Many deep-sea charters now practice catch-and-release for billfish, a practice we highly recommend because these majestic lords of the deep are being disastrously overfished. See p303 for a glossary of Spanish fish names.

When & Where to Fish

You can catch fish in these waters year-round, but in general the biggest catches occur from April to July and October to December. Keep in mind that summer and late fall is also prime tropical storm and hurricane season.

Mazatlán (p107), 'the billfish capital of the world,' is famous for marlin, while Puerto Vallarta (p64) is known for sailfish; both offer big catches of yellowfin tuna, *dorado* (dolphinfish or mahimahi), red snapper and black sea bass. In Zihuatanejo (p183) sailfish, marlin, dorado, roosterfish and wahoo are caught most of the year, and the biggest tuna catches are in spring. In Bahías de Huatulco (p257) swordfish, sailfish and dorado are caught year-round, while marlin are caught mostly from October to May; roosterfish season is April to August.

Plenty of other light-tackle fish are caught year-round along the entire coast, including yellowtail, grouper, Spanish mackerel, sea bass, halibut and wahoo.

Charters

Fishing charters are available in all major resort towns, and you'll find reputable local companies listed throughout this book. Always ask what's included in the rates. Fishing licenses, tackle, crew and ice are standard, but sometimes charters also include bait, cleaning and freezing, meals, drinks and tax. Live bait – usually available dockside for a few dollars – should be checked for absolute freshness. Tips for the crew are at your discretion, but M$150 to M$200 (per angler) for a successful eight hours is considered adequate. Bring along a hat, sunscreen, polarized sunglasses and Dramamine (or equivalent) whether or not you suffer from seasickness. Make sure the toilet situation is up to your standards of privacy.

Prices depend on boat type, size and season. The most comfortable is the cruiser, usually 8.6m to 14m (26ft to 42ft) in length and equipped with everything from fighting chairs (to reel in the big fish) to fish-finders and a full head (toilet). Prices range from M$2500 to M$5000 per boat for an eight-hour day.

The cheapest boats are *pangas*, the vessel of choice of Mexican commercial fishermen, as they put you right up close with the sea. About 6m to 8m (18ft to 24ft) long, these sturdy skiffs hold three to four people and cost between M$1500 and M$2000 per day. Super-*pangas* are larger, accommodate four to six fishers comfortably and often feature toilets and a canvas top for shade. Rates start around M$3000 per day per boat.

Licenses & Bag Limits

Anyone aboard a private vessel carrying fishing gear, both on the ocean and in estuaries, must have a Mexican fishing license whether they're fishing or not. Licenses are almost always included on charters, but you'll need your own if you choose to hire a local fisherman to take you out. In Mexico licenses are issued by the Oficina de Pesca, which has offices in most towns. Licenses can also be obtained in the USA from the **Mexican Fisheries Department** (☎ 619-233-4324; fax 233-0344; www.conapescasandiego.org; Ste 101, 2550 Fifth Ave, San Diego, CA 92103). The cost of the license at the time of research was US$25.80/US$37/US$48.20 per week/month/year. Write, call or fax to request an application form.

The daily bag limit is 10 fish per person with no more than five of any one species. Billfish, marlin, sailfish, shark and swordfish are restricted to one per day per boat, while for dorado, tarpon and roosterfish it's two.

The website www .ontheroad.com is a great source for trailer parks and camping sites along the Pacific coast and elsewhere in México.

Surf Fishing

No license is required when fishing from land, as many Mexicans still make their livelihood this way. You don't have to bring a pole – just find a local tackle shop (they're in any sizable fishing town, and some are listed in this book) and purchase a hand reel (a small piece of wood wrapped with fishing line) or *rollo de nylon* (spool of nylon) and some hooks, lures and weights. Some tackle shops sell live bait and *carnada* (raw bait), and it's often sold near the town pier. Shrimp and other raw baits are sold cheaply in the central markets.

Surf fishing is widely enjoyed on rocky shorelines throughout the region. With your hand reel in one hand let out some line, grab it with the other hand, swing it around your head (this takes practice) and let it go. Even if you fail horribly, it's a good way to meet local fishers who might give you a few tips.

Earthfoot (www.earth foot.org/mx_pc.htm) presents small-scale, locally produced, low-impact ecotours worldwide and maintains a page dedicated to specialist guides in Pacific Mexico.

KAYAKING, CANOEING & RAFTING

The coastal lagoons and sheltered bays of the Pacific coast are magnificent for kayaks and canoes. If you have your own boat, you'll be in heaven. If you don't, don't worry – many places rent kayaks and provide guides and transportation to boot. Parque Nacional Lagunas de Chacahua (p234), Laguna de Manialtepec (p244), Barra de la Cruz (p263), La Manzanilla (p145) and Barra de Navidad (p150) are all places with brackish, bird-filled, mangrove-fringed lagoons just waiting to be paddled. In many of these smaller areas, you may or may not be able to rent a kayak locally – it's largely dependent on the whim of

A Gringo's Guide to Mexican Whitewater by Tom Robey details 56 kayak, canoe and raft runs on 37 different rivers.

local entrepreneurs – but you can normally arrange a tour from a neighboring city, and you can certainly bring your own boat. Outfitters in San Blas (p122), Mazatlán (p108), Puerto Vallarta (p68) and La Manzanilla (p145) take folks on some excellent kayaking trips. You can also rent kayaks and/or canoes and paddle off on your own at these and other places, including La Cruz de Huanacaxtle (p92), Barra de Potosí (p188) and Pie de la Cuesta (p208).

White-water rafting is practiced from June to November on the Copalita and Zimatán Rivers near Bahías de Huatulco (p259); several outfitters there offer excursions.

WILDLIFE- & BIRD-WATCHING

Teeming with birdlife, lined with mangroves and sometimes even crawling with crocodiles, the coastal lagoons of Pacific Mexico are wonderful spots to see wildlife. Many of them are flanked by a small village or two and have docks where you can hire a local fisher to buzz you around in the cool of the morning. They'll point out birds and iguanas, crocs and turtles, maybe even a boa or two, and they'll let you fish, or stop at an island beach for a swim and a snack. See p43 for additional information on the creatures that inhabit the coast.

Sea Turtle–Watching

For great information on surfing, diving and other adventure sports in Jalisco, Colima and Oaxaca click on www.tomzap.com.

Seven of the world's eight sea turtle species are found in Mexican waters, and four of those make it to the Pacific shores of mainland Mexico (the others are found around Baja California and the Gulf of Mexico). Getting a glimpse of these majestic creatures is truly a highlight. There are numerous places to spy on sea turtles, but you have to know where and when to go looking. In order to protect the turtles, some beaches (most notably Playa Escobilla, p44) are guarded during nesting season and are off-limits to tourists. But chances of seeing the turtles at other beaches are still quite high. See the boxed text, p45, for tips on how to avoid disrupting nesting turtles if you happen to find yourself on a nesting beach.

Whale-Watching

Between November and March, humpback whales migrate to Pacific Mexico to mate and calve. Puerto Vallarta's Bahía de Banderas (p66) is one of their most popular stomping grounds, and a whale-watching trip from one of the city's many operators can bring you almost within kissing distance. Mazatlán is another possibility for keen whale-watchers (p108). Other great places for whale-watching (all of which have outfits offering seasonal trips out to sea) include Chacala (p129), La Cruz de Huanacaxtle (p92), Punta de Mita (p93) and Rincón de Guayabitos (p131), all near Puerto Vallarta. Even from the shore, it's not uncommon to see breaching whales along the entire coast during the first few months of the year.

Bird-Watching

Avidly read by birders, Fat Birder (www.fatbirder.com) covers bird-watching worldwide and provides general information about the pursuit in Mexico.

Bird-watchers flock here year-round for the great variety of birds on offer. A morning float around one of the coast's many lagoons, with abundant birdlife, is an unforgettable experience. And if you do it in winter, not only will you see the native waterfowl, you'll see the North American and Alaskan species that migrate here as well. See p44 for some of the birds you might see.

The swamp forests and lagoons around San Blas (p122) are ideal for bird-watching, and there's a bird sanctuary in the nearby San Cristóbal estuary. The island of Isla Isabel (p122), four hours from San Blas by boat, is a bird-watcher's dream, and from Mazatlán (p108) you can organize a bird-watching tour of the coastal wetlands. Laguna de Manialtepec (p244)

TOP TURTLE-WATCHING AREAS

The following coastal areas are where you're most likely to encounter sea turtles:

- **Playa San Francisco** (p135) The southern coast of Nayarit is home to Grupo Ecológico de la Costa Verde, which offers volunteer opportunities and releases more than 25,000 hatchlings each year to the sea.
- **Cuyutlán** (p162) Just south of Manzanillo, the Centro Tortuguero operates a thriving turtle-release program and a visitors center with baby turtles on display.
- **Playa Maruata** (p165) Black turtles come ashore nightly from June to December to lay their eggs at this isolated beach.
- **Puerto Escondido** (p239) Turtle-spotting tours on Bahía Principal often encounter the elusive loggerhead turtle.
- **San Agustinillo** (p252) Once the site of large-scale turtle slaughter, today this village is known for its turtle-viewing boat trips.
- **Mazunte** (p253) Home to the Centro Méxicano de la Tortuga, a turtle aquarium and research center with specimens of all seven of Mexico's marine turtle species.
- **Bahías de Huatulco** (p258) This area's terrific dive sites feature frequent close encounters with sea turtles.

in Oaxaca is another wetland bird habitat that will truly send you over the edge. There are estuary wetlands flapping with birds near La Cruz de Loreto (p141), Playa La Ticla (p164) and Barra de Potosí (p188). In Oaxaca, the pair of giant lagoons in Parque Nacional Lagunas de Chacahua (p234), and the tiny lagoon of Barra de la Cruz (p263) are two other places offering plenty of chances. Inland, near Tepic, Laguna Santa María del Oro (p129), an idyllic lake at 750m elevation in a 100m-deep volcanic crater, is home to some 250 species of bird, and its mountainous surroundings make a wonderful contrast to coastal ecology.

Most outfitters that offer bird-watching tours don't provide binoculars, so pack your own if this activity is on your agenda.

HIKING

Mexico's beaches make for outstanding hiking. The 13km beach in Parque Nacional Lagunas de Chacahua (Oaxaca), Playa Larga (near Zihuatanejo), and the endless, empty beaches of Michoacán are great for stretching the legs. Many villages on the coast have back roads or nearby trails you can explore by foot.

Some great hikes can be had inland too (if you can drag yourself away from the beach). Near Tepic, Laguna Santa María del Oro (p129) and the terrain around the extinct Volcán Ceboruco (p129) both offer superb settings for various levels of hiking. Parque Nacional Volcán Nevado de Colima (p157), in Colima, has more good hiking. The Valles Centrales of Oaxaca (p223) are popular for guided hikes (p219 and p223) between mountain villages.

MOUNTAIN BIKING

Shops rent mountain bikes up and down the coast, but you're usually left to your own intuition about where to explore. Troncones (p172), Zihuatanejo, Manzanillo, Playa Azul, San Blas, Sayulita, La Crucecita (Bahías de Huatulco) and many other coastal towns have bike rentals and are small enough places that you can navigate through town and into open terrain without the fear of being run down. You can often ride from one fishing village to another, stopping in each for a beer or a bite to eat (Troncones to La Saladita comes to mind here). Oaxaca (p219), Mazatlán

A Hiker's Guide to Mexico's Natural History by Jim Conrad and Backpacking in Mexico by Tim Burford are both must-reads for intrepid explorers planning a tour along the coast.

(p108) and Puerto Vallarta (p67) have become very popular for mountain biking, and several operators listed in these chapters will take you for some beautiful rides along old mountain roads to visit tiny villages.

HORSEBACK RIDING

Planeta (www.planeta
.com) has a 'Mexico
Biking Guide,' while
Spanish-language site
Ciclismo de Montaña en
México (Mountain Biking
in Mexico; www
.mountainbike.org.mx)
is a great resource for
bilingual pedalheads.

Horses are rented on countless beaches along the coast. Mazatlán (p107), Puerto Vallarta (p66), Troncones, Zihuatanejo (p182), Pie de la Cuesta (p208) and Bahías de Huatulco (p259) are just a few of the places where you can mount up for about M$150 to M$300 per person for a two- to three-hour guided ride. Some places will allow you to take horses on your own if you leave a small deposit and an ID. Mexican horses tend to be a bit smaller, more worn out and less inclined to run than their North American and European counterparts, but they can still be fun. Keep in mind that if a guide accompanies you, the money he or she makes is often primarily what riders tip them; around M$50 per person is usually sufficient.

GOLF & TENNIS

Mazatlán (p108), Puerto Vallarta (p67), Ixtapa (p177), Acapulco (p199) and Bahías de Huatulco (p258) all have world-class golf courses where you can swing the old irons to some spectacular views. But you'll pay a pretty price to do it: green fees run anywhere from M$800 to M$2500. Carts and caddies – which are often required – can cost an additional M$300 to M$500, depending on the course.

These same resorts all have numerous tennis clubs, many of which are found in the luxury hotels. Nonhotel guests are almost always welcome to use the courts for about M$200 per hour and can rent racquets on the spot.

OTHER ACTIVITIES

The two-stroke
engines found on jet
skis discharge as much
as one third of their fuel
and oil unburned into the
sea and can also prove
detrimental to wildlife.

Water-skiing, parasailing and banana-boat riding are widespread resort activities, especially in Acapulco, Puerto Vallarta, Zihuatanejo, Mazatlán and Bahías de Huatulco. Many of the larger resort hotels – if they're located on a bay – rent sailboats and catamarans, too. Laguna de Coyuca (p208), at Pie de la Cuesta, is famous for water-skiing and has several operators who will zip you around the lagoon. Always cast an eye over the equipment before taking off.

Adrenaline junkies can bungee jump from a platform over sea cliffs near Puerto Vallarta (p68) or from a crane top in the middle of the hotel district in Acapulco (p200) – great for those margarita hangovers!

Puerto Vallarta

Set against a backdrop of verdant coastal mountains, Puerto Vallarta hugs a vast, glistening shoreline along the crescent-shaped Bahía de Banderas (Bay of Flags), one of the largest bays in the world. Millions of visitors come here each year to laze around on alluring sandy beaches, dine at slick waterfront restaurants and indulge in margarita-soaked revelry.

And with some of the best scuba-diving sites along the Pacific coast, dense jungles with cascading waterfalls, and remote beach villages only accessible by boat, it's perfectly understandable if you forget what your hotel room looks like.

Most of the action centers on the cobblestone streets of the historic center, where the Río Cuale (Cuale River) dramatically splits the town, known simply as 'Vallarta' or 'PV,' in two. There you can browse through contemporary galleries, take sunset strolls along the *malecón* (boardwalk) and shake your booty to electronica and pop tunes in rip-roaring discos.

Exploring beyond Vallarta's city limits pays big rewards. To the southwest are the aforementioned coastal villages, and in the opposite direction awaits Bucerías, with a surprising offering of international cuisine and cozy hotels. Further north you'll find quality R&R in the tranquil fishing village of La Cruz de Huanacaxtle, a town so chill it makes Bucerías look like a boomtown. On the northern peninsula, surfers flock to Punta de Mita to savor long breaks and easy living.

Outdoor activities abound in Vallarta: whale-watching excursions, horseback riding, sportfishing, golf and scenic booze cruises – it's all here. Boredom is simply not an option.

HIGHLIGHTS

- Going primitive on the restful beach cove of **Playa Majahuitas** (p99)
- Catching a water taxi and chilling on the soft sands of **Yelapa** (p98) and **Quimixto** (p98), remote beaches only accessible by boat
- Dining and cherishing the diverse flavors of the charismatic **Zona Romántica** (p76)
- Rolling with the tranquil vibe and living the good life in **Bucerías** (p87)
- Plunging into the clear waters of **Los Arcos** (p65) and **La Corbeteña** (p65) and exploring a colorful underwater world at two of Vallarta's premier scuba-diving sites

- AVERAGE JANUARY DAILY HIGH: 26°C | 78°F
- AVERAGE JULY DAILY HIGH: 33°C | 91°F
- TELEPHONE CODE: 322 / POPULATION: 220,000

HISTORY

Present-day Puerto Vallarta once belonged to pre-Hispanic Aztatlán, a term that refers to similar cultures that inhabited the region extending from Colima to Sinaloa. Archaeological evidence indicates these indigenous peoples had sophisticated agricultural techniques and were skilled ceramists. Historians know that Aztatlán flourished from around 900 to 1200, but little is known about its downfall.

Later came the so-called 'Banderas' (flags) era. Legend has it that in 1524 a contingent of 100 Spaniards led by Spanish conquistador Francisco Cortés de Buenaventura, the nephew of Hernán Cortés, found themselves in a standoff with about 20,000 Indians brandishing standards adorned with colorful plumage. The Spaniards were carrying a banner of their own bearing the image of the Holy Virgin. As the story goes, a ray of light miraculously struck the banner, casting a resplendent glow. Purportedly the natives were in such awe that they laid down their arms. At that point the area was christened the Bahía de Banderas (Bay of Flags).

In 1918 the settlement was named Vallarta, in honor of Ignacio Luis Vallarta, a former governor of the state of Jalisco.

Tourists started to trickle into Puerto Vallarta back in 1954 when Mexicana airlines started a promotional campaign and initiated the first flights here, landing on a dirt airstrip in Emiliano Zapata, an area that is now the center of Vallarta. A decade later, John Huston chose the nearby deserted cove of Mismaloya as a location for the film of Tennessee Williams' play *The Night of the Iguana*. Of his first visit, Huston later wrote: 'When I first came here, almost 30 years ago, Vallarta was a fishing village of some 2000 souls. There was only one road to the outside world – and it was impassable during the rainy season. I arrived in a small plane, and we had to buzz the cattle off a field outside town before setting down.' As production on the film commenced, Hollywood paparazzi descended on the town to report on the tempestuous romance between Richard Burton and Elizabeth Taylor, and Burton's co-star, Ava Gardner, also raised more than a few eyebrows. Puerto Vallarta suddenly became world-famous, with an aura of steamy tropical romance.

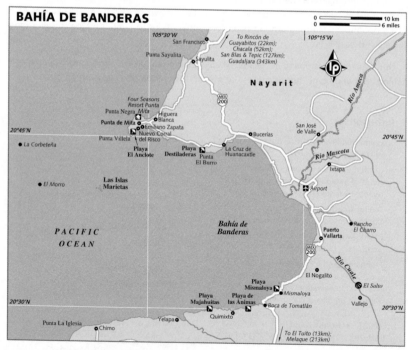

BAHÍA DE BANDERAS

BAHÍA DE BANDERAS

The Bay of Flags' coastline spans an impressive 96km, extending 60km along the shores of Jalisco and 36km into the bordering state of Nayarit. One of the largest bays in the world, it was supposedly formed by an extinct volcano slowly sinking into the ocean. It now has a depth of some 1800m and is home to an astounding variety of marine life.

Like many people reading this book, humpback whales come here to mate during the winter months. They leave their feeding grounds in Alaskan waters and show up in Mexico from around November to the end of March. Once they arrive, they form courtship groups, mate, or bear the calves that were conceived the year before. Although the mating rituals of humpbacks remain a mystery, they are thought to be promiscuous breeders. By the end of March, the whales' attention turns to the long journey back to their feeding grounds up north.

With the humpbacks gone, the giant manta rays take their turn. During the month of April you may catch sight of their antics as they jump above the water's surface, flashing their 4m-wide wings in acrobatic displays that you can sometimes see from boats or even from the shore.

Guillermo Wulff, an engineer from Mexico City, fell under Vallarta's spell in the late 1950s and began building houses in what would become known as Gringo Gulch and Mismaloya. In the late 1960s, as more and more visitors came to soak up the sun and expatriates put down roots, Jalisco governor Francisco Medina Ascencio took his vision for Puerto Vallarta's emergence as a world-class destination to President Gustavo Díaz Ordaz. The president enthusiastically embraced the plan.

Construction began on bridges and highways, banks were open for business and hotels sprouted from the sands of Playa Olas Altas.

When the peso was devalued in 1980, causing economic hardship for most of Mexico, large resort towns such as Puerto Vallarta prospered as tourists with pockets full of dollars streamed in for bargain vacations. Between 1980 and 1990 Puerto Vallarta's population doubled to reach 112,000. Through it all, the town's historic center managed to retain its vintage character, as new development was centered around the Marina Vallarta, completed in 1993. Today, Puerto Vallarta, a city of 220,000 people, has cemented its position on the A-list of international beach resorts, attracting nearly four million visitors per year.

ORIENTATION

Puerto Vallarta's historic center is bisected by the Río Cuale, which splits to encircle the long and narrow Isla Río Cuale. Two short road bridges, two rickety suspended bridges and a new beachside pedestrian bridge allow easy passage between the Zona Romántica and the Zona Centro.

North of the Río Cuale lies the more modern part of town, the Zona Centro, whose heart is the seaside Plaza Principal. The crown-topped steeple of the cathedral perches nearby. On a few long blocks paralleling the beachless *malecón* (waterfront street) are many modern boutiques, galleries, cafés, bars and restaurants, along with a few hotels. Avs Morelos and Juárez are Puerto Vallarta's two principal thoroughfares.

South of the Río Cuale is Puerto Vallarta's most picturesque district, the Zona Romántica (also called Old Town or Olas Altas), with hotels, boutiques, restaurants and bars. It has the only two beaches in the city center: Playa Olas Altas (which doesn't have 'high waves,' despite the name) and Playa de los Muertos (Beach of the Dead), which takes its strange name from a fierce fight there in the late 19th century.

North of the city is the Zona Hotelera, a strip of giant luxury hotels; Marina Vallarta, a large yachting marina (6.5km from the center); the airport (10km); the bus terminal (10.5km); and Nuevo Vallarta, a new resort area of hotel and condominium development (15km). To the south of the city, in a more natural setting than Zona Hotelera, are more large resorts and some of the most beautiful beaches in the area.

For details on getting to and from the airport, see p86.

Maps

Guía Roji publishes a detailed *Ciudad de Puerto Vallarta* map; it's available from major internet booksellers. Tourist maps are available at the tourist office (p60) and in many hotel lobbies.

INFORMATION

Puerto Vallarta is in Jalisco state, one hour ahead of nearby Nayarit, so set your watches forward an hour. Also note that any opening hours or days listed in this chapter, especially for restaurants or shops, reflect the busy winter season; in other seasons, hours and days tend to be more limited, with some businesses even closing down altogether.

Bookstores

A Page in the Sun Bookshop-Café (Map pp62-3; ☎ 222-36-08; cnr Olas Altas & Diéguez; ☼ 7am-midnight) Has the best selection of English-language books in town and brews a good cup of joe.

Librería Limón (Map pp62-3; ☎ 222-24-52; Carranza 315; ☼ 9am-8pm Mon-Sat) A small section of books in English, mostly of the best-seller variety.

Cultural Centers

Centro Cultural Cuale (☎ 223-00-95; Isla Río Cuale; ☼ 8am-8pm Mon-Fri, 9am-2pm Sat) Beautifully situated on Isla Río Cuale, this cultural center offers fine-arts workshops and music classes, such as lessons teaching you how to play Latin American instruments. Check out the schedule posted in the office for upcoming courses.

Emergency

The tourist police corps, dressed in white safari outfits with matching helmets, are easy to spot. You'll see the bilingual officers buzzing proudly around town in shiny

---

PUERTO VALLARTA IN...

Two Days

Breakfast on **Isla Río Cuale** (p61), then stop in at the **Museo del Cuale** (p61) or linger beneath shady rubber trees on the **Isla Río Cuale River Walk**. Spread out a towel on **Playa Olas Altas** (p61) or join the happy throng on the waterfront *malecón* and enjoy the **public sculptures** (p67). Linger over dinner at one of Vallarta's splendid **restaurants** (p76) and then hit one of the raucous late-night **dance clubs** (p81).

On day two get up early (yeah, right) and continue indulging in the pleasures of the city by **shopping** (p83) at markets and boutiques, or browsing at an **art gallery** (p84). Otherwise, take your pick from the many **outdoor adventures** (p64) on offer. Top things off with a candlelit meal at the **Marina Vallarta** (p79) and relish a panoramic bay view over nightcaps at the **El Faro Lighthouse Bar** (p81).

Four Days

To the two-day itinerary add an overnight trip to **Yelapa** (p98) or **Playa Majahuitas** (p99), remote getaways on the southern shores of Bahía de Banderas. Luxuriate in the sand, enjoy fresh *mariscos* (seafood), or perhaps take a rejuvenating hike to a waterfall. Along the way, stop in at the seaside communities of **Quimixto** (p98) and **Las Ánimas** (p98) for more snorkeling, hiking or beach bumming. All four beaches are accessible only by boat. If you decide to make a day trip to these beaches, set aside some time to visit a seasonal **sea-turtle camp** (p68), or venture out on a **whale-watching excursion** (p66).

One Week

Add on a day enjoying Puerto Vallarta's epic landscapes from astride a **mountain bike** (p67) or a **horse** (p66). Explore underwater at one of the area's great **diving** and **snorkeling sites** (p64) or test your skills while enjoying some world-class **sportfishing** (p64). For a restful retreat, head 6km southeast of Vallarta to El Nogalito and rid your body of party toxins at a *temascal* steam bath, a pre-Hispanic cleansing treatment (p95).

Take a day or two to enjoy one or more of the small waterfront communities north of town. Find new ways to relax in **Bucerías** (p87) with its less-crowded beaches or in **La Cruz de Huanacaxtle** (p92), a simple fishing village. Alternatively, learn or practice the art of surfing at **Playa El Anclote** (p93).

One Month

Start looking for an apartment.

PUERTO VALLARTA & AROUND

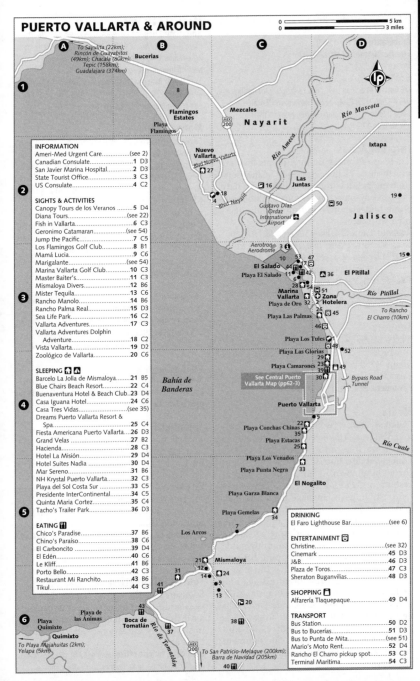

0 — 5 km
0 — 3 miles

To Sayulita (22km);
Rincón de Guayabitos
(49km); Chacala (80km);
Tepic (158km);
Guadalajara (374km)

Bucerías

Flamingos Estates

Playa Flamingos

Mezcales

Nayarit

Río Mascota

Ixtapa

Nuevo Vallarta

Blvd Nuevo Vallarta

Río Ameca

Las Juntas

Blvd Nayarit

Gustavo Díaz Ordaz International Airport

Jalisco

Aerotron Aerodrome

El Salado
Playa El Salado

Marina Vallarta

Zona Hotelera

Playa de Oro

El Pitillal

Río Pitillal

To Rancho El Charro (10km)

Playa Las Palmas

Playa Los Tules

Playa Las Glorias

Playa Camarones

See Central Puerto Vallarta Map (pp62-3)

Bypass Road Tunnel

Puerto Vallarta

Bahía de Banderas

Playa Conchas Chinas

Playa Estacas

Río Cuale

Playa Los Venados

Playa Punta Negra

El Nogalito

Playa Garza Blanca

Playa Gemelas

Los Arcos

Playa de las Ánimas

Playa Quimixto

Quimixto

To Playa Majahuitas (2km);
Yelapa (5km)

Boca de Tomatlán

Río de Tomatlán

Mismaloya

To San Patricio-Melaque (200km);
Barra de Navidad (205km)

INFORMATION
Ameri-Med Urgent Care................(see 2)
Canadian Consulate..........................1 D3
San Javier Marina Hospital................2 D3
State Tourist Office...........................3 C3
US Consulate....................................4 C2

SIGHTS & ACTIVITIES
Canopy Tours de los Veranos 5 D4
Diana Tours................................(see 22)
Fish in Vallarta................................6 C3
Geronimo Catamaran...................(see 54)
Jump the Pacific...............................7 C5
Los Flamingos Golf Club..................8 B1
Mamá Lucia.....................................9 C6
Marigalante................................(see 54)
Marina Vallarta Golf Club...............10 C3
Master Baiter's................................11 C3
Mismaloya Divers...........................12 B6
Mister Tequila.................................13 C6
Rancho Manolo................................14 B6
Rancho Palma Real..........................15 D3
Sea Life Park...................................16 C2
Vallarta Adventures........................17 C3
Vallarta Adventures Dolphin
  Adventure...................................18 C2
Vista Vallarta..................................19 D2
Zoológico de Vallarta......................20 C6

SLEEPING
Barcelo La Jolla de Mismaloya........21 B5
Blue Chairs Beach Resort................22 C4
Buenaventura Hotel & Beach Club..23 D4
Casa Iguana Hotel...........................24 C6
Casa Tres Vidas...........................(see 35)
Dreams Puerto Vallarta Resort &
  Spa...25 C4
Fiesta Americana Puerto Vallarta...26 D3
Grand Velas....................................27 B2
Hacienda..28 C3
Hotel La Misión..............................29 D4
Hotel Suites Nadia 30 D4
Mar Sereno.....................................31 B6
NH Krystal Puerto Vallarta.............32 C3
Playa del Sol Costa Sur...................33 C5
Presidente InterContinental............34 C5
Quinta Maria Cortez......................35 C4
Tacho's Trailer Park........................36 D3

EATING
Chico's Paradise..............................37 B6
Chino's Paraíso...............................38 C6
El Carboncito 39 D4
El Edén...40 C6
Le Kliff..41 B6
Porto Bello.....................................42 C3
Restaurant Mi Ranchito..................43 B6
Tikul...44 C3

DRINKING
El Faro Lighthouse Bar...................(see 6)

ENTERTAINMENT
Christine.....................................(see 32)
Cinemark..45 D3
J&B...46 D3
Plaza de Toros................................47 C3
Sheraton Buganvilias......................48 D3

SHOPPING
Alfarería Tlaquepaque.....................49 D4

TRANSPORT
Bus Station.....................................50 D2
Bus to Bucerías...............................51 D3
Bus to Punta de Mita....................(see 51)
Mario's Moto Rent..........................52 D4
Rancho El Charro pickup spot.........53 C3
Terminal Marítima..........................54 C3

ATVs (all-terrain vehicles) and on foot along the *malecón*.

Ambulance (☎ 222-15-33)
Fire Department (☎ 223-94-76)
Police (☎ 060)
Red Cross (☎ 065)
US Consulate (Map p59; ☎ 222-00-69, 24hr hotline 0133-3268-2145; Paseo de los Cocoteros 85, Local L-7, Paradise Plaza shopping center, Nuevo Vallarta; ⏱ 8:30am-12:30pm Mon-Fri)

Internet Access

There are so many internet places they are practically a plague, especially in the Zona Romántica. All of the places listed here have high-speed connections and air-conditioning. Some budget hotels and most midrangers offer wi-fi access.

Aquarius (Map pp62-3; Juárez 523; per hr M$15) A 24hr, air-conditioned cybercafé with long-distance phone service.
Ciber Milenium (Map pp62-3; Madero 370; per hr M$10; ⏱ 9am-10:30pm) Fast, cheap and cool.
PVC@fe.com (Map pp62-3; Olas Altas 250; per hr M$35; ⏱ 7am-1am) Wireless access, fast machines, good coffee and cheap internet calls.

Laundry

There are many laundries around town, most of which are closed on Sunday. They charge about M$50 per load.

Lavandería Cisne (Map pp62-3; Madero 407A)
Lavandería Elsa (Map pp62-3; Olas Altas 385)

Media

Vallarta Today (www.vallartatoday.com) and *Vallarta Tribune* (www.vallartatribune .com) are free, informative daily papers conceived for tourists; you'll find them throughout town in hotel lobbies and at restaurants. *Puerto Vallarta Lifestyles* is a quarterly English-language magazine with good maps, in-depth restaurant reviews, a complete real-estate section and information on shopping, art galleries, activities and tours. *Bay Vallarta* is a free monthly guide with useful culture and shopping listings. *Vallarta Map & Dining Guide* is the official guide for the local restaurant association, including a lengthy directory of restaurants and plenty of maps. *Gay Guide Vallarta* is an up-to-date, definitive guide to gay businesses and events. Good sources for info on hotels, tours, culture and entertainment options are www.visitpuertovallarta.com and www.pvmirror.com.

Medical Services

Ameri-Med Urgent Care (Map p59; ☎ 226-20-80; Plaza Neptuno, Marina Vallarta) A modern American-style hospital charging American-style fees. It advertises that US medical insurance is accepted.
San Javier Marina Hospital (Map p59; ☎ 226-10-10; Av Ascencio 2760) Vallarta's best-equipped hospital. You'll find it near Marina Vallarta.

Money

Most businesses in Vallarta accept US dollars as readily as they accept pesos, though the exchange rate is usually more favorable in banks. Several banks can be found around Plaza Principal, but they often have long queues. Most of the banks also have ATMs.

Vallarta has many *casas de cambio* (exchange houses); it may pay to shop around, since rates differ. Most are open around 9am to 7pm daily, sometimes with a 2pm to 4pm lunch break. Look for them on Insurgentes and Vallarta and along main thoroughfares.

Banamex (Map pp62-3; cnr Zaragoza & Juárez; ⏱ 9am-5pm Mon-Fri, 9am-2pm Sat) On the south side of the plaza (Western Union is also situated here).
Banorte ATM (Map pp62-3; cnr Díaz Ordaz & Domínguez)
Las Marietas Agencia de Cambio (Map pp62-3; Vallarta 247; ⏱ 9am-9pm) Gives decent exchange rates.

Post

Main post office (Map pp62-3; ☎ 222-63-08; Colombia 1014; ⏱ 8am-6pm Mon-Fri, 9am-1pm Sat) Send your postcards home from here.

Telephone

Vallarta has many *casetas telefónicas* (public telephone call stations), including one on Plaza Lázaro Cárdenas and another at Cárdenas 267. Public card phones are plentiful everywhere in town. Calling Canada or the USA isn't cheap – expect to pay at least M$10 per minute. The cheapest option is an internet café (see left).

Telecomm (Map pp62-3; Hidalgo 582; ⏱ 8am-7:30pm Mon-Fri, 9am-12:30pm Sat & Sun) Offers money transfers, faxes and phone service.

Tourist Information

Sponsored by the visitors bureau and tourist board, www.puertovallarta.net provides a wealth of information regarding lodging, activities, attractions, and vacation and car rentals.

Municipal tourist office (Map pp62-3; ☎ 226-80-80, ext 230; Municipal bldg, Juárez s/n; ⏱ 8am-8pm

Mon-Sat, 8am-6pm Sun) Vallarta's busy but competent office, at the northeast corner of Plaza Principal, has free maps, multilingual tourist literature and bilingual staff.

State tourist office (Dirección de Turismo del Estado de Jalisco; Map p59; ☎ 221-26-76, 221-26-80; www .visita.jalisco.gob.mx, in Spanish; Plaza Marina, Local 144 & 146; ☼ 9am-5pm Mon-Fri) In Marina Vallarta, this is the place to go for information about attractions throughout the state of Jalisco.

DANGERS & ANNOYANCES

Puerto Vallarta has an extraordinarily low crime rate, but police occasionally stop and frisk locals and tourists, checking for drugs.

Expect to be approached by the omnipresent touts who are intent on reeling in potential buyers to timeshare presentations. If you choose to attend a presentation – perhaps swayed by the promise of a free meal, tour or cruise – be prepared to fend off the 'hard sell.' And if you're tempted to buy, make absolutely sure you know what you're getting yourself into, lest you be paying off your vacation years into the future.

SIGHTS

With about 60km of precious coastline, it's no great secret why millions of visitors come to Puerto Vallarta each year. As one would expect, most of the action centers around the water, with activities such as scuba diving, deep-sea fishing, whale-watching, sailing and scenic cruises. The city also offers a growing number of museums, horseback riding in the mountains, and various cultural festivals throughout the year. Try fitting all that into a weeklong vacation.

Beaches

Only two beaches, **Playa Olas Altas** and **Playa de los Muertos** (Beach of the Dead) are handy to the city center; they're both south of the Río Cuale.

The most significant of the two is Playa de los Muertos, a mile-long stretch of yellow sand dotted by *palapa* (thatched-roof) restaurants and beachfront hotels. The surf is gentle and there's rarely an undertow, making for good swimming and family-friendly conditions. From the recently constructed pier at the terminus of Francisca Rodriguez, water taxis depart for destinations including Yelapa, Quimixto, Playa las Ánimas and Los Arcos islands. According to local legend, the Beach of the Dead was named for a grisly

battle fought here over a century ago between smugglers working in the gold and silver mines of the Río Cuale and the natives who tried to take their stolen booty from them. When the fight was over, or so the story goes, the beach was strewn with bodies (much as it is today!).

Trendy gay men head to the section of beach called **Blue Chairs**, at the southern end of Playa de los Muertos (there are blue, green and yellow chairs here). There are several gay hotels and bars there. For a more isolated gay beach, see p66.

North of town, the shoreline curves to the west all the way to Punta de Mita, many miles away. Beaches along the way include **Playa Camarones**, **Playa Las Glorias**, **Playa Los Tules**, **Playa Las Palmas** and **Playa de Oro**. Further north, at Marina Vallarta, is **Playa El Salado**. Nuevo Vallarta also has beaches and there are others, less developed, right around the bay to Punta de Mita. These places have a much more laidback vibe than Vallarta's main beaches.

For beaches further north or south of town, see North of Puerto Vallarta (p87) and South of Puerto Vallarta (p95).

Isla Río Cuale

The Río Cuale splits in two as it flows past the shores of this small island in the middle of town. During the rainy season, it's an impressive sight to see the twin rivers swell along the restaurant-dotted riverbank. The quiet island is a charming place shaded by old *hule de oro* (rubber) trees and it's where the city's earliest residents built their humble homes.

The **Museo del Cuale** (Map pp62-3; Paseo Isla Río Cuale s/n; admission free; ☼ 10am-6pm Tue-Sat), near the western end of Isla Río Cuale, has a collection of beautiful pottery, grinding stones, clay figurines and other ancient objects. Text panels are in Spanish and English.

Upstream you'll notice two rickety cable **suspension bridges** connecting the island to the Zona Romántica. As you pass over them, you'll need your sea legs: the bridges tend to buck and sway, particularly when some little rascal starts to shake it just as you reach the center.

You'll find it hard to resist the **Mercado de Artesanías** (p83), on the adjacent riverbank, as you progress up the island. Further on is **Plaza John Huston**, where a stoic bronze sculpture of the film icon sitting in his director's chair holds court.

CENTRAL PUERTO VALLARTA

0   0.2 miles
0   400 m

INFORMATION
A Page in the Sun Bookshop-Café....1 C7
Aquarius...2 E3
Banamex...3 D4
Banorte ATM...4 E2
Caseta Telefónica.................................5 D6
Centro Cultural Cuale...................(see 18)
Ciber Milenium..............................6 E6
Las Marietas Agencia de Cambio....7 D6
Lavandería Cisne.................................8 E6
Lavandería Elsa....................................9 C7
Librería Limón....................................10 D6
Main Post Office.................................11 F1
Municipal Tourist Office....................12 D4
PVC@fe.com..13 C7
Telecomm..14 E3

SIGHTS & ACTIVITIES
La Parroquia de Nuestra Señora de
 Guadalupe.......................................15 D4
Andale on the Bay Café....................16 C8
Banderas Scuba...................................17 C6
Centro Cultural Cuale.......................18 E5
Centro Cultural Vallartense..............19 E5
Centro de Estudios Para Extranjeros..20 D5
Eco Ride..21 E4
Ecotours de Mexico...........................22 D6
International Friendship Club............23 D5
Museo del Cuale.................................24 C5
Museo Histórico Naval......................25 D4
Plaza John Huston..............................26 E5
Voladores de Papantla.......................27 D3

SLEEPING
Abbey Hotel..28 C8
Casa Amorita......................................29 E4
Casa Andrea..30 C8
Casa de los Cuatro Vientos..............31 E3
Casa Dulce Vida.................................32 E3
Estancia San Carlos............................33 D6
Hacienda San Angel..........................34 E4
Hotel Ana Liz.....................................35 E6
Hotel Azteca......................................36 F6
Hotel Belmar......................................37 E6
Hotel Bernal.......................................38 E6
Hotel Cartagena de Indios................39 E6
Hotel Eloísa..40 C6
Hotel Emperador................................41 C8

River Cafe...91 D5
Steak House Brasil.............................92 C7
Trattoria Michel..................................93 C8
Trío..94 D5
Vista Grill..95 F8
Vitea..96 C4

DRINKING
Apaches...97 C8
Big Kahuna...98 C7
Burros Bar...99 C6
Café San Angel................................100 E2
Carlos O'Brian's................................101 E2
El Barril...102 D4
Encuentros..103 D6
Frida..104 E6
Funiculi...105 D6
La Bodeguita del Medio..............(see 76)
Los Molcajetes.................................106 D6
Memories Café.................................107 D3
Organic Café....................................108 E3
Steve's Sports Bar............................109 D7

ENTERTAINMENT
Anthropology....................................110 C5
Bar Sheona..111 E2
De Santos..112 D3
Hilo..113 D3
Kit Kat Klub......................................114 C8
La Cantina...115 D5
La Iguana..116 D6
La Noche...117 D6
La Regadera......................................118 E2
La Revolución...................................119 D5
Malafama..120 D3
Mañana..121 D7
Mandala..122 E2
Mariachi Loco...................................123 D6
Paco's Ranch.....................................124 D7
Palm..125 E1
Party Lounge.....................................126 C8
Sama Bar...127 C8
Santa Barbara Theater.....................128 C7
Zoo..129 E2

SHOPPING
Artesanías Flores..............................130 D6
Artículos Religiosos La Asunción....131 D5

Galería Omar Alonso........................138 E2
Galería Pacífico................................139 E3
Galería Uno......................................140 D3
Galería Vallarta................................141 D4
Huichol Collection............................142 D3
La Playa Vinos y Licores..................143 E2
Lucy's Cucu Cabaña.........................144 E7
Mercado de Artesanías....................145 D5
Mundo de Azulejos..........................146 E6
Mundo de Cristal.............................147 E7
Olinalá..148 D6
Patti Gallardo...................................149 D7
Peyote People...................................150 D4
Puerco Azul Galería.........................151 D7
Serafina...152 D7

Parque Hidalgo

Millennium

La Nostalgia

Nature as
Mother

Bahía de
Banderas

In Search
of Reason

Triton and
Nereida

Friendship
Fountain

Las Arcos &
Aquiles Serdán
Amphitheater

Plaza
Principal

Zona
Centro

La Rotunda
del Mar

Malecón

To Airport (9km),
Bus Station (11km),
Tepic (176km)

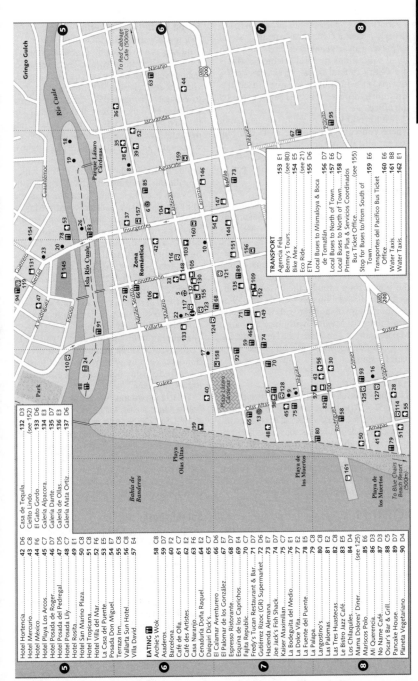

Continuing up the island, pay a visit to the gallery at **Centro Cultural Vallartense**, a small volunteer-run arts center offering classes and small exhibitions by local talent. Nearby is the **Centro Cultural Cuale** (8am-8pm Mon-Fri, 9am-2pm Sat), which offers classes in fine arts and music. Course schedules are posted by the office.

Just beyond is the rocky tip of the island, where you can gaze up the clear running stream and enjoy the refreshing breeze. If you're lucky, you'll catch a glimpse of a slow-moving iguana slinking through the trees.

Cathedral

On Hidalgo, one block from Plaza Principal, stands **La Parroquia de Nuestra Señora de Guadalupe** (Map pp62–3), named for Mexico's favorite – and the city's patron – saint. The simple brick architecture might seem austere were it not for the audacious crown that sprouts like a jaunty mushroom from the tower. Interestingly, the crown is modeled after that of Empress Carlota, the 19th-century Belgian-born royal who briefly administered Mexico with her husband, Maximilian, at the behest of Napoleon III. The cathedral's doors are unlocked from 9am to 5pm.

Naval Museum

The new **Museo Histórico Naval** (Map pp62-3; ☎ 223-53-57; Zaragosa 4; admission free; 9am-7:30pm Tue-Fri, 10am-2pm & 3-7:30pm Sat & Sun) on the boardwalk chronicles Mexico's maritime heritage and it's arrrrghuably the best place to practice bad pirate puns. Here you can check out maps charting 16th-century explorers' routes, old cannons, and models of Spanish galleons and modern Mexican naval ships.

ACTIVITIES

Puerto Vallarta is chock-full of activities. Head toward the sea for diving, snorkeling, windsurfing, fishing and sailing. (Most activities can be arranged on the beaches in front of any of the large hotels.) Parasailing is also very popular, but there have been some accidents in the past and the activity should be considered potentially hazardous. Turn inland to ride horses, play golf, drive off-road or do some mountain biking. For the sedate, wildlife-watching boat tours and scenic cruises are a good option; some include meals and plenty of drinks.

Scuba Diving & Snorkeling

Below the warm, tranquil waters of Bahía de Banderas is a world of stingrays, tropical fish and garishly colored corals. The most spectacular spots for diving are Los Arcos (opposite), the rocky islands in the bay just south of town (now a protected ecological zone), and Las Islas Marietas (right), at the entrance to the bay, surrounded by impressive reefs, underwater caves, tunnels and walls. Dolphins, whales and giant manta rays are often sighted between December and April. Most folks get to Los Arcos via a boat tour or a hired skiff.

Vallarta has several diving operators. Most dives include transportation, gear and light meals. Water is clearest from May to November, with peak clarity in October and November. Operators also offer certification courses and snorkeling trips (which usually means snorkelers tag along with divers).

Banderas Scuba (Map pp62-3; ☎ 223-41-03; www .mexicoscuba.com; Cárdenas 230; snorkeling M$250, 2-tank dive trip M$750-1500, PADI open-water certification M$2900) specializes in small-group excursions to both well- and lesser-known sites. It offers lessons from beginning to advanced levels. For a challenging dive, inquire about trips to La Corbeteña (M$1350 minimum three divers). Banderas recommends you have at least 30 dives under your belt before venturing out to La Corbeteña.

Vallarta Adventures (Map p59; ☎ 297-12-12; www .vallarta-adventures.com; Marina Vallarta; 2-tank dive trip M$850-1250, PADI open-water certification M$5720) has 'gold-palm' instructors who take you to Islas Marietas and Caletas. It also does tours (p69) for more experienced divers to El Morro and La Corbeteña, locations known for their steep walls, deep canyons and waters teeming with colorful tropical fish.

Sportfishing

Deep-sea fishing is popular all year, with a major international sailfish tournament held every November. Prime catches are sailfish, marlin, tuna, red snapper and sea bass. Fishing trips can be arranged dockside at Marina Vallarta or in many of the surrounding municipalities. Moreover, *pangas* (motorized skiffs) can be hired on the beach in front of several major hotels, including Hotel Playa Los Arcos (Map pp62–3) on Playa de Los Muertos and NH Krystal (Map p59) on Playa de Oro. The going rate runs between M$400 and M$500 per hour for trips of two to three

TOP DIVING SITES

Puerto Vallarta is regarded as one of the Pacific coast's finest diving destinations. Any diving provider here worth its salt offers trips to the following roundly celebrated diving sites.

El Morro

Just beyond the northernmost waters of the bay, 42km north of Puerto Vallarta, this secluded dive site (Map p56) offers thrills to advanced divers. Humpback whales, sailfish, dolphins and even the occasional whale shark are spotted here. Equally grand is the underwater landscape, characterized by a good collection of pinnacles and caves.

Las Islas Marietas

These beautiful islands (Map p56), nearly 34km from Puerto Vallarta on the north side of the bay, are a diver's dream. Underwater caves and coral reefs shelter great hordes of tropical fish, and whale, dolphin and giant manta-ray sightings are common. Invariably, divers are monitored by personable blue-footed boobies watching from the rocks. Between dives, the divers stretch out on Playa del Amor and count their blessings.

Los Arcos

Far and away the most popular diving destination in Bahía de Banderas, and a protected National Underwater Park, Los Arcos (Map p59) is a picturesque spot that features gnarly granite formations rising from the sea. Near the largest of the arches you'll enjoy good visibility and depths ranging from 8m to 20m. Follow the shelf to the edge and hover over the abyss of Devil's Canyon, which drops off to a jaw-dropping 600m.

Playa Majahuitas

At the southern end of the bay and accessible only by boat is the hidden cove of Majahuitas (Map p56). In between dives you'll disembark and linger on the beach at Quimixto over lunch. Back in the water, divers commonly spot manta rays, dolphins, any number of brightly colored tropical fish, and eels darting in and out of black coral.

Chimo

You're not likely to have to mingle with those pesky snorkelers at the dive sites near this small fishing village (Map p56), which lies 42km from Puerto Vallarta on the bay's southern coast. Giant manta rays are plentiful during the winter months, and great swarms of tropical fish are a sure bet all year long. Its most remarkable feature, however, is the amazing pinnacles rising from a wide underwater plateau called Torrecillas.

La Corbeteña

Considered one of the choicest diving spots, this group of rocky pinnacles lies about 56km northwest of Vallarta, or roughly 1½ hours by boat. Instructors recommend this spot for experienced divers only. Visibility often exceeds 30m, allowing you to spot giant manta rays, moray eels, tuna and the occasional hammerhead shark. Best of all, since amateur divers steer clear of these waters, you're likely to have the area entirely to yourself.

hours. Equipment and bait is included, but you may have to negotiate for cold drinks!

The good folks at **Master Baiter's** (Map p59; ☎ 222-40-43; www.masterbaiters.com.mx; Paseo de la Marina 245, Local 118, Marina Vallarta; charters M$2750-14,000) say, 'We won't jerk you around.' Silly taglines aside, these guys take their sportfishing seriously. Prices vary considerably depending on the size of the charter boat, the location and the number of hours you want to spend at sea. The company strongly promotes catch-and-release fishing for billfish.

Again, prices at **Fish in Vallarta** (Map p59; ☎ 209-18-81, in the US & Canada 619-241-4851; www.fishinvallarta.com; Las Palmas 1, Local 19, Marina Vallarta; 8hr per boat M$5500-8000) fluctuate depending on what kind of charter you have in mind. Most people opt for an eight-hour trip on an 11m

(36ft) Allure or a 10m (32ft) Bertram. Also on offer are luxury packages for more experienced fishers. Rates include live bait, lures, Shimano and Penn gear, and fishing licenses. The family-run operation has experienced, bilingual captains.

See p87 for information on hiring private yachts or *pangas*.

Cruises

Vallarta's daytime, sunset and evening cruises usually involve eating and drinking, and lots of it! Some cross the bay to the nearby beaches of Yelapa and Las Ánimas, while some head further out to Las Islas Marietas. Prices start at M$400 for sunset cruises and beach trips. Longer trips lasting four to six hours, with meals and bottomless cocktails, will set you back M$750 to M$850. To pick the right cruise, ask your fellow travelers or inquire at the tourist office.

Marigalante (Map p59; ☎ 223-03-09; www.marigalante.com.mx; Díaz Ordaz 770, Marina Vallarta; adult/child M$850/350; ☼ day cruise Mon-Sat 9am-3:30pm, night cruise 6-10pm; ☗) is a reproduction Spanish galleon that hosts pirate-themed booze cruises on the bay. The price of admission includes an open bar and typical swashbuckler fare such as barbecued chicken and shrimp brochettes. On the day cruise you can get some snorkeling in at Playa Majahuitas. The evening cruise, which is more geared toward adults, features a pre-Hispanic show and culminates with a mock pirate attack and an onboard fiesta. The boat departs from the Terminal Maritima, opposite Sam's Club. Get there one hour prior to departure.

On Thursday **Diana Tours** (Map p59; ☎ 222-50-40; ☼ 9:30am-5pm) offers an all-day gay and lesbian cruise to Playa las Animas and Los Arcos, with plenty of food, snorkeling and an open bar (M$750). Not that you'll need another drink, but if you do, join your group for a post-cruise cocktail on the rooftop bar of the Blue Chairs Beach Resort (p75).

Geronimo Catamaran (Map p59; ☎ 222-49-35; www.puertovallartatours.com; Marina Vallarta; tours adult/child M$800/400) sails a large two-hulled vessel to Las Islas Marietas. The seven-hour tour includes continental breakfast, lunch, open bar, snorkeling gear and kayaking on the beach. It departs from the Terminal

Maritima. Get there at 8:30am and be sure to reserve in advance.

Dolphin- & Whale-Watching

A frequent, year-round visitor to Bahía de Banderas, the Pacific bottlenose dolphin is often seen leaping out of the water or gliding along the bows of boats. Kids and adults can enjoy close encounters with Pacific bottlenose dolphins, in either a lagoon or a special pool, courtesy of Vallarta Adventures Dolphin Adventure (p68). There's something for tots here too.

Whale-watching trips operate from December to March, when humpback whales are in the bay mating, bearing young and caring for new calves (p57). Vallarta Adventures (p69) does 4½-hour whale-watching trips (M$1105). A spotter plane stays in contact with the boat operators, which nearly guarantees whale sightings.

Horseback Riding

Explore Vallarta's jungly mountains from the privileged perspective of horseback. Most stables charge around M$150 per hour or roughly M$1000 for a full-day excursion.

For a short ride suitable for children, there are sometimes horses for rent around Playa Olas Altas, near the western end of Carranza.

Rancho El Charro (Map p56; ☎ 224-01-14; www.ranchoelcharro.com; ride M$610-1200; ☗) is recommended for its healthy horses and scenic three- to eight-hour trots into the Sierra Madres. Several rides are conceived for kids. Setting this ranch apart from its competitors is the all-inclusive four-day excursion, which includes meals and lodging at the colonial-style Hacienda Jalisco (M$8750). The tour requires a four-person minimum and is offered from November to May. Reaching Rancho El Charro is difficult without a car. You can call El Charro and make arrangements to be picked up at the **Collage Club** (Calle Proa s/n), off Blvd Ascencio, at the entrance of Marina Vallarta.

In the village of Las Palmas, 40 minutes by car northeast of Puerto Vallarta, **Rancho Palma Real** (Map p59; ☎ 222-05-01; Carretera Vallarta-Tepic; rides from M$800) offers two off-the-beaten-track routes and a popular excursion to **El Salto**, a lovely jungle waterfall. Its office is on Carretera Vallarta, about five minutes north of the airport.

Golf

Vallarta has many attractive options for a day on the links. Most acclaimed is the Jack Nicklaus–designed **Four Seasons Punta Mita** (Map p56; ☎ 291-60-00; www.fourseasons.com/puntamita/golf .html; green fees M$3612), where golfers are blissfully distracted from the challenging course by sweeping ocean vistas. One hole is on a natural island and requires the use of an amphibious golf cart.

Home of the 2002 World Cup tournament, **Vista Vallarta** (Map p59; ☎ 290-00-30; www.vistavallar tagolf.com; Circuito Universidad 653; green fees M$2522) has two 18-hole, par-72 courses designed by golf legends Jack Nicklaus and Tom Weiskopf.

Designed by famed golf-course architect Joe Finger, **Marina Vallarta Golf Club** (Map p59; ☎ 221-00-

73; www.marinavallartagolf.com; Paseo de la Marina 430; green fees M$1130-1526) has an exclusive 18-hole, par-71 course, just north of Marina Vallarta.

Los Flamingos Golf Club (Map p59; ☎ 329-296-50-06; www.flamingosgolf.com.mx; Hwy 200 s/n; green fees M$1210) is a recently renovated 72-par championship course, with nine water hazards and 43 bunkers. You'll find it 13km north of town.

Mountain Biking

Head to Vallarta's verdant hillsides for some adrenaline-fueled pedaling.

The adventure-loving **Eco Ride** (Map pp62-3; ☎ 222-79-12; www.ecoridemex.com; Miramar 382; rentals per day M$250, tours M$500-1400) leads guided cycling tours suited to beginners and badasses alike. All are one-day rides. The most challenging

---

BOARDWALK STROLL

Puerto Vallarta's *malecón,* the broad seawall boardwalk that stretches the length of downtown Vallarta, woos hopeless romantics with its enticing sunset strolls. Even if you're not feeling the love, join the cheerful throng anyway. You can walk off all those guilty indulgences as you check out the collection of bronze public sculptures. Or there's the less taxing option of taking a seat at the open-air theater and watching the clowns and mimes work the crowd.

You'll find the **Aquiles Serdán Amphitheater**, also known as **Los Arcos** (The Arches), on the south end of the beachfront boulevard. In addition to clown routines, there's often live music and folkloric dance.

Just north are the three leaping dolphins known as the **Friendship Fountain**, by California artist James 'Bud' Bottoms. It was installed in 1987 as a gift to Vallarta from sister city Santa Barbara.

Every seaside city on Mexico's Pacific coast has at least one mermaid statue, but few are as lovely as Italian artist Carlos Espino's **Triton and Nereida**, depicting two wistful lovers reaching for each other. Triton, son of Neptune, and his sea nymph mate, Nereida, took their place on the *malecón* in 1990.

Vallarta's most recognizable statue is Rafael Zamarripa's **Caballero del Mar** (the Seahorse), featuring a naked boy riding bareback on a 3m-tall seahorse. The original sculpture, once located at the end of Playa de los Muertos, was tossed into the drink by Hurricane Kenna in 2002, and was so missed that Zamarripa was quickly commissioned to create a new one.

With the installation of Guadalajara artist Sergio Bustamente's **In Search of Reason** in 1990, *malecón* statuary took a sharp left turn into surrealism. Two pillow-headed children climb a ladder leading to nowhere, as their robed mother directs them from the sidewalk. Passersby are irresistibly drawn to follow the puff-headed imps up the rungs.

Similarly interactive and even more bizarre is Alejandro Colunga's transcendent installation **La Rotunda del Mar**. Six mutant alien sea-creatures with clawed feet, serrated spines and prodigious posteriors take the shape of high-backed chairs; to sit on one of these bizarre thrones is an oddly mystical – or perhaps just odd – experience. Nearby is a bench seemingly composed of eyes, ears and feet.

Representing the cycle of life and death, Tapatio Adrian Reynoso's **Nature as Mother** offers a spiraling wave on a snail for your reflection. Further on is Ramiz Barquet's well-loved **La Nostalgia**, a romantic bronze rendering of the artist and his wife.

The stroll concludes at one of Vallarta's most audacious sculptures, Mathis Lídice's **Millennium**, adjacent to the Hotel Rosita. Depicting a host of mythic figures emerging from a wave and crowned by a buxom nude offering a dove to the sky, the whole thing looks like it's about to topple into the sea.

is a 50km hair-raising expedition from El Tuito, a small town at 1100m elevation, through Chacala and down to the beach in Yelapa. The views are stunning along the way. Other tours include an easy trip to Vallejo, a typical local village, and a technical ride to El Salto waterfall.

Bike Mex (Map pp62-3; ☎ 223-18-34; Guerrero 361; ⏱ 8:30am-4pm Mon-Sat) runs quite a few hiking and mountain-biking tours using experienced bilingual guides. Tours are tailored to your level of fitness and experience. A four-hour bike ride takes you up into the mountains along the Río Cuale (M$680). Mountain-bike rentals are available for M$300 per day. Oscar, the owner, is a virtual Puerto Vallarta encyclopedia.

Bungee Jumping

Jump the Pacific (Map p59; ☎ 228-06-70; www.val larta-action.com; jump M$600; ⏱ 10am-6pm) promises that 'If the cord breaks, your next jump is free.' Even better, survivors get the second jump for half-price. From a platform jutting out over the sea cliffs, it's a 40m plunge. It's 9km southwest of Puerto Vallarta on the road to Mismaloya.

COURSES

Centro de Estudios Para Extranjeros (CEPE; Map pp62-3; ☎ 223-20-82; www.spanish-spanish.info; Libertad 105-1) Courses range from M$1240 for a week of basic tourist Spanish to M$5000 for a month of university credit courses. Private instruction costs M$250 per hour. The center, associated with the Universidad de Guadalajara, provides lodging for M$400 per night and also arranges homestays with local families. Two 'content courses' are offered in English: one focuses on Mexican culture from an anthropological standpoint, the other on modern Mexican history. After class, hit the streets and put the day's lesson into practice.

PUERTO VALLARTA FOR CHILDREN

Kids go hog wild with all the animal attractions in Vallarta.

Ecotours de Mexico (Map pp62-3; ☎ 222-66-06; www.ecotoursvallarta.com; Vallarta 243; adult/child M$520/390) From August through December this operator leads visitors to a crocodile habitat and a sea-turtle camp in one fell swoop. The trip begins at El Quelele, a marshy lagoon home to the American crocodile. Later you head to the coast to observe olive ridley sea-turtle hatchlings scurrying into the sea. The meeting point is at Ecotours'

downtown office at 4:30pm. Kids also get a big kick out of Ecotours' wild dolphin-watching trips (adult/child M$750/550).

Sea Life Park (Map p59; ☎ 297-07-08; www .sealifeparkvallarta.com; Hwy 200, Km 155; adult/child M$180/140; ⏱ 10am-6pm) Here kids can swim and interact with dolphins and sea lions, and shoot down 10 different water slides.

Vallarta Adventures Dolphin Adventure (Map p59; ☎ 297-12-12; www.vallarta-adventures.com/dolphins; Av Las Palmas 39, Nuevo Vallarta) You and the little ones can experience thrilling close encounters with Pacific bottlenose dolphins in either a lagoon or a special pool, ranging in price from M$800 to M$2800. A new offering is the Dolphin Kids program for tots aged four to eight, where participants enjoy a thrilling, educational encounter with dolphin babies and their proud mothers.

Zoológico de Vallarta (Map p59; ☎ 228-05-01; www .zoologicodevallarta.com; Camino al Eden 700; adult/child M$100/50; ⏱ 10am-6pm) Carved out of the surrounding jungle, this small zoo houses about 350 animals, including black jaguars, crocodiles and the endangered golden eagle. It's a short run through the zoo, but children get to feed and pet some of their new furry friends along the way.

TOURS

Canopy Tours de los Veranos (Map p59; ☎ 223-05-04; www.canopytours-vallarta.com; cnr Insurgentes & Diéguez; adult/child M$798/585; ⏱ hourly 9am-2pm) This operator takes you to an extensive zip-line course at an ecopark near Mismaloya. The tour includes swimming and lunch at a riverside seafood restaurant.

Ecotours de Mexico (Map pp62-3; ☎ 222-66-06; www .ecotoursvallarta.com; Vallarta 243) One of Vallarta's first ecotour operators. Professional guides lead you on a wide range of outings, including five-hour sea-kayaking trips (adult/child M$900/670), four-hour whale-watching excursions (adult/child M$960/720) and bird-watching outings in the mountains of Mismaloya (M$800).

International Friendship Club (Map pp62-3; ☎ 222-54-66; www.ifcpv.com; Libertad 13; ⏱ office 9am-1pm Mon-Fri) Offers five-hour tours on Thursdays that take you to the lovely Puerto Vallarta Botanical Gardens, where you can see more than 3000 plant species in a mountainous setting. It's also an ideal spot for bird-watching. The excursion includes lunch at the gardens and stops at some of Vallarta's most luxurious private homes. If you just want to visit the homes, go on the three-hour tour (M$350) on Wednesday. The weekly outings are on offer from November through April. Transportation departs from Andale on the Bay Café (Map pp62–3; Olas Altas 503) at 10:30am. Get there earlier to purchase tickets.

Puerto Vallarta Tours (☎ 222-49-35, in the US 866-217-9074; www.puertovallartatours.net) For an ample offering of land and water tours, call or visit the website.

Vallarta Adventures (Map p59; ☎ 297-12-12, in the US 888-303-2653; www.vallarta-adventures.com; Marina Vallarta) Offers canopy adventures (adult/child M$1027/385), wild dolphins and snorkeling trips (adult/child M$910/455) and romantic dinner shows including open bar on Las Caletas beach (M$850). On the four-hour canopy tour, thrillseekers can whoosh from tree to tree on zip lines strung high above the forest floor, among hanging wild orchids, native birds and reptiles.

FESTIVALS & EVENTS

In March the Vallarta Yacht Club presents the **J/24 World Sailing Championship** on the bay, drawing many boating aficionados from Mexico and abroad.

Semana Santa (Holy Week), running from Palm Sunday to Easter Sunday, is the busiest holiday of the year in Puerto Vallarta. Hotels fill up and hundreds (or thousands) of excess visitors camp out on the beaches and party. Prepare to suffer through many hangovers.

Festival Cultural de Mayo, a city-wide fair with cultural and sporting events, music concerts, carnival rides and art exhibits, is held throughout May.

In September Puerto Vallarta stages several events commemorating **Mexican independence**. On **Charro Day** (September 14), Mexican men and women on horseback ride with great élan through the streets wearing traditional *charro* (cowboy) attire. In the evening at various *charro* rings, there are bullfights, calf-roping and other spectacles. The lively **Independence Eve** celebration takes place on the 15th. From a balcony at city hall, the mayor oversees the lighting of the flame of independence and then leads a parade through town. At 11pm the central plaza fills with revelers belting out the traditional *grito* (shout; ¡*Viva México!*), followed by

an impressive fireworks display over the bay. The next day, a national holiday, sees more colorful parades and festivities in the streets.

November is a busy month for the local cultural calendar, with the city-wide **Festival de las Artes**, featuring a month-long series of gallery exhibitions and beachside theater performances. Gourmets come from far and wide to celebrate the annual 10-day **Puerto Vallarta Gourmet Festival** (www.festivalgourmet.com), held mid-month. Showcasing the talents of local chefs and guest chefs from around the world, the festival features gourmet cooking classes, wine tastings and other delicious events.

Día de Santa Cecilia (November 22) honors the patron saint of mariachis, with all the city's mariachis forming a musical procession to the cathedral in the early evening. They come playing and singing, enter the church and sing homage to their saint, then go out into the plaza and continue to play. During the entire day one or another group of mariachis stays in the church making music.

Held each year in mid-November, the **Torneo Internacional de Pez Vela y Marlin** (International Sailfish & Marlin Tournament; www.fishvallarta.com) celebrated its 50th anniversary in 2005; dates vary according to the phase of the moon, which must be right for fishing.

In December the city hosts the **Puerto Vallarta Film Festival** (www.vallartafilmfestival.com), with screenings of Mexican and international movies. All Mexico celebrates **Día de Nuestra Señora de Guadalupe** (December 12) in honour of the country's patron saint, the Virgen de Guadalupe. In Puerto Vallarta the celebrations are more drawn out, with pilgrimages and processions to the cathedral day and night from December 1 until the big bash on the 12th.

AERIALISTS OF THE GODS

Bringing considerable excitement to the *malecón*, the **Voladores de Papantla** (Papantla Flyers) enact a pre-Hispanic religious ritual wherein four men attached by ropes swing upside down with open arms from an 18m pole. A fifth man balanced at the pole's zenith plays a hand-carved flute to represent the songs of birds, or beats a *tambor* (drum) to evoke the voice of God. The ritual is tied to an ancient Totonaca legend in which the gods commanded 'You shall dance. We will watch.'

The four men signify the four cardinal points, and the pole represents the fertility goddess Tlazoleotl. Each of the four *voladores* flies 13 times around the pole for a total of 52 revolutions, evoking the 52 years of the Mayan calendar's solar cycle. Thus, the ritual is performed as a spiritual gift to the gods so that a new sun can be born.

The Voladores de Papantla perform every half-hour Monday through Friday from 7pm to 11pm and on Saturday and Sunday from 6pm to 11pm.

SLEEPING

Vallarta's hotels cater to all tastes and budgets. Some of the best deals in town can be found in the Zona Romántica and north of the Río Cuale. If you've got the urge to splurge, check out the luxurious digs in Marina Vallarta, Mismaloya and Nuevo Vallarta. Many of the pricier hotels offer all-inclusive meal plans and mainly target package tours. These are best reserved through a travel agent or on the internet, as rates are considerably lower than the 'walk-in' rates quoted in this book. The true gems at the top end are Puerto Vallarta's good selection of special, small and stylish places, which provide a good alternative for those looking for something more intimate.

Prices here reflect the mid-December to mid-April high season; low-season rates can fall 20% to 50%. For accommodation at Vallarta's busiest times – during Semana Santa or at Christmas and New Year's – reserve in advance, and be prepared to pay 20% to 40% more than the prices listed here. The most expensive hotels will most likely tack on almost 18% in taxes, so ask beforehand if these are included. Many budget and some midrange establishments only charge the IVA and ISH taxes if you require a receipt. And remember, if you plan on staying a week or more, negotiate for a better rate; monthly rates can cut your rent by half.

South of the Río Cuale

BUDGET

South of the Río Cuale on Calle Madero are clustered many of Vallarta's most economical hotels, ranging from gloomy to good. They are a bit far from the action, but the prices are right.

Hotel Azteca (Map pp62-3; ☎ 222-27-50; Madero 473; s/d/tr/apt M$250/300/400/500) This old-timer has seen better days, but you can't shake a stick at the price. The rather dark rooms surround an intimate, shady palm-potted courtyard. Some of the larger setups have kitchens, dining tables and desks. All have fans, old tile floors and small bathrooms, and they're kept fairly clean. On the roof are a few simple chairs and tables, affording tremendous views over the town and into the mountains. Also on the roof is a small and bright apartment with a kitchen and two beds, offering privacy.

Hotel México (Map pp62-3; ☎ 223-56-12; Carranza 466; s/d/tr M$300/350/450; 🖵) The bright orange entry-

way of this recently remodeled budget hotel feels like summertime all year round. Inside you'll find a sunny, albeit austere, courtyard surrounded by 21 rooms with simple furnishings, fans and cable TV. With the exception of those facing the street, most of the rooms, unfortunately, are rather dark. Looking at the glass half-full, this serves to keep down the temperature.

Hotel Cartagena de Indias (Map pp62-3; ☎ 222-69-14; hotelcartagenapv@yahoo.com.mx; Madero 428; s/d/tr M$300/350/400) It's bare basics here, but at least you get cable TV and air-conditioning if you're willing to cough up an additional M$100. Ask for a room with a balcony; they're brighter and more pleasant than the interior digs. Singles are tiny, however. The hotel provides no internet access and, as you may have guessed, no chocolate on the pillow at turndown.

Other cheapies:

Hotel Ana Liz (Map pp62-3; ☎ 222-17-57; Madero 429; s/d M$250/350) Look on the bright side: the dark, less-than-stellar digs here get you out of the hotel room.

Hotel Bernal (Map pp62-3; ☎ 222-36-05; Madero 423; s/d M$300/350) An old standby with dark rooms around a courtyard.

MIDRANGE

Hotel Hortencia (Map pp62-3; ☎ 222-24-84; www.hotel hortencia.com; Madero 336; s/d/tr/q M$400/450/500/550; 🖵) The attentive service at this family-run hotel puts it several notches above the other older hotels in the neighborhood. An excellent budget option, this place offers 23 pleasant rooms on three floors set around a plain, open courtyard. Each room comes with at least one double bed, cable TV and ceiling fan, and some have a fridge. The front rooms have balconies but suffer from street noise; if you crave quiet, take one of the inside rooms. The more expensive rooms have air-con, and one on offer features a kitchen. In the small lobby, you'll find the family chatting with the guests over coffee.

Hotel Villa del Mar (Map pp62-3; ☎ 222-07-85; www .hvilladelmar.com; Madero 440; s/d/tr/apt M$400/455/510/580) This one-of-a-kind budget place resembling a brick fortress came into its own in the 1970s and hasn't changed much since. Along the way someone applied an awful lot of paint that is not quite orange and not quite pink. The owners keep this hotel spick-and-span – the air is heavy with disinfectant. The cheapest rooms are tiny and dour with little light; you're better off dropping an extra couple of bucks for one with a terrace. On the roof are two desirable apartments with kitchenettes, a moon deck and nooks and crannies good for relaxing with a book. Bring the laptop; there's wi-fi.

Hotel Posada Lily (Map p62-3; ☎ 222-00-32; Badillo 109; s/d M$400/600) So you want to reserve your limited funds for two-for-one margaritas at dusk? Well, you could choose to slumber in one of the very cheap guesthouses several blocks from the beach, or you could spend a few pesos more and take up residence at this amazingly priced option just off the beach. It's a no-brainer. Sure, it's plain, but the 18 rooms are clean and pleasant with fridge, TV and good light. The larger rooms have three beds – bring your friends! – and there are small balconies overlooking the street. The simple, hand-painted decorations and chintzy paintings are icing on the cake. Just don't ask for room service.

Posada Don Miguel (Map pp62-3; ☎ 222-45-40; www .posadadonmiguel.com.mx; Insurgentes 322; s/d M$400/650; ✄ ✿) This place has rooms so large you can do three cartwheels down their length. They'd be better if stocked with more furniture, but remain a good deal. Kitchenettes, air-con and TV are available for extra, but there's no internet. Have a splash in the small pool.

Hotel Belmar (Map p62-3; ☎ 223-18-72; www.belmar vallarta.com; Insurgentes 161; s/d/tr M$450/600/700, with air-con add M$60; ✄ ✿) One of the choicest budget places in town, this colorful hotel near the Río Cuale offers clean and comfy rooms with few frills but plenty of personality. The Belmar has long served budget-minded travelers with rooms providing simple comfort. They have tiled floors, TVs with cable, ceiling fans and miniature bathrooms; they are a bit small but cozy in their austerity. Snag one with a balcony or, better yet, one of the corner units to take advantage of cross-ventilation. Well-chosen art and simple decor add a small flourish. The brightly painted lobby devotes considerable wall space to extravagant original works of art, and the owners will gladly act as your emissaries to Puerto Vallarta's thriving art scene.

Hotel Posada de Roger (Map pp62-3; ☎ 222-06-39; www.hotelposadaderoger.com; Badillo 237; s/d/tr/q M$600/650/700/800; ✄ ✿) This four-story guesthouse comes with some good guest hangout spots, such as a 2nd-floor pool and plant-filled courtyards. Mazelike outside hallways surround clean rooms with TV, dark wood furniture and – if you're lucky – a balcony.

This was one of the first backpacker haunts in town, and folks still talk about the lascivious free spirits that used this place as their hive in the 1970s. The large and shady courtyard with its dripping fountain is a perfect place to escape the heat and compare tales with other travelers. On the 2nd floor, the motif of repose is extended with a small pool and plenty of chaise longues. The rooms are pleasant enough, with phones, well-worn furniture, diminutive TVs and creaky ceiling fans. For brightness and cross-ventilation, choose the rooms overlooking the street. The posada has been gradually remodeling its rooms as it replaces aging air-con units and spruces up the bathrooms. There's wi-fi access in the lobby.

Hotel Emperador (Map pp62-3; ☎ 222-17-67; www.ho telemperadorpv.com; Amapas 114; d M$733-800, ste M$1356-2778; ✄ ✿ ✿) This up-to-date beach hotel on Playa de los Muertos gives a lot of bang for your buck with thoughtfully designed rooms and suites, many with incomparable views of the coast. The fresh oceanfront rooms celebrate the sea with large balconies complete with dining tables and kitchenettes for preparing and eating food alfresco. Each tiled unit is furnished with fridge, king-sized bed and sleeper couch, as well as air-con, cable TV and in-room phones. The hotel recently added a rooftop Jacuzzi overlooking an ideal swimming beach, where mariachi bands stroll about looking for business and drum circles coalesce in the sweaty heat of the afternoon.

Vallarta Sun Hotel (Map pp62-3; ☎ 223-15-23; www .vallartasunsuites.com; Rodríguez 169; d M$790; ✄ ✿ ✿) Perched atop a quiet hill just two blocks from the beach, this adults-only hotel has 20 units done up with rustic wood furnishings, tiled floors and hand-carved headboards. They are spiffy and attractive, with fridges, microwaves and two double beds, or a queen-sized bed and sofa bed. Six open up to an attractive pool, while the brighter upstairs units have balconies, several offering terrific sea views. The hillside location catches the ocean breezes, providing a measure of relief on scorching-hot days. It has secure covered parking, wireless internet and frequent promotions.

Hotel Eloisa (Map pp62-3; ☎ 222-64-65; www.hoteleloisa .com; Cárdenas 179; s/d/tr/ste M$840/924/994/1680; ✄ ✿) With a great location just off the beach, this recently renovated hotel, with 69 rooms and eight luxury suites, has an understated charm. The standard rooms are pleasingly decorated with rustic furniture, tiled floors and two double beds. The suites have eye-catching tiled bathrooms and kitchens, and bright sitting areas, good for entertaining. Some feature terrific sea views. Up on the roof, you'll find a small pool, plenty of room for luxurious sunbathing, and gratifying views over the town. Rooms with air-conditioning and TVs cost an additional M$108.

Hotel Suites Nadia (Map p59; ☎ 222-52-52; www .hotelsuitesnadia.com; Uruguay 127; s/d/tr M$925/1075/1225 ﹡ ﹡) A romantic new boutique hotel overlooking the beach. All 10 suites here have modern kitchenettes, comfortable queen-sized beds and luxurious bathrooms. For an ocean view, ask for a room on the 3rd or 4th floor. If those rooms are taken, you can still enjoy the spectacular scenery on the chic rooftop terrace, where you'll find a small café and a blue-tiled hot tub and an infinity pool. TV junkies will love the plasma screens in the bedroom and living room.

Terraza Inn (Map pp62-3; ☎ 223-54-31; www.terraza inn.com; Amapas 299; r M$950-1000; ﹡) Terraced up a hillside with lush vegetation and just one block from Playa de los Muertos, this little gem has a class and style all its own, providing a welcome change from the homogenous beach hotels. With only 10 *cabaña*-style units, the owners have devoted themselves to making each unique, comfortable and attractive. With romantic hand-carved furniture and comfortable lounge chairs on the deck, the individually named rooms come with a double bed, cable TV and a kitchenette. All have interesting architectural features, such as arched doorways, columns and brick ceilings with exposed timbers.

TOP END

Estancia San Carlos (Map pp62-3; ☎ 222-54-84; Constitución 210; d/q M$1110/1450; ﹡ ﹡ ﹡) This old favorite provides exceptional value, especially if you're traveling in a group or with the family. Spacious, fully equipped apartments surround a peaceful courtyard with a swimming pool embellished with double cascades and a smaller wading pool for tots. The large two-bedroom apartments come with kitchens, small balconies and wireless internet access. Sweetening the deal are comfortable king-sized beds, dining areas and bathrooms decked out with inviting hand-painted tiles. Ask about discounts for longer stays.

Hotel Tropicana (Map pp62-3; ☎ 222-09-12; www .hoteltropicana.com/tropicana_puerto_vallarta; Amapas

214; d M$1200-1400, ste M$1600; ﹡ ﹡) On one of the quieter streets of beachfront Vallarta, this venerable, 160-room beach hotel is a multilevel affair sporting views of swaying palms and the ocean extending to the horizon. The ground level is immaculately landscaped with brick terraces, a large fountain, open-air bars and a splendid pool. The standard rooms are furnished with king-sized beds and cable TV, and all have private balconies. The suites are larger, but are not really worth the extra expense. You're better off splurging on a standard with an ocean view.

Casa Andrea (Map pp62-3; ☎ 222-12-13; www.casa -andrea.com; Rodríguez 174; 1-/2-bedroom M$1200/2250; ﹡ ﹡ ﹡) Here's that gorgeous little tropical retreat you've been longing for. All 11 of these beautifully decorated apartments overlook a flowery garden patio with palm trees, hibiscus plants and an inviting swimming pool. The rooms have high ceilings with exposed wood beams, tiled floors and tasteful rustic touches throughout. Some may like that the apartments have no TVs, but if you just can't live without it, you'll find a largescreen model downstairs in the well-stocked lending library. Other amenities include a complimentary daily breakfast, laundry facilities and a recently added internet room. Make reservations well ahead of time.

Hotel Playa Los Arcos (Map pp62-3; ☎ 226-71-01, in the US 800-648-2403; www.playalosarcos.com; Olas Altas 380; d M$2450, ste M$2750-3004; ﹡ ﹡ ﹡) This long-standing beachside darling underwent a colonial-chic makeover, adding a touch of rustic elegance to the rooms and lobby area. Rooms and suites are divided between three buildings, one smack dab on the beach and two more on the other side of Calle Olas Altas. All of the rooms are spacious and bright, with aircon, cable TV, room safes and other amenities you would expect at this price level. The suites include fully equipped kitchens with dining tables. An all-inclusive plan is available.

Hotel San Marino Plaza (Map pp62-3; ☎ 222-30-50; www.hotelsanmarino.com; Gómez 111; all-inclusive d M$3000, ste M$3190-3290; ﹡ ﹡ ﹡ ﹡) Don't expect the type of all-inclusive plan that you'll find in some of the fancier hotels offering food at all hours. Instead, the San Marino provides three daily buffet-style meals and an open bar that closes at 10pm. Built in a 1960s cram-'em-in style pioneered in Acapulco, it's not the most attractive hotel in town, but it's right on the beach and kids seem to love it. Oceanfront rooms are sizable, with large balconies and amazing views over the beach and down the coast.

South of the City Center

TOP END

Playa del Sol Costa Sur (Map p59; ☎ 226-80-50; www .playadelsolpv.com; Hwy 200, Km 4.5; ste M$1590-2550; P ✿ ☐ ✿ ✿) All 208 suites at this towering 14-story hotel have private balconies with striking ocean views and fully equipped kitchens. The large two-bedroom, with one queen-sized, two doubles and a sofa bed, sleeps up to six. The hotel built a breakwater on the beach, making it ideal for children to take a dip in the ocean. On-site facilities and services include two pools, a spa and *español* classes three times a week.

Quinta Maria Cortez (Map p59; ☎ 221-53-17; www .quinta-maria.com; Calle Sagitario 132; ste incl breakfast M$1980-3860; ✿ ☐ ✿) Just south of town off Hwy 200, this is perhaps the most atmospheric and sophisticated place to stay near Vallarta. The seven spacious and romantic suites, all different sizes, are furnished with a distinct style the proprietor calls 'Mexiterranean.' Most come with kitchen, fireplace and sea views, and breakfast is served in a terraced, *palapa*-covered common space. The suites are equipped for comfort and convenience, with direct-dial phones, fluffy towels and bathrobes, fancy soaps and shampoos, and in-room safes. Definitely reserve in advance.

Presidente InterContinental (Map p59; ☎ 228-01-91; www.intercontinental.com/puertovallarta; Hwy 200, Km 8.5; d M$6130-6861, ste M$7657-20,423; P ✿ ☐ ✿) This luxurious five-star behemoth pampers its guests with rejuvenating luxury. The chic suites feature timbered ceilings, huge bathrooms with separate tub and shower, spacious dressing and sitting areas, and balconies. Standard rooms come equipped with DVD and CD players, and they're stocked with all-natural, ooh-la-la French beauty products. If you really want to put on the ritz, you can take advantage of a full-service spa or the international water and pillow menus. Three good restaurants feature healthy international and Mexican fare. Recreational activities include kayaking and grass-court tennis, and as you'd expect, the pool and beach areas are divine.

Dreams Puerto Vallarta Resort & Spa (Map p59; ☎ 226-50-00; www.dreamsresorts.com; Hwy 200, Km 3.5; all-inclusive d M$6360, ste M$7620-19,060; P ✿ ✿ ☐ ✿) This storied luxury property recently emerged

from a splendid makeover. Sitting pretty before a jungle backdrop and with one of Vallarta's most beautiful beaches, the hotel offers a sense of luxury and privacy. All rooms have sweeping views of the ocean and all the luxury amenities one would expect from a first-rate hotel. Daytime activities include rappelling, kayaking and yoga, while at night you can party down on salsa and karaoke nights. Five restaurants and four bars keep the food coming and the glasses full.

Casa Tres Vidas (Map p59; ☎ 221-58-15; www .casatresvidas.com; Calle Sagitario 126; villas M$8777-9360; ✿ ☐ ✿) Right next door to the Quinta Maria Cortez, this property offers three luxurious beachfront villas providing a ridiculous amount of space. The most impressive villa of the trio, 'Vida Alta,' is a rather humble 465-sq-meter penthouse with three levels, three bedrooms, five bathrooms, Jacuzzi and private rooftop pool. It accommodates up to six guests, or up to 10 when combined with the adjoining villa. Meals are not included in rates, but an on-site chef is standing by to take your order.

North of the Río Cuale

MIDRANGE

Hotel Posada del Pedregal (Map pp62-3; ☎ 222-06-04; A Rodríguez 267; s/d/ste M$500/700/800; ✿) On a busy mercantile street with a mixture of tourist and local shops, this hotel offers simple rooms overlooking an old courtyard. It's a basic but pleasant hotel with 21 rooms, only a stone's throw from the handicrafts market and the picturesque Río Cuale. On offer are streetfront studio suites sporting small kitchens, a balcony and small but bright standard rooms. All units come with fridges, tile floors and attractive, up-to-date bathrooms. Rooms with air-con cost considerably more.

Casa Dulce Vida (Map pp62-3; ☎ 222-10-08; www.dulce vida.com; Aldama 295; ste M$700-2500; ✿ ✿) With the look and feel of an Italian villa, this collection of seven spacious suites with modern kitchens and private entrances offers graceful accommodations and delicious privacy. Most have private terraces and gratifying views of Bahía de Banderas. Back in the 1950s, this part of Vallarta was favored by the many cultural luminaries who came here from *el norte* to familiarize themselves with the pleasures of genteel Mexican repose. Noted American painter Edith Hoyt was a frequent guest, leaving behind several paintings that are on display to this day. The tastefully appointed suites boast airy rooms with 4m-high ceilings and plentiful windows, with sunny living areas and extra beds for groups. Even when the place is fully booked it retains a quiet and intimate atmosphere. It has a well-situated pool and manicured tropical gardens. Book well in advance for the holiday season.

Casa de los Cuatro Vientos (Map pp62-3; ☎ 222-01-61; www.cuatrovientos.com; Matamoros 520; r/ste M$724/848; 🖳) Thriving in its hilly residential location, this guesthouse harbors peaceful, friendly rooms above a garden patio. The rooftop bar is an attraction unto itself, affording terrific views of the cathedral and the entire bay. Common spaces are shared with Sushi and Sake, a duo of Siamese cats. Rooms on the upper level have partial views. Though not large, the colorful digs are rather cozy, with hand-painted trim and red-tiled floors. Each has a double bed and is cooled by a fan and afternoon breezes. The corner rooms are preferable for natural light and cross-ventilation. For those wanting more space, there's a two-room suite with a large bedroom and two daybeds. The rooms have no TVs, but you'll find wi-fi internet and a pool to while away the time.

TOP END

Hotel Rosita (Map pp62-3; ☎ 222-10-33; www.hotelrosita.com; Paseo Díaz Ordaz 901; d/tr M$1090/1650; 🏊 🖳 🖳) The Rosita was one of the first hotels in town and therein lies its charm. While some other Vallarta hotels have been renovated into mind-numbing homogeneity, this old place looks like it hasn't changed a whit since opening in 1948. Ask for one of the recently remodeled rooms, preferably one away from the noisy street. All of the rooms have cable TV, fans and balconies. The terrace has a ho-hum pool – it would be a nice place to look out to sea if it weren't for the chain-link fence blocking the view.

La Casa del Puente (Map pp62-3; ☎ 222-07-49; www.casadelpuente.com; Insurgentes s/n; apt M$1100) Owned by the grandniece of American naturalist John Muir, these beautifully appointed apartments, behind La Fuente del Puente restaurant, make you feel like you're deep in the jungle. Here you can wake up to the relaxing sights and sounds of birds chirping in tall trees and the steady flow of the Río Cuale passing below. The large apartments come complete with Mexican-style kitchens, tiled bathrooms,

tasteful rustic furnishings and period antiques. You couldn't ask for a more pleasant terrace in which to mingle with other guests as you take in the gorgeous scenery. There are just two apartments available, so make reservations well in advance for the high season.

Casa Amorita (Map pp62-3; ☎ 222-49-26; www.casaamorita.com; Iturbide 309; r M$2050-2160; 🖳) This romantic B&B is hands-down one of Vallarta's most unique and luxurious accommodations. Rita Love, your friendly American host, practically designed the place herself, and her attention to architectural detail shows throughout the house – part of the outdoor pool extends into the living room. With just five rooms, you can be assured that you will be treated to lavish hospitality; Rita gets up bright and early to prepare gourmet breakfasts. The two 2nd-floor rooms catch the sea breezes; one opens up to a mammoth mango tree while the other affords expansive views. The beds are very comfortable, with imported German mattresses and down comforters and pillows. You'll also find a shady rooftop bar with privileged views of the town, and a friendly rottweiler named Maya.

Hacienda San Angel (Map pp62-3; ☎ 222-26-92; www.haciendasanangel.com; Miramar 336; ste M$3900-7070; 🅿 🏊 🖳 🖳) This colonial-style hotel elicits oohs and ahs from most guests, but for others the eye candy is a bit too sweet. Enough already with the soothing dripping fountains and statues of angels playing saxophones! But after a while, even the most jaded grump may be won over by the thoughtful attentions of the staff and the culinary magic practiced in the oh-so-colonial kitchen. The 16 suites are individually decorated and undeniably luxurious, and the pools afford tremendous views. You'll also get breakfast brought to your door each morning, and live Mexican folk music in the dining area at night. No kids allowed.

North of the City Center
BUDGET

Tacho's Trailer Park (Map p59; ☎ 224-21-63; www.tachostrailerpark.com; Prisciliano Sa'nchez s/n; tent or RV sites M$290; 🖳) This large and agreeable RV park offers grassy spots and plenty of shady trees. Added perks include a swimming pool and wi-fi internet. To find it, turn east at Sam's Club on Hwy 200; Tacho's is approximately 1km away on the left. Ask about weekly and monthly rates.

MIDRANGE

Hotel La Misión (Map p59; ☎ 222-71-04; Av México 1367; d/tr/ste M$568/702/802; ❄ ☐ ☑) Far enough removed from the party strip to give you some peace and quiet, this affordable hotel offers good deals for two or more guests. Of course, some visitors may find the rooms' pastel colors and whimsical artwork a bit too much, but the lobby and adjoining restaurant certainly have a unique sense of appeal. The more expensive apartments, ideal for families, feature fully equipped kitchens and glass-topped dining tables. Head to the roof for sun worship, where you'll enjoy the views while soaking in an impossibly tiny pool.

TOP END

Hacienda (Map p59; ☎ 226-66-77; www.hacienda online.com.mx; Blvd Ascencio 2699; s/d M$1056/2112; ☐ ❄ ☐ ☑) A colonial-style hotel with thoughtful touches of old-world charm, this place has one of the best all-inclusive deals in town. The spacious suites overlook a tropical garden with a large pool and swim-up bar, a rocky waterfall and a pleasant open-air restaurant. The rustic-chic rooms come with two double beds or a king, ample closet space, large bathrooms and private balconies. The hotel sits a couple blocks from the ocean, so you'll have to take a short walk to the private beach club. Opt for the all-inclusive plan since it costs roughly the same as the non-inclusive.

Buenaventura Hotel & Beach Club (Map p59; ☎ 226-70-00; www.hotelbuenaventura.com.mx; Av México 1301; s/d/tr M$1570/1800/2030; ❄ ☐ ☑) This high-quality beach hotel offers appealing rooms and impressive hacienda-style architecture. The tile-floored rooms and suites have neutral tones, contemporary Mexican furnishings, and either two double beds or one king. Superior rooms up the ante with whirlpool baths, balconies and ocean views; suites add a kitchenette and living area. Two large pools and plenty of lush greenery are used to positive effect. The beach isn't the biggest in town, but the waters are gentle and you can enjoy a measure of privacy.

Fiesta Americana Puerto Vallarta (Map p59; ☎ 224-20-10; www.fiestaamericana.com; Blvd Ascencio, Km 2.5; d M$3554, ste M$4996-14,175; ☐ ✕ ❄ ☐ ☑) This hotel is one of the nicest in the Zona Hotelera, with a stunning lobby ringed by an artificial

---

GAY & LESBIAN RESORTS & INNS

Come on 'out' to gay-friendly Vallarta. The *Gay Guide Vallarta* (www.gayguidevallarta.com) booklet has tons of information and a helpful map and directory with gay business listings. Other useful websites include www.discoveryvallarta.com and www.doinitright.com.

Villa David (Map pp62-3; ☎ 223-03-15; www.villadavidpv.com; Galeana 348; r with breakfast M$1250-1600; ❄ ☐ ☑) This colonial-style gay B&B bills itself as the only 'clothing optional' guesthouse in town. Each room has well-appointed furnishings and they are individually designed around different themes. The rooftop Jacuzzi affords an extraordinary view of the city at night. Reservations essential.

Hotel Mercurio (Map pp62-3; ☎ 222-47-93; www.hotel-mercurio.com; Rodríguez 168; s M$1320, d M$1470-1573; ❄ ☐ ☑) On offer at this three-story gay-owned hotel are 28 rooms around a pleasant courtyard with a stylish pool area and small bar. The rooms have fridges, wi-fi internet access, cable TV and double or king-sized beds with fine linens. The new day welcomes you with a complimentary gourmet breakfast.

Abbey Hotel (Map pp62-3; ☎ 222-44-88; www.abbeyhotelvallarta.com; Púlpito 138; s/d/ste M$1520/1640/2200; ❄ ☐ ☑) This remodeled tower has changed ownership and now flies the rainbow banner. All rooms have private balconies, wi-fi access and spacious bathrooms, and they're clean as a whistle. Suites sleep up to four people. Lively social circles form around the poolside bar and Jacuzzi.

Blue Chairs Beach Resort (Map p59; ☎ 222-50-40; www.hotelbluechairs.com; Almendro 4; d M$2000-2400, ste M$2500-2600; ❄ ☑) Smack in the heart of Vallarta's gay zone, this resort is a good place to let it all hang out (although officially the beach has a 'no nudity' policy). Amenities are conducive to socializing: there are bars and restaurants on the beach and roof, with a pool on the roof as well. The rooftop bar is particularly raucous, with nightly live entertainment, including a 'dirty bitches' drag show on Wednesday and Sunday at 7:30pm. The breezy and attractive rooms have cable TV and private balconies; suites have kitchenettes. The resort offers a full menu of tours and spa services.

stream and sitting pretty under a giant *palapa* roof said to be the largest in the world. The wide and wonderful yellow-sand beach is one of Vallarta's loveliest, with limpid waters ideal for swimming. The nine-story terracotta high-rise houses 291 rooms looking over the pool and out to sea. The tile-floored rooms have private balconies and deluxe amenities. The massive pool is enhanced by a huge fountain and beguiling swim-up bar. Three restaurants and a lobby bar with nightly live music help ensure that most guests never leave the property.

NH Krystal Puerto Vallarta (Map p59; ☎ 226-07-00; www.nh-hotels.com; Av de las Garzas s/n; r M$3822-4940 P ⊠ 🖳 ⏾) Big would be an understatement at this 13-hectare hacienda-style sprawl. In fact, with 512 rooms, six Jacuzzis, four swimming pools, two tennis courts and an on-site disco, this megaresort feels more like a small village. Tall palms line grassy gardens overrun with large iguanas. Rooms come with modern furnishings, tile floors, large bathrooms and garden or ocean views. Some guests have complained about the hotel's renovation projects, saying they make for a noisy stay, but on grounds this huge the front desk should be able to find you a quiet room removed from the racket.

Grand Velas (Map p59; ☎ 226-80-00; www.grand velas.com; Av Paseo de los Cocoteros 98 Sur, Nuevo Vallarta; all inclusive s/d M$11,900/13,200; P ⊠ ⊠ 🖳 ⏾ 🐬) Make no mistake: this posh all-inclusive is about as pricey as they come, but it's pampering at its best. All of the lavish suites feature elegant teak furnishings, queen-sized beds with white down comforters and pillows, and terraces with dazzling oceanfront views. For dining, choose between four on-site restaurants offering gourmet French, Mexican, Italian-Mediterranean and international cuisine. Other strong draws include a world-class spa, an enormous infinity pool, a tennis court, a kids' club, and the list goes on.

EATING

Dining options in Vallarta range from affordable taco joints and family-run eateries to upscale cosmopolitan restaurants specializing in a wide array of international cuisine. Like many of Mexico's top tourist resorts, Vallarta attracts renowned chefs from Mexico and abroad, making it a truly diverse culinary experience. For a romantic night out, pull up to a candlelit table along the Río Cuale, or hit the waterfront restaurants along Playa de los Muertos or the marina. If you're hankering for homestyle Mexican cooking and looking to pinch your pesos, hit the *cenadurías* or the Mercado de Artesanías (p83), just north of the river, where economical traditional fare is whipped up. Locals will tell you some of the tastiest grub is best served on a plastic plate from the street stalls slinging tacos, and rightly so. Hygiene is often a crapshoot (no pun intended), but the stall food is a delicious proposition nonetheless. When all else fails, the old standbys fronting the boardwalk offer fine views of the bay with mostly tourist-oriented food, and plenty of drink specials on offer to wash it all down.

South of the Río Cuale
BUDGET
If you're watching your budget, look for taco stands that sprout in the Zona Romántica early in the evenings – they serve some of the best and cheapest food in town. For inexpensive fish and seafood, try the corner of Serdán and Constitución. There are also a few small, economical, family-run restaurants along Madero. Women sell delicious tamales and flan along Insurgentes at dusk.

El Calamar Aventurero (Map pp62-3; ☎ 222-64-79; Serdán 130; tacos M$15-20; ⏰ 9am-7pm Mon-Sat) The Frisky Squid, as it's known in gringo-speak, prepares tasty fish, shrimp, manta ray and marlin tacos. Be sure to ask for the zesty *chile de arbol* and garlic-based *salsa mulata*. The eatery also has good shrimp cocktails. Service is speedy here, so don't worry about missing that pressing appointment on the beach.

Pancake House (Map pp62-3; ☎ 222-62-72; Badillo 289; mains M$30-50; ⏰ 8am-2pm) You may have to wait in line here because the amazing array of pancakes has made this place more than popular. There are other breakfast goodies to choose from if you can resist the lure of a stack of steaming hotcakes.

Las Tres Huastecas (Map pp62-3; ☎ 222-30-17; cnr Olas Altas & Rodríguez; mains M$32-95; ⏰ 7am-8pm) This is the place for delicious Mexican favorites in a homey atmosphere at local prices. The charming owner, hailing from the Huasteca region of San Luis Potosí, is a poet who calls himself 'El Querreque.' He recites verse as readily as he does the house specialties.

Fredy's Tucan Restaurant & Bar (Map pp62-3; ☎ 223-07-78; cnr Badillo & Vallarta; mains M$40-70; ⏰ 8am-3am; ⊠) With breakfast specials like pancakes, waffles and omelets, this spick-and-span eatery is a tourist magnet. If you're really hungry, go for the *campesino* breakfast, with a big portion of tender skirt steak and *chilaquiles* (fried tortilla strips cooked with a red or green chili sauce, and sometimes meat and eggs). It also serves lunch, dinner, snacks and drinks, and at night this place turns into a buzzing bar.

MIDRANGE

Planeta Vegetariano (Map pp62-3; ☎ 222-30-73; Iturbide 270; buffet M\$65; ☯ 8am-10pm; Ⓥ) A vegetarian's delight through and through, this warm tropical-themed restaurant serves up superb all-you-can-eat buffets at every meal. All of the dishes are made from scratch and the menu changes daily.

Mama Dolores' Diner (Map pp62-3; ☎ 223-58-97; Olas Altas 534B; mains M\$65-155; ☯ 8am-1pm, 4-11pm Tue-Sun) This popular diner recently changed ownership, but the new owners wisely decided to keep the cook around. It's the only place in town to get good meatloaf, liver and onions, and fried chicken. Don't miss turkey-dinner night on Sunday. It also slings hearty breakfasts.

Café de Olla (Map pp62-3; ☎ 223-16-26; Badillo 168A; mains M\$65-210; ☯ 9am-11pm Wed-Mon) This small, busy and very pleasant tourist-oriented restaurant serves great traditional Mexican food at good prices.

Langostino's (Map pp62-3; ☎ 222-08-94; Diéguez 109, at Playa de los Muertos; mains M\$65-225; ☯ 7am-11pm) This tropical-themed restaurant serves salads,

seafood, ribs, burgers, tacos and frogs' legs. The real reason you're here, however, is to eat on the beach under a shady *palapa*.

Joe Jack's Fish Shack (Map pp62-3; ☎ 222-20-99; Badillo 212; mains M\$80-150; ☯ noon-11pm) Fresh is the operative word at the shack, where you can delight in tasty Baja-style fish and shrimp tacos and excellent *ceviche* (marinated seafood and lime dish – the house specialty). The *mojito* (a rum drink with mint and lime) is arguably Vallarta's best. Have a few of them and you may find yourself practicing the Spanish-language pick-up lines listed on the menu.

Red Cabbage Café (off Map pp62-3; ☎ 223-04-11; Rivera del Río 204A; mains M\$80-200; ☯ 5-10:30pm; ☒ ☒ Ⓥ) Though the atmosphere is casual, with fabulous eclectic and bohemian artwork, the food is serious Mexican *alta cocina* (haute cuisine). This is the only nonsmoking restaurant in town. Try the subtle mole or hearty vegetarian dishes. To get there from the Zona Romántica, begin at Insurgentes and then follow Cárdenas east five long blocks. Take a right turn before the green bridge and go approximately one more block. Reservations are recommended.

Mariscos Polo (Map pp62-3; ☎ 113-03-64; Madero 376; mains M\$80-240; ☯ noon-10pm Wed-Mon) This small unassuming restaurant does artfully prepared seafood treats. Try the coconut shrimp with mango and mild pepper sauce, or the generously served combo plate with grilled lobster, garlic scallops and skewered shrimp.

Trattoria Michel (Map pp62-3; ☎ 223-20-88; Olas Altas 507; mains M\$80-260; ☯ 6-11pm) All of the traditional Tuscan dishes at this romantic trattoria are prepared *a la minute*. Translation? Have patience, my friend, it's worth the wait. Signature dishes include Italian gnocchi with pesto and the *bistecca florentina,* a tender steak that serves two. The restaurant buys mostly organic ingredients from local farmers and producers.

Hacienda Alemana (Map pp62-3; ☎ 222-20-71; Badillo 378; mains M\$95-175; ☯ 11:30am-11pm) Take a break from the seafood routine and dive into this hacienda-style restaurant's traditional Bavarian fare, such as veal bratwurst with fried onions, and schnitzel, or for more conventional tastes there's the filet mignon in red-wine sauce. On Wednesday and Saturday it has an all-you-can eat spread with draft beer included (M\$225).

Archie's Wok (Map pp62-3; ☎ 222-04-11; Rodríguez 130; mains M\$95-199; ☯ 2-11pm Mon-Sat) The setting here is elegant but urban. The menu features fine pan-Asian cuisine, with specialties such as spicy pad Thai noodles, hoisin ribs and grilled dorado wrapped in banana leaves. You dine to live harp and flute music and jazz tunes Thursday through Saturday.

Fajita Republic (Map pp62-3; ☎ 222-31-31; Badillo 188; mains M$104-178; ⏰ 5-11pm) With pleasant open-air dining on a leafy, atmospheric patio, this popular fajita factory grills up generous portions of shrimp, vegetables, steak and chicken with plenty of guacamole. Top it off with a mango margarita.

Espresso Ristorante (Map pp62-3; ☎ 222-32-72; Vallarta 279; pizza M$109-179; ⏰ noon-1:30am Tue-Sun) Come to this two-story Italian restaurant for brick-oven pizza and fine pastas. The spaghetti neptuno is prepared with fresh seafood and a homemade red or white sauce. The feel is upscale and open, and the downstairs bar area is a nice spot to grab a drink and chew the fat.

Asaderos (Map pp62-3; ☎ 222-19-55; Badillo 223; buffet M$115; ⏰ 10am-11pm) Bottomless pits get their fill at this sports bar and grill with all-you-can-eat barbecued chicken, steak, ribs and Mexican sausage. Salad is included to give you a little roughage, but tack the drinks onto the restaurant's profits.

El Palomar de los González (Map pp62-3; ☎ 222-07-95; Aguacate 425; mains M$120-300) The superb view over the city and bay is a big draw at this hillside restaurant, especially at sunset. Jumbo shrimp and fillet steak are specialties. It's a steep climb up here, so get a taxi or work up an appetite.

TOP END

Daiquiri Dick's (Map pp62-3; ☎ 222-05-66; Olas Altas 314; mains M$135-255; ⏰ 9am-10:30pm) An elegant dining establishment, despite its name. Nibble roast duck with scalloped sweet potatoes, bite into the sesame-encrusted tuna or wrestle with lobster tacos. Southwest colors, soft music and a beautiful view help it all go down easy.

Casa Naranjo (Map pp62-3; ☎ 222-35-18; Naranjo 263; mains M$135-265; ⏰ 5:30-11:30pm) This family-run favorite has an unabashed predilection for the color orange and a dining room that wraps around its exposed kitchen. On the menu is delicious, fussed-over fare like saffron mussels, ginger-grilled scallops and invigorating cold soups.

Kaiser Maximilian (Map pp62-3; ☎ 222-50-58; Olas Altas 380B; mains M$168-260; ⏰ 8am-midnight Mon-Sat) Get your well-prepared wiener schnitzel or veal scallopini with twice-baked potatoes

at this upscale Austrian restaurant. It also offers good coffee, desserts, snacks and meals, all with an Austrian flavor. It's popular for evening drinks.

Steak House Brasil (Map pp62-3; ☎ 222-29-09; Carranza 210; women/men M$180/200; ⏰ 1-11pm) Carnivores rejoice! Here the meat-hungry masses devour gut-busting portions of sirloin, filet mignon, ribs and turkey. One price gets you all you can eat, including a choice of three salads, soup and veggies.

La Palapa (Map pp62-3; ☎ 222-52-25; Púlpito 103; mains M$250-410; ⏰ 8am-11:30pm) This is elegant beach dining at its best. Sea bass with macadamia crust and seared scallops with orange miso sauce are just some of the delicacies here. Tables are positioned to take full advantage of the sea views, making it a particularly marvelous spot at sunset or breakfast.

North of the Río Cuale
BUDGET

The Mercado de Artesanías, just north of the river, has simple stalls upstairs serving typical Mexican market foods. You'll find the following eateries north of the Río Cuale in El Centro.

El Carboncito (Map p59; ☎ 223-17-03; Honduras 5; tacos M$10; ⏰ 9pm-3am Tue-Sun) Vallarta's undisputed champ of spit-roasted *tacos al pastor* (with marinated pork), this family-run *taqueria* has terrific late-night snacks awaiting. The tacos are prepared on handmade tortillas and topped with onion, cilantro, fresh pineapple and great salsas. Bet you can't eat just one.

Cenaduría Doña Raquel (Map pp62-3; ☎ 222-30-25; Vicario 131; mains M$43-81; ⏰ 2:30-11:30pm Wed-Mon) Best known for its *pozole* (hominy stew), this local haven serves traditional Mexican basics, which can be smelled from a block away. Friendly atmosphere and friendly prices.

Los Chilaquiles (Map pp62-3; ☎ 223-94-82; Zaragoza 160; mains M$48-99; ⏰ 8am-11pm) With a privileged view of the boardwalk and the ocean beyond, this new restaurant is a great place to start the day with good coffee and a traditional Mexican breakfast. The *chilaquiles* are the house specialty, or you can go for something lighter.

Esquina de los Caprichos (Map pp62-3; ☎ 222-09-11; cnr Miramar & Iturbide; tapas under M$50; ⏰ 1-10pm Mon-Sat) This Spanish-Mexican tapas eatery serves delicious garlic-heavy gazpacho, buttery grilled scallops and much more, all in a tiny, intimate dining area with just six tables.

MIDRANGE

Barcelona (Map pp62-3; ☎ 222-05-10; cnr Matamoros & 31 de Octubre; tapas M$38-139; ☺ noon-11:30pm) Requires a walk up a hill and some stairs, but the grand view and excellent tapas are worth it. Lamb, duck, seafood paella and vegetarian dishes are also served. Try to get a table on the patio up top, and by all means order the homemade ice cream, or better yet, a sangria!

La Fuente del Puente (Map pp62-3; ☎ 221-11-41; Insurgentes 107; mains M$45-190; ☺ 9am-9pm Mon-Sat, 9am-4pm Sun) Perched over the Río Cuale at the bridge, this delightfully situated café serves traditional regional specialties from all corners of Mexico. It's particularly charming for breakfast in the morning, when the birds along the river turn up the volume and iguanas pass noiselessly in the trees overhead.

Las Palomas (Map pp62-3; ☎ 222-36-75; cnr Paseo Díaz Ordaz & Aldama; mains M$45-350; ☺ 8am-midnight) Looking over the *malecón* from its comfortable perch, Las Palomas is a popular place for people-watching. The menu lists seafood, chicken crepes and authentic Mexican specialties, and the decor is smart and festive. Soft music serenades loud and happy gringo voices – perhaps they scored a 'free margarita' coupon?

No Name Café (Map pp62-3; ☎ 223-25-08; Morelos 460; mains M$50-285; ☺ 9am-1am) Serving all-American favorites, this restaurant and sports bar has 31 (count 'em) TV sets. Obviously, it's a good place to catch your choice of game. No Name claims to serve the best ribs in Mexico: you be the judge. Phone for free delivery.

La Bodeguita del Medio (Map pp62-3; ☎ 223-15-85; Paseo Díaz Ordaz 858; mains M$70-150; ☺ 11am-2:30am) The writing's literally on the walls at this cheerful Cuban joint, and it promises good times. Here you can try favorites like roast pork, fried plantains and the politically incorrect *moros y cristianos* (Moors and Christians), a black beans and rice dish. Wash it all down with a *mojito*.

Vitea (Map pp62-3; ☎ 222-87-03; Libertad 2; mains M$75-225; ☺ 8am-midnight) Owned by the same people who created Trio (right), this oceanside bistro serves up an eclectic mix of surf, turf and pasta dishes in a casual setting. Start with the shrimp tempura to ease your way into the crab cannelloni or the vegetarian lasagna with three cheeses and white-wine sauce. The outdoor dining area overlooking the boardwalk lends itself to some great people-watching.

La Dolce Vita (Map pp62-3; ☎ 222-22-04; Paseo Díaz Ordaz 674; mains M$98-135; ☺ noon-2am Mon-Sat, 6pm-midnight Sun) Overlooking the boardwalk in party central, this lively *ristorante* does wood-fired pizzas and fresh pastas. On Friday night there's handmade gnocchi. *Molto delizioso!*

Mi Querencia (Map pp62-3; ☎ 222-20-30; Morelos 426; mains M$98-279; ☺ 8am-midnight) *Ceviche* – the marinated seafood and lime dish that makes an appearance on nearly every Pacific coast menu – gets gussied up here with variations featuring coriander, pineapple, beet juice and oranges. Similar liberties are taken with the shrimp dishes.

TOP END

Trio (Map pp62-3; ☎ 222-21-96; Guerrero 264; mains M$150-290; ☺ 6-11:30pm) The two European chefs put a lot of passion into the seasonal menu at this elegant restaurant-bar-bistro. Exceptional Mediterranean flavors prevail in dishes like rack of lamb with ravioli with lamb ragout, chili-roasted snapper, or Lebanese salad with marinated goat's cheese. The rooftop-bar area is choice for an after-dinner libation.

our pick Café des Artistes (Map pp62-3; ☎ 222-32-28; Sánchez 740; mains M$179-385; ☺ 6-11:30pm; ☒) This cosmopolitan restaurant has a romantic ambience to match its exquisite French cuisine. Choose a three-course meal from famed chef Thierry Blouet's selection, or go à la carte with artfully prepared dishes such as roasted sea bass fillet with potato slices or roasted duck glazed with quince and ginger. After the meal, hit the cigar and cognac bar or the sophisticated Constantini wine bar and take in some live jazz and blues music. Wining and dining doesn't come cheap here, but it's worth every last peso. Reservations are recommended.

Vista Grill (Map pp62-3; ☎ 222-35-70; Púlpito 377; mains M$200-500; ☺ 6:30-11:30pm) Sitting on a prime hillside location with a breathtaking view of the bay, this popular gourmet restaurant serves international cuisine in an elegant dining room with thoughtful art deco touches. Rack of lamb, Chilean sea bass and grilled New York steak are among some of the house favorites. After the meal, head to the chic lounge bar for live jazz and cocktails.

North of Puerto Vallarta

North of town, you can dine in fine waterfront restaurants in Marina Vallarta or stuff your face at a finger-lickin' all-you-can-eat barbecue. Recommended places:

TOP END

Porto Bello (Map p59; ☎ 221-00-03; Marina Sol, Local 7, Marina Vallarta; mains M$130-395; ⌚ noon-11pm) Considered one of Vallarta's finest Italian restaurants, this elegant place on the marina is best known for its vitello Porto Bello (veal cutlets), or try the fusilli topped with artichoke, black olives, lemon juice, garlic and basil-accented olive oil, the signature pasta dish.

Tikul (Map p59; ☎ 209-20-10; Paseo de la Marina 245, Local 113, Marina Vallarta; mains M$160-365; ⌚ 5:30-11pm) Set in a classy gold- and amber-toned dining area with teak chairs, this waterfront gem prepares interesting Asian-accented creations like Singapore pepper-rubbed duck breast, grilled curry and ancho chili shrimp, and macadamia-encrusted Chilean sea bass. There are tables outside overlooking the marina and live sax music at night.

Isla Río Cuale

TOP END

The riverside setting of the restaurants on the island makes for a romantic and relaxing dining experience.

Oscar's Bar & Grill (Map pp62-3; ☎ 223-07-89; Isla Río Cuale 1; mains M$100-250; ⌚ 8am-midnight) Overlooking the mouth of the river, this romantic open-air spot offers impressive scenery for a sunset meal. The main draw here are fish and seafood dishes, such as baked mahimahi topped with basil and parmesan cheese, or jumbo shrimp sautéed in garlic, olive oil and red-pepper sauce.

Le Bistro Jazz Café (Map pp62-3; ☎ 222-02-83; Isla Río Cuale 16A; mains M$110-300; ⌚ 9am-midnight Mon-Sat;) Overlooking the river, this swanky spot is good for a martini but even better for its scrumptious cuisine, pleasant jazz recordings and beautiful tropical scenery. The menu is replete with gourmet fare like mahimahi with achiote, tempura-style coconut shrimp, and grilled or garlic lobster. For breakfast try the savory crepes and eggs Benedict.

River Café (Map pp62-3; ☎ 223-07-88; Isla Río Cuale 4; mains M$210-265; ⌚ 9am-11:30pm) Imaginative seafood dishes are a highlight of this well-regarded and delightfully situated restaurant. Indulge in shrimp encrusted with pecans and coconut, or grilled filet mignon with wild mushrooms. There's live jazz Thursday to Sunday.

Self-Catering

Cater your own picnic and save some beer money.

Gutiérrez Rizoc (GR; Map pp62-3; cnr Constitución & Aquiles Serdán; ⌚ 7am-11pm) A well-stocked, air-con supermarket. Inside you'll find an ATM and a bulletin board with various ads placed for weekly and monthly apartment rentals and Spanish classes.

DRINKING

Not surprisingly for a city where lounging around is one of the preferred activities, Vallarta has many choice spots for sipping a strong coffee or tipping a tipple. Coffee shops open early and close late, and most bars keep 'em coming well after midnight.

Coffee Shops

Rest assured, you won't need to walk far to get an early-morning caffeine fix.

Café San Angel (Map pp62-3; ☎ 223-12-73; Olas Altas 449; M$20-30) Start your day in this artsy, relaxed café. Its sidewalk tables are filled with gringos sitting pretty, sipping their black coffee and nibbling on snacks and sweets. For some extra kick, try a cup of joe laced with whiskey, tequila or Kahlua (M$63).

Big Kahuna (Map pp62-3; ☎ 222-16-93; Badillo 162; coffee M$15-30, bagels M$20-35) For a light snack and good java, this air-conditioned coffee shop has a wide assortment of bagels and cream cheeses to go on top. It also does sandwiches.

Funiculi (Map pp62-3; ☎ 222-06-07; Cárdenas 292; coffee M$15-20, pastas M$90-120) This small *caffé* has great coffee and sandwiches prepared on *filone* bread. It imports all its products from Italy for its pastas dishes. The Mexican owner learned how to cook Italian food while living in Italy and returned to Mexico with homestyle recipes and an Italian husband to boot.

Organic Café (Map pp62-3; Corona 185; coffee M$12-25; ⌚ 7am-10pm) Pours organic Mexican coffee grown in the highlands of Chiapas. The white chocolate frappé goes down nicely on a hot day, and the place has sweets if you want to double up on your sugar intake.

Bars

It's easy to become inebriated in Puerto Vallarta, where two-for-one happy hours are as reliable as the sunset and the margarita glasses look like oversized snifters. The following bars are preferred watering holes.

Burros Bar (Map pp62-3; ☎ 222-01-22; Olas Altas 401; ⌚ 10am-10pm) This oceanfront joint rains buckets of beer and pours two shots of tequila in its large mango margaritas. One too many of those bad boys and you'll be braying like a donkey.

La Bodeguita del Medio (Map pp62-3; ☎ 223-15-85; Paseo Díaz Ordaz 858) With good eats and a view over the *malecón*, this graffiti-marred Cuban joint has live music and famous rum-and-mint *mojitos*.

El Faro Lighthouse Bar (Map p59; ☎ 221-05-41, 221-05-42; Royal Pacific Yacht Club, Marina Vallarta; ☽ 6pm-2am) How often do you get the chance to toss back drinks in a lighthouse? Smooth jazz sounds and panoramic views of the bay in the moonlight are a surefire prelude to a kiss.

Steve's Sports Bar (Map pp62-3; ☎ 222-02-56; Badillo 286) Aging hippies share space with purple-haired ladies at this friendly little joint. Here you can watch sporting events, play board games and catch an occasional live music act. The kitchen does your typical American pub grub like fish 'n' chips and burgers.

Los Molcajetes (Map pp62-3; Madero 279) This is *not* the kind of place where you'll find Tom Cruise types twirling their cues and kicking shit. It's large, full of pool tables and downright seedy. Get drunk and challenge the locals (all male) to a game.

Other possibilities:

Carlos O'Brian's (Map pp62-3; ☎ 222-14-44; Paseo Díaz Ordaz 786) A favorite drinking hole for rabble-rousing gringos.

El Barril (Map pp62-3; ☎ 223-21-55; Guerrero 225) Grab a table on the terrace and strike up a conversation with locals over cheap beers. It's mostly a drinking-man's bar.

Memories Café (Map pp62-3; Mina & Juárez; ☽ 7pm-2am) If you like classic rock along the lines of Pink Floyd and the Beatles, you'll dig this spot.

ENTERTAINMENT

You've probably already heard a thing or two about Puerto Vallarta's happening nightscene. Lining the *malecón* are plenty of romantic open-air restaurants and heaps of riotous bars. Entertainment is often on tap in the amphitheater by the sea (opposite Plaza Principal), and at discos near the Marina Vallarta.

Clubs & Discos

Along the *malecón* are a bunch of places where teen and 20-something (or even older) tourists get trashed and dance on tables. On a good night, some of the establishments stay open to about 5am. You can see from the street which

---

GAY & LESBIAN CLUBS & NIGHTSPOTS

Head to the Zona Romántica for the most hopping gay bars and nightclubs. Sorry ladies, unfortunately Vallarta has slim pickings for lesbians.

Apaches (Map pp62-3; ☎ 222-40-04; Olas Altas 439; ☽ 5pm-2am) One of the few lesbian options in PV, Apaches is a friendly little martini joint with an intimate neighborhood bar feel. Plop yourself on a stool at the bar and shoot the breeze with Dutch bartendress Endra: she's a laugh a minute.

Paco's Ranch (Map pp62-3; ☎ 222-18-99; www.pacosranch.com; Vallarta 278; cover M$50; ☽ 10pm-6am) With a Mexican-themed disco and a rooftop cantina, this venerable institution is most famous for its transvestite revues.

Mañana (Map pp62-3; ☎ 222-77-22; www.elclubmanana.com; Carranza 290; cover M$50-100; ☽ noon-6am) Pool party by day, wild dance club by night, Mañana stages strip shows in its flashy disco, while out by the pool transvestites do amusing Madonna and Britney Spears impersonations.

Anthropology (Map pp62-3; Morelos 101) Hot male bodies are on display for one another, and if you're lucky, salsa beats will be on tap. If you're not so lucky, you'll get heavy techno thump. Check out the dark, more intimate rooftop patio.

Palm (Map pp62-3; ☎ 223-39-13; Olas Altas 508; cover M$50, before 9pm free) A different show is held every night, including variety acts, drag-queen performances and striptease. Spinning lights, snazzy colors and palm decor make it all seem like a dream.

Depending on the alignment of the stars, the following gay bars are mostly mellow. **Kit Kat Klub** (Map pp62-3; ☎ 223-00-93; Púlpito 120; ☽ 6pm-2am) is an ultrahip spot with wicked martinis and a 'divas' dinner show on Tuesday. **Sama Bar** (Map pp62-3; ☎ 223-31-82; Olas Altas 510; ☽ 5pm-2am) is a likable small place with big martinis. **La Noche** (Map pp62-3; ☎ 222-33-64; Cárdenas 257; ☽ 7pm-3am) is well loved for its convivial atmosphere and buff bartenders. **Encuentros** (Map pp62-3; ☎ 223-06-43; Cárdenas 312; ☽ 6pm-2am) is a candlelit lounge bar that draws a mixed crowd. It has an extensive martini menu and tasty thin-crust pizza. **Frida** (Map pp62-3; ☎ 044-322-112-93-42; Cárdenas 361; ☽ 1pm-2am) is a Frida Kahlo–themed friendly neighborhood watering hole.

LOCATION IS EVERYTHING

The Night of the Iguana put Vallarta on the map as a highly attractive location for Hollywood productions. American director John Huston shot the picture in the early 1960s on the beach cove of Mismaloya, about 12km south of the city. The site is now dominated by the 317-room hotel, Barceló La Jolla de Mismaloya (p97), and the buildings used in the film (look toward the south side of the cove) live on as seafood restaurants.

Since then numerous crews from Tinseltown have headed south to work their magic in and around Vallarta's lush jungles and sparkling coastline.

In the 1970s, director James Goldstone and company hit the northern shore to shoot the pirate-themed adventure movie *Swashbuckler*, starring James Earl Jones and Robert Shaw (of captain Quint fame in *Jaws*). About a decade later Arnie found himself in the thick of the Mismaloya jungle on the set of *Predator* (p97) and there's no denying the extraterrestrial suit and camouflage paint provided the perfect cover against the mountainous backdrop.

Later came director Tony Scott's turn with the Kevin Costner–starrer *Revenge*. Scenes for the thriller were shot at the Quinta Maria Cortez (p73), a lovely B&B on Playa Conchas Chinas. Vallarta's locations list is long and it includes recent productions such as Quentin Tarantino's *Kill Bill: Vol 2* and Disney's talking pooch flick, *Beverly Hills Chihuahua*. Though Mexico pales in comparison to Canada in luring runaway production, the eye-catching scenery in Vallarta and many other coastal towns has made significant contributions to the Hollywood movie machine.

one has the most action. Usually there's no cover charge, but drinks are on the expensive side, except during the 'happy hours,' which can be any time from 8pm to 11pm. On the backstreets you'll find numerous bars with a slightly lower-key vibe.

De Santos (Map pp62-3; ☎ 223-30-52; Morelos 771; ⏰ 6pm-5am) Co-owned by the drummer of Mexican rock band Maná, Vallarta's choicest nightspot combines a Mediterranean restaurant with an animated weekend disco upstairs and an open-air rooftop bar that invites you to chill out on oversized beds with martini in hand.

Bar Shelona (Map pp62-3; ☎ 223-80-37; Juárez 712; ⏰ 8pm-4am Tue-Thu, 8pm-6am Fri & Sat) This minimalist lounge bar features resident and guest DJs from abroad, and it's the in place to bug out electronica-style. On Friday they have open bar night (men/women M$180/80); on Saturday bring a friend on two-for-one martini nights.

Malafama (Map pp62-3; ☎ 044-322-779-9314; Juárez 464; ⏰ 11pm-4am Fri & Sat) One of the few places in Vallarta where you can sample an underground scene, this graffiti-marred lounge bar features DJs spinning minimal techno grooves. The bar has a cozy loft area, a patio for dancing and comfy beanbag chairs on the floor.

Zoo (Map pp62-3; ☎ 222-49-45; Paseo Díaz Ordaz 638; weekend cover M$100-150) Sports an animal scene, and we're not just talking about the decor.

Grilled windows resemble cages, so if you're up for a wild time step inside – carefully. You may be greeted with all-the-margaritas-you-can-drink hour.

Hilo (Map pp62-3; ☎ 223-53-61; Paseo Díaz Ordaz 588; weekend cover M$100; ⏰ 4pm-6am) Just look for the imposing statue of the *adelita* (a term used for women who fought during the revolution). At this thumping disco you can get a groove on into the wee hours of the morning.

La Regadera (Map pp62-3; ☎ 222-39-76; Morelos 664) Prepare yourself for some pretty bad karaoke sessions, though the clamato-, tamarind- and pineapple-flavored beers certainly help to ease the suffering.

La Cantina (Map pp62-3; ☎ 222-17-34; Morelos 709) Certainly not the most original name, but this large place really packs them in with a young and uninhibited crowd, especially on Wednesday nights when you pay a M$50 cover and get *cervezas* for a mere M$11 a pop.

La Revolución (Map pp62-3; ☎ 222-06-06; Matamoros 235) A cool and casual local joint attracting a good mix of gringos and Mexicans. It's one of the oldest bars in Vallarta: Liz Taylor and Richard Burton hung out here. At last visit, the owners were looking to sell the place.

Party Lounge (Map pp62-3; Av México 993; ⏰ 9pm-4am) You'll hear the blaring music from a block away. The name of this tropical-themed bar pretty much sums it up; it's a big hit with the younger crowd. Downstairs, jumbo mixed drinks to go are prepared.

Christine (Map p59; ☎ 224-69-90; ☻ 10pm-5am)
At the NH Krystal Puerto Vallarta (p76), this flashy dance club is occasionally explosive, with cutting-edge sound and lighting systems. Cover charges (M$350 with open bar) fluctuate depending on your gender and the night. Terraced levels, spinning spotlights and hip-hop music delight well-dressed dancers downing overpriced and weak drinks. Still, it's flashy, modern and lively.

J&B (Map p59; ☎ 224-46-16; Francisco Ascencio, Km 2.5; admission Wed-Sun M$90, Mon-Tue free; ☻ 9pm-6am) Great spot to practice your salsa, *cumbia* and merengue steps. On Friday and Saturday at 8pm you can take a two-hour dance class for M$50, then stick around for the live bands to strut your stuff on the dance floor.

Mandala (Map pp62-3; Paseo Díaz Ordaz 640; ☻ 8am-6am; cover M$50-100) With 30 plasma screens and towering Hindu statues looking on, this raucous dance club keeps things going until the break of dawn. For a breath of fresh air, hit the rooftop bar upstairs and take in the spectacular ocean view. The fashion police at the door enforce a strict dress-code policy, prohibiting shorts, sandals, baseball hats and tank tops.

Fiestas Mexicanas
These fun folkloric shows give tourists a crash course in not-very-contemporary Mexican culture.

La Iguana (Map pp62-3; ☎ 222-01-05; http://laiguanapv .com; Cárdenas 311; adult/child M$670/330; ☻ 7-11pm Thu & Sun) Said to be the original of this much-copied tourist entertainment. The deal here includes a Mexican buffet, open bar, live music, folkloric dances, mariachis, cowboy rope tricks, bloodless cockfights and a piñata.

Mariachi Loco (Map pp62-3; ☎ 223-22-05; cnr Cárdenas & Vallarta; cover M$50; ☻ shows 10.30pm) Usually attracting an exuberant all-Mexican crowd, this restaurant-bar presents an entertaining (if slightly amateur) show of music, comedy and mariachi every night. It's a great bit of local color, but you'll need good Spanish to get the jokes.

Sheraton Buganvilias (Map p59; ☎ 226-04-04; Francisco Ascencio 999; buffet M$270; ☻ 9am-2pm Sun) Has Sunday champagne brunch with live mariachi music.

Cinemas
Cinemark (Map p59; ☎ 224-89-27; Av de los Tules 178; adult/child M$44/39) A multiplex in Plaza Caracol screening recent Hollywood releases. Theaters here have stadium seating and digital sound. When buying tickets, ask if the film is *subtitilada* (subtitled) or *doblada* (dubbed).

Theater
Santa Barbara Theater (Map pp62-3; ☎ 223-20-48; www .santabarbaratheater.com; Olas Altas 351; admission M$220, with dinner M$350) This cabaret-style community theater stages plays, musicals and live-music events put on mostly by expats from the US and Canada. Performers usually take the stage at 8pm. The dinner show includes, you guessed it, American food.

Bullfights
Every Wednesday from the third week of November to June, *matadores* and *novilleros* (professional and amateur bullfighters) step into the ring to put their bravery to the test at Vallarta's small bullfighting ring, **Plaza de Toros** (Map p59; ☎ 221-04-14; Blvd Ascencio, Km 2.5; admission M$350; ☻ 5pm). It isn't pretty, unless of course you share bullfighting aficionado Ernest Hemingway's view that the *corrida de toro* is an art form.

SHOPPING
Shops and boutiques in Puerto Vallarta sell fashion clothing, beachwear and just about every type of handicraft made in Mexico, but prices are high, as they target tourists' pocketbooks.

Markets
There are a few markets concentrating on craft stalls, and these are the places to go for cheaper prices and some hard bargaining.

Mercado de Artesanías (Map pp62-3; ☎ 223-09-25; A Rodríguez 260) A maze of more than 150 craft stalls, this market offers touristy T-shirts, Taxco silver jewelry, sarapes (cloaks) and *huaraches* (leather sandals), wool wall-hangings, painted pottery and blown glass, among many other things. Tons of other shops line Agustín Rodríguez, facing the market. Bargain like your life depended on it: walk away and prices plummet.

The most atmospheric handicraft district, however, is the shady and tropical strip on Isla Río Cuale, where stands sell crafts daily for comparable prices.

Shops & Boutiques
Olinala (Map pp62-3; ☎ 222-49-95; Cárdenas 274) This excellent gallery displays authentic Mexican

dance masks, folk art, rural antiques, fine guitars and contemporary paintings.

Serafina (Map pp62-3; ☎ 223-45-94; Badillo 260) A bit funky, with a good and crowded selection of pottery virgins, clothing, bags (leather, cloth, plastic) and jewelry.

Puerco Azul Galería (Map pp62-3; ☎ 222-86-47; Constitución 325) This beguiling, well-curated shop tempts with a treasure trove of movie posters, quirky original art, 'kitsch mexicana' and delightful curios.

Cielito Lindo (Map pp62-3; ☎ 222-40-78; Badillo 274) Come here for all your beach needs, including funky sunglasses, Panama hats and excellent straw hats and beach bags. It also specializes in creative and original jewelry. There's a considerate sofa on which the hubbies can wait.

Huichol Crafts

Puerto Vallarta is a prime place to shop for indigenous Huichol beadwork, yarn art (made by pressing thread into a wax-covered board) and jewelry. The following stores sell quality work.

Peyote People (Map pp62-3; ☎ 222-23-02; www .peyotepeople.com; Juárez 222) This fair-trade co-op sells high-quality Huichol yarn and bead art, masks, ceramic bowls and authentic ritual pieces. The owner, Kevin Simpson, has been traveling around Mexico for more than a decade collecting folk art. In addition to the Huichol pieces, the store stocks fantastic *alebrijes*, colorful wood sculptures from the state of Oaxaca.

Huichol Collection (Map pp62-3; ☎ 223-21-41; Morelos 490) Here you'll find a wide variety of jewelry, yarn art and lovely beadwork.

Artesanías Flores (Map pp62-3; ☎ 223-07-73; Cárdenas 282) Has much of the same Huichol bead and yarn art and also sells black clay pottery from Oaxaca.

Home Decor

Alfarería Tlaquepaque (Map p59; ☎ 223-21-21; Av México 1100) This large showroom has been in business for decades, offering the best prices and selection of baked earthenware, blown glass and ceramics.

Mundo de Cristal (Map pp62-3; ☎ 222-41-57; Insurgentes 333) Stocks an incredible selection of hand-blown glass and many other interesting breakables.

Lucy's CuCu Cabaña (Map pp62-3; ☎ 222-12-20; Badillo 295; ◷ 10am-8pm) Lucy's offers fine, fun

crafts from all over the country – Oaxacan wood animals, papier-mâché masks and recycled metal arts – among a lot of other things. The owners started an animal rescue program in Vallarta.

Mundo de Azulejos (Map pp62-3; ☎ 222-26-75; Carranza 374) This place has to have the best selection of artistic tiles in Vallarta. The tiles aren't cheap, but Mundo de Azulejos can custom-make whatever you can think up.

Artículos Religiosos La Asunción (Map pp62-3; ☎ 222-31-86; Libertad 319) This is the place to come for all sorts of religious paraphernalia. The calendars make great souvenirs.

Tequila & Cigars

Casa de Tequila (Map pp62-3; ☎ 222-20-00; Morelos 589) This store pours high-quality tequila shots…for free. They also sell the stuff, so they don't appreciate moochers. It's a good place for information on the national drink, if you're curious.

La Playa Vinos y Licores (Map pp62-3; ☎ 223-18-18; Morelos 803) Here's a good liquor store to buy the two bottles of tequila you're allowed to take back into the USA.

El Gato Gordo (Map pp62-3; ☎ 223-52-82; Vallarta 226) This small cigar shop has a fine selection of Cuban, Nicaraguan and Mexican cigars.

Art Galleries

Puerto Vallarta has more than its fair share of contemporary fine art galleries. The following are some of the best known for their consistent quality and selection:

Galería Alpacora (Map pp62-3; ☎ 222-30-77; www .galeriaalpacora.com; Corona 179) Sells intricately designed gourds from Peru, handmade pottery from Mata Ortiz, alpaca wool clothing, sculptures, mirrors, and magnificent tapestries by renowned weaver Maximo Laura.

Galería Dante (Map pp62-3; ☎ 222-24-77; www .galleriadante.com; Badillo 269) Contemporary paintings and sculptures by Mexican artists.

Galería de Ollas (Map pp62-3; ☎ 223-10-45; www .galeriadeollas.com; Corona 176) Displays beautiful pottery from Mata Ortiz.

Galería Mata Ortiz (Map pp62-3; ☎ 299-14-58, 222-74-07; Cárdenas 268A) Very small, but sells some of the finest pottery in Mexico.

Galería Omar Alonso (Map pp62-3; ☎ 222-55-87; www.galeriaomar.com; Vicario 249) Mostly contemporary art and photography.

Galería Pacífico (Map pp62-3; ☎ 222-19-82; www .galeriapacifico.com; Aldama 174) Open since 1987, with an emphasis on contemporary works by regional artists.

THE PSYCHADELIC ART OF THE HUICHOL

For centuries the Huichol have resisted efforts by missionaries to convert them and to this day they have managed to keep their traditions and culture intact. Their isolation has been a key factor, as they live in some of the furthest-flung and most inaccessible areas of Jalisco and Nayarit, a rugged region of about 39,000 sq km straddling the Sierra Madre Occidental. Believed to be direct descendants of the Aztecs, there remain approximately 8000 Huichol living where they have for centuries in five autonomous mountain communities.

Steeped in symbology, Huichol art is a window into another world, where deer, scorpions, salamanders and wolves speak to shamans; arrows carry prayers; serpents bring rain; and pumas carry messages from the gods. With no written language, the Huichol document and encode their legends and spiritual knowledge in beautiful and elaborate works including yarn art, brightly colored beaded bowls and carvings such as puma heads and serpents. Their undeniably beautiful work is never merely decorative: each piece manifests an aspect of tradition and belief, drawn from lifelong participation in rites and ceremonies.

The hallucinogenic peyote cactus, known as *hikuri*, is sacred to the Huichol, who consider it a gift from the gods and use it to acquire shamanic powers or to approach enlightenment. Each year, for the ritual use of peyote, the Huichol do a pilgrimage to La Sierra Quemada, their sacred ground in the state of San Luis Potosí. Peyote is a prime influence on Huichol art, inspiring its vibrant color and fantastic design but also appearing as a symbol for what scholar Angela Corelis called 'the essence, the very life, sustenance, health, accomplishment, good fortune of the Huichol.'

Originally all forms of Huichol art were made as *ofrendas,* or prayer offerings to the gods. Today, some of their art is also made to sell, providing the Huichol people with a livelihood that encourages them to maintain and preserve their cultural and spiritual identity. In recent decades some 4000 Huichol have descended from the highlands to sell their art in cities such as Tepic, Guadalajara and Mexico City. In Puerto Vallarta fine examples are offered for sale at several locations (opposite).

Visiting Huichol territory on your own is difficult since most of the communities are far removed from Vallarta. However, **Banderas Bay Tour & Travel** (☎ 329-296-5587; www.banderasbaytravel.com; adult/child M$1375/688) offers a one-day tour to the mountain hamlet of Nueva Valey, a small Huichol community outside Compostela, Nayarit. The trip includes pickup at your hotel and stops for breakfast and lunch. The residents present a music and dance ceremony, and you can buy their colorful crafts.

A more interesting option is chartering a plane to the remote mountain village of San Andres Coamihata, a Huichol religious and political center. The charter costs M$30,000 round-trip for up to 12 passengers and it departs from the **Aerotron** (Map p59; ☎ 226-84-46; www.aerotron.com.mx) hangar next to the Puerto Vallarta international airport (below).

To learn about efforts to preserve Huichol culture or to find outlets for artwork, contact the **Huichol Center** (☎ 457-983-7054; www.huicholcenter.org; Calle Victoria 24, Huejuquilla El Alto, Jalisco 46000).

Galería Uno (Map pp62-3; ☎ 222-09-08; Morelos 561) Mexican fine art in all mediums since 1971.

Galería Vallarta (Map pp62-3; ☎ 222-02-90; www.galeriavallarta.com; Juárez 263) Paintings by Mexico's most collected painters and unique handcrafted jewelry.

Patti Gallardo (Map pp62-3; ☎ 222-57-12; www.pattigallardo.com; Badillo 250) Specializes in mixed media paintings by Canadian artist Patti Gallardo.

GETTING THERE & AWAY

Air

Puerto Vallarta's **Gustavo Díaz Ordaz International Airport** (PVR; Map p59; ☎ 221-13-25), on Hwy 200

about 10km north of the city, is served by several national and international airlines. Inside are many duty-free shops, exchange houses (including Amex; good rates) and car-rental stalls (again, better rates than in town). There are also some expensive bars, restaurants and souvenir shops; bring a small bottle of water to save yourself a couple of thirsty pesos.

Aeroméxico (☎ 224-27-77) Direct service to Mexico City and Guadalajara, with connections to most major cities in the US and Mexico.

Alaska Airlines (☎ 221-13-50, in the US 800-426-0333) Direct service to Los Angeles and San Francisco.

American Airlines (☎ 221-17-99; in the US 800-433-7300) Flies nonstop to Dallas and Chicago.

Continental (☎ 221-10-25, in the US 800-231-0856) Direct service to Houston and Newark.

Delta Airlines (☎ 01-800-123-4710, in the US 800-221-1212) Nonstop flights to Los Angeles.

Frontier (☎ in the US 800-432-1359) Direct service to Denver and Kansas City.

Mexicana (☎ 224-89-00, in the US 800-531-7921) Direct service to San Francisco, Los Angeles and Mexico City.

US Airways (☎ 221-13-33, in the US 800-428-4322) Direct flights to Phoenix connect to Las Vegas and San Diego.

Bus

Vallarta's long-distance **bus station** (Map p59; ☎ 290-10-09; Carretera Puerto Vallarta-Tepic, Km 9) is just off Hwy 200, about 10km north of the city center and 2km north of the airport.

Most intercity bus lines have offices south of the Río Cuale, where you can buy tickets without having to make a trip to the station. They include ETN, Primera Plus and Servicios Coordinados, at Cárdenas 268 (Map pp62–3); and Transportes del Pacífico, at Insurgentes 282 (Map pp62–3). North of the river, **Agencia Fela** (Map pp62-3; ☎ 223-34-07; Morelos & 31 de Octubre) sells tickets for Primera Plus and TAP to Mexico City, Guadalajara, Mazanillo and other long-distance destinations.

Daily departures from the main terminal include the following:

Barra de Navidad (M$185, 3½ hours, four 1st-class; M$155, four hours, five 2nd-class) Same buses as to Manzanillo.

Guadalajara (M$280 to M$320, 5½ hours, frequent 1st-class)

Manzanillo (M$231, five hours, 1st-class; M$195 2nd-class)

Mazatlán (M$320, eight hours, 1st-class) You can also take a bus to Tepic, where buses depart frequently for Mazatlán.

Mexico City (M$797, 14 hours, frequent 1st-class) To Terminal Norte.

Rincón de Guayabitos (M$70, 1½ hours 2nd-class) Same buses as to Tepic.

San Blas (M$118, 3½ hours, 2nd-class) Or take a bus to Tepic for transfer.

San Patricio-Melaque (M$180, 3½ hours, four 1st-class; M$150, four hours, four 2nd-class) Same buses as to Manzanillo.

Sayulita (M$33, one hour, 10 2nd-class)

Tepic (M$140, 3½ hours, frequent 1st- and 2nd-class)

Car & Motorcycle

Starting at about M$750 per day, car rentals are pricey during high season, but deep discounts are offered during other times, particularly if you book online.

Due to immediate competition from the neighbors, showing up in person at the airport car-rental counters can result in the best deals (watch out for those tricky downtown timeshares; they can be mistaken for rental-car companies). Negotiating is always a possibility.

Check with your credit-card company back home to see if car insurance for a rental abroad is covered (to be covered, you must use that credit card to pay for the rental); sometimes the coverage is limited to rentals of less than two weeks. Paying cash is often cheaper, and you won't be forced to use the rental companies' self-favored rate of exchange (check the fine print on the contract). For more information about renting cars in Mexico, see p289.

The following car-rental agencies are at the airport:

Avis (☎ 221-16-57)

Budget (☎ 221-17-30)

Hertz (☎ 221-14-73)

National (☎ 221-12-26)

Mario's Moto Rent (Map p59; ☎ 221-71-13; Av Ascencio 998), opposite the Sheraton Buganvilias hotel, rents out trail bikes (M$150 per hour) and scooters (M$120 per hour).

GETTING AROUND
To/From the Airport

The cheapest way to get to/from the airport is on a local bus for M$5.50. 'Aeropuerto,' 'Juntas' and 'Ixtapa' buses from town all stop right at the airport entrance; 'Centro' and 'Olas Altas' buses go into town from beside the airport entrance. A taxi from the city center costs around M$80.

From the airport to town, fixed-fare taxis inside the airport charge different prices depending on where you want to go: they charge approximately M$120/140/160 to Marina Vallarta/Centro/Zona Romántica (also called Old Town or Olas Altas).

Bicycle

If you're after a two-wheeled buzz, **Bike Mex** (Map pp62-3; ☎ 223-16-80, 223-18-34; Guerrero 361) and **Eco Ride** (Map pp62-3; ☎ 222-79-12; Miramar 382) rent mountain bikes for guided or self-guided tours starting at M$250 per day. See p67 for more information.

Boat & Water Taxi

In addition to taxis on land, Vallarta also has water taxis to beautiful beaches, accessible only by boat, on the southern side of the bay.

Water taxis departing from the pier at Playa de los Muertos head south around the bay, making stops at Playa Las Ánimas (25 minutes), Quimixto (30 minutes) and Yelapa (45 minutes); the round-trip fare is M$220 for any destination. Boats depart at 10am, 11am, 11:30am, 12:30pm, 4pm and 5:30pm. Purchase tickets at **Benny's Tours** (Map pp62-3; Diéguez 109), next to Langostino's.

A water taxi also goes to Yelapa from the beach just south of Hotel Rosita, on the northern end of the *malecón*, departing at 11:30am Monday to Friday (M$140 one way, 30 minutes).

If you buy a return ticket from any particular water taxi, you have to return with the same boat at the time the boat operator has set to return. If you buy just a one-way ticket, you can take any boat back with any boatman. If you go to more isolated places, however, you should probably buy a return ticket so someone knows to come back for you.

Cheaper water taxis *(pangas)* to the same places depart from Boca de Tomatlán, south of town, which is easily reached by local bus.

Private yachts and *lanchas* (fast, open, outboard boats) can be hired from the south side of the Playa de los Muertos pier. Expect to pay about M$350 per hour or up to M$1500 per day. They'll take you to any secluded beach around the bay, and many have gear aboard for snorkeling and fishing. *Lanchas* can also be hired privately at Mismaloya and Boca de Tomatlán, but they're expensive.

Bus

Local buses that are marked 'Ixtapa' and 'Juntas' go to the bus station; 'Centro' and 'Olas Altas' buses run into town from beside the long-distance bus station parking lot.

Local buses operate every five minutes from 5am to 11pm on most routes and cost M$5.50. Plaza Lázaro Cárdenas at Playa Olas Altas is a major departure hub. Northbound local bus routes also stop a half-block from the Hotel Belmar, on Insurgentes near the corner of Madero.

Northbound buses marked 'Hoteles,' 'Aeropuerto,' 'Ixtapa,' 'Pitillal' and 'Juntas' pass through the city heading north to the airport, the Zona Hotelera and Marina Vallarta; the 'Hoteles,' 'Pitillal' and 'Ixtapa' routes can take you to any of the large hotels north of the city.

Southbound 'Boca de Tomatlán' buses pass along the southern coastal highway through Mismaloya (M$5.50, 20 minutes) to Boca de Tomatlán (M$8, 30 minutes). They depart from Constitución near the corner of Badillo every 15 minutes from 6am to 11pm.

Taxi

There's no such thing as a cheap cab in Vallarta. Fares are generally fixed and determined by how many zones you cross. A typical trip from downtown to the Zona Hotelera costs M$80, to Mismaloya it's about M$130, and to move about around downtown expect to pay M$60. Always agree on the price of the ride before you get in.

AROUND PUERTO VALLARTA

Vallarta's appeal reaches far beyond its city limits. All around Bahía de Banderas you'll find gorgeous beaches and impressive green mountains. So what are you waiting for? Pack that day-trip bag and hit the road.

NORTH OF PUERTO VALLARTA

North of town, in the Zona Hotelera, are the sandy stretches of Camarones, Las Glorias, Los Tules, Las Palmas, Playa de Oro and, past the marina, El Salado. Nuevo Vallarta, an expansive land of all-inclusive behemoth beach hotels, is just past here. And beyond that, up toward the roof of the bay, are the day-trip destinations of Bucerías, La Cruz de Huanacaxtle and Playa El Anclote (at Punta de Mita), with more beaches dotted between.

Remember that as you travel from Jalisco state to Nayarit state (the border is between Marina Vallarta and Nuevo Vallarta) you need to set your watch back an hour. Any business hours listed in the following towns reflect winter high-season hours; in summer, hours and days are often cut back, but hotel prices go down as well.

Bucerías

☎ 329 / pop 11,1000

Visitors looking to escape from the hustle and bustle of Puerto Vallarta can rest easy

PUERTO VALLARTA

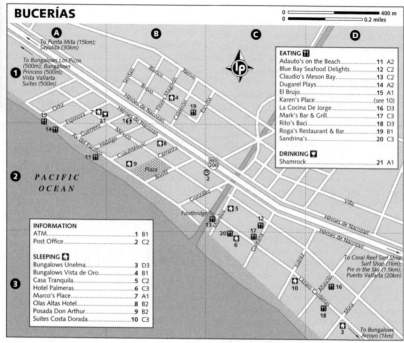

BUCERÍAS

EATING		
Adauto's on the Beach	11	A2
Blue Bay Seafood Delights	12	C2
Claudio's Meson Bay	13	C2
Dugarel Plays	14	A2
El Brujo	15	A1
Karen's Place	(see 10)	
La Cocina De Jorge	16	D3
Mark's Bar & Grill	17	C3
Rito's Baci	18	D3
Roga's Restaurant & Bar	19	B1
Sandrina's	20	C3

DRINKING		
Shamrock	21	A1

PACIFIC OCEAN

INFORMATION		
ATM	1	B1
Post Office	2	C2

SLEEPING		
Bungalows Unelma	3	D3
Bungalows Vista de Oro	4	B1
Casa Tranquila	5	C2
Hotel Palmeras	6	C3
Marco's Place	7	A1
Olas Altas Hotel	8	B2
Posada Don Arthur	9	B2
Suites Costa Dorada	10	C3

in this small-scale resort town about 15 minutes northwest of the PV airport. From the freeway, Bucerías looks like another road-straddling town you'd just as soon zoom by on your way to somewhere else. But head toward the coast and you'll find bougainvillea-lined streets dotted with cozy hotels, excellent restaurants and a smattering of watering holes frequented mostly by foreigners. A dry riverbed cuts through the middle of town. On the northwest side you'll see the main plaza, several beachfront *palapa* restaurants and a touristy outdoor market. Hotels and restaurants predominate on the quieter southeast side.

Bucerías consists of just a few very long blocks paralleling the beach and Hwy 200. It's a four-stoplight town. The **post office** (Héroes de Nacozari, btwn González & Bonfil) faces the highway. Internet service is available at **Sandrina's** (☎ 298-02-73; Cárdenas 33) for M$20 per 30 minutes (or free, if you purchase breakfast or lunch). There's an ATM on the western edge of the highway near the corner of Guerrero.

The big local celebration is **Fiesta de la Virgen de la Paz**, held each year in mid-January to honor the town's patron saint, Nuestra Señora de la Paz. Local boatmen deck their launches out with palm fronds, paper streamers, flowers and balloons in anticipation of a blessing from the priest.

ACTIVITIES

Coral Reef Surf Shop (☎ 298-02-61; www.surf-mexico .com/sites/coralreef; Héroes de Nacozari 114; 9am-9pm Mon-Sat) is a full-service shop that rents longboards (M$200 per day) and boogie boards (M$75 per day). Long- and short-boards are for sale; after you've broken them in you can bring them back for repairs. Surf lessons are also offered.

SLEEPING

Many of Bucerías nicer hotels offer large bungalows and suites geared toward families and small groups. If you're rolling with the crew, these accommodations are very affordable. You'll also find a decent offering of budget and midrange options several blocks from the beach. Prices quoted here are for high season. If you're planning to stay around for a while, check out the vacation rentals posted at www.sunworx.com or www.las-palmas-travel.com.

Budget

Bungalows Vista de Oro (☎ 298-03-90; cnr Flores Magnón & Bravo; d/q M$350/700; 🏊) Terraced up a hillside, this friendly, funky-flavored and pink-themed place is a block east of the highway on the inland side of town (look for the red pagoda and cross the highway). The big, fan-cooled bungalows are good but basic and work well for large, unfussy groups. One downside: it's a bit of a hike to the beach, though.

Midrange

Posada Don Arthur (☎ 298-09-95; texmexnay1@hotmail .com; Av del Pacífico 6; d/q M$480/580; 🏊) The manager initially seems a tad gruff, but once you get to know him you'll find that he's merely discriminating. The location is central and the six rooms are large and OK for this budget, with kitchens, air-con and cable TV. It's good for longer stays, as there's a fair-sized apartment with kitchen suitable for a cozy couple or four good friends.

Olas Altas Hotel (☎ 298-04-07; cnr Héroes de Nacozari & Cuauhtémoc; s/d M$380/500; 🏊) This bright-green no-frills hotel offers the most affordable digs

---

DETOUR: GUADALAJARA & TEQUILA

Colonial Guadalajara, Mexico's second-largest city, offers quite a change of scenery from the sandy beaches of Puerto Vallarta. The home of mariachi music, tequila, *charreadas* (rodeos) and the Mexican hat dance, the state capital of Jalisco boasts some of Mexico's most cherished traditions. It's also known for its riveting cultural scene, with a bountiful offering of contemporary art, alternative music and folkloric ballet.

Short-term visitors spend most of their time basking in the ambience of the Centro Histórico, with its many leafy plazas, 400-year-old cathedral and stunning murals by José Clemente Orozco. For the classic Guadalajara cantina experience in the Centro, just off the main square, drop by **La Fuente** (Suárez 78; 🕐 1pm-3am) for cheap beers and live piano and violin music played with old-school flair.

Just a hop, skip and a stumble away, on the square's south side, **Hotel Francés** (☎ 33-3613-1190; www.hotelfrances.com; Maestranza 35; s/d M$643/678) has been offering rooms since 1610, making it Guadalajara's oldest hotel. There's live music in its central arched stone courtyard, and all of downtown's main attractions are within walking distance.

If time permits, check out the nearby municipality of Tlaquepaque, known for its quality arts-and-crafts stores and great little restaurants. Or go straight to the source at Tonalá, where most of the ceramics and blown-glass objects sold in Tlaquepaque are produced.

Guadalajara is 374km from Puerto Vallarta (six hours by car or bus). If driving, head north from town on Hwy 200 to its end at Chapatilla, then south on Hwy 15. Frequent 1st-class buses leave throughout the day from the long-distance bus terminal (M$280 to M$320). Direct air service from Puerto Vallarta to Guadalajara is provided by Mexicana and Aeroméxico (p85).

While in the area, consider taking a side trip to the small town of Tequila, home to Mexico's top distilleries. Tequila lies about 50km northwest of Guadalajara. Lining the streets are small stores selling a wide range of tequila, ranging from watered-down, hangover-inducing spirits sold in plastic bottles to high-quality varieties of 100% agave. Sample the many different flavors and enjoy the wild ride. Contrary to what one might think, Tequila has a remarkably low-key vibe. Rarely will you see drunks face down on the sidewalk, as you might find in other small towns, and most of the bars tend to shut down by midnight. If you decide to stick around for a night, **Mision Tequillan** (☎ 374-742-32-32; www.tequillan.com.mx; Abasolo 47; s/d/tr M$395/612/700, ste M$730 🅿 🏊) has spotless, reasonably priced rooms with modern furnishings and comfortable beds.

To get to Tequila from Guadalajara, catch a bus (they depart frequently) from the Antigua Central Camionera, near Parque Agua Azul.

A more entertaining option for tequila tasting is the **Tequila Express** (adult/child M$950/450) train. Departing from Guadalajara's train station on Saturdays at 11am, the choo-choo chugs along to Amatitán, about 10km shy of Tequila. The trip includes a tour of the **Herradura distillery**, lunch, a lively mariachi performance and open bar. The train conductor will be your designated driver for the trip back to Guadalajara.

in town. The large rooms are a tad musty, but they're clean and come with air-con and TV.

our pick **Casa Tranquila** (☎ 298-17-67; www.casa tranquila-bucerias.com; Morelos 7A; d M$600-700; ✗ ✗ ✗) *Tranquila* is the operative word at this breezy, casual hideaway run by Patricia Mendez and Joann Quickstad, an affable iced-tea–loving couple who will make you feel right at home. The five one-bedroom units are cozy and individually decorated. Each comes with a well-equipped kitchen and feels like home right away. On site is a bookstore and a coffee shop, and Joann offers therapeutic massages (M$450 per hour).

Hotel Palmeras (☎ 298-12-88; www.hotelpalmeras .com; Lázaro Cárdenas 35; r M$650-1300; ✗ ✗ ✗ ✗) In proximity to some of the town's best restaurants, this well-run hotel provides 21 smoke-free one- and two-bedroom kitchenette apartments, all well appointed and modern. The hotel also has wireless internet and a leafy patio with a large pool. The larger suites sleep up to six.

Marco's Place (☎ 298-08-65; www.marcosplacevil las.com; Espinoza 6A; r M$750, ste M$850-950; ✗ ✗) This squeaky-clean hotel offers 18 rooms and suites, all of which have kitchenettes and cable TV. The larger rooms, which come with sofa beds and sleepers, accommodate up to six people. All rooms surround a quiet pool area, while those on 3rd floor afford a glimpse of the ocean about a block away.

Top End

Bungalows Princess (☎ 298-01-00; http://bungalows -princess.com; Retorno Destiladeras, Playas de Huanacaxtle; d/ste M$800/1600, bungalow M$2200-2800; ✗ ✗ ✗) With two rooms, two bathrooms and a sofa bed, the beachfront bungalows here can accommodate up to eight people, making this a real deal for families and small groups. More affordable single rooms are available as well. The pool with water slide, game room and play areas will keep the little ones out of your hair.

Bungalows Arroyo (☎ 298-02-88; http://bunga lowsarroyobucerias.com; Lázaro Cárdenas 500; bungalows M$1000-1200; ✗ ✗ ✗ ✗ ✗) A popular home-away-from-home five blocks east of Hotel Palmeras, this hotel offers 15 two-bedroom apartment-style units half a block from the beach. The comfortable units, arranged around a palm-shaded swimming pool, sport king-sized beds, balcony, kitchen and living and dining areas. They fill up quickly in the winter, so book early.

Suites Costa Dorada (☎ 298-00-46; www.scostado rada.com; Lázaro Cárdenas 156 Sur; ste M$1000-2900; ✗ ✗) This six-story hotel looks big in this small town, and even the smallest of suites is fit for a king, or a very large family. They come with fully equipped kitchens, satellite TV and ocean-view terraces. The oceanfront restaurant provides breathtaking sunset views and the pool area is a big hit with the kids.

Vista Vallarta Suites (☎ 298-03-61; www.vistaval lartasuites.com; Av los Picos 87, Playas de Huanacaxtle; ste M$1350-2600; ✗ ✗ ✗ ✗) On offer at this all-suites hotel are bright, well-appointed apartments arranged around a shady beachside pool. The spacious two-bedroom suites include dining areas, kitchenettes and ocean-view balconies. The place empties out in the summer, when the proprietors are apt to make a deal on the price.

Bungalows Los Picos (☎ 298-04-70; www.lospicos .com.mx; Av Los Picos & Retorno Pontoques, Playas de Huanacaxtle; 1-/2-/3-bedroom bungalow M$1529/2189/3289; ✗ ✗ ✗ ✗) This beachfront complex delivers the goods with excellent large bungalows ideal for groups of four to eight. The largest of the bunch enjoy sweeping ocean views and have pleasant eating and living areas. All units have cable TV, but only some come with air-con. Two pools and ample garden areas make this an ideal place to hole up for a while and practice the art of relaxation.

Bungalows Unelma (☎ 298-00-80; unelma@prodigy .net.mx; Lázaro Cárdenas 51; d M$1600; ✗) This unique, tropical hideaway offers a little slice of paradise with its two beachside bungalows surrounded by lush, manicured gardens. Each has an outdoor living room and kitchenette. A manicured lawn leads to the beautiful beach with a private sunbathing area and comfortable deck chairs. The bungalows are very private and secured day and night from both the street and the beach. Kitchens are fully equipped and one unit comes with air-con. Boogie boards, sea kayaks and hammocks are part of the deal.

EATING & DRINKING

For such a small town, Bucerías sure has a lot of excellent eating options. Menus consist mostly of seafood dishes, and many expat-owned establishments offer top-quality Western food.

Blue Bay Seafood Delights (☎ 298-22-64; Galeana 12; M$20-70; ⏱ noon-9pm Mon-Sat) Pull up a plastic chair on the sidewalk of this unassuming eatery and enjoy delish Baja-style fish and shrimp tacos. The menu also features *ceviche tostadas*, burritos, seafood salad and other light snacks.

Pie in the Sky (☎ 298-08-38; Héroes de Nacozari 202; pie slice/whole M$30/295; ☺ 8am-10pm) On the highway at the first stoplight coming into town from Puerto Vallarta. The *besos* (brownies M$30), chocolate mousse and mango pie are so good you'll want to spend a small fortune on goodies to go. Gourmet coffees are also served.

La Cocina de Jorge (☎ 298-06-13; Abasolo 5; breakfast M$50, lunch M$45-80; ☺ 9am-noon & 2-4:30pm Tue-Fri, 9am-noon Sat) This is the place for economical, homestyle Mexican cooking. The menu has the usual breakfast suspects and the poor man's lunch favorite, the *comida corrida* (M$45), a complete meal with drink included.

Claudio's Meson Bay (☎ 298-16-34; Lázaro Cárdenas 17; mains M$60-200; ☺ 11am-11pm) All-you-can-eat salad bars are few and far between, but this beachside *palapa* sets out an endless supply of shrimp and fish on Monday, fine cuts of steak on Wednesday, and Mexican favorites and margaritas on Friday night.

Karen's Place (☎ 298-31-76; Lázaro Cárdenas 156 Sur; mains M$75-195; ☺ 9am-9pm Tue-Sat, 9am-3pm Sun) The Sunday champagne brunch with live music gets top billing at this oceanfront restaurant at the Suites Costa Dorada hotel. The menu offers fish and seafood dishes, such as mahi-mahi and coconut shrimp, and it has a fair share of comfort food for finicky foreigners. On Monday, Wednesday and Friday evenings live classical-guitar music fills the air.

Sandrina's (☎ 298-02-73; Lázaro Cárdenas 33; mains M$75-210; ☺ 3-10:30pm Wed-Mon) Savor the Mediterranean flavor in this restaurant's delightful courtyard, where you can also catch live flamenco dancing and classical guitar twice a month on Tuesday. The menu features Greek salads, lasagna and Mediterranean chicken. After the meal, drop by Sandrina's gift shop and check out the colorful Mexican folk art. There's free internet service for customers.

Adauto's on the Beach (☎ 298-29-70; Av del Pacífico 11A; mains M$85-225; ☺ noon-10pm) One of the most popular restaurants in town, Adauto's has moved to a beautiful new oceanfront location under a palm-thatched roof. Adauto Ramos, the friendly proprietor, will be happy to show you old newspaper clippings confirming that he was once director John Huston's house boy. While you're at it, give him a wink and

ask for a shot of his special *raicilla* (agave distillate). Grab a table right on the beach or take in the new-age ambience in the airy dining room. The menu features fish and seafood treats such as grilled mahimahi, red snapper drenched in garlic butter, and a burrito stuffed with lobster tail and all the fixings.

Dugarel Plays (☎ 298-17-57; Av del Pacífico s/n; mains M$90-230; ☺ 10am-10pm) In case you might be wondering, the funky name was intended to be something more along the lines of 'Dugarel's Place.' Sitting on a rickety-looking wooden deck with great sea views, you'd do well to go for the jumbo shrimp, lobster or fresh red snapper. They also make a mean margarita.

El Brujo (☎ 298-04-06; Av del Pacífico 202A; mains M$95-210; ☺ noon-9pm) This seafood restaurant has been such a big hit in Puerto Vallarta that the owners recently opened a beachfront location in Bucerías. The menu offers mostly fish and seafood dishes, but it also has several beef and chicken options. The tables on the deck out back offer an ocean view. The portions come generously served here, so you might want to go easy on the chips and guacamole that are brought to the table when you sit down.

Rito's Baci (☎ 298-01-40; Lázaro Cárdenas 51; mains M$129-169; ☺ 1-11pm) Kindhearted Rito Calzada, the man behind these authentic freshmade pasta dishes, inherited a love for cooking from his Italian-born grandfather. Specialties include pizzas, lasagna with béchamel sauce, and Rito's favorite, an Italian sausage sandwich with onions, bell peppers and melted mozzarella. Rito's delivers if you feel like staying in.

Roga's Restaurant & Bar (☎ 298-15-65; Bravo 26; mains M$140-240; ☺ 2-11pm Mon-Sat) This swanky spot perched on a cliff overlooking the town is a tequila-lover's dream – it keeps a cellar stocked with the stuff and a rare agave distillate called *raicilla* (which may induce a slightly psychedelic state). The menu is grounded in seafood dishes like tequila shrimp and barbecued oyster fajitas. To get there, you can slog up Calderón or take the elevator from the highway.

our pick **Mark's Bar & Grill** (☎ 298-03-03; Lázaro Cárdenas 56; mains M$165-315; ☺ noon-10:30pm) Mark's Mediterranean- and Asian-inspired menu has won many fans over the years, and it's not hard to see why. Notable dishes served in the elegant, breezy dining room include New

Zealand rack of lamb, miso-marinated beef salad and pan-roasted Bay lobster in the shell. It's not exactly a cheap night out, especially if you indulge in wine, but few would argue that it's one of the finest dining experiences in town.

Shamrock (☎ 298-30-73; Av Mexíco 22; ⊗ 11am-1am) Recite some old Irish blessings and you're sure to earn some brownie points with the owners here. The pub offers the best of both worlds, with Irish stew, Guinness beer and live *cumbia* and salsa music three nights a week.

GETTING THERE & AWAY

There are buses every 20 minutes from Puerto Vallarta, leaving from across from the Sheraton Buganvilias in the Zona Hotelera. The trip takes 30 minutes and costs M$11; in Bucerías, get off at the second stoplight and walk in-land to the plaza (unless you're only going to Bucerías for brownies at Pie in the Sky; in this case, get off at the first stoplight).

La Cruz de Huanacaxtle
☎ 329 / pop 2600

Travelers are just starting to catch on to the traditional little Mexican fishing town of La Cruz de Huanacaxtle. Fidgety sorts may find the pace of life here underwhelming, but those who enjoy simple pleasures might fall under its spell. Get to know the locals or hear the interesting stories of the expats who've made this home. Hold court in the pretty plaza, conjugating verbs beneath a shady tree, or watch a fisherman skillfully throwing his net out from the shore.

Local lore puts forth that the town earned its name when the body of an indigenous woman was buried at the base of a giant *huanacaxtle* tree. In tribute a large cross, 2m by 1m, was carved into the trunk of the tree.

The town puts on its best face during its lively annual fiesta in early May, when the church bells toll for patron saint Santa Cruz, the streets fill with food stands and games, and there's a big fireworks show over the bay.

La Cruz supports a growing selection of cosmopolitan restaurants and a pleasant yacht harbor where many gringos anchor for free. Fishermen sell their catch at the dockside every morning, and there's a village market on Wednesday from 9am to 1pm. Traffic is rare but tourism is starting to pick up – enjoy it while you can.

ACTIVITIES

Acción Tropical (☎ 329-295-50-87; www.acciontropical .com.mx; Langosta 3; ⊗ 9am-2pm & 4-8pm) is a friendly operation that rents surfboards (M$300 per day) and kayaks (M$120 per hour); offers surfing lessons (two hours, M$900) and surfing trips (from M$400); and also leads snorkeling excursions to Las Islas Marietas (up to eight people M$1400). Whale-watching, boating and fishing trips are available as well. Another branch is at Punta de Mita.

SLEEPING

La Cruz's accommodation scene is dominated by long-term villa rentals, with only a few traditional hotels.

Bungalows Sukasa (☎ 295-59-92; Coral 25; s/d M$350/500; ✕ ⊛) This small hotel in the heart of town offers eight well-priced and decent rooms, each with kitchen and air-conditioning. There's a small pool in the grassy courtyard.

La Cruz Inn (☎ 295-58-49, in the US 707-202-4693; www.lacruzinn.com; r/apt M$1100/1300; ✕ ⊛) A charming and exceedingly peaceful accommodation situated next to the church just off the plaza. On offer are four tastefully furnished apartments with open-air kitchens, sitting areas and hand-carved furniture. For a more economical option, check out the 'dream weaver' room, though you'll have to get by without a kitchen. Guests can use the inn's kayaks and bicycles, and there's also an attractive pool with chaise longues around a leafy patio area.

Villa Bella Bed & Breakfast Inn (☎ 295-51-61, in the US 877-273-6244; www.villabella-lacruz.com; r M$1170, ste M$2100-2900, house M$7950; ℗ ✕ ⌨ ⊛) Perched atop a hill with a striking view of the Bay of Banderas and the Sierra Madres, this upscale retreat offers comfortable adjoining rooms, spacious suites with king-sized beds, and a large house that accommodates up to eight adults and two children. Sumptuous breakfasts are served on the terrace, where you can also enjoy a panoramic lap pool. Additionally, the B&B arranges ecotours, fishing and golf trips.

EATING & DRINKING

Like its neighbor Bucerías, La Cruz supports several stylish expat-run restaurants in addition to typical Mexican eateries. On Saturday and Sunday nights near the plaza, family-run taco stands are set up serving delicious corn tortillas and all the fixings, and the whole town turns out to mingle.

Café Galería Arte Huichol (☎ 295-50-71; www.hikuri .com; Coral 66; breakfast M$30-50; ☒ 8am-5pm) Situated in a very peaceful courtyard with a gurgling fountain and shady trees, this is a great, easy-going hangout – and more than just a café. Wayland and Aruna are Brits with a one-of-a-kind story of designing and building their own boat (with money made by selling tacos on the streets of London), having a baby, then sailing around Central America for 10 years before finally settling in at La Cruz de Huanacaxtle. Here they established a T-shirt printing shop, carpentry workshop, Huichol crafts-center store and café. Wayland also started a project of building and distributing spinning wheels for the Huichol locals to weave more efficiently. You can see Huichol sandals being made, and a sale percentage of the Huichol-designed T-shirts sold are donated to Huichol projects in Mexico. If that isn't enough to make you feel all fuzzy inside, try the delicious Mexican dishes, salads, baguettes, iced lattes or lemonades.

Philo's (☎ 295-50-68; Delfín 15; mains M$59-179; ☒ 10am-1am Tue-Sun; ☒) Philo's is a little bit of everything: restaurant, bar, music studio and cultural center. Here's the line-up: Monday is football night, Wednesday is ciné club, on Friday and Saturday live blues and rock bands jam, and on Sunday there's more football. Burgers and grilled sandwiches cost M$60, and yoga and Spanish classes are offered as well.

La Cruz Yacht Club (☎ 295-55-26; Marlín 39A; mains M$75-205; ☒ 8am-10:30pm) Don't worry, it's not as snooty as it sounds. Overlooking the new marina harbor, the restaurant serves fish, seafood and international cuisine. After the meal, head upstairs to the open-air lounge bar and take in the panoramic view over a few cocktails.

Black Forest (☎ 295-52-03; Marlín 16; mains M$85-189; ☒ 6-10pm Sun-Fri) A trip to La Cruz wouldn't be complete without trying chef Winfried Küffner's famous schnitzel, Hungarian goulash, or mouthwatering desserts. To get things started, go for the potato bisque with smoked summer sausage. The live flamenco music on Friday evenings creates a festive air.

Restaurante La Glorieta de Enrique (Coral 26; breakfast M$40-75, dinner M$95-185; ☒ 9am-8pm) A simple palapa restaurant on the roundabout, this local haunt is a fine place to while away a long morning over coffee and a paperback.

Frascati (☎ 295-61-85; Langosta 10; mains M$109-208; ☒ 5-11pm) You know La Cruz is officially on the tourist circuit when a chain restaurant rolls into town. In all fairness, Frascati is a small chain that prepares respectable Italian cuisine. The menu includes wood-oven gourmet pizzas, homemade pastas and grilled steaks served in a rustic-smart, open-air dining area.

Britannia Bar (Coral 68; ☒ 6pm-midnight Tue-Sun) With the look of a wannabe medieval castle, this watering hole and social hall is the only place in town to draw a cool Guinness.

GETTING THERE & AWAY

It's easy to reach La Cruz de Huanacaxtle: simply hop on a north-pointing Punta de Mita bus anywhere along Puerto Vallarta's Zona Hotelera (M$14, every 15 minutes).

Punta de Mita, Playa El Anclote & Around

☎ 329 / pop 2000

Surfers' paradise Punta de Mita sits pretty on a scenic peninsula on the northern tip of Bahía de Banderas. Life moves so deliciously slow in these parts that you just might decide to stick around for a while, as many expats have done. Here and about lie creamy strands of beaches, including Playa El Anclote, the main attraction for surfers and bodyboarders. Ubiquitous seafood palapa restaurants on the beach offer great views of the bay and a distant Puerto Vallarta. Not a bad deal for those who also come to enjoy the beach, go on boat trips or try their balance in the surf.

Playa El Anclote is in the village of Nuevo Corral del Risco. To get there, head downhill from the main road; at the T-junction at the bottom is the beachside road Av Anclote, where most of the local businesses operate. Occupying higher ground just to the east is its sister village Emiliano Zapata, where many accommodations are to be had. You can walk from one end of town to the other in about 15 minutes.

ACTIVITIES

Playa El Anclote is justifiably famous for surfing. At **Acción Tropical** (☎ 291-66-33; Av El Anclote s/n, Nuevo Corral del Risco) local surfing honcho Eduardo del Valle Ochoa provides his considerable expertise from a shady spot across from the palapa restaurants on the beach road. Here you can book surfing lessons (two hours,

M$900) and boat trips in the bay, including snorkeling at Las Isla Marietas (two hours, M$1400) and whale-watching in season. You can also rent kayaks and surfboards.

Tranquilo Surf Adventures (☎ 291-64-75; www.tran quilosurf.com; Pez Vela 130, Nuevo Corral del Risco), a small company promoting low-impact surfing, operates a surf school (two hours M$1500) from November through April catering to individuals and small groups in pursuit of 'a liquid foundation to surfing.' They also can arrange boats trips for inshore and offshore fishing and snorkeling trips.

Formerly a fishing cooperative, **Caseta Cooperativa Corral de Riscos Servicios Turisticos** (☎ 291-62-98; Anclote 17; ☷ 8am-4pm Mon-Sat) offers snorkeling tours to Las Islas Marietas (M$1200 per two hours), fishing trips (M$600 to M$700 per hour), and whale-watching (M$1200 per two hours) from December to March.

SLEEPING & EATING

Hotel Coco's (☎ 291-63-75; cocosmita@yahoo.com; Av de las Pangas 4, Nuevo Corral del Risco; s/d M$250/350) Think of this budget hotel as a convenient place to crash if you're looking to save some pesos. The eight clean rooms are a tad dark, but what would you expect from the cheapest digs in town?

Punta Mita Hotel (☎ 291-62-69; Hidalgo 5, Emiliano Zapata; d with/without kitchen M$500/400; ☷ ☐ ☷) This old-school hotel has austere rooms with aging furnishings that take you back in time. The beach is about 50m from the property. Unfortunately, some recently built condos now block the hotel's ocean view, but it's still a good budget option if you plan to spend most of the day on the beach.

Meson de Mita Bungalows (☎ 291-63-30; meson demita@yahoo.com; Av El Anclote 200; s/d M$550/750; ☷ ☷) With a big *palapa* restaurant and a privileged location right on Playa El Anclote, this hotel offers clean, simple rooms and a small pool just a stone's throw from the beach.

Casa Las Palmas (☎ 291-63-04; www.casalaspalmas .net; Francisco Madero s/n, Emiliano Zapata; 1-/2-bedroom apt M$600/900; ☷ ☷) Immaculate and welcoming, this well-run operation in Emiliano Zapata offers five large brick-and-stucco apartments in a garden setting. Guests enjoy access to a large swimming pool, Jacuzzi and barbecue grill, as well as kayaks, snorkeling gear and surfcasting poles. With wireless internet, free phone service to the US and Canada, satellite

TV, DVD players, a large book-lending library and even a telescope for whale-watching, you may decide to extend your vacation.

Hotel Villas las Olas (☎ 291-53-37; www.villaslas olas.com.mx; Madero s/n, Emiliano Zapata; 1-/2-bedroom apt M$650/850; ☷ ☐) The spacious apartments at this place go fast, so make reservations well ahead of time. The one-bedroom sleeps up to five people, while the two-bedroom houses seven comfortably, making it a great option for families and groups. Prepare your own meals in the large kitchens, or your kind host Lisa will whip something up for an extra charge. Las Olas offers all the modern conveniences: satellite TV, wireless internet and free phone calls to the US and Canada. It also rents surfboards and bodyboards (M$150/100 per day).

Hotel la Quinta del Sol (☎ 291-53-15; in Canada or the US 888-425-2824; www.laquintadelsol.com; Hidago 162, Emiliano Zapata; d M$900-1020; ☷ ☐) Just a short walk from Playa El Anclote, this tranquil surfers' haven offers seven stylish rooms with attractive rustic furnishings, kitchens, ceiling fans and red-tiled floors. Terraces outside the rooms have an ocean view and comfortable handmade wood chairs with leather backrests. On the scenic rooftop you can bask in the sun and use the barbecue grill for afternoon cookouts. If you want to hit the crashing surf, the hotel rents surfboards, bodyboards and kayaks (M$100/50/50 per day).

Hotel des Artistes (☎ 291-50-05, in the US 866-628-6293; www.hoteldesartistesdelmar.com; Av El Anclote 5; 2-bedroom ste M$6487-7488, 3-bedroom M$9815; ☐ ☷ ☷) The choicest option in town, this new luxury boutique hotel has 12 suites decorated with impeccable taste. All units come with contemporary furniture, fully equipped gourmet kitchens, laundry rooms, dining and living rooms, lots of closet space and large balconies with ocean views. The units sleep up to four persons. On-site amenities include a fitness club and spa, two pools (including a rooftop infinity pool), and a gourmet bistro with a menu designed by award-winning chef Thierry Blouet. On display in the lobby are contemporary paintings from the Thierry Blouet Fine Art Collection. The hotel provides many activities, such as kayaking, horseback riding, snorkeling and yoga classes.

El Dorado (☎ 291-62-96; Av El Anclote 7, Nuevo Corral del Risco; mains M$73-298; ☷ 9am-10pm) With tables right on the beach, this popular seafood restaurant is the oldest in town, meaning it enjoys first pick from the fishermen's daily catch. The house specialty is the *filete dorado*, a baked fish fillet stuffed with shrimp and topped with a creamy white sauce.

Tino's (☎ 291-64-73; Av El Anclote 64; mains M$108-330; ☯ noon-9:30pm) This popular oceanfront restaurant has an extensive fish and seafood menu ranging from shrimp tacos and seafood soup to a delightful *pescado zarandeado*, grilled fish served with tortillas and a zesty salsa. Another treat is the *camarones especial tinos,* a shrimp dish prepared with béchamel sauce, white wine, mushrooms, bacon and almonds.

GETTING THERE & AWAY

To get to Playa El Anclote, simply take any Punta de Mita bus roaming north on the Zona Hotelera (M$20, every 15 minutes) and get off at Nuevo Corral del Risco, the town above Playa El Anclote.

SOUTH OF PUERTO VALLARTA

South of town, off scenic Hwy 200, are the beaches of Conchas Chinas, Estacas, Los Venados, Punta Negra, Garza Blanca and Gemelas. Above this lovely shoreline (and blessed with stunning sea views) perch upscale hotels, timeshare condos, and villas owned by the very rich and very lucky.

Near these beaches and also located further south are the hamlets of **El Nogalito**, **Playa Mismaloya**, **Boca de Tomatlán**, **Las Ánimas**, **Quimixto**, **Playa Majahutias**, and **Yelapa** – these last four are reachable only by boat. There are also quite a few upscale restaurants, both near the highway and further inland, which for some folks are a worthy destination in themselves.

El Nogalito
pop 170

Just 5km south of Vallarta and 1km inland, the lush tropical hillsides of El Nogalito offer a gorgeous river, dense jungles ideal for hiking, rarely visited waterfalls and a charming little spa and resort with *temascal* steam baths. And here's even better news: tourism hasn't taken a strong foothold here, so it's the perfect place to relax and enjoy some peace and quiet. To get there, take a coastal bus and tell the driver you want to get off at El Nogalito, then follow the rutted dirt road into town.

Contacto Natural Health Spa and Resort (☎ 221-60-10; www.contactonatural.com; Naranjo 123; all-inclusive M$680, without meals M$300; 🔊 Ⓥ) is a restful

retreat for the body and senses. Here you can truly relax in quiet, wooded surroundings and be rejuvenated by a long menu of body therapies and massage. The all-inclusive rate includes three meals with the option of selecting strictly vegetarian fare. You also choose one daily service from the spa menu, including hydrotherapy treatment, *temascal* steam bath, deep-tissue massage and facials. The *temascal* steam bath, an ancient healing method used by the Aztecs, is a real treat and a great way to rid your body of party toxins. Nonguests can enjoy the service for M$300. The 12 rooms are rustic but comfortable.

Heavy on primate-themed decor, **Casa de los Monos** (☎ 221-64-16; www.micasadelosmonos.com; Gavilanes 10; r M$720; 🔊) is a nice little B&B to monkey around in for a few days. Set against a backdrop of verdant mountains, all four of the bright rooms have tiled floors, exposed wood beams, kitchenettes and queen-sized beds.

For a good, atmospheric meal, spend an afternoon luxuriating at the jungle ranch **El Nogalito** (mains M$90-200; ☯ noon-5:30pm). The property is awash in the sound of the river burbling by and is surrounded by abundant vegetation, ideal for bird-watching. The menu offers a good selection of international dishes in addition to several local delicacies, including coal-grilled shrimp and snapper *zarandeado,* cooked whole with spices and vegetables.

Mismaloya
pop 922

It's no wonder location scouts for *The Night of the Iguana* were so impressed when they laid their eyes on Mismaloya. Backed by lush mountains, the surrounding jungles and bayside scenery are captivating. Today the imposing Barceló La Jolla de Mismaloya resort occupies a large chunk of beachfront property. There are also plenty of tourist shopping stalls and people enjoying many water activities – not quite the scene for those seeking enlightenment, at least in the traditional vein. To reach Playa Mismaloya take the coastal bus and hop off right after the La Jolla de Mismaloya.

From Mismaloya you can head inland along a riverside dirt road to a couple of rustic yet upscale restaurants notable for their lush outdoor locations and for being able to function without electricity or telephone. Along the way you can do some tequila tasting at two family-run distilleries. Horses can be hired at Mismaloya for the ride up. Take insect repellent.

SIGHTS

Rising from the sea, offshore to the north beyond the cove, are the intriguing rocky islands known as Los Arcos (p65), a protected marine park and ecological preserve. It's one of the best snorkeling spots in the Puerto Vallarta area.

Mamá Lucia (Map p59; ☎ 296-51-89; 5 de Mayo 542; ☒ 10am-5pm), a family-run distillery, has been passing down secrets of the tequila-producing trade for three generations. Drop by for a tour and learn about the process from start to finish. A guide explains how, after a long life of repose lasting eight to 10 years, the agave plant has its heart *(piña)* carved out by harvesters called *jimadores*. Resembling a wooden pineapple, it's then halved or quartered and roasted in an adobe oven for 24 to 36 hours. Next comes the satisfying moment everyone's been waiting for: the *piña* is crushed to release the sweet (and so hard to come by) agave nectar, which is distilled twice in a large round kettle for a total of about six hours, and then aged in sweet old bourbon barrels. The demonstration is free, but of course the good people at Mamá Lucia would love it if you'd take some of their delicious product home with you. Choose a delicate *añejo* or perhaps an almond-flavored agave liqueur.

Next door to Mamá Lucia, **Mister Tequila** (Map p59; ☎ 228-05-34; 5 de Mayo 115; ☒ 9am-5pm Mon-Sat, 9am-2:30pm Sun) is a veritable tequila superstore, with an incredible selection of boutique tequilas from all corners of Jalisco and Nayarit. Be careful, the free tastings can quickly get out of hand.

ACTIVITIES

On the dirt road leading to the beach you'll find **Mismaloya Divers** (Map p59; ☎ 228-00-20), a tourism provider offering three- to four-hour tours to Los Arcos, Las Animas, and Quimixto (up to eight people M$2000), and in-season whale-watching tours (four hours M$2500). True to its name it also offers diving trips (one-/two-tank dive M$650/800) and snorkeling excursions to Los Arcos (M$200 per person).

Rancho Manolo (Map p59; ☎ 228-00-18), located beneath the Mismaloya bridge, on the opposite side from the resort, is a cheerful operation that keeps 25 horses and ponies fat and happy. Its two most popular tours are jaunts through an exuberant jungle landscape to Chino's Paradise restaurant (1½ hours, M$150) and to another remote jungle restaurant, El Edén (three hours, M$300). Double saddles are available for kids.

From Playa Mismaloya, launches can be hired for snorkeling tours or passage to the nearby islands. At last visit, the going rate was M$400 per hour, or M$1500 for a full day for up to eight persons.

Canopy Tour El Eden (☎ 222-25-16; Vallarta 228; adult/child 7-10yr M$810/610) has a dozen zip lines crisscrossing high above the jungle. Tour includes transportation from Vallarta, a tequila-producing demonstration and a 10% discount at the restaurant.

SLEEPING

Mar Sereno (Map p59; ☎ 228-08-79, in the US 888-302-3662; www.marsereno.com; Hwy 200, Km 15; s/d/ste M$1000/1250/1200; P ☒ ☐ ☒) Offering quite a bargain, this 11-story hotel with 30 oceanfront suites lives up to its 'serene' name. The rooms and overall appearance are quite appealing, and the panoramic views from the lobby restaurant and pool area are undeniably seductive. There's no beach to speak of, but there is a saltwater pool carved out of the rocks below. Other amenities include free scuba-diving lessons, a large Jacuzzi and a massage center. You'll find it between Mismaloya and Boca de Tomatlán.

Casa Iguana Hotel (Map p59; ☎ 228-01-86; www.casaiguanahotel.com; Av 5 de Mayo 455, Mismaloya; ste M$1400-1785; P ☒ ☐ ☒) A superb mid-sized hotel nestled against the jungles of Mismaloya, this place offers eminently pleasant suites, perfect for families and those who eschew ostentatious hullabaloo. The place is well run, with a feeling of style and substance throughout. If you're traveling with kids, the two-bedroom suites offer the possibility for mom and dad to get some privacy behind closed doors. Each of the 50 units is painted in warm hues of orange and yellow, with good-natured art and rattan furniture. Well-equipped kitchens and large dining tables make home-cooked meals a pleasure. The compact grounds are lushly gardened with a fish pond and large elevated hot tub. Extras include spa, gym, on-site mini-market and internet café.

Barceló La Jolla de Mismaloya (Map p59; ☎ 226-06-60; www.barcelo.com; Hwy 200, Km 11.5; all-inclusive ste M$3864-4830; P ☒ ☒ ☒ ☒ ☒) Built on the site of the sets for John Huston's *The Night of the Iguana,* this big resort has undergone quite a makeover since it was purchased by Spanish hotel chain Barceló several years ago. The remodeled suites sport sitting areas, offering much more space than before, and the neutral tones and white marble floors add a contemporary-chic touch. All rooms feature balconies looking out over the expansive courtyard, four impressive pools and scores of coconut palms. Activities include tennis, snorkeling and kayaking, and there's also a full-service spa. With four pools, a free kids' club, ping-pong tables and live shows, mom and dad can rest easy here knowing the young ones are well entertained.

EATING

Chino's Paraíso (Map p59; ☎ 225-52-71; mains M$120-360; ☾ 10am-6pm) Located where relaxing tiers of *palapa*-covered tables decorate rocky ledges on both sides of a river (cross a footbridge), this place is about 2.8km south of Mismaloya. There's a swimming hole too – bring your swimsuit and towel. Seafood and meats are on the menu, but try to avoid being here between 1pm and 3pm, when hungry tour groups arrive for lunch. Look for iguanas – they'll be checking you out.

El Edén (Map p59; ☎ 222-25-16; mains M$130-280; ☾ 11am-5pm) Nestled away in a jungle where *Predator* was filmed (look for the helicopter skeleton used on the set), this riverside seafood restaurant is worth it if you've hired a horse or taxi, or have wheels; only serious hikers will enjoy the long and dusty walk up (5.5km further upriver from Chino's Paraíso, and about 7km total from Mismaloya and the highway). It's still airy but more closed in than Chino's. A tour company offers zip-line canopy adventures above the jungle and waterfalls of the Río Mismaloya, and guess where they all eat?

Le Kliff (Map p59; ☎ 224-09-75; Carretera 200, Km 17.5; mains M$245-425; ☾ 1-8:30pm) Back on the highway, going south toward Boca de Tomatlán, is Le Kliff, which brags about being the best whale-watching spot in Vallarta…and that may be right. Its dramatic cliff-hanging location south of town is matched by a super menu – try the braised pork shoulder and roasted rack of pork or go all the way with

the lobster tail. Down on the ocean, Le Kliff's seaside 'terrace of love' wedding gazebo serves as a scenic spot to get hitched.

GETTING THERE & AWAY

Grab a cab, drive or hop on a 'Mismaloya' or 'Boca' bus (M$15); they leave Puerto Vallarta from the corner of Constitución and Badillo.

Boca de Tomatlán
pop 570

Many visitors just pass through this fishing village to catch boats to Yelapa, Quimixto and Las Animas, a group of remote beaches west of Boca de Tomatlán. Some, however, find the time to enjoy the small bayside restaurants and absorb the eye-catching tropical scenery.

On the beach, **Restaurant Mi Ranchito** (☎ 228-07-07; mains M$65-120; ☾ 8am-6pm) provides a pleasant spot to eat while you wait for your boat. It sells the much-loved local specialty *pescado zarandeado* (a charcoal-broiled fish stuffed with onion, tomatoes, peppers and spices) by the kilogram.

If you like what you see and decide to stick around, **Casa Tango** (☎ 224-73-98; www.tangorentals .com; house daily/weekly M$1500/7000) has an attractive two-bedroom bayfront house surrounded by dense jungle. It's owned by a friendly Argentine and his Scottish partner, who also offer a good selection of other vacation rentals in the area and orchestrate personalized tours, including private boat trips, canopy tours and whale-watching excursions.

The highway swings inland from Boca, and you can follow it 5km to **Chico's Paradise** (Map p59; ☎ 223-60-05; Hwy 200, Km 20; mains M$90-240; ☾ 10am-6pm), which perches above the Río de Tomatlán. Dining areas under rustic *palapas* look down to idyllic swimming holes and small waterfalls, and you can sunbathe on large boulders while enjoying the lush jungle backdrop. The menu, predictably, speaks of seafood and Mexican dishes. It's a tad pricey, but most of these touristy jungle restaurants are.

GETTING THERE & AWAY

Take a bus marked 'Boca' (M$15) from the corner of Constitución and Badillo in Puerto Vallarta.

Pangas carrying up to eight passengers depart from the beach here to Las Ánimas, Quimixto and Yelapa.

Las Ánimas, Quimixto, Yelapa & Playa Majahuitas

A stay in Puerto Vallarta without an excursion to the tropical havens of Las Ánimas, Quimixto, Yelapa or Playa Majahuitas would be a serious oversight. Beyond the reach of roads, they are accessible only by boat – getting there is half the fun. Along the coastline verdant mountains rise from the sea and deserted beaches and picturesque coves beckon. Yelapa and Playa Majahuitas provide the opportunity to spend the night.

Wear your waterproof sandals, as landings are often wet, and by all means carry insect repellent just in case the mosquitoes are in the mood to swarm.

Water taxis carrying up to eight passengers depart from Boca de Tomatlán hourly from 9am to 11am and 1pm to 4pm to Playa Las Ánimas, Quimixto, Yelapa and Playa Majahuitas. The fares run around M$60 to M$120 for a round-trip, about half of what it costs for the boats departing from Puerto Vallarta (p87).

PLAYA LAS ÁNIMAS
pop 25

Beach of the Spirits, a 20-minute ride by boat from Boca de Tomatlán, is a lovely stretch of sugary sand fronting a small fishing village. An afternoon spent here provides the most delicious sort of escapism. Your culinary needs will be simply but marvelously met by the good selection of *palapa* restaurants offering ultrafresh seafood such as shrimp empanadas or whole fried red snapper. Dessert is provided by the pie ladies who wander the beach with coconut or lemon meringue pies for sale. Should you decide to pry yourself from the sands and ease into the water you'll discover some superlative **snorkeling** opportunities along the rocky shoreline at the far end of the beach. Or you may wish to shake the sand off with an hour-long hike through the rainforest to Quimixto, via an adventurous coast trail.

The neighboring beach east of Las Ánimas, informally known as **El Caballo**, is a gorgeous, albeit small, stretch of sand edged by high palms. Walk over there and check out the scenery: you just might have the entire beach to yourself.

When you get dropped off, let the boatman know what time you'd like to be picked up. But if he doesn't show up, there are always fishermen on hand ready to transport you for a slight markup in price.

QUIMIXTO
pop 423

A 30-minute boat ride from Boca, the equally lovely Quimixto has a sandy beach lined with seafood restaurants against a jungle backdrop. Just east, past a rocky point, is a pretty and deserted little beach. Lounge on the beach and gorge on *mariscos,* but don't leave without making the undemanding half-hour inland hike to a beautiful **waterfall** and **swimming hole**. The hike requires four to five shallow river crossings (wear waterproof sandals). Alternatively – and by doing so you'll be supporting local families whose livelihood depends on it – you can hire a horse to take you up for M$100. At the falls, two rustic restaurants sell somewhat pricey refreshments. To avoid crowds, make the trip as early in the day as possible.

Further on along the same trail, perhaps another 40 minutes by foot, is yet another **waterfall** that you are likely to have all to yourself. Along the way, you'll enjoy beautiful vistas and ever-changing scenery as you pass through the lush vegetation along the river.

YELAPA
pop 715

Furthest from town, Yelapa is one of Vallarta's most popular boating destinations – so popular it's overrun with tourists during high season. Yelapa is home to a sizable colony of foreign residents in addition to 100 or so Mexican families. Its picturesque beach cove with turquoise-colored waters is lined with crowded *palapa* restaurants during the day, but it empties out when the boats leave in the late afternoon. There are plenty of horses for rent and hikes to beaches and waterfalls (head upriver), but just a walk around the funky little town, most of which overlooks the cove, is pleasant.

There are now payphones scattered throughout the village and even a couple of internet cafés. An up-to-date compendium of information about Yelapa can be accessed at www.yelapa.info.

Sleeping

There are quite a few places to stay here, particularly if you're willing to book for three or more days. You can usually find a place to stay by inquiring on the beach, or for vacation rentals visit the **Palapa in Yelapa** (☎ 209-50-96; www.palapainyelapa.com) office at the southern end of the beach. Prices can rise if you miss the last boat. During the peak season, it's safest to reserve in advance.

Apartamentos La Barca (☎ 209-50-73; per night/week M$200/1400) Budget accommodations can be had at this Spartan option by the Río Tuito, which offers a rustic open-air apartment sleeping up to six, with hot water and a utility kitchen. Your host, Valentín, can often be found on the beach.

Casa Milagros (☎ 209-51-79; www.casamilagros.net; s/d M$400/580; 🖳) Up a lush hillside overlooking the still cove, this family-run guesthouse offers 10 simple rooms. For most rooms, guests must share bathroom facilities. There's a communal kitchen, but no meal service. Over the years, the peaceful house has become a popular retreat for yoga groups and visitors seeking quiet time. Just a short walk away, there's a waterfall in the jungle.

Blue Moon Hotel (☎ 209-50-62; javier_rodriguez@yahoo.com; r M$550-600) Right on the beach, this simple hotel offers a good selection of rooms with comfortable beds and hot water. Inquire at Chico's restaurant.

La Joya de Yelapa (☎ 209-52-33; www.cabanas yelapa.com; d per day/week M$780/5460) Located behind Marlin Restaurant, these rustic fan-cooled wood cabins are sweet and simple, and they're just a few steps from the beach. Under the thatched roof you get two double beds, a hammock, a coffeemaker, hot water and earthen floors. You can cook your own food in the kitchenette, but you'll probably wind up eating at the scenic beachfront *palapa* restaurants.

Hotel Lagunita (☎ 209-50-56; www.hotel-lagunita .com; d M$900-1500; 🏊) The nicest midrange place in Yelapa, this hotel offers rustic-chic *cabañas* with one or two double beds, private bathrooms with hot water, electricity and fan. The 32 units are breezy and welcoming, painted in strong colors with plenty of local flair. It also has a pleasant restaurant bar, a well-kept pool, therapeutic massage and the occasional yoga class. Prices drop precipitously during the low season.

Verana (☎ 222-08-78, in the US 310-455-2425; www .verana.com; d villa M$3200-4800; 🍴 🏊) Even if you can't afford to stay in this hidden gem, the long hike through a lush jungle with magnificent bay views along the way is worth the trip. Perched atop a high hillside peak, this getaway offers eight beautifully designed private guesthouses that *Architectural Digest* magazine saw fit to swoon over. Each of the houses has its own personality; some completely enclosed with air-con, others with open-air spaces. The Tea House, the newest and most expensive accommodation, has a sophisticated Japanese design and a private plunge pool. Verana also offers a full-service spa and a much-ballyhooed chef to help you achieve the restive state of bliss you paid good money for. It has a five-day minimum for reservations, and a mandatory food plan (M$800 per person) providing breakfast and dinner.

Eating
Yelapa supports some 20 restaurants catering both to locals and visitors. The atmosphere in all of the restaurants is decidedly casual.

Vortex Café (mains M$40-80; 🕙 breakfast & lunch) This friendly eatery serves delicious international breakfasts and lunches, including espresso, bagels, baked goods, seafood, and pizzas baked in a wood-fired oven. It often remains open in the evenings, and recently added terminals provide internet access.

Brisas (mains M$60-120; 🕙 9am-2pm) Follow your nose along the hillside to this small bakery and restaurant, where you can enjoy fresh-baked banana bread, cinnamon rolls and seafood dishes with rice, veggies and handmade tortillas.

Chico's (☎ 209-50-58; mains M$60-200; 🕙 lunch) This old favorite was among the first to open for business on the beach and has been setting the standard ever since. You'll do well to order a steaming plate of giant shrimp served with the requisite garlic, butter and spices, or fresh red snapper with handmade tortillas.

PLAYA MAJAHUITAS
Tucked away in a small, serene cove between Yelapa and Quimixto, the paradisiacal beach here puts you about as close as you'll ever come to heaven on earth. Relax on the white sands, go snorkeling and kayaking, or head into the verdant hills and explore the abundant wildlife and nearby waterfalls. Make it all happen at a rustic-chic, off-grid hotel on the beach.

our pick **Ecolodge Majahuitas** (☎ 293-45-06; www.majahuitas-resort.com; Playa Majahuitas; casita s/d M$3510/4400) makes for an extremely romantic retreat. Nestled against a lush hillside, eight electricity-free, solar-powered houses overlook a secluded beach. There are no telephones and no TVs, but who needs the outside world when surrounded by such stunning natural beauty? Prices include three meals a day, snorkeling gear, use of kayaks and a guided hiking tour through the jungle to a waterfall near Quimixto beach. The hotel also will arrange fishing, diving and zip-line canopy tours. Playa Majahuitas is only reachable by boat. Reservations recommended.

Getting There & Away

Most visitors arrive via water taxi from either Puerto Vallarta (p87) or Boca de Tomatlán (p97).

From 8:30am to 5pm, water taxis depart for Puerto Vallarta and Boca de Tomatlán from the small pier next to the Yacht Club and from the beach. Before departing they cruise slowly down the beach to pick up anybody who is waiting.

El Tuito
pop 2800

This small town makes for a nice little provincial getaway from the hustle and bustle of Puerto Vallarta. After passing Boca de Tomatlán, Hwy 200 curves inland and climbs through high pine forests. Then, about 45km south of Puerto Vallarta, it reaches El Tuito, which stretches east about 2km. While not incredibly impressive from the highway, it's a pleasant spot if you want to explore a completely untouristy, practically traffic-free and very Mexican place. It's also distinctive in that the church is behind the cute plaza and not on it. While in town, hit one of the stores along the narrow streets selling *raicilla*, a regional alcoholic beverage similar to mezcal and tequila (careful though, this stuff packs a mean punch). Be prepared for curious stares, as not many gringos stop here.

There's a unique restaurant nearby, about 2km south past El Tuito and just off the highway. Look for signs leading to **Rancho Altamira** (☎ 269-00-35; Km 167; ☯ 11am-7pm). The open but covered restaurant sits on a lofty knoll overlooking green brushy hills, some agave fields and a pond full of ducks and geese. Deer, peacocks and ostriches (that's right) scamper around in the distance, and from your aerie a gentle breeze caresses you while you wolf down the very generous dishes of meat and seafood (M$80 to M$230). Afterward, cocktails and tequila shots will wriggle and twitch your whiskers (if you happen to have any). The restaurant offers fishing and horseback tours (M$120 per hour) as well.

If you need to spend the night, back in town and on the highway there's the decent, modern **Hotel Real de Valle** (☎ 269-00-11; hotel reald@yahoo.com.mx; r M$400, ste M$550; ☷ ☯), with rooms arranged around a shady garden and an astonishing airbrushed mural in the lobby.

Buses to El Tuito depart Puerto Vallarta from the corner of Carranza and Aguacate (Map pp62–3).

Mazatlán

At first glance Mazatlán may seem like your typical resort offering standard-issue tourist fare, but beyond the posh hotels and thumping discos awaits an old port city with intriguing local flavor. Dubbed the 'Pearl of the Pacific,' Mazatlán is a place of many faces. On the south side, revamped Old Mazatlán has emerged as the center of a thriving new cultural movement, while scores of contemporary galleries, sidewalk restaurants and hip bars sprout up along the narrow streets of the new-look historic center.

Southeast of Old Mazatlán, and just a five-minute boat ride away, you couldn't ask for a lovelier place to while away the time than the coconut grove–edged beach of Isla de la Piedra (Stone Island). The hardest decision you'll have to make here is deciding which *palapa* seafood restaurant you want to eat at. Head north of Old Mazatlán and you'll hit party central in the Zona Dorada, a vibrant tourist playground where the agenda consists mostly of fine dining, boozing and uninhibited dancing. While in the 'hood, be sure to visit one of several venues that stage live *banda* concerts. Mazatlán is the birthplace of the brass-band sounds of *banda sinaloense*, making it a treat to see a live performance.

If time allows, make a special point of checking out the surrounding areas. For an invigorating breath of mountain air, venture out to the small mining towns of Copala and Cosalá. And just about 30 minutes northeast of the city, you can enjoy a joyful slice of rural life on the cobblestone streets of El Quelite.

So much to do, so little time.

HIGHLIGHTS

- Wining, dining and soaking up the cultural offerings in revamped **Old Mazatlán** (p104)
- Bopping and swinging your partner to the beat of Mazatlán's famed **banda music** (p114)
- Strolling along the cobblestone streets of the friendly mountain villages of **Copala** (p116) and **Cosalá** (p117)
- Boating through mangrove swamps and beach bumming at **Teacapán** (p118)
- Swimming in calm waters and spending a lazy day under a beachfront *palapa* restaurant at **Isla de la Piedra** (p107)

- AVERAGE JANUARY DAILY HIGH: 28°C | 82°F
- AVERAGE JULY DAILY HIGH: 33°C | 91°F
- TELEPHONE CODE: 669 / POPULATION: 404,000

MAZATLÁN

HISTORY

Researchers have found numerous petroglyphs (images carved into rocks) in nearby areas, some of which date back 10,000 years. In pre-Hispanic times Mazatlán (which means 'place of deer' in Nahuatl) was populated by the Totorames, who lived by hunting, gathering, fishing and agriculture. They also were accomplished ceramic artisans.

On Easter Sunday in 1531, an army of about 150 Spaniards and 8000 Indians led by Nuño de Guzmán officially founded a settlement here, but almost three centuries elapsed before a permanent colony was established in the early 1820s. German immigrants played a crucial role in developing Mazatlán's port, which established its first customs office in 1828. In 1848 US forces blockaded the port during the Mexican-American war. Commercial trade started to flourish in the latter part of the 19th century with the arrival of the railroad.

Today Mazatlán ranks among Mexico's largest ports and is home to one of the biggest fishing fleets in the nation. Tourists started coming in the 1930s, mainly for fishing and hunting, and some hotels appeared along Playa Olas Altas, Mazatlán's first tourist beach, in the 1950s.

From the 1970s onward, a long strip of modern hotels and tourist facilities had extended north along the coast. As large resort hotels spread like wildfire in the Zona Dorada, Old Mazatlán, which dates from the 19th century, was abandoned for decades. Yet in recent years, thanks to an ambitious renovation program, the historic center has reclaimed its glorious past.

ORIENTATION

Old Mazatlán, the city center, is near the southern end of a peninsula, bounded by the Pacific Ocean on the west and the Bahía Dársena channel on the east. The center of the 'old' city is Plaza Principal, surrounded by a rectangular street grid. Several blocks southwest of the plaza lies the Plazuela Machado, a restaurant zone and the heart of Mazatlán's cultural renaissance.

Heading north from Old Mazatlán, the beachside boulevard Paseo Olas Altas becomes Av del Mar along the coast of Playa Norte. Once you hit the hotel zone in Zona Dorada, the avenue converts into Camarón Sábalo, which extends north to the marina.

Continuing north from the marina along Sábalo-Cerritos, you'll pass some new hotels and timeshare developments before arriving at surfers' paradise Playa Brujas at the end of the road.

On the southern end of the city, at the tip of the peninsula, El Faro (the Lighthouse) stands on a rocky prominence overlooking Mazatlán's sportfishing fleet and La Paz ferry terminal. East of the peninsula are the cruise-ship docks, the ferry terminal and a boat operator offering rides to Isla de la Piedra.

Maps

Guía Roji publishes a detailed *Ciudad de Mazatlán* map that's available from major internet booksellers. Basic tourist maps are available at the tourist office and most hotels.

INFORMATION

Opening hours reflect winter schedules; summer hours may be more limited.

Bookstores

Mazatlán Book & Coffee Company (Map p106; ☎ 916-78-99; Camarón Sábalo 610; ☺ 9am-7pm Mon-Sat) Across from Hotel Costa de Oro and hidden behind Banco Santander, this store has more than 6000 titles in English. It also buys and trades used books.

Sanborns (Map p103; ☎ 992-01-91; La Gran Plaza; ☺ 7:30am-1am) Spanish-language books, maps and guidebooks.

Emergency

Ambulance, fire department, police (☎ 066)

Internet Access

Internet cafés are plentiful in Mazatlán, with prices ranging between M$15 and M$35 per hour. All places listed here have speedy connections and air-con.

Café Internet Online (Map p105; Sixto Osuna 115; per hr M$16; ☺ 11am-8:30pm Mon-Sat) High-speed internet and fax service.

Cyber Café (Map p106; Camarón Sábalo 610; per hr M$35; ☺ 9am-8pm Mon-Fri, 1-7pm Sat & Sun) Pricey but fast and convenient.

Italian Coffee Company (Map p103; Av del Mar 1020; ☺ 7am-10pm Mon-Sat, 10am-10pm Sun) Free wireless access and good java.

Laundry

Lavamar (Map p106; Playa Gaviotas 214; per kg M$70)

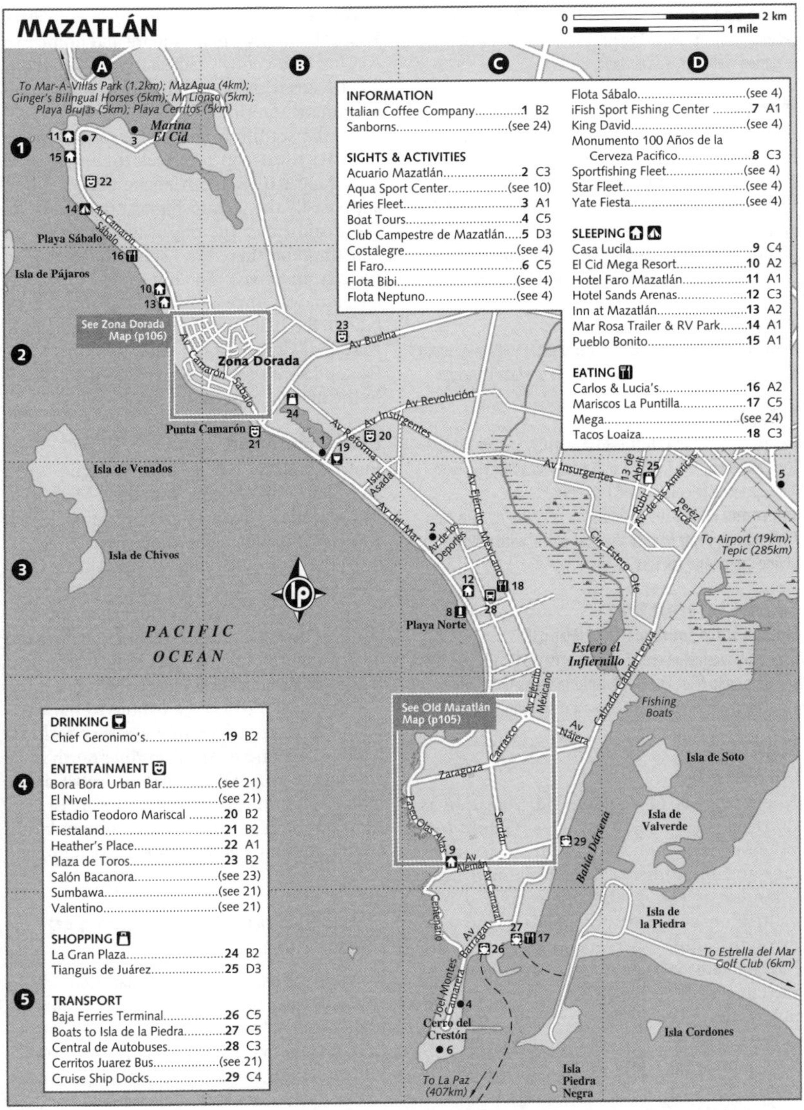
MAZATLÁN
0 2 km
0 1 mile
To Mar-A-Villas Park (1.2km); MazAgua (4km); Ginger's Bilingual Horses (5km); Mr Lionso (5km); Playa Brujas (5km); Playa Cerritos (5km)
Marina El Cid
Playa Sábalo
Isla de Pájaros
See Zona Dorada Map (p106)
Zona Dorada
Av Camarón Sábalo
Punta Camarón
Av Buelna
Av Revolución
Av Insurgentes
Av Reforma
Isla de Venados
Isla Asada
Av del Mar
Av de los Deportes
Av Ejército Mexicano
13 de Abril
Rubí
Av de las Américas
Peréz Arce
Circ Estero Ote
To Airport (19km); Tepic (285km)
Isla de Chivos
PACIFIC OCEAN
Playa Norte
Estero el Infiernillo
Calzada Gabriel Leyva
See Old Mazatlán Map (p105)
Av Nájera
Fishing Boats
Isla de Soto
Carrasco
Zaragoza
Paseo Olas Altas
Serdán
Isla de Valverde
Bahía Dársena
Av Alemán
Av Camaraí
Centenario
Av Barragán
Joel Montes Camarena
Isla de la Piedra
To Estrella del Mar Golf Club (6km)
Cerro del Crestón
Isla Cordones
To La Paz (407km)
Isla Piedra Negra
INFORMATION
Italian Coffee Company 1 B2
Sanborns (see 24)
SIGHTS & ACTIVITIES
Acuario Mazatlán 2 C3
Aqua Sport Center (see 10)
Aries Fleet 3 A1
Boat Tours 4 C5
Club Campestre de Mazatlán 5 D3
Costalegre (see 4)
El Faro 6 C5
Flota Bibi (see 4)
Flota Neptuno (see 4)
Flota Sábalo (see 4)
iFish Sport Fishing Center 7 A1
King David (see 4)
Monumento 100 Años de la Cerveza Pacifico 8 C3
Sportfishing Fleet (see 4)
Star Fleet (see 4)
Yate Fiesta (see 4)
SLEEPING
Casa Lucila 9 C4
El Cid Mega Resort 10 A2
Hotel Faro Mazatlán 11 A1
Hotel Sands Arenas 12 C3
Inn at Mazatlán 13 A2
Mar Rosa Trailer & RV Park 14 A1
Pueblo Bonito 15 A1
EATING
Carlos & Lucia's 16 A2
Mariscos La Puntilla 17 C5
Mega (see 24)
Tacos Loaiza 18 C3
DRINKING
Chief Geronimo's 19 B2
ENTERTAINMENT
Bora Bora Urban Bar (see 21)
El Nivel (see 21)
Estadio Teodoro Mariscal 20 B2
Fiestaland 21 B2
Heather's Place 22 A1
Plaza de Toros 23 B2
Salón Bacanora (see 23)
Sumbawa (see 21)
Valentino (see 21)
SHOPPING
La Gran Plaza 24 B2
Tianguis de Juárez 25 D3
TRANSPORT
Baja Ferries Terminal 26 C5
Boats to Isla de la Piedra 27 C5
Central de Autobuses 28 C3
Cerritos Juarez Bus (see 21)
Cruise Ship Docks 29 C4

Media

Most hotels have city maps, restaurant and activity advertisements, and free English-language newspapers such as *Pacific Pearl* (www.pacificpearl.com) and *Mazatlán Interactivo* (www.mazatlaninteractivo.com). In Old Mazatlán pick up the free bilingual *Viejo Mazatlán* (www.viejo-mazatlan.com), or monthly arts and entertainment newspaper *M!*.

Medical Services

There are several clinics on Camarón Sábalo, in the Zona Dorada, that cater to gringos who come down with a case of indigestion or worse.

Clínica Balboa (Map p106; ☎ 916-79-33; Camarón Sábalo 4480; ☒ 24hr) English is spoken at this well-regarded walk-in medical clinic.

Money

Banks, ATMs, and *casas de cambio* (exchange bureaus) are bountiful in Mazatlán. There are Bancomer and Banamex branches near Plaza Principal (Map p105) and a **Banco Santander** (Map p106; Camarón Sábalo 610) in the Zona Dorada. **American Express** (Map p106; Centro Comercial Balboa, Camarón Sábalo s/n) is in the Zona Dorada.

Post

Main post office (Map p105; Juárez s/n; ☒ 8am-5:30pm Mon-Fri, 9am-1pm Sat) On the east side of Plaza Principal.

Telephone

Caseta Telefónica Hermes (Map p105; Serdán 1510; ☒ 9am-8pm) The friendly staff here will assist you with long-distance telephone and fax services. **Telecomm** (Map p105; Juárez s/n; ☒ 9am-7:30pm Mon-Fri, 9am-noon Sat) Next to the post office, with private phone cabins and fax service.

Tourist Information

Sinaloa State Tourism Office (Map p105; ☎ 981-88-83; www.vivesinaloa.com, in Spanish; Paseo Olas Altas 1501; ☒ 9am-5pm Mon-Fri) Helpful information about hotels, attractions and events in Mazatlán and surrounding areas.

SIGHTS
Old Mazatlán

After decades of neglect Old Mazatlán is sporting a new look these days. Thanks to a sweeping renovation project, historic buildings and monuments have reclaimed their splendor as the downtown revival drives a thriving cultural movement. Thursday through Sunday, streets surrounding the **Plazuela Machado** (Map p105; cnr Carnaval & Constitución) are closed off to traffic to make room for musicians playing in front of crowded sidewalk restaurants. Contemporary galleries, museums and trendy bars line the nearby streets.

The center of attention is the **Teatro Ángela Peralta** (Map p105; ☎ 982-44-46; www.culturamazatlan .com, in Spanish; Carnaval 47), half a block south of the plaza. Reopened in 1992 after a thorough restoration, this elegant 19th-century theater has played a crucial role in Mazatlán's cultural revival. Events of all kinds are presented here (see p114), and the opulent interior is open for viewing most days.

A short walk northeast brings you to **Plaza Principal**, the city's main square and home to a soaring 19th-century **cathedral** (Map p105; cnr Juárez & 21 de Marzo) with high, yellow twin towers and a dramatic interior.

At the southern end of the peninsula, a tall rocky outcrop provides the base for **El Faro** (Map p103), 135m above sea level and supposedly the second-highest lighthouse in the world (after the one in Gibraltar). You can climb up there for a spectacular view of the city and coast. The hill, called Cerro del Crestón, was once an island, but a causeway built in the 1930s now joins it to the mainland. Mazatlán's sportfishing fleet, the ferry to La Paz and some tourist boats (see p108) dock in the marina, east of the causeway.

Quirky Mazatlán

Puerto Vallarta has its high-art sculptures, and Manzanillo its epic Swordfish Memorial. But Mazatlán's audacious collection of kitsch statuary is in a category of its own.

At the north end of Playa Olas Altas is **Carpe Olivera** (Map p105), a statue of a buxom mermaid in pike position, drawing passersby irresistibly down the stairs to the rocks below and a saltwater dipping pool (see p108). Nearby is the small **Monumento al Venado** (Monument to the Deer; Map p105) – a tribute to the city's Nahuatl name – depicting a rather forlorn-looking deer on a pedestal. Further north is the kitsch masterpiece **Monumento a la Continuidad de la Vida** (Monument to the Continuity of Life; Map p105), featuring a nude, gesticulating couple with big hair and nine rusty dolphins.

ASK A LOCAL: THE OLD MAZATLÁN MAKEOVER

About 15 years ago, Old Mazatlán was totally abandoned; it was almost spooky. Everything began to change once they renovated the Teatro Ángela Peralta. After that the neighborhood really began to grow with restaurants, cafés and art galleries.

We don't want a party zone like the Zona Dorada. This is where the city's roots are and we don't want to lose the essence of the historic center. The best thing, of course, is that a new cultural movement has come out all this.

Miguel Ruiz Contreras is the owner of Casa Etnika (p115)

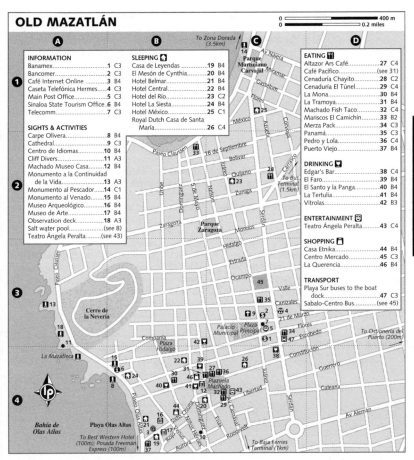

OLD MAZATLÁN

0 ——————— 400 m
0 ——————— 0.2 miles

INFORMATION
Banamex..............................1 C3
Bancomer............................2 C3
Café Internet Online...........3 B4
Caseta Telefónica Hermes....4 C3
Main Post Office..................5 C3
Sinaloa State Tourism Office.6 B4
Telecomm...........................7 C3

SIGHTS & ACTIVITIES
Carpe Olivera......................8 B4
Cathedral............................9 C3
Centro de Idiomas.............10 B4
Cliff Divers.........................11 A3
Machado Museo Casa........12 B4
Monumento a la Continuidad
de la Vida.......................13 A3
Monumento al Pescador....14 C1
Monumento al Venado......15 B4
Museo Arqueológico.........16 B4
Museo de Arte...................17 B4
Observation deck...............18 A3
Salt water pool.................(see 8)
Teatro Ángela Peralta.......(see 43)

SLEEPING
Casa de Leyendas 19 B4
El Mesón de Cynthia..........20 B4
Hotel Belmar......................21 B4
Hotel Central......................22 B4
Hotel del Río......................23 C2
Hotel La Siesta...................24 B4
Hotel México......................25 C1
Royal Dutch Casa de Santa
María...............................26 C4

EATING
Altazor Ars Café.................27 C4
Café Pacífico....................(see 31)
Cenaduría Chayito.............28 C2
Cenaduría El Túnel.............29 C4
La Mona.............................30 B4
La Tramoya.........................31 B4
Machado Fish Taco.............32 C4
Mariscos El Camichín.........33 B2
Merza Pack.........................34 C3
Panamá..............................35 C3
Pedro y Lola.......................36 C4
Puerto Viejo.......................37 B4

DRINKING
Edgar's Bar.........................38 C4
El Faro................................39 B4
El Santo y la Panga............40 B4
La Tertulia..........................41 B4
Vitrolas..............................42 B3

ENTERTAINMENT
Teatro Ángela Peralta........43 C4

SHOPPING
Casa Etnika........................44 B4
Centro Mercado.................45 C3
La Querencia......................46 B4

TRANSPORT
Playa Sur buses to the boat
dock...............................47 C3
Sabalo-Centro Bus...........(see 45)

MAZATLÁN

From a nearby platform **cliff divers** (*clavadistas*; Map p105) cast their bodies into the ocean swells below for your enjoyment. Tip accordingly. They usually perform around lunchtime and in the late afternoon, but they won't risk their necks until a crowd has been assembled. Also here is an unnamed **observation deck** (Map p105) perched atop a stony precipice. It takes considerable nerve to scale the arching brick stairway – it has no rail and it's a long drop to open sea on either side – but it's even more unsettling going back down.

Overlooking the southern end of Playa Norte is the **Monumento al Pescador** (Monument to the Fisherman; Map p105). This bully pigeon perch depicts a nude fisherman with Tin Tin hair and enormous feet.

Elsewhere are statues of a dapper chap on a motorcycle, a mermaid getting directions from a cherub, a copper beer tank commemorating the first century of Pacífico beer, and a memorial to local songbird Lola Beltrán. Take a walk – you can't miss 'em.

Museums

The **Museo Arqueológico** (Map p105; ☎ 981-14-55; Sixto Osuna 76; admission M$29, free Sun; ☼ 10am-6pm Mon-Sat, 10am-3pm Sun) has temporary exhibits and a permanent collection of artifacts from around Sinaloa state, including pre-Hispanic objects and ceramic vessels. Opposite, the **Museo de Arte** (Map p105; ☎ 985-35-02; cnr Sixto Osuna & Carranza; admission free; ☼ 10am-2pm & 4-7pm Mon-Fri, 10am-2pm Sat & Sun) showcases works by famous Mexican artists such as Rufino Tamayo, Francisco Toledo and José Luis Cuevas.

Also worth a peek is the **Machado Museo Casa** (Map p105; Constitución 79; adult/child M$20/10; ☺ 9am-6pm), a beautifully restored 19th-century house filled with French and Austrian furniture, clothing and other antiques. The museum's projection room screens an English-language video that chronicles the history of Mazatlán.

Beaches & Zona Dorada

With more than 20km of beaches, it's easy to find a quiet stretch of sand. The following beaches are listed in geographic order, from south to north.

In Old Mazatlán, the crescent-shaped **Playa Olas Altas** (Map p105) is where tourism first flourished in the 1950s. The small beach is a grand place to watch the sun drop into the sea. Signs on the faded '50s hotels along the seafront road commemorate some of the area's first visitors, such as writer Jack Kerouac and photographer Tina Modotti (p33).

Flanked by a broad *malecón* (boardwalk) popular with joggers and strollers, the golden sands of **Playa Norte** (Map p103) begin just north of Old Mazatlán and arc toward **Punta Camarón** (Map p103), a rocky point dominated by the castlelike Fiestaland nightclub complex. The traffic circle here marks the southern end of the **Zona Dorada**, an unabashedly touristy precinct of hotels, restaurants, bars and souvenir shops.

The most luxurious hotels face the fine beaches of **Playa Las Gaviotas** (Map p106) and **Playa Sábalo** (Map p103), which extends north of the Zona Dorada. Sheltered by picturesque islands, the waters here are ideal for water sports; on offer are sailing excursions, water-skiing, banana-boat rides and parasailing. To reach these beaches from downtown, just hop on a 'Sábalo-Centro' bus; these originate at the market on Juárez and travel along Av del Mar.

Further north, past the ever-evolving Marina Mazatlán, are the undeveloped beaches of **Playa Brujas** (Witches' Beach) and **Playa Cerritos** (off Map p103). Both sport a few excellent seafood restaurants and are well loved by surfers. To get there by bus, catch a 'Cerritos Juárez' bus from the Fiestaland complex or from along Camarón Sábalo in the Zona Dorada.

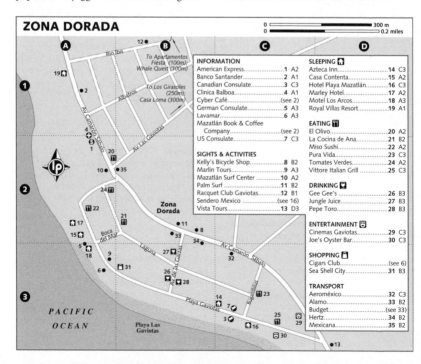

ZONA DORADA

0 —————— 300 m
0 —————— 0.2 miles

INFORMATION
American Express.......................**1** A2
Banco Santander......................**2** A1
Canadian Consulate.................**3** C3
Clinica Balboa............................**4** A1
Cyber Café..............................(see 2)
German Consulate....................**5** A3
Lavamar.......................................**6** A3
Mazatlán Book & Coffee
  Company............................(see 2)
US Consulate...............................**7** C3

SIGHTS & ACTIVITIES
Kelly's Bicycle Shop.................**8** B2
Marlin Tours................................**9** A3
Mazatlán Surf Center **10** A2
Palm Surf..................................**11** B2
Racquet Club Gaviotas...........**12** B1
Sendero Mexico ....(see 16)
Vista Tours................................**13** D3

SLEEPING
Azteca Inn................................**14** C3
Casa Contenta.........................**15** A2
Hotel Playa Mazatlán..............**16** C3
Marley Hotel.............................**17** A2
Motel Los Arcos.......................**18** A3
Royal Villas Resort...................**19** A1

EATING
El Olivo......................................**20** A2
La Cocina de Ana.....................**21** B2
Miso Sushi.................................**22** A2
Pura Vida...................................**23** C3
Tomates Verdes........................**24** A2
Vittore Italian Grill **25** C3

DRINKING
Gee Gee's..................................**26** B3
Jungle Juice..............................**27** B3
Pepe Toro..................................**28** B3

ENTERTAINMENT
Cinemas Gaviotas....................**29** C3
Joe's Oyster Bar.......................**30** C3

SHOPPING
Cigars Club.............................(see 6)
Sea Shell City...........................**31** B3

TRANSPORT
Aeroméxico...............................**32** C3
Alamo..**33** B2
Budget....................................(see 33)
Hertz...**34** B2
Mexicana..................................**35** B2

Islands

Those three photogenic land masses jutting from the sea are Mazatlán's signature islands. **Isla de Chivos** (Goat Island; Map p103) is on the left, and **Isla de Pájaros** (Bird Island; Map p103) is on the right. The most visited is the one in the middle, **Isla de Venados** (Deer Island; Map p103). It's designated a natural reserve for the protection of native flora and fauna, and its secluded beaches are wonderful for a day trip and its limpid waters ideal for snorkeling.

A five-hour excursion to Isla de Venados leaves from the marina at **El Cid Mega Resort** (Map p103; ☎ 913-33-33, ext 3490; www.elcid.com; Camarón Sábalo s/n; ☺ 9:30am Tue-Sat; ☲). The guided trip costs M$420 per person, lasts five hours and includes a banana-boat ride, snorkeling equipment, kayaks and lunch.

ISLA DE LA PIEDRA

Escape artists love Stone Island for its long, sandy beach edged by coconut groves, and anyone with an appetite sings the praises of its rustic *palapa* restaurants.

To get there, take a **small boat** (Map p103; round-trip M$20; ☺ every 10min 7am-6pm) from the Playa Sur embarcadero near the Baja Ferries terminal. You'll be dropped off at a jetty a short walk from the beach. 'Playa Sur' buses leave for the boat dock from a bus stop on the corner of Serdán and Escobedo, two blocks southeast of Plaza Principal.

If you miss the last boat, you can stay overnight at Stone Island Gardens Hotel (p110).

ACTIVITIES
Surfing

With a season lasting from late March through November, Mazatlán has several noteworthy surfing sites and a couple of great surf shops. The most famous waves include two that break near downtown. Off **Punta Camarón** is a dependable right-hander, and north of the old fort is a famous lefty known as the **Cannon**. The Cannon is about 500m south of Monumento al Pescador (Map p105). Off **Isla de la Piedra** (Map p103) you'll find a beach break with perfect peaks, but unless there's a decent swell you're better off grabbing a beer and watching from the beach. Rolling in at **Playa Brujas** each morning is a big right that you can set your watch to.

The longest-established surf shop in town is **Mazatlán Surf Center** (Map p106; ☎ 913-18-21; www.mazatlansurfcenter.com; Camarón Sábalo 500-4; board rentals per day/week M$250/1200, lessons per hr M$325; ☺ 10am-9pm Mon-Sat, 1-9pm Sun), known for its popular surfing lessons and expert advice. **Palm Surf** (Map p106; ☎ 914-06-87; www.palmsurf.com .mx; Camarón Sábalo 333; board rentals per day M$250, lessons per hr M$400; ☺ 10am-8pm Mon-Sat) also has boards for rent and surf excursions to far-flung spots like Patolé, Celestinos and Mármol.

Other Water Sports

The **Aqua Sport Center** (Map p103; ☎ 913-04-51; El Cid Mega Resort) is the place to go for water sports, including scuba diving (M$600 one-tank dive); snorkeling rentals (M$120 per day); jet-skiing (M$50 per half-hour); parasailing (M$400); and kayak rentals (M$150 to M$250 per hour).

Horseback Riding

If you love to canter on the beach, or dream of doing so, your best bet is with **Ginger's Bilingual Horses** (off Map p103; ☎ 988-12-54; www .mazinfo.com/gingershorses; Playa Brujas; per hr M$250; ☺ 10am-4pm Mon-Sat). Unlike at some other Mexican stables, here the horses are eager to stretch their legs on the trails leading through coconut plantations on to the open beach. Children five and older are welcome. Take a 'Cerritos Juárez' bus from Zona Dorada to Playa Brujas.

Short rides can also be arranged on Isla de la Piedra at Restaurant Puesta de Sol (M$70).

Sportfishing

Mazatlán is world-famous for its sportfishing – especially for marlin, swordfish, sailfish, tuna and shark. January through April is the best time of year to hook sailfish and striped marlin. It can be an expensive activity (M$4000 to M$4500 for a day in an 11m cruiser with four people fishing), though small-game fishing from a 7m super-*panga* (motorized skiff) is less expensive (M$2500 to M$2750 with up to six people fishing). All operators should offer tag-and-release options. For the winter high season, make fishing reservations far in advance.

Boats leave from the El Cid Resort marina and from Marina Mazatlán, but the best deals are found with the operators on the peninsula on Calz Camarena.

Aries Fleet (Map p103; ☎ 916-34-68; www.elcid.com; El Cid Marina)
Flota Bibi (Map p103; ☎ 913-10-60; www.bibifleet .com; Calz Camarena s/n)

MAZATLÁN

Flota Neptuno (Map p103; ☎ 982-45-65; Calz Camarena s/n)
Flota Sábalo (Map p103; ☎ 981-27-61; Calz Camarena s/n)
Star Fleet (Map p103; ☎ 982-26-65; Calz Camarena s/n)

Freshwater large-mouth bass fishing is also caching on, particularly at scenic Lake El Salto, one hour north of town. **iFish Sport Fishing Center** (Map p103; ☎ 913-33-08; www.ifishmexico.com; Camarón Sábalo 1504) runs day trips starting at M$2800 per private boat, with equipment included. It also has three-day package deals with lodging, meals and transportation for M$4650 to M$29,000.

Golf & Tennis

If you'd like to swing the clubs, you'll find **Club Campestre de Mazatlán** (Map p103; ☎ 988-66-91; Hwy 15; green fees 9/18 holes M$250/350), east of town; **Estrella del Mar Golf Club** (off Map p103; ☎ 915-83-00; www.estrelladelmar.com; Isla de la Piedra; green fees 9/18 holes M$740/1100), south of the airport by the coast; and **El Cid Mega Resort** (Map p103; ☎ 913-33-33; Camarón Sábalo s/n; green fees 9/18 holes M$483/667), north of the Zona Dorada.

Play tennis at the **Racquet Club Gaviotas** (Map p106; ☎ 913-59-39; cnr Río Ibis & Bravo; per hr M$155), or at El Cid Mega Resort.

COURSES

Centro de Idiomas (Map p105; ☎ 985-56-06; www.spanishlink.org; Aurora 203; 3/5 1hr classes per week M$3750/4000) offers Spanish courses Monday through Friday with a maximum of six students per class. You can begin any Monday and study for as many weeks as you like; registration is every Saturday morning from 9am to noon. Homestays (shared/private room M$2000/2775 per week) can be arranged with a Mexican family and include three meals a day.

MAZATLÁN FOR CHILDREN

Kids love this town, if only for the many opportunities to get wet. One of the most economical and enjoyable places to accomplish this is at the delightful, all-natural **saltwater pool** (Map p105) on Paseo Olas Altas. Here kids and adults splash around as waves crash over the pool's seaward edge. There are bathrooms and changing rooms.

Splashing around is also the featured activity at **MazAgua** (off Map p103; ☎ 988-00-41; Entronque Habal-Cerritos s/n; admission M$120; ☽ 10am-6pm Mar-Dec),

where kids can go hog wild with water toboggans, a wave pool and other amusements. The 'Cerritos-Juárez' bus takes you there from anywhere along the coastal road.

Acuario Mazatlán (Map p103; ☎ 981-78-15; www.acuariomazatlan.gob.mx; Av de los Deportes 111; adult/child M$75/50; ☽ 9:30am-5pm), a block inland from Playa Norte, recently launched the largest saltwater aquarium in Latin America. The 1.6-million-liter tank holds lemon sharks, olive ridley turtles and manta rays. In all, the park has 53 aquariums with 250 species of freshwater and saltwater fish. Sea-lion and bird shows are presented four times daily.

During whale-watching season from December through March, bilingual biologists at Onca Explorations lead visitors on **Whale Quest** (off Map p106; ☎ 913-40-50; www.whalewatchingmazatlan.com; Rio de la Plata 409, Frac Gaviotas, Zona Dorada), four-hour tours to observe migrating humpback whales. Boats depart at 9am and the cost includes hotel transfers (adult/child six to 12 years M$850/650). For reservations, contact oxinfo@gmail.com.

TOURS

Bicycle Tours

Kelly's Bicycle Shop (Map p106; ☎ 914-11-87; www.kellys-bikes.com; Camarón Sábalo 204; tours M$295, mountain-bike rental per day M$185; ☽ 10am-2pm & 4:30-8pm Mon-Sat) leads wild off-road mountain-bike tours, including a 20km ecoride that meanders through thick jungle and along the coast. Kelly's also offers custom trips on some of Sinaloa's most scenic paved routes.

Kayak Tours

King David (Map p103; ☎ 914-14-44; Calz Camarena s/n) has 1½-hour guided tours in two-person kayaks to Cactus Island, departing from Stone Island (adult/child M$250/200).

Ecotours

Tour operator **Sendero Mexico** (Map p106; ☎ 940-86-87; Playa Gaviotas 202; www.eduventura.com) offers 3½-hour bird-watching trips (M$450) to the coastal wetlands and foothills of the Sierra Madres. It also does a kayaking, snorkeling and hiking outing (M$750) to Isla de los Venados.

Boat Tours

In addition to trips to **Isla de Venados** (see p107), several boats do 2½-hour sightseeing tours, mostly leaving from the docks off Calz

Camarena at 11am (M$200 including hotel transfers and open bar). Two-hour sunset cruises, sometimes called 'booze cruises,' include hors d'oeuvres and open bar (M$300). To find out what's going on, talk to a tour agent or call boat operators such as **Costalegre** (Map p105; ☎ 982-31-30; Calz Camarena s/n) and **Yate Fiesta** (Map p105; ☎ 981-71-54; www.yatefiesta.com; Calz Camarena 7).

Land Tours

Several companies offer interesting tours in and around Mazatlán. Prices vary slightly from company to company for the same tours: M$250 for a three-hour city tour, M$450 to M$550 for a colonial tour to the foothill towns of Concordia and Copala, and M$400 for a tequila factory tour that includes a visit to the village of La Noria. If you make reservations, tour operators will pick you up from your hotel. Recommended agencies:

Marlin Tours (Map p106; ☎ 913-53-01; www.toursin mazatlan.com; Playa Gaviotas 417A) Friendly and long-standing, with tours to Copala, Concordia and La Noria.

Vista Tours (Map p106; ☎ 986-86-10; www.vistatours .com.mx; Camarón Sábalo 51) Bigger range to choose from, including Cosalá, the San Ignacio missions and El Quelite.

FESTIVALS & EVENTS

If you happen to be in town during the third week of February, prepare yourself for Mazatlán's wildest fiesta of the year during **Carnaval** celebrations. People from around Mexico (and beyond) pour in for music, dancing and general revelry. Be sure to reserve a hotel room in advance and prepare to pay steep rates during the weeklong event. The party begins late February/early March and ends abruptly on the morning of **Ash Wednesday**.

Famous for its billfish, Mazatlán hosts two important sportfishing contests in November: the prestigious **Bisbee's Classic** and the annual **Sailfish Tournament**. In June anglers descend on the marina to compete in the **International Sportfishing Tournament**.

Golf tournaments, food fairs and various cultural festivals are held throughout the year; the tourist office has details.

The **Sinaloa Arts Fair**, featuring local talent and troupes traveling from afar, is staged at the Teatro Ángela Peralta and other local venues during the month of October.

On December 12 the day of the **Virgen de Guadalupe** is celebrated at the cathedral. Children come in colorful costumes.

SLEEPING

Mazatlán offers a mixed bag of lodging options ranging from cheap digs in the downtown area to expensive megaresorts in the touristy Zona Dorada. In both areas you'll have no problem finding family-friendly midrange hotels with old-style Mexican ambience. Bad news for backpackers, though: you'll be hard-pressed to find a youth hostel. If you're looking to dive into the party scene, the Zona Dorada's vivacious discos and crowded bars are just stumbling distance from the hotel strip. For a slower pace, Old Mazatlán is the ticket. Some hotels offer a third night for free during low season, but many do not openly advertise promotions, so don't be afraid to ask.

Budget

Head to Old Mazatlán for the most affordable rooms in the city. Some hotels give discounts for longer stays.

Hotel México (Map p105; ☎ 981-38-06; México 201; s/d M$100/150) Holing up in one of the cheapest hotels in town has the obvious drawbacks of dark rooms and rundown bathrooms. However, cash-strapped travelers on the go are willing to overlook the shortcomings since the hotel is so close to the beach.

Hotel del Río (Map p105; ☎ 982-44-30; Juárez 2410; d/q M$250/500; ⚡) If only all budget hotels were this clean. Just three blocks from the Playa Norte boardwalk, this place is a good value for travelers looking to stretch their pesos. Looking to practice Spanish? The hotel's friendly working-class neighborhood provides *muchas oportunidades*.

Hotel Belmar (Map p105; ☎ 985-11-12/13; www.hotel belmar.com.mx; Paseo Olas Altas 166 Sur; r interior/sea view M$400/450; ⓟ ⚡ 🖥) Some people love the retro appeal of this totally faded 1960s classic, but others can't look past the rough edges. Interior rooms don't get much sunlight and the pool has seen better days, but the oceanfront location and reasonable rates work in the hotel's favor.

Hotel Central (Map p105; ☎ 982-18-66; Domínguez 1607; d/tr M$400/465; ⚡ 🖥) Within walking distance of the Plazuela Machado, this old-timer in the heart of downtown keeps things simple, clean and affordable. Some of the rooms are showing their wear, but the air-con and cable TV make up for any deficiencies.

The trailer parks are near the beaches toward the north end of the town. The following places offer weekly and monthly discounts.

Mar Rosa Trailer & RV Park (Map p103; ☎ 913-61-87; mar_rosa@mzt.megared.net.mx; Camarón Sábalo 702; tent M$220, trailer M$310-450) Lacks sufficient shade but the location is hard to beat.

Mar-A-Villas Park (off Map p103; Playa Cerritos s/n; sites M$320) Set on a quiet, lovely beach, north of Quinta del Mar condominiums. Spots here go fast in the high season. There's no telephone, so you'll have to drop by and try your luck.

Midrange

Rooms and apartments in this price bracket are a considerable step up from the budget hotels. Many of these places have fully equipped kitchenettes, a nice bonus if you're traveling with the family.

Apartamentos Fiesta (off Map p106; www.mazatlanapartments.com; Río Ibis 502; studio/1-bedroom M$375/560, 2-bedroom M$700-850; P) This place has 13 apartments, all different in size and layout. All have kitchens and pleasing decor and are peacefully located in or near the leafy garden area. English is spoken.

Stone Island Gardens Hotel (☎ 981-92-74; www.stoneislandgardens.com; Av Principal Las Palmas; d M$500-650, ste M$1200; P) Located on Isla de la Piedra, this place has clean, comfy rooms with wireless internet and satellite TV. It's possible to camp on the beach, too.

Hotel La Siesta (Map p105; ☎ 981-26-40, 800-711-52-29; www.lasiesta.com.mx; Paseo Olas Altas 11 Sur; r with/without view M$649/531; P) Sporting an excellent ocean view, a pleasant courtyard draped with long vines, and bright rooms with modern decor, La Siesta arguably offers the best bang for your buck. The hotel has a travel agency and a restaurant that specializes in shrimp dishes.

Los Girasoles (off Map p106; ☎ 913-52-88; Playa Gaviotas 709; apt M$650; P) If you're after some peace and quiet, this hotel offers spacious apartments with kitchenettes, a well-tended pool and friendly staff. Keep in mind, though, that the nearest beach is about a five-minute walk away.

Azteca Inn (Map p106; ☎ 913-44-77; www.aztecainn.com.mx; Playa Gaviotas 307; s/d M$700/750; P) A fairly affordable option in the Zona Dorada, the Azteca Inn has simple rooms with warm colors and comfy beds. Vacationing barflies gravitate toward the quaint air-conditioned sports bar in the pool area.

Royal Dutch Casa de Santa María (Map p105; ☎ 981-43-96; www.royaldutchcasadesantamaria.com; Constitución 627; d with/without breakfast M$1100/900;) The royal treatment you get at this small B&B

will knock your socks off. Mexican-Dutch couple Alicia and Wim go out of their way to make their guests feel at home in their splendid 18th-century abode, and they'll even find time to show you around town. Choose from three lovingly and tastefully decorated rooms. Reservations essential.

El Mesón de Cynthia (Map p105; ☎ 136-05-60; www.mesondecynthia.com; Sixto Osuna 408; r/ste M$900/1150;) Just a stone's throw from the happening Plazuela Machado, this B&B has cozy rooms with kitchenettes, wireless internet access, cable TV and stylish rustic furnishings. An added bonus is the rooftop Jacuzzi. Kids under 12 not permitted.

Marley Motel (Map p106; ☎ 913-55-33; http://travelbymexico.com/sina/marley; Playa Gaviotas 226; 1/2 beds M$950/1130; P) This small motel offers pleasant seafront apartments with well-equipped kitchens, and best of all, it has privileged beach access and sits in a relatively quiet area of the Zona Dorada.

Hotel Sands Arenas (Map p103; ☎ 982-00-00; www.sandsarenas.com, in Spanish; Av del Mar 1910; d/tr M$950/1020; P) If your kids are impressed by swimming pools with a spiraling water slide, they may find happiness here. Rooms are spotless, modern and large and come with satellite TV and refrigerator. Best of all, the beds are firm.

Casa Contenta (Map p106; ☎ 913-49-76; www.casacontenta.com.mx; Playa Gaviotas 224; apt/house M$990/2360; P) Not too keen on the nearby megaresorts? Casa Contenta has intimate apartments with partial ocean views, a small pool and a tranquil beach sporting a striking view of three rocky islands.

Top End

Rooms at Mazatlán's top-end hotels can be reserved quite economically as part of a holiday package – see your travel agent or poke around online.

ourpick Casa de Leyendas (Map p105; ☎ 981-61-80; www.casadeleyendas.com; Carranza 4; d M$1170-1400; P) This was once a former Mazatlán mayor's home and a 19th-century storage place for gold bullion. Legend has it that precious metal is still buried under the hotel, hence the name House of Legends. Today the building houses one of the city's most charming B&Bs. The large house has six intimate rooms and many appealing common areas conducive to hanging out with other guests, such as a terrace with an ocean view, a courtyard and pool area, and an airy living room with a library. Glen and Sharon, your kind hosts, offer hearty homestyle breakfasts and a well-stocked 'honor bar,' providing you replace the booze you consume. Tack on an additional M$150 for one-night stays. Kids under 12 not permitted.

Best Western Posada Freeman Express (off Map p105; ☎ 985-60-60; www.posadafreemandelrio.com; Paseo Olas Altas 79; r M$1239-1357, ste M$1900; **P** ✕ ✖ ▣ ☎) Towering over Old Mazatlán's waterfront, this hotel is all about the ocean views, whether you're tossing back drinks in the Sky Room bar, swimming in the rooftop pool, or just kicking back in a seaside room. Rates include a free daily breakfast buffet.

Motel Los Arcos (Map p103; ☎ 913-50-66; www.motel losarcos.com; Playa Gaviotas 214; s/d/ste M$1260/1390/1410; **P** ✖ ☎) This attractive hotel features good-value suites with kitchenettes and commanding sea views. They're very comfortable, spacious and clean, and the beach is right there.

Hotel Faro Mazatlán (Map p103; ☎ 913-11-11; www .faromazatlan.com.mx; Punta de Sábalo s/n; s & d M$934, ste M$1524; **P** ✕ ✖ ▣ ☎) Perched atop a small cliff overlooking a private beach, this appealing hotel exudes peace and tranquility. All of the bright and spacious rooms offer an ocean or marina view. Guests spend considerable time at the pleasant beachfront restaurant and bar. An all-inclusive plan is available, starting at M$1507/1884 for a single/double and M$2114 for a suite.

Inn at Mazatlán (Map p103; ☎ 913-55-00; www.innat maz.com; Camarón Sábalo 6291; r M$1652-2478, ste M$2300-5133, penthouse M$7611-9912; ✕ ✖ ▣ ☎) The 215 bright, cheerful rooms and suites – all with ocean views, private balconies or terraces, and decked out with amenities – are agreeable for longer stays. The three-bedroom, eight-person penthouse makes for royal digs if you're traveling with a group. It's right on the beach.

El Cid Mega Resort (Map p103; ☎ 913-33-33; www .elcid.com.mx; Camarón Sábalo s/n; r M$1850-2150, ste M$3800-6770; **P** ✕ ✖ ▣ ☎ ♿) Decked out in 1980s-style luxury, this 967-room, 2.9-sq-km mini-city has it all – seven pools, several dive shops, restaurants, travel agencies, kids' areas, gyms and more. Given the hotel's size, the service at times can be a bit slow. Discounts are abundant if you reserve ahead of time.

Hotel Playa Mazatlán (Map p106; ☎ 989-05-55; www.playamazatlan.com.mx; Playa Gaviotas 202; garden view/ocean view/ste M$1714/1955/3002; ✖ ▣ ☎) A

long-standing favorite in the Zona Dorada, all of this establishment's 408 well-appointed rooms come with a terrace or private balcony. If you want to flush out those party toxins, the hotel has a unique spa featuring a *temascal* steam bath and man-made *cenotes* (sinkholes) for swimming.

Casa Lucila (Map p103; ☎ 982-11-00; www.casalucila .com; Olas Altas 16; ste M$1900-3400; ✕ ✖ ☎) A honeymooners' haven through and through, this classy boutique hotel boasts eight suites with high ceilings, custom-made Italian doors and windows, and sophisticated furnishings. Most rooms offer an ocean view, as does the small infinity pool on the 3rd floor. A jazz bar and intimate restaurant on the main floor add a nice touch to the refined setting.

Pueblo Bonito (Map p103; ☎ 989-89-00; www .pueblobonito.com; Camarón Sábalo 2121; ste from M$2395; **P** ✕ ✖ ▣ ☎) Overlooking a nearly private stretch of sandy beach, this upscale hotel has an elegant colonial facade, two fantastic freeform pools and all the facilities you'd expect at the top end. The spacious rooms have comfortable sitting areas and private balconies with an ocean view.

Royal Villas Resort (Map p106; ☎ 916-61-61, 800-696-70-00; www.royalvillas.com.mx; Camarón Sábalo 500; ste/1-/2-bedroom M$2595/3658/6254; **P** ✕ ✖ ▣ ☎) Don't let this hotel's facade fool you: the elegant suites here are absolutely fabulous and the private balconies afford a stunning ocean view. All rooms have kitchens and dining rooms, and they sleep at least four.

EATING

Foodies fantasize about places like Mazatlán. Among the culinary treats, a must-try is the traditional *pescado zarandeado*, a whole fish marinated and grilled to perfection. Mazatlán also claims fame as 'the shrimp capital of the world.' Along the coast the tasty little crustacean is prepared in so many different ways that it would have made *Forrest Gump*'s Bubba proud.

With a few exceptions, restaurants in the Zona Dorada cater primarily to the tourist trade. Make no mistake: dining in many of these establishments will set you back a pretty peso, but the area has some of the finest places in town.

For a sublime dining experience head to Old Mazatlán's Plazuela Machado, where you'll find cosmopolitan restaurants with outdoor tables and plenty of romance in the air.

The most centrally located downtown supermarket is **Merza Pack** (Map p105; Serdán & Flores), but for serious replenishment head to the **Mega** (Map p103; Buelna 128) superstore.

Old Mazatlán & Around
BUDGET

Panamá (Map p105; ☎ 985-18-53; Juárez s/n; sweet bread & pastries M$10-40; ☒ 7am-11pm) For a thoroughly satisfying sweet-tooth fix, indulge in some of the best *pan dulce* (sweet bread) in Mazatlán at this popular restaurant and bakery.

Cenaduría Chayito (Map p105; ☎ 982-67-23; Azueta 2407; mains M$30-80; ☒ 7am-11pm Tue-Sun) Find out for yourself why locals rave about the home-style cooking at this popular mom-and-pop eatery. Favorites include the *asado* (a beef-and-potatoes dish), beef tostadas and *pozole* (hominy soup).

Machado Fish Taco (Map p105; Sixto Osuna 34; mains M$40-100; ☒ 9am-midnight) For a quick bite drop by this sidewalk restaurant on the Plazuela Machado for some tasty fish or shrimp tacos served with a sweet slaw and spicy *chile de arbol* salsa. It's fast food done right.

Cenaduría El Túnel (Map p105; Carnaval 1207; mains M$35-60; ☒ 5pm-midnight) This atmospheric cheapie has been serving local favorites such as Sinaloa-style *pozole* and smoked marlin enchiladas in a long, narrow dining room for over 50 years.

MIDRANGE & TOP END

Puerto Viejo (Map p105; ☎ 982-18-86; Paseo Olas Altas 25; mains M$35-95; ☒ 11am-11pm Sun-Thu, 11am-1am Fri & Sat) This super-casual, inexpensive sea-food restaurant and watering hole is popular with both locals and expats, especially in the evening when the karaoke mike comes out and the voices warm up.

Pedro y Lola (Map p105; ☎ 982-25-89; Carnaval 1303; mains M$70-180; ☒ 6pm-1am) Named after beloved Mexican singers Pedro Infante and Lola Beltrán, this popular sidewalk restaurant-bar serves seafood, burgers and toned-down Mexican favorites. It's good for big groups or romantic couples.

Altazor Ars Café (Map p105; ☎ 981-55-59; Constitución 517; mains M$55-130) This trendy side-walk café offers deli sandwiches, various sea-food dishes and has a steady offering of live music at night. Altazor boasts, 'None of our bands suck.'

La Tramoya (Map p105; ☎ 985-50-33; Constitución 509; mains M$63-135; ☒ 8am-2am) Here hearty Mexican meat dishes are set out on spacious sidewalk tables. Feeling adventurous? Try the *carne azteca*, a steak stuffed with *huitlacoche* (corn truffle, a fungus that grows on maize) served on a bed of *nopales* (cactus).

Mariscos El Camichín (Map p105; ☎ 985-01-97; Paseo Claussen 97; mains M$65-130; ☒ noon-7pm) Facing Playa Norte, this popular patio res-taurant serves delicious seafood and *pescado zarandeado* under a cool *palapa* roof. In the afternoon *norteño* and *banda* groups offer their services in the dining area for a pricey M$70 a song.

La Mona (Map p105; ☎ 981-56-10; Niños Heroes 1508; mains M$65-180; ☒ 1pm-2am) Set in a lovely old downtown building, this pizzeria and cantina specializes in brick-oven pizza and has an extensive wine and beer list.

Mariscos La Puntilla (Map p103; ☎ 982-88-77; Flota Playa Sur s/n; mains M$79-155; ☒ 8am-6:30pm) Popular with Mexican families for the week-end breakfast buffet, this open-air eatery has a relaxed atmosphere and fantastic *pescado zarandeado*. It's near the Isla de la Piedra ferries.

Café Pacífico (Map p105; ☎ 985-20-60; Constitución 501; mains M$95-195; ☒ Noon-2am; ☒) This resto-bar comes alive on Thursday karaoke nights and has a pool table in the back room if you want to escape from the amateur crooners. The extensive menu offers international and Mexican cuisine, and of course, Mazatlán's own Pacífico beer.

Zona Dorada & Around
BUDGET

Tacos Loaiza (Map p103; Ejército Mexicano 2205; tacos M$11; ☒ 7:30pm-3am) About a block from the bus station, the grilled beef tacos at this popular street stand make a great snack before heading out to your next destination.

La Cocina de Ana (Map p106; ☎ 916-31-19; Laguna 49; mains M$30-70; ☒ noon-4pm Mon-Sat) Fine home cooking is the order of the day at this small eatery, where the daily lunch buffet offers di-verse dishes like *asado* and chili con carne. Since you pay by the kilogram, the cost of a meal depends on just how much you chow down.

Pura Vida (Map p106; ☎ 916-10-10; Bugambilias 18; fresh juice M$30, mains M$37-65; ☒ 8am-11pm; ☒) This health mecca squeezes out fresh juices and serves vegetarian fare ranging from buck-wheat pancakes and veggie omelets to salads and garden burgers.

Tomates Verdes (Map p106; ☎ 913-21-36; Laguna 42; mains M$38-50 ⏰ 9am-5pm Mon-Sat) This unassuming lunch spot offers a daily menu featuring flavorful soups such as cream of corn, to accompany main dishes such as beef tamales and stuffed chicken breast. With beverage, a complete meal costs a mere M$50.

MIDRANGE

Miso Sushi (Map p106; ☎ 913-02-99; Playa Gaviotas 17; sushi rolls M$35-140; ⏰ 1-11pm) Mazatlán has several sushi restaurants, but none as cosmopolitan as this trendy newcomer. It's recommended for its stylish urban decor, good music and super-fresh, well-presented fare.

Carlos & Lucia's (Map p103; ☎ 913-56-77; Camarón Sábalo s/n; mains M$50-200; ⏰ 8am-11pm Tue-Sun) Here husband-and-wife team Carlos and Lucia mix it up with Mexican and Cuban flavors from their respective homelands. Toothsome dishes like picadillo and imperial shrimp go down nicely with the exemplary *mojito*, a refreshing rum-and-mint drink.

our pick **Mr Lionso** (off Map p103; ☎ 988-04-25; Sábalo Cerritos s/n, Playa Brujas; mains M$60-180; ⏰ 9am-10pm) The be-all, end-all seafood restaurant, this pleasant and casual spot serves magnificent food at reasonable prices. Even if you're not hungry, the open-air oceanfront dining area is a great place to unwind over a strawberry daiquiri. One look at the menu, though, and you just might work up an appetite for some coconut shrimp with a mango dipping sauce, or another tempting treat, the bacon-wrapped imperial shrimp and grilled lobster combo plate. Located on Mazatlán's northernmost end, it's about a 15-minute cab ride from the Zona Dorada. Bring a bathing suit and make a day out of it.

El Olivo (Map p106; ☎ 916-30-23; Las Gaviotas 205; mains M$69-145; ⏰ V) This upscale café and deli serves pastas, strong coffee, crepes and incredible salads, and it has an outstanding bakery.

TOP END

Vittore Italian Grill (Map p106; ☎ 986-24-24; Playa Gaviotas 100; mains M$86-210; ⏰ noon-midnight) This popular spot is a fine choice for an elegant night out. The service is rather formal and the menu heavy on delicious calorie-rich pasta dishes and many other Italian-leaning delectables, such as rack of lamb with stuffed eggplant.

Casa Loma (off Map p106; ☎ 913-53-98; Las Gaviotas 104; mains M$139-249; ⏰ 1:30-10:30pm; ❈) Its devoted clientele ranks this secluded restaurant as one of the very best in Mazatlán. Escape the tourist scene and enjoy the homey atmosphere and high-quality dishes such as veal shank with capers, shrimp scampi and Pacific lobster.

DRINKING

Edgar's Bar (Map p105; ☎ 982-72-18; cnr Serdán & Escobedo; ⏰ 9am-midnight) This old-school downtown cantina has been serving suds since 1949. Unlike some of the neighborhood's seedier, male-dominated drinking holes, a sign on the door boasts that Edgar's welcomes women.

La Tertulia (Map p105; ☎ 983-16-44; Constitución 1406; ⏰ closed Sun) Adorned with stuffed bullheads and old *torero* posters, this taurine-themed cantina is a festive spot to grab some *cervezas* while mingling with locals and expats.

The following spots are ideal for heavy partying and youthful exploits:

Chief Geronimo's (Map p103; ☎ 984-24-77; Av del Mar s/n) Popular with college students for its generous drink specials and shrimp and ribs served by the kilogram.

El Santo y La Panga (Map p105; ☎ 985-41-24; Niños Heroes 1505) Hip lounge bar and restaurant that pays tribute to El Santo, Mexico's most beloved masked wrestler.

Gee Gee's (Map p106; ☎ 913-50-65; Av de las Garzas 12) A trendy restaurant and bar where you can rock out to alternative tunes over margaritas.

Jungle Juice (Map p106; ☎ 913-33-15; Av de las Garzas 101) A cantina-style place with exotic fruit drinks and a breezy nook upstairs.

Gay Bars

Mazatlán doesn't offer much of a gay bar scene, but there are a few options.

Pepe Toro (Map p106; ☎ 914-41-76; www.pepetoro .com; Av de las Garzas 18; ⏰ Thu-Sun; ❈) A festive gay disco attracting a fun-loving mixed crowd. The club stages weekly transvestite strip shows and the staff spin a good mix of danceable grooves.

Vitrolas (Map p105; ☎ 985-22-21; www.vitrolasbar .com; Frias 1608; ⏰ 6pm-1am Tue-Sun) A gay bar and restaurant in a beautifully restored downtown building with high ceilings and an elegant brass-edged bar. Overall this spot is more button-down than mesh muscle shirt.

ENTERTAINMENT

Mazatlán has more to offer than fun in the sun. Choose from a wide variety of nightspots, live music, theater or sporting events. And for drunken debauchery, the name pretty much says it all at Fiestaland. If boisterous merrymaking isn't your thing, cultural options abound in Old Mazatlán.

Theater

Teatro Ángela Peralta (Map p105; ☎ 982-44-46; www .culturamazatlan.com, in Spanish; Carnaval 1024) The restored Italian Renaissance–style auditorium, named after the world-famous Mexican opera singer Ángela Peralta, stages a variety of events, including concerts, opera, theater, dance and film screenings. Drop by the box office for event listings. The schedule is most interesting during the annual Sinaloa Arts Fair (p109).

Nightclubs

Fiestaland (Map p103; ☎ 989-16-00; Av del Mar s/n) That ostentatious white castle on Punta Camarón, at the southern end of the Zona Dorada, is home to several of Mazatlán's most popular nightspots. The scene starts percolating around 9pm, boiling over after midnight. Valentino's (Map p103; cover M$50 to M$80) draws well-dressed Mexican and foreign tourists to its throbbing dance floors. For bar-top dancing and drunken misbehaving Bora Bora Urban Bar (Map p103) does the trick. Escape from the loud, steamy clubs at Sumbawa (Map p103), a chic open-air lounge bar just behind the Fiestaland complex. There's a swimming pool there if you need to cool off from the hot dancing.

Joe's Oyster Bar (Map p106; ☎ 983-53-33; Playa Gaviotas 100) Near Fiestaland, behind Hotel Los Sábalos, this popular spot is fine for a quiet drink until early evening, but it goes ballistic after 11pm when it's packed with college kids dancing on tables, chairs and each other.

Live Music

If you get a chance, try to hear a rousing traditional *banda sinaloense* – a boisterous brass band unique to the state of Sinaloa and especially associated with Mazatlán. Watch for announcements posted around town or broadcast from slow-moving cars with speakers mounted on top. Venues and bars to try include the following:

Salón Bacanora (Map p103; ☎ 989-16-00; Buelna s/n; admission M$80-200; 🕑) First-rate *banda* acts frequently take the stage at this large venue next to Plaza de Toros.
El Nivel (Map p103; ☎ 987-16-00; Fiestaland, Av del Mar s/n; cover M$50-100; 🕑) A cantina-style bar where you can swing to *banda sinaloense* Thursday through Sunday.
Ostionería del Puerto (off Map p105; ☎ 982-22-49; Barragán 1109; 🕑 9am-11pm) A lively outdoor restaurant-bar with live *banda* groups playing from 4pm to 9pm. The food is subpar but the music is great.
Heather's Place (Map p103; ☎ 914-29-99; Camarón Sábalo 300) Professional artists do their best Vegas-style impersonations of Elvis, Bowie and Roy Orbison from Friday to Sunday at 7pm.

Sports

BULLFIGHTS & RODEOS

Plaza de Toros (Map p103; ☎ 989-16-00; Buelna s/n) Just inland from the Zona Dorada traffic circle, the bullring hosts *corridas de toros* once a month on Sundays from mid-December to Easter; the 'Sábalo-Cocos' bus will drop you there. Tickets for bullfights and information are available at major hotels and the Fiestaland box office. *Charreadas* (rodeos) are also infrequently held at the Plaza de Toros.

BASEBALL

Los Venados (www.venadosdemazatlan.com) Mazatlán's baseball team makes its home at the large and modern Estadio Teodoro Mariscal (Map p103); the season starts in early October and continues through March. The box office opens at 10am on game days (tickets M$15 to M$105).

Fiesta Mexicanas

The Fiesta Mexicana is a corny spectacle providing a reductive view of Mexican culture, but it's all in good fun. For three hours, guests are treated to a floor show of folkloric dance and music, a generous buffet dinner and an open bar. Several of the largest luxury hotels stage these extravaganzas, but the hands-down favorite is the one at **Hotel Playa Mazatlán** (Map p106; ☎ 989-55-55; Playa Gaviotas 202; adult/child M$306/180; 🕑 7pm Sat; 🕑).

Cinemas

Cinemas Gaviotas (Map p106; ☎ 983-75-45; Camarón Sábalo 218; admission M$35, Wed M$25; 🕑) Six screens here show recent releases, mostly with English subtitles.

SHOPPING

Crafts stores and galleries in Old Mazatlán sell pottery, clothes, sculptures and many other goodies. In the Zona Dorada you'll find shops and boutiques along Playa Gaviotas specializing in souvenirs and high-end jewelry.

Sea Shell City (Map p106; ☎ 913-13-01; Playa Gaviotas 407; ☺ 9am-7pm) This 'city' is packed with an unbelievable assortment of you-know-what. Upstairs there's a small museum with a cool fishpond adorned with seashell mosaics.

Tianguis de Juárez (Juárez Flea Market; Map p103) Stalls lining the street at this outdoor market sell everything from bootleg CDs and DVDs to used clothes, housewares and even tacos. To get there from the Zona Dorada, grab the 'Cerritos-Juárez' bus heading east. The *tianguis* is held every Sunday, starting at an early-bird 5am.

Centro Mercado (Map p105; cnr Ocampo & Serdán) Here in Old Mazatlán you can enjoy a classic Mexican market experience, complete with vegetable and food stalls and shops selling bargain-priced crafts.

Cigars Club (Map p106; Playa Gaviotas 214-5; ☺ 9am-7pm) Good selection of Cuban and Mexican cigars.

La Querencia (Map p105; ☎ 981-10-36; Domínguez 1502; ☺ 9am-8pm Mon-Sat) This large gallery sells a wide array of colorful crafts hailing from various Mexican regions, including ceramics, jewelry, wood sculptures and Day of the Dead paraphernalia.

Casa Etnika (Map p105; ☎ 136-01-39; Sixto Osuna 50; ☺ 9am-7pm Mon-Sat) A one-stop-shop for arts and crafts, here you'll find handmade jewelry, trendy housewares, clothes and wildlife photography, and they've got great coffee, too.

GETTING THERE & AWAY

Air

Rafael Buelna International Airport (MZT; ☎ 982-23-99), 27km southeast of the Zona Dorada, is served by the following carriers:

Aeroméxico (Map p106; ☎ 982-34-44; Camarón Sábalo 310) Service to Atlanta via Mexico City and to Los Angeles, Phoenix and Tucson via Mexico City or Hermosillo. Direct service to Tijuana, La Paz, Guadalajara and Mexico City.

Alaska Airlines (☎ tin the US 800-252-7522) Direct service to Los Angeles and connecting flights to San Francisco and Seattle.

Continental Airlines (☎ 800-900-50-00) Direct service to Houston.

Mexicana (Map p106; ☎ 913-07-72; Camarón Sábalo 359) Direct flights to Los Angeles, Mexico City and Los Cabos, and connecting service to Chicago, Denver, Miami, New York and San Antonio.

US Airways (☎ 981-11-84, in the US 800-428-43-22) Nonstop to Phoenix.

Boat

Baja Ferries (Map p103; ☎ 982-55-88; www.bajaferries.com; adult/child aged 3-11yr M$825/425; ☺ ticket office 8am-4pm Mon-Sat, 9am-1pm Sun) operates ferries between Mazatlán and La Paz in Baja California Sur (to the port of Pichilingue, 23km from La Paz).

The 12-hour ferry to Pichilingue departs at 5pm (you should be there with ticket in hand at 3pm) on Monday, Wednesday and Friday from the terminal at the southern end of town (off Av Barragan, near the Playa Sur embarcadero). Tickets are sold from two days in advance until the morning of departure. Passage for vehicles (M$1600/2150/11,900 for a motorcycle/car/trailer up to 9m) is available, as are cabins and suites (M$760 to M$1200).

Bus

The **Central de Autobuses** (main bus station; Map p103; ☎ 982-19-49; Jose Ángel Ferrusquilla s/n) is three blocks inland from the northern end of Playa Norte, near Ejército Méxicano. It's a full-service station with authorized taxi stands and a left-luggage service. All bus lines operate from separate halls in the main terminal. Local buses to small towns nearby operate from a smaller terminal, behind the main terminal. There are several daily long-distance services:

Culiacan (M$135, 21 hours, eight 1st-class)
Durango (M$300, eight hours, six 1st-class)
Guadalajara (M$370, nine hours, frequent 1st-class)
Manzanillo (M$630, 12 hours, one 1st-class)
Mexico City (M$850, 18 hours, 12 1st-class) To Terminal Norte.
Monterrey (M$658, 17 hours, four 1st-class)
Puerto Vallarta (M$320, seven hours, two 1st-class) Or take a bus to Tepic, where buses depart frequently for Puerto Vallarta.
Tepic (M$150, two hours, 24 1st-class)
Tijuana (M$820, 24 hours, three 1st-class)

To get to San Blas (290km), go first to Tepic then get a bus from there.

GETTING AROUND
To/From the Airport

Colectivo (shared) vans and a bus operate from the airport to town, but not from town to the airport. Taxis are about M$260.

Bus

Local buses run daily from 6am to 10:30pm. A trip on the regular white buses costs M$5.50, while air-con green buses cost M$8. A useful route for visitors is the Sábalo-Centro, which travels from the Centro Mercado (Map p105) in the center to Playa Norte via Juárez, then north on Av del Mar to the Zona Dorada and further north on Camarón Sábalo. Another is Playa Sur, which travels south along Ejército Méxicano near the bus station and through the city center, passing the market, then to the ferry terminal and El Faro.

To get into the center of Mazatlán from the bus terminal, go to Ejército Méxicano and catch any bus going south (to your right if the bus terminal is behind you). Alternatively, you can walk 500m from the bus station to the beach and take a 'Sábalo-Centro' bus heading south to the center.

Car & Motorcycle

Shop around for the best rates, which range between M$400 to M$700 per day during the high season. There are several rental agencies in town:

Alamo (Map p106; ☎ 913-10-10; Camarón Sábalo 410)
Budget (Map p106; ☎ 913-20-00; Camarón Sábalo 413)
Hertz (Map p106; ☎ 913-60-60; Camarón Sábalo 314)

Various companies on Camarón Sábalo in the Zona Dorada rent out motor scooters – you'll see the bikes lined up beside the road. Prices are somewhat negotiable, ranging from M$150 to M$500 per day. You need a driver's license to hire one; a license from any country will do.

Pulmonía & Taxi

Mazatlán has a special type of taxi called a *pulmonía*, a small open-air vehicle similar to a golf cart – usually a modified VW. There are also regular red-and-white taxis and green-and-white taxis called 'ecotaxis.' A typical cab fare around town runs about M$60, or less, depending on your bargaining skills, the time of day and whether there is a cruise ship in port or not.

AROUND MAZATLÁN

Several small, picturesque colonial towns in the Sierra Madre foothills make pleasant day trips from Mazatlán. Note that if you visit on a Sunday, many things will be shut down. In rural La Noria you can visit a tequila distillery, or in nearby El Quelite catch a pre-Hispanic ball game. South of Mazatlán, the long, secluded beaches of Teacapán await.

Getting There & Away

Buses to all these places depart from the small bus terminal at the rear of the main bus station in Mazatlán.

Concordia (M$20, 1½ hours, every 15 minutes 6am to 6pm)
Copala (M$40, two hours, three 1st-class)
Cosalá (M$100, three hours, two 2nd-class)
El Quelite (M$30, 45 minutes, five 2nd-class)
La Noria (M$30, 45 minutes, four 2nd-class)

Tours to these spots are available as well (see p108).

CONCORDIA
Pop 27,000

Founded in 1565, Concordia has an 18th-century church with a baroque facade, elaborately decorated columns and a daily market around it. The village is known for its manufacture of high-quality pottery and hand-carved furniture. It's about a 45-minute drive east of Mazatlán; head southeast on Hwy 15 for 20km to Villa Unión, turn inland on Hwy 40 (the highway to Durango) and go another 20km.

COPALA
Pop 377

Also founded in 1565, the charming little town of Copala, 25km past Concordia on Hwy 40, was one of Mexico's first mining towns. It has a colonial church (1748), red-tiled houses and a tiny museum, and local urchins sell donkey rides while pigs and chickens roam the cobbled streets. There are a couple of hotels; try the quaint **Copala Butter Company** (☎ 200-124-4876; r M$200) if you decide to spend the night, though you can visit both Concordia and Copala in a day – even on public transportation. Take an *auriga* (transport pickup) between the two towns (M$25, 30 minutes). On your way out, drop by **Daniels** (☎ 044-669-926-2380; ☼ 9am-6pm) for

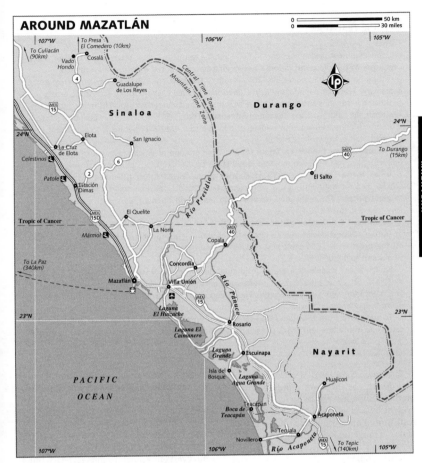

AROUND MAZATLÁN

lunch and its 'world-famous' banana cream coconut pie.

COSALÁ
Pop 6800

In the mountains north of Mazatlán, Cosalá is a beautiful colonial mining village dating from 1550. It features several hotels, a 17th-century church, an even older chapel, and a colonial mansion that houses a mining museum. Attractions nearby include **Vado Hondo**, a *balneario* (bathing resort) with a large natural swimming pool and three waterfalls, 15km from town; **La Gruta México**, a large cave 18km from town; and the **Presa El Comedero** reservoir, 20km from town, where you can hire rowboats for fishing.

To get to Cosalá, head northwest on Hwy 15 for 113km to the turnoff (opposite the turnoff for La Cruz de Elota on the coast) and then go about 45km up into the mountains. If taking the direct bus, consider staying the night, since bus schedules are such that you only get one hour in town before needing to head back the same day. A good option is **Hotel Quinta Minera** (☎ 696-965-0222; Hidalgo 92; r M$750; 🅿), a lovely old hacienda with rustic-chic rooms and a lovely pool and garden area.

EL QUELITE
Pop 1700

A day trip to the colonial village of El Quelite wouldn't be complete without a meal at **El Mesón de los Laureanos** (☎ 965-41-43; mains M$80-115;

DETOUR: TEACAPÁN

☎ 695 / pop 4000

With development plans under way to build a mega tourist resort twice the size of Cancun, you'd better get to this place fast before the secluded beaches become overrun with tourists.

Sitting on an isolated peninsula 126km south of Mazatlán and surrounded by a rich mangrove ecosystem, Teacapán's long palm grove–lined beaches are prime territory for escape artists.

Boating excursions into the mangrove swamps can be arranged with local fishermen at Boca de Teacapán, the natural marina. **Teacapán Adventure Tours** (☎ 954-53-93) offers boat trips (M$650) to nearby islands teeming with wildlife, or a jungle tour (M$2000) that leads to an ancient 25m pyramid built entirely of seashells.

Nearby beaches include **La Tambora**, with a smattering of *palapa* restaurants and camping opportunities, and the even more secluded spots Las Cabras, Las Lupitas and Los Angeles.

Villas Maria Fernanda (☎ 954-53-93; www.villasmariafernanda.com; r/ste/house M$690/1000/2200; ✂ ✂) is a romantic little resort with comfortable rooms, spacious suites and a house for up to eight people. The manicured gardens, two pools and open-air restaurant area make for a very pleasant stay.

Restaurant & Bungalows Señor Wayne (☎ 954-56-95; r/cabaña M$300/450; P ✂), a family-run operation just next door, has nine simple rooms and one economical *palapa*-roofed *cabaña*. Also on the premises is Teacapán's best restaurant (mains M$80 to M$140), serving big breakfasts, steaks and seafood.

Smack in the middle of a grassy residential development, **Hotel Villas Coral** (☎ 954-54-77; ste M$800; P ✂ ✂) has a pool, a restaurant and four large suites with kitchens, satellite TV and bathrooms laid with Talavera tile. They sleep up to four people. You'll find the hotel about 500m before entering town.

To get there from Mazatlán's 2nd-class bus terminal (adjacent to the main bus terminal), catch one of the frequent buses to Escuinapa (M$50, 2½ hours) and transfer there for Teacapán (M$35, one hour).

8am-6pm), a traditional Mexican restaurant that doubles as the town museum. Owner Marcos Osuna has rather eccentric taste, as evident by a pig-shaped urinal in the men's restroom. Tours groups (p109) will often make arrangements for you to watch an *ulama* match (a pre-Hispanic ball game still practiced today).

LA NORIA
Pop 1300

The colonial town of La Noria, about 30km northeast of Mazatlán, is known for its hand-made leather goods, but the main draw is the **Los Osuna** tequila distillery, 15km southeast of town. Here you can tour the factory and sample the final product. Legally, Los Osuna must call the beverage a *'destilado de agave'* (agave spirit) since the state of Jalisco claims Denomination of Origin on tequila, but everyone knows it's the same darn thing. Buses to La Noria run infrequently, so you might want to consider a tour that includes stops at the factory and the **Huana Coa** (☎ 990-11-00) canopy adventure park. You can reserve by calling the park's office.

Nayarit

Once one of the best-kept secrets of the Pacific coast, pristine Nayarit has unsurprisingly emerged as one of Mexico's hottest tourist destinations. After all, it was just a matter of time before beach bums and nature buffs would start spreading the word about the scenic fishing villages, secluded beaches and lush mountains and wetlands teeming with natural wonders.

The state is drawing so much tourism attention these days that the government seized the opportunity to brand a 60km stretch of coastline the 'Riviera Nayarit.' From the gringo-friendly resort of Nuevo Vallarta in the south to the sleepy fishing town of San Blas in the north, once-isolated beach communities, for better or worse, now find themselves sitting on prime real estate.

Despite the ongoing development boom, life on the beach continues to move at a leisurely pace. In Punta de Mita and Sayulita, surfers flock to warm waters with primo breaks, while further north the calming effect of San Francisco, Lo de Marcos and Chacala puts even the most neurotic traveler at ease. In San Blas, tour boats glide through mangroves with hundreds of exotic bird species.

Nayarit is also awash in history and culture. The man-made island of Mexcaltitán is believed by some to be none other than the ancestral homeland of the Aztecs. In the state capital, Tepic, well-preserved historic buildings and several interesting museums dot the streets.

Distances from one town to the next are relatively short in Nayarit, making traveling a breeze. Of course, once you've found that special place, the hardest part is packing your bags.

NAYARIT

HIGHLIGHTS

- Boating through mangroves and gazing at exotic bird species in **San Blas** (p122)
- Letting your imagination run wild on the island village of **Mexcaltitán** (p121), the legendary homeland of the Aztecs
- Watching tiny olive ridley turtles scurry into the sea at **Playa San Francisco** (p135)
- Hanging loose at the surfers' paradise of **Sayulita** (p135)
- Unwinding on the picture-perfect beaches in and around **Chacala** (p129)

- SAN BLAS JANUARY DAILY HIGH: 21°C | 70°F
- SAN BLAS JULY DAILY HIGH: 30°C | 86°F

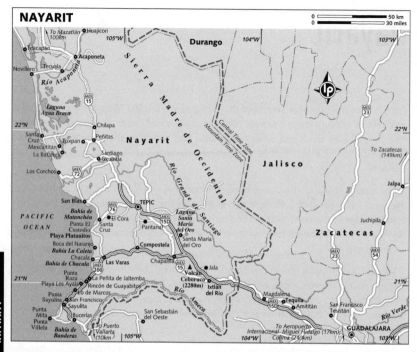

NAYARIT

SANTIAGO IXCUINTLA

☎ 323 / pop 17,000

OK, so Santiago Ixcuintla won't be making any must-see lists anytime soon, but it serves just fine as a jumping-off point for the historic island village of Mexcaltitán. You'll find the best hotels within several blocks of the main square.

The **tourist office** (☎ 235-05-95; 9am-3pm Mon-Fri) and internet services are on the *zócalo* (main plaza), while banks with ATMs and money exchange are nearby.

Indigenous Huichol artists make colorful bead and yarn art at **Centro Huichol** (☎ 235-11-71; cnr Av 20 de Noviembre 452 & Constitución; 10am-7pm Mon-Sat), a handicrafts center about 10 blocks northwest of the city center. It's on the road to Mexcaltitán and there's a *mariscos* (seafood) restaurant next door if you want to grab a bite before heading out.

Hotel Casino Plaza (☎ 235-08-50; Ocampo 40; s/d/tr M$275/320/380; P 🔀) has modern rooms with cable TV and wireless internet. Street-facing rooms are much brighter than those around the interior parking lot. The hotel's Los Vitrales restaurant offers a surpris-

ingly good breakfast and lunch buffet in an air-conditioned space.

Hotel Plaza Los Reyes (☎ 235-42-57; Av 20 de Noviembre 89; d/tr M$377/425, ste M$542; 🔀), one of the newest hotels in town, sports modern rooms with rustic furnishings, cable TV and internet access. High rollers can opt for spacious suites with partial views of the plaza.

Getting There & Away

Santiago Ixcuintla is about 8km west of the Hwy 15 *crucero* (turnoff).

Buses from Tepic leave frequently for Santiago Ixcuintla. You also can take direct buses from Guadalajara or San Blas; however, some lines let passengers off at Las Peñas, a highway town about 10km before the Santiago Ixcuintla *crucero*, so ask if the bus goes '*directo*' to save yourself the hassle of taking a taxi into town.

Three bus lines operate in town, each within several blocks of each other and about three blocks east of the *zócalo* near the intersection of Avs Zaragoza and 20 de Noviembre. Various long-distance buses leave daily from Santiago:

Guadalajara (M$180, five hours, 11pm departure, Transportes Norte de Sonora)
Mazatlán (M$115, four hours, Rápido del Sur)
Puerto Vallarta (M$134, 4½ hours, Transportes Norte de Sonora)
San Blas (M$35, two hours, Transportes Norte de Sonora)
Tepic (M$40, two hours, every half-hour, Transportes Norte de Sonora)

Combis (minibuses) from Santiago Ixcuintla to La Batanga (the departure point for boats to Mexcaltitán) depart from the *taxis foráneos* pickup spot on Juárez, between Allende and Morelos, about two blocks north of the *zócalo*, at 7am, 10am, noon and 2pm. The trip costs M$20.

MEXCALTITÁN
☎ 319 / pop 895

The jury's still out on whether the island village of Mexcaltitán was once Aztlán, the mythical homeland of the Aztecs, but you can't help but let your imagination run wild.

As the story goes, the Aztecs left the island in 1091 to embark on a long migration that eventually led them to Tenochtitlán (present-day Mexico City) in 1325. While there's no denying the striking similarities between the cruciform design of Mexcaltitán's streets and the urban layout of Tenochtitlán, some skeptics dismiss the myth as a clever ploy to draw tourism.

Even if you're not buying into the legend, the stunning natural beauty around the friendly shrimp-fishing hamlet makes it all worthwhile. Visitors arrive via a 10-minute boat ride that motors through mangrove channels full of fish and dozens of bird species.

On the island, you'll find waterside restaurants, a small museum, a lone hotel in need of maintenance and loads of shrimp set out to dry out on narrow sidewalks. Given the island's lack of sleeping options, most people make a day trip out of it. Keep in mind that during the rainy season, from May to mid-October, heavy rains often flood the streets. If you can't find someone to take you around in a canoe, you may be swimming with the shrimp.

Orientation & Information
Mexcaltitán is delightfully free of cars, filled instead with bicycles and handcarts. The main street rings the center of the island, which is a small oval, about 350m from east to west, 400m from north to south. The central *zócalo*

has a church on its east side, and the museum on its north side. The hotel is a block behind the museum.

Sights & Activities
The **Museo del Origen** (admission M$5; ⏰ 9am-2pm & 4-7pm), on the northern side of the plaza, is small but enchanting. Among the exhibits are many interesting ancient objects and a reproduction of a fascinating long scroll, the Códice Ruturini, telling the story of the peregrinations of the Aztec people, with notes in Spanish. Rendered in a vaguely cartoonish style, the scroll reminds one of an outtake from *The Simpsons*.

You can arrange for **boat trips** (about M$70 per hour) on the lagoon for bird-watching, fishing and sightseeing – every family has one or more boats.

Festivals & Events
Semana Santa (Holy Week) is celebrated in a big way here. On Good Friday everyone takes to the streets and the normally placid town comes to life. After a life-sized crucifix is carried through the streets, sound systems are fired up and the central plaza becomes party central until dawn. For the **Fiesta de San Pedro Apóstol**, celebrating the patron saint of fishing on June 28 and 29, statues of Sts Peter and Paul are taken out into the lagoon in decorated *lanchas* (fast, open, outboard boats) for the blessing of the waters. Festivities start around June 20, leading up to the big day.

Sleeping & Eating
Hotel Ruta Azteca (☎ 235-60-20; Venecia 5; s/d/tr M$200/300/450) is the best, worst and only hotel in town. Rooms are dark, simple and marginally clean; insist on one in the back with a view of the lagoon.

The *tamales de camarón* (shrimp tamales) sold from a wheelbarrow on the streets in the morning are a local culinary highlight.

On the east shore, accessible by a rickety wooden walkway, **Restaurant Alberca** (☎ 235-60-27; mains M$60-120; ⏰ 7am-6pm) has a great lagoon view and a menu completely devoted to shrimp. Try the local specialty, *albóndigas de camarón*, battered and fried shrimp balls served in a savory broth. For an even better view, take a free boat ride to a small island across the lagoon and grab a bite at **Mariscos Kika** (☎ 235-60-54; mains M$70-130; ⏰ 9am-6pm), which makes a mighty fine shrimp pâté.

Getting There & Away

From Santiago Ixcuintla (p120), take a *combi* or bus to La Batanga, a small wharf from which boats depart for Mexcaltitán. The arrival and departure times of the *lanchas colectivas* are coordinated with the bus schedule. The boat journey takes 10 minutes and costs M$10 per person. If you miss the *lancha colectiva,* you can hire a private one for M$40 per person (one way), between 8am and 7pm.

SAN BLAS

☎ 323 / pop 9100

The old port town of San Blas seduces surfers and ecotourists with its long, soothing beaches and estuaries brimming with wildlife. It was an important Spanish port from the late-16th to the 19th centuries, and a fortress was built here to protect *naos* (trading galleons) from marauding British and French pirates. Later, Romantic poet Longfellow saw fit to honor the town and its bells in a long poem, completed just days before he keeled over. Sadly there's no bringing back the swashbuckling days of yore, but you can visit the old fort and stay in a semi-pirate-themed hotel if you're overcome with nostalgia.

On the downside, the town boasts a pernicious proliferation of *jejenes,* tiny gnatlike insects with huge appetites for human flesh. Looking at the glass half-full, the little buggers have kept large-scale tourism development at bay. Just make sure to check the screens in your hotel room, carry insect repellent, and stay indoors at dawn and dusk when the *jejenes* are out in full force.

Orientation

San Blas sits on a tongue of land situated between Estuario El Pozo and Estuario San Cristóbal, with Playa El Borrego on the Pacific Ocean on the southern side. A 36km paved road connects San Blas with Hwy 15, the Tepic–Mazatlán road. This road goes through town as Juárez, the town's main east–west street. At the small *zócalo* it crosses Batallón de San Blas (Batallón for short), the main north–south street, which heads south to the beach.

Information

Alfa y Omega (Canalizo 194; per hr M$10; ☉ 9am–11pm) Speedy internet access.

Banamex (Juárez s/n) Has an ATM.

Caseta Telefónica (☎ 285-12-04; Canalizo 5; ☉ 9am–9pm)

Health Clinic (☎ 285-02-32; cnr Teniente Azueta & Campeche; ☉ 24hr)

Post office (cnr Sonora & Echeverría)

Tourist office (☎ 285-00-05; Palacio Municipal; ☉ 9am–4pm Mon–Fri) On the east side of the *zócalo,* this basic tourist office has maps and brochures about the area and the state of Nayarit.

Sights & Activities

For a change of scenery from the main beach, take a boat tour through a captivating estuary system, visit some historical sites, or enjoy scuba diving and camping on a pristine island.

From December to May, **Diving Beyond Adventures** (☎ 285-14-18; in the US 415-235-3789; www .divingbeyond.com; Juárez 187B) organizes and leads various adventure experiences, including diving and bird- and whale-watching trips. The 'extravaganza' tour is a three-day diving, fishing and camping trip to **Isla Isabel National Park**, a paradise for bird-watchers and divers. There you can dive or snorkel among giant rays and observe magnificent frigate birds and blue-footed boobies. The inclusive trip with meals costs M$4620 per person for up to four guests. There's also a more affordable package, without meals, for about half the cost. A diving tank and gear runs an additional M$400 (arrive with proof of diving certification).

Additionally, Diving Beyond Adventures does four- and five-hours trips to the lovely mountain village of El Cora, just outside Tepic, where you can visit a 21m waterfall that cascades into a deep swimming hole. There's a cave behind the falls. The trip costs M$200 per person for a minimum of four people.

On January 30 the commemoration of Mexican Independence hero, Father José María Mercado, livens up San Blas with a march by the Mexican navy and a parade that ends on the hilltop of La Contaduría Fort. On the evening of January 31 the celebration culminates with a fireworks show.

BOAT TRIPS

A boat trip through the jungle to the freshwater spring of **La Tovara** is a real San Blas highlight. Small boats (maximum 13 passengers) depart from the embarcadero. Boats go up Estuario San Cristóbal to the spring, passing thick jungle vegetation and mangroves rife with exotic birds. The limpid waters of

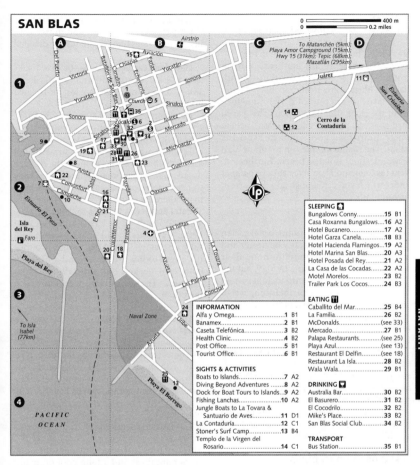

La Tovara are gorgeous to behold, but resist taking a dip: a swimmer was attacked by a crocodile here in 2006.

For a few pesos more, you can extend the trip from La Tovara to the **Cocodrilario** (crocodile nursery), where the reptiles are reared in captivity for later release in the wild. For a group of up to four people, it costs M$90 per person to go to La Tovara (3½ hours) and M$110 to also visit the Cocodrilario (four hours). Shorter boat trips to La Tovara can be made from docks near Matanchén village, further up the river.

The mangrove ecosystem surrounding San Blas is a sanctuary for 300 species of birds – you don't have to be a birder to get a thrill from an encounter with the flamingo-like roseate spoonbill. A five-hour bird-watching trip up the Estuario San Cristóbal to the **Santuario de Aves** (Bird Sanctuary) can be arranged at La Tovara embarcadero by the bridge (M$150 per person).

Other boat trips depart from a landing on Estuario El Pozo. They include a trip to **Piedra Blanca** (M$250 per hour), a large rock, to visit a statue of the Virgin; to the **Isla del Rey** peninsula (M$20), just across from San Blas; and to **Playa del Rey**, a 20km beach on the other side of Isla del Rey. From here you can also hire boatmen to take you on bird-watching excursions.

Boatmen also offer fishing and sightseeing trips from small boats docked on Campeche, on the edge of the estuary. The going rate is about M$300 per boat.

BEACHES

The beach closest to town is **Playa El Borrego**, at the end of Azueta. Broad waves roll in with bravado at this popular surfers' hangout.

The best beaches are southeast of town around Bahía de Matanchén, starting with **Playa Las Islitas**, 7km from San Blas. To get there, take the road toward Hwy 15, and turn off to the right after about 4km. This paved road goes east past the village of Matanchén, where a dirt road goes south to Playa Las Islitas. The road continues on to follow 8km of wonderfully isolated beach. Further on, **Playa Los Cocos** and **Playa Miramar** have *palapas* under which you can lounge and drink fresh coconut milk.

SURFING

With many beach and point breaks, San Blas is the place where many beginner and intermediate surfers choose to hone their skills. The surf season starts in May, but the waves are fairly mellow until October when the south swell brings amazingly long waves curling into **Bahía de Matanchén**. Popular surf spots include El Borrego, Second Jetty, La Puntilla, Stoner's, Las Islitas and El Mosco.

At Playa El Borrego, **Stoner's Surf Camp** (☎ 285-04-44; www.stonerssurfcamp.com; Playa El Borrego; boogie-board/surfboard rental per hr M$20/30, per day M$80/100, lessons per hr M$150) offers surf classes from long-board champion 'Pompis' Cano. Also available are five rustic cabins (M$100 to M$300), camping sites (M$30) and tent and bike rentals (M$20/60).

CERRO DE LA CONTADURÍA

Just west of the bridge over Estuario San Cristóbal, the road passes the Cerro de la Contaduría. Climb up the hill and see the ruins of the 18th-century Spanish **La Contaduría Fort** and **Templo de la Virgen del Rosario**; there's a fine view from the top.

Sleeping

San Blas has a wide offering of accommodations, from affordable air-conditioned rooms to roomy suites and bungalows with kitchens.

BUDGET

Campers at Los Cocos and Playa Amor should be prepared for the swarms of insects, especially at sunset.

Trailer Park Los Cocos (☎ 285-00-55; Azueta s/n; tent/RV sites M$80/130) Pleasant and grassy with just enough trees but a haven for the dreaded *jejenes*.

Playa Amor Campground (Playa Los Cocos; tent/RV sites M$100/145) An attractive trailer park, about 15km east of town, overlooking an isolated beach.

Motel Morelos (☎ 285-13-45; Batallón 108; r M$200-250) Austere rooms surround a central courtyard at this friendly family-owned hotel. An old pelican, which has become somewhat of a local celebrity, resides on the patio. About a decade ago the proprietors nursed him back to health following an injury and he's been living there ever since.

Hotel Bucanero (☎ 285-08-05; Juárez 117; s/d/tr M$250/400/500; P ⊠ ⊠) This hotel has seen better days but it still sparkles with old, salty character. The dark, rough-around-the-edges rooms are set around a big leafy courtyard decked out with 19th-century cannons. There's a lively weekend disco next door.

MIDRANGE & TOP END

Bungalows Conny (☎ 285-09-86; www.bungalowsconny.com; Chiapas 26; r M$400, bungalow M$500-600; ⊠ ⊠) In a quiet part of a quiet town, this place rests easy with modern rooms and bungalows. The largest bungalow is fresh and feels like a small apartment, with a separate bedroom and large kitchen. The pool area provides plenty of relaxation.

Casa Roxanna Bungalows (☎ 285-05-73; www.casaroxanna.com; El Rey 1; bungalows M$550-650; P ⊠ ⊠) This gay-friendly haven provides four capacious bungalows and a long pool on manicured grounds. Discounts are offered for longer stays.

Hotel Posada del Rey (☎ 285-01-23; Campeche 10; d/tr M$600/650; ⊠ ⊡ ⊠) The recently remodeled rooms in this low-key hotel are sporting new beds with firm mattresses, sparkling tiled floors in the bathrooms, and upgraded TVs. All rooms overlook a tranquil courtyard with a clean swimming pool.

La Casa de las Cocadas (☎ 285-09-60; www.etcbeach.com; Juárez 145; s/d/t M$750/850/1535; ⊠ ⊡) Conveniently located near the boat docks and just a short walk from the beach, this intimate boutique hotel offers 10 airy rooms with slick rustic furnishings. The rooms come with a private balcony, cable TV and wireless internet.

ourpick **Hotel Hacienda Flamingos** (☎ 285-09-30; www.sanblas.com.mx; Juárez 105; ste M$890-1365; ⊠ ⊠) This gorgeous 19th-century hacienda provides the classiest accommodations in town but beware: rumor has it ghosts are lurking in the courtyard. The large suites have private terraces, TVs with DVD players and rustic-chic furnishings. Some rooms overlook a pleasant green garden and pool.

Hotel Marina San Blas (☎ 285-14-37; www.sanblas .com.mx; Cuauhtémoc 197; s/d M$990/1240, ste M$1500-2500; ⓟ ⊠ ⊠) Gaze out at the El Pozo estuary and the old lighthouse from a private terrace at this waterfront hotel. The large suites are a good deal for a family or group of four. The hotel also has kayaks that guests can use for free.

Hotel Garza Canela (☎ 285-01-12; www.garza canela.com; Paredes 106 Sur; s/d/ste M$1076/1359/1935; ⓟ ⊠ ⊠) The Garza Canela may seem a tad pricey by San Blas standards, but you're paying for spacious, modern rooms with satellite TV and an attractive pool area. It's also home to El Delfín, the best restaurant in town.

Eating

Restaurants in San Blas cater mainly to tourists; however, you'll be able to find a few places with fairly reasonable prices, especially in the *mercado* (market) on Sonora and Batallón. For fresh fish and seafood, hit the *palapa* restaurants on the beach.

Playa Azul (☎ 285-04-44; Playa El Borrego; mains M$40-60, at Stoner's Surf Camp; ⓥ) A traveler hangout with good music, lots of hammocks and well-prepared fare (including vegetarian).

La Familia (☎ 285-02-58; Batallón 16; mains M$65-90) This quaint family restaurant asks moderate prices for delicious Mexican and seafood dishes, such as a fish-and-shrimp concoction called the *merequetengue*. The 19th-century building, which has a charming little courtyard, is one of the oldest homes in San Blas.

Restaurant La Isla (☎ 285-04-07; cnr Paredes & Mercado; mains M$70-120; ⓥ 2-9pm Tue-Sun; ⊠) La Isla grills near-perfect seafood, but it's also worth coming in just to check out the overdone seashell decor – it's so tacky it's cool. Try the 'Especial Alberto,' grilled mahimahi with shrimp, grilled onions, bell pepper and cheese.

Wala Wala (☎ 285-08-63; Juárez 117; mains M$70-150; ⓥ 7am-10pm Mon-Sat) This attractively decorated restaurant serves tasty, homestyle Mexican meals and has a few specialties such as *pollo*

con naranja (chicken with orange) and *camarones al vino blanco* (shrimp sautéed in white wine), accompanied by rice and steamed veggies.

McDonalds (☎ 285-04-32; Juárez 36; mains M$78-120; ⓥ 7am-10pm) We know what you're thinking, but this isn't the fast-food joint of Big Mac fame. Instead, you get hearty breakfasts and generously served daily lunch and dinner specials here.

Caballito del Mar (☎ 285-04-07; Playa El Borrego; mains M$85-170) Cooks up remarkably sophisticated seafood dishes and *pescado zarandeado* (filleted fish marinated with spices and herbs and grilled).

ourpick **Restaurant El Delfín** (☎ 285-01-12; Paredes 106 Sur; mains M$105-169; ⊠) For gourmet international cuisine you can't get any better than this elegant restaurant at Hotel Garza Canela. Chef Betty Vazquez, who studied at the Cordon Bleu culinary school in France, designed a diverse menu that includes a delicious shrimp dish with fine herbs, chipotle and plantain. If there's room for dessert, indulge in the chocolate cake.

Drinking & Entertainment

Most of San Blas' watering holes close at midnight, so don't expect any all-nighters in this low-key town. You'll find these places within a block or so of the main square.

San Blas Social Club (cnr Juárez & Canalizo; ⓥ 9am-3pm, 7pm-midnight) Old jazz records line the walls in this friendly bar and grill. It has live music Friday and Saturday, fish and chips for the munchies, and good strong coffee every morning.

Mike's Place (Juárez 36) Restaurant and bar owner Mike McDonald and friends get together about five nights a week to play a good mix of blues and '60s rock music. The lively bar is on the 2nd floor, above McDonalds restaurant.

El Cocodrilo (Juárez 6) This old favorite still attracts gringos in the evening, using well-priced cocktails as bait. If you get hungry, it also has steak, seafood and pasta dishes.

Australia Bar (Juárez 34) The long bar of this upstairs pool room is dotted with cool youths and grungy foreigners throwing drinks back.

El Basurero (Paredes s/n) How 'bout some local flavor? The neighborhood barflies in this rustic old cantina will keep you entertained for hours on end, and the *cerveza* is dirt cheap.

DETOUR: PLAYA PLATANITOS

Tucked away in a beautiful cove surrounded by striking mountain terrain, you couldn't ask for a lovelier spot to enjoy a quiet beach and excellent fresh fish. Several *palapa* restaurants line the beach, but **Ruiz** (mains M$80-150) is king of the *pescado zarandeado*, a grilled whole fish marinated in a zesty barbecue sauce. After the meal, take a stroll to Playa Venecia, about 1km north. You can reach the beach by hopping across a stretch of slippery-when-wet rocks, or walk down a winding trail from the highway. Once you arrive, it's just you, the sand crabs and the palm trees.

To get there, take a Puerto Vallarta–bound bus from San Blas and ask the driver to let you off at Platanitos. To return, ask the driver what time you need to be waiting on the highway to flag down the last bus, or you can make arrangements in San Blas for a taxi to pick you up at a designated hour. If you get stranded, the simple rooms at **Bungalows Alex** (r M$400, bungalow M$600; ⚡) are a welcome sight.

Getting There & Around

The little **bus station** (cnr Sinaloa & Canalizo) is served by Transportes Norte de Sonora and Estrella Blanca 2nd-class buses. For many destinations to the south and east, it may be quicker to go to Tepic first. For Mazatlán, transfer in Tepic. There are daily departures to various destinations:

Guadalajara (M$180, five hours, one 2nd-class, 7am)
Puerto Vallarta (M$118, 3½ hours, four 1st-class)
Santiago Ixcuintla (M$40, one hour, two 2nd-class)
Tepic (M$42, 1½ hours, 2nd-class hourly 6am-8pm)

Second-class buses departing from the station also serve all the villages and beaches on Bahía de Matanchén.

Taxis line up along Canalizo, next to the bus station. They'll take you around town and to nearby beaches. A trip to Playa El Borrego will set you back about M$40. Rent bicycles from Wala Wala (per hour/day M$15/100) or Stoner's Surf Camp (per day M$60).

TEPIC

☎ 311 / pop 336,000 / elevation 920m

Founded by the nephew of Hernán Cortés in 1524, the colonial city of Tepic is old even by Mexican standards. Today the capital of Nayarit is a forward-thinking, predominantly middle-class place, retaining few vestiges of its distant past. Many travelers pass through the outskirts of town without looking back, but those who take a day to nose around may come to appreciate the provincial hustle and bustle playing out on its narrow streets. Indigenous Huichol are seen here wearing their colorful traditional clothing.

Orientation

Plaza Principal, with the large cathedral at the eastern end, is the heart of the city.

Av México, the city's main street, runs south from the cathedral to Plaza Constituyentes, past restaurants, the state museum and other places of interest. The bus station is on the southeastern side of the city, about 2km from Plaza Principal, with plenty of buses serving the center.

Information

The **state tourist office** (☎ 214-80-71, 214-80-72; www.visitnayarit.com; cnr Av México & Calz del Ejército; ⊗ 8am-3pm, 6-8pm) is a great resource with free maps and extensive information about Tepic and the state of Nayarit.

This busy downtown **Tepic tourist office** (☎ 216-55-15; Puebla Nte & Nervo Pte; ⊗ 8am-8pm) has a tourist module with maps of the city and other useful information.

Banks (with ATMs) and *casas de cambio* line Av México Nte between the two plazas; you'll find the post office at the corner of Durango Nte and Morelos.

Access the internet at **@net.com** (Av México Nte s/n, Plaza Milenio; per hr M$10).

Sights

Construction on the large **cathedral** on Plaza Principal began in 1804 and the neo-Gothic towers were completed in 1896. On the other side of the plaza from the cathedral is the **Palacio Municipal** (city hall). On Av México Nte, south of the plaza, look inside the Nayarit state government buildings – **Palacio de Gobierno** and the **Cámara de Diputados** – to see some impressive and colorful **murals**.

The 16th-century **Templo de la Cruz de Zacate** and the 18th-century **Ex-Covento** (cnr Av México & Calz del Ejército; ⊗ 8am-8pm Mon-Fri) are about 2km south of the cathedral. It was here in

1767 that Father Junípero Serra organized his expedition that established the chain of Spanish missions in the Californias; you can visit the room where he stayed.

MUSEUMS

Housed in a palatial 18th-century residence with a lovely courtyard, **Museo Regional de Nayarit** (☎ 212-19-00; Av México 91 Nte; admission M$35; ☉ 9am-6pm Mon-Fri, 9am-3pm Sat) concerns itself primarily with pre-Hispanic objects, including ancient pottery and tomb artifacts, as well as exhibits that shed light on Huichol art and cosmology.

A couple of interesting museums are housed in impressive restored colonial residences. The **Casa y Museo Amado Nervo** (☎ 212-29-16; Zacatecas 284 Nte; admission free; ☉ 9am-2pm Mon-Fri, 10am-2pm Sat) celebrates the life of famed poet Amado Nervo, born in this house in 1870. The house is lovely to behold.

Casa Museo Juan Escutia (☎ 212-33-90; Hidalgo 71 Ote; admission free; ☉ 9am-2pm & 4-7pm Mon-Fri, 10am-2pm Sat) was the home of Juan Escutia, one of Mexico's illustrious Niños Héroes (child heroes), who died in 1847 at age 17 defending Mexico City's Chapultepec Castle from US forces during the Mexican-American War. It's simply furnished and evocative of early 19th-century Mexico.

The **Museo de los Cuatro Pueblos** (☎ 212-17-05; Hidalgo 60 Ote; admission free; ☉ 9am-2pm & 4-7pm Mon-Fri, 9am-2pm Sat) displays contemporary popular arts of Nayarit's Huichol, Cora, Nahua and Tepehuano peoples, including clothing, yarn art, musical instruments, ceramics and beadwork. It also offers crafts workshops.

Aramara (☎ 216-42-46; Allende 329 Pte; admission free; ☉ 9am-3pm Mon-Fri) is a small museum of visual arts about 1.5km west of the town center.

Sleeping

Tepic's downtown area pretty much offers it all, from no-frills digs and reasonable midrange options to an elegant colonial-style hotel.

Trailer Park Los Pinos (☎ 210-27-28; Blvd Tepic-Xalisco 150; RV/tent sites per person M$150/40) About 5km south of town, this spacious park has 24 trailer spaces with full hookups and wireless internet. The leafy, grassy grounds make tent camping a pleasure.

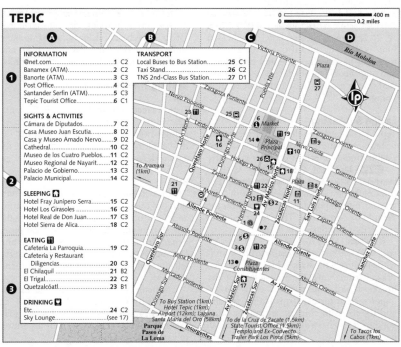

Hotel Tepic (☎ 213-13-77; fax 210-05-45; Dr Martinez 438 Ote; s/d/ste M$225/300/420; P ⊠ 🖳) With clean rooms, wireless internet and a restaurant/bar, this modern hotel next to the bus station makes for a comfortable stopover point if you're just passing through.

Hotel Los Girasoles (☎ 216-26-51; www.hotel-los -girasoles.com; Lerdo 181 Pte; s/d/tr/q M$335/368/400/420; ⊠ P) Just a few blocks from the main square, this clean hotel offers modern rooms with checkerboard-pattern tiled floors, cable TV and firm mattresses. It's one of the best deals in town but the walls can be pretty thin.

Hotel Sierra de Alica (☎ 212-03-22; Av México 180 Nte; s/d M$485/625; P ⊠) An old favorite in the heart of downtown, this 1950s hotel has 60 spacious rooms with satellite TV and phones. The front-desk service leaves a bit to be desired but overall it's an enjoyable stay.

our pick **Hotel Fray Junípero Serra** (☎ 212-25-25; www.frayjunipero.com.mx, in Spanish; Lerdo 23 Pte; s/d/tr/ste M$908/1003/1097/2124; P ⊠ 🖳) If you can score one of the recently remodeled rooms overlooking the main square, you'll have one of the finest views in town. Rates include free access to the on-site gym, and in the lobby there's a nice restaurant with a salad bar.

Hotel Real de Don Juan (☎ 216-18-88; www.real dedonjuan.com.mx; Av México 105 Sur; r/ste M$1265/2035; P ⊠ 🖳) Tepic's classiest hotel, the old Don Juan is done up in antique replica furniture and has marble-accented bathrooms and huge beds. The hotel has a good restaurant on the ground floor and a chic rooftop lounge bar.

Eating & Drinking

Tepic has a healthy selection of vegetarian restaurants, natural food stores and seafood establishments offering nutritious local fare.

our pick **Tacos Los Cabos** (☎ 111-68-11; Av Universidad 115; tacos M$14; ☺ 10am-4pm Mon-Sat) For some of the best shrimp, marlin and fish tacos around, hit this popular street stand near the Templo de San Rafael. They're served with zesty salsas and Baja-style fixings.

El Chilaquil (☎ 217-66-83; Allende Pte & Querétaro Nte; mains M$23-90; ☺ 8am-3pm, 7pm-3am) Black-and-white photos of the stars of Mexico's 'Golden Era of Cinema' cover the walls at this popular breakfast joint. The specialty here is the *chilaquiles*, fried tortilla strips bathed in salsa and topped with chicken, shrimp or other goodies. It also has a dinner menu and a small bar upstairs.

Cafetería y Restaurant Diligencias (☎ 212-15-35; Av México 29 Sur; mains M$25-60; ☺ breakfast, lunch & dinner) Diligencias serves up quality coffee and dishes out homestyle Mexican meals all day long in a vintage dining hall.

Quetzalcóatl (☎ 212-99-66; León 224 Nte; mains M$28-75; ☺ 8:30am-5pm Tue-Sat; V) The main draw here is the vegetarian buffet, which comes with drink and dessert, or you can order light, healthy dishes off the menu.

Cafetería La Parroquia (☎ 124-53-03; Nervo 18 Ote; mains M$29-79) On the northern side of the plaza, upstairs under the arches, this place is very pleasant for breakfasts, drinks and inexpensive light meals. It also does good coffee.

El Trigal (☎ 216-40-04; Veracruz 112 Nte; mains M$33-70; ☺ 8:30am-7pm Mon-Fri; V) This inexpensive vegetarian restaurant has a daily buffet and does up whole-wheat quesadillas and veggie burgers.

Sky Lounge (☎ 216-18-80; Av México 105 Sur; ☺ 7pm-2am Mon-Sat) Grab a few drinks and take in the panoramic view at this hip lounge bar on the 5th floor of the Hotel Real de Don Juan. Sourpuss doormen strictly enforce a dress code, meaning no shorts, grimy sneakers or tattered rags.

Etc (☎ 217-09-88; Av Mexico 55 Nte; ☺ 6pm-1am Sun-Wed, 6pm-3am Thu-Sat) Middle-class 20-somethings gather in this beautiful downtown bar to shoot some stick and listen to live *trova* music and *rock en español* over beers and mixed drinks.

Getting There & Away

AIR

Tepic's **airport** (TPQ; ☎ 214-18-50) is in Pantanal, 12km (or a 20-minute drive) from Tepic, going toward Guadalajara. **Aeromar** (☎ 210-26-84; Airport) offers three daily flights to Mexico City with connections to other cities.

BUS

The bus station is on the southeastern outskirts of town; local buses marked 'Central' and 'Centro' make frequent trips between the bus station and the city center; local buses depart from the corner of Nervo Pte and Durango Nte. The bus station has a cafeteria, left-luggage office, tourist information and an ATM.

The main bus companies are Elite, Estrella Blanca (EB), Ómnibus de México (OB; all 1st-class), and Transportes del Pacífico (TP; 1st- and 2nd-class). There are daily departures to various destinations:

Guadalajara Elite (M$200, 3½ hours, frequent 1st-class); Futura (M$174, 3½ hours, frequent 1st-class)
Mazatlán Elite (M$170, 4½ hours, hourly 1st-class); TP (M$147, 4½ hours, hourly 2nd-class)
Mexico City OB (M$640, 10 hours, four 1st-class) To Terminal Norte.
Puerto Vallarta TP (M$140, 3½ hours, five 1st-class; M$125, 3½ hours, frequent 2nd-class)

TNS (Transportes Norte de Sonora) operates a small terminal north of the cathedral near the Río Mololoa with 2nd-class service to San Blas (M$42, two hours, hourly from 5am to 7pm) and Santiago Ixcuintla (M$30, 1½ hours, half-hourly from 6am to 7pm).

Getting Around

Local buses operate from around 6am to 9pm (M$4). *Combis* operate along Av México from 6am to midnight (M$4.50). There are also plenty of taxis, and a taxi stand on the south side of Plaza Principal. A typical cab fare runs M$20.

AROUND TEPIC
Laguna Santa María del Oro

Surrounded by steep, forested mountains, idyllic Laguna Santa María del Oro (elevation 730m) fills a volcanic crater 2km around and thought to be over 100m deep. The clear water takes on colors ranging from turquoise to slate. A walk around the lake and surrounding mountains makes for great bird-watching, with some 250 species inhabiting the area. You can also climb to an abandoned gold mine, swim, kayak on the lake, or fish for black bass and perch. A few small restaurants serve fresh fish.

Koala Bungalows & RV Park (☎ 311-264-36-98; http://geocities.com/cfrenchkoala; Santa María del Oro; per person tent/r/bungalow M$40/400/500, cabin M$700-800) is an attractive, peaceful park with a restaurant, campsites and well-maintained bungalows in several sizes. It's owned and operated by a friendly Englishman, who's an excellent source of information about the lake.

To get there, take the Santa María del Oro turnoff about 40km from Tepic along the Guadalajara road; from the turnoff it's about 10km to Santa María del Oro, then another 8km from the village to the lake. Buses in Tepic depart frequently from the 2nd-class bus station (M$30, one hour).

Volcán Ceboruco

This extinct 2280m volcano, with a number of old craters, interesting plants and volcanic forms, has several short, interesting walks at the top. There's plenty of vegetation growing on the slopes, and the 15km cobbled road up the volcano passes lava fields and fumaroles (steam vents). The road begins at the village of Jala, 7km off Hwy 15D, between Tepic and Guadalajara; the *crucero* is 76km from Tepic. There's no public transportation, so you'll need your own wheels.

Ixtlán del Río
☎ 324 / pop 22,000

The small town of Ixtlán del Río, about 1½ hours (88km) south of Tepic along Hwy 15D, is unremarkable in itself, but fans of controversial author Carlos Castaneda will remember that this is where Don Juan took Carlos in the book *Journey to Ixtlán*. Outside Ixtlán, the **Los Toriles** archaeological site has an impressive round stone temple, the **Templo a Quetzalcóatl** (admission M$35; ☺ 9am-5pm). If you decide to stay the night, **Hotel Plaza Hidalgo** (☎ 243-21-00; Av Hidalgo 101; s/d M$527/579; **P** **⚡**) has clean rooms and a good coffee shop. Any bus between Tepic and Guadalajara will drop you at Ixtlán.

CHACALA
☎ 327 / pop 277

You gotta love the small-town feel of this picturesque fishing village. Sitting pretty along a gorgeous cove backed by verdant slopes, Chacala's mesmerizing beach and scenic surroundings will hold you in a state of bliss. More and more people have discovered Chacala in recent years, but at last visit the town remained untouched by large-scale tourism.

Chacala has just one main, sandy thoroughfare and a few cobbled side streets. There are no banks or ATMs in town, so plan accordingly.

If time permits, the dense jungles and nearby beaches are worth exploring. Tour guides offer their services for horseback riding, snorkeling, fishing and whale-watching outings; that is, if you can pull yourself away from the celestial beach.

Activities

Hereabouts, the sea provides most of the action. The waters of **Bahía Chacala** are calm and clear most days, allowing for relaxing water sports and exemplary snorkeling. Local boat operators, easily encountered

NAYARIT

on the beach, will take you to favorite spots like **Bahía La Caleta**, 15 minutes north by boat. Here surfers rejoice to find a fine left-breaking point break.

You can also hike through the jungle to **Playa La Caleta**, about 1½ hours to the north; it's a challenging but rewarding slog with a happy ending on a deserted beach known for its big waves. Along the way, you're likely to see exotic birds such as the West Mexican chachalaca or the Pacific slope flycatcher. You can arrange to have a boat pick you up on the beach for transportation back to Chacala.

Inquire about kayaking and snorkeling tours at the **Mar de Jade** (☎ 219-40-00; www .mardejade.com; Playa Chacala s/n) resort. There you can also make arrangements for seasonal whale-watching excursions from November through March.

Sleeping

In Chacala you can stay in budget inns, guesthouses or upscale hotels.

Techos de México (www.techosdemexico.com; r M$150-400) Folks interested in getting to know some locals should check out this place, a series of six homes with room for up to four people. Rooms are updated but basic and are separate from the host home. You'll find the homes' contact info on the website.

Casa Mirador (☎ 219-40-73; Océano Pacífico 10; r M$250-350) The beds at this inn could use new mattresses, but the rooms are decent enough and you couldn't ask for nicer hosts. Casa Mirador also operates Chacala Adventures, a family-run ecotour service that provides whale-watching and sportfishing excursions.

Posada Guadalajara (☎ 219-40-11; Av Chacalilla 500; r M$600) This two-story hotel offers 15 clean rooms with two double beds, air-conditioning, TV and DVD players. The front desk loans Hollywood and Mexican flicks.

Las Brisas (☎ 219-40-15; Av Chacalilla 4; r M$650) Right on the beach and home to the best *palapa* seafood restaurant. Rooms here come complete with two double beds, cable TV and wireless internet access.

Casa de Tortugas (☎ 219-40-18; www.casadetortugas.com; Océano Pacífico 4; r/house M$850/4000; 🖭) On offer at the quaint House of Turtles are three rooms with large beds, air-con and ocean views, and a three-bedroom house that sleeps up to 12. A heated infinity pool overlooks the ocean, and on the 3rd floor there's a communal kitchen.

Villa Celeste (☎ 219-41-14; www.villacelestechacala .com; r M$900-1000) Done up in warm yellow and orange tones, this hillside hotel offers nine guest rooms facing a rustic courtyard and a lush garden dotted with tall palms. The clean rooms come with kitchens, DVD players and boomboxes. If available, ask for one with a bayside view.

our pick **Majahua** (☎ 219-40-53; www.majahua.com; Playa Chacala s/n; ste M$1462-3217) Super-chic and tucked away in the unspoiled jungle overlooking the edge of the cove, this earthy ecolodge sports six beautifully designed rooms and a fantastic outdoor restaurant. Ask about two- and three-night packages that include meals and spa services. It's a five-minute walk along the beach from Mar de Jade.

Mar de Jade (☎ 219-40-00; www.mardejade.com; Playa Chacala s/n; s/d M$1670/2760, ste M$1670-2010, d ste M$3330; 🖭 🖳) Part holistic healing center, part vacation retreat, Mar de Jade provides everything from yoga classes and community workshops to spa treatments and Spanish classes. Three healthy meals are served under a breezy open-air pavilion overlooking the sea, and the well-appointed rooms face a beautiful garden. If you like large, luxurious bathrooms, check out the goods in the romantic suite.

Casa Pacífica (☎ 219-40-67; www.casapacificachacala .com; d per week M$4500) At this relaxing midrange option, three large, beautiful suites come with queen-sized beds and a kitchen. Unfortunately they're only available as weekly rentals. Owner Susana Escobido is exceptionally knowledgeable about the area and she has the best breakfast joint in town.

Eating

You'll find about a dozen thatched-roof *palapa* restaurants lining the sandy beach. For super-fresh seafood, head to the dock early in the morning and buy your own fish; some hotels will cook it up for a small fee.

Mauna Kea Café (☎ 219-40-67; breakfast M$40-60; 🕙 8-10am Mon-Sat) A tiny, unconventional and casual rooftop café at Casa Pacífica (above), Mauna Kea serves up full, hearty breakfasts, good coffee and Hawaiian-style waffles.

Las Brisas (☎ 219-40-15; mains M$55-150; 🕙 8am-10pm) The best option on the beach, Las Brisas does good morning coffee and seafood prepared the local way. Try the house specialty *camarones al coco*, coconut shrimp served with a pineapple dipping sauce. You'll be in seventh heaven.

Getting There & Away

To reach Chacala, get off the bus at Las Varas (any 2nd-class bus will stop here, as will most – but not all – 1st-class buses) and take a *taxi colectivo* (shared taxi) to Chacala (M$15, 15 minutes). A private taxi sets you back about M$100.

AROUND CHACALA

Hidden in the mountains up a rough dirt road lie the hot springs of **Jamurca** (admission M$20; 🕙 9am-5pm Thu-Tue). It is said the Huichol *marakames* (shamans) once took ritual baths to purify their bodies and souls. You can do the same in three concrete pools. You'll need your own wheels to get there; on Hwy 200 look for the swimmer pictograph 2km north of Las Varas at a town called Las Cuatas, then head south about 4km.

RINCÓN DE GUAYABITOS

☎ 327 / pop 1900

Known simply as 'Guayabitos,' this beach-resort town is first and foremost a Mexican family affair. In the winter months, many German and Canadian tourists head to Guayabitos' warm beach to escape the cold-weather blues of home. The town shows its weathered age, but that's part of its appeal. Restaurants, hotels and stores selling beach-wear and touristy knick-knacks line the main avenue, while two blocks north you'll find a festive beach atmosphere with families picnicking on the sand and vendors selling tasty grilled fish on a stick. Guayabitos gets overrun during holiday periods. In the low season, the crowds thin out considerably and hotels give generous discounts.

Orientation & Information

Rincón de Guayabitos is on the coast just west of Hwy 200. At the north entrance to town, a high-water tower emulates an elongated mushroom. Turn into town here, or along Jacarandas if you're coming from the south, and soon you'll be on Guayabitos' main street, Av Sol Nuevo. The most appealing restaurants and hotels sit along the beach, one block over – they're reached by side streets, as there's no road along the waterfront.

The nearest bank is in La Peñita de Jaltemba, 3km north of Guayabitos, but there's a **Bancomer ATM** (Retorno Laureles) just outside Villas Buena Vida. Access the internet

and send faxes at **Reflecta** (☎ 274-30-62; Sol Nuevo 2; per hr M$20), in front of the church.

Near the water tower, **Modulo de Información Turistica** (☎ 274-06-93; Sol Nuevo s/n; 🕙 9am-2pm & 4-6pm Mon-Sat, 9am-2pm Sun) provides tourist information on the local area and the state of Nayarit. The **post office** (🕙 8am-2pm Mon-Fri) is on the main square.

Sights & Activities

From the beach you can take a *panga* (motorized skiff) or a glass-bottom boat (up to five people M$450) out to the gorgeous snorkeling nirvana **Isla Islote** (a few kilometers offshore), where you can rent snorkeling gear and eat in a simple restaurant. From November to March, **Fiesta Guayabitos** (☎ 274-04-53; outing M$200) leads three-hour whale-watching outings. You can hire its services on the beach, but try to agree on a reasonable price as some agents tack on a commission.

North of Guayabitos, **Boca del Naranjo** beckons, with wild waves crashing onto the beach and mangroves ideal for kayaking and bird-watching. To get there, drive 6km north from the turnoff to Chacala on Hwy 200 and take the signed left to the village of La Lima de Abajo and continue a short distance further to the beach.

For something different, climb the 224 steps to **Cerro de la Santa Cruz** (Hill of the Holy Cross), known locally as La Cruz. From here you'll enjoy fantastic views of Bahía de Jaltemba. Pilgrims make the climb en masse at Easter, but the rest of the year you're likely to have the lookout to yourself. You'll find the path at the southern terminus of Av Sol Nuevo.

Sleeping

Many hotels in town are geared toward accommodating families and groups, hence the multiple beds and fully equipped kitchens, yet lone travelers and couples will have no problem finding smaller setups.

Paraíso del Pescador Trailer Park & Bungalows (☎ 274-00-14; www.guayabitos.com/paraisodelpescador; Retorno Ceibas; tent & RV sites M$300, r M$650) Stark and basic, but right on the beach.

Posada Jaltemba (☎ 274-01-65; cnr Sol Nuevo & Laureles; d/q M$450/600, 4-person bungalows M$500, 6-person bungalows M$950; P ⬚ ⬚ ⬚) With clean, spacious rooms, friendly staff and poolside barbecues, it's no wonder so many visitors return to this affordable family-run inn

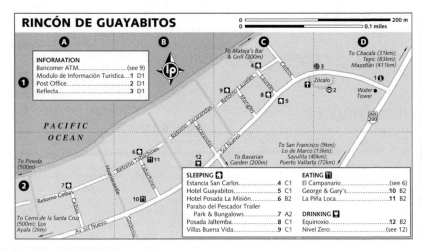

RINCÓN DE GUAYABITOS

0 — 200 m
0 — 0.1 miles

INFORMATION
Bancomer ATM..............................(see 9)
Modulo de Información Turística....**1** D1
Post Office.....................................**2** D1
Reflecta...**3** D1

To Mateja's Bar
& Grill (200m)

To Chacala (31km);
Tepic (83km);
Mazatlán (411km)

Zócalo

Water
Tower

PACIFIC
OCEAN

To Pineda
(500m)

To Cerro de la Santa Cruz
(500m); Los
Ayala (2km)

To San Francisco (9km);
Lo de Marco (13km);
Sayulita (40km);
Puerto Vallarta (72km)

To Bavarian
Garden (200m)

SLEEPING 🛏
Estancia San Carlos.....................**4** C1
Hotel Guayabitos.........................**5** C1
Hotel Posada La Misión................**6** B2
Paraíso del Pescador Trailer
   Park & Bungalows....................**7** A2
Posada Jaltemba.........................**8** C1
Villas Buena Vida........................**9** C1

EATING 🍴
El Campanario.............................(see 6)
George & Gary's..........................**10** B2
La Piña Loca...............................**11** B2

DRINKING 🍷
Equinoxio...................................**12** B2
Nivel Zero..................................(see 12)

year after year. If you're feeling homesick, you can make free phone calls to the US and Canada.

Hotel Guayabitos (☎ 274-09-20; Sol Nuevo 17; d/q M$600/950, bungalows M$700-1100; P 🅿 ❄ 🛜) Always buzzing with activity, this family-friendly hotel has great deals on air-conditioned bungalows with fully equipped kitchens. There's just one catch: expect an early-morning wake-up call from excited kids running around the pool and lobby area.

Hotel Posada la Misión (☎ 274-08-95; www.guaya bitos.com/lm; Retorno Tabachines 6; d/tr M$780/845, bungalows M$865-1385; P ❄ 🖥 🛜) This hotel has a colonial theme going, with beautiful tiles lining open halls in front, great sea views out back and an amoeba-shaped pool in the middle. Rooms are nice and quaint, and bungalows have balconies.

ourpick Estancia San Carlos (☎ 274-01-55; www .estanciasancarlos.com; Retorno Laureles s/n; q/bungalows M$1235/1682; P ❄ 🛜 👶) A good option for vacationing families, the 'standard' rooms at this cheerful hotel sleep up to four and come with a kitchenette, ocean view and cable TV. Children dig the kiddie pool and grown-ups take a strong liking to the beachfront bar.

Villas Buena Vida (☎ 274-02-31; www.villasbuena vida.com; Retorno Laureles 2; r M$1598, ste M$2097-2662; P ❄ 🛜) Ahh, the good life. With manicured grounds and a well-tended pool, Buena Vida offers just that, along with roomy suites that accommodate four to six guests. The hotel also arranges sportfishing, snorkeling and horseback-riding trips.

Eating & Drinking

On the main drag you'll find many economical spots to grab a bite; local tastes tend to gravitate toward *pollo asado* (grilled chicken) and fried fish, along with plenty of shrimp dishes.

La Piña Loca (☎ 274-11-84; Retorno Tabachines 4; mains M$50-140; 🕑 7am-10pm) This homey restaurant has an extensive menu of Mexican dishes such as coconut shrimp and *sopa azteca*. It also offers daily specials (M$110) including dessert and a margarita.

George & Gary's (☎ 274-04-00; Sol Nuevo s/n; breakfast M$50; 🕑 7am-9:30pm) G&G's pours *the* best cup of joe in town and has a small breakfast and lunch menu featuring muffins, waffles and BLTs. There's also a book exchange.

Mateja's Bar & Grill (☎ 044-322-147-6383; www .matejasmexico.com; Emiliano González 11; mains M$50-115; 🕑 11am-7pm) It home of the 10-peso beer and Sunday beach parties, and a fun-loving, middle-aged crowd has a riotous time here with live music, dancing and drinking contests. The menu features comfort-food standbys like ribs and burgers.

Pineda (☎ 274-21-42; Carretera Los Ayala; mains M$80-120; 🕑 11am-7pm) The *pescado zarand-eado*, a grilled fish specialty, is a smash hit at this bayside seafood joint, and it goes down oh-so-nicely with a large *michelada* (beer, lime and salt). With sand floors and plastic chairs, it's nothing fancy, but the place has character.

ourpick Bavarian Garden (☎ 274-21-36; Hwy 200; mains M$80-115; 🕑 3-10pm Mon-Sat, 8am-3pm Sun)

NAYARIT

German transplant Petra Huerta serves authentic homestyle Bavarian cuisine at this open-air roadside restaurant at the entrance to town. House specialties include *jagerschnitzel* (breaded pork loins) and *rouladen* (beef stuffed with pickles, bacon, onion and cheese). There's live music on Wednesday and Friday nights.

El Campanario (☎ 274-08-95; Retorno Tabachines 6; mains M$80-150; ☺ 1-10pm) Best known for its fajitas and barbecue ribs, which you can nibble on in airy, casual surroundings that are beautifully tiled and set with hanging ceramic parrots. It's at the Hotel Posada la Misión.

Try these places for late-night action:

Equinoxio (☎ 274-01-76; Sol Nuevo s/n; cover M$50; ☺ 9am-3pm) Brush up on your reggaeton and *banda* moves at the snazziest disco in town.

Nivel Zero (☎ 274-01-76; Sol Nuevo s/n; ☺ 6pm-3am) Karaoke, anyone? The bar's stiff mixed drinks will help you find the courage.

Getting There & Away

Rincón de Guayabitos doesn't have a bus terminal. Second-class buses coming from Puerto Vallarta (M$65, 1½ hours, 72km) or Tepic (M$70, two hours, 83km) will drop you on the highway at Rincón de Guayabitos or a few kilometers north at La Peñita. *Colectivo* vans operate frequently between La Peñita and Guayabitos (M$6, 10 minutes) during daylight hours, or you can take a taxi (M$30).

AROUND RINCÓN DE GUAYABITOS

There are many pleasant little beach towns south of Rincón de Guayabitos that make good day trips from either Guayabitos or Puerto Vallarta. The sleepy Playa Los Ayala (Km 96) beckons about 2km south of Guayabitos, while the two pleasant beach towns of Lo de Marcos and San Francisco also await, 9km and 13km respectively. Be careful about swimming at these beaches: waves and currents are changeable, so ask if it's safe to enter the water during your time there.

First- and 2nd-class buses traveling along Hwy 200 will drop you at the *crucero* for Lo de Marcos or San Francisco, about 1km from the edge of each town.

Playa Los Ayala
☎ 327 / pop 370

Considerably earthier and more sedate than its neighbor Guayabitos, Playa Los Ayala is shared by sun-worshippers and fishermen who spend much of the day sitting in a kind of manly sewing circle, mending their nets. Boats are for hire on the beach for snorkeling trips to Isla Islote and Boca del Naranjo. A 15-minute jungle hike over the headlands at the southern end of the beach will drop you down into a secluded cove and beach called **Playa del Beso** (Beach of the Kiss).

Overlooking the beach, **Villas Minerva** (☎ 274-11-10; Coral 42; r M$700-900, ste M$1500; P ☒ ☎) is a well-run hotel offering homey rooms sleeping up to six, and suites with kitchens and balconies. It has an appealing beachside pool and patio.

Right next door, **Villas Corona** (☎ 274-11-34; www.guayabitos.com.mx/villascorona; Coral 44; ste M$1000-1600; P ☒ ☎) sports large one- and two-bedroom suites with kitchens, satellite TV and balconies with ocean or garden views. The villas sleep four to eight people.

DETOUR: PLAYA PUNTA RAZA

If you're up for a 3km hike from the town of Monteón, about 5km south of Guayabitos, the pristine sands of Punta Raza await. Ringed by a lush jungle, the long-sloping beach here offers glorious quiet time and outstanding wildlife-watching. The crashing surf makes things a bit hairy for swimmers, so enter with caution. An elusive, edge-of-the-world charm means you'll want to stay at least as long as your sunscreen holds out.

Punta Raza provides the ideal setting in which to pitch a tent, or you can crash at the seasonal **Hotel Rincón del Cielo** (☎ in Monteón 274-70-70; d M$700-900). The oceanfront, off-grid rooms are lit by lanterns or candles. An additional M$250 per day gets you two delicious meals at the small beachside restaurant; from your table you can watch blue-footed boobies and magnificent frigate birds crash headfirst into the sea.

To get there, look for the El Monteón sign on Hwy 200. Turn to the west, pass through the village, then turn right at Calle Punta Raza. The rutted dirt road passes over a scenic ridge and through lush old-growth forest.

Playa Lo de Marcos
☎ 327 / Pop 1600

Playa Lo de Marcos, 9km south of Guayabitos, is a small village with a beautiful beach beloved by Mexican travelers and snowbirds from *el norte*. There are a couple of decent restaurants along the beach and simple bungalows if you decide to spend the night. One choice is **Villas and Bungalows Tlaquepaque** (☎ 275-00-80; Av Echeverría 44; d/q M$1000/2750; RV hookup per week M$2000; P ⚓ ♿), which has pleasant, spacious rooms decorated with religious iconography and an RV park well located by the beach. It also has grassy areas and playgrounds for kids.

On a quiet beach, **El Caracol Bungalows & Trailer Park** (☎ 275-00-50; Camino a las Minitas; RV hookup M$230, d M$950-1050, q M$1150-1250; ⚓) has roomy bungalows and a small circular pool. Before deciding on a room, check out the options, as some are more accommodating than others.

Just 2km to 3km south from Lo de Marcos you'll find **Playa Los Venados** and **Playa Miñitas**, two more beaches with restaurants. You'll also find a few trailer parks along the side road there.

Playa San Francisco
☎ 311 / pop 1500

You just might leave your heart in San Francisco. Known locally as San Pancho, this is one of those traditional fishing towns where roosters still strut the streets and the slow-paced lifestyle is downright contagious. Less overrun with tourists than nearby Sayulita, San Francisco's long expanse of sandy beach offers plenty of quiet spots for some quality R&R. As San Pancho grows more and more popular, many terrific new restaurants and hotels have sprouted up in recent years. You'll find most of the action on the beach and along Av Tercer Mundo, the main avenue cutting through the center of town.

From September 26 to October 4 the town dresses up and takes part in the nine-day festival called San Pancho Days. There is a **casa de cambio** (exchange bureau; cnr Av Tercer Mundo & Av America Latino) and two ATMs; the most convenient one at the entrance of town, across from Gallo's Pizza.

SLEEPING
Calandria Realty (☎ 258-42-85; www.calandriarealty .com; Av Tercer Mundo 50) manages several bungalow and villa rentals in town.

Palapas Las Iguanas (☎ 258-42-85; www.calandria realty.com/palapas_iguanas.htm; Av Tercer Mundo s/n; palapa/ apt M$600/900) With two flavors of accommodation, here you can choose between perpetually breezy, romantic open-air *palapa* units with kitchenettes and mosquito nets over the bed, and more traditional units with kitchenettes. You'll find it half a block from the beach.

Hotel Cielo Rojo (☎ 258-41-55; www.hotelcielorojo .com; Asia 6; r/ste M$950/1500; ♿) Health-conscious travelers will find exceptional value at this ecofriendly B&B with an organic bistro serving up wholesome meals. Choose from seven well-appointed rooms and two suites artfully furnished with handmade furniture and vibrant native touches. It has a small sitting pool, a communal kitchen and a garden patio where continental breakfasts are served. Additionally, the hotel offers Swedish massages and a babysitting service.

ourpick **Lydia Bungalows** (☎ 258-43-37; www.bun galowslydia.com; ste M$1050-1900; ⚓) Overlooking two hidden beaches and surrounded by nearly 2000 palm trees that the owners planted themselves, this restful cliff-side haven is as idyllic as it gets. On offer are four fan-cooled suites with kitchenettes and a spacious one-bedroom bungalow that sleeps four. Two of the apartments afford a stunning ocean view and there's a nice little pool at the edge of the cliff. Once you get settled in head down to the beach and splash around in a delightful saltwater pool.

Roberto's Bungalows (☎ 258-43-75; America Latina 777; s/d M$1250/1500; ♻ ⚓) Five bungalows with open-air kitchens, rustic furnishings and ample patio space surround a leafy courtyard and swimming pool at this delightful boutique hotel. Each room has a different color scheme, but there are plenty of neutral tones throughout to offset the primary colors.

Costa Azul Adventure Resort (☎ 258-41-20; www .costaazul.com; ste/villa M$1500/1690, all-inclusive d M$2200-2760; P ♻ ⚓ ♿) Perfect for a splurge, this eco-chic resort with a private beach is well suited to travelers too antsy to spend their vacations on the beach. Surfing lessons and excursions take full advantage of the multiple point, reef and beach breaks nearby; there are also kayaking, mountain-biking and snorkeling trips. Retire to your big, bright room or to Wahoo's, the *palapa* restaurant. Activities are included in the all-inclusive rate. To get there, from the main village road, Av Tercer Mundo, take the signed right turn two blocks shy of the beach. From here it's a bumpy 2km ride.

Casa Obelisco Bed & Breakfast (☎ 258-43-15; www.casaobelisco.com; d M$2750; 🔀 🔊) Located 1km south of Costa Azul, this romantic, Mediterranean-style B&B offers four luxurious, richly decorated suites with ocean-view balconies overlooking a manicured jungle garden and pool. A generous breakfast, prepared by your American hosts, is included in the price. Children under 16 are not allowed and reservations are essential.

EATING

La Cocina de Mel (☎ 258-4157; Argelia 6; mains M$30-55; ☯ 5-11pm Fri-Wed) Good ol' Mel gives you your money's worth at this small family-run eatery. Try the filling shrimp burrito or a marlin quesadilla on a handmade tortilla.

Restaurante Marias (☎ 258-44-39; Av Tercer Mundo 103; mains M$45-75; ☯ 7:30am-10pm) The menu at this affordable family-owned restaurant consists of Baja-style fish tacos and a wide selection of yummy homestyle Mexican dishes. It also has a good selection of wines.

Gallo's Pizza (☎ 258-41-35; Av Tercer Mundo 7; mains M$70-150; ☯ 5-10pm Wed-Sun) Drop by Gallo's, an expat-favored hangout on the edge of town, for thin-crust pizza, buckets of beer and live Mexican regional music several nights a week.

Restaurante Las Palmas (☎ 258-40-35; mains M$60-150; ☯ 8am-9pm) Even on Mexican beach time, the service seems a bit slow at this oceanside seafood eatery, so just kick back and enjoy the view. This place celebrates shrimp in a big way, and if you never care to eat another crustacean, try the spicy octopus.

Mar Plata (☎ 258-44-24; Palmas 130; mains M$100-320; ☯ 5-10pm Tue-Sun) Some consider this upscale steak-and-seafood house one of Mexico's finest restaurants. Specialties here include shrimp croquettes, choice Argentine steaks and Belgian chocolate fondue with tropical fruits. You'll find it near the Costa Azul resort.

GETTING THERE & AWAY

San Francisco is off Hwy 200, 13km south of Guayabitos and 8km north of Sayulita, at Km 118. Any 2nd-class bus heading north or south on Hwy 200 will drop you at the crossroads, 2km from the beach. From there, take a *combi* (M$20) or private taxi (M$40).

SAYULITA

☎ 329 / pop 2300

The secret's out on this cheerful little beach town. Once a tranquil surfers' hideaway, Sayulita now gets top billing as one of Nayarit's star attractions. It's no wonder so many tourists come here these days. The restaurant-laden

---

TURTLE AID

Driven by primeval impulse, thousands of olive ridley sea turtles arrive on the pristine beaches of Pacific Mexico for a few months each year to lay their leathery, ping-pong-ball-sized eggs in the sand. Six to 10 weeks later, turtle hatchlings emerge from the shell to scamper into the water, dodging numerous predators. Despite their numbers, they have slim chances of surviving.

Playa San Francisco provided prime nesting grounds for marine turtles well into the 1970s. By 1992, however, their numbers started to plummet as coastal development, shrimp fishing and poaching reduced the numbers of nests from thousands to a scant 72.

This was the year that the **Grupo Ecológico de la Costa Verde** (☎ 258-41-00; www.project -tortuga.org; America Latina 102, Playa San Francisco) built its first marine nursery to provide large-scale protection of sea turtles. Today the group incubates and releases more than 70,000 hatchlings each year to the sea.

During the summer and fall months, visitors are invited to tour the nursery, and from late August through December they can attend release events as turtle hatchlings scurry into the Pacific Ocean for the first time. On Thursday nights at 7pm, Grupo Eco puts on a multimedia presentation about local efforts to protect marine turtles at the Costa Azul Adventure Resort (opposite), or sometimes at Gallo's Pizza (above).

The group gladly accepts volunteers to collect nests from six different beaches in the dark of night and relocate them to the nursery. Volunteers must pay their own expenses (about M$3000 per month). No special skills or education are necessary – only the willingness to work in adverse weather at 3am!

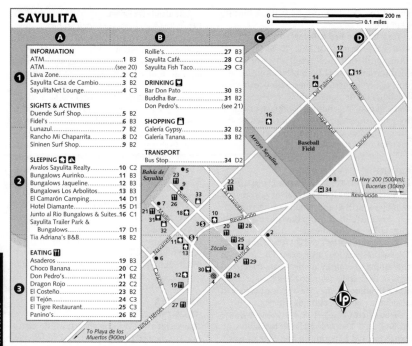

SAYULITA

0 — 200 m
0 — 0.1 miles

INFORMATION	
ATM	1 B3
ATM	(see 20)
Lava Zone	2 C2
Sayulita Casa de Cambio	3 B2
SayulitaNet Lounge	4 C3

SIGHTS & ACTIVITIES	
Duende Surf Shop	5 B2
Fidel's	6 B3
Lunazul	7 B2
Rancho Mi Chaparrita	8 D2
Sininen Surf Shop	9 B2

SLEEPING	
Avalos Sayulita Realty	10 C2
Bungalows Aurinko	11 B3
Bungalows Jaqueline	12 B3
Bungalows Los Arbolitos	13 B3
El Camarón Camping	14 D1
Hotel Diamante	15 D1
Junto al Rio Bungalows & Suites	16 C1
Sayulita Trailer Park & Bungalows	17 D1
Tia Adriana's B&B	18 B2

EATING	
Asaderos	19 B3
Choco Banana	20 C2
Don Pedro's	21 B2
Dragon Rojo	22 C2
El Costeño	23 B2
El Tejón	24 C3
El Tigre Restaurant	25 C3
Panino's	26 B2

Rollie's	27 B3
Sayulita Café	28 C2
Sayulita Fish Taco	29 C3

DRINKING	
Bar Don Pato	30 B3
Buddha Bar	31 B2
Don Pedro's	(see 21)

SHOPPING	
Galería Gypsy	32 B2
Galería Tanana	33 B2

TRANSPORT	
Bus Stop	34 D2

main square sits two short blocks from the attractive beach, making it all too easy to settle into a carefree slacker lifestyle. Sayulita's long waves still draw quite a few boarders. Several surf shops in town rent boards by the hour and there's even a surfer campground where you can hang out and talk about the day's big rides. Some businesses close from May through November, but that practice has become less common as many proprietors warm up to the idea of pesos rolling in year-round.

Information

Sayulita has no tourist office, but www.sayulita life.com and www.sayulita.com have maps and all kinds of useful information on restaurants, hotels, vacation rentals and activities. The town has a currency exchange and two ATMs, one on the main plaza next to Choco Banana and another on Marlín, near Revolución.

Lava Zone (Mariscal; wash & dry 6kg M$60; ☟ 8am-6pm Mon-Sat) The place to spin and tumble your washables.

Sayulita Casa de Cambio (Delfín 44; ☟ 10am-2pm, 4-8pm Mon-Sat) Near the *zócalo;* offers so-so rates.

SayulitaNet Lounge (☎ 291-34-44; Marlín 12; per hr M$40; ☟ 8am-6pm) Try this place to log on over a tipple.

It doubles as a chic bar serving well-made concoctions and imported beers.

Sights & Activities

Sayulita's central beach can get pretty crowded during the high season. If you're looking for a quieter setting, head south along the coast road, past the Villa Amor hotel and Playa de los Muertos, a popular picnic spot for Mexican families. Continue along the dirt road and you'll find some isolated beaches further south.

Here are some other options to get you out and about:

Fidel's (☎ 291-35-63; www.sayulitalife.com/business /fidel/htm; cnr Navarrete & Caracol; 4-5hr per person M$2000) Offers fishing excursions and snorkeling trips to Isla Marietas.

Rancho Mi Chaparrita (☎ 291-31-12; www .michaparrita.com; Sánchez 14; ☟ 8am-4pm) Leads you on horseback rides to Los Muertos and Carrisitos beaches (one hour, M$275) and offers a zip-line canopy tour through the treetops (M$825).

SURFING

Surfing is a way of life in Sayulita. With decent waves pouring into Bahía de Sayulita from both the left and the right, you can practice your well-honed moves with an audience, or even take up the sport for the first time. Try these full-service surf shops, all open from 8am until sundown:

Duende Surf Shop (rentals per hr/day M$50/250, lessons per 1½hr M$450) Next to El Costeño restaurant on the beach.

Lunazul (☎ 291-20-09; Marlín 4; surfboard/bodyboard rental per day M$200/150, lessons per 1½hr M$500)

Sininen Surf Shop (☎ 291-31-86; Delfín 4A; rentals per day/week M$200/1500, lessons per 1½hr M$500)

Sleeping

Many hotels here offer 'bungalows' (suites with kitchens) and there are several budget options near the beach. If you arrive during holiday periods, when everything's booked up, try **Avalos Sayulita Realty** (☎ 291-31-22; www .move2sayulita.com; Revolución 46), which has more than 100 vacation rentals.

El Camarón Camping (Del Palmar 100; sites per person/huts M$60/125) Surfers and 20-something hippies find cheap accommodations and plenty of easy living at this grassy oceanside camping ground north of town. Its beach is the only place in town to enjoy left and right breaks, and while this may come as a surprise, it's a pretty happening party spot.

Hotel Diamante (☎ 291-31-91; www.hoteldiamante sayulita.com; Miramar 40; s/d/q M$375/425/750; 🖭) Diamante has downright basic rooms – but has a pool, laundry service, wireless internet and a communal kitchen. A good option for thrifty travelers.

Sayulita Trailer Park & Bungalows (☎ 390-27-50; www.pacificbungalow.com; Miramar s/n; trailer sites M$180-280, r/bungalow/ste M$380/650/950) This attractive, palm-shaded property beside the beach offers 34 RV spaces with full hookups and simple bungalows that can sleep up to six people. Discounts are offered for long stays.

Bungalows Jaqueline (☎ 291-30-27; www.bunga lowsjaqueline.com; Revolución 52; bungalow M$650-750; 🗱) Just a few blocks from the beach, these reasonably priced bungalows vary in size, some accommodating up to four guests. All rooms come with large kitchens, tasteful rustic furnishings and sitting areas. Some have air-conditioning for an additional M$150.

Tia Adriana's B&B (☎ 291-30-29; cnr Delfín & Navarrete; ste incl breakfast M$650-1600) This friendly B&B offers vibrant suites with kitchenettes and ceiling fans; top ones are open to breezes (no

walls!) and have views. Other suites also have special touches. The camaraderie-inducing hearty breakfasts are served in an airy lobby with a hammock.

Junto al Rio Bungalows & Suites (☎ 291-34-16; www.juntoalrio.com; Del Palmar 10; ste/bungalow M$825/1210; 🗵) By the edge of the arroyo on the beach, this place has six airy suites, two spacious bungalows and two additional suites under enclosed tents, each with a queen-sized bed, two twin beds and a kitchen. It also rents mountain bikes and surfboards.

our pick **Bungalows Aurinko** (☎ 291-31-50; www .sayulita-vacations.com; Marlín 7; 1-/2-bedroom bungalows M$1053/1651, ste M$1378; 🗱) The lush vegetation and the orange and yellow hues in these attractive rustic bungalows will make you feel warm all over. The spacious digs have smooth river-stone floors, open-air kitchens, exposed raw beams and Oaxacan linen covering the beds. In addition, the hotel provides wi-fi internet, free bike use and discounts on surfboard rentals.

Bungalows Los Arbolitos (☎ 291-31-46; www.sayu litabungalows.com; Marlín 20; ste M$1500; 🗱) Six luxurious suites with queen-sized beds, kitchens and craftsman touches overlook a lush garden at this quaint hotel. Free wi-fi available in lobby area.

Eating

Numerous eateries around the main square prepare very good Mexican and international cuisine. For a pleasant meal with an ocean view, hit the beachside restaurants and *palapas*.

our pick **Sayulita Fish Taco** (☎ 291-32-71; Mariscal 13; tacos from M$20; 🕙 10am-10pm Mon-Sat) This place has perhaps the tastiest fish tacos in Mexico. It also does shrimp and fish burritos served Baja-style, or with a pineapple and garlic sauce. The terrace upstairs affords a bird's-eye view of the main plaza.

Rollie's (Revolución 58; breakfast M$45-70, dinner M$80-130; 🕙 7:30am-noon daily, 5:30-9pm Tue-Sun) This is *the* place for breakfast. Rollie and friends lovingly serve Western breakfasts with an occasional Mexican twist. The restaurant now opens for dinner. Try the paella, Rollie's signature rice dish.

Choco Banana (☎ 291-30-51; cnr Revolución & Delfín; breakfast M$45-75; 🕙 6am-6pm; 🖤) This busy sidewalk café on the *zócalo* does great breakfast, the best burger in town and tasty homemade brownies and muffins. Vegetarians will find options here, and milkshake fanatics just might find heaven.

El Tejón (Mariscal 9; mains M$70-140; ☯ 10am-3pm, 6pm-1am) Marcelo, an affable Argentine expat who has called Sayulita home for over a decade, recently launched this small sidewalk restaurant that comes up big on Mediterranean and Middle Eastern fare. A surefire favorite is the lamb gyro, topped with a tasty yogurt and garlic sauce.

Sayulita Café (☎ 291-35-11; Revolución 37; mains M$80-140; ☯ 5-11pm) With an atmospheric dining room and candlelit sidewalk tables, this place serves hearty Mexican fare and splendid fresh seafood dishes. The house specialty is *chile relleno*, a chilipepper stuffed with shrimp or other fixings of your choice.

El Tigre Restaurant (zócalo; mains M$80-150; ☯ 6pm-1am) Some locals think the town's best seafood is grilled here. Surf videos play while you wrestle with your lobster in the bar area upstairs. After the meal, toss back some drinks and chill to reggae tunes.

Don Pedro's (☎ 291-30-90; Marlín 2; meals M$110-235; ☯ restaurant 5-11pm, bar & grill 8am-11pm) Overlooking the beach, Don Pedro's is two eateries in one: a fine restaurant upstairs offering elegant dining choices, and a bar and grill downstairs serving woodfired pizza, salads and a terrific grilled-fish sandwich (M$110).

Other recommendations:

Asaderos (☎ 291-35-17; Niños Héroes 2; mains M$50-70; ☯ 8am-midnight) The homestyle *carne en su jugo* (beef in its juice) and grilled beef tacos served on hand-made tortillas are easy on the wallet.

Dragon Rojo (☎ 291-32-01; cnr Las Gaviotas & Navarrete; mains M$89-125; ☯ 9am-midnight) Reasonably good Chinese fare and live salsa and reggae five nights a week.

El Costeño (☎ 291-30-45; Delfín; mains M$50-100; ☯ noon-9pm) Right on the beach; the tables on the sand get packed with gringos enjoying seafood.

Panino's (Delfín 1; coffee M$15-35, pastries & sandwiches M$12-69; ☯ 6am-7pm) Fresh-baked bread, tasty 'panini' sandwiches and to-die-for apple strudel.

Drinking & Entertainment

Sayulita's not a place to paint the town red, but there are a few places where you can kick out the jams.

Don Pedro's (Marlín 2; ☯ restaurant 6-11pm, bar & grill noon-11pm) Get your salsa and flamenco dancing on at this oceanside bar.

Bar Don Pato (Marlín 12; ☯ 6pm-1am) Overlooking the town square, this friendly bar is a great place to blow off some steam after a hard day at the beach. Belly up to the bar and sample the *raicilla*, an alcoholic beverage similar to mezcal. It's got quite a kick.

Buddha Bar (☎ 291-37-77; Marlín 10; ☯ 6pm-1am) This groovy Asian-accented bar and restaurant sports an ocean view from its romantic open-air lounge. DJs spins tunes nightly and the menu includes an extensive offering of mixed drinks, sushi and seafood dishes.

Shopping

Several crafts stores in Sayulita sell interesting folk art and knick-knacks.

Galería Tanana (☎ 291-38-89; Navarrete 8; ☯ 9am-9pm) Offers fine Huichol handicrafts such as colorful bead jewelry, yarn art and wood sculptures. The crafts you buy help support the nonprofit Huichol Center for Cultural Survival.

Galería Gypsy (☎ 291-33-85; Marlín 10; ☯ 9am-9pm) Here you'll find hand-tooled leather bags, ceramics and a wide selection of trendy Mexican folk art.

Getting There & Away

Sayulita is about 35km northwest of Puerto Vallarta, just west of Hwy 200. Second-class buses leave frequently from the long-distance terminal in Puerto Vallarta (M$33, one hour). The bus stop is on Revolución by the bridge crossing the arroyo. Some buses will leave you at the crossroads. Taxis on the opposite side of the road will take you into town.

Buses headed for Puerto Vallarta leave every 30 minutes between 5:30am and 6:45pm (M$20 to M$33, one hour).

Jalisco, Colima & Michoacán Coasts

This lost coast is wild and lonely, an arching firmament of rock, honey-sand beaches, rolling coastal hills, picturesque fishing villages, bird-choked lagoons and a few larger-than-life resort areas set against the ever-present waves and seemingly endless sunsets of the Pacific Ocean.

This is still relatively virgin territory, with large-scale resort development taking place in just a few select towns like Manzanillo and Barra de Navidad. Outside these pockets, unassuming beach towns where 20 pesos buys a palm-thatched camping spot for the night will delight travelers, as will plentiful surf breaks and locals who say *hola* and invite you over for a *cerveza*.

Traveling south from Puerto Vallarta, Hwy 200 jaunts inland through the state of Jalisco past Cabo Corrientes before heading back to the welcoming arms of the Pacific. This is the beginning of the Costa Alegre, where low-fi tourism development is taking place in towns like Playa Pérula, Tenacatita and La Manzanilla, before hitting grander notes in the Bahía de Navidad, home to one of the region's stand-out coastal cities, Barra de Navidad.

Further south is the Colima coast, known mostly for the aging resort town of Manzanillo, and a few decent surfing and snorkeling spots. As the coast continues its march southeast, you hit the state of Michoacán. For the intrepid soul, this is the stuff of dreams: forgotten beaches, big surf, few travelers and a low-key defiance toward the march of time and 'progress.'

HIGHLIGHTS

- Soaking up some Vitamin D on the impossibly perfect bleached-blonde beaches of **Bahía Tenacatita** (p143) before heading out on a birding expedition in the neighboring **mangrove lagoon** (p143)

- Sucking down margaritas and shrimp cocktails after a hard day lounging in the mocha-chocolata sand of **Barra de Navidad** (p150), a chic and laid-back mini-resort

- Leaving the coast for a few days to explore the sights and sounds of the colonial capital of **Colima** (p157) or the verdant hills of the **Manantlán Biosphere** (p161)

- Starting your never-ending surf session on the adrenaline-charged breaks of **Boca de Pascuales** (p162), **La Ticla** (p164) or **Barra de Nexpa** (p166)

- Witnessing the circle of life as sea turtles come ashore in summer and fall to lay precious eggs at **Playa Maruata** (p165)

MANZANILLO JANUARY DAILY HIGH: 27°C | 80°F ■ MANZANILLO JULY DAILY HIGH: 30°C | 86°F

JALISCO, COLIMA & MICHOACÁN COASTS

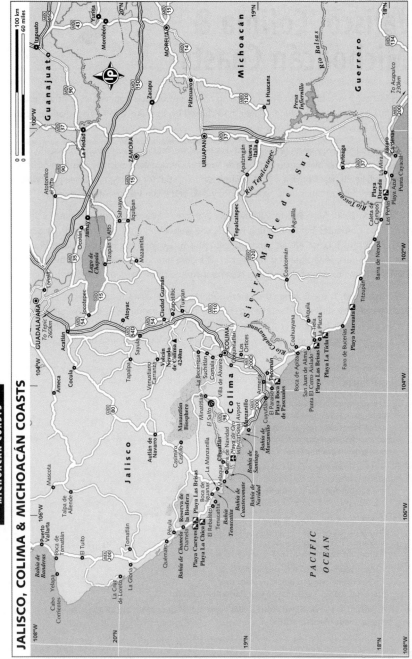

JALISCO

Arching delicately south and east from Puerto Vallarta to Barra de Navidad, the Jalisco Coast offers something for every taste, with most of the action happening around the protected bays of Chamela and Tenacatita on the Costa Alegre, and further south in the Bahía de Navidad. Along the way travelers will delight to low-key development, good protected swimming spots and a few chic boutiques.

COSTA ALEGRE

The northern stretch of the Jalisco coast, known as the Costa Alegre, has a beach for every taste and desire. The kilometer distances mentioned for destinations are measured on Hwy 200, heading northwest from the junction of Hwys 200 and 80 (the road to Guadalajara) at Melaque.

La Cruz de Loreto
☎ 322

The village of La Cruz de Loreto, west of Hwy 200 and 90km south of Puerto Vallarta, is next to a wetland estuary and nature reserve. It's also the closest village to one of Mexico's most attractive, ecofriendly and expensive all-inclusive hotels. Love for nature and luxury are in the air at **Hotelito Desconocido** (☎ 281-40-10, in the US 800-851-4130; www.hotelito.com; La Cruz de Loreto; r from M$9980, ste from M$11,640; 🏊), an unforgettable solar-powered resort. As the sun sets, the candles are lit and the evening orchestra of frogs, birds and cicadas begins, you'll find yourself drunk with relaxation. Take a dip in the saltwater pool before slipping into the ever-so-smooth sheets in your lagoon-side bungalow on stilts. In the morning simply raise a flag and the staff will bring you coffee in bed. There's 65km of beach, excellent bird-watching, and a sea-turtle protection project that operates from June to February; guests can set baby turtles free from September to December. Rates include all meals and activities such as horseback riding, kayaking, windsurfing, yoga, and wildlife-watching excursions. Spa services will cost you extra.

Quémaro
☎ 322

At Km 83 is the sign for Quémaro, a small, dusty village of dirt roads and shabby housing. But just past this village, on a short gravel road toward the coast, is one of Mexico's fanciest resorts. At **Las Alamandas** (☎ 285-55-00, in the US 888-882-9616; www.alamandas.com; Hwy 200, Km 83.5; r from M$4880, ste M$9580-13,720; 🏊), luxurious and colorful suites nestle in six separate adobe buildings, all simply beautiful with private terraces or patios. Most have stunning sea views and are surrounded by spacious, well-manicured and palm-studded grounds. Reservations are a must; without them you won't get past the security gate.

Playa Pérula
☎ 315

Down a side road from Km 76, toward the north end of tranquil 11km-long Bahía de Chamela, lies the rather bleak town of Pérula. Its beach, however, is long, flat and sheltered – great for swimming, boogie-boarding and extended walks. There are only a few *palapa* restaurants, the sands aren't overrun with tourists, and islands offshore break the ocean's horizon. In winter, whales bask in the warm bay waters, and you can always hire a boat from the beach for fishing trips. For those who can deal with few luxuries and services in an unassuming Mexican beach town, this could end up being quite a pleasant stop.

Red Snapper RV Park & Restaurant (☎ 333-97-84; redsnapperrv@hotmail.com; tent/trailer M$60/120) occupies a prime stretch of beach. This well-run RV haven has 12 spaces, five of which front the beach. The casual restaurant is a good hangout. Monthly and weekly discounts available. Get here by heading into town 3km from the highway; after the first *tope* (speed bump) turn left.

Although **Hotel y Bungalows Playa Dorada** (☎ 333-97-10; www.playa-dorada.com.mx; Tiburón 40; d M$900, bungalow M$1000; 🍴 🏊) won't win any architecture prizes, it's right on the beach overlooking a particularly glorious stretch of yellow sand. The rooms are basic, clean and freshly painted, and come with up-to-date fixtures. Bungalows up the ante with air-con, a full kitchen and a small living room. Also on offer are a dozen trailer spots with full hookups (M$120).

A stone's throw from the beach, the budget **Hotel Las Palmas** (☎ 333-99-51; Independencia 30; r M$200) offers nine dark and cool rooms arranged around a shady courtyard. Meet like-minded souls in the communal kitchen.

Long-distance buses don't head straight into Pérula; they stop at the highway crossroads known as 'El Super.' From there, call

---

OUR FAVORITE BEACHES ON THE COSTA ALEGRE

The following beaches, listed from north to south, are sure to satisfy even the pickiest beach connoisseur.

- **Playa Pérula** (Km 76; p141) This scenic stretch of honeyed sand, located at the northern end of 11km Bahía de Chamela, is known for its tranquil waters, which are ideal for swimming and fishing. There is a good selection of *palapa* restaurants, plus affordable accommodations and *panga* (motorized skiff) captains looking for passengers intent on snorkeling and fishing excursions.

- **Playa Tecuán** (Km 33; opposite) Located 10km off the highway near an abandoned resort, this deserted white-sand beach has no facilities but has tremendous opportunities for camping, beach hiking and advanced surfing. A nearby lagoon is rife with birds, crocodiles and the occasional ocelot.

- **Playa Tenacatita** (Km 28; opposite) Crystal-clear waters, terrific *palapa* restaurants, a fair selection of accommodations and a merry community of return visitors make this 3km white-sand beach on Bahía Tenacatita enduringly popular.

- **Playa Cuastecomate** (Km 3; p146) Located 3km west of Melaque, this tiny cove within Bahía de Cuastecomate is one of the most scenic beaches on the entire Pacific coast. Calm waters make for safe swimming and good snorkeling.

---

a taxi – if you're lucky there will be cheaper *taxis colectivos* (shared taxis). It's about a 10-minute drive to Pérula.

Playas La Negrita & Chamela
☎ 315

Near the Km 64 highway marker, a dirt road leads to a couple of isolated and relaxing beaches nestled in the south end of Bahía de Chamela, a great spot for day trips from neighboring Pérula. Playa Chamela has a calm shore with small waves and is home to a handful of *palapa* restaurants and some fishing boats. The feel is small and local, so if you don't want to see any gringos, this is a good bet. A five-minute walk from here, just past a rocky point, is La Negrita, 50m of tiny cove beach with one small restaurant. Neither of these places is built up, so no accommodation is available (other than possibly camping – ask first).

To find these little havens, take the dirt road just 30m south of the yellow 'Chamela principal' bridge. Go about 1km along this road – you'll pass a small village and then a lagoon. Don't follow the fork up to the left, unless you want to see some abandoned condominiums. Where it forks right is Playa Chamela; at the stony end just past this fork is La Negrita.

Playa Careyes
☎ 315

Another small and beautiful beach is Careyes, sheltered in a dune cove and sloping steeply

to the water. Here you'll find only friendly locals, a snack and beer shack and some fishing cooperative boats. A big pink *palapa* building sits as a landmark on the hillside above.

Careyes is 200m down a dirt road just south of the white Careyes bridge (*not* the nearby Careyitos bridge) at Km 52. Look for a bus-stop shed and an '*acceso publico*' (public access) sign signifying the turnoff.

At Km 53.5, taking full advantage of the amazing scenery, is the terrifically romantic **El Careyes Beach Resort & Spa** (☎ 351-00-00, toll free in Mexico 01-800-433-3989; www.elcarayesresort.com; Hwy 200, Km 53.5; r M$3685, ste M$4500-12,340; ✦ ✦). A bottle of champagne and an overflowing fruit basket welcomes honeymooners and lovebirds to flower-filled suites with private, ocean-view plunge pools. You can relax to the sounds of the tranquil bay on sheltered, pillow-piled outdoor beds, or enjoy a massage before indulging in a sunset dinner at La Lantana, the on-site restaurant with a menu featuring 'food of the sea gods.'

Playas Las Brisas & La Chica
☎ 315

These two beaches head off in opposite directions from the village of **Arroyo Seco**, about 4km down a dirt road from the highway at Km 36.

When you find the schoolyard with a mural of Snow White, turn right and go 1.5km past farmland and a red gate. Playa La Chica, a nice beach with latte-colored sand, no services and few people awaits between two headlands.

To get to Las Brisas, turn left at the schoolyard and right at the fork. Go past farmland about 1.5km and you'll reach the sea. Here too there are no services, though camping and RV parking are possible in the palm-tree-shaded area (someone may turn up to collect a small property-use fee). The long, flat beach has very surfable waves and little competition for them.

Playa Tecuán

About 10km off the highway at Km 33 lie the pristine shores of Playa Tecuán. High above the beach is the abandoned resort of Hotel Tucuán, a spooky skeleton of doorless rooms, broken windows and caved-in beamed hallways just waiting to be turned into the snazziest youth hostel in existence. Horror-film buffs might know this as the location for the slasher flick *I Still Know What You Did Last Summer*. You can still see steel kitchen freezers and bats in the pantries. It's a cool experience and worth getting to if you've got wheels – but remember to be respectful, as it's still considered private property.

The 2km road going south along Playa Tecuán is part of an old landing strip. It passes a private housing complex on the mountain and eventually peters out at the edge of a pretty lagoon.

Bahía Tenacatita

☎ 315 / pop 2400

A laid-back crescent of gleaming sand with tranquil waves and an off-the-grid allure, Bahía de Tenacatita gives travelers three towns to choose from, each with its own unique vibe. On the western promontory of Bahía Tenacatita – a longtime favorite destination

of snowbirds and escape artists – the town of Tenacatita (below) is a sometimes crowded but always beguiling beach destination with a long, curving white-sand beach and safe conditions for extended camping. Further south, Boca de Iguanas (p144) has limited lodging options, but is the least visited of the three. Still further down the coast is the mellower-than-Jello town of La Manzanilla (p145), a great place to study Spanish for a week.

TENACATITA

As you drive the 8.5km into Tenacatita from the highway, you get to take your pick of three luscious beaches, passing **Playa Mar Abierto** on the right, which extends for kilometers back to the north toward Playa Tecuán. You then hit **Playa Tenacatita** itself, which is lined with *palapa* seafood restaurants but remains beautiful, wide and calm. And over to the right a bit, just over a small hill and tucked into some headlands in between these two larger beaches, are the tiny twin shores of **Playa Mora**. The snorkeling is great in the crystal-clear waters around the protected rocks here. The bay here is protected by a series of islands, the largest of which is known as La Ampolla, or 'the little water bubble.' Arrange sportfishing trips out to La Ampolla from Restaurant Fiesta Mexicana, which is on the main road in the center of town.

A mangrove lagoon backing onto Playa Tenacatita is home to scores of birds and sunning reptiles. Boat tours of **El Manglar** (the Mangrove) are available; ask at Restaurant Fiesta Mexicana. Trips take one hour and cost M$350 per boatload for up to 10 people. Bring insect repellent.

For groceries or phone service, head to the village of **El Rebalsito**, 3km from the beach on the Hwy 200–Tenacatita road. Just 1.5km

---

COCOS FRIOS: 10 PESOS!

What says 'tropical' more than lying on beachside hammock and sipping the transparent and mildly sweet milk from a freshly opened coconut? *Cocos* are available at many beachside restaurants or road stalls; the dead giveaway is a shady pile of them near a chopping block (often a section of palm tree) cleaved by a large machete. And, unlike some of Mexico's tap water, it's safe to drink. Some huge specimens can store up to 1L of liquid, though most probably hold about half that.

Prices vary from M$5 to M$15, but most cost around M$10. In tourist areas and fancier restaurants, expect to pay at least this. The price may include a final few whacks to split the fruit's hulk in half after you've finished the milk. Have the coconuteer add chili, lime juice and salt, grab a spoon, and enjoy scooping out the tender, meaty flesh…a great quick snack anytime!

before Tenacatita, **Rancho El Cono** (☎ 100-10-06) is a micro-distillery that brews up *raicilla*, a local firewater derived from the maguey cactus. It offers tours and tastings.

Sleeping & Eating

Stretching north from Punta Tenacatita along a particularly fine stretch of sand is a 3km-long sand dune where RVs set up camp for the winter. RV campers can try the unofficial free sites at Playa Mora – space is limited here, so be considerate. Camping is good on the main beach, though you may need to ask permission (check with the proprietors of the nearest beachfront restaurant). The majority of hotels are south of the main junction. Seafood *palapas* provide most of the nourishment here. They cater to day-trippers and thus tend to close at 6pm or 7pm.

Hotel Paraíso de Tenacatita (☎ 314-102-03-89; dobie@prodigy.net.mx; d with fan/air-con from M$300/350, tr with air-con M$800; 🅿 ⏚) Just across from the ocean, this hotel offers 23 adequate rooms, hot water and a pool out back. Room 7 has the best sea views. The restaurant here, open until 10pm, is the only place in town to get a meal after the sun goes down.

Hotel Los Amigos (☎ 314-102-93-02; d/q M$550/800; 🅿 ⏚) The best buy for clean freaks, this bright and cheery yellow hotel, one block from the beach across from Restaurant Fiesta Mexicana, has rock-hard beds and a small pool (open for nonguests for M$20). Prices drop precipitously during the low season, and discounts are offered for longer stays.

Hotel Mision del Sol (☎ in Guadalajara 333-681-35-59; d M$600, bungalow M$1600; 🅿 ⏚) On the main road in El Rebalsito, this hotel has more creature comforts than the ocean-front spots in Tenacatita. There's a big pool, and the *cabañas* are perfect for families, with kitchens and sitting areas.

Restaurant Fiesta Mexicana (☎ 338-63-16; mains M$45-98; ⏱ 8am-7pm) This is Tenacatita's most visible – and best – restaurant, serving delectable seafood dishes with a twist. Try the signature dish, *rollo del mar* (a fish fillet stuffed with shrimp, wrapped in bacon and smothered in an almond cream sauce; M$98). Also, here you can try *raicilla*.

Getting There & Away

Tenacatita is 8.5km from Hwy 200 (Km 28) via a good paved road. The easiest way to get here is to take a major bus running between Manzanillo and Puerto Vallarta (around M$60). Ask the driver to leave you at the El Rebalsito exit in Aguas Calientes, where you can take a M$60 taxi into town. Taxis and *combis* (minibuses) operate between El Rebalsito and Tenacatita. There are daily buses to and from Melaque (M$25, one hour) departing Tenacatita at 6:30am and from Melaque at 5pm.

BOCA DE IGUANAS

Smack in the middle of Bahía Tenacatita lies the wide, long and very pleasant **Playa Boca de Iguanas** (Km 19). The surf is mild, the sand is hot and wonderful, and the beach is quite shallow for a long way out, making it good for a swim (just don't go past the rocky point, as a dangerous riptide kicks in). The palm-fringed bay curves uninterrupted all the way around to La Manzanilla, providing a tranquil one-hour walk along a firm waterline. An abandoned hotel nearby adds visual interest and curiosity (clue: propane explosion), and there's a nearby lagoon that's home to one very large crocodile (maybe two).

There are fewer lodging options here than elsewhere on the bay: one ridiculously expensive 'ecolodge' and a beachside RV park. Plans are in the works to build condos around here, so the very face of the town may be changing as you read this. There's a small store in town, just at the edge of the beach, but it's only open in high season, so consider bringing food with you.

To get there, take the paved road about 2.5km from the highway at Km 19, or ask your long-haul bus driver to stop here. *Taxis colectivos* regularly pick up and drop off passengers at the highway turnoff; a ride into town will set you back M$10.

Sleeping & Eating

Hotel Boca de Iguanas (☎ 100-89-55; www.bocadeiguanas.com; d or bungalow M$3515; 🅿 🖳 ⏚) Opened in 2008, this spalike 'eco-retreat' has essentially bought all of Boca de Iguanas – save for the Boca Beach Campground – with plans to build condos, implement green technology (like solar panels) and expand the small lodge. The hotel's rooms are sophisticated and chic, but lack ocean views, making them a bit overpriced. Down by the beach, you'll find a large pool, a *cabaña* perfect for larger groups and a small spa and restaurant. Follow signs from the main road to get here.

DON'T FEED THE CROCODILES!

At the northern end of the main road in La Manzanilla is a lagoon filled with conspicuously large crocodiles. These mega-predators have been evolving into perfect killing machines over the past 200 million years – the dinosaurs became extinct just 65 million years ago. But a recently built viewing platform over the lagoon, intended to prevent folks from getting too close to the crocs, may be having a detrimental effect on the health and ultimate survival of these crocs and their ecosystem. The problem is that too many people are feeding the crocodiles, something that many biologists believe can throw the delicate balance of nature out of whack. So think twice before you toss one of these marvelous creatures the leftovers from your *tacos al pastor* – they'd rather bask in the sun while they await the next fish to swim by, anyway.

Boca Beach Campground (bocabeach@hotmail.com; camping per person M$100, trailer sites M$250) Boca Beach has more than 60 palmy sites right by the water.

LA MANZANILLA & AROUND

At the sheltered, southern end of Bahía Tenacatita basks the peaceful, dusty little town of La Manzanilla (Km 13). It's home to some decent restaurants, a rather rocky beach, a few expat residents and a crocodile-infested lagoon. Tourism still hasn't quite caught on here (there's no internet café yet), but the town has grown mightily during the past few years.

Activities

Get out on the water or into the bush with **Immersion Adventures** (☎ 351-53-41; www.immersion adventures.com), an ecologically minded provider offering sea kayaking, snorkeling, birding and cultural tours to many corners of the Costa Alegre. Half-day tours cost M$450 to M$750 per person, while full-day tours cost M$1150 to M$1200. Prices include kayaks, snorkeling gear and a snack or lunch; all experience levels are accommodated. Custom tours are also possible. You can also just rent kayaks (M$100 to M$150 per hour), snorkeling gear (M$80 per day) and surfboards (M$300 to M$400 per day). Dave, the manager, has his office at his home, on the road into town (look for the A-frame sign).

Courses

La Catalina Natural Language School (☎ 351-53-62; www.lacatalinaschool.com; Montana del Mar; per week M$1350) offers one- to four-week courses for beginners right through to advanced students, and a Spanish camp for kids aged five to 12 (M$1350 per week). In addition to daily classes, the school provides many opportunities to learn Spanish outside the classroom through volunteer work and cultural events, and it also arranges guided excursions to local areas of interest. Homestays with local families – the best way to really learn a language – are available for M$700 to M$1750 per week, depending on the number of meals. As it sometimes closes during the summer months, call ahead.

Sleeping

RV parking (sites M$30) At the northern end of town, just past the crocodile lagoon. There are no hookups or services. Find a pleasant shady site that appeals, and pay the man snoozing under a palm.

Campamento Ecológico (campsites per person M$35) A 10-minute walk further down the beach from the RV site; rates include basic showers and toilets.

Hotel y Bungalows Michel (☎ 351-53-53; Asunción 63E; s/d/bungalow M$300/450/700; 🅿 P) Michel offers nice budget digs right by the center plaza. The fan-cooled rooms are clean and you get off-street parking.

Hotel Posada de Tonalá (☎ 351-54-74; posadatonala@ hotmail.com; Asunción 75; s/d/tr M$300/600/650; 🅿) In the middle of town, the Tonalá has clean, modern rooms with nice wood details and pleasing architecture. Spacious rooms include a TV and whimsically carved wooden furniture. Most face into a modern *palapa* patio area.

La Casa de María (☎ 351-50-16; www.lacasamaria.com; cnr Los Angeles Locos & Conca Molida; apt M$700) This place has five peaceful, artistically decorated and very spacious apartments, all with private patios. María is the gracious host and opens her rooftop *palapa* terrace to community teaching projects such as art, yoga, meditation, cooking or dance (teachers with project ideas can contact her). Her house is one street south of the main road into town. There's wi-fi for the laptop crowd.

Palapa Joe's Restaurant & Bungalows (☎ 351-52-67; www.jjsantanavacationrentals.com; Asunción 163; bungalows d/tr M$750/800; 🆒) For choice digs in the somnambulant heart of downtown La Manzanilla, commandeer one of these two big bungalows with kitchenettes in a peaceful backyard garden. The decor is refined, there's cable TV and you can hang out in the cool covered rooftop terrace, which has an unheated Jacuzzi.

Casa Maguey (☎ 351-50-12; www.casamaguey .com; bungalows M$950-1250) Perched above the southern end of the beach and surrounded by a lush, hilly garden, Casa Maguey's three bungalows are all charmingly different. Each is like a home and is wonderfully decorated with Mexican tiles. Book early for high season (November through April).

Casa Danza del Sol (☎ 351-52-67; www.jjsantana vacationrentals.com; Asunción s/n; d/q M$1000/1250; 🆒) Between the ocean and the main street, this little beach house offers three units with warm and unassuming decor, a kitchen and a spacious dining area well suited to dinner parties. A fully enclosed garden has plenty of chairs and tables for seating and its own outdoor shower. Advance reservations are recommended.

El Tamarindo Golf Resort & Spa (☎ 351-50-31, in the US 866-717-4316; www.eltamarindoresort.com; Hwy 200, Km 7.5; villas M$8200-31,100; P 🆒 🖥 🏊) Bringing considerable luxury and panache to the southern tip of Bahía Tenacatita, this resort is the ultimate in romantic getaways, with three secluded beaches on 8 sq km of breathtaking wilderness. Visitors disappear into 28 warmly appointed, private bungalows with plunge pools and poolside beds. Oceanside massage *palapas* and double spa-treatment rooms make relaxing with your companion effortless. El Tamarindo also has a stunning golf course – think skinny dipping between birdies – and is located 7km north of Melaque.

Eating

Activity in La Manzanilla winds down to the speed of molasses in the summer, and some of the restaurants close down altogether.

Loncheria Mi Casita (tacos M$7, tortas M$19; 🕒 8am-4pm, closed Tue) This little lunch spot offers cheap *tortas* (Mexican-style sandwiches made with rolls) and tacos just steps from the *zócalo*.

Mariscos Rincón (☎ 351-71-97; Playa Blanca; mains M$35-90; 🕒 9am-6pm, closed Thu) Two blocks south of the entrance road, this beachfront *palapa* has rough-hewn wood tables and features a broad selection of seafood. The shrimp tacos and the catch of the day are both recommended.

Palapa Joe's Restaurant & Bungalows (Asunción 163; mains M$45-80; 🕒 noon-10pm Tue-Sun) Joe's offers tasty food, such as roasted herb chicken or beer-battered shrimp, plus CNN on TV.

Quinta Valentina (mains M$55-115; 🕒 9am-6pm, closed Wed) A big sprawling joint overlooking the sea just north of town, this is a great place to stop for a shrimp cocktail. It has some of the friendliest service in town.

Restaurant Martín (☎ 351-51-06; Playa Blanca; mains M$75-190; 🕒 8am-11pm, closed Tue in low season) Probably the best eatery in town, this rustic-chic restaurant, affording a pleasing view of the sea through swaying palms, prepares wonderful gourmet seafood, meats, soups, salads and fajitas. At breakfast, it's omelets, crepes and nicely arranged fruit platters. The 2nd-floor open *palapa* is romantically lit at night, and service is first-rate. Enjoy a Cuban cigar, if you must, but by all means save room for the flambéed bananas. The restaurant is on the main road at the south end of town.

Getting There & Away

To get to La Manzanilla by bus, travel first to Melaque and then catch a local bus (M$10) at the depot. Local buses headed to Melaque (M$10) leave from the *zócalo* (main plaza) at 8am, 11am, 4pm and 5pm. A taxi costs about M$100 to Melaque, and around M$20 to the crossroads, where you can flag down Manzanillo- or Puerto Vallarta–bound buses. A taxi to/from Playa de Oro International Airport (64km from Manzanillo) costs M$300 to M$400, depending on your bargaining skills.

Playa Cuastecomate

About 3km west of Melaque, Cuastecomate's maple-hued beach is probably the best around. The little cove it inhabits is knock-down gorgeous, and is nearly enclosed by the embrace of craggy mountains. At its opening in the far distance, strange rock formations rise from the sea in silhouette. Calm waters make for safe swimming and good snorkeling, and you can explore the village and surrounding hills. There's a full line-up of *palapa* restaurants, but really no nice place to stay, making this a better day trip than overnighter. (A word to the wise: beware the mother of all speed bumps on the road as it descends into town.)

The only place to stay is the overpriced resort-wannabe **Hotel Solamar** (☎ 315-355-50-85; www.solamarinncuastecomate.com; d/ste M$900/1800; P ≋ 오), a homely concrete hotel with rooms that are clean but clinical, though they feature rewarding views of the bay. The large, slightly dingy pool overlooks the beach.

BAHÍA DE NAVIDAD
☎ 315

The tight arc of Bahía de Navidad is ringed by deep, honey-colored sand with two resort towns at either end, waving amiably at each other. Situated 5km apart, Barra de Navidad and Melaque (also known as San Patricio-Melaque) are siblings with distinct personalities. Barra is beloved for its attractive cobbled streets and aura of good living, while Melaque, the scrappier of the two, draws budget-minded travelers seeking to get back to basics in a place that shuns pretension.

GETTING THERE & AWAY
Barra de Navidad and Melaque are served by Playa de Oro International Airport (ZLO), 26km southeast of Barra de Navidad on Hwy 200, which also serves Manzanillo. To get to each town from the airport, take a taxi (M$250, 30 minutes), or take a bus 15km to Cihuatlán and a cheaper taxi from there.

Both towns maintain separate bus terminals. See p149 and p153 for information on routes and pricing.

Melaque
pop 6300

A kick-back no-frills beach resort on Bahía de Navidad that hasn't lost its 'authentic Mexico' charm, Melaque (meh-*lah*-keh) – the greater metropolitan area of some 12,000 inhabitants is known to map-makers and census-takers as San Patricio-Melaque – is a popular beach destination for Mexican families. Less expensive and much more ragged

---

than its neighbor to the south, Melaque offers better deals for budget travelers, and has become a popular winter hangout for snowbirds (principally Canadians). The town is famous for its weeklong Fiesta de San Patricio in March.

The crumbling ruins of the Casa Grande Hotel are an imposing reminder of the destructive 1995 earthquake and the subsequent *maremotos* (tidal waves) that severely damaged the region.

ORIENTATION
Melaque is compact and walkable. Most hotels, restaurants and public services are concentrated on or near the east–west Gomez Farías, which runs parallel to the beach, and north–south López Mateos, the main Hwy 200 exit. Barra de Navidad is 5km southeast of Melaque via Hwy 200 or 2.5km by walking 30 to 45 minutes along the beach.

INFORMATION
The tourist office (p150) in Barra de Navidad has some basic information on Melaque.

Banamex (Gomez Farías s/n) Has an ATM but will not change US and Canadian dollars (unless you have an account there!); traveler's checks are changed from 9am to noon only.

Casa de Cambio Melaque (Pasaje Comercial 11, Gomez Farías s/n) Changes cash and traveler's checks at so-so rates.

El Navegante (Gomez Farías 48; internet per hr M$15; ⏲ 9am-2:30pm & 5-9pm Mon-Sat, 10am-2pm Sun) Air conditioned.

Post office (Orozco) Near the intersection with Corona.

Telecomm (Morelos 53; ⏲ 9am-2:30pm Mon-Fri) Offers the usual fax and phone services. See Map p148 for other *casetas telefónicas* (public telephone call stations).

Total Laundry Service (Gomez Farías 26; per kg M$12)

Tourist Police (☎ 355-50-80) Give them a call if you get in a jam.

SIGHTS & ACTIVITIES
The main activities are swimming, lazing on the beach, watching pelicans fish at sunrise and sunset, climbing to the *mirador* (lookout) at the bay's west end, prowling the plaza and public market, or walking the beach to Barra de Navidad. A *tianguis* (indigenous people's market) is held every Wednesday starting around 8am; it's on Orozco two blocks east of the plaza.

The Only Tours (☎ 355-67-77; raystoursmelaque@yahoo .com; Las Cabañas 26) is a small operation running popular snorkeling tours (M$250) and tours to

---

> **STUCK IN THE SAND? TRY A PALM FROND**
>
> If you ever drive your car onto the beach and get mired in sand, try this little trick: grab yourself a few fronds and stick them under the stuck tire, for traction. Often they're the only material on hand, and can save your ass surprisingly well.

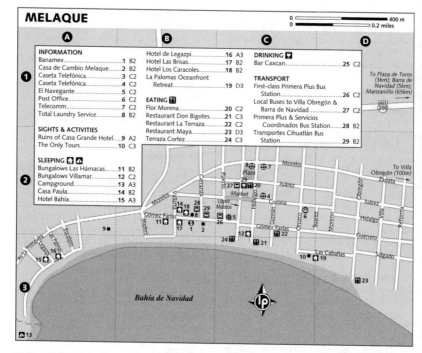

MELAQUE

0 | 400 m
0 | 0.2 miles

INFORMATION
Banamex...................................1 B2
Casa de Cambio Melaque.......2 B2
Caseta Telefónica....................3 C2
Caseta Telefónica....................4 C2
El Navegante............................5 C2
Post Office...............................6 C2
Telecomm................................7 C2
Total Laundry Service............8 B2

SIGHTS & ACTIVITIES
Ruins of Casa Grande Hotel.....9 A2
The Only Tours......................10 C3

SLEEPING
Bungalows Las Hámacas........11 B2
Bungalows Villamar...............12 C2
Campground...........................13 A3
Casa Paula.............................14 B2
Hotel Bahía............................15 A3

Hotel de Legazpi....................16 A3
Hotel Las Brisas......................17 B2
Hotel Los Caracoles..............18 B2
La Palomas Oceanfront
   Retreat...............................19 D3

EATING
Flor Morena............................20 C2
Restaurant Don Bigotes.........21 C3
Restaurant La Terraza............22 C2
Restaurant Maya....................23 D3
Terraza Cortez.......................24 C3

DRINKING
Bar Caxcan...........................25 C2

TRANSPORT
First-class Primera Plus Bus
   Station...............................26 C2
Local Buses to Villa Obregón &
   Barra de Navidad...............27 C3
Primera Plus & Servicios
   Coordinados Bus Station....28 B2
Transportes Cihuatlán Bus
   Station...............................29 B2

To Plaza de Toros
(3km); Barra de
Navidad (5km);
Manzanillo (65km)

To Villa
Obregón (100m)

Bahía de Navidad

Colima (M$500). It also rents mountain bikes
(half-/full-day M$60/100), snorkeling gear and
bodyboards (each M$100 per day).

FESTIVALS & EVENTS

Melaque's biggest annual celebration is the
Fiesta de San Patricio (St Patrick's Day Festival;
March 17), honoring the town's patron saint.
A week of festivities – including all-day parties, rodeos, a carnival, music, dances and
nightly fireworks – leads up to the big day,
which is marked with a Mass and the blessing
of the fishing fleet. Take care when the *bor-
rachos* (drunks) take over after dark.

COURSES

At La Paloma Oceanfront Retreat, **La Paloma
Art Center** (☎ 355-53-45; www.lapalomamexico.com; Las
Cabañas 13; ⏰ 2-4pm Mon-Fri) offers drawing, paint-
ing or mask-making classes.

SLEEPING

Rates vary greatly depending on the season; the following prices are for November
through April. Discounts are common for
longer stays.

Budget

The Ejidal beachfront **campground** (sites M$20), at
the west end of town, has no facilities but inhabits an undeniably beautiful setting. Many
of the nearby *enramadas* (thatch-covered
open-air restaurants) charge a nominal fee
for showers and bathroom usage.

Casa Paula (☎ 355-50-93; Vallarta 6; s/d M$100/200)
Staying here is like staying with the sweetest
grandma ever. In this simple home there are
four basic rooms, with TVs and a fridge, set
around a courtyard. It's very quiet and a family atmosphere pervades the place.

Bungalows Villamar (☎ 355-50-05; Hidalgo 1;
r M$350; ⌘) The Villamar has five spacious
but worn garden bungalows with kitchens, a
porta-pool and a beachfront terrace. Its owner
Roberto speaks English.

Hotel Bahía (☎ 355-68-94; Legazpi 5; r M$350, bun-
galow M$300-500; ⌘) Just half a block from the
beach, this family-run place is one of Melaque's
best deals. It's clean, very well maintained and
has a communal open-air kitchen. Four of the
23 units have private kitchens.

Bungalows Las Hámacas (☎ 355-51-13; Gomez
Farías 13; d/q M$400/870; ⓟ ⌘ ☖) Ideal for larger

groups and families, the beachfront Las Hámacas has chipping paint, and worn but big rooms with full kitchens.

Midrange

Hotel de Legazpi (☎ 355-53-97; hoteldelegazpi@prodigy .net.mx; Las Palmas 3; d/tr M$490/550; P ⊠) Right on the beach, the Legazpi has bright, if slightly worn and institutional-feeling, rooms. It's very popular for the rooms with ocean views; they cost the same but are hard to get.

Hotel Los Caracoles (☎ 355-73-08; www.loscaracoles .com.mx; Gomez Farías 26; r M$700) This fresh new hotel is not on the beach but makes amends with clean but cramped modern rooms with hand-painted headboards and tiled desks. The lack of air-con can make for a hot night.

Hotel Las Brisas (☎ 355-51-08; Gomez Farías 9; r M$800; ⊠ ⊠) The beachfront Las Brisas has one of the nicest pools in the neighborhood, outdoor communal cooking facilities, friendly staff and a small library. All rooms have fridge, air-con and TV.

La Paloma Oceanfront Retreat (☎ 355-53-45; www .lapalomamexico.com; Las Cabañas 13; studios M$800-1000; P ⊠ ⊠ ⊠) Original art abounds at this unique boutique resort, which doubles as an art center. The singular, comfortable studios have kitchens and terraces with rewarding ocean views. Lush gardens, a 25m beachside swimming pool, complimentary breakfasts, a well-stocked library and internet access make an extended stay here extremely tempting. Reservations are a must.

EATING & DRINKING

Of an evening, from about 6pm to midnight, food stands serve inexpensive Mexican fare a block east of the plaza along Juárez. A row of pleasant *palapa* restaurants (mains M$40 to M$110) stretches along the beach at the west end of town.

Flor Morena (Juárez s/n; mains M$15-45; ⊗ 6-11pm Tue-Sun; Ⓥ) You may have to wait to get a seat in this tiny place, but it's worth it. Everything is made fresh, there are plenty of vegetarian options and even the house specialty, shrimp *pozole* (hominy soup),costs less than M$40.

Restaurant La Terraza (☎ 355-53-13; Guzmán 4; mains M$25-50; ⊗ 7am-10pm) This warm, family-run spot serves organic coffee and a full breakfast menu in the morning, and home-made bread, salads, salsa and traditional Mexican food for lunch and dinner. It offers internet access and a breezy 2nd-floor terrace,

where on Friday nights you'll find a buf-fet (M$120 to M$150) and a traditional dance performed by students from the local secondary school.

Terraza Cortez (López Mateos 1; mains M$30-90; ⊗ 8am-6pm) This low-key beachfront joint has some of the friendliest service in town – and the fajitas ain't bad either.

Restaurant Don Bigotes (☎ 100-76-72; Hidalgo 1; mains M$50-120; ⊗ 8am-9pm) Seafood is the spe-cialty at this pleasant beachfront *palapa;* try the *guachinango a la naranja* (red snapper à l'orange) or *camarones al cilantro* (cilantro shrimp). The two-for-one happy hour (2pm to 8pm) is popular.

Restaurant Maya (Obregón 1; www.restaurantmaya .com; mains M$70-150; ⊗ 6-11pm Wed-Sun & 10:30am-2pm Sun) The menu changes regularly, but the qual-ity at this Asian-fusion beachside hot spot is consistently excellent. Dinners include a range of gourmet salads, grilled meats and fish with exotic sauces, and there are appetizers like tequila lime prawns. Western favorites such as eggs Benedict and rich omelets with Brie rule the brunch menu.

Bar Caxcan (cnr López Mateos & Juárez) This young-lin's spot thumps out techno beats, and has a pool table and an extended happy hour.

ENTERTAINMENT

During the winter and spring, *corridas de toros* (bullfights) occasionally liven up the Plaza de Toros, 3km southeast of town off Hwy 200, near the Barra turnoff. Watch for flyers promoting *charreadas* (Mexican rodeos), and keep an ear out for cruising, megaphone-equipped cars scratchily announcing *béisbol* games and *fútbol* (soccer) matches.

GETTING THERE & AWAY

Bus

Melaque has three bus stations. Transportes Cihuatlán and Primera Plus/Servicios Coordinados are on opposite sides of Carranza at the corner of Gomez Farías. Both have 1st- and 2nd-class buses and ply similar routes for similar fares. The 1st-class Primera Plus bus station is a block east on Gomez Farías. Buses trundling daily out of these stations serve the following destinations:

Barra de Navidad (M$11 to M$15, 10 minutes, every 15 minutes 5am to 11:30pm) Or take any southbound long-distance bus.

Guadalajara (M$259, five to 7½ hours, nine 1st-class; $219, five to 7½ hours, 12 2nd-class)

Manzanillo (M$52, one to 1½ hours, eight 1st-class; M$44, one to 1½ hours, 2nd-class at least hourly 5am-11:30pm)
Puerto Vallarta (M$180, 3½ to five hours, departing 9:30am and 1:30pm 1st-class; M$150, 3½ to 5 hours, 11 2nd-class)

Local buses for Villa Obregón (M$5, 1km) and Barra de Navidad (M$5, 15 to 20 minutes, 5km) stop near the plaza by the Paletería Michoacán every 15 minutes.

Taxi

A taxi between Melaque and Barra should cost no more than M$50, or as little as M$35, depending on how well *tu hablas espanglish*. A taxi to the Manzanillo airport runs around M$390 one way.

Barra de Navidad

☎ 315 / pop 3500

The charming town of Barra de Navidad (usually simply called 'Barra') is squeezed onto a sandbar between Bahía de Navidad and the Laguna de Navidad. The traffic-free cobblestone streets of the town center make this one of the most pleasant cityscapes on the Jalisco coast. Unfortunately, the hard-packed brown-sand beach is almost impossibly steep, making for dangerous swimming conditions.

Barra de Navidad first came to prominence in 1564 when its shipyards produced the galleons used by conquistador Miguel López de Legazpi and Father André de Urdaneta to deliver the Philippines to King Philip of Spain. By 1600, however, most of the conquests were being conducted from Acapulco, and Barra slipped into sleepy obscurity (a state from which it has yet to fully emerge).

ORIENTATION

Legazpi, the main drag, runs parallel to the beach. Veracruz, the town's other major artery and the highway feeder, runs parallel to Legazpi before merging with it at the southern end of town, which terminates in a finger-like sandbar. Buses drop passengers at offices on Legazpi.

INFORMATION

Banamex ATM (Veracruz s/n)
Beer Bob's Book Exchange (Tampico 8; ☾ noon-3pm Mon-Fri) You can exchange, but not buy, books here.
Ciber@Money (Veracruz 212C; per hr M$25; ☾ 9am-7pm Mon-Sat, 9am-5pm Sun in high season) Has a decent internet connection, and can exchange foreign currency.

Lavandería Mary (Veracruz s/n; ☾ 8am-8pm Mon-Sat, 8am-1pm Sun) Washes your clothes for M$10 per kilogram.
Mini-Market Hawaii (Legazpi at Sonora; ☾ noon-10pm) Telephone and fax services.
Post office (cnr Sinaloa & Mazatlán)
Regional tourist office (☎ 355-51-00; www.costa alegre.com; Jalisco 67; ☾ 9am-5pm Mon-Fri) Free maps and information about more than just Barra; it also runs an information kiosk on the jetty during the high season.
Spiaggia (Veracruz s/n; per hr M$15; ☾ noon-9pm Mon-Fri, 10am-3pm Sat) Another good bet for internet.
Telecomm (Veracruz 212B; ☾ 9am-3pm Mon-Fri) Phones and fax. See Map p151 for locations of *casetas telefónicas* (public telephone call stations).

ACTIVITIES

Barra's steep and narrow beach is lovely to behold. But with its steep slope, waves crash close to shore, and conditions can get rough for swimming. The gentlest waves arrive in the early mornings. Head over to the lagoon for shallow clear waters perfect for swimming. Small but surfable right and left breaks are snatched up by determined souls at the southernmost end of the beach near the jetty.

Boards can be rented from **Crazy Cactus** (☎ 355-60-91; crazycactusmx@yahoo.com; Veracruz 165; ☾ 9:30am-6pm Mon-Sat), as can snorkeling gear, kayaks and bicycles, not to mention cars and apartments – call first, however, as it was planning on moving at press time.

Nauti-Mar dive shop (☎ 355-57-90; www.seatosierra .com; Veracruz 204) rents out outfits for all manner of aquatic sports, and arranges biking (M$250), horseback (M$500) and diving (M$850) trips.

Boat Trips

Boat trips into the Laguna de Navidad are a Barra highlight for most travelers. The boat operators' cooperative, **Sociedad Cooperativa de Servicios Turísticos** (☎ 107-76-99; Veracruz 40; ☾ 7am-9pm), offers boat excursions, ranging from half-hour trips around the lagoon (M$200 per boat) to all-day jungle trips to Tenacatita (M$2500 per boat). Prices (for up to eight people) are posted at the open-air lagoon-side office. The cooperative also offers fishing (from M$400 per hour for up to four people), snorkeling (from M$250) and diving trips.

For a short jaunt out on the water, an appealing option is to catch a **water taxi** from a nearby dock and head over to the Grand Bay

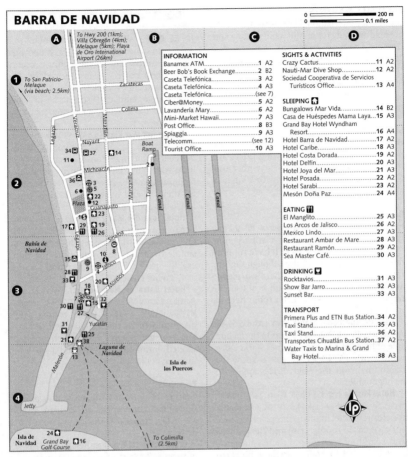

BARRA DE NAVIDAD

0 ——————— 200 m
0 ——————— 0.1 miles

To Hwy 200 (1km);
Villa Obregón (4km);
Melaque (5km); Playa
de Oro International
Airport (26km)

To San Patricio-
Melaque
(via beach; 2.5km)

Zacatecas

Colima

Nayarit

Boat
Ramp

Michoacán

Plaza

Cuanajuato

Bahía de
Navidad

Sinaloa

Jalisco

Sonora

Yucatán

Laguna de
Navidad

Malecón

Isla de
los Puercos

Jetty

Isla de
Navidad

Grand Bay
Golf Course

To Colimilla
(2.5km)

INFORMATION
Banamex ATM...........................**1** A2
Beer Bob's Book Exchange...........**2** B2
Caseta Telefónica.........................**3** A2
Caseta Telefónica.........................**4** A3
Caseta Telefónica....................(see 7)
Ciber@Money.............................**5** A3
Lavandería Mary.........................**6** A2
Mini-Market Hawaii.....................**7** A3
Post Office.................................**8** B3
Spiaggia....................................**9** A3
Telecomm.............................(see 12)
Tourist Office............................**10** A3

SIGHTS & ACTIVITIES
Crazy Cactus.............................**11** A2
Nauti-Mar Dive Shop..................**12** A2
Sociedad Cooperativa de Servicios
  Turísticos Office.......................**13** A4

SLEEPING
Bungalows Mar Vida....................**14** B2
Casa de Huéspedes Mama Laya...**15** A3
Grand Bay Hotel Wyndham
  Resort....................................**16** A4
Hotel Barra de Navidad...............**17** A2
Hotel Caribe..............................**18** A3
Hotel Costa Dorada....................**19** A2
Hotel Delfin..............................**20** A2
Hotel Joya del Mar.....................**21** A3
Hotel Posada.............................**22** A3
Hotel Sarabi..............................**23** A3
Mesón Doña Paz........................**24** A4

EATING
El Manglito...............................**25** A3
Los Arcos de Jalisco...................**26** A2
Mexico Lindo.............................**27** A3
Restaurant Ambar de Mare...........**28** A3
Restaurant Ramón......................**29** A3
Sea Master Café.........................**30** A3

DRINKING
Rocktavios................................**31** A3
Show Bar Jarro...........................**32** A3
Sunset Bar................................**33** A3

TRANSPORT
Primera Plus and ETN Bus Station.**34** A2
Taxi Stand................................**35** A3
Taxi Stand................................**36** A2
Transportes Cihuatlán Bus Station.**37** A2
Water Taxis to Marina & Grand
  Bay Hotel...............................**38** A3

Hotel Wyndham Resort on Isla de Navidad, or to Colimilla (M$20 round-trip). At Colimilla, you can laze your afternoon away at one of the pleasant restaurants, all with super-fresh *mariscos* (seafood) and rewarding views of the lagoon.

Walking
For a pleasant day of intensive beach strolling, you can pad the sands all the way to Melaque, 2.5km north at the other end of Bahía de Navidad. Start early in the morning with the sun at your back, and carry water and sun protection. At the far end of Melaque you'll find a trail leading beneath the cliff to a wonderfully craggy spot at the tip of the bay with splendid tide pools.

Sportfishing
The waters near Barra are rife with marlin, swordfish, albacore, dorado (dolphinfish), snapper and other more unusual catches. Fishing trips can be arranged at the boat operators' cooperative (see p150) for about M$400 per hour, including gear.

Golf
Golfers will be ecstatic. **Grand Bay Golf Course** (☎ 355-50-50; Grand Bay Hotel Wyndham Resort, Isla de Navidad; green fees 18/27 holes M$2000/2500), on Isla de Navidad, is a celebrated 27-hole course with excellent vistas and greens carved into ocean dunes against a backdrop of mountains. Caddies and golf clubs are available for hire.

FESTIVALS & EVENTS

Big-money international fishing tournaments are held annually for marlin, sailfish, tuna and dorado. The most important, the three-day **Torneo Internacional de Pesca**, is held around the third week in January. The two-day **Torneo Internacional de Marlin** is held during late May or early June, with another two-day tournament in mid-August.

SLEEPING

Barra has fewer beachfront rooms than its neighbor Melaque. The following prices are for the high season (between November and May). A bungalow is a room with a kitchen and sleeps at least three.

Budget

Hotel Caribe (☎ 355-59-52; Sonora 15; s/d/tr/q M$200/300/350/400) The popular Caribe is one of Barra's better budget deals. It has a rooftop terrace, hot water and 18 clean though slightly musty rooms. Downstairs there's a pleasant garden offering respite on a hot afternoon. You'll be lucky to get a room here in the winter.

Casa de Huéspedes Mama Laya (☎ 355-55-88; Veracruz 69; s/d/tr/q M$200/250/300/350) On the lagoon side of town, the Mama Laya has stark, worn rooms with TV. Expect to get to know the family that runs the place. Prices appear to be negotiable.

Hotel Posada (☎ 355-69-68; Veracruz s/n; s/d with fan M$250/300, d with air-con M$400; P ❌) Arguably the cleanest hotel in town, this place has nice sitting areas in rooms, crisp and clean sheets and sparkling baths. Alas, there's no pool, so you'll need to hoof it a whole block to the beach.

Midrange

Hotel Sarabi (☎ 355-82-23; www.hotelsarabi.com; Veracruz 196; s/d/tr M$350/450/550, bungalow M$800-1000; P ❌) Clean and efficiently run, this is probably your last-ditch midrange option – after the Joya del Mar. Ask about the 'third night free' promotion.

Hotel Costa Dorada (☎ 355-64-10; Veracruz 174; bungalow M$400-700; P ❌ ❒) This welcoming option offers 24 whimsically tiled bungalows with diminutive TVs and good, firm mattresses. The rooms could use a good scrub, but are a decent value nonetheless. Grab an upstairs unit to benefit from the cross-breeze.

our pick **Hotel Delfín** (☎ 355-50-68; www.hotel delfinmx.com; Morelos 23; d/tr/q/apt M$495/595/695/1200; P ❒ ❒ ❒) With large, pleasant rooms that open onto shared balconies, a grassy pool area and an exercise room, the Delfín is one of Barra's best hotels – it just feels right. The large apartments, complete with kitchens, are a good bet for families. Discounts are available for longer stays, but repeat customers fill the place in winter.

Bungalows Mar Vida (☎ 355-59-11; www.tomzap .com/marvida.html; Mazatlán 168; apt M$650; ❌ ❒ ❒) While it's a bit away from the action, the fine little Mar Vida has five newly remodeled studio apartments, all with satellite TV, cheerful tilework and hand-carved doors. Some English is spoken.

Hotel Joya del Mar (☎ 355-69-67; joyadelmar@ yahoo.com; Veracruz 209; s/d/ste M$450/550/950; ❌) Overpriced for what you get, the cramped and simple rooms at the 'Jewel of the Sea' don't exactly sparkle. The hotel's central location is its saving grace.

Hotel Barra de Navidad (☎ 355-51-22; www .hotelbarradenavidad.com; Legazpi 250; d/tr/bungalow M$1000/1040/1550; ❌ ❒) The rooms are a bit rundown in this bulging white hotel, but you get Barra's best beach access, a shaded, intimate courtyard and a small but inviting pool.

Top End

Getting away from it all is a matter of considerable luxury on Isla de Navidad, a short water-taxi ride across the lagoon from Barra de Navidad.

Grand Bay Hotel Wyndham Resort (☎ 314-331-05-00; www.wyndham.com; Rinconada del Capitán s/n, Isla de Navidad; d from M$2230; ❌ ❒ ❒ ❒) This super-luxury resort is self-consciously magnificent and very large. The same adjectives apply to the rooms, which feature marble floors, hand-carved furniture and bathrooms big enough to herd sheep in. If the weather's not quite hot enough for you, spend some time in your suite's steam bath or, better yet, at the pool's convenient swim-up bar. Justifying the hefty price tag are oodles of extras, including three grass tennis courts, golf packages, a 'kids' club' day-care center and big fluffy bathrobes. Book online for cheaper rates and golf packages.

Mesón Doña Paz (☎ 314-337-90-00; www.meson donapaz.com; Rinconada del Capitán s/n, Isla de Navidad; d from M$3000; ste from M$4600; ❌ ❒ ❒) For something really special, check into this gorgeous colonial-style lodge where every room has a balcony facing the languid lagoon. The grounds are graced by a tranquil private bay, lookout point and lush landscaping. All-inclusive plans and golf packages are available. Be sure to ask about low-season and promotional rates.

EATING

Simple, small and inexpensive indoor-outdoor places line Veracruz in the center of town. However, most are open only in the high season.

Mexico Lindo (Legazpi 138; mains M$30-65; 9am-midnight) With simple plastic tables under a corrugated tin roof, this place somehow manages to feel romantic and intimate at night. The menu features regional favorites like savory tortilla soup, quesadillas, garlic fish tacos and shrimp *ceviche*; a good selection of drinks and cocktails seals the deal.

Los Arcos de Jalisco (355-70-30; Veracruz 170; mains M$40-110; 8am-10pm) Sit outside to enjoy people-watching as you indulge in simple, authentic Jalisceño fare at this central eatery. The *tacos dorados* (M$40) are a great deal.

Restaurant Ramón (355-64-35; Legazpi 260; mains M$50-90; 7am-11pm) This casual, down-home eatery serves excellent fish tacos among other local and gringo favorites.

Sea Master Café (355-51-19; cnr Legazpi & Yucatán; mains M$65-120; 11am-11pm) With a hip lounge 'chic-tatmosphere' perfect for tossing back cocktails, this place scores points with diners by taking liberties with seafood. For instance, a dish called 'piña sea master' fills a pineapple with shrimp, peppers, mushrooms and a buttery Kahlua sauce. Who needs dessert after that?

El Manglito (355-85-90; Veracruz s/n; mains M$70-100; 8am-7pm) An exuberantly decorated *palapa* overlooking the lagoon, El Manglito is a grand place to while away a hot afternoon watching the *lanchas* (open, outboard boats) come and go. The service is slow but the seafood served is so good you'll soon forget about this minor inconvenience.

ourpick Restaurant Ambar de Mare (355-81-69; Legazpi 158; mains M$90-290; 5:30pm-midnight, closed Mon in low season) With a great menu featuring Italian and French cuisine, and arguably the best wood-fired pizza pie in town, this is the best restaurant in Barra. The cozy European atmosphere extends to the seaside patio, which offers simply delightful views. There's even a decent wine list.

DRINKING

Sunset Bar (355-52-17; Jalisco 140; noon-2am) The waiter at this seaside saloon claims that 'the sunset' was named after the bar, and not the other way around. Humongous drink specials are served daily from 2pm to 10pm. A DJ spins nightly during the high season.

Rocktavios (Legazpi 154A; 10am-2am) With its tough motorcycle-bar look and loud live music on weekends (from 9pm), this is the place to rock. The friendly owner, Octavio, was a former *lucha libre* (big-time wrestling) star.

Show Bar Jarro (Veracruz; 9pm-4am) Near the corner of Veracruz and Yucatán, this down-to-earth, gay-friendly disco has pool tables and lagoon views.

GETTING THERE & AROUND
Bus

The long-distance buses stopping at Melaque (p149) also stop at Barra de Navidad (15 minutes before or after). Transportes Cihuatlán's station is at Veracruz 228; Primera Plus and ETN operate from small terminals nearby, on the opposite side of Veracruz. Primera Plus has service to Manzanillo (M$44, one hour) and Puerto Vallarta (M$154, four hours), among other destinations.

In addition to the long-distance buses, colorful local buses connect Barra and Melaque (M$5, every 15 minutes, 6am to 9pm), stopping in Barra at the long-distance bus stations (buses stopping on the south-bound side of the road loop round Legazpi and back to Melaque).

Boat

Water taxis operate on demand 24 hours a day from the dock at the southern end of Veracruz, offering service to the hotels on Isla de Navidad (M$20), the marina, the golf course and Colimilla. Also see p150 for information on boat tours.

Taxi

Catch **taxis** (355-57-60) from the taxi stands at the corners of Veracruz and Michoacán, and Sinaloa and Legazpi. One-way taxi fares: Melaque (M$50), La Manzanilla (M$200), Manzanillo Airport (M$300), Manzanillo (M$400) and Tenacatita (M$300).

COLIMA

Trips to Colima's coast generally begin and end in the large city of Manzanillo, home to one of Mexico's most important ports and a thriving tourism scene. South of town are the sleepy towns of Cuyutlán and El Paraíso, and Playa Boca de Pascuales, a legendary surf spot.

MANZANILLO

☎ 314 / pop 137,000

With a port that recently surpassed Veracruz to become the busiest in Mexico, these are heady times in Manzanillo. Nowhere is the upbeat attitude more prevalent than downtown, where the waterfront has been enhanced with a 3km boardwalk along the ocean and a capacious seaside *zócalo*. Providing a dramatic setting for a promenade, at dusk swarms of starlings do their best to blot out the sunset, while the giant Swordfish Memorial creates an imposing silhouette. The port and powerplant that overlook town are noticeable eyesores, making Manzanillo feel a bit too industrial to be a true vacation destination.

Away from the center, miles of steeply sloped beaches ring nearby Bahía de Santiago and Bahía de Manzanillo. They are not the perfect swimming or sunning spots, but find a nice corner and you'll know what to do. The lagoons surrounding the town offer good bird-watching, and there are a few decent snorkeling and diving spots nearby. Befitting the city's deep-sea-fishing reputation, fans call Manzanillo the 'World Capital of Sailfish,' and each year fishing tournaments draw hopeful anglers from all around.

Orientation

Manzanillo extends 16km from northwest to southeast. The resort hotels and finest beaches begin at Playa Azul, across the bay from Playa San Pedrito, the closest beach to the center. Further around the bay is the Península de Santiago, a rocky outcrop holding Las Hadas Resort and Playa La Audiencia. Just west of the peninsula, Bahía de Santiago is lined with excellent beaches. Hwy 200 runs from Playa Miramar down to Playa Las Brisas through the Zona Hotelera, and is also called Blvd Miguel de la Madrid.

Central Manzanillo is bound by Bahía de Manzanillo to the north, the Pacific Ocean to the west and Laguna de Cuyutlán to the south. Av Morelos, the main drag, runs along the north edge of the town center, beside the sea. At its east end it meets Av Niños Héroes, which leads to Hwy 200.

Information

Aeroviajes Manzanillo (Map p156; ☎ 332-74-16; Av México 43) Arranges flights, tours and bus tickets.

Banks Several banks with ATMs are scattered around the city center.

Caseta Telefónica (Map p156; Av Morelos 144; ☉ 9am-10pm) Long-distance telephone and fax service. Public telephones are plentiful around the center.

HSBC (Map p156; Av México s/n) Offers currency exchange.

Lavandería Savi (Map p156; Bocanegra 44; ☉ 9am-8pm Mon-Sat) Washes clothes for M$10 per kilogram.

Members.com (Map p156; Juárez 116; per hr M$15) Offers fast net connections in a comfortable atmosphere.

Post office (Map p156; Galindo 30)

Tourist office (Map p155; ☎ 333-22-77; www.visita colima.com.mx; Blvd Miguel de la Madrid 875A, Km 8.5; ☉ 9am-7pm Mon-Sat Sat) Dispenses information about Manzanillo and the state of Colima.

Tourist police (Map p156; ☎ 332-10-04) Stationed behind the Presidencia Municipal.

www.gomanzanillo.com Has good information on tours and activities in the area.

Sights & Activities

MUSEO UNIVERSITARIO DE ARQUEOLOGÍA

The University of Colima's **archaeological museum** (Map p156; ☎ 332-22-56; cnr Niños Héroes & Glorieta San Pedrito; admission M$15; ☉ 10am-2pm & 5-8pm Tue-Sat, 10am-1pm Sun) presents interesting objects from ancient Colima state and rotating exhibits of contemporary Mexican art. At the time of research the museum was undergoing renovation; it should be open again by the time you read this.

BEACHES

Playa San Pedrito, 1km northeast of the *zócalo*, is the closest beach to town. The next closest stretch of sand, spacious **Playa Las Brisas**, caters to a few hotels. **Playa Azul** stretches northwest from Las Brisas and curves around to **Playa La Escondida** and the best beaches in the area: **La Audiencia**, **Santiago**, **Olas Altas** and **Miramar**. Miramar and Olas Altas have the best surfing and bodysurfing waves in the area; surfboards can be rented at Miramar at Bara's Bar. Playa La Audiencia, lining a quiet cove on the west side of Península de Santiago, has more tranquil water and is popular for water-skiing and other noisy motorized water sports.

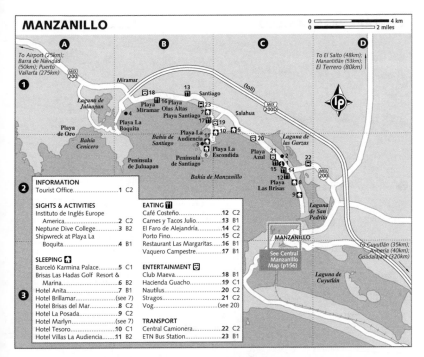

MANZANILLO

0	4 km
0	2 miles

To Airport (25km);
Barra de Navidad
(50km); Puerto
Vallarta (275km)

MEX 200

Miramar

To El Salto (48km);
Manantitlán (53km);
El Terrero (80km)

MEX 200D

Laguna de
Juluapan

Playa
Miramar

Santiago

Playa
Olas Altas

Salahua

Playa
de Oro

Playa La
Boquita

Playa Santiago

Bahía de
Santiago

Playa La
Audiencia

Laguna de
las Garzas

Bahía
Cenicero

Península
de Juluapan

Península
de Santiago

Playa La
Escondida

Playa
Azul

MEX 200

Bahía de Manzanillo

Playa
Las Brisas

Laguna
de San
Pedrito

INFORMATION
Tourist Office..........................1 C2

MANZANILLO
See Central
Manzanillo
Map (p156)

To Cuyutlán (35km);
Armería (40km);
Guadalajara (320km)

SIGHTS & ACTIVITIES
Instituto de Inglés Europe
America................................2 C2
Neptune Dive College.............3 B2
Shipwreck at Playa La
Boquita................................4 B1

SLEEPING
Barceló Karmina Palace..........5 C1
Brisas Las Hadas Golf Resort &
Marina................................6 B2
Hotel Anita............................7 B1
Hotel Brillamar...................(see 7)
Hotel Brisas del Mar...............8 C2
Hotel La Posada.....................9 C2
Hotel Marlyn.....................(see 7)
Hotel Tesoro........................10 C1
Hotel Villas La Audiencia......11 B2

EATING
Café Costeño........................12 C2
Carnes y Tacos Julio.............13 B1
El Faro de Alejandría.............14 C2
Porto Fino...........................15 C2
Restaurant Las Margaritas.....16 B1
Vaquero Campestre..............17 B1

ENTERTAINMENT
Club Maeva...........................18 B1
Hacienda Guacho..................19 C1
Nautilus...............................20 C2
Stragos................................21 C2
Vog..................................(see 20)

TRANSPORT
Central Camionera................22 C2
ETN Bus Station....................23 B1

Laguna
de
Cuyutlán

Getting to these beaches from the town center is easy: local buses marked 'Santiago,' 'Las Brisas' and 'Miramar' head around the bay to San Pedrito, Salahua, Santiago, Miramar and beaches along the way. 'Las Hadas' buses take a more circuitous, scenic route down Península de Santiago. These buses pick up passengers from local bus stops, along the length of Calle 21 de Marzo, and from the main bus station, every 10 minutes from 6am to 11pm.

WATER SPORTS

Snorkeling, windsurfing, sailing, water-skiing and deep-sea fishing are all popular around the bay. The scuba diving in Manzanillo can be spectacular, and there are many sites to explore – either off one of the beaches or out on the bay. See the boxed text 'Ask a Local' (p158) for more details on the area's snorkeling and diving spots.

The best diving operator is the well-established **Neptune's Dive College** (Map p155; ☎ 334-30-01; www.neptunesdiving.com; Calle Las Palmas 59, Peninsula de Santiago), which specializes in dive-instructor training, but also offers diving and snorkeling trips.

SPORTFISHING

Sailfish and dorado are found in the waters off Manzanillo during every season of the year, while marlin and tuna are generally in the area from November to March.

Ocean Pacific Adventures (☎ 335-06-05, www.gomanzanillo.com/fishing) supports Manzanillo's only catch-and-release program. This well-run operation offers fishing trips on an 8m (26ft) and 12m (40ft) cruiser (M$2000/2600); prices are for the whole boat and include gear, drinks and having your fish cooked up for dinner.

Courses

Instituto de Inglés Europe America (Map p155; ☎ 333-27-94; euroamer1@prodigy.net.mx; Hwy 200 No 1317) provides individual Spanish instruction from M$150 per hour.

Tours

Colima Magic (☎ 312-310-74-83; www.colimamagic.com) is a Colima-based operator that runs day trips from Manzanillo up to the towering Volcán Nevado de Colima. Trips cost from M$70 to M$1200.

JALISCO, COLIMA & MICHOACÁN COASTS

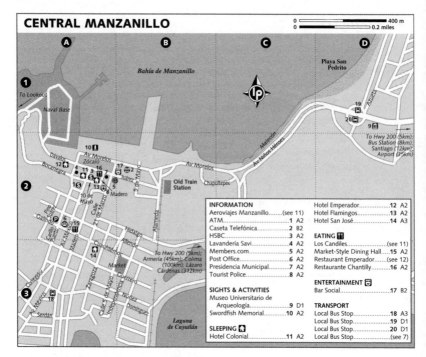

CENTRAL MANZANILLO

INFORMATION	
Aeroviajes Manzanillo........(see 11)	
ATM....................................1 A2	
Caseta Telefónica.................2 B2	
HSBC.................................3 A2	
Lavandería Savi....................4 A2	
Members.com......................5 A2	
Post Office...........................6 A2	
Presidencia Municipal...........7 A2	
Tourist Police........................8 A2	

SIGHTS & ACTIVITIES	
Museo Universitario de	
Arqueología.......................9 D1	
Swordfish Memorial...........10 A2	

SLEEPING	
Hotel Colonial....................11 A2	

Hotel Emperador...............12 A2	
Hotel Flamingos.................13 A2	
Hotel San José...................14 A3	

EATING	
Los Candiles.....................(see 11)	
Market-Style Dining Hall.....15 A2	
Restaurant Emperador.......(see 12)	
Restaurante Chantilly...........16 A2	

ENTERTAINMENT	
Bar Social..........................17 B2	

TRANSPORT	
Local Bus Stop...................18 A3	
Local Bus Stop...................19 D1	
Local Bus Stop...................20 D1	
Local Bus Stop..................(see 7)	

JALISCO, COLIMA &
MICHOACÁN COASTS

Hectours (☎ 333-17-07; www.hectours.com) offers a half-day tour of Manzanillo (M$300) and a full-day excursion to Colima and the colonial town of Comala (M$700). The tour prices include transportation from your hotel.

Ventanas Adventures (☎ 333-70-35; www.ventanasadventures.com) offers ATV excursions (for the nonecologically-minded set), as well as hiking, biking, climbing, kayaking and zip-line tours.

Festivals & Events

The **Fiestas de Mayo** (May 1 to 10) celebrate the founding of Manzanillo in 1873 by holding sporting competitions and other events popular with locals.

The **Fiesta de Nuestra Señora de Guadalupe** is held from December 1 to 12 in honor of Mexico's revered manifestation of the Virgin Mary, here as elsewhere in Mexico.

Sailfish season runs November to March, with marlin, red snapper, sea bass and tuna also plentiful. The biggest international tournament is held in November, with a smaller national tournament in February.

Sleeping

Central Manzanillo has the town's best cheap options within a block or two of the *zócalo*. There are more places in the rundown area a few blocks south of the city center. Around the bay, where the better beaches are, hotels are naturally more expensive; Playa Santiago, half an hour away by bus, is the exception, with budget beachfront digs on offer.

BUDGET

Hotel Emperador (Map p156; ☎ 332-23-74; Dávalos 69; s/d M$200/250) Half a block from the *zócalo*, this simple but clean refuge has some top-floor rooms that are marginally brighter than the rest. The hotel's restaurant is good and is one of the cheapest in town.

Hotel San José (Map p156; ☎ 332-51-05; Cuauhtémoc 138; s/d/tr M$300/400/500) In the frenetic market area, this is one of the cleanest budget digs in town. All the rooms have fans, and there's a big water cooler up front to help keep our landfills water-bottle free. A little white poodle provides security by licking intruders to death.

Hotel Marlyn (Map p155; ☎ 333-01-07; Playa Santiago s/n; d/ste from M$350/1400; ⊠ ⓡ) The oceanfront Marlyn has pleasant rooms with TVs and fans. The ones you want have sea views and balconies, and consequently cost more. Six-person kitchen suites are available.

MIDRANGE

All the following hotels – except Hotel La Posada – overlook Playa Santiago, and are a winding 15-minute walk (or five-minute bus ride) from Santiago town, down the road leading off Hwy 200 past the ETN bus station. The hotels perch on a bluff overlooking the beach, and all have beachfront swimming pools.

OUR PICK **Hotel Colonial** (Map p156; ☎ 332-10-80; www.hotelcolonialmanzanillo.com; Bocanegra 100; s/d from M$340/500; ⓟ ⊠) This atmospheric, old-fashioned hotel in the heart of downtown retains the character of a bygone hacienda. Big rooms, blue-tiled outdoor hallways and a thick colonial ambience make it the best deal in town. It has limited underground parking and a quality restaurant-bar on the premises.

Hotel Flamingos (Map p156; ☎ 332-56-85; Madero 72; s/d M$350/450) On a quiet side street, this old cheapie is a last resort, at best. Run-down and a bit dark and dingy, the hotel offers 30 basic rooms with soft beds. Some can be musty; ask for one with two beds and an outside window.

Hotel Brillamar (Map p155; ☎ 334-11-88; Playa Santiago s/n; d/q from M$400/900; ⊠ ⓡ) Brillamar has air-con and TV, though, unforgivably, some toilets may be missing their seats and the beds aren't very comfortable. Rooms are otherwise reasonable, but small. Large bungalows with kitchen are also available.

DETOUR: COLIMA CITY

If knocking around in the heart of Manzanillo has aroused in you a taste for the urban experience, consider a day trip or an overnighter to the pleasant inland capital city of Colima. Overshadowed by the imposing, actively puffing Volcán Nevado de Colima (4240m) – 30km to the north – this attractive (and growing) city is graced by lively plazas and several noteworthy examples of preserved colonial buildings. Standing proud over the heart of the city and Plaza Principal, the **cathedral** (Santa Iglesia) dates back to 1527 but was rebuilt in the original style after a cataclysmic 1941 earthquake. Next to the cathedral is the **Palacio de Gobierno**, built between 1884 and 1904, which also houses a small tourism office. Local artist Jorge Chávez Carrillo painted the murals on the stairway to celebrate the 200th anniversary of the birth of independence hero Miguel Hidalgo y Costilla (p23), who was once parish priest of Colima. The murals depict Mexican history from the Spanish conquest to independence. There's also a **museum** (admission free; ⏰ 10am-6pm Tue-Sun) with engrossing painting, currency and arms exhibits.

Equally edifying is the **Museo Regional de Historia de Colima** (☎ 312-312-92-28; Portal Morelos 1; admission M$37; ⏰ 9am-6pm Tue-Sat, 5-8pm Sun), displaying an excellent collection of ceramic vessels and figurines and an impressive reconstruction of a shaft tomb, and the must-see **University Museum of Popular Arts** (☎ 312-312-68-69; cnr Barreda & Gallardo; admission M$10, free Sun; ⏰ 10am-2pm & 5-8pm Tue-Sat, 10am-1pm Sun), about 1km north of Plaza Principal. On display are folk-art exhibits from Colima and other states, with a particularly grand collection of costumes and masks used in traditional Colima dances.

Spend the night in style at **Hotel Ceballos** (☎ 312-316-01-00; www.hotelceballos.com; Portal Medellín 12; r from M$1300; ⓟ ⊠ ⓛ ⓡ), a stately five-star hotel on the north side of Plaza Principal, or more economically at one of the good, modern rooms at **Hotel Buena Aventura** (☎ 136-12-46; Juarez 70; d from M$350; ⓟ ⊠).

No visit to Colima is complete without visiting the volcano, which has erupted dozens of times in the past four centuries and as recently as June 2005. A visit to the **Parque Nacional Volcán Nevado de Colima**, 87km from Colima on roads of varying quality, will get you up close and personal. Bring your hiking boots to enjoy the well-tended trails. The easiest way to make the trip is with a tour operator such as **Colima Magic** (☎ 312-310-74-83; www.colimamagic .com; tours M$750-1200).

Colima is 45km from the coast, but quite a bit cooler and less humid. Getting there by car or bus from Manzanillo is a breeze. It's about an hour's drive on the four-lane Hwy 54; 20 1st-class buses make the journey daily from Manzanillo's Central Camionera.

ASK A LOCAL: THE BEST DIVING & SNORKELING SPOTS IN MANZANILLO

A very calm, extremely nice place to go is **Carrisales**. It's very pretty and tranquil with rock coral, manta rays, spotted grunts and moray eels. In season – from about November through February – you can see humpback and gray whales here. And, while it's only accessible by boat, this is a good snorkeling spot as well, as the depth ranges from 3m to 30m (9ft to 100ft).

Another good dive is called **Orejas del Caballo** (Ears of the Horse). This advanced dive is only accessible by boat, and takes you to 18m to 30m (60ft to 100ft). It is known for its eagle rays and the unusual abundance of local fauna.

At **Roca del Elefante** (Elephant Rock), you get pretty much the same flora and fauna as at Carrisales, but it's closer – though you still have to take a boat – and is still a good snorkel spot.

And snorkelers won't want to miss the **Shipwreck at Playa La Boquita**. To get here, go to Club Santiago, on the side road to Playa La Boquita. From there, you hit a dirt road and a series of good restaurants. The old freighter that sunk in 1959 is about 100m out to sea.

Jorge Sosa is owner of Neptune's Dive College (p155)

Hotel Anita (Map p155; ☎ 333-01-61; Playa Santiago s/n; d M$430, tr M$530-800) Even though it's run-down, we still love this budget spot on Playa Santiago. It's nothing spectacular, but most of the 36 large, faded rooms have ocean views, and some even have balconies. And the ramshackle styling somehow just works: a welcome anachronism in a town hell-bent on modernization.

Hotel Villas La Audiencia (Map p155; ☎ 333-08-61; www.villaslaaudiencia.com.mx; Península de Santiago; r/villas from M$837/1289 [P] [X] [图] [图]) Near Playa Audiencia, but a bit far from the beach, this moderately priced hotel has seen better days, but is still a good value, especially for families. All the villas come with a kitchen, air-con and satellite TV.

Hotel La Posada (Map p155; ☎ 333-18-99; www.hotel-la-posada.info; Cárdenas 201; s/d with continental breakfast M$580/790; [P] [图]) Right on the beach, this friendly, passionate-pink posada has spacious rooms with Mexican architectural touches. There's a breezy, well-appointed common area ideal for reading a book or chatting with the amiable staff.

TOP END

Most of Manzanillo's upmarket hotels are on or near the beaches outside the city center. Many sprawl along the beach side of the main road near Playa Azul. The 'rack rate' listed in these reviews is easily improved by booking online.

Hotel Brisas del Mar (Map p155; ☎ 334-11-97; www.brisasdelmarmanzanillo.com; Playa Las Brisas; s/d/ste M$1500/1595/2160; [P] [X] [图] [图]) A sprawling white complex with a long arching stretch of beach at its doorstep, Brisas del Mar

recently underwent a renovation, and is trying in earnest to go upmarket. It's not quite there, but the sleek rooms, decked out in all-white modern-deco decor, are a good starting point, though they could be a bit cleaner given the price. Three pools, including an adults-only infinity pool, add to the hotel's appeal.

Hotel Tesoro (Map p155; ☎ 331-22-00; www.tesororesorts.com; Av de la Audiencia 1, Playa La Audiencia; all-inclusive d from M$2400; [P] [X] [图] [图] [图] [图]) This blindingly white, sterile hotel is beautifully situated above Playa La Audiencia. It's not ultraluxurious, but is pleasant enough for most vacationers. And with pools and activities aplenty, it's a good family place.

Barceló Karmina Palace (Map p155; ☎ 331-13-00; www.barcelo.com; Vista Hermosa 13; all-inclusive per person M$1750; [P] [X] [图] [图] [图] [图]) Conceived to evoke Mayan pyramids, the architecture of this posh 324-unit all-inclusive hotel is unintentionally silly – the Maya lived nowhere near here, after all – but after a day or two in your deluxe suite, you may come to appreciate it. The amenities are extravagant, from the his-and-hers black-marble sinks in the swanky bathrooms to the eight connected swimming pools. Youngsters dig the kids' club so much that you may not see them for the rest of your vacation.

Brisas Las Hadas Golf Resort & Marina (Map p155; ☎ 331-01-01; www.brisas.com.mx; Vista Hermosa s/n, Playa La Audiencia; r from M$3000, ste M$5500-6500; [P] [X] [图] [图] [图]) This resort sits like a Moroccan kingdom, so bright and white you'll need sunglasses just walking around. Las Hadas has a choice of 232 spacious rooms and suites with marble floors, all-white furnishings and plentiful amenities; some even have their own private pool. Hard-core film buffs may know this is where the Bo Derek film *10* was made. There's also a golf course. And two very good restaurants, which are open to the public.

Eating

CENTRAL MANZANILLO

The best budget eats are found in the downtown area.

Market-Style Dining Hall (Map p156; cnr Madero & Cuauhtémoc; mains M$20-50; ⏰ 7am-6pm) This spot has a number of inexpensive food stalls to choose from.

Restaurant Emperador (Map p156; ☎ 332-23-74; Dávalos 69; mains M$20-50) Good, cheap and simple, this intimate ground-floor restaurant in the Hotel Emperador is popular with locals and budget travelers. Highlights here are the set breakfasts and the meat-and-seafood *comida corrida* (set-price lunch or dinner menu).

Restaurante Chantilly (Map p156; ☎ 332-01-94; Juárez 44; mains M$30-99; ⏰ 7:30am-10:30pm) This crowded *cafetería* and *nievería* (ice creamery) has reasonably priced meals and snacks, plus a generous *comida corrida*, genuine espresso and good ice cream.

Los Candiles (Map p156; ☎ 332-10-80; Bocanegra 100; mains M$40-110; ⏰ 10am-11pm) Hotel Colonial's restaurant opens onto a pleasant patio, features surf-and-turf fare and has a full bar; sports dominates the satellite TV.

ZONA HOTELERA

Upscale eateries – and a few fast-food chains – sit on either side of Hwy 200 as it passes through the Zona Hotelera.

Café Costeño (Map p155; ☎ 333-94-60; Lázaro Cárdenas 1613, Playa Las Brisas; mains M$30-45; ⏰ 9am-2pm & 5-10:30pm Mon-Sat, 5-10:30pm Sun) This friendly café with a chilled-out garden patio offers great breakfasts – French toast, hotcakes and omelets are cheerfully served along with its espresso and cappuccino – and decent light snacks like tacos and quesadillas for dinner.

Carnes y Tacos Julio (Map p155; ☎ 334-00-36; Hwy 200, Km 14.3; Playa Olas Altas; mains M$30-125; ⏰ 8am-midnight) Savory grilled meat is the specialty at this lively place, but breakfast, pasta and other tourist-friendly fare won't disappoint.

Restaurant Las Margaritas (Map p155; ☎ 333-25-40, ext 67; Hwy 200, Km 15.5; Playa Miramar; mains M$60-145; ⏰ 8am-10pm) Sitting on a rocky promontory above Playa Miramar, this tourist-oriented restaurant has a great list of international and local dishes – there's basically an option for everyone. Amazing sunset views and courteous service add to the appeal.

Vaquero Campestre (Map p155; ☎ 334-14-48; Playa La Audiencia; mains M$80-155; ⏰ 2-10:30pm Tue-Sat) Near Las Palmas, this place serves pitchers of margaritas and sangria to help lubricate those servings of grilled beef and seafood. *Palapa* roofs and a few animal heads and skins surround diners.

Porto Fino (Map p155; ☎ 333-13-33; Hwy 200 No 923; Playa Azul; mains M$80-185; ⏰ 2pm-midnight Tue-Sun) Arguably the best Italian joint on the strip, this beachfront eatery has a rustic Italian feel with checked tablecloths and warm lighting. The menu features all the usual suspects, plus a few welcome additions like a salmon fillet in Chianti sauce.

El Faro de Alejandría (Map p155; ☎ 333-77-48; Hwy 200 No 865; Playa Azul; mains M$85-260; ⏰ 1pm-1am) One of the more upscale joints in town, El Faro specializes in international fare, with a smorgasbord of pasta dishes on offer. It offers live music on the weekends, and good ocean views.

Entertainment

If you're in town on a Sunday evening, stop by the *zócalo*, where multiple generations come out to enjoy an ice cream and the warm evening air. On the most atmospheric of nights, a band belts out traditional music from the gazebo, and every night around sunset you can hear the cacophony of the resident *zanates* (blackbirds), a regular bomb squad – don't stand under any electrical wire for too long. And be sure to check out the *golondrinas* (swallows) perching on the wires later in the evening; it's eerily reminiscent of the Hitchcock classic *The Birds*.

Behind the doors of **Bar Social** (Map p156; cnr Calle 21 de Marzo & Juárez; ⏰ noon-midnight Mon-Sat) is a world frozen in the past; it's not scary, but it is odd.

Tourist nightlife starts in Playa Azul, with theme discos like **Vog** (Map p155; ☎ 333-18-75; Hwy 200, Km 9.2; cover women/men M$100/150; ⏰ Fri & Sat night) and **Nautilus** (Map p155; ☎ 334-33-31; Hwy 200, Km 9.5; cover M$150; ⏰ Fri & Sat night), and continues northwest around the bay. Near Hotel Fiesta Mexicana, **Stragos** (Map p155; ☎ 333-19-90; Hwy 200, Km 8.5) offers live music and dancing.

Near Vaquero Campestre, **Hacienda Gaucho** (Map p155; ☎ 334-19-69; Playa Santiago) features *carne asada* (grilled beef) and dance music. On Playa Miramar, **Club Maeva** (Map p155;

(☎ 331-08-00) houses Disco Boom Boom and the casual Solarium Bar, which has a pool table; phone for reservations.

Getting There & Away

AIR

Playa de Oro International Airport lies between a long and secluded white-sand beach and tropical groves of bananas and coconut, 35km northwest of Manzanillo's Zona Hotelera on Hwy 200.

Alaska Airlines (☎ in the US 800-252-7522; www .alaskaair.com) Direct service to Los Angeles.

Continental (☎ in the US 800-523-3273; www .continental.com) Direct service to Houston.

US Airways (☎ in the US 800-428-4322; www.usair ways.com) Direct service from Phoenix.

For direct service to Mexico City:
Aeroméxico (☎ 800-021-4010; www.aeromexico.com)
Mexicana (☎ 800-801-2010; www.mexicana.com)

BUS

Manzanillo's new, airportlike, full-service Central Camionera (Map p155) is northwest of the center near Playa Las Brisas, just off Blvd Miguel de la Madrid (Hwy 200). It's an organized place with two tourist offices, phones, eateries and left luggage. There are several daily departures:

Armería (M$30, 45 minutes, 2nd-class services at least hourly)

Barra de Navidad (M$44, one to 1½ hours, three 1st-class; M$50, one to 1½ hours, 10 2nd-class)

Colima (M$50, 1½ to two hours, 20 1st-class)

Guadalajara (M$202, 4½ to eight hours, frequent 1st-class services; M$140 to M$180, 4½ to eight hours, 19 2nd-class)

Lázaro Cárdenas (M$202, six hours, 1st-class at 2am & 6am; M$170, six hours, four 2nd-class)

Mexico City (M$667, 12 hours, four 1st-class; M$550, four 2nd-class) To Terminal Norte.

Puerto Vallarta (M$197, five to 6½ hours, four 1st-class; M$180, five to 6½ hours, 10 2nd-class)

San Patricio-Melaque (M$44 to M$50, one to 1½ hours) Same services as to Barra de Navidad.

ETN (☎ 334-10-50; www.etn.com.mx, in Spanish) offers deluxe and 1st-class service to Barra de Navidad (M$66, one to 1½ hours, three daily), Colima (M$85, 1½ to two hours, seven daily) and Guadalajara (M$310, seven daily) from its own bus station near Santiago at Hwy 200, Km 13.5. ETN also offers daily service to the international airport in Guadalajara (M$310).

Getting Around

There is no local or regional bus service to or from Playa de Oro airport. Most resorts have shuttle vans. **Transportes Turísticos Benito Juárez** (☎ 334-15-55) shuttles door-to-door to/from the airport. The fare is M$300 for private service (one or two people) or M$80 per person when three or more people share the ride. A taxi from the airport to Manzanillo's center or most resort hotels costs around M$300.

Local buses heading around the bay to San Pedrito, Salahua, Santiago, Miramar and beaches along the way depart every 10 minutes from 6am to 11pm from the corner of Madero and Domínguez, from Calle 21 de Marzo near the *zócalo*, from the roundabout on Niños Héroes and Azueta, and from the Central Camionera. Fares (pay the driver as you board) are M$5, depending on how far you're going.

Taxis are plentiful in Manzanillo. From the bus station buy a prepaid ticket for a *taxi colectivo* to ensure the best price. Taxis from the Zona Hotelera to the center cost around M$35, from Playas Santiago and Audiencia they cost around M$40. Be sure to agree on a price before you get in.

CUYUTLÁN & EL PARAÍSO
☎ 313

The laid-back black-sand-beach resort towns of Cuyutlán and El Paraíso are popular with Mexicans but see very few tourists. Gentle waves and fun-in-the-sun activities, such as swimming, people-watching and boogie-boarding, can be savored on or about the charcoal-colored sands. Cuyutlán has a better selection of hotels, but the beach is less crowded and more tranquil in El Paraíso.

Orientation & Information

Cuyutlán is at the southeastern end of Laguna de Cuyutlán, 40km southeast of Manzanillo and 12km west of Armería. Sleepy El Paraíso is 6km southeast of Cuyutlán along the coast, but 12km by road.

Cuyutlán has a post office (El Paraíso does not), but neither town has a bank; for this you'll have to visit Armería. Both towns have public telephones and long-distance *casetas* near their *zócalos*.

The beachfront accommodations here are cheaper than they are at other coastal resorts. The high season is Christmas and Semana

---

DETOUR: EL SALTO FALLS & SIERRA DE MANANTLÁN BIOSPHERE

While it seems incredible, some people actually grow weary of gorgeous sandy beaches and crystalline ocean waters. For them, an excursion to the cool cascades of El Salto waterfall and the highland cloud forests of Manantlán Biosphere provides a lovely respite from the insufferable pressures of beach life.

The one-hour drive from Manzanillo to El Salto on Hwy 98 takes you over meandering mountain roads through dense tropical deciduous forest and a few typical small villages. You'll pass by the Peña Colorada strip mine at the top of a mountain and the 27km blue pipeline used to move iron ore all the way back to the outskirts of Manzanillo.

One kilometer past the company town where the miners live is the entrance to **El Salto Park** (admission M$10). Beyond the gate, you'll find a new-fangled picnic area and water park with three spring-fed pools and an impressive water slide. Just down the road, across an iron bridge, is a nicer spot to lunch overlooking the falls, which cascade over two 10m steps into a series of inviting pools. Descend the stone steps and jump in! From the base of the falls, it's possible to float 100m downstream on your back beneath the canyon walls to where there's a beach of sorts. On weekends hungry masses devour tacos from a simple stand, but the rest of the week you'll likely have the place to yourself (and have to rely on the contents of your picnic basket). Overnight camping is allowed.

Back on the road, continue north 5km to the pleasant town of Minatitlán, which supports a good, traditional restaurant called La Herradura. Another 16km brings you to the entrance of **Manantlán Biosphere** (☎ 317-381-01-54, in Spanish), an ecological reserve that gives refuge to more than 2900 plant species, half of which are endemic. A very bumpy but navigable road ascends 16km through exceptionally scenic territory to the 2700m summit and the small indigenous ranchito of **El Terrero**. Here you can spend the night in a rustic cabin shelter or at a shady campground with picnic tables, potable water and an outhouse. Even if there are no other people around, you may not be camping alone – the biosphere is home to a staggering 588 vertebrate animals including ocelots, pumas, boa constrictors, jaguars and lynxes. If this unnerves you, see if you can't get your hands on some locally brewed *pulque* (an ancient form of fermented agave) to calm your nerves.

If you've developed a taste for adventure, the road that brought you to El Terrero continues down the other side of the mountain into more unspoiled territory uncharted by this or any other guidebook.

Your journey begins in Manzanillo at the traffic circle near Km 4 on the main highway, where the highway to Minatitlán peels off to the north. From here it's 48km to El Salto and another 16km to the entrance of Manantlán Biosphere (keep an eagle eye out for the sign reading 'Estación Biosfera'). You'll travel another slow 16km on bumpy roads to El Terrero. Departing from Manzanillo's Central Camionera (main bus station), 2nd-class buses bound for Minatitlán will drop you at El Salto, but you'll need a car to make it to El Terrero.

Santa (Holy Week), when Cuyutlán's hotels are booked solid by Mexican families.

Getting There & Away

Cuyutlán and Paraíso are connected to the rest of the world through Armería, a dusty but friendly little service center on Hwy 200, 46km southeast of Manzanillo and 55km southwest of Colima. From Armería, a 12km paved road heads west to Cuyutlán; a similar road runs 8km southwest from Armería to El Paraíso.

To reach either place by bus involves a transfer in Armería. Two bus lines – Sociedad Cooperativa de Autotransportes Colima Manzanillo and Autotransportes Nuevo Horizonte – have offices and stops just off Armería's main street. They both operate 2nd-class buses to Manzanillo every 15 minutes from 6am to midnight (M$30, 45 minutes) and to Colima every half-hour from 5:45am to 10:30pm (M$31, 45 minutes). Buses go every 20 minutes to Tecomán (M$10, 15 minutes), where you can connect with buses heading southeast on Hwy 200 to Lázaro Cárdenas and elsewhere.

Buses to Cuyutlán and El Paraíso depart from Armería's market, one block north and one block east of the long-distance bus depots. To Cuyutlán, they depart every half hour from 6am to 7:30pm (M$8.50, 20 minutes). To El Paraíso, they go every 45 minutes (M$8, 15 minutes).

No buses shuttle directly between Cuyutlán and El Paraíso. To go by bus, you must return to Armería and change buses again. However, you can take a boat from the Centro Tortuguero (below) between the hours of 9am and 4:30pm; the scenic 45-minute trip through the Palo Verde estuary costs M$65 per person.

Cuyutlán
pop 926

The long stretch of fine-grained, black-sand beach here attracts Mexican vacationers like bears to honey. Rickety wooden paths make walking the hot black sands tolerable, there are plenty of seaside restaurants, and hundreds of colorful, rentable beach chairs and umbrellas keep the scorching sun off.

Cuyutlán is known for its **ola verde** (green wave), which appears just offshore in April and May. It's supposedly caused by little green phosphorescent critters, but it's the subject of much local debate.

Don't miss the **Centro Tortuguero** (☎ 328-86-76; adult/child M$25/20; ☼ 10am-4pm winter, 10am-6pm summer, closed Wed; ⚲), about 4km toward Paraíso. This ecological center, founded in 1993, has incubated and released 500,000 baby sea turtles into the sea. On display are various small pools containing many of the endearing reptiles as well as some crocodile and iguana enclosures. Guides speak English, and there are educational talks almost hourly. Bring your swimsuit if you want to splash in the pool.

Lagoon trips lasting 40 minutes on the **Palo Verde estuary** – featuring passage through a mangrove 'tunnel' – leave from the Centro Tortuguero and cost M$40 per person. You can also take a boat from here to El Paraíso (see right). Get there by car or taxi, or walk 4km southeast along the beach.

SLEEPING & EATING

You can camp on the empty sands on either side of the hotels. Several of the beachfront *enramadas* rent showers. Most hotels have decent restaurants, and some even require meal plans. Other than that, head to the beachfront restaurants and snack stands for fresh seafood and cold drinks. Or grab a snack at one of the simpler places near the *zócalo*.

Hotel Morelos (☎ 326-40-13; Hidalgo 185 at Veracruz; r per person with 3 meals M$360; ⚲) Just a block from the beach, this simple hotel has moderately clean rooms and a pool. The enthusiastically decorated restaurant (open 7am to 10pm) offers a M$50 *comida corrida* that's worth a try. In the high season, it only offers the three-meal plan. In low season, you can negotiate a much better deal.

Hotel María Victoria (☎ 326-40-04; mvcuyutlan@hot mail.com; Veracruz 10; s/d/tr/q M$468/500/680/800; ℗ ⚲) This beachfront hotel has a giant spacecraft-inspired structure in the airy lobby – see it for yourself. The rooms are somewhat dirty, but you get ocean views from some, and the restaurant serves fresh typical Mexican fare at high-roller prices.

Hotel San Rafael (☎ 326-40-15; Veracruz 46; r per person with 2 meals M$450; ⚲) Offering the cleanest rooms in a town that has an obvious hygiene problem, the San Rafael is your best budget bet. Adding to the allure are a pleasant swimming pool and a good beachfront restaurant and bar.

El Paraíso
pop 189

As the crow flies, the small, rustic fishing village of El Paraíso is just 6km southeast of Cuyutlán, but by road it's more like 12km. Like its larger neighbor, it harbors a fine, salt-and-pepper beach that attracts mostly Mexican families. Unlike its larger neighbor, there are fewer decent places to stay, which makes for a less crowded and more tranquil beach. An unending line of seafood restaurants sits on the sands.

The nicest hotel in town, **Hotel Paraíso** (☎ 322-43-05; www.portaldearmeria.com, in Spanish; r M$350-425; ℗ ⚲) has 60 decent rooms and is to the left of the T-junction at the entrance to town. Ask for a new room. Otherwise, you can camp on the beach or string up a hammock at one of El Paraíso's beachfront *palapas*. All the *palapas* serve basically the same food at similar prices; expect to spend M$50 to M$100 per person for a full, fresh meal.

PLAYA BOCA DE PASCUALES
☎ 313 / pop 58

Playa Boca de Pascuales, 3km south of El Paraíso, is a legendary surf spot where aggressive, surfable barrel swells ranging from 2m to 5m in height arrive in the summer season. This is a heavy beach break, and if you're a neophyte surfer, don't try your luck. But Pascuales isn't just for surfers. With a chilled-out air and a groovalicious scene, nonsurfers will also enjoy a few days of watching the waves crash and soaking in the 'dudetastic' atmosphere.

Otherwise known as Edgar's Place, **Hotel Real de Pascuales** (☎ 133-18-32-53; www.pascualessurf .com.mx, in Spanish; r M$300-400, camping M$30; ⚡) is the local surfing nexus. Proprietor Edgar Álvarez welcomes surfers from all over the world and fixes their boards when they get munched. You can also buy new boards here. Everyone calls each other 'bro' at Edgar's, where the rooms are Spartan to the extreme. But that's the way the 'bros' seem to like it. 'Non-bros' will enjoy the rooms with air-con, wi-fi and ocean-view balconies.

To get to Pascuales, travel first to the town of Tecomán, 3km south of Cuyutlán. If driving, follow the sign from downtown about 10km to the beach. Taxis or *combis* provide transportation from Tecomán to Pascuales.

MICHOACÁN

This lost coast remains wild and unspoiled, and intrepid travelers may feel as if they discovered the place. Mango, coconut, papaya and banana plantations line the highway, while the Sierra Madre del Sur mountains form a verdant backdrop to this lost ribbon of coastline. There are few tourists and only a smattering of down-at-heel accommodations, but there are plenty of campsites to choose from, and an 'authentic' air that reminds you of what the rest of the Pacific coast must have looked like before Señor Frog's and Carlos & Charlies took over.

The Purépecha people (also known as the Tarascos) have lived in the state of Michoacán for more than a thousand years. And a fly-by-the-seat-of-your-pants journey to the interior may take you to Purépecha enclaves, the enchanting capital city of Morelia and a smattering of pre-Colombian ruins. On the coast, there is a handful of Nahua communities.

BOCA DE APIZA
☎ 313 / pop 225
Near the Michoacán-Colima border, at the mouth of the Río Coahuayana, basks this dusty little fishing town lined with egret-filled mangrove lagoons. A 300m line of competing

seafood *enramadas* crowd the beach. To get to Boca de Apiza, turn off Hwy 200 at the town of Coahuayana (Km 228) and continue about 4km to the beach.

There's another side to Boca de Apiza, literally. Across the river (and across the Michoacán-Colima border) is where Mexican families have built many *palapa* shelters for Sunday picnics. Here a long beach heads northward, with a sandy access road going inland 6.5km to meet up with the highway. There are no services here, so bring your own supplies.

Thinking about sticking around? Try **Hotel Solar** (☎ 329-96-24; r M$150), a roughish place at the entrance to town. Just down the road, Hotel Vero offers equally disenchanting digs.

SAN JUAN DE ALIMA
☎ 313
About 20km south of Boca de Apiza, near where the highway meets the coast, lie the concrete bumps of San Juan de Alima (Km 211). It's a town still defining itself: half-finished constructions attest to continuing growth. However, there are reasons to come: plenty of hotels, small stores and beachfront restaurants service the tourists and are spread out along the coast where creamy breakers curl and fall. Be careful of swimming out too far, though, where heavier currents lurk.

Sleeping & Eating
The restaurants you want to eat at are on the beach, and they're just like the ones up and down the rest of the coast, so don't expect any surprises.

OUR FAVORITE BEACHES ON THE MICHOACÁN COAST

Adventurers looking for desolate expanses of golden sand and mostly undeveloped coastal towns will discover them all here along the scenic 250km coast of Michoacán. Kilometer markers begin counting down from Km 231 at the state border with Colima.

Plenty of Michoacán's coves and beaches are not listed in this or any guidebook. Have fun finding them on your own.

■ **Playa La Ticla** (Km 183; below) is a good surfing spot with beachfront *cabañas* for rent.

■ **Faro de Bucerías** (Km 173; opposite) is known for its clear, pale-blue waters, yellow sand and rocky islands. It's a good spot for camping, swimming and snorkeling, and the local Nahua community prepares fresh seafood.

■ **Playa Maruata** (Km 150; opposite) is one of Michoacán's most beautiful beaches, with white sands and clear turquoise waters. This is the principal Mexican beach where black sea turtles lay their eggs.

Hotel Coral (☎ 328-80-06; d/tr beds M$150/250) This pepto-pink option has worn, comfortable rooms. The otherwise-empty ground floor is marked by supporting pillars, giving a somewhat bleak, tidal-wave-ready feel to the whole place. Small pink rooms greet you up the concrete stairs.

Hotel Villas de San Juan (☎ 327-90-64; r M$300) These centrally located villas to the right of the town entrance are painted an indescribable shade of blue. Inside the high wing, there are super-clean sea-view rooms, making this the best deal in town. Bungalows with kitchens may be available.

Hotel San Juan (☎ 327-90-11; hotelsanjuan1@hot mail.com; r with/without air-con M$500/450; 🏊) To the right of the town's entrance, this hotel is well overpriced considering the beds don't have top-sheets and toilets don't have seats. But it's relatively clean, and you get air-con and TV in most rooms. The *palapa* restaurant with well-made fare is watched over by rowdy parrots.

Hotel Hacienda (☎ 327-92-00; www.hotelhacien datrinidad.com.mx, in Spanish; r M$2100; 🏊) San Juan de Alima's only upscale offering, the Hacienda has decent rooms and the best pool in town. The high-season prices are ridiculous, but you can get decent deals the rest of the year. The restaurant is one of the nicest in town.

LAS BRISAS

The road south from San Juan de Alima affords one tremendous scenic overlook where visitors can survey desolate sandy beaches as far as the eye can see. The tiny community of Las Brisas, 1.5km down a dirt road from the

highway (Km 204), is accented by just a few *palapa* restaurants and one big-ass, incongruous midrange hotel – the only solid building on the beach. It's very peaceful, with swaying palms and a long, wide, flat beach with fine, firm dark sand. The wind tends to kick up (as the name implies) and a nice bird-filled lagoon is nearby. Camping and RV parking (no hookups) are exceptionally pleasant here. To get here by bus, travel first to La Placita and then commandeer a taxi.

Unless you camp, you'll be staying at the moderately priced **Hotel Brisas del Verano** (☎ 313-327-90-55; s/d M$600/900; 🅿 🏊 🐾), where 30 large, modern and thoughtfully appointed rooms are on offer with cable TV and air-con. While there's some paint chipping, this hotel ain't bad at all, and you get a crystal-clear pool, clean rooms and uber-friendly service.

LA PLACITA

Here's a cute little highway town (Km 199) with a leafy plaza and surrounding *comedores* (inexpensive restaurants) and, if you're going south, the last Pemex gas station until Caleta de Campos, about 150km away. Fill up here, and if you can't find a roof to sleep under in nearby Playa La Ticla (below), try Hotel Reyna, a basic cheapie near the highway.

PLAYA LA TICLA

At Km 186 a newly paved road peels off and leads over a hill and down to Playa La Ticla, another prime surfing destination. In the early morning, calm seas near the shore give birth to curving arcs of gorgeous, misty-edged waves, simply beautiful to watch – but even better to ride. Head over to the river mouth for the best waves. The quaint pueblo of La Ticla, hiding behind a small coastal mountain, draws mostly foreign surfers with their own vehicles. They also bring their own boards and camping equipment, since beach services are fairly undeveloped and the quiet little town isn't yet geared toward tourism of any sort. A nearby palm-ringed lagoon provides bird-watching possibilities, salt-free swimming and a variation in landscape.

You can camp (per person M$20) under flimsy *palapa* shelters at the northern edge of town. Your other option is **Parador Turístico La Ticla** (☎ 424-488-00-24; www.playaticla.com; r M$800, cabañas M$1800-2000), offering well-kept, thatch-roofed *cabañas* on stilts, some of which sleep up to 10 people, making this an affordable spot for larger groups. If you snag a tiny room, don't expect much privacy or peace: the ceiling is shared and your neighbors will be young surfers, dude, so bring earplugs. Perhaps the interesting burning smells in the air will aid entry into a dreamlike state.

Restaurant Serrano (mains M$30-80), nearest the lagoon's mouth, is popular for breakfast and seafood. You can camp for free if you eat there often enough.

You have a choice of two paved roads that lead to Playa La Ticla, at Km 183 or 186. Don't forget sunscreen and insect repellent.

FARO DE BUCERÍAS

About 2km down a paved road at Km 173 lies a calm cove, which has decent snorkeling and is wonderful for swimming. Known for its clear, pale-blue waters, soft yellow sand and rocky islands, Faro de Bucerías is also good for camping and having a spot of lunch with the Nahua community. A picturesque square red-and-white lighthouse sits high up on the hill, and there's some good tide-pooling behind the lofty restaurant Palapa Miramar – just be careful getting around the

rocky point, and never turn your back on those ocean waves.

The only hotel in town is **El Parador Turístico** (r M$300-500, camping per person M$40). Run by the local Nahua community, this beachfront joint offers three simple, clean rooms and camping under well-crafted *palapas*. There's no air-con, but you get fans and a good ocean breeze.

There are a number of open-air seafood restaurants; lobsters are plentiful, well priced and beautifully prepared here.

PLAYA MARUATA

About 1km west of Km 150, past the town's bleak plaza, lies this paradise for beach lovers and rustic campers. Playa Maruata is three beaches in one: two climbable rocky heads, riddled with small caves and tunnels, separate three white-sand crescents. Each has a different size and character: the one on the right (northernmost) is about 1km long and has the roughest waters (don't try swimming here); the middle arc is more intimate and OK for strong swimmers; the one on the left is 3km long and decorated with fishing boats and is where most camping shelters and their snack sheds lie. There are also shallow, palm-ringed lagoons to explore, often visited by vultures looking for fish scraps (you can get mighty close to the birds on the ground). Two simple *palapa* restaurants and some camping shelters dot the varied landscape, but there are very few concrete structures. It's a pleasant and tranquil place to hang out with your sweetie or a large stack of paperbacks.

Playa Maruata is also the principal Mexican beach where black sea turtles lay their eggs – from June to December they come ashore nightly. Hatchlings of these and other species of sea turtles are set free here each year by conservation programs.

Camping shelters are all pretty much the same and most charge M$20 to M$25 per

JALISCO, COLIMA & MICHOACÁN COASTS

HIGHWAY 200, MICHOACÁN STYLE

Be prepared for some slower driving along the stretch of coast from Km 74 to Km 134, somewhere between Barra de Nexpa and Faro de Bucerías. This area isn't the highest priority for Mexican highway funds, and the road is mostly curvy with some minor rough spots. Give yourself a couple more hours of daylight to cover this stretch, and make sure your vehicle is full of gas: there are no Pemex stations between La Placita (Km 199) and Caleta de Campos (Km 50), though you'll pass dinky little towns where signs may offer a few liters for sale. Also, don't expect much solid accommodation when the sun gets low: unless you're camping, you won't run across many places to stay, though there will be a few eateries along the way.

person. You can also string up a hammock, or rent one at some shelters. Those who need four semi-solid walls can try one of the few rustic, two-bed *cabañas* for M$200 to M$300, but honestly, you're better off camping. RV drivers have several discrete spots in which to park. For simple groceries such as fruit, ramen, cereal or beer, there's a small store at the end of the southernmost beach past all the *palapa* shelters.

BARRA DE NEXPA
☎ 753 / pop 112

At Km 55.5, just north of Puente Nexpa bridge and 1km from the highway down a cobbled road, lies Barra de Nexpa. The salt 'n' pepper bar of sand here, and a good number of healthy waves – which build up and curl sharply in the mornings – bring in surfers from around the world. Rustic *cabañas*, good campsites and some decent restaurants add comfort to the mix. A laid-back feel completes the recipe for a perfectly peaceful stay.

A long point break wave curls in from the left. The longest are about 150m, and 50m waves are common. As long as there's not an organized surfing tour in town, there are enough waves for everyone. Beginners hone their chops in winter but make way for more advanced surfers when the big swells hit, from March through October. With its rocky shoreline and strong surf, Nexpa is not ideal for swimming.

Twenty minutes by foot along the river and into the mountains, the fluorescent-blue **El Troncon** waterfall makes for a refreshing hike. Engage a local guide to lead the way for a small tip.

Jorge's y Helen's Tienda (☎ 555-150-92-43; helennex@hotmail.com) rents surfboards (M$100/500 per day/week) and sells gear. It also has telephone service and internet access (M$20 per hour), and sells groceries. Pablo's Palapa, near Restaurant Chichos, repairs and sells boards. There's a larger surf shop in the nearby Caleta de Campos (right); a taxi will take you there for about M$40.

Sleeping & Eating

Río Nexpa Rooms (☎ 115-88-44; www.surf-mexico.com/sites/nexpa; d/tr/q M$350/400/450; (P)) This beautifully crafted Southeast Asian–style *palapa* about 200m inland along the river has four comfortable rooms with three full-sized beds and a loft.

It has a shared kitchen, lagoon-side garden area and tranquil communal sitting room.

Hotel Mar de Noche (☎ 118-39-31; www.nexpasurf.com; r M$800, cabaña M$1500; (P) (X)) Right at the town's entrance, this hacienda-style hotel has the swankiest rooms in town.

Villas Cheyos (☎ 110-30-93; r M$800; (P) (X)) Along with beachside bungalows, this place also offers simple rooms with air-con and TV. For the price you are better off at Mar de Noche, but this isn't a bad option.

La Isla Restaurant (mains M$30-120) This restaurant cooks up the best Western breakfasts around, with good cappuccinos and the largest fruit plate on the coast. A taxi service and a casual book exchange are available, as are rooms (M$200 to M$350).

Restaurant Chicho (mains M$35-70) Chico has tables perched just right for watching surfers cut waves nearby. The food is good, and there are basic rooms (M$250 to M$300). The owners may let you camp here.

CALETA DE CAMPOS
☎ 753 / pop 2000

A friendly town on a bluff overlooking a lovely azure bay, 'Caleta' (Km 50), also known as Bahía de Bufadero (Blowhole Bay), is a quiet place, but it has a handful of good, clean hotels and several satisfying places to eat. Caleta's paved main drag has all the essentials, including a telephone *caseta*, late-night *taquerías* (taco stalls) and *torta* shops, a pharmacy and grocery stores. The southern side of the bluff has perfect waves for novice surfers. From near Hotel Los Arcos, you can look down at the bay's namesake blowhole, but don't get too close, large waves can come up at any minute.

Just off the main drag, near Hotel Yuritzi, is **Surf y Espuma** (☎ 531-52-55; surfboard rental per day M$100), which sells and rents surf gear. It also carries surfwear, does fishing charters and washes your laundry (M$15 per kilogram).

Just 1km before the town entrance (Km 51.25), **Parador Turistico** (☎ 531-51-01; www.partourcaleta.com, in Spanish; r M$920; (X) (R)) is the best hotel in the area, offering great views out to the sea, and clean hacienda-style rooms with private porches.

A bit odiferous, but nice and clean, **Hotel Yuritzi** (☎ 531-50-10; www.hotelyuritzi.com, in Spanish; Corregidora 10; s/d with air-con M$550/650, s/d with fan M$450/500; (P) (X) (Q) (R)) counts as its customers business travelers, beach bums and families.

Hotel Los Arcos (☎ 531-50-38; r from M$300; P X) affords dramatic sea views and bright rooms. It's toward the ocean, at the end of the main drag, and is a bit run-down, but the view of Bahía de Bufadero's blowhole is brilliant.

Large, well-appointed **Villa Tropical** (☎ 531-52-55; www.caletadecampos.com; r M$500, villa M$3500) can sleep up to 12 and is thus a sweet deal. Individual rooms are also for rent if the entire villa is not rented out. The owner, who also operates Surf y Espuma, is happy to negotiate, particularly when the house is empty. The breezy roof deck with views of the lighthouse is the ultimate party nook.

Hourly buses depart Caleta for Lázaro Cárdenas from 5am to 7pm (M$49, 1½ hours). A taxi between Caleta de Campos and Barra de Nexpa costs M$40.

LAS PEÑAS

A small cove at Km 18 is home to eight *enramadas* and one wide but cozy beach, punctuated by rocky headlands. Around the southern point is a much longer beach called **Playa Dorada**, dotted with a few rustic restaurants of its own and stretching as far as you can see. No accommodations are available, but camping may be possible – ask around at Playa Dorada or just pick an isolated spot.

PLAYA AZUL

☎ 753 / pop 3000

Playa Azul is a sleepy, dusty and rather ugly beach resort backed by lagoons fed by tributaries of the Río Balsas. It's usually quiet, with a trickle of foreign travelers enjoying the long beach and surfable waves. A strong undertow makes swimming touch-and-go; swimming is better (when it's not mosquito season) at Laguna Pichi, a couple of kilometers east along the beach, where boat trips take visitors to view the plants, birds and other animals that inhabit the surrounding mangrove forest.

You can string up a hammock at most of the beachfront *enramadas*; otherwise there are a couple of reasonable hotels, all with private bathrooms, in town.

The 42 large and comfortable balconied rooms at **Hotel María Teresa** (☎ 536-00-05; www .hotelmariateresa.com, in Spanish; Independencia 626; s/d M$565/792; X ☒) are fresh and up-to-date, making this a good bang-for-your-buck option. A poolside *palapa* restaurant-bar comes with an attractive patio area. Look for this place two blocks north of the plaza.

On the far (east) side of the plaza and a bit worn around the edges, **Hotel María Isabel** (☎ 536-00-16; antoniocampos1306@hotmail.com; Madero s/n; s/d without air-con M$350/450, d with air-con M550; P X ☒) has impeccably clean and very peaceful rooms, and a slightly down-trodden pool area.

The upmarket, 73-room **Hotel Playa Azul** (☎ 536-00-88; www.michoacan-hotels.com; Carranza s/n; r with/without air-con M$1000/700, camping/RV sites M$170/200; P X ☒ ☒) has a small trailer park and enjoyable though slightly dirty rooms around a garden courtyard with an inviting pool. There's also a water slide out back (open to the public for M$20).

The *malecón* (waterfront street) is lined by informal restaurants with beachside seating. One of the most laid-back is **Yupanky** (mains M$40-100; ☽ 8am-6pm), remarkable for its utter idleness. Hammocks are strung up throughout and the sound of the pounding surf often mixes with the melancholy music of Playa Azul's elderly mariachis. The menu features seafood, of course, and there's invariably a pile of coconuts waiting to be cracked open.

Locals recommend Restaurant Galdy and Restaurant Familiar Martita, both on the market street near Madero, around the corner from Hotel Playa Azul. Both serve freshly squeezed juices and good cheap grub (*comida corrida* from M$35).

Get funky at the Oasis Disco, at the corner of the plaza and the beach, pretty much the only nightlife option in town.

Combis run every 10 minutes from 5am to 9pm between Playa Azul and Lázaro Cárdenas (M$16, 30 minutes, 24km). Taxis between Playa Azul and Lázaro Cárdenas cost around M$120.

LÁZARO CÁRDENAS

☎ 753 / pop 75,000

Industrial Lázaro isn't of interest to travelers, but it is the terminus of several bus routes, so some travelers may end up stranded here for the night. Once here, you can change buses, stock up on provisions and head 24km west to Playa Azul (left). If you must spend the night, several adequate hotels are near the bus stations.

Hotel Reyna Pio (☎ 532-06-20; Corregidora 78; s/d M$290/350; X) is a good, friendly budget hotel with clean, spacious rooms. It's on the corner of Av 8 de Mayo, a block west of Av Lázaro Cárdenas, near the bus terminals.

Hotel Casablanca (☎ 537-34-80; www.hcasablanca.com.mx, in Spanish; Nicolás Bravo 475; s/d/tr/ste M$600/760/832/1080; [P] [🗙] [🖳] [🖳]) has air-con, TV, a pool with a Jacuzzi and secure parking. The 56 modern rooms with balconies and wide windows overlook the city or inland mountains. Look for this high-rise a block east of Av Lázaro Cárdenas.

Many cheap restaurants cluster around the bus terminals. Locals recommend **Restaurant El Tejado** (Lázaro Cárdenas s/n; mains M$45-100), between Corregidora and Javier Mina, for meats, seafood, six styles of frogs' legs and four pages of drinks.

Getting There & Away

Lázaro has four bus terminals, all a few blocks from each other. **Galeana** (☎ 532-02-62) and **Parhikuni** (☎ 532-30-06), with services northwest to Manzanillo and inland to Uruapan and Morelia, share a **terminal** (Lázaro Cárdenas 1810 at Constitución de 1814). Opposite, Autovias, La Línea, Omnibus and Sur de Jalisco share another **terminal** (☎ 537-18-50; Lázaro Cárdenas 1791) and serve the same destinations, plus Colima, Guadalajara and Mexico City.

The terminal for **Estrella Blanca** (EB; ☎ 532-11-71; Francisco Villa 65) is also the home base for Cuauhtémoc and Elite. From here buses head southeast to Zihuatanejo and Acapulco; up the coast to Manzanillo, Mazatlán and Tijuana; and inland to Uruapan, Morelia and Mexico City. The **Estrella de Oro terminal** (☎ 532-02-75; Corregidora 318) serves Acapulco, Cuernavaca, Mexico City and Zihuatanejo.

Daily buses from Lázaro Cárdenas:

Acapulco EB (M$200, six to seven hours, 12 1st-class); M$170, six to seven hours, hourly 2nd-class); Estrella de Oro (M$200, six to seven hours, three 1st-class; M$160, six to seven hours, 11 2nd-class)

Caleta de Campos Galeana (M$49, 1½ hours, 10 2nd-class); Sur de Jalisco (M$49, 1½ hours, four 2nd-class)

Colima Autobuses de Jalisco (M$194, four to 6½ hours) Same buses as to Guadalajara.

Guadalajara Autobuses de Jalisco (M$446, nine to 11 hours, five 1st-class); Sur de Jalisco (M$300, nine to 11 hours, four 2nd-class)

Manzanillo Elite (M$202, seven hours, four 1st-class); Galeana (M$180, six to seven hours, four 2nd-class); Autobuses de Jalisco (M$270, six to seven hours, 2nd-class at 2:30pm and 5:30pm)

Mexico City Vía Plus (M$500, 12 hours, five 1st-class); Futura (M$500, five 1st-class); Estrella de Oro (M$490, two 1st-class) To Terminal Sur.

Morelia Futura (M$347, four to eight hours, five 1st-class); Parhikuni 'Plus' (M$347, four to eight hours, one executive; M$300, 14 2nd-class); Futura (M$300, four to eight hours, five 1st-class)

Puerto Vallarta (M$370, 12 hours, four 1st-class Elite)

Uruapan (M$150, three to six hours) Same buses as to Morelia.

Zihuatanejo (M$68, two to three hours) Same buses as to Acapulco.

Combis to Playa Azul via La Mira trawl Av Lázaro Cárdenas every 10 minutes from 5am to 9pm (M$16, 30 minutes, 24km), stopping outside the Autobuses de Jalisco terminal, opposite Galeana. A taxi from Lázaro Cárdenas to Playa Azul costs around M$120.

Ixtapa, Zihuatanejo & the Costa Grande

A glowing halo of bleached-blonde sand shimmers brilliantly along the 325 kilometers of Guerrero state's Costa Grande. Beyond the 'Great Coast's' heavenly crescent of beatified beach, small islands rocket from the azure-dream waters like angel's tears, while on terra firma, tawny resorts like Ixtapa and Troncones strut their wares. For beach lovers and chuck-it-all escapists, this could be the entrance to the 'Pearly Gates.'

This lightly developed coast extends southeast from the Río Balsas at the Michoacán border all the way down to Acapulco. The verdant hills of the Sierra Madre del Sur protect the tropical forests of the northwest corners of this region, giving way to coconut plantations and a handful of estuaries in the southeast.

Most folks visiting this region will begin their adventures from the Ixtapa-Zihuatanejo area. These twin cities – alike in geography alone – couldn't be more different. Ixtapa is a beach resort that kicks, screams, parties and purges all day and all night without feeling a drop of regret, while her demure sister, just miles away, hides an interesting history, great swimming spots, an intimate downtown area and some top-flight clifftop hotels and restaurants.

Just a half-hour drive northwest of Zihua, Troncones and Majahua offer buxom and beautiful beaches, good waves for surfing and a laid-back cool that even Miles Davis could dig. Southeast from Zihuatanejo on your way down to Acapulco, travelers will delight at deserted beaches, bird-choked estuaries and fishing villages forgotten by time and the sweep of development.

HIGHLIGHTS

- Leaving your all-inclusive Ixtapa resort for the day to explore the mangrove-fringed lagoon at **Barra de Potosí** (p188)

- Letting loose at the hopping bars and discotheques of **Zihuatanejo** (p179) and **Ixtapa** (p174)

- Dreaming of buying a second home in the sleepy beachside town of **Troncones** (p171), before heading out for a day of surfing, snorkeling or suntanning

- Chartering a **sailboat** (p183) in Zihuatanejo for an afternoon of sailing and snorkeling

- Slipping into a peeling roller at great surf spots like **La Saladita** (p174), **El Rancho** (p171), **La Boca** (p171), **Playa Linda** (p176) or **Playa Escolleras** (p176)

■ AVERAGE JANUARY DAILY HIGH: 29°C | 84°F   ■ AVERAGE JULY DAILY HIGH: 32°C | 90°F

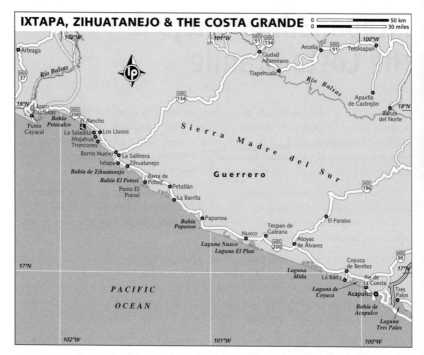

IXTAPA, ZIHUATANEJO & THE COSTA GRANDE

History

Humans have been living (and vacationing) on the Costa Grande since 2500 BC. And while the area's archaeological sites have largely been left unprotected, archaeologists have found ceramic shards and architectural remnants at Soledad de Maciel (near Petatlán) and Puerto Marqués (near Acapulco). Unlike those found along the coastal areas to the north, these archaeological markers indicate the region had contact with the Olmecs and later with Teotihuacán. Still, settlements always remained small and widely dispersed.

Tourism, so to speak, goes back a long way. The Purépecha (aka Tarascos), who ruled what is now Michoacán from the early 15th century until the arrival of the Spanish, had an early king named Calzontzin who liked Bahía de Zihuatanejo so much that he decided to build a winter 'retreat' on the point at Playa Las Gatas. If tales are true, the retreat included an artificial reef (still there) constructed to form something of a swimming pool for Calzontzin and his many wives.

When the Spanish arrived in the early 16th century, the region was loosely controlled by the Aztecs. Following the conquest, Hernán Cortés set his sights on developing a maritime route between Mexico and Asia, and in 1523 he established the shipyard and port of Puerto Santiago (present-day Zacatula) on the Río Balsas. Álvaro Saavedra de Cerón sailed from Zihuatanejo in search of a trade route in 1527, never to return. When a return trade route from Asia was finally established in 1565 between Acapulco and Manila (Philippines), Zihuatanejo's importance fizzled, with just a few English and Dutch pirates using the bay as a hideout before they attacked treasure-filled galleons en route to Acapulco.

After independence, and the subsequent completion of the Acapulco–Manila maritime route, Zihuatanejo remained a sleepy fishing village until the 1970s when Fonatur, a government tourism organization, developed Ixtapa.

Information

Ixtapa and Zihuatanejo are the gateway cities to this region. Though they're right next door to each other, they still feel worlds apart. With its purpose-built infrastructure, Ixtapa clearly exists only to accommodate tourists, while Zihuatanejo offers much more for locals and visitors alike.

Packed with useful information in Spanish and English are the **Ixtapa-Zihuatanejo municipal website** (www.ixtapa-zihuatanejo.com), **Zihua.net** (www.zihua.net) and **ZihuaRob's Travel Guide and Directory** (www.zihuatanejo.net). All three focus primarily on Zihuatanejo and Ixtapa, but also provide information on Troncones and other Costa Grande destinations.

Getting There & Away

See p187 for specifics. A few airlines fly direct to Zihuatanejo from US cities; most other flights involve transfers in Mexico City. Regular 1st-class buses connect Zihuatanejo with Mexico City, and there's even more frequent service to Lázaro Cárdenas and Acapulco, to the northwest and southeast respectively.

Getting Around

Regular 2nd-class buses run along the entire length of Hwy 200 through Guerrero state and will drop you either at your destination or at points where you can catch local transport. For car-rental agencies in Zihuatanejo and Ixtapa, see p179.

TRONCONES

☎ 755 / pop 593

About 35km northwest of Zihuatanejo, Troncones' coastline has several kilometers of vacation homes, B&Bs and guest inns, the majority gringo-owned. It also has some amazing surfing, good swimming and snorkeling, and various terrestrial activities such as bird-watching and mountain biking. Though accommodations are moderately expensive, the place is addictively relaxed and friendly.

Families generally fill Troncones' lodgings through the winter, but the place changes face in summer, when prices fall, the waves pick up and surfers roll in from all over. Many restaurants close during the summer months.

Orientation

The village of Troncones is about 100m from the beach at the end of a 3km paved road from Hwy 200 – but most of what you'll be interested in is along the unpaved beachfront road. From its T-junction with the road from the highway, the dirt road stretches along Playa Troncones in both directions. About 2km to the south (left) it ends, while to the north

(right) from the T, it runs some 4km past Troncones Point to reach the calmer waters of Playa Manzanillo. The road continues a short way to the small village of Majahua, a 10-minute walk past Playa Manzanillo. From Majahua, the road (rough in wet season) continues about 6km to meet Hwy 200 near Km 32.

Information

Abarrotes Gaby (☽ 7:30am-9pm) Has a long-distance telephone service. It's just off the coast road in Troncones village.

Café Sol (☽ 8am-10pm, closed Tue) Has a book exchange.

Casas Canela & Canelita (☎ 553-28-00; www.tronconestropic.com/canela.html) Does your laundry for M$15 per kilogram.

ZihuaRob's Troncones website (www.troncones.com.mx) Chock-full of useful information.

Activities

SURFING

With more than a dozen breaks within 20km of Troncones, short-boarders, long-boarders, rookies and rippers will all find something to ride. As usual, it's best to get out before the breeze picks up (usually around 11am), or around sunset when it gets glassy once again. The waves are biggest May to October.

Troncones itself has several world-class breaks. The beach breaks here can be excellent in summer, but the wave to chase is the left at **Troncones Point**. When it's small, the take-off is right over the rocks (complete with sea urchins), but when it's big, it's beautiful and beefy, and rolls halfway across the bay.

La Saladita (p174) has a blissfully long, rolling left, perfect for long-boarders. Yet another endless left and some rights can be had at the reef break of **El Rancho**. It's about 45 minutes northwest of La Saladita by car (standard drive OK in dry season), but it's easier (if pricier) by boat. **La Boca**, a river mouth just north of Majahua (via the beach and an easy-to-miss dirt track) and some 6km northwest of the Troncones T-junction, is best in summertime when the sandbar breaks, and both rights and lefts are consistent.

In Troncones, 100m north of the T-junction, **Mexcalli** (☎ 101-39-04) rents surfboards for M$250 per day and offers a rental, lesson combo for M$500 per day. For a better selection, head to the surf shop at the **Inn at Manzanillo Bay** (☎ 553-28-84; www.manzanillobay.com;

IXTAPA, ZIHUATANEJO & THE COSTA GRANDE

Playa Manzanillo), which rents short- and long-boards (from M$240 per day) as well as boogie boards (M$110 per day). It also offers surf lessons starting at M$500, buys and sells boards, and arranges guided boat trips (from M$1500) to many of the best local surf spots.

OTHER ACTIVITIES

There's good **snorkeling** at Troncones Point off Playa Manzanillo, and you can rent equipment for M$50 per half-day at the Inn at Manzanillo Bay (p171), which also rents **mountain bikes** for about M$200 per day; a good ride heads north along the beach as far as La Saladita. **Costa Nativa Eco Tours** (☎ 044-755-100-74-99; costanativa@hotmail.com) leads various bicycle tours around the Troncones area from M$200 per person (mountain bike and all equipment included).

Other activities include **fishing**, **hiking**, **bird-watching** and **sea turtle–spotting**; many hoteliers can help arrange these activities or contact the captain of the **Margarita II** (☎ 554-53-71) for charter information. The Present Moment Retreat (opposite) offers **yoga classes** for M$120, along with dance and meditation seminars.

Sleeping

Reservations are necessary almost everywhere in Troncones during the high season (November through April); several places also require multiple-night stays. Prices at other times can be as much as 50% lower than those listed here, but be aware that many business owners aren't around in the low season. Two Troncones residents who between them manage several properties are Tina Morse at **Casa Ki** (☎ 553-28-15; casaki@yahoo.com) and Anita LaPointe at the **Tropic of Cancer Beach Club** (☎ 553-28-00; casacanela@yahoo.com). With some advance notice, they can usually set you up with anything from an affordable room to a luxurious house.

BUDGET

The first two listings are a bit inland from the T-junction; the final two are not far south of the T. Strictly speaking, the high-season prices of Quinta and El Burro are a smidge outside our definition of 'budget', but that's only for a few weeks a year. Outside these times, they're the best budget options in town.

Miscelánea Yasmín (☎ 553-28-40; r with fan/air-con M$300-500; ✸) Behind the in-town *abarrotes* (small grocery), this place has a few OK rooms,

most with tinted windows. The fan rooms are nicer overall; some share a large balcony.

Hotel Costa Mar (☎ 553-29-46; d with fan/air-con M$400/600; ✸ ✿) For the price, you are certainly better off someplace else. But if everywhere else in town is full, hunker down in these cramped and hot rooms for the night.

Quinta d'Liz (☎ 553-29-14; www.playatroncones.com; d with breakfast M$500) These six simple but stylish bungalows are just off the beach and come with fans and good beds, plus use of a communal kitchen. The combination of price, facilities, location and mellow management by the surfing owner make this one of the best deals in town.

El Burro Borracho (☎ 553-28-34; www.tronconesburro .com; r with fan/air-con M$500/600; ✸) Just 100m south of the T, this beachfront spot offers clean and comfortable rooms. Breakfast is included and you have direct access to the beach, making this the second-best 'budget' deal in town.

MIDRANGE & TOP END

The following accommodations are spread out along the beachfront road. Going north from the T-junction you first reach Casa Escondida, then Casa Ki, Present Moment Retreat, the Delfín Sonriente, Casas Gregorio, the Inn at Manzanillo Bay, Posada de los Raqueros and Hacienda Edén. South from the T are Puesta del Sol and Casas Canela & Canelita.

Casas Canela & Canelita (☎ 553-28-00; www.tron conestropic.com/canela.html; r M$300, house M$1050-1687) Across the road from the beach, this two-building garden property is an affordable, comfortable option. Casa Canela, the house in front, sleeps six and has a large kitchen and a hammock-strewn front porch, a good spot for families. Casa Canelita is a much more modest duplex with rooms that can be rented individually. The rooms share a kitchen and terrace. All options require a three-night stay in high season.

La Puesta del Sol (☎ 553-28-15; www.thepuestadelsol .com; r M$400-1050, penthouse M$1950) This attractive four-room, three-story *palapa* (thatched-roof shelter) offers a simple 'surfers' room' on up to a super-luxurious penthouse apartment.

Casa Delfín Sonriente (☎ 553-28-03, in the US 831-688-6578; www.casadelfinsonriente.com; r/ste/villa M$850/1190/4890; ✸ ✿) A striking Mediterranean-style seaside villa, this offers a variety of well-furnished B&B accommodation. It's not quite as upscale as its neighbors, but it's nonetheless quite pleasant and is a budget-busting deal most of the year. Some rooms have air-con available (for an additional fee), while others are nearly open-air, with hanging beds. All units have access to the gorgeous swimming pool, the communal master kitchen and art supplies galore.

our pick **Casa Ki** (☎ 553-28-15; www.casa-ki.com; bungalow with breakfast M$950-1150, house M$2200) A charming retreat, Ki features a thoughtfully furnished main house sleeping up to six people, and three colorful free-standing bungalows with private porches and access to a communal kitchen. All are set on a verdant beachside property. Some rooms have minimum stays, so call ahead for reservations.

Hacienda Edén (☎ 553-28-02; www.edenmex.com; r M$1050, bungalows M$1050-1150, air-con ste M$1400, all with breakfast; **P** **X**) On Playa Manzanillo, 4km north of the T-junction, this tranquil beachfront gem has lovingly decorated bungalows, rooms and suites, a gourmet restaurant and a full bar. Tropical hardwoods, Talavera tiles and other touches are used everywhere to great advantage, and screens are first-rate, including over the otherwise roofless showers attached to the bungalows, which give bathers the sensation of showering under the open sky (without the bug bites).

Casas Gregorio (☎ 553-29-36; www.casasgregorio .net; per week bungalow/house M$8000/16,000; **X**) At the northern end of Playa Troncones, Gregorio has two spacious two-bedroom, two-bathroom houses beachside. Each has a fully equipped kitchen. The two bungalows are set back a bit and share a small kitchen. With cleverly constructed king-sized concrete 'bunkbeds,' each will accommodate four people. During the winter months Gregorio only offers weekly stays.

Posada de los Raqueros (☎ 553-28-70; www .raqueros.com; Playa Manzanillo; r M$1150, bungalows M$1450-1750; **X**) This posada offers three split-level bungalows, each with beds above and a living room, kitchen and bathroom below. Two other private rooms have a shared kitchen, and the latest offering is a two-bedroom house with air-con. All are stylishly designed and open onto a sand-and-grass area leading to the beach. It's peaceful here; the name refers to beachcombers, not musicians.

Inn at Manzanillo Bay (☎ 553-28-84; www.manzanillo bay.com; bungalows M$1280-1580; **P** **X** **X**) The inn has 10 well-appointed, thatched-roof bungalows with room safes, good mattresses, ceiling fans, mosquito nets and hammock-bedecked terraces. Other pluses are a popular restaurant, a full surf shop and easy access to the primo break at Troncones Point.

Casa Escondida (☎ 553-28-79; www.tronconesbeach .com; r/bungalows/houses M$1250/1750/4250; **X**) A bit overpriced, Casa Escondida is about 500m north of the T-junction. Each room has a kitchen in this rustic beachfront hotel, highlighted by traditional Mexican blankets and homey hacienda styling.

Present Moment Retreat (☎ 103-00-11; www.pre sentmomentretreat.com; bungalows with 3 meals & classes M$3975-5555; **X**) Just north of Casa Ki, this yoga retreat has immaculately manicured grounds and well-appointed *palapa*-covered rooms. Massive beds and mosquito nets add to the charms of this rustic and chic atavism. And it's this back-to-basics philosophy that makes Present Moment the perfect Zen getaway. Non-yogis will find it freakishly quiet.

Eating & Drinking

Be prepared to pay M$20 per beer in most places.

La Cocina del Sol (mains M$40-90) The renowned chef, Christian, turns out some sublime dishes here at Hacienda Edén's restaurant, wielding goat's cheese, arugula and *jamón serrano* (cured ham) with equal dexterity. The kitchen is open for all meals (one dinner seating only, at 6:30pm, reservations recommended); on Sundays it puts on a rib barbecue.

Inn at Manzanillo Bay (mains M$75-130) At the inn's restaurant you can choose from Mexican dishes, American favorites (think cheeseburgers and hickory-smoked pork ribs) and such fusions as 'Thai-style' deep-fried shrimp tacos or a seared ahi-tuna sandwich with wasabi mayonnaise.

Café Sol (breakfasts M$25-38, sandwiches M$38-55; ☽ 8am-10pm, closed Tue) The breakfasts come with a view at this two-story open-air place run by the peripatetic chef from La Cocina del Sol. It's a short way north of the T-junction and serves great egg dishes, homemade bread, smoothies, good espresso drinks and gelato, plus sandwiches; at night it morphs into a taco bar.

El Burro Borracho (☎ 553-28-34; mains M$50-100; ☽ 8am-10pm) Since 1993 – and that's a long time in these here parts – the drunken burro has been slinging out yummy fajitas and international grub in its zero-pretension beachfront restaurant.

Troncones and Majahua proper each have a few taco stands where you can eat well for under M$35, as well as some beachfront *enramadas* (thatch-covered open-air restaurants) where M$120 goes a long way. Good beachfront restaurants include Costa Brava, north of the T-junction, and Doña Nica's Enramada, just south of the T-junction. A few steps south of Doña Nica's is the **Tropic of Cancer** (mains M$40-90; ☺ closed Tue), a popular restaurant-bar–beach club with swimming pool.

In Majahua, Marta has an ideal bayside location and makes a *machaca* (dried seafood, often shark, made into a hash; M$40) like no other in all of Mexico – it's a must for adventurous eaters.

Getting There & Away

Driving from Ixtapa or Zihuatanejo, head northwest on Hwy 200 toward Lázaro Cárdenas. Just north of Km 30 you'll see the marked turnoff for Troncones; follow this winding paved road 3km west to the beach.

Second-class buses heading northwest toward Lázaro Cárdenas or La Unión from Zihua's long-distance terminals will drop you at the turnoff for Troncones (M$25, 40 minutes) if you ask. You can also catch La Unión–bound buses from the lot a couple of blocks east of Zihua's market. You can save money by taking a truck to Zihua from the Troncones turnoff (M$12)

White *colectivo* (shared transportation) vans and microbuses shuttle between Hwy 200 and Troncones roughly every half-hour or so between 7am and 9am and from 2pm to 6pm (M$5 to M$15). In a pinch you would probably have no problems hitching in either direction.

A taxi from Ixtapa or the Zihua airport to Troncones costs around M$500 to M$780, depending on where you're headed. It's cheaper to take a bus or even a cab from the airport to Zihua and then catch a cab to Troncones. Taxis from Troncones back to Zihuatanejo may be even cheaper.

LA SALADITA

☎ 755 / pop 21

Around 7km northwest of Troncones, La Saladita has a long, gentle left, perfect for long-boarding. The beach itself stretches far to the northwest and makes for blissful walks. The area has become increasingly popular with surfers from the States, some of whom have bought land and built houses and rental units here.

Restaurant Jacqueline serves mind-blowing lobster (some swear it's the best on the coast; others make the same claim for the handmade tortillas), beer and other seafood dishes. One lodging option is the beachfront *cabañas* at **Saladita Surfing Resort Camp** (www.saladita.com; 1-/2-bedroom bungalow M$650/950). Each contains bathroom, screens, fan, coffeemaker, and private deck with hammock. Make reservations far in advance for May to October; you may get lucky simply showing up the rest of the year.

Some restaurants allow people to camp or sleep in a hammock and use bathrooms and showers for free, provided you eat regularly in the restaurant.

To get to La Saladita from Troncones, take Hwy 200 north and turn left at the town of Los Llanos (around Km 140); follow the road to the fork near the convenience stores, hang a right and follow the dirt road 5km to the beach. Any northbound 2nd-class bus will drop you at Los Llanos; bussing is only feasible if you plan to stay more than a day.

IXTAPA

☎ 755 / pop 6400

Ixtapa (eeks-*tah*-pah), 240km northwest of Acapulco and next door to Zihuatanejo, is a glitzy, government-planned luxury resort with some fine beaches, a marina, golf courses, discos and several fairly expensive hotels.

Ixtapa was a coconut plantation and nearby Zihuatanejo a sleepy fishing village until 1970, when Fonatur – the Mexican government's tourism-development organization – decided that the Pacific coast needed a Cancún-like resort complex. Ixtapa was selected for its proximity to the USA, average temperature of 27°C (81°F), tropical vegetation and lovely beaches. Fonatur bought up the coconut plantation, laid down infrastructure and rolled out the red carpet for hotel chains and real-estate developers.

Orientation & Information

Most of the services or stores you'll need in Ixtapa are found in the outdoor *centros comerciales* (shopping centers), all within walking distance of each other on the main drag, Blvd Ixtapa. There are a few banks and *casas de cambio* (money-changing bureaus, in the commercial malls) where you can change US dollars and traveler's checks; some hotel

---

'IXTAPA' SOUNDS SO MUCH NICER

As in many other parts of the world, several place-names around the Zihuatanejo area have colorful stories behind them. 'Zihuatanejo' itself comes from the Nahuatl *cihuatlán*, meaning 'place of women.' Depending on whose version you believe, this is derived from the fact that old Zihua was inhabited by a matriarchal society. Or that it was a ceremonial center which, like Isla Mujeres off the Yucatán Peninsula, was used for female-deity worship. Or – least plausibly – that when the Spanish first arrived, the local menfolk had stashed their women here and gone off to hide. (Wouldn't it have a Spanish name, then?) In any case, the conquistadors added the diminutive suffix '-ejo,' supposedly to express their opinion of Zihua's insignificance. 'Ixtapa,' also from Nahuatl, means roughly 'covered in white,' and refers to the area's sands, or the white guano left by seabirds on the rocky islands just offshore. Coulda been worse.

The names of beaches lining Bahía de Zihuatanejo also tell stories. Playa Madera (Wood Beach) was so dubbed after the timber that was once milled on its shore, loaded aboard ships and carried to various parts of the world; at one time there was also a shipyard here. Playa Las Gatas does not have a history involving pussycats; it's named for the gentle nurse sharks that once inhabited the waters, called 'gatas' because of their whiskers. And finally, the name of Playa La Ropa (Clothing Beach) commemorates the occasion when a Spanish galleon coming from the Philippines was wrecked and its cargo of fine silks washed ashore.

---

lobbies have ATMs. The banks give the best rate of exchange; the *casas de cambio* give a slightly less favorable rate but they're open longer hours. The town lacks a post office, but you can mail letters from any big hotel. The only official tourist office in the area is located in Zihuatanejo, but nearly any local is happy to help with recommendations.

Bancomer (Centro Comercial La Puerta; 9am-5pm Mon-Fri) Behind Señor Frog's.

Hotel Tropicana (553-21-59, Centro Comercial La Puerta) Does laundry for a fraction of what other hotels charge: M$20 per kilogram.

Kaldhi Café (553-19-17; Centro Comercial La Puerta; 8am-11pm) Has free wi-fi if you order a coffee, and internet access for M$30 per hour.

Tourist police (553-20-08; Centro Commercial La Puerta)

Sights & Activities
BEACHES

Ixtapa's big hotels line **Playa del Palmar**, a long, broad stretch of white sand teeming with families, strolling beach vendors and sunburnt honeymooners. Be very careful if you swim here: the waves crash straight down and there's a powerful undertow. The western end of this beach, just before the entrance to the lagoon, is known as **Playa Escolleras** and is a favorite spot for surfing. Further west, past the marina, are three small beaches that are among the most beautiful in the area: **Playa San Juan**, **Playa Casa Blanca** and **Playa Cuatas**. Unfortunately,

they've all been effectively privatized by new developments, so unless you can gain access by skiff or helicopter they are out of bounds – public access, required by Mexican law, appears to have been overlooked.

To the northwest, past Punta Ixtapa, are **Playa Quieta** and the long, wide **Playa Linda**. The latter has several decent seafood *enramadas* and a few shops selling souvenirs, snacks and beer, all at the beach's southern end, near the pier.

ISLA IXTAPA

Just offshore, Isla Ixtapa is a small, wooded island with four pocket-sized beaches and several seafood *enramadas* that feed the island's steady stream of visitors. It's home to deer, raccoons, armadillos, iguanas and numerous species of birds, as well as the flipper-footed humans who migrate here daily for the excellent snorkeling. You can rent snorkeling gear for about M$60 a day (M$120 if you add a life jacket).

Playa Cuachalalate, the main beach, has plenty of restaurants and the island's main pier, but with fishing boats anchored along the beach and jet-skiers zipping around just offshore, it's the least appealing for swimming. No matter – the smaller but equally beautiful **Playa Varadero** is only a short walk away. The best snorkeling is at **Playa Coral**, directly behind Varadero, where you will see numerous species of tropical fish, including blowfish, butterfly fish, angelfish and, as

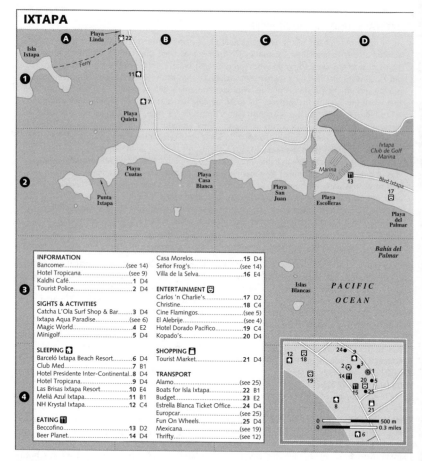

IXTAPA

the name suggests, lots of coral. **Playa Carey** is the most isolated beach of all and is accessible only by boat, usually from the pier at Cuachalalate.

Boats zip over to the island every few minutes (less frequently in the low season) from the Playa Linda pier and drop visitors at Playa Cuachalalate or Playa Varadero. The return boat ride (five minutes each way) will set you back M$30; boats operate 9am to 5pm daily. A boat also goes to Isla Ixtapa from the Zihuatanejo pier, but only when there are eight passengers or more. It departs at 11am, and leaves the island at around 4pm. The trip (M$120 return) takes an hour each way. The ticket office is at the foot of the pier.

SURFING

The best bet for waves in the immediate area is the beach break at **Playa Linda**, directly in front of the parking lot at the end of the Playa Linda road. In winter, when it's pancake-flat everywhere else, it can be chest-high and fun. Further down the beach, the river mouth is good during the rainy season after the river breaks through the sandbar. For both spots, take a Playa Linda bus to the pier and walk up the road (or the beach) to the parking lot. Another local favorite for its proximity to town is **Playa Escolleras**, a jetty-side beach break in Ixtapa favoring rights and, on weekends, crowds. It's at the western end of Playa del Palmar next to (and thanks to) the marina; bring your short-board.

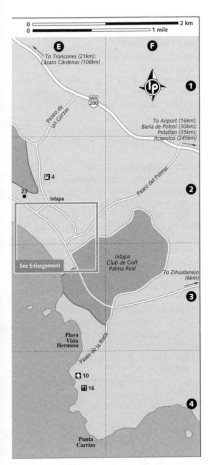

north of Ixtapa, through the Aztlán Eco Park practically into Zihuatanejo. Mountain bikes can be rented at several places (see p179). If you'd prefer not to pedal, you can go **horseback riding** on Playa Linda (you can arrange this on the beach).

Ixtapa Aqua Paradise (☎ 555-20-78; www.ixtapaaqua paradise.com) is a PADI-certified dive operation working out of the Barceló Ixtapa Beach Resort. For more information on snorkeling and diving, see p182.

The **Ixtapa Club de Golf Palma Real** (☎ 553-10-62) and the **Club de Golf Marina Ixtapa** (☎ 553-14-10) both have 18-hole courses, tennis courts and swimming pools.

The area also has some great sportfishing (p183).

IXTAPA FOR CHILDREN
Brush up on your putting at the **minigolf** near Ixtapa's Cine Flamingos cinema, or get wet at **Magic World** (☎ 553-13-59; admission M$80; ☷ 10:30am-5:30pm), an aquatic park beside Hotel Ixtapa Palace. It has rides, water slides, toboggans and other amusements.

Sleeping
Ixtapa's resorts are all top-end, with the cheapest running around M$1250 a night in the winter high season (January to Easter). Some drop their rates by 25% or more at other times of the year. The best buys are had by arranging a package deal through a travel agent, including airfare from your home country, or online. Otherwise, Zihuatanejo's accommodations are generally cheaper.

Hotel Tropicana (☎ 553-21-59; Centro Comercial La Puerta; s/d M$550/700) If you simply must stay in Ixtapa, but want to save some ducats, then the Tropicana may be right for you. Across from the beach in the Centro Comercial La Puerta, this simple hotel has back-to-basics accommodations, though budget-busters are still better off in Zihua.

Las Brisas Ixtapa Resort (☎ 553-21-21; www .brisas.com.mx; Playa Vista Hermosa; d from M$2400; Ⓟ ☒ ☒ ☐ ☒ ☷) Enormous Brisas (423 rooms) sits alone on the small, lovely Playa Vista Hermosa, essentially laying claim to it. The main structure's design looks a bit dated, but gives all rooms a terrace with first-rate ocean views. Arguably the best hotel in town – especially for non-partiers – Brisas has a great lobby bar, a plethora of pools and restaurants, a fitness center, kids' club and tennis courts.

The best surf shop around is **Catcha L'Ola Surf Shop & Bar** (☎ 553-13-84; www.ixtapasurf.com; Centro Comercial Kiosko, Local 12, Ixtapa; ☷ 9am-9pm), owned by Masters Division national champ Leonel Pérez, who is a great source of information. Behind the movie theater in Ixtapa, it's well stocked and likely your best bet for board repairs. Leon rents short- and longboards for M$200 per day, and will drive you out to Playa Linda or up to Troncones or La Saladita. Guided tours with a board rental cost M$500 per day. The shop is good for cheap beer and gossip.

OTHER ACTIVITIES
Bicycling is a breeze along the 15km *ciclopista* (bicycle path) that stretches from Playa Linda,

NH Krystal Ixtapa (☎ 553-03-33; www.nh-hotels .com; Blvd Ixtapa s/n; all-inclusive per person M$1683, all-inclusive ste per person M$2000; P ⊗ ⊗ ⊛ ⊛) Resort life is good at the Krystal. Sit in the wet bar, head out to the beach, or simply stay in the well-appointed rooms and order room service. The rugrats will love the highly regarded children's club, Krystalitos. European plans, where your meals aren't included, are also available.

Hotel Presidente Inter-Continental (☎ 553-00-18, in the US 800-327-0200; www.intercontinental .com/ixtapa; Blvd Ixtapa s/n; d all-inclusive M$4000; P ⊗ ⊗ ⊛ ⊛ ⊛) Despite looking like the Ministry of Peace from George Orwell's *1984*, the Intercontinental is one of the most popular hotels on the beach, with a gym, sauna, tennis courts, five restaurants and a kids' club that teaches the little ones basic Spanish on top of all the other activities. While the rooms are quite nice, the Krystal's are better.

Barceló Ixtapa Beach Resort (☎ 555-20-00, in the US 800-227-2356; www.barcelo.com; Blvd Ixtapa s/n; all-inclusive per person M$2750; P ⊗ ⊗ ⊛ ⊛) Another good family choice, the Barceló has especially fine pool and patio areas, as well as tennis courts and a gym. Its all-inclusive plan covers three meals, alcoholic beverages, gym use, tennis courts, room service and child care.

Two resorts on Playa Linda, a bit removed from central Ixtapa, do business almost exclusively through all-inclusive packages: **Club Med** (☎ 01-800-022-6060; www.clubmed.com; d all-inclusive from M$2400; ☺ closed Sep 15-Oct 31) and **Meliá Azul Ixtapa** (☎ 550-00-00; www.solmelia.com; d all-inclusive from M$2500).

Eating

Ixtapa has plenty of restaurants in addition to those in the big hotels. But it's always worthwhile to take a taxi or bus over to Zihua for a more authentic experience.

Casa Morelos (☎ 553-05-78; Comercial La Puerta Lote 9; M$75-270; ☺ 8am-midnight) Open since 1996 – veritably Jurassic in Ixtapa years – this cozy restaurant features lots of Mexican seafood dishes like shrimp enchiladas and *cazuela de mariscos* (shellfish stew). If it's too pricey, you can always head next door to Señor Frog's for cheaper (and worse) food and drinks.

Villa de la Selva (☎ 553-03-62; Paseo de la Roca Lote D; mains M$150-230; ☺ 7pm-late) Reservations are a must at this elegant Italian/Mediterranean restaurant in the former home of Mexican president Luis Echeverría. Near Las Brisas

resort (p177), the cliffside villa overlooks the ocean (sunsets are superb). Offerings include glazed salmon with couscous, duck breast, several pastas with and without shellfish, and a good wine list.

Beccofino (☎ 553-17-60; Veleros Lote 6, Ixtapa Marina Plaza; mains M$158-288; ☺ 9am-11pm) Indoor-outdoor Beccofino enjoys a good reputation for delicious (if pricey) northern Italian cuisine, especially seafood and pastas. Several other good restaurants ring the marina.

Entertainment

All the big hotels have bars and nightclubs. Many also have discos; in low season most of these charge less and open fewer nights.

Beer Planet (Comercial La Puerta) Behind Señor Frog's this open-air bar fills up with locals nightly.

Christine (☎ 553-04-56; Blvd Ixtapa s/n; admission to M$250) Right next to the NH Krystal, Christine has the sizzling sound and light systems you'd expect from one of the most popular discos in town.

Kopado's (☎ 553-20-00; Comercial La Puerta) This locals' favorite sits in a *palapa*-covered perch just south of Señor Frog's, and has some good drink specials and super-friendly waiters. There's live music on occasion.

El Alebrije (☎ 553-27-10; Paseo de las Garzas s/n; admission for women/men M$200/250) A fog machine, banks of computerized lights, pop, rock, house, salsa and merengue, open bar – what more do you want?

Carlos 'n' Charlie's (☎ 553-00-85; Paseo del Palmar s/n) Things can get wild on this chain restaurant's dance floor right above the beach; on weekends it fills with hard-partying young tourists and locals alike.

Also deserving mention are the Barceló Ixtapa Beach Resort's Sanca Bar, where you can shake it to Latin music, and the excellent lobby bar at Las Brisas resort.

Several of Ixtapa's big hotels hold evening 'Fiestas Mexicanas,' which typically include a Mexican buffet and open bar, entertainment (traditional dancing, mariachis and bloodless cockfighting demonstrations), door prizes and dancing; the total price is usually M$350 to M$450. The Barceló Ixtapa Beach Resort holds fiestas year-round; in the high season several other hotels, including **Hotel Dorado Pacífico** (☎ 553-20-25), also present fiestas. Reservations can be made directly or through travel agents.

Cine Flamingos (☎ 553-24-90; admission M$50), behind the tourist office and opposite Plaza Ixpamar and the minigolf, shows two films nightly, usually in English with Spanish subtitles.

Shopping

Tourist Market (Blvd Ixtapa s/n; ☉ 9am-10pm) Though this market is packed with everything from tacky T-shirts to silver jewelry and hand-painted pottery, shopping is much better in Zihuatanejo (see p187).

Getting There & Around

Private *colectivo* vans provide transportation from the airport to Ixtapa for M$100 per person, but not in the other direction. A taxi to the airport costs M$110 to M$150 from Ixtapa.

Mexicana (☎ 553-20-25), with an office in the Hotel Dorado Pacífico, flies to Mexico City.

Estrella Blanca (☎ 553-04-65; www.estrellablanca .com.mx, in Spanish; Paseo Av Gaviota, Andador Punta Carrizo) has a ticket office in Ixtapa. There's also a ticket office for Autovias, Parhikuni, La Linea and Omnibus service next to Fun On Wheels in the Centro Comercial Los Patios.

Local 'Directo' and 'B Viejo' buses run frequently between Ixtapa and Zihua, a 15-minute ride. They depart every 15 minutes from 5:30am to 11pm (M$7). In Ixtapa, buses stop all along the main street, in front of all the hotels. In Zihua, buses depart from the corner of Juárez and Morelos. Buses marked 'Zihua-Ixtapa-Playa Linda' continue through Ixtapa to Playa Linda (M$7), stopping near Playa Quieta on the way; they operate from 7am to 7pm.

Ixtapa has plenty of taxis. Always agree on the fare before climbing into the cab; between Zihua and Ixtapa it should be around M$55. For prearranged service call **Radio Taxi UTAAZ** (☎ 554-33-11).

CAR & MOTORCYCLE

Ixtapa has several places renting motorbikes (around M$200 per hour, M$900 per day), including **Fun on Wheels** (☎ 553-02-59; ☉ 9am-8pm), in the Centro Comercial Los Patios, which also rents mountain bikes for M$50/200 per hour/day. You usually need a driver's license and a credit card to rent; if you're not an experienced motorcycle rider, Mexico is *not* the place to learn.

There are several car-rental companies in Ixtapa. Try to reserve ahead of time, but be warned that this won't always guarantee you a vehicle.

Alamo Ixtapa (☎ 553-02-06; Centro Comercial Los Patios); Airport (☎ 554-84-29)

Budget Ixtapa (☎ 553-03-97; Centro Comercial Ambiente, Local 10); Airport (☎ 554-48-37)

Europcar (☎ 553-10-32; Centro Comercial Los Patios)

Hertz Airport (☎ 554-29-52)

Thrifty Ixtapa (☎ 553-30-19; Hotel NH Krystal, Ixtapa); Airport (☎ 553-70-20)

ZIHUATANEJO
☎ 755 / pop 62,300

Like its sister city Ixtapa, Zihuatanejo (see-wah-tah-*neh*-ho) is quite touristy. Nevertheless, it retains an easygoing coastal ambience, and its setting on a beautiful bay with several fine beaches makes it a gratifying place to visit. Small-scale fishing is still an economic mainstay; if you stroll down by the pier early in the morning, you can join the pelicans in greeting successful fisherfolk and inspecting the morning's catch. Needless to say, seafood is superb here. Several cobblestone streets downtown have been closed to traffic, making for one of the best pedestrian zones on the coast, and budget travelers can still find reasonably priced accommodation here.

Orientation

Though Zihua's suburbs are extensive, spreading around Bahía de Zihuatanejo and climbing the hills behind town, in the city's center everything is compressed within a few blocks. It's difficult to get lost; there are only a few streets and they're clearly marked.

Information
EMERGENCY

General emergency (☎ 060; ☉ 24hr)

Hospital (☎ 554-36-50; Av Morelos) Near Mar Egeo.

Tourist police (☎ 554-20-40; Juan Alvarez 72) On the plaza.

INTERNET ACCESS

Zihuatanejo is crawling with internet cafés, most charging around M$10 per hour.

El Navegante Internet (Bravo 41)

LAUNDRY

Lavandería del Centro (☎ 554-97-91; Guerrero 17; ☉ 8am-8pm Mon-Sat, 10am-4pm Sun) Charges M$16 per kilogram; self-service also available.

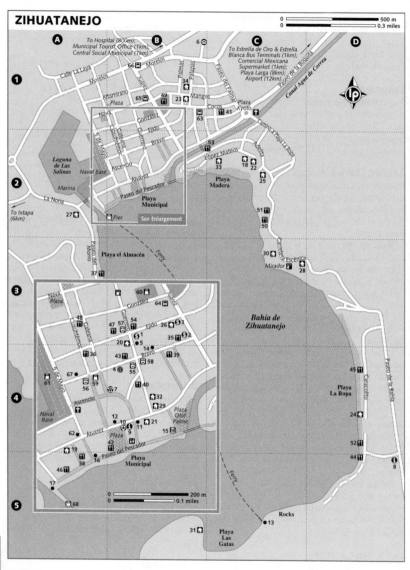

ZIHUATANEJO

MONEY

Zihuatanejo has many banks and *casas de cambio* where you can change US dollars and traveler's checks. The following banks have air-conditioned ATMs:

Banamex (cnr Ejido & Guerrero)

Bancomer (cnr Juárez & Bravo; 8:30am-4pm Mon-Fri, 10am-2pm Sat)

Banorte (cnr Juárez & Ejido; 9am-4pm Mon-Fri, 10am-2pm Sat)

POST

Post office (8am-6pm Mon-Fri, 9am-1pm Sat) Located off Morelos, this is well signed but still hard to find. Note that several hotels and stores in town also sell stamps.

TELEPHONE & FAX

Long-distance telephone and fax services are available at several telephone *casetas*, including two on the corner of Galeana and Ascencio. Public Lada phones are all around town. **Telecomm** (8am-6pm Mon-Fri, 9am-1pm Sat), inside the post office, has a fax service.

TOURIST INFORMATION

Municipal tourist office (554-20-01; www.ixtapa
-zihuatanejo.com; Zihuatanejo Pte s/n, Colonia La Deportiva; 8am-4pm Mon-Fri) Upstairs in the *ayuntamiento* (city hall), 2km northeast of the town center. Local buses between Ixtapa and Zihuatanejo stop out front.

Tourist branch office (8am-4pm Mon-Fri) Near the southern end of Playa La Ropa.

Tourist kiosk (Álvarez s/n; 9am-8pm) Operates in high season in the heart of town and offers free information, maps and brochures.

TRAVEL AGENCIES

Various agencies provide travel services and arrange local tours.
Viajes Bravo (554-88-90; Alvarez 8)

Dangers & Annoyances

A study published in 2003 by the Mexican government's environmental protection agency, Profepa, cited 16 of the country's beaches as having unacceptably high levels of bacterial contamination. At the top of the list were Playas La Ropa, Las Gatas and Municipal, all on Bahía Zihuatanejo. This is a result of insufficiently treated sewage flowing into the bay. Ocean currents in winter keep the bay flushed out, but at other times of year (particularly late summer and during periods of rain), you should use discretion (and your nose) when deciding whether to swim.

From late fall to early spring as many as four cruise ships a week anchor in the bay. When their passengers are in port, prices have a tendency to inflate, especially for things like cab rides and souvenirs.

Sights & Activities

See p175 for activities on offer in nearby Ixtapa.

MUSEO ARQUEOLÓGICO DE LA COSTA GRANDE

This small but recommended **archaeology museum** (554-75-52; Paseo del Pescador at Plaza Olof Palme; admission M$10; 10am-6pm, closed Mon) houses exhibits on the history, archaeology and culture of the Guerrero coast, with Spanish captions; a free English-language brochure has translations.

BEACHES

Waves are gentle at all Bahía de Zihuatanejo's beaches. If you want big ocean waves, head west toward Ixtapa, only a few minutes away by local bus.

Fishing *pangas* (motorized skiffs) line the sands of the **Playa Municipal**, which buzzes with activity when the fishermen haul in their catch in the early morning. This beach is the least appealing for swimming, especially when the seasonal, polluted Agua de Correa Canal is flowing into the bay. Standing on this beach you can see several other beaches spread around the bay, starting with Playa Madera, just past the rocky point on your left, then the long white stretch of Playa La Ropa past that. Directly across the bay lies the enticing Playa Las Gatas.

Playa Madera was once isolated from Playa Municipal by two rocky points, but now a concrete pathway over the rocks makes it an easy five-minute walk from town. It's better for swimming than the municipal beach and has several decent seafood restaurants.

From Playa Madera, walk over the hill along the Camino a Playa La Ropa (about 20 minutes) and you reach the broad expanse of **Playa La Ropa**, bordered by palm trees and lined with low-level hotels, seafood restaurants and sun beds. It's a pleasant walk, with the road rising up onto cliffs that offer a fine view over the bay. The first road to the beach is beside La Casa Que Canta hotel. Most restaurants along the beach require a minimum consumption of M$50 to M$80 of food or drink for use of their sun beds, but once you hit the minimum, you can stay all day – and feel pretty confident that someone is guarding your goodies while you swim. That said, La Ropa is hardly prone to theft. Arguably the most beautiful beach on the bay, La Ropa is great for swimming, parasailing, water-skiing, banana-boat rides and beach soccer. You can also rent sailboards and sailboats.

Opposite Zihuatanejo, **Playa Las Gatas** is a protected beach, crowded with sun beds and restaurants. It's a good spot for snorkeling (there's some coral) for children to swim at, but beware of sea urchins. According to legend, Calzontzin, a Purépecha king, built a stone barrier here in pre-Hispanic times to keep the waves down and prevent sea creatures from entering, making it a sort of private swimming pool. Beach shacks and restaurants rent snorkeling gear for around M$50 per day.

Boats to Playa Las Gatas depart frequently from the Zihuatanejo pier from 9am to 5pm daily. Buy tickets (M$35 round-trip) at the booth at the foot of the pier; one-way tickets can be bought on board. You can also extend your trip, by visiting Isla Ixtapa (p175).

South of Zihuatanejo

About 10km south of Zihuatanejo, halfway between town and the airport, **Playa Larga** has big waves, beachfront restaurants and **horseback riding**. To reach Playa Larga, take a 'Coacoyul' *combi* (minibus; M$7) from Juárez, opposite the market, and get off at the turnoff to Playa Larga. Another *combi* will take you from the turnoff to the beach, about 3km along a paved road through a coconut plantation.

Forty minutes south of town, **Barra de Potosí** (p188) has a mangrove lagoon and makes an excellent day trip.

SNORKELING & SCUBA DIVING

The ocean waters here enjoy an abundance of species because of a convergence of currents, and can offer great visibility, sometimes up to 35m. There are more than 30 dive sites nearby, offering conditions for beginners and advanced divers. Migrating humpback whales pass through from December to February, and manta rays can be seen all year, though there's greater likelihood of seeing them in summer, when the water is clearest, bluest and warmest.

A 40-minute boat ride southeast from Zihua, the granite rocks of **Los Morros del Potosí** offer some of the most fascinating diving along the coast, with submarine caves, walls, canals and tunnels; the high currents require experience. Isla Ixtapa offers numerous shallow- and deep-water dives for all skill levels. Experts can explore the nearby **Islas Blancas**, just off Playa del Palmar, with coral-covered walls, caves, canals and abundant sea life.

Snorkeling is good at **Playa Las Gatas**, the home of **Carlo Scuba** (☎ 554-60-03; www.carloscuba .com; Playa Las Gatas), which offers a variety of PADI courses and dives (M$650/850 for one/two tanks). You're picked up at the Zihuatanejo pier, and dropped off there as well, or at Playa Las Gatas if you prefer.

Adventure Divers (☎ 112-17-79; cnr Alvarez & Cuauhtemoc) offers cheaper diving trips (M$500/750 for one/two tanks). But cheaper isn't always better, especially when you are 50m underwater.

SPORTFISHING

Lugging a cooler full of beer onto a fishing boat and bringing it home full of fish (or empty of both) is one of Zihua's favorite tourist attractions. See our interview with Captain Moses Pelaez (right) for more on the area's fishing. Many captains now maintain a strict catch-and-release policy for billfish (especially sailfish and marlin). Deep-sea-fishing trips for four people cost anywhere from M$1800 to M$3500 and up, depending on the size of the boat. Trips generally last six to eight hours and leave the Zihuatanejo pier no later than 7am.

Prices quoted by operators include equipment and usually include fishing license, bait, beer and water – always ask. You can also walk along the pier and talk with the various fishermen, many of whom speak some English.

Among the fishing cooperatives near Zihuatanejo's pier are the **Sociedad Cooperativa José Azueta** (☎ 554-20-56) and **Sociedad de Servicios Turísticos** (☎ 554-37-58).

SURFING

The only surf in Zihuatanejo is the point at **Playa Las Gatas**. Just inside the bay, it requires a big swell to break, but when it does, it's reportedly a perfect hollow left, rarely more than 1.5m (5ft); take a boat over from the Zihua pier. Ixtapa has more surf and better facilities; see p176. Troncones (p171) is an easy day trip away, and has the best swells on the coast.

CRUISES

A few sailboats offer cruises of local waters that often include snorkeling as part of the package. One of these is **Picante** (☎ 554-26-94, 554-82-70; www.picantecruises.com), a 23m catamaran based in Bahía de Zihuatanejo that offers a couple of different excursions, including a sail-and-snorkel excursion and a 2½-hour sunset cruise. Prices range from M$500 to M$700. Reservations are required; private charters are also available.

Courses

Everest Academia de Idiomas (☎ 554-33-08; Bravo 26) offers Spanish courses.

Sleeping

The most reasonably priced hotels are in Zihuatanejo proper, with top-end hotels gravitating toward Playa La Ropa. Playa Madera is

> ### ASK A LOCAL: SPORTFISHING NEAR ZIHUATANEJO
>
> I own my own boat, *La Diosa*. I take people out fishing and we just have a good time. Sailfish are caught here all year. And there are marlin (March to May), wahoo (October), mahimahi (November to December), roosterfish (September to October), Spanish mackerel (December), and more.
>
> *Captain Moses Pelaez can be contacted at ☎ 101-72-045, or charter a boat through one of the fishing cooperatives near the pier.*

a good middle ground and has some excellent midrange hotels, many with kitchens, all with great views.

During the December-to-April high season many hotels here fill up, so phone ahead to reserve a room; if you don't like what you get, you can always look for another room early the next day. The busiest times of year are Semana Santa (Holy Week) and the week between Christmas and New Year; at these peak times you *must* reserve a room and be prepared to pony up extra pesos. Tourism is much slower and rates are often negotiable from mid-April to mid-December.

BUDGET

The budget establishments listed here are in central Zihuatanejo.

Angela's Hotel & Hostel (☎ 554-47-48; angelashostel@hotmail.com; Mangos 25; dm/d M$100/250, d with air-con M$350; 🖳 🐾) Friendly, convenient and helpful, this hostel is hard to beat. Rooms are dark and crowded, but it's off a quiet street and offers a shared kitchen and internet access (M$10 per hour).

Casa de Huéspedes Elvira (☎ 554-20-61; Álvarez 32; r M$150-200) This simple family place offers eight rooms on two floors surrounding an open courtyard. Upstairs rooms are much better, with more light and privacy, but they are accessible only via a rickety spiral staircase.

MIDRANGE

Most of these hotels are in the town center, but folks looking for a bit more quiet should check out the Playa Madera offerings.

Hotel Bugambilias (☎ 554-58-15; Mangos 28; s/d with air-con M$300/550, with fan M$250/500; P 🐾) Cramped as hell, the Boog has clean, bright rooms next to the market, in a less touristy but quite lively part of town. It's a good value; balconied Room 110 is the best of the lot.

Hotel Susy (☎ 554-23-39; cnr Guerrero & Álvarez; d with fan/air-con M$400/600; **P** **⊠**) Close to Playa Municipal, this well-located place has good-sized but unremarkable and even cheerless rooms – avoid the ground-floor ones, which are dark and musty.

Posada Citlali (☎ 554-20-43; Guerrero 4; s/d/tr M$450/550/600) This pleasant older posada features small rooms that are basic but well kept and have good ventilation and light. It has a dark, leafy central courtyard.

Hotel Posada Michel (☎ 554-74-23; www.zihua tanejo.net/hotels.html; Ejido 14; r with fan/air-con M$500/550; **P** **⊠**) The tight, dark halls and rooms of this small hotel will have you feeling like you are stowing away on a train. But the rooms are clean enough, and it's relatively affordable.

Hotel Ámueblados Valle (☎ 554-20-84; luisavall@ prodigy.net.mx; Guerrero 33; apt with fan/air-con M$500/600; **⊠** **♨**) While it's no great shakes, you do get a kitchen in each room, making this a good deal for groups or families. Some rooms even have balconies with partial mountain views. There's a wonderful sunny rooftop area, and three-bedroom apartments are also available. Ask the lady who runs the place about other apartments in town and on Playa La Ropa, which may be cheaper, especially for longer stays.

Zihua Inn Hotel (☎ 554-39-12; Palapas 119; r M$695; **P** **⊠** **♨**) Near the market, the Zihua has four floors of big blue rooms that will have you feeling like you landed in Fairyland. It also has a decent pool with a kiddy section and a covered parking area.

Bungalows Ley (☎ 554-40-87; www.bungalowsley .com; López Mateos s/n, Playa Madera; 1-/2-bedroom bungalows M$800/1600; **P** **⊠**) Well-kept and spacious – with unbeatable views and beach access – these bungalows are only a short walk from the center. In short, a great value. They're not fancy, but all have terraces, room safes, air-con and kitchens or kitchenettes (some outdoors), and the biggest has a living room, dining room and two bathrooms.

Hotel Ávila (☎ 554-20-10; hotelavila68@yahoo.com .mx; Álvarez 8; r with/without sea view M$900/700; **P** **⊠**) Fronting Playa Municipal, the Ávila has 27 spacious but forgettable rooms with cable TV – get one with a balcony overlooking the bay if you want to remember something.

Hotel Raúl Tres Marías (☎ 554-67-06; www.3marias .net; La Noria 4; r M$950) Across the lagoon footbridge, this popular option comes with clean, spacious rooms – though the baths could use a good scrubbing. Its best features, however, are the large terraced patios dotted with chairs and hammocks and boasting great views of the pier.

Posada Pacíficos (☎ 554-21-12; www.bungalowspacifi cos.com; López Mateos s/n, Playa Madera; bungalows M$1000) The six large bungalows have ample sea-view terraces with greenery, good bathrooms and fully equipped kitchens. The owner, a long-time Zihua resident, is a gracious and helpful hostess who speaks English, Spanish and German. Though maintenance is slipping a bit, clever construction maximizes breezes throughout all the rooms.

TOP END

Hotel Palacios (☎ 554-20-55; www.zihuatanejo.net /hotelpalacios, in Spanish; Adelita s/n, Playa Madera; d M$1050; **P** **⊠** **♨**) Overlooking the eastern end of Playa Madera, pleasant Hotel Palacios is a family place with a swimming pool and beachfront terrace. Some rooms are on the smaller side, and not all have views, but they do all have air-con and good beds, baths and screens. For your money, you are probably better off at another hotel in town, but with its beach-level location, you avoid the stair-climbing of other Playa Madera hotels.

Las Gatas Beach Club (☎ 554-63-96; www.lasgatas beachclub.com; bungalows M$1150) Four large free-standing bungalows sit on peaceful grounds at the edge of the bay, where at night you'll hear only the rhythmic sound of the surf and the sea breezes rustling through the palms. The unique, somewhat rustic bungalows are made of natural building materials and some sleep up to eight people. The last public-boat service from Zihuatanejo to Playa Las Gatas is at 5pm or 6pm (depending on the time of year), so you're under a bit of a curfew if you don't want to shell out bucks for private service.

Hotel Casa del Mar (☎ 554-38-73; www.zihua-casa delmar.com; Caracolito; r with fan M$1170, with air-con M$1400; **P** **⊠** **♨**) This hideaway at the southern end of Calle Caracolito, on Playa La Ropa, has garden and beachfront rooms, the latter with good air-con, and all with OK beds and baths. Crocodiles, fed by the manager, inhabit the mangrove-lined waterway bordering the property. Good thing the small pool is above ground.

ourpick **Hotel Brisas del Mar** (☎ 554-21-42; www
.hotelbrisasdelmar.com; López Mateos s/n, Playa Madera; d from
M$1920; ❄ ▣ ⊛) Great common areas, a little
pool and big sea views make this attractive red
adobe-style hotel one of the best boutique hotels in town. It has a spa with sauna and steam
room and a small gym. All rooms have safes,
minibars, coffeemakers, exquisite ocean-view
terraces, and some even have whirlpool tubs.

La Casa Que Canta (☎ 555-70-00; www.lacasaquecanta
.com; Carretera Escénica s/n; ste from M$5730; Ⓟ ❄ ▣ ⊛)
Perched on the cliffs between Playa Madera
and Playa La Ropa, this award-winner uses
gorgeous Mexican handicrafts, furniture and
textiles to great effect throughout. All rooms
have terraces, full sea views and amenities
galore. Down by the beach you'll find a freshwater and saltwater pool. If you've got the
dough, this is the best hotel in town.

Eating

Guerrero is famous for its *pozole* (a hearty
broth with hominy and pork, chicken, shrimp
or other seafood), which is on most menus in
town (especially on Thursday) and well worth
a try. Seafood in Zihuatanejo is excellent, and
you can always buy some fresh fish at the
Playa Municipal and fry it up later on the
beach or in your hotel if you have a kitchen.

PASEO DEL PESCADOR

Seafood here is fresh and delicious; many
popular (if touristy) fish restaurants run parallel to Playa Municipal. The following are
the best options.

A FRESH SPIN ON CEVICHE

Tiritas (slivers of raw fish quickly marinated
in lemon juice, onion and green chili) are
a local specialty. The dish originated with
local fishermen: it was a quick snack
requiring no cooking, easily prepared in the
boat or on the beach after a morning at
sea. *Tiritas* were just too damn good, however, to remain a treat for fishermen alone.
You can find them at seafood stands in the
market, at carts near the bus stations and
at some of the smaller seafood restaurants
around town (ask – they're often not on
the menu). They're served cold with soda
crackers and *salsa picante* (hot chili sauce)
on the side and make a great snack on a
hot day.

El Cafecito (Paseo del Pescador; mains M$35-40; ❨ 8am-
10:30pm) Just west of the plaza, this little café
bakes up yummy cakes and crepes, as well
as smoothies.

La Sirena Gorda (☎ 554-26-87; Paseo del Pescador
90; mains M$65-210; ❨ 8:30am-10:30pm Thu-Tue)
Close to the pier, the Fat Mermaid is a casual and popular open-air restaurant that's
good for garlic shrimp, curry tuna and fish
tacos, as well as burgers and traditional
Mexican dishes.

Casa Elvira (☎ 554-20-61; Paseo del Pescador 8; mains
M$65-165; ❨ 1-10:30pm) This old hand turns out
some tasty food such as oysters Rockefeller,
jumbo steamed shrimp, and broiled octopus
with garlic. Vegetarians will appreciate the
soup, salad and spaghetti choices. Order the
coconut custard for dessert.

CENTRAL ZIHUATANEJO – INLAND

Many good, inexpensive options lie a couple
of blocks from the beach. Hearty, cheap
breakfasts and lunches can be had in the
market (Juárez btwn Nava & González; ❨ 7am-6pm).

Cenaduría Antelia (☎ 554-30-91; Bravo 14 at
Andador Pellicer; meals under M$32; ❨ 9am-2:30pm &
6pm-midnight) Antelia's popular and friendly
eatery has been dishing out tasty *antojitos
Mexicanos* (traditional Mexican snacks)
and desserts since 1975. Tuck into a *tamal
de chile verde* or a bursting bowl of daily
pozole and top it off with *calabaza con leche*
(squash in milk) for dessert.

ourpick **Tamales y Atoles Any** (☎ 554-73-73;
Guerrero 38; mains M$20-105) This super-friendly
place serves some of the most consciously
traditional Mexican cuisine in town under
its big *palapa* roof, and does a first-rate job
of it. For something different, try the *caldo
de mi patrón* (literally, 'my boss's soup': soup
with chicken liver, feet and gizzard), pineapple tamales or the squash blossoms with
cheese; less exotic dishes are easy to find on
the bilingual menu. The several varieties of
atole (a corn-based drink usually served hot)
are worth sampling as well.

Banana's (☎ 554-47-21; Bravo 9; mains M$45-70;
❨ 8am-4pm Mon-Sat, 8am-1pm Sun) This small,
airy restaurant offers a pretty fair selection
of Mexican dishes, Western breakfasts and
tasty *licuados* (fruit usually blended with
milk, sometimes just with ice).

Doña Licha (☎ 554-39-33; Cocos 8; mains M$50-90;
❨ 8am-6pm) Licha is known up and down the
coast for its down-home Mexican cooking,

casual atmosphere and excellent prices. There are always several *comidas corridas* (set-price lunch menus) to choose from, including one delicious specialty, *pollo en cacahuate* (chicken in a peanut sauce). All come with rice, beans and handmade tortillas. Breakfasts are huge.

Cafetería Nueva Zelanda (☎ 554-23-40; Cuauhtémoc 23-30; mains M$39-100) Step back in time at this spotless diner, where you can order a banana split or chocolate malt with your shrimp taco and chicken fajitas. This place is great for breakfast, everything is available *para llevar* (to go) and it steams a decent cappuccino. There are entrances on both Cuauhtémoc and Galeana.

Los Braseros (☎ 554-87-36; Ejido 21; mains M$30-100; ☼ 9am-1am) The *tacos al pastor* (with sliced, rotisserie-cooked, marinated pork) are this open-fronted eatery's crowning glory. It specializes in grilled and skewered meat and veggie combinations, served in a festive, hangar-like space.

Mariscos El Acacio (Galeana 21; mains M$40-120; ☼ 11am-8pm Mon-Sat) A simple little seafood eatery, this place offers authentic *tiritas* (see boxed text, p185), shrimp cocktails and fried fish, among other tasty treats. Prices are unbeatable and the shady sidewalk tables are fine. It's open Sunday during the high season.

Il Paccolo (☎ 559-08-38; Bravo 38; mains M$60-110; ☼ 4pm-midnight) Aching for Italian? This is the place to come. Order delicious pizzas, pastas, meats and seafood dishes, and consider the caramel crepe for dessert. The atmosphere is dark and low-key, and the bar is friendly.

AROUND THE BAY
Salvador's (Adelita s/n; mains M$20-45; ☼ 8am-9pm) This little taco joint in the laid-back Madera neighborhood serves up yummy, cheap, authentic fare.

Casa Bahía (☎ 544-86-66; Paseo del Morro s/n; mains M$88-180; ☼ 3-11:30pm) The CB has an exquisite location overlooking the bay from Punta El Morro. To reach it, cross the footbridge over the lagoon, turn left (south) and head about 350m up the road. The food is well prepared and leans to Italian, with several pastas on offer as well as carpaccio. The menu also has sashimi, burgers, steaks, seafood and some Mexican dishes. It's a romantic spot for dinner.

Coconuts (☎ 554-25-18; Ramírez 1; mains M$110-220; ☼ noon-11pm) For a romantic dinner this upscale place is hard to beat. Fairy lights fill the outdoor courtyard, service is attentive and dishes include garlic snapper, leg of duck, *chiles rellenos* (stuffed peppers), vegetable tart and herb chicken.

Puerta del Sol (☎ 554-83-42; Carretera Escénica s/n; mains M$75-180; ☼ 5pm-midnight) Reservations are recommended in high season at this romantic restaurant hanging on the cliffs between Playa Madera and Playa La Ropa. Spectacular bay and sunset views accompany the varied international menu, which features a lot of flambés. Ever seen a flaming saltimbocca?

La Casa Que Canta (☎ 554-70-30; Carretera Escénica s/n; mains M$140-300; ☼ 6:30-10:30pm) The views and food are fab at this intimate, multilevel, open-air hotel restaurant. Dishes range from Asian fusion and Mexican specialties to standards such as lobster and rack of lamb. Reservations are required, as is 'casual elegant' attire.

Restaurant Kau-Kan (☎ 554-84-46; Carretera Escénica 7; mains M$140-300; ☼ 5pm-midnight) High on the cliffs, this renowned gourmet restaurant enjoys stellar views. Making a selection is exhausting when faced with choices like stingray in black butter sauce, marinated abalone or grilled lamb chops with couscous.

On Playa La Ropa, a M$5 bus ride from downtown Zihua, **Rossy's** (☎ 554-40-04; mains M$50-190; ☼ 9am-9pm), **La Perla** (☎ 554-27-00; mains M$75-150) and **La Gaviota** (☎ 554-38-16; mains M$85-300; ☼ noon-9pm) are all good seafood restaurants. Playa Las Gatas has several restaurants offering fresh seafood as well.

SELF-CATERING
The enormous Comercial Mexicana supermarket is behind the Estrella Blanca bus station.

Drinking
Many beachfront bars have an extended happy hour.

Hotel Royal Sotavento (☎ 554-20-32; Carretera Escénica s/n; ☼ 3-11pm, happy hour 6-8pm) Tucked into the hillside over Playa La Ropa, the Sotavento is a great spot to watch the sunset. Its relaxed bar affords a magnificent view over the whole bay.

Entertainment
For big-time nightlife, head to Ixtapa. Zihuatanejo is all about being mellow.

Central Social Municipal (Morelos s/n; ☺ from 7pm) Hosts theater and art shows in the Casa de la Cultura, as well as the occasional *lucha libre* (big-time wrestling) match.

Black Bull Rodeo (☎ 554-11-29; cnr Bravo & Guerrero; ☺ from 9pm) This corner discotheque claims to have the best *norteño* (one of Mexico's versions of country-and-western) band in town. There is also *cumbia*, merengue, salsa, electronica and reggae music on offer.

Ventaneando (Guerrero 24; ☺ 8pm-4am) Across the street from the Black Bull Rodeo, this stuffy upstairs bar is a popular spot that attracts karaoke-loving crowds.

Sacbé (cnr Ejido & Guerrero; cover on weekends) Things heat up late at night at this disco and lounge. And, just in case you didn't know, *sacbé* were the ceremonial roads that connected Mayan cities in Mexico's Yucatán Peninsula.

Cine Paraíso (☎ 554-23-18; Cuauhtémoc; admission M$40) Near Bravo, this cinema shows two films nightly, usually in English with Spanish subtitles.

Shopping

Zihua offers abundant Mexican handicrafts, including ceramics, *típica* (characteristic of the region) clothing, leatherwork, Taxco silver, wood carvings and masks from around the state of Guerrero.

El Jumil (☎ 554-61-91; Paseo del Pescador 9; ☺ 9am-2pm & 5-9pm Mon-Sat) This shop specializes in authentic *guerrerense* masks. The state of Guerrero is known for its variety of interesting masks, and El Jumil stocks museum-quality examples, many starting from around M$150, as well as cheaper but delightful coconut-shell masks.

Mercado Turístico La Marina (Calle 5 de Mayo; ☺ 8am-9pm) This market has many stalls selling clothes, bags and knick-knacks.

Mercado Municipal de las Artesanías (González near Juárez; ☺ 9am-8pm) Similar to La Marina, but smaller.

Several shops along Cuauhtémoc sell Taxco silver. **Alberto's** (☎ 554-21-61; Cuauhtémoc 12 & 15; ☺ 9am-10pm Mon-Sat, 10am-3pm Sun) and **Pancho's** (☎ 554-52-30; Cuauhtémoc 11; ☺ 9am-9pm Mon-Sat) have the best selection of quality pieces.

Keep your eyes peeled, especially in the central market, for *dulces de tamarindo* (gooey dark-brown sweets made from tamarind pulp) and *dulces de coco* (coconut sweets, sold in countless shapes and flavors, a specialty of this coconut-producing region).

Getting There & Away

AIR

The Ixtapa/Zihuatanejo **international airport** (☎ 554-20-70) is about 13km southeast of Zihuatanejo, a couple of kilometers off Hwy 200 heading toward Acapulco. Note that there are far fewer flights in the off season. **Aeroméxico** (☎ 554-20-18, airport 554-22-37, 554-26-34; www.aeromexico.com; Álvarez 34) flies to Mexico City, with many onward connections. **Alaska Airlines** (☎ 554-84-57, 800-252-7522; www.alaskaair.com) flies to Los Angeles and San Francisco, **American** (☎ in the US 800-433-7300; www.aa.com) flies to Dallas, **US Airways** (☎ in the US 800-428-4322; www.usairways.com) flies to Phoenix and Las Vegas, **Mexicana** (airport ☎ 554-22-27; Zihuatanejo ☎ 554-22-09; www.mexicana.com; Bravo 64) flies to Mexico City. **Continental** (☎ 01-800-900-5000, in the US 800-523-3273; www.continental.com) flies to Houston and Minneapolis and **Northwest** (☎ in the US 800-692-6955; www.nwa.com) to Houston and Los Angeles.

BUS

Both long-distance bus terminals are on Hwy 200 about 2km east of the town center (toward the airport): the **Estrella Blanca terminal** (Central de Autobuses; ☎ 554-34-76/77) is a couple of hundred meters further from the center than the smaller **Estrella de Oro terminal** (☎ 554-21-75). Bus services include the following:

Acapulco Estrella Blanca (M$124, four hours, 1st-class hourly 5am to 7:30pm; M$90, four hours, 2nd-class hourly); Estrella de Oro (M$104, four hours, three 1st-class daily; M$90, four hours, 13 2nd-class 5:30am to 5pm)

Lázaro Cárdenas Estrella Blanca (M$68, 1½ hours, 1st-class hourly 5am to 7:30pm; M$50, two hours, 2nd-class hourly 9am to 10pm); Estrella de Oro (M$46, two hours, 11 2nd-class daily)

Manzanillo Estrella Blanca (M$316, eight hours, 1st-class at 10am, 10:50am, 8pm)

Mexico City Norte Estrella Blanca (M$484, nine to 10 hours, 1st-class at 6:45pm, 8pm)

Mexico City Sur Estrella Blanca (M$484, eight to nine hours, deluxe at 10:30pm; M$420, eight to nine hours, five 1st-class daily); Estrella de Oro (M$550, eight to nine hours, deluxe at 10pm and 10:55pm; M$483, eight to nine hours, nine 1st-class daily)

Petatlán Estrella Blanca (M$24, 30 minutes, 1st-class every hour 3:45am to 11:20pm); Estrella de Oro (M$15, 30 minutes, 13 2nd-class buses 5:30am to 6pm) Or take a local bus (M$14, 30 minutes) from the bus lot a couple of blocks east of the market in Zihuatanejo.

Manzanillo-bound buses continue to Puerto Vallarta (M$500, 14 hours, 718km) and Mazatlán (M$720, 24 hours, 1177km).

Getting Around

If you want your own set of wheels, Ixtapa has a number of car-rental agencies; see p179.

TO/FROM THE AIRPORT

The cheapest way to get to the airport is via a public 'Aeropuerto' *colectivo* (M$7) departing from Juárez near González between 6:20am and 10pm. Private *colectivo* vans provide transportation from the airport to Ixtapa or Zihua (M$100 per person), but they don't offer service to the airport. Taxis from Zihua to the airport cost around M$90.

BUS

Ixtapa, 8km northwest, is easily reached by local bus. Local 'Directo' and 'B Viejo' buses run frequently between Ixtapa and Zihua, a 15-minute ride. They depart every 15 minutes from 5:30am to 11pm (M$7). In Ixtapa, buses stop all along the main street, in front of all the hotels. In Zihua, buses depart from the corner of Juárez and Morelos. Buses marked 'Zihua-Ixtapa-Playa Linda' continue through Ixtapa to Playa Linda ($7), stopping near Playa Quieta on the way, and operate from 7am to 7pm.

The 'Correa' route goes to the Central de Autobuses from 5:30am to 9:30pm (M$5). Catch it on Juárez at the corner of Nava.

'Playa La Ropa' buses head south on Juárez and out to Playa La Ropa every half-hour from 7am to 8pm (M$5).

'Coacoyul' *colectivos* heading toward Playa Larga depart from Juárez near the corner of González, every five minutes from 5am to 10pm (M$6).

TAXI

Cabs are plentiful in Zihuatanejo. Always agree on the fare before getting in. Approximate sample fares (from central Zihua) include M$40 to Ixtapa, M$30 to Playa La Ropa, M$50 to Playa Larga and M$20 to the Central de Autobuses. If you can't hail a taxi street-side, ring **Radio Taxi UTAAZ** (☎ 554-33-11).

BARRA DE POTOSÍ

☎ 755 / pop 396

About 34km (a 40-minute drive) southeast of Zihuatanejo, lovely Barra de Potosí has an endless fine-sand beach and a large lagoon teeming with birdlife (bring repellent; it teems with other flying things, too). You can swim, take boat trips, rent a canoe and paddle around the estuary, or go horseback riding or hiking on local trails. In winter, when the waves are small, the ocean makes for sublime swimming outside the breakers, an almost divine experience as you gaze back at the dramatic backdrop of the cloud-capped Sierra Madre del Sur. The beach itself stretches north for miles, unbroken as far as Playa Larga, near Zihuatanejo. You can still see residents mending nets in the village, about 100m inland from the beach.

The area is beginning to change as outsiders buy up and develop land; the most notable example is 'Betseyville,' pricey lodgings built by American designer Betsey Johnson.

Exploring the lagoon is best in the cool of the morning, when bird-watching is good and the sun is gentle. Single and double kayaks and traditional wooden canoes can be rented at several restaurants. **Enramada Leticia** (⏰ 8am-7pm), to the left as you approach the beach, has a good selection, charging M$50 and M$120 per hour for one-person and two-person kayaks respectively, and M$60 for three hours' use of canoes that hold up to three people. Boat tours aboard covered fishing *pangas* cost about M$50 per person for a 30-minute buzz around the lagoon.

Horses are sometimes available for rent, at about M$150 per hour; check at Enramada Leticia, or with Laura at Casa del Encanto (below); she can give you information on bird-watching as well.

Low-season rates at the following places drop by between 20% and 40% from the prices listed here.

Casa del Encanto (☎ 100-14-46; www.casadelencanto .com; with breakfast d M$900-1000, bungalow M$1150, all incl breakfast) is a knockout B&B three blocks inland from Tendejón Lupita (grocery store). Private yet open-air rooms blend interior with exterior to keep things as cool and relaxed as possible, aided by numerous hammocks and fountains. The six spacious rooms have good baths and super-comfy beds; a separate bungalow (with full kitchen) holding up to four is perfect for families.

Several seafood *enramadas* line the beach and lagoon, and most are open between 8am or 9am and 7pm. The first in line, La Condesa, is one of the best. Try the *pescado a la talla*

(broiled fish fillets) or *tiritas,* both local specialties, and don't pass up the savory handmade
tortillas. Tendejón Lupita is a small grocery
store at the edge of town as you enter.

To reach the village, head southeast on Hwy
200 toward Acapulco; turn off at the town of
Los Achotes, 25km from Zihua, and drive
another 9km. Any bus heading to Petatlán
(they depart frequently from both of Zihua's
main terminals, and from the stop a couple
of blocks east of Zihua's market; see Map
p180) will drop you at the turnoff. Tell the
driver you're going to Barra de Potosí; you'll
be let off where you can catch a *camioneta*
(pickup truck) going the rest of the way. The
total cost is about M$25 if you go by bus; a
taxi from Zihua costs around M$350/450 one
way/round-trip (negotiable).

PETATLÁN
☎ 758 / pop 20,700

An unprepossessing town 30 minutes southeast of Zihuatanejo, Petatlán is best known for
its **Santuario Nacional del Padre Jesús de Petatlán**,
a large, modern sanctuary attracting pilgrims
from near and far, who leave votive offerings
(often the tiny gold trinkets that are sold at
shops across the street from the church's entrance) to the statue of Christ inside. Legend
has it that the statue was found floating in a
nearby stream shortly after Petatlán's con-
gregation took up a collection to purchase
a new one.

The archaeological site of **Soledad de Maciel**,
known as **La Chole,** is about 5km up a signed
road that takes you seaward from Hwy 200,
about 6km north of Petatlán; you can visit
on your own (ask for a guide in the village)
or go as part of a tour from Zihuatanejo. The
site contains some unexcavated mounds, a
ball court, some large carved stones and a
cave with carvings. The villagers of Soledad
de Maciel display some artifacts at a modest
museum; others are in Zihuatanejo's archaeological museum (p181).

During Semana Santa, Petatlán has a traditional fair with food, music and handicrafts
exhibitions. Petatlán's religious festival is held
on August 6.

Several restaurants flank the plaza, but
the best-value deals are in the *fondas* (small

restaurants) beside the church. They all
charge around M$25 for the *comida corrida*
and serve fresh, handmade tortillas to ac-
company the meal.

Petatlán is on Hwy 200, 32km southeast of
Zihuatanejo. For bus information, see p187.

LA BARRITA
☎ 758 / pop 60

La Barrita (Km 187) is a shell-sized village on an attractive, rocky beach an hour
southeast of Zihua off Hwy 200. Not many
tourists stop here, but surfers might want to
check the beach breaks here and 3km north
at **Loma Bonita**. Several restaurants have very
basic rooms for rent, the best probably being
those at **Restaurant Las Peñitas** (d/q M$150/200); you
can escape the evening heat of your room by
dozing in the restaurants' hammocks.

Second-class buses heading south from
Zihua or north from Acapulco will drop you
at La Barrita.

One of the more dramatic stretches of
highway in Guerrero starts about 4km south
of La Barrita, running along clifftops above
beaches and crashing surf. Several roadside
restaurants offer opportunities to enjoy the
view for a spell.

PLAYA CAYAQUITOS & OJO DE AGUA

At Km 160 (78km southeast of Zihuatanejo),
Hwy 200 rolls through the nondescript town
of **Papanoa**, where you can gas up and purchase
basic provisions. At the southern outskirts
of town, **Hotel Club Papanoa** (☎ 742-422-01-50;
www.hotelpapanoa.com; Hwy 200, Km 160; r from M$100;
P ⊠ ⊡) overlooks the beautiful, and almost
always deserted, Playa Cayaquitos. The hotel
is overpriced, but it's your only option.

Even if you don't plan to stay the night,
Playa Cayaquitos is a beautiful place to spend
the day. The main access is just north of the
Hotel Club Papanoa sign. The beach is long
and the swimming is good in winter when the
waves are gentle. At the southern end of the
beach, a tiny headland separates Cayaquitos
from Ojo de Agua, a picture-perfect little cove
with several beachfront seafood *enramadas.*
Ojo de Agua is more sheltered and the restaurants will allow you to use their services if
you eat their food.

Acapulco & the Costa Chica

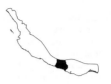

Acapulco is a cantankerous dame. She slurs and swears, and certainly was never known to pull a punch. Back in the '50s and '60s, when the Hollywood jet set came here to slurp down margaritas, she was a comely little number. But the years haven't been good for old Acapulco. Along her drooping shores, decades of waste pollute the bay. And the main strip, where you'll find the best hotels in town, is a six-lane highway plagued by traffic jams, honking horns, and even a few pimps and pushers. But one thing she still knows how to do is party. And partying it up at the languid cantinas of the old town and the barbarous discos found up on the precipitous hills is about the only reason to come here. Oh, and there's the toned cliff divers who slice the air with the precision of a surgeon's scalpel, and a couple of interesting museums and forts in the downtown area. There's also the rip-roarious spring-breakers who descend on the city each year. While they certainly bring the chaos level up to fever pitch, they have also put this city back on the map, breathing new life into the nightlife and dining scene.

Just minutes away, Pie de la Cuesta offers relief from the din of Acapulco. Here, you can take an early-morning birding expedition, or while away the afternoon sipping *mojitos* on the beachfront. To the southeast of Acapulco is Guerrero's Costa Chica, a lightly developed coast that takes day-trippers through cattle country, dwarf jungle and some absolutely spectacular beaches like Playas Ventura and Bocana. This land bears a unique cultural footprint, with many Afro-mestizos calling it home. Stop by the museum at Cuajinicuilapa to learn more, or simply strike up a conversation over sunset *cervezas* – this coast harbors secrets centuries old.

HIGHLIGHTS

- Letting your heart skip a beat as you marvel at the bravado of Acapulco's famous **cliff divers** (p196), or putting your money where your mouth is by taking a dive of your own at the oceanfront **bungee jump** (p200)

- Living *la vida loca* at Acapulco's thumping **discos** (p204) as you discover the true heartbeat of the city

- Getting up early for a birding expedition at **Pie de la Cuesta** (p208) or a **snorkel-and-scuba adventure** (p198) somewhere along this coast

- Escaping the chaos for a day or a week on the forgotten beaches of the Costa Chica, stopping for seaside snacks at **Playas Ventura** (p210), **La Bocana** (p210), and **Las Peñitas** (p210)

- Unraveling the traditions of the Costa Chica's Afro-mestizos at the museum in **Cuajinicuilapa** (p210)

- AVERAGE JANUARY DAILY HIGH: 31°C | 88°F 　　- AVERAGE JULY DAILY HIGH: 33°C | 91°F

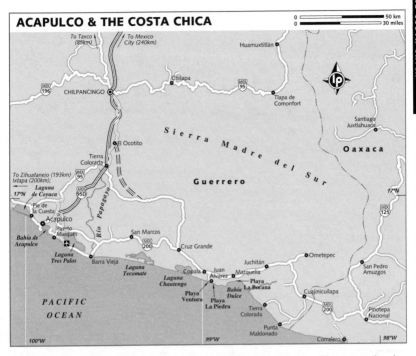

ACAPULCO & THE COSTA CHICA

Getting There & Around

Regular 1st-class buses and more frequent 2nd-class buses connect Acapulco with Zihuatanejo and points in between. Estrella Blanca (EB) has the most departures, and also offers frequent service to all points to the southeast on Hwy 200 along the Costa Chica. Several EB buses continue into Oaxaca state at least as far as Puerto Escondido.

ACAPULCO

☎ 744 / pop 717,000

Acapulco offers little to see or do for the indie traveler – even resort-goers seeking a relaxed beach vacation will be sorely disappointed by the crowds and clamor – but if a Bacchanalian brawl is what you are after, then you may have just found your spot. Acapulco is all about the nightlife. Sure, there's the golden beaches, death-defying cliff divers and towering resort hotels, but the true pulse of the city only gets going well after sunset. Whether you decide to hit the foam party at Disco Beach, or just suck down a few relaxed sunset margaritas at Hotel Los Flamingos, there's a party scene for every taste. And being one of Mexico's most gay-friendly towns, there's a diversity in the nightlife here not seen in smaller cities along the coast.

This sprawling megalopolis has been attracting more and more visitors in recent years, reversing a decline that began in the late 1970s. And new touristic and cultural life is being breathed into the city, in part by American university students who come to spend their spring break in a more economical environment than Cancún.

A bustling and relatively gay-friendly city, Acapulco offers pockets of calm, from romantic cliffside bars and restaurants to the old town's charming, shady *zócalo* and impressive 16th-century fort. The arc of beach that sweeps around many kilometers of Bahía de Acapulco (Bay of Acapulco) can be a good place to relax as well – if you take the beach vendors in your stride – but step off it and you'll find much of the rest of the city a bedlam of clogged traffic, crowded sidewalks and smoggy fumes (which at least make for a nice sunset).

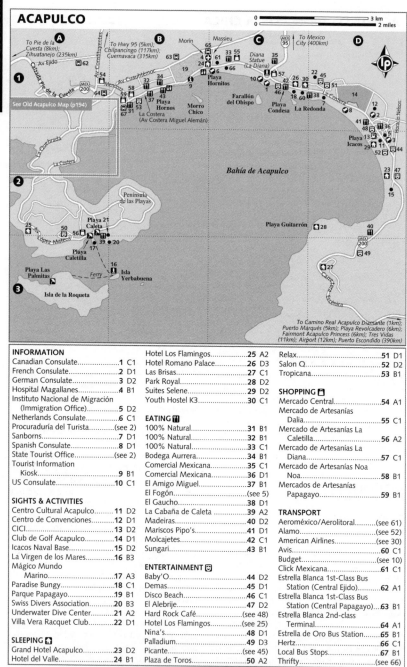

ACAPULCO

Afternoon showers are common from June to September but rare the rest of the year.

HISTORY

The name 'Acapulco' is derived from ancient Nahuatl words meaning 'where the reeds stood' or 'place of giant reeds.' Archaeological finds show that when the Spanish 'discovered' Bahía de Acapulco in 1512 people had already been living in the area for some 2000 years.

The Spanish quickly established port and shipbuilding facilities in the substantial natural harbor, and in 1523 Hernán Cortés and two partners financed a road between Mexico City and Acapulco. This 'Camino de Asia' became the principal trade route between Mexico City and the Pacific; the 'Camino de Europa,' from Mexico City to Veracruz on the Gulf coast, completed the overland leg of the route between Asia and Spain.

Acapulco became the only port in the New World authorized to receive *naos* (Spanish trading galleons) from China and the Philippines. By the 17th century, trade with Asia was flourishing, and English and Dutch privateers were busily looting ships and settlements along the Pacific coast. To fend off these pirates, the Fuerte de San Diego was built atop a low hill overlooking Bahía de Acapulco. It was not until the end of the 18th century that Spain permitted its American colonies to engage in free trade, ending the monopoly of the *naos*.

Upon gaining independence Mexico severed most of its trade links with Spain and Spanish colonies, and Acapulco declined as a port city. It became relatively isolated from the rest of the world until a paved road linked it with Mexico City in 1927. As Mexico City flourished, its citizens began vacationing on the Pacific coast. A new international airport was built, Hollywood filmed a few flicks here, and by the '50s Acapulco was becoming a glitzy jet-set resort.

Over the next few decades Acapulco's population climbed and development soared, the bay became polluted, and by the '80s foreign tourists were looking elsewhere to spend their cash. Vacationers continued to come from Mexico City and Guadalajara, and cruise ships brought in cargoes of American tourists, but thousands of hotel rooms stayed empty.

The city has poured millions into cleanup efforts since the 1990s, and the bay has benefited greatly, but many locals and visitors still refuse to swim there (the state and local governments have declared the waters to be acceptably clean; federal authorities do not always agree). Spring-breakers, attracted by discounted rooms and a welcoming hotel industry, began coming to Acapulco in droves in 2002, and don't show signs of letting up.

ORIENTATION

Acapulco is on a narrow coastal plain along the 11km shore of Bahía de Acapulco. Reached by Hwy 200 from the east and west and by Hwys 95 and 95D from the north, it is 400km south of Mexico City and 240km southeast of Zihuatanejo and Ixtapa.

Acapulco's tourist industry divides the city into three parts: Acapulco Viejo (Old Acapulco, more commonly called 'el centro'), Acapulco Dorado (Golden Acapulco) and Acapulco Diamante (Diamond Acapulco). Acapulco Viejo is the old part of town on the west side of the Bahía de Acapulco. Acapulco Dorado, usually called the Zona Dorada, wraps around the bay from Playa Hornos to the Icacos naval base. Acapulco Diamante is the relatively new, luxury-resort area that stretches 10km from the peninsula on the southern tip of Puerto Marqués – a bay situated about 18km southeast of Acapulco proper – down Playa Revolcadero to the international airport.

At the west end of Bahía de Acapulco, the Peninsula de las Playas juts south from central Acapulco. South of the peninsula is the popular Isla de la Roqueta. From Playa Caleta on the southern edge of the peninsula, Av López Mateos climbs west and north to Playa La Angosta and Playa La Quebrada before curling east back toward the city center.

Playa Caleta also marks the beginning of Av Costera Miguel Alemán. Known simply as 'La Costera' or as 'Miguel Alemán,' it's Acapulco's principal bayside avenue. Addresses along La Costera don't follow an entirely sequential numbering scheme. From Playa Caleta, La Costera cuts north-northwest across the Península de las Playas and then hugs the shore all the way around the bay to the Icacos naval base at the east end of the city. Most of Acapulco's major hotels, restaurants, discos and other points of interest are along or just off La Costera.

ACAPULCO &
THE COSTA CHICA

OLD ACAPULCO

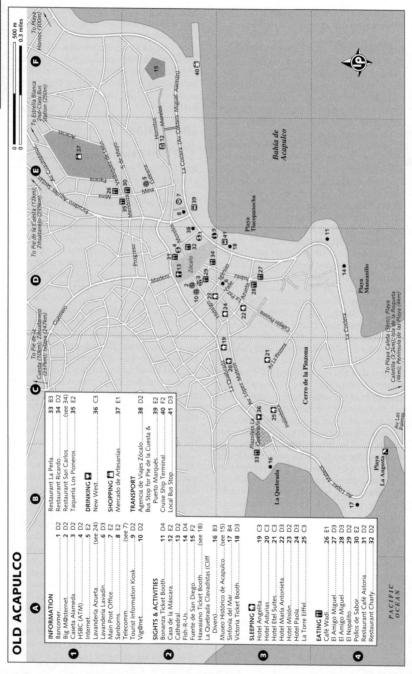

INFORMATION	
Bancomer............................1	D2
Big M@sternet....................2	D2
Caseta Alameda..................3	D2
HSBC (ATM)........................4	D2
Internet..............................5	E2
Lavandería Azueta..........(see 24)	
Lavandería Lavadín.............6	D3
Main Post Office.................7	E2
Sanborns............................8	E2
Telecomm......................(see 7)	
Tourist Information Kiosk.....9	D2
Vig@net...........................10	D2

SIGHTS & ACTIVITIES	
Bonanza Ticket Booth.........11	D4
Casa de la Máscara............12	E2
Cathedral..........................13	D2
Fish-R-Us..........................14	D4
Fuerte de San Diego...........15	F2
Hawaiano Ticket Booth....(see 18)	
La Quebrada Clavadistas (Cliff	
Divers)...........................16	B3
Museo Histórico de Acapulco...(see 15)	
Sinfonía del Mar................17	B4
Victoria Ticket Booth..........18	D3

SLEEPING	
Hotel Angelita...................19	C3
Hotel Asturias...................20	C3
Hotel Etel Suites................21	C3
Hotel María Antonieta.........22	D3
Hotel Misión.....................23	D2
Hotel Paola.......................24	D3
La Torre Eiffel...................25	C3

EATING	
Café Wadi.........................26	E1
El Amigo Miguel................27	D3
El Amigo Miguel................28	D3
El Nopalito.......................29	D2
Pollos de Sabor.................30	E2
Restaurant Café Astoria......31	D2
Restaurant Charly...............32	D2

Restaurant La Perla.............33	B3
Restaurant Ricardo.............34	D2
Restaurant San Carlos.....(see 34)	
Taquería Los Pioneros.........35	E2

DRINKING	
New West..........................36	C3

SHOPPING	
Mercado de Artesanías........37	E1

TRANSPORT	
Agencia de Viajes Zócalo.....38	D2
Bus Stop for Pie de la Cuesta &	
Puerto Marqués...............39	E2
Cruise Ship Terminal...........40	F2
Local Bus Stop...................41	D3

PACIFIC
OCEAN

Bahía de
Acapulco

To Playa
Hornos (300m)

To Estrella Blanca
2nd-Class Bus
Station (250m)

To Pie de la Cuesta (12km);
Zihuatanejo (239km)

To Pie de la
Cuesta (10km); Zihuatanejo
(237km); Ixtapa (247km)

To Playa Caleta (3km); Playa
Caletilla (3.2km); Isla de la Roqueta
(4km); Península de las Playa (4km)

500 m
0.3 miles

After the naval base, La Costera becomes La Carretera Escénica (the Scenic Highway) and, 9km further on, intersects the road to Hwy 200 on the left and the road to Puerto Marqués on the right. The airport is about 3km past this intersection.

INFORMATION
Bookstores
For its size, Acapulco is woefully lacking good bookstores. The shop in the Fuerte de San Diego (p196) maintains a good supply of art, architecture and history books, though most are in Spanish.

Sanborns La Costera 1260 (Map p192; ☎ 481-24-80; La Costera 1260; ☯ 7am-1am); La Costera 209 (Map p194; ☎ 482-61-67; La Costera 209; ☯ 7am-11pm) You can almost always find a small selection of books and magazines in English at these department stores, as well as good road and city maps for all of Mexico.

Emergency
Locatel (☎ 481-11-00) Operated by Sefotur; 24-hour hotline for all types of emergencies.
Tourist police (☎ 440-70-22)

Immigration
Instituto Nacional de Migración (Immigration Office; Map p192; ☎ 484-90-14; cnr La Costera & Elcano; ☯ 9am-1pm Mon-Fri)

Internet Access
It's impossible to walk more than a few blocks without passing a cybercafé in Acapulco's major hotel districts; most have quick connections and charge around M$10 per hour.

Big M@sternet (Map p194; Hidalgo 6; ☯ 9am-midnight) Family-run with air-con.
Internet (Map p194; Galeana 13; ☯ 10am-11pm) Fifteen computers and loud music.
Vig@net (Map p194; Hidalgo 8; ☯ 8am-midnight) Keeps more reliable hours than some.

Internet Resources
www.allaboutacapulco.com Good source of general information.
www.visitacapulco.com.mx Decent info is found on this Visitors Bureau site.

Laundry
Lavandería Azueta (Map p194; Azueta 14A; per kg wash & dry M$15; ☯ 9am-7pm Mon-Fri) Below Hotel Paola.
Lavandería Lavadín (Map p194; ☎ 482-28-90; cnr La Paz & Iglesias; 3kg min, per kg wash & dry M$15; ☯ 8am-10pm Mon-Sat)

Left Luggage
The three 1st-class bus stations have luggage-storage facilities. See p206.

Medical Services
Hospital Magallanes (Map p192; ☎ 485-61-94; Massieu 2)

Money
Omnipresent banks (many with ATMs) give the best exchange rates, and many will change US-dollar traveler's checks and euro banknotes. Conspicuous *casas de cambio* (exchange bureaus) pay a slightly lower rate, but are open longer hours and are less busy than banks; shop around, as rates vary. Banks and *casas de cambio* cluster around the *zócalo* and line La Costera. Hotels will also change money, but their rates are usually painful.

Post
Post office (Map p194; ☎ 483-53-63; La Costera 125, Palacio Federal; ☯ 8am-5:30pm Mon-Fri, 9am-1pm Sat)

Telephone
You can make long-distance calls from the many Telmex card phones throughout the city, or from private telephone *casetas* (with signs saying '*larga distancia*'). These abound near the *zócalo* and along La Costera.
Caseta Alameda (Map p194) Telephone and fax services. West side of the *zócalo*.
Telecomm (Map p194; ☎ 484-69-76; La Costera 125) Fax, telephone and limited internet service. At main post office.

Tourist Information
The city maintains an **information kiosk** (Map p194; ☯ 8:30am-10pm) on the waterfront sidewalk across from the *zócalo*, and another **kiosk** (Map p192; ☯ 8:30am-10pm) on the boardwalk opposite Parque Papagayo on La Costera. The following offices on the grounds of the Centro de Convenciones all provide tourist information and assistance. The first is in the yellow building out front.
Procuraduría del Turista (Map p192; ☎ 484-45-83; www.guerrero.gob.mx; La Costera 4455; ☯ 8am-11pm) This government dispenser of visitor information will also try to resolve complaints and problems with documents.
State tourist office (Sefotur; Map p192; ☎ 484-24-23; sefotur@yahoo.com; La Costera 4455; ☯ 9am-9pm Mon-Fri) Inside the Centro de Convenciones; provides basic information on Acapulco and the state of Guerrero.

DANGERS & ANNOYANCES

Acapulco is certainly not the safest city on the planet – but then again neither are New York or London. All travelers should use common sense when staying here: avoid buying drugs, or taking part in other illegal activities, and be wary of leaving the main tourist areas late at night. The inland neighborhoods are also best avoided.

Most of Acapulco's crime is drug-related, with warring cartels battling for lucrative shipping routes from South America to the US. A 2006 report ranked Acapulco fifth among Mexican cities for the number of crimes committed per capita, which surpassed Mexico City. And in 2007 two Canadian tourists were grazed on the legs by bullets while standing in the lobby of a Costera hotel. Recent news reports indicate a decline in violence, perhaps on the back of President Felipe Calderón's 2007 deployment of 24,000 troops nationally, 7000 of which were originally sent to the Acapulco area.

Travelers probably have more to fear from traffic on La Costera, the rough surf at Playa Revolcadero (which does claim lives) and the raw sewage that flows into the bay following rain.

Regarding crimes against property, there are many reports from visitors who have suffered thefts from their hotel rooms in the area around the *zócalo*. Secure your valuables!

Some Acapulco police are notoriously corrupt, and often stop tourists for 'shakedowns.' If you are stopped by a cop on trumped-up charges, keep your cool. They will often take your identification or driver's license, so leave your passport in the hotel safe, taking a photocopy with you instead. The most common scam is to stop a driver for speeding (or a partyer for public drunkenness), take your ID and then offer the unpleasant alternatives of going to jail, waiting at the municipal office to pay the fine, or paying it on the spot (a pleasant enough euphemism for a bribe). Bribing a police officer is a crime in Mexico, but a canvass of locals revealed that this in not uncommon, and that the standard bribe given is somewhere between M$100 and M$200. This being Mexico, they always negotiate. The Policía Federal – they drive cool Dodge Charger cop cars – are reputed to be less corrupt than the local cops, as are the tourist police. If you get in a serious jam, contact your consulate (p272) or the state tourist office (p195).

SIGHTS

Acapulco may not have a wealth of colonial architecture, but it does have an interesting history and a growing arts, music and dance scene that extends well beyond the beach.

La Quebrada Cliff Divers

The famous *clavadistas* of **La Quebrada** (the Ravine; Map p194; adult/child M$35/10; ☻ shows at 12:45pm, 7:30pm, 8:30pm, 9:30pm & 10:30pm) have been dazzling audiences since 1934, diving with fearless finesse from heights of 25m to 35m into the rising and falling swells of the narrow ocean cove below. Understandably, the divers pray at small clifftop shrines before leaping over the edge. The last show usually features divers making the plunge with a torch in either hand. For a view from below the jump-off point, walk up Calle La Quebrada from the *zócalo* or catch a cab; either way, you climb down about 60 steps to the viewing platform. Get there at least 30 minutes early to get a spot on the edge. La Quebrada is also an excellent place to watch the sunset.

La Perla restaurant-bar (p204) provides a great view of the divers from above, plus two drinks, for M$200. Dinner costs M$330.

Fuerte de San Diego

This handsomely restored, five-sided fort (Map p192) was built in 1616 atop a hill just east of the *zócalo* to protect the *naos* that conducted trade between the Philippines and Mexico from marauding Dutch and English buccaneers. Thanks in no small part to the fort's effectiveness, the trade route – which

---

ASK A LOCAL: THE ART OF CLIFF DIVING & LOCAL HOT SPOTS

Cliff diving is a family tradition that is passed from generation to generation. A family member started me on it when I was 16 years old. From there, I started learning my trade.

The best things about Acapulco are its beaches and its people. And people should definitely start their trip at La Quebrada (above), then Pie de la Cuesta (p208), and from there, head out to the discos to have even more fun. My favorite clubs are Disco Beach (p205) and El Alebrije (p205).

Ángel David Castrejón is an Acapulco cliff diver

was a crucial link between Europe, Nueva España and Asia – lasted until the early 19th century. It was also strong enough to forestall independence leader Morelos' takeover of the city in 1812 for four months. The fort had to be rebuilt after a 1776 earthquake damaged most of Acapulco, fort included. It remains basically unchanged today, except for having been restored to top condition by the Instituto Nacional de Antropología e Historia (INAH). The panorama of Acapulco you get from the fort's surroundings is free, and it alone is worth the trip.

The fort is home to the **Museo Histórico de Acapulco** (Map p194; ☎ 482-38-28; Morelos s/n; admission M$35; 🕑 9:30am-6pm Tue-Sun). It explains the story of the Yopes and Tepuztecos, the native inhabitants at the time of the Spanish arrival in the early 16th century. Most of the museum recounts Acapulco's historical importance as a port, with exhibits explaining the *torna-vuelta* (the fastest return route from Manila to Nueva España), the galleons and the treasure they carried, and the famous buccaneers who tried to capture that treasure and take it home to England or the Netherlands. On fine days during high season, the museum puts on an evening sound-and-light show (8pm Friday and Saturday).

Casa de la Máscara

This lovely **mask museum** (Map p194; Morelos s/n; admission by donation; 🕑 10am-4pm Tue-Sun) is near the Fuerte de San Diego, on the pedestrian portion of Morelos. It has an amazing collection of masks from around Mexico – including some by Afro-mestizos on the Costa Chica – as well as masks from Cuba, Italy and Africa. A central room displays modern creations. The scant signage is in Spanish.

Centro Cultural Acapulco

Set around a garden just southeast of CICI water park down La Costera, this **complex** (Casa de la Cultura; Map p192; ☎ 484-38-14; La Costera 4834; 🕑 9am-9pm) houses a groovy café-art gallery, a handicrafts shop, an open-air theater and an indoor auditorium, as well as the **Salon de Fama de los Deportistas de Guerrero** (Guerrero Sports Hall of Fame; admission free).

Centro de Convenciones

Acapulco's **convention center** (Map p192; ☎ 484-71-52, 484-70-98; La Costera 4455) is a huge complex with a permanent crafts gallery (Galería de Artesanías), temporary special exhibitions, a large plaza, theaters and concert halls. The grounds have reproductions of statuary from archaeological sites throughout Mexico. Phone the center to ask about current offerings.

Beaches

Visiting Acapulco's beaches tops most visitors' lists of things to do here. During the December to April high season, you can bank on the beaches being Speedo-to-Speedo, with rental chairs, umbrellas, vendors, sun-soakers, jet skis and parasailers dominating the view. That's Acapulco.

ZONA DORADA

The beaches (Map p192) heading east around the bay from the *zócalo* are the most popular. If you jump on a bus in the old town and head east, the first beach you'll pass is **Playa Hornos**, a narrow strip of sand crowded with fishing boats and families. In the morning it's abuzz with activity as the fishers haul in their catch, but the Costera sits right on its shoulder, making it noisy in the afternoon. At **Playa Hornitos** the beach widens, and from here east it's flanked by high-rise hotels and restaurants. The beach narrows in front of Parque Papagayo before opening up again at **Playa Condesa**, the trendiest of Acapulco's beaches, where you go to show it all off – and watch others do the same. Playa Condesa is also home to Acapulco's most outwardly gay beach. **Playa Icacos** is the easternmost stretch of sand on the bay, backed by more hotels and restaurants. Nearly all the beaches east of Playa Hornos are good for swimming and great for sunbathing, and various entrepreneurs set up stands to rent chaise longues and umbrellas. These are also the beaches where you can parasail, ride banana boats and waterski; mobile outfitters set up shop all down the beach. City buses constantly ply La Costera, the beachside avenue, making it easy to get up and down this long arc of beaches.

PENÍNSULA DE LAS PLAYAS

The beaches on the southwestern shores of Bahía de Acapulco (Map p192) have a markedly different feel than those to the east; they're smaller, more sheltered, lack the glitz of the Zona Dorada, and are often even more crowded due to their smaller size. They're well worth a visit for their old-time feel. **Playas Caleta** and **Caletilla** are two small, protected beaches beside one another in a cove on the south side of the Península de las Playas. They're lined end-to-end with cheap seafood *enramadas* (thatch-covered open-air restaurants). During Sunday afternoons they're the epitome of family fun: the shallow water chaotic with splashing children, anchored fishing *pangas* (small motorized skiffs) and paddling vendors selling trinkets. Music blares over it all from Mágico Mundo Marino, an aquarium on the spit of land separating the two beaches. Boats to Isla de la Roqueta leave frequently from near the aquarium.

All buses marked 'Caleta' heading down La Costera stop here, though it's a pleasant 30-minute walk; take the *malecón* (waterfront street) from the *zócalo* and then follow the Costera and the signs from there.

Playa La Angosta ('Narrow Beach'; Map p194) is in a thin, protected cove nestled between two high cliffs on the west side of the peninsula. It has a few seafood *enramadas* and the only stretch of sand in Acapulco with a view of the sunset on the water. From the *zócalo* it takes about 30 minutes to walk there, either along the Costera (turn right on Av Las Palmas and walk another block), or along the cliffside walkway heading downhill from La Quebrada, a more strenuous but also more scenic route. The latter takes you past the **Sinfonía del Mar**, perhaps the best spot in Acapulco for sunsets.

Isla de la Roqueta

This island (p192) offers a popular (that means crowded) beach with decent snorkeling and diving possibilities. You can rent snorkeling gear, kayaks and other water-sports equipment on the beach.

From Playas Caleta and Caletilla, boats make the eight-minute one-way trip every 20 minutes or so (M$40 round-trip). The alternative is a glass-bottomed boat that makes a circuitous trip to the island, departing from the same beaches but traveling via **La Virgen de los Mares** (the Virgin of the Seas), a submerged bronze statue of the Virgen de Guadalupe; visibility varies with water conditions. The round-trip fare is M$70; the trip takes about 45 minutes, depending on how many times floating vendors accost your boat. You can alight on the island and take a later boat back, but find out when the last boat leaves (usually around 5pm).

ACTIVITIES

As one might expect, Acapulco's activities are largely beach-based. There are nonbeach things to do, but generally everything is in the mega-vacation spirit, with once-in-a-lifetime adventure and/or adrenaline rush promised.

Water Sports

Just about everything that can be done on, or below, the water is done in Acapulco. On Bahía de Acapulco, water-skiing, boating, 'banana-boating' and parasailing *(paracaída)* are all popular activities. To partake in any of these, walk along the Zona Dorada beaches and look for the usually orange kiosks. They charge about M$70 for snorkel gear, M$250 for a five-minute parasailing flight, M$300 for a jet-ski ride and M$550 for one hour of water-skiing. The smaller Playas Caleta and Caletilla have sailboats, fishing boats, motorboats, pedal boats, canoes, snorkel gear, inner tubes and water bicycles for rent.

Though Acapulco isn't a scuba destination in itself, there are some decent dive sites nearby. At least two outfitters offer quality services. **Underwater Dive Center** (Map p192; ☎ 181-57-10; www.underwateracapulco.com; Playa Caleta) has PADI-certified instructors and offers several certification courses and guided day trips. All prices include gear, a boat and refreshments. Intro dives cost M$900, two-tank dives run M$700, and snorkeling from the boat is M$350.

Swiss Divers Association (SDA; Map p192; ☎ 482-13-57; www.swissdivers.com; La Costera 100) is a first-rate shop at the Hotel Caleta that also offers PADI and NAUI instruction – in Spanish, English and German – with a variety and prices similar to those of Underwater Dive Center.

The best **snorkeling** is off small Playa Las Palmitas on Isla de la Roqueta (left). Unless you pony up for an organized snorkeling trip, you'll need to scramble over rocks to reach it. You can rent gear on the Isla or on Playas Caleta and Caletilla, which also have some decent spots. Both scuba operations mentioned above do half-day snorkeling trips for around M$350 per person, including boat, guide, gear, food and drink, and hotel transportation.

Sportfishing is very popular in Acapulco and many companies offer six- to seven-hour fishing trips; book at least a day in advance and figure on a 6am or 7am departure time. **Fish-R-Us** (Map p194; ☎ 482-82-82; www.fish-r-us.com; La Costera 100) offers fishing trips starting at around M$2500 (for the entire eight-person

---

ESCAPE FROM ACAPULCO

Several beaches and interesting towns can be seen on a day (or quick overnight) trip from Acapulco. Here are our favorites.

■ **Puerto Marqués** (off Map p192) This beach lies on a striking little bay of the same name about 18km southeast of old Acapulco. It's a madhouse on weekends when families pour in to devour seafood prepared in the countless restaurants that have come to be Puerto Marqués' main attraction. Midweek it can be quiet. If you're going to Puerto Marqués from La Costera, take an eastbound 'Puerto Marqués' bus (M$5) from the west end of Playa Hornos; they pass every 30 minutes or so, less frequently on weekends.

■ **Playa Revolcadero** (off Map p192) This long, wide beach, a bit past Marqués, is home to Acapulco's grandest luxury resorts. They're spread out, however, so you rarely feel crowded here. It has the only surf in Acapulco; though it's best as a big-wave break, there are people out chasing waves all year. Swimming can be very dangerous here: mind the warning flags. Horseback riding along the beach is popular. The best way to get here is by taxi (around M$20).

■ **Pie de la Cuesta** (p208) This little town is about 10km northwest of Acapulco, and is an excellent sunset spot. Get up early for a birding expedition on the lagoon.

■ **Cuajinicuilapa** (p210) This Afro-mestizo stronghold has a tidy little museum dedicated to the unique history and culture of these people.

■ **Mexico City** Chilangos (people from Mexico City) make the five-hour trip to Acapulco all the time. So why not reverse the trend, and head to the capital of the Latino world for a weekend blaster? You can get information to ease your way into this 19-million-person maelstrom at www.lonelyplanet.com or www.allaboutmexicocity.com.

■ **Taxco** Just four hours away – you may be able to do it in one long day – this colonial gem, famous for its silver, takes you a world away from the steroid-pumped glitz of Acapulco. Visit www.taxco.com.mx for a good listing of hotels (you'll need some Spanish to understand).

---

boat, gear and bait). If you don't have a group large enough to cover the boat, the captain can often add one or two people to an existing group for M$700 to M$800 per person.

Cruises

Various boats and yachts offer cruises, most of which depart from near Playa Tlacopanocha or Playa Manzanillo (Map p194) near the *zócalo*. Cruises (from M$120 for 90 minutes to M$250 and up for four hours) are available day and night. They range from glass-bottomed boats to multilevel craft with blaring salsa music and open bars, to yachts offering quiet sunset cruises around the bay. Most offer a lunchtime cruise (around 11am to 3:30pm) and a sunset cruise (around 4:30pm to 7pm, later in winter). Some offer moonlight cruises (10:30pm to 2am), complete with dancing. A typical trip heads from Tlacopanocha around Península de las Playas to Isla de la Roqueta, passes by to see the cliff divers at La Quebrada, crosses over to Puerto Marqués and then returns around Bahía de Acapulco.

The **Victoria** (Map p194; ☎ 495-47-46), **Hawaiano** (☎ 482-21-99) and **Bonanza** (Map p194; ☎ 482-20-55) cruise operations are all popular; you can make reservations directly or through travel agencies and most hotels. Both Victoria and Bonanza have ticket booths along the old-town section of La Costera.

Other Activities

Acapulco has squash courts, tennis courts, public swimming pools, gymnasiums, tracks and facilities for other sports. The tourist office stays abreast of most sport-related opportunities and events and is a good source of information.

For tennis, try **Club de Golf Acapulco** (Map p192; ☎ 484-12-25; La Costera s/n), Club de Tenis Hyatt at the Grand Hotel Acapulco (p203), **Villa Vera Racquet Club** (Map p192; ☎ 484-03-33; Lomas del Mar 35) or Fairmont Acapulco Princess Hotel (p202).

Acapulco has many 18-hole golf courses, among them the **Club de Golf Acapulco** (Map p192; ☎ 484-65-83; La Costera s/n), next to the convention center on La Costera; **Tres Vidas** (off Map p192; ☎ 444-51-26) in Acapulco Diamante near the

> **SEARCHING FOR THE PERFECT SUNSET**
>
> Finding the perfect sunset – the kind that lasts for hours as the sun dips its golden toes ever so lovingly into the Pacific – is basically what a vacation to this region is about. But despite all the ocean-front real estate here, it can be challenging to find that perfect spot. Here are some places to get you started.
>
> First off, think Old Acapulco. The only place you can sit on the sand (within the city limits) and watch the sun set on the water is Playa La Angosta (p198), a sliver of a beach on the Península de las Playas. The bar at Hotel Los Flamingos (p202), perched high on the peninsula's western cliffs, has an almost dizzying perspective of the event, always aided by hoisting a few to the fading sun. **Plazoleta La Quebrada**, near where the divers perform, is another great spot; the parking lot fills with people around sunset. One of the finest views of all is at the small **Sinfonía del Mar** (Symphony of the Sea), a stepped plaza built on the edge of the cliffs just south of La Quebrada. Its sole purpose is to give folks a magical view. If you really feel like chasing the sunset, you should head over to Pie de la Cuesta (p208), about a half-hour's ride northwest of Acapulco. Its long, wide beach and hammock-clad restaurants are famous for spectacular sunsets.

airport; and the Fairmont Acapulco Princess Hotel, also in Diamante. Those courses in Diamante front Playa Revolcadero and have spectacular views.

The 50m-high bungee tower at **Paradise Bungy** (Map p192; ☎ 484-75-29; www.paradisebungy.com.mx; La Costera 107; ☯ 1pm-2am) is easy to spot on La Costera, and for M$600 you can throw yourself (bungee included) from its platform.

ACAPULCO FOR CHILDREN
Acapulco is very family-friendly (if not wallet-friendly), with many amusement options designed for children, but fun for adults too.

Parque Papagayo
This large **amusement park** (Map p192; La Costera; admission free; ☯ 8am-8pm, rides operate 3-10pm) is full of tropical trees and provides access to Playas Hornos and Hornitos. Its attractions include a go-kart track, a lake with paddleboats, a children's train, mechanical rides, animal enclosures with deer, rabbits, crocodiles and turtles, an aviary, a restaurant-bar and a hill affording an excellent view. A 1.2km 'interior circuit' pathway is good for jogging. The park is between Morín and El Cano and has entrances on all four sides.

CICI
On the east side of Acapulco, the **CICI** (Centro Internacional de Convivencia Infantil; Map p192; ☎ 484-19-70; La Costera 101; admission M$100; ☯ 10am-6pm) is a family water-sports park. Dolphins perform several shows daily, and humans occasionally give diving exhibitions. You can also enjoy an 80m-long water toboggan, a pool with artifi-

cial waves and the Sky Coaster ride (M$150 per person), which simulates the Quebrada cliff-diving experience. Children who are two years and up pay full price, plus you'll need to rent a locker (M$30), and an inflatable ring (M$25 to M$35) to use the toboggan.

Any local bus marked 'CICI,' 'Base' or 'Puerto Marqués' will take you there.

Mágico Mundo Marino
This **aquarium** (Map p192; ☎ 483-12-15; adult/child 3-12yr M$60/30; ☯ 9am-6pm) stands on a small islet just off Playas Caleta and Caletilla. Highlights include a sea-lion show, swimming pools, water toboggans and the feeding of crocodiles, turtles and piranhas.

COURSES
Centro Cultural Acapulco (Casa de la Cultura; Map p192; ☎ 484-38-14; La Costera 4834; ☯ 9am-9pm) offers occasional art and dance classes.

FESTIVALS & EVENTS
Acapulco hits its height of merry-making during the three weeks around **Semana Santa** (Holy Week), when the city fills with tourists, the discos stay packed every night of the week and the beaches are crammed.

The **Festival Francés** (French Festival), celebrating French food, cinema, music and literature, began in 2004 and is held in March. More long-standing is the **Tianguis Turístico** (www.tianguisturistico.com), Mexico's major annual tourism trade fair, held the second or third week in April. The **Festivales de Acapulco**, held for one week in May, feature Mexican and international music at venues around town.

Aviation fans shouldn't miss the **Acapulco Air Show**, which takes place over three days around the beginning of November. It features everything from biplanes to F-16s, plus wing-walking, parachute teams, precision aerobatics and high-speed fighter maneuvers over the bay and between the hotels. The USAF Thunderbirds team appeared at the show for the first time in 2005.

The festival for Mexico's favorite figure, the **Virgen de Guadalupe**, is celebrated all night on December 11 and all the following day; it's marked by fireworks, folk dances and street processions accompanied by small marching bands. The processions converge at the cathedral in the *zócalo*, where children dressed in costumes congregate.

SLEEPING

Acapulco has a plethora of hotels (more than 30,000 rooms) in every category imaginable. What part of town you choose to stay in will depend on your budget and your interests. The cheapest hotels are near the *zócalo* and uphill along La Quebrada, and generally charge per person, rather than per room type. This also happens to be the part of town with the most historical character, cheaper restaurants and easily accessible services and bus lines. The Zona Dorada hotels are more expensive, but are on or near the beaches and closer to the clubs and bars. Some of the hotels on the Península de las Playas are extremely relaxing and offer a romantic, old-time-Acapulco feel, but they are a fair distance from other restaurants and services.

Rooms are priciest from mid-December until a week or so after Semana Santa, and through the July and August school holidays. Reservations are recommended between Christmas and New Year's Day and around Semana Santa. Unless specified, the following prices are high season; they can drop 10% to 40% when business is slow.

Head to the internet for the best deals on midrange and top-end hotels.

Budget

Most of Acapulco's budget hotels are concentrated around the *zócalo* and on La Quebrada; the latter catch more breezes.

Hotel Angelita (Map p194; ☎ 483-57-34; La Quebrada 37; r per person M$150) Clean, spacious rooms – each with at least one fan, a hot-water bath-

room and good screens – are set back along a narrow, plant-filled courtyard. A paper-back library augments the small TV room in front, where doña Angelita, the hotel's lovely grandmotherly owner, occasionally holds court.

Hotel Paola (Map p194; ☎ 482-62-43; Azueta 16; r per person M$150) This positively pink hotel might as well be called the hotel 'Pepto' on account of its color scheme. Dark hallways and dirty baths make this a last-ditch budget buy. But it certainly is cheap.

Hotel Asturias (Map p194; ☎ 483-65-48; gerardomancera@aol.com; La Quebrada 45; r per person M$170; P ⋈ ⛱) This friendly, family-run hotel is clean and well-tended, with mostly pleasant rooms on a courtyard (the beds are just a bit concave), cable TV in the lobby, a small swimming pool and a book exchange.

Hotel María Antonieta (Map p194; ☎ 482-50-24; Azueta 17; r per person with fan/air-con M$200/300; ⋈) The 'Ma Antonieta' has 38 sterile budget rooms. They're very plain, but clean and good-sized, and guests have use of a communal kitchen.

La Torre Eiffel (Map p194; ☎ 482-16-83; hoteltorreeiffel@hotmail.com; Inalámbrica 110; s/d M$200/400; P ⛱) Perched on a hill above Plazoleta La Quebrada, the popular Eiffel has a small swimming pool, huge shared balconies and some spectacular sunset views. It's right near the Quebrada, and the friendly, helpful management, good baths and comfortable beds help make the climb worth it.

Youth Hostel K3 (Map p192; ☎ 481-31-11; La Costera 116; www.k3acapulco.com; dm/r with continental breakfast M$200/480; ⋈ ▣) It's shared bathrooms only, and the rooms have almost a Japanese capsule-hotel feel. But both dorms and private rooms have air-con, there's a shared kitchen and the terrace, bar and game room provide ample space for socializing. Most importantly, it's right across La Costera from the beach.

ourpick Hotel Misión (Map p194; ☎ 484-36-43; hotelmision@hotmail.com; Valle 12; r per person with fan/air-con M$250/300; P ⋈) Acapulco's oldest hotel certainly looks it from the outside, but step into the colonial compound's leafy, relaxing courtyard and things get much nicer, making this one of the best buys for the price. Basic rooms feature colorful tiles, heavy Spanish-style furniture and comfortable beds in a variety of configurations. A big water cooler in the lobby does its part to keep our planet green by reducing water-bottle usage.

Midrange

Most of the high-rise hotels along La Costera tend to be expensive. But there are some good deals in older places around town. A few places offer rooms with fully equipped kitchens.

Hotel Los Flamingos (Map p192; ☎ 482-06-90; www .flamingosacapulco.com; Av López Mateos s/n; r/ste M$650/1000; Ⓟ ⓧ ⓡ) Perched 135m over the ocean on the highest cliffs in Acapulco, this single-story classic boasts one of the finest sunset views in town, as well as a bar and restaurant. Rooms themselves are modest and comfortable, with great baths, good screens and a long shared lounging terrace. John Wayne, Johnny Weissmuller (best movie Tarzan ever!) and some of their Hollywood pals once owned the place. The 'Round House' is a two-room circular house surrounded by trees with its own small pool, private entry and a stone walkway down to a tiny parapet on the cliff's edge. Weissmuller died here in 1984, of natural causes. You can rent it out, if you dare.

Hotel del Valle (Map p192; ☎ 485-83-36; cnr Morín & Espinoza; r with fan/air-con M$700/877; Ⓟ ⓧ ⓡ) On the east side of Parque Papagayo, near La Costera and popular Playa Hornitos, the del Valle has reasonably comfortable rooms and a small swimming pool. Things can get a bit noisy here, and the beds will put a spring in your back, rather than in your step.

Suites Selene (Map p192; ☎ 484-29-77; suitesselene@ hotmail.com; Colón 175; d M$819, ste with/without kitchen M$1755/936; Ⓟ ⓧ ⓡ) One door from the sands of Playa Icacos, Selene is a decent option for long-stay self-caterers. Though a little worn, it has fine, firm beds, good air-con (though only fans in the dining room/kitchens), good baths, a nice deep pool and cable TV throughout.

Hotel Etel Suites (Map p194; ☎ 482-22-40; etelsuites@terra.com.mx; Av La Pinzona 92; s/d M$700/1000; Ⓟ ⓧ ⓡ ⓕ) High atop the hill overlooking Old Acapulco, the Etel offers service with a snarl and oh-so-70s bebop styling. The spotless suites and apartments all sleep at least three people, and most have expansive terraces with views of La Quebrada and the Pacific to one side and the bay to the other. Amenities include full kitchens, well-manicured gardens, a children's play area and at least one swimming pool.

Top End

The original high-rise zone begins at the eastern end of Parque Papagayo and curves east around the bay; new luxury hotels have been springing up on Playa Revolcadero, east of Puerto Marqués. Most of the establishments listed here offer at least a couple of rooms set up for disabled guests, and recreation programs for children (though these may be available only on weekends and at school vacation times).

Off-season package rates and special promotions can be less than half the standard rack rates – hit the internet for the best deals year round. All prices given here are high-season rack rates.

Hotel Romano Palace (Map p192; ☎ 484-77-30, 800-090-15-00; www.romanopalace.com.mx; La Costera 130; r M$1530; Ⓟ ⓧ ⓡ) It's a bit costly for a place without ocean frontage, but nonetheless, this 22-story hotel offers passable accommodations: slightly smoky-smelling rooms have private balconies, air-con and floor-to-ceiling windows with great bayfront views (ask for an upper-story room). The faintly Asian decor is dated, whereas the marble bathrooms still look good, and the Romano has multiple restaurants and a beach club.

Las Brisas (Map p192; ☎ 469-69-00, in the US 800-223-6800; www.brisas.com.mx; Carretera Escénica 5255; casitas with continental breakfast from M$2300; Ⓟ ⓧ ⓛ ⓡ) Classic Las Brisas commands some amazing views from its vantage point high above the bay, making it our favorite high-end option. Built in the late '50s, the place has great bones, including a lot of lovely stonework and tile floors. Each of the 236 'casitas' has a private terrace or balcony and either a private swimming pool or one shared with at most two other casitas. The hotel's beach club is nestled far below in a rocky cove.

Camino Real Acapulco Diamante (off Map p192; ☎ 800-901-2300, in the US 800-722-6466; www.cami noreal.com; Carretera Escénica, Km 14; r from M$2800; Ⓟ ⓧ ⓧ ⓛ ⓡ ⓕ) The CR lies down a steep, gated 1km access road off the Carretera Escénica, directly above its own small, rocky stretch of Playa Pichilingue on the calm bay of Puerto Marqués. Each of the 157 luxuriously appointed rooms has a terrace or balcony looking out on the bay, and their showers put out enough filtered water to drown a hippo in no time flat. The well-designed, multilevel hotel has a spa, a gym, three shallow swimming pools and the usual multiplicity of bars and restaurants.

Fairmont Acapulco Princess (off Map p192; ☎ 469-10-00, in the US 800-441-1414; www.fairmont.com; Playa Revolcadero s/n; r from M$2800; Ⓟ ⓧ ⓧ ⓛ ⓡ ⓕ)

This Aztec-themed place on Playa Revolcadero is BIG. Its core 'pyramid' has a towering, 15-story atrium lobby and is one of three huge structures that hold a total of 1015 guestrooms and suites. The 194 hectares of lush landscaped grounds also contain a golf course, nine tennis courts, five swimming pools, two fitness centers and a dozen bars and restaurants. Rooms come with varying views, but all have a high standard of comfort and lots of nice touches like ironing boards, hairdryers, dual sinks and digital room safes.

Park Royal (Map p192; ☎ 440-65-65; www.parkroyal hotels.com.mx; Costera Guitarrón 110; r per person all-inclusive from M$2000; P X 🍴 🖥 🏊) The Park Royal opened for business in its present incarnation in 2003, and remodeling continues on the former Radisson resort. Its 218 rooms are spread out on various levels and floors, but only about 40 of them have sea views. Most standards have two beds, a really big TV, great air-con and a bathroom done up in lovely subdued brown marble. A tram carries guests down to a large swimming pool sitting just above the hotel's relatively secluded stretch of beach. Rack rates cover three meals a day and all the drinks you want.

Grand Hotel Acapulco (Map p192; ☎ 469-12-34, 800-005-00-00, in the US 800-492-8804; www.grandhotelacapulco .com; La Costera 1; r from M$2850; P X 🍴 🖥 🏊 ♿) The Grand is right on the beach and at the middle of La Costera's action. Its 638 plush rooms and suites have marble bathrooms, and most have private balconies. Two inviting swimming pools, a passel of palm trees, a bevy of bars and restaurants (one serving kosher food from December to February) and an on-site synagogue round things out.

EATING

For inexpensive, down-home Mexican cooking, the eateries around the *zócalo* offer the best pop for your peso. For finer dining and a more celebratory atmosphere, try something on La Costera.

Old Acapulco

Café Wadi (Map p194; ☎ 482-09-14; cnr Mina & Velásquez; coffee M$10-20; 🕑 8am-8pm Mon-Sat) This is a great morning stop for good fresh-roasted espresso drinks before hitting the nearby artisan market.

Taquería Los Pioneros (Map p194; ☎ 482-23-45; cnr Mendoza & Mina; 5 tacos for M$25, mains M$25-95; 🕑 9am-3am) The tacos are tiny but their various fillings are tasty, plus you can load up on accompaniments: jalapeños, pickled carrots, onions, cilantro and so forth. The food comes with plenty of open-air atmosphere, too, at the sweaty, busy, noisy intersection. Hang with locals and watch the elaborately painted buses go by (with luck you'll spot the vomiting scene from *The Exorcist*).

Pollos de Sabor (Map p194; cnr Mina & 5 de Mayo; quarter/half/whole fowls approx M$22/44/88; 🕑 11am-8pm) For eat-in or takeout rotisserie-roasted chicken, head to this corner restaurant. There's nothing like tearing a hot bird limb from limb, dumping on the salt and chowing down.

Restaurant San Carlos (Map p194; Juárez 5; mains M$30-60) An open-air patio, good traditional Mexican fare and a M$30 *comida corrida* (set menu). Want more? OK: the menu has an endless list of Mexican standards, including green and white *pozole* (a hearty pork and hominy soup).

Restaurant Ricardo (Map p194; Juárez 9; mains M$40-50) A couple of doors further from the *zócalo*, Ricardo's is another good choice for cheap *comidas corridas* and tasty house specials like *camarones en ajo* (shrimp with garlic) or *pollo en salsa de cacahuete* (chicken in peanut sauce), all served under bright fluorescent light shining onto white tile.

El Nopalito (☎ 483-84-76; cnr La Paz & Ramírez; mains $40-60; 🕑 7am-8pm) Reader-recommended, the 'Little Cactus' serves inexpensive and filling fish and meat dishes (*pozole* on Thursday) and a good *menú del día* (lunch special).

Restaurant Charly (Map p194; Carranza s/n; 4 tacos M$22, set meal M$39) Just steps east of the *zócalo*, on the pedestrian alley of Carranza, economical Charly has shady sidewalk tables and offers up *barbacoa de chivo* (goat) as both a main dish and taco.

Restaurant Café Astoria (Map p194; zócalo, Edificio Pintos 4C; snacks M$18-45, mains $50) This friendly café has indoor and outdoor tables in a shady, semiquiet spot just east of the cathedral. It serves some OK espresso drinks, including a massive *tarro* (cup) of cappucino for M$20.

El Amigo Miguel (Map p194; ☎ 483-69-81; Juárez 31 & Juárez 16; 🕑 10am-9pm; mains M$70-200) This cheery open-air restaurant is one of the busiest, featuring cheap and delicious seafood. Miguel has two restaurants opposite one another, at the same intersection, with other branches around town (the branch on La Costera, Map p192, is open from 11am to 8pm). Several other good seafood places are nearby.

La Costera

Dozens of restaurants line La Costera heading east toward the high-rise hotels; most specialize in fresh seafood or flashy gimmicks. Stroll along, browse the posted menus, and take your pick.

100% Natural (Map p192; ☎ 485-52-79; La Costera 34; mains M$40-90; **V**) This health-conscious chain has other branches at La Costera 112 and 200, and elsewhere in town, all with a mellow ambience and good, friendly service. The food is consistently good, mostly vegetarian fare, including wholegrain breads and rolls (the rolls on the table aren't free) and a large variety of fruit and veggie juice blends, *licuados* (smoothies) and shakes. The restaurant at La Costera 200 is open 24 hours.

El Fogón (Map p192; ☎ 484-50-79; La Costera 10; mains M$45-100) Another chain, El Fogón serves its traditional Mexican dishes at several La Costera branches. Many fast-food chains also dot La Costera, especially near the east end.

ourpick Molcajetes (Map p192; La Costera s/n; mains M$60-100; ☯ 5pm-2am) Dig in to the home-toasted tortillas – there's a big stone toaster in the middle of the restaurant – at this little beachside joint on the Costera. It has cheap beer and great home cooking, a rarity amid the dense fog of overdevelopment hanging over the rest of the area. There's no pretensions here. And that's the way (ah-ha-unh-ha) we like it.

Sungari (Map p192; ☎ 486-14-23; La Costera s/n; mains M$80-130, 3-course meal M$90; ☯ 1-11pm) This beachfront Chinese joint offers well-priced meals and standard Chinese fare. It even delivers.

Mariscos Pipo's (Map p192; ☎ 484-17-00; cnr La Costera & Nao Victoria; mains M$80-250; ☯ 1-9pm) Pipo's has a varied menu that includes baby shark quesadillas, freshwater bass, grilled crawfish and scallop cocktail, all served in a large dining area with a simple, nautical theme.

El Gaucho (Map p192; ☎ 484-17-00; Hotel Presidente, La Costera 8; mains M$80-250; ☯ 5pm-midnight) The Gaucho is upscale but not stuffy, and one of the top spots in town for a steak (though you pay dearly for it). All the meat is grilled in the true Argentine style. Less carnivorous or extravagant folk can choose from an assortment of pasta dishes. The short but decent wine list includes Mexican, Chilean, Spanish and, of course, Argentine selections.

Outskirts

La Cabaña de Caleta (Map p192; ☎ 469-85-53; López Mateos s/n, Playa Caleta; mains M$46-165; ☯ 9am-9pm)

This little beach club and restaurant is a good spot to check out the chaos of Playa Caleta without actually having to take part in it.

Restaurant La Perla (Map p194; ☎ 483-11-55; Hotel El Mirador, Plazoleta La Quebrada 74; dinner M$330; ☯ 7-11pm) First-rate views of the death-defying *clavadistas* (see La Quebrada Cliff Divers, p196) justify the high price of a meal here; candlelit terraces and sea breezes are a bonus. The three-course menu is meat-heavy but includes several fish choices and a couple each of chicken and pasta dishes.

Madeiras (Map p192; ☎ 446-56-36; Carretera Escénica 33; prix-fixe dinner M$400; ☯ 7-9:30pm Mon-Fri, 7-10:30pm Sat & Sun) A great spot for a romantic meal, Madeiras has been in operation for more than 25 years. You construct a four-course meal from the fairly wide menu of offerings that blend Old World favorites with Mexican flourishes, such as tournedos with Roquefort and *huitlacoche* (corn truffle, a fungus that grows on maize), accompanied by a sauce made with *guajillo* chilies and Madeira. Decor is appealingly simple, but it can't compete with the spectacular terrace views over Bahía de Acapulco.

Self-Catering

The huge air-conditioned Comercial Mexicana, Bodega Aurrera and Bodega Gigante combination supermarkets (Map p192) and big-box discount department stores are along La Costera between the *zócalo* and Parque Papagayo, among other places. Aside from the fresh produce and all manner of groceries, you can find some pretty high-quality, ready-to-eat stuff in the bakery and deli departments.

ENTERTAINMENT

Acapulco's active nightlife probably outdoes its beaches as the city's main attraction. Much of the entertainment revolves around discos and nightclubs.

Discos

Most of the discos open around 10:30pm (but don't get rolling till midnight or later) and stay open till 4am or later. Cover charges vary seasonally and nightly; when they include an open bar, you still usually need to tip your server. Dress codes prohibit shorts, sneakers and the like.

Palladium (Map p192; ☎ 446-54-90; Carretera Escénica s/n; cover & open bar women/men M$330/430)

Hailed by many as the best disco in town, Palladium attracts a 20s-to-30s crowd with fabulous views from giant windows and a range of hip-hop, house, trance, techno and other bass-heavy beats emanating from an ultraluxe sound system. Dress up, and expect to wait in line.

Baby'O (Map p192; ☎ 484-74-74; La Costera 22; cover M$100-380) Very popular with the upscale crowd, Baby'O has a laser-light show, Wednesday theme nights and spins rock, pop, house and 'everything but electronica.' Drinks are not included in the cover charge.

El Alebrije (Map p192; ☎ 484-59-02; La Costera 3308; cover & open bar women/men M$260/360) This disco-concert hall bills itself as 'one of the largest and most spectacular discos in the world.' Less spectacular than big, it's usually packed with a young Mexican crowd. The music is middle-of-the-road Latin rock and pop; open bar between 1am and 5am.

Disco Beach (Map p192; ☎ 484-82-30; La Costera s/n, Playa Condesa; cover & open bar women/men M$250/300; ☼ Wed-Sat) This popular spot is in the line of beachfront restaurant-bars, right on Playa Condesa (the beach forms part of the dance floor). Dress policy is more relaxed here than at most other clubs, and the place draws a fairly young crowd. Music is house, disco, techno, hip-hop, '70s and '80s; women get in (and drink) free Wednesday, and the Friday foam parties can be wild. Check out Ibiza Lounge next door, too.

Live Music & Bars

Most of the big hotels along La Costera have bars with entertainment, be it quiet piano music or live bands; head to the following for something different.

Nina's (Map p192; ☎ 484-24-00; La Costera 41; cover & open bar M$250) Nina's is one of the best places in town for live *música tropical* (salsa, *cumbia*, cha-cha, merengue etc); it has a smokin' dance floor, variety acts and impersonators.

Salon Q (Map p192; ☎ 484-32-52, 481-01-14; La Costera 3117; cover M$120, with open bar M$250) This *'catedral de la salsa'* gives Nina's a run for its money, with first-rate salsa singers and bands, celebrity impersonators and a Carnaval atmosphere. Reservations are recommended; discounts for groups are available.

Tropicana (Map p192; Playa Hornos; cover M$50) Like Nina's, Tropicana has a full spectrum of live *música tropical,* only without the bells and whistles, and a much cheaper cover.

Hotel Los Flamingos (Map p192; ☎ 482-06-90; López Mateos s/n) The one quiet spot in this rowdy bunch, Los Flamingos' clifftop bar has the hands-down best sunset-viewing/drinking spot in Acapulco. Not a car or hustler in sight, and you can sip *cocos locos* to your heart's content.

New West (Map p194; ☎ 483-10-82; La Quebrada 81) This popular local bar has cheap beer, rodeo videos and a jukebox blaring *música ranchera: norteño, banda, tejano* and a smattering of US country-and-western hits. You WILL see cowboy hats and big belt buckles.

Hard Rock Café (Map p192; ☎ 484-00-47; La Costera 37; ☼ noon-2am) It's hard to miss the Hard Rock. Just west of CICI, the chain's Acapulco branch has live music from 10pm to 2am.

Dance, Music & Theater

The city's not all booze and boogying. The **Centro de Convenciones** (Map p192; ☎ 484-71-52; La Costera s/n) presents plays, concerts (by the Acapulco Philharmonic, among others), dance and other performances, as does the **Centro Cultural Acapulco** (Map p192; ☎ 484-38-14; La Costera 4834). **Parque Papagayo** (Map p192; La Costera btwn Morín & El Cano) sometimes hosts alfresco events.

Bullfights

Bullfights take place at the Plaza de Toros (Map p192), southeast of La Quebrada and west of Playas Caleta and Caletilla, every Sunday at 5:30pm from January to March; for tickets, try your hotel, a travel agency or the **bullring box office** (☎ 482-11-81) between 10am and 2pm. The 'Caleta' bus passes near the bullring.

ACAPULCO &
THE COSTA CHICA

SHOPPING

Mercado de Artesanías (Map p194; btwn Acacias & Parana)
Bargaining is the rule at this 400-stall *mercado*, Acapulco's main craft market, especially as the sellers often find soft touches among the many cruise-ship passengers. It's paved and pleasant, and is an OK place to get better deals on everything that you see in the hotel shops – sarapes (cloaks), hammocks, jewelry, *huaraches* (sandals), clothing and T-shirts.

Mercado Central (Map p192; Mendoza s/n) A truly local market, this sprawling indoor-outdoor bazaar has everything from *atole* to *zapatos* (not to mention produce, hot food and souvenirs). Any eastbound 'Pie de la Cuesta' or 'Pedregoso' bus will drop you there; get off where the sidewalk turns to tarp-covered stalls.

Other artisan markets include the **Mercados de Artesanías Papagayo**, **Noa Noa**, **Dalia** and **La Diana** (near the statue of the same name), all on La Costera, and **Mercados de Artesanías La Caletilla** at the west end of Playa Caletilla (all on Map p192).

GETTING THERE & AWAY
Air

Acapulco has a busy **airport** (off Map p192; ☎ 466-94-34) with many international flights, most connecting through Mexico City or Guadalajara – both short hops from Acapulco. All flights mentioned here are direct; some are seasonal. **Aeroméxico/Aerolitoral** (Map p192; ☎ 485-16-00; www.aeromexico.com; La Costera 1632, Local H12) flies to Guadalajara, Mexico City and Tijuana, and **US Airways** (☎ 466-92-75, in the US 800-428-4322; www.usairways.com; Airport) to Los Angeles and Phoenix. **American Airlines** (Map p192; ☎ 481-01-61, in the US 800-433-7300; www.aa.com; La Costera 116, Plaza Condesa, Local 109) flies to Dallas and Chicago. **Aviacsa** (☎ 01-800-771-6733; www.aviacsa.com.mx; Airport) flies regularly to Oaxaca, Mexico City and Tijuana. **Continental Airlines** (☎ 01-800-900-5000; www.continental.com; Airport) flies to and from Houston, Minneapolis and Newark, while **Mexicana/Click Mexicana** (Map p192; ☎ 486-75-70; www.mexicana.com; La Costera 1632, La Gran Plaza) serves Mexico City, and **Northwest** (☎ in the US 800-692-6955; www.nwa.com; Airport) travels between Acapulco and Houston.

Bus

There are two major 1st-class long-distance bus companies in Acapulco: Estrella de Oro and Estrella Blanca. The modern, air-condi-tioned **Estrella de Oro bus station** (Map p192; ☎ 01-800-900-01-05; www.autobus.com.mx; Av Cuauhtémoc 1490), just west of Massieu, has free toilets, a Banamex ATM and a ticket machine that accepts bank debit cards (left luggage M$4 per hour per piece). Estrella Blanca has two 1st-class terminals: **Central Papagayo** (Map p192; ☎ 469-20-80; Av Cuauhtémoc 1605) just north of Parque Papagayo (left luggage M$4 per hour per piece) and **Central Ejido** (☎ 469-20-28/30; Av Ejido 47). Estrella Blanca also has a **2nd-class terminal** (off Map p194; ☎ 482-21-84; Av Cuauhtémoc 97) that sells tickets for all buses, but only has departures to relatively nearby towns. Estrella Blanca tickets are also sold at several agencies around town, including **Agencia de Viajes Zócalo** (Map p194; ☎ 483-56-86; La Costera 207, Local 18).

Both companies offer frequent services to Mexico City, with various levels of luxury; journey durations depend on whether they use the faster *autopista* (Hwy 95D) or the old federal Hwy 95.

The following destinations are among those served from Acapulco:

Chilpancingo Frequent 1st-class services to Estrella de Oro (M$76, 1¾ hours). Several 1st-class services (M$85, 1¾ hours) and 2nd-class services every half-hour from the Central Ejido and 2nd-class terminal, from 5am to 7pm (M$60, three hours).

Cuernavaca Seven daily 1st-class services (M$292, four to five hours) and frequent *semi-directo* services (M$200, five hours) to Estrella de Oro. Three daily 1st-class services to Central Papagayo on Estrella Blanca (M$290, four to five hours).

Iguala Has 18 daily 1st-class services (M$170, three hours) and frequent *semi-directo* services (M$130, 3½ hours) to Estrella de Oro. Hourly 1st-class services to Central Ejido on Estrella Blanca (M$170, four hours).

Mexico City (Norte) Seven daily 1st-class services to Estrella de Oro (M$347, six hours). Also has one deluxe daily service (M$500, six hours) and several daily 1st-class services (M$347, six hours) to Central Papagayo on Estrella Blanca, and two daily 1st-class services from the Central Papagayo.

Mexico City (Sur) Many daily 1st-class services (M$347, five hours) and six deluxe services daily (M$500, five hours) to Estrella de Oro. Four daily deluxe services (M$500, five hours) and frequent daily 1st-class services (M$347, five hours) to Central Papagayo on Estrella Blanca, and eight daily 1st-class services (M$347, five hours) from Central Ejido.

Puerto Escondido Five daily 1st-class services (M$192, seven hours) and five 2nd-class services (M$180, 9½ hours) to Central Ejido on Estrella Blanca.

Taxco Two daily 1st-class services to Estrella de Oro (M$165, four hours). Three daily 1st-class services to Central Ejido on Estrella Blanca (M$165, four hours).
Zihuatanejo Has 10 daily 1st-class services (M$180, four to five hours) and 13 daily Primera Plus services (M$200, four to five hours) to Central Ejido on Estrella Blanca. Has three 1st-class daily services (M$180, four to five hours) and 12 2nd-class services, hourly from 5am to 5:30pm (M$90, four to five hours) to Estrella de Oro.

The 2nd-class Estrella Blanca buses depart Central Ejido roughly half-hourly to Costa Chica destinations southeast of Acapulco along Hwy 200, including Copala (M$60, 2½ hours, 120km), Marquelia (M$70, three hours, 133km) and Cuajinicuilapa (M$80, 3½ hours, 200km).

Car & Motorcycle

Many car-rental companies rent Jeeps as well as cars; several have offices at the airport as well as in town, and some offer free delivery to you. Note that rental rates are more expensive at the airport. Shop around to compare prices, or find good deals via the internet ahead of time. Consider waiting until you're finished with Acapulco before you pick up your vehicle; it's not very practical to try to get around town by car. Parking time is limited on the Costera, and you'll generally have to pay a surcharge at your hotel to park. Rental companies include the following.

Alamo (Map p192; ☎ 484-33-05, 466-94-44; La Costera 2148)
Avis (Map p192; ☎ 466-91-90; Fiestamericana Hotel, La Costera 97)
Budget (Map p192; ☎ 481-24-33; La Costera 121)
Hertz (Map p192; ☎ 485-89-47; La Costera 137)
Thrifty La Costera (Map p192; ☎ 486-19-40; La Costera 139); Airport (☎ 466-92-86)

Drivers heading inland on Hwy 95D need to have some cash handy. The tolls to Chilpancingo, about 117km north, total M$250, including M$65 just to get through the 'Maxi Túnel' beyond the edge of town. If you've been driving in Acapulco much, it may seem a small price to pay for being on the open road again.

There are several military checkpoints along the coast southeast of Acapulco. Keep your cool, and there should be no problem. And, for God's sake, don't bring drugs with you.

GETTING AROUND
To/From the Airport

Acapulco's airport is 23km southeast of the *zócalo*, beyond the junction for Puerto Marqués. Arriving by air, you can buy a ticket for transportation into town from the *colectivo* desk at the end of the domestic terminal; it's about M$80 per person for a lift to your hotel (a bit more if it's west of the *zócalo*).

Leaving Acapulco, phone **Móvil Aca** (☎ 462-10-95) 24 hours in advance to reserve transportation back to the airport; depending on where your pickup is, the cost varies from M$150 to M$200 per person or M$300 to M$400 for the whole vehicle, holding up to five passengers. Taxis from the center to the airport cost from around M$180 to M$250, depending on the amount of luggage. Always negotiate the price before you get in a taxi.

Bus

Acapulco has a good bus system (especially good when you get an airbrushed beauty with a bumping sound system). Buses operate from 5am to 11pm daily and cost M$5 with air-con, M$4 without.

From the *centro*, a good place to catch buses is the stop opposite Sanborns department store on La Costera, two blocks east of the *zócalo* – it's the beginning of several bus routes (including to Pie de la Cuesta), so you can usually get a seat.

There are several useful city routes:
Base–Caleta From the Icacos naval base at the southeast end of Acapulco, along La Costera, past the *zócalo* to Playa Caleta.
Base–Cine Río–Caleta From the Icacos naval base, cuts inland from La Costera on Av Wilfrido Massieu to Av Cuauhtémoc. Heads down Av Cuauhtémoc through the business district, turning back to La Costera just before reaching the *zócalo*, continuing west to Playa Caleta.
Puerto Marqués–Centro From opposite Sanborns, along La Costera to Puerto Marqués.
Zócalo–Playa Pie de la Cuesta From opposite Sanborns, to Pie de la Cuesta (see p209 for details).

Taxi & Car

Hundreds of blue and white VW cabs scurry around Acapulco like cockroaches, maneuvering with an audacity that borders on the comical. Drivers sometimes quote fares higher than the going rate, so ask locals what a fair price for your ride is, and agree on the fare with the cabbie before you climb in.

If you can possibly avoid driving in Acapulco, do so. The streets are in poor shape, the anarchic traffic is often horridly snarled and some traffic cops are overtly corrupt.

AROUND ACAPULCO
Pie de la Cuesta
☎ 744 / pop 626

About 10km northwest of Acapulco – it could take a good hour-and-a-half if the traffic is bad – Pie de la Cuesta is a narrow 2km strip of land bordered by the beach and ocean on one side and the large, freshwater Laguna de Coyuca on the other (where Sylvester Stallone filmed *Rambo II*). Compared to Acapulco, it's quieter, cleaner, closer to nature and much more peaceful. Swimming in the ocean at Pie de la Cuesta can be dangerous due to a riptide. Laguna de Coyuca, three times larger than Bahía de Acapulco, is better for swimming; in the lagoon are the islands of Montosa, Presidio and Pájaros. Pájaros is a bird sanctuary.

Pie de la Cuesta has many beachside restaurants specializing in seafood, and it's a great place for watching the sunset. There's no nightlife, so if you're looking for excitement you may be better off staying in Acapulco.

There's one main road, with two names: Av de la Fuerza Aérea Mexicana or Calzada Pie de la Cuesta. **Netxcom** (per hr M$10; ☼ 9am-10pm) has fast internet connections.

ACTIVITIES
Pie de la Cuesta has been famous for waterskiing for decades. The glassy morning waters of the enormous Laguna de Coyuca are perfect for the sport, and several clubs, including **Club de Ski Chuy** (☎ 460-11-04; Calzada Pie de la Cuesta 74), will gladly pull you around the lagoon from their speedboats. They all charge approximately M$500 per hour, which includes boat, driver and ski equipment.

Wakeboarding is another possibility; try **Club Náutico Cadena X Ski** (☎ 460-22-83; cadenax@ yahoo.com; Calzada Pie de la Cuesta s/n).

Boat trips on the lagoon provide a glimpse of its attractions, though bird-watching is often reduced to a minimum because of speedboats and jet skis. Still, if you can convince someone to take you early enough, chances are high you'll spot storks, herons, avocets, pelicans, ducks and other waterfowl. Stroll down to the boat launch along the southeast end of the lagoon and you'll be greeted by independent captains ready to take you for a

tour. Restaurant **Coyuca 2000** (☎ 460-56-09; Playa Pie de la Cuesta; ☼ 9am-2am Dec-Apr, 8am-10pm Mar-Nov) offers 3½-hour tours (M$250 per person) that generally leave at 11:30am, though you can negotiate an early departure, looking at bird habitat, flora, a small zoo area, fisherfolk's homes and the like. **Quinta Erika** (☎ /fax 444-41-31; www.quintaerika.de.vu; Playa Luces) arranges kayak, windsurfing and sailing trips.

Finally, **horseback riding** on the beach runs at around M$150 an hour.

SLEEPING
For accommodation, Pie de la Cuesta is a decent alternative to Acapulco, and every hotel provides safe car parking. High-season dates are approximately December 15 to around Easter. There are 15 or so hotels lining the single, 2km road along the lagoon; take a quick drive to check them out. More lie beyond to the northwest, one of which is listed here.

Acapulco Trailer Park & Mini-Super (☎ 460-00-10; acatrailerpark@yahoo.com.mx; campsites for 2 people M$200, RV sites M$250; ⊜) Beachside with big spaces, clean facilities, friendly management that speaks English and just enough shade, this is the nicest camping ground in the Acapulco area. You can usually negotiate discounts for long stays.

Hotel Parador de los Reyes (☎ 460-01-31; Av Fuerza Aérea 305; d M$350; P ⊜) This clean, economical choice is right beside the road and has a small courtyard swimming pool and rock-hard beds. It has 11 large, no-frills rooms.

Villa Nirvana (☎ 460-16-31; www.lavillanirvana .com; rear Av Fuerza Aérea 302; d M$350-800, q M$1000; P ⊒ ⊜) Villa Nirvana's friendly American owners have thoughtfully landscaped and expanded this cheerful property. It has a variety of accommodations, some with ocean views, all comfortable and decorated with local crafts. A beachside swimming pool, and pleasant open-air bar and restaurant (breakfast only) round out the good-value offering.

Hotel Restaurante Rocío (☎ 460-10-08; hotelrocio@ hotmail.com; Av Fuerza Aérea 9; s/d M$450/550; P) The beds at this beachfront hotel-restaurant-bar are a bit springy and the place could use some sprucing up, but newer oceanside rooms cost the same as the others, and the laptop set gets wi-fi.

Quinta Erika (☎ /fax 444-41-31; www.quintaerika .de.vu; Playa Luces; s/d/bungalow M$550/600/1300; P ⊜) Located 6km northeast of Pie de la Cuesta at Playa Luces, on 2 hectares of lagoon-side land, this quality seven-room lodging is one of the region's best places to relax for a few days. Rooms come with many amenities. The owner, who speaks German, Spanish and a little English, rents kayaks and sailboats, and takes great pride in his place. Reservations are strongly suggested.

Bungalows María Cristina (☎ 460-02-62; Av Fuerza Aérea s/n; d M$800; **P**) Run by English-speaking Enrique and his friendly family, this is a clean, well-tended, relaxing place with a barbecue and hammocks overlooking the beach. This is a good budget choice, with excellent low-season rates, though the beds do feel just a bit 'plasticy.'

Hotel & Restaurant Casa Blanca (☎ 460-03-24; casablanca@prodigy.net.mx; Av Fuerza Aérea s/n; r M$800-1500; **P** 🍴 📶) This well-tended beachfront place has some of the best rooms in town and a modern boutique-hotel feel. The restaurant retains a homey atmosphere, and you can check your email on the wi-fi network.

EATING & DRINKING

Restaurants here are known for fresh seafood. Plenty of open-air places front the beach, though some close early in the evening. Most of the hotels and guesthouses have restaurants, as do many of the water-skiing clubs. Dining out tends to cost more here than in Acapulco, so it may be worth bringing some groceries and getting a room with kitchen access.

Restaurante Rocío (☎ 460-10-08; Av Fuerza Aérea 9; mains M$30-110) Serves a limited menu of a few seafood dishes and simple Mexican fare, such as quesadillas, under *palapas* (thatched-roof shelters) on the beach.

Coyuca 2000 (☎ 460-56-09; Playa Pie de la Cuesta; mains M$40-150; 🕙 9am-2am Dec-Apr, 8am-10pm Mar-Nov) Pull up a chair on the sand, watch the waves and enjoy good fish *al mojo de ajo* (with garlic sauce) or in fajitas, plus other tasty seafood and meat dishes, in a casual atmosphere. The owner is known for concocting new cocktails and offers several margaritas and numerous tropical drinks.

Club de Ski Tres Marías (☎ 460-00-13; Calzada Pie de la Cuesta 375; mains M$80-220; 🕙 8am-7pm) Said to have the best food on the strip, though service can be lax. It's a comfy lagoon-side restaurant and the closest you'll come to upscale dining in town.

Steve's Hideaway/El Escondite (mains M$80-200; 🕙 9am-11pm) Esteban, the owner, serves

drinks, steaks and seafood at a bar on stilts over the water; the view up the lagoon is great. On the southeast side of the lake.

GETTING THERE & AWAY

From Acapulco, catch a 'Pie de la Cuesta' bus on La Costera across the street from the Sanborns near the *zócalo* (main plaza; Map p194). Buses go every 15 minutes from 6am until around 8pm; the bumpy, roundabout 35- to 50-minute ride costs M$4. Buses marked 'Pie de la Cuesta–San Isidro' or 'Pie de la Cuesta–Pedregoso' stop on Hwy 200 at Pie de la Cuesta's arched entrance; those marked 'Pie de la Cuesta–Playa Luces' continue all the way along to Playa Luces, 6km further along toward Barra de Coyuca. *Colectivo* (shared) vans (M$5) continue on from Barra de Coyuca back out to Hwy 200.

Colectivo taxis to Pie de la Cuesta operate 24 hours along La Costera, and elsewhere in Acapulco's old town, and charge M$15 one way. A private taxi from Acapulco costs anywhere from M$80 to M$120 one way (more after dark).

COSTA CHICA

Guerrero's Costa Chica is far less traveled than its Costa Grande (the stretch of coast from Acapulco northwest to the border of Michoacán), though it has some spectacular beaches and a unique cultural history, with Afro-mestizos – people of mixed African, European and indigenous descent – comprising a large portion of the population.

When Guerrero state tourist brochures refer to the Costa Chica ('small coast'), they're usually referring to the coast of Guerrero from Acapulco southeast to the border of Oaxaca. The Costa Chica actually stretches as far south as Puerto Ángel in Oaxaca, though even that boundary varies depending on whom you talk to, what you read, or what radio station you're tuned to. This section covers the Costa Chica as far as the Oaxaca border. The coast south of there is described in the Oaxaca chapter.

SAN MARCOS & CRUZ GRANDE

San Marcos (population 12,000), 65km east of Acapulco, and Cruz Grande (population 10,700), about 40km past that, are both unremarkable towns, but they provide basic services including banks, gas and simple

---

REVEALING AFRO-MESTIZO TRADITIONS

Afro-mestizos make up a large portion of the population here. Also called *morenos*, they come from African, indigenous and European descent. The region was a safe-haven for Africans who escaped slavery, some from the interior, others (it's believed) from a slave ship that sank just off the coast.

---

hotels. They're the only two towns of significant size before Cuajinicuilapa near the Oaxaca border.

PLAYA VENTURA
☎ 744

About 2½ hours southeast of Acapulco, Playa Ventura is a long, beautiful beach with soft white and gold sand, decent swimming and a number of simple beachfront fish restaurants and places to stay. From Playa Ventura you can walk or drive about 1.5km southeast through the tiny village of **Juan Álvarez** (population 600) to an even more spectacular beach, **Playa La Piedra** (stone beach), so named for the golden, wave-sculpted rock formations at its north end and the jagged rocks that accent its long, sandy shoreline as it disappears from sight to the south. The rock formations are known as La Casa de Piedra ('house of stone'). On weekdays it's possible to have both beaches all to yourself, a blissful condition that makes leaving extremely difficult. A small **museum** in the town center reveals a bit of the local history – if it's open.

Sleeping & Eating

Most restaurants will allow you to camp beneath their beach *enramadas* (palm-frond shelters) and use their toilet and shower (if they have one), provided you patronize the restaurant. If you plan to cook your own food, bring it with you; the several little *mini-supers* (convenience stores) stock little beyond snacks, cold drinks and, on a good day, fruit. There are several good places to stay, all of them cheaper in the May-to-November low season and midweek during high season.

Restaurant y Hotel Celsa (r M$250; P ⚓) Just follow the road straight into town until you hit the beach, where you'll find this good, clean budget option.

La Caracola (☎ 101-30-47; www.playaventura.com; r M$400-500; P ⚓) This funky beachfront joint is located about 1.5km north of the church, and is the nicest spot in town.

Getting There & Away

You won't find Playa Ventura on most maps, which only show Juan Álvarez. To get there from Acapulco, take a bus heading southeast on Hwy 200 to Copala (M$60, 2½ hours, 120km; see p116), a small town on Hwy 200. Ask the driver to drop you there or at *el crucero,* the turnoff to Playa Ventura just southeast of town. In Copala, *combis* (microbuses) and *camionetas* (pickups) depart for Playa Ventura about every half-hour (M$15, 30 minutes, 13km) from just east of the bus stop.

If you're driving, the signed turnoff to Playa Ventura is at Km 124, about 3km past Copala, to the southeast.

PLAYAS LA BOCANA & LAS PEÑITAS

The same buses that depart from Acapulco for Copala continue 13km east on Hwy 200 to **Marquelia** (M$7, three hours). It's a market town with a population of 6600. It has travelers' services, including several inexpensive hotels, and offers access to an immense stretch of beach backed by coco palms, which follows the coastline's contours for many kilometers in either direction.

From Marquelia's center you can take a *camioneta* (M$5 shared, M$30 private; 3km) to a section of the beach known as **Playa La Bocana**, where the Río Marquelia meets the sea and forms a lagoon. The lagoon has rich birdlife and makes for great morning exploration and bird-watching. Except during large swells, ocean swimming is excellent outside the breakers. La Bocana has some *cabañas*, as well as *comedores* (simple, inexpensive eateries) with hammocks that diners can spend the night in. Another portion of the beach, **Playa Las Peñitas**, is reached by a 5km road heading seaward from the east end of Marquelia. Las Peñitas has two small hotels and some *cabañas* that also offer camping spaces.

CUAJINICUILAPA
☎ 741 / pop 9000

Cuajinicuilapa (kwah-hee-nee-kwee-*lah*-pah), usually shortened to Cuaji (*kwah*-hee), is the nucleus of Afro-mestizo culture on the Costa Chica and well worth a stop if you're at all interested in the mixed African-indigenous heritage that is unique to this region. Hwy 200 is the main drag in Cuaji, and gas, food and lodging are all available right off its dusty shoulders.

If you're only stopping for a few hours, be sure to visit the interesting **Museo de las Culturas Afromestizas** (Museum of Afro-mestizo Cultures; ☎ 414-03-10; cnr Manuel Zárate & Cuauhtémoc; admission M$10; ☽ 10am-2pm & 4-7pm Tue-Sun), a tribute to the history of African slaves in Mexico and, specifically, to local Afro-mestizo culture. Behind the museum are three examples of *casas redondas,* the round houses typical of West Africa that were built around Cuaji until as late as the 1960s. The museum is a block inland from the Banamex just west of the main plaza.

Hotel Lozano (☎ 414-07-08; Ignacio Zaragoza 19A; r M$200-350) is the best hotel in town, owned by the amiable Dr Enrique, the local dentist. It's half a block inland from Hwy 200, and the bathroom in its deluxe suite features a Jacuzzi and steam cabinet!

Las Siete Flores, near the bus terminal on the inland side of the highway, is a great, rickety *palapa* restaurant serving inexpensive daily specials for breakfast, lunch and dinner. The Thursday bowls of *pozole* are huge and delicious.

Coming from Acapulco, buses to Cuaji depart hourly, 5am to 6:30pm (M$119, 3½ hours, 200km), from Estrella Blanca's Central Ejido terminal.

PUNTA MALDONADO
☎ 741 / pop 692

The last beach worth checking out before crossing the Oaxaca border is at Punta Maldonado (also known as El Faro), a remote fishing village about 31km down a partially paved road from Hwy 200. It's a ramshackle little place, almost eerie in its isolation, at the base of dramatic cliffs on a small bay. The swimming is good, and the surfing, on occasion, is excellent; the break is a reef/point favoring lefts. Punta Maldonado has a few seafood restaurants on the beach. The town's lone hotel is hardly worth the pesos.

To reach Punta Maldonado by bus, you first must get to Cuajinicuilapa. Then take one of the *camionetas* that leave Cuaji every half-hour or so (M$20, 45 minutes) from just off the main plaza. A taxi from Cuaji is also possible. If you're driving, the turnoff from Hwy 200 is just east of Cuaji. Unless the washed-out bridge a couple of kilometers in on this road is rebuilt, don't attempt the drive immediately following rains.

Oaxaca

Oaxaca… The concussive, guttural name alone conjures images of swirling, visceral mountain vistas, proud and resilient indigenous enclaves, laissez-faire beach towns, remarkable cuisines, mole and mezcal – a spirit and essence far removed from the glitter and glam of the coasts to the north. At the heart of this ancient southern state, pronounced wah-*hah*-kah, is Oaxaca city. This delightful capital dates back to pre-Colombian times, and to this day the mishmash of indigenous groups and settlers that call this land home retain many of the traditions of their forebears. In the hills that encircle the city, you'll find numerous pre-Colombian ruins, including the region's largest archaeological site at Monte Albán.

Heading down from the capital, travelers arrive at the lyrical and rhythmic Oaxacan coast. Even the biggest draw here, Puerto Escondido, retains a peaced-out cool. Further south is a free-loving series of beach towns, including Puerto Ángel, Zipolite and Mazunte. While surfing is one of the region's biggest draws, there's plenty to do for everyone. And a visit to the numerous lagoons that dot the coast is not to be missed.

But the spirit of Oaxaca extends well beyond the coast. A visit to the Isthmus of Tehuantepec, one of the last strongholds of the Zapotec people, reveals the ancient heartbeat that keeps this area as vital today as it was more than a thousand years ago.

HIGHLIGHTS

- Getting high – on life – as you let the winds of the gods blow past you beachside in the chiller-than-chiva town of **Zipolite** (p249), before spending an afternoon with the turtles at nearby **Mazunte** (p253)

- Rambling through the labyrinthine markets of **Oaxaca city** (p228) to pick up all the fixings – grasshoppers, chocolate and chilipeppers – for an afternoon picnic at the ancient Zapotec capital of **Monte Albán** (p232)

- Going big at Mexico's very own Pipeline at **Puerto Escondido** (p235), or simply sitting on shore and marveling at the moves and bravado of the toned gods and goddesses charging these leviathan waves

- Skipping across the waves to the desolate bays around **Bahías de Huatulco** (p255), where pristine beaches, and prolific plant and animal life prevail

- Taking a week away from the travails of modern life to study yoga in **Puerto Ángel** (p248), Spanish in **Oaxaca city** (p219), or the currents of modern Zapotec life in **Tehuantepec** (p263) – you are sure to leave the wiser

---

■ AVERAGE JANUARY DAILY HIGH: OAXACA CITY: 25°C	77°F, PUERTO ESCONDIDO: 32°C	90°F;	■ AVERAGE JULY DAILY HIGH: OAXACA CITY: 28°C	82°F, PUERTO ESCONDIDO: 35°C	95°F

History

The Valles Centrales (Central Valleys) have always been the hub of Oaxacan life, and the pre-Hispanic cultures here reached heights rivaling those of central Mexico. The hilltop city of Monte Albán became the center of the Zapotec culture, which extended its control over much of Oaxaca by conquest, peaking between AD 300 and 700. Monte Albán declined suddenly, for reasons still unknown, and by about 750 it was deserted, as were many other Zapotec sites in the Valles Centrales. From about 1200, the surviving Zapotecs came under the growing power of the Mixtecs, renowned potters and metalsmiths from Oaxaca's northwest uplands. Mixtec and Zapotec cultures became entangled in the Valles Centrales before the Aztecs conquered them in the 15th and early 16th centuries.

The Spaniards had to send at least four expeditions before they felt safe enough to found the city of Oaxaca in 1529. Cortés munificently donated large parts of the Valles Centrales to himself and was officially named Marqués del Valle de Oaxaca. In colonial times, the indigenous population dropped disastrously as a result of introduced diseases and mistreatment by the Spanish. The population of the Mixteca (the mountainous western region) is thought to have fallen from 700,000 at the time of the Spanish arrival to about 25,000 in 1700. Rebellions continued into the 20th century, but the indigenous peoples rarely formed a serious threat.

Benito Juárez, the great reforming leader of mid-19th-century Mexico, was a Zapotec. He served two terms as Oaxaca state governor before being elected Mexico's president in 1861.

Through the close of the 19th century, tobacco planters set up virtual slave plantations in northern Oaxaca, and indigenous communal lands were commandeered by foreign and mestizo (of mixed European and American Indian ancestry) coffee planters. After the Mexican Revolution, plantations were dissolved and about 300 *ejidos* (peasant landholding cooperatives) were set up, effectively returning lands to the people who worked them. However, land ownership and poverty – this is one of Mexico's poorest states – remain a source of conflict even today. Oaxaca made international headlines in 2006 when a teachers' strike (p216) boiled over, leading to a seven-month state of siege in the downtown area of Oaxaca city. With the teachers' strike long gone, Oaxaca city is trying to regain lost ground, but tourism figures remain at about 60% of their pre-siege numbers.

The Land

The Sierra Madre del Sur (average height 2000m) runs parallel to the Pacific coast. It meets the Sierra Madre de Oaxaca (average height 2500m), which runs down from Mexico's central volcanic belt, roughly in the center of the state. Between them lie the three Valles Centrales, which converge at the city of Oaxaca. In Oaxaca city December and January are the coldest months, with average lows between 8°C and 9°C and highs around 25°C; March through May are the hottest months, with average highs around 30°C. The valleys are warm and dry, with most rain falling between June and September. The coast and low-lying areas are hotter and a bit wetter.

Situated in a region where temperate and tropical climatic zones and several mountain ranges meet, Oaxaca has spectacularly varied landscapes and a biodiversity greater than any other Mexican state. The inland highlands still have cloud forests and big stands of oak and pine, while lower-lying areas and Pacific-facing slopes support deciduous tropical forest.

Internet Resources

Oaxaca's Tourist Guide (www.oaxaca-travel.com) is an excellent photo-filled website with everything from information on beaches and hotels to regional recipes and biographies of famous Oaxacans. **Oaxaca's Forum** (http://bbs.oaxaca.com) is a bulletin board where you can look for rented accommodation or shared transportation or ask any old question.

Dangers & Annoyances

Buses and other vehicles traveling along isolated stretches of highway, including the coastal Hwy 200 and Hwy 175 from Oaxaca city to Pochutla, are occasionally stopped and robbed. Though incidents have decreased in recent years, it's still advisable not to travel at night. Robberies aside, this is a good rule of thumb in all of Mexico, particularly on the winding mountain roads connecting the coast to Oaxaca city.

Getting There & Around

Oaxaca city has good bus links with Mexico City and Puebla to the north, and a few daily services to/from Veracruz, Villahermosa,

OAXACA

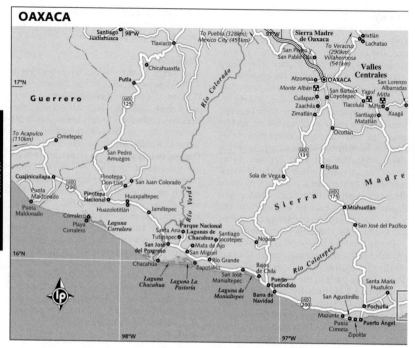

Tuxtla Gutiérrez and San Cristóbal de Las Casas. Services between the city and the state's main coastal destinations are fairly frequent though mostly 2nd-class. Plenty of buses (again mostly 2nd-class) also travel the length of the Oaxaca coast along Hwy 200 from Acapulco and Chiapas.

Several daily flights link Oaxaca city with Mexico City. Further flights go east to Tuxtla Gutiérrez, Tapachula, Villahermosa and beyond. Small planes hop over the mountains between Oaxaca city and the coastal resorts Puerto Escondido and Bahías de Huatulco, which you can also reach direct from Mexico City.

OAXACA CITY

☎ 951 / pop 258,000 / elevation 1550m

Zapotecs mingle peacefully with Mohawk-shorn university students, Teva-ed travelers and starched businessmen along the coiled cobblestone streets of this cosmopolitan city, while in the back alleys and up into the bucolic neighborhoods that stretch to the edge of the sierra, artisans still work their looms to create intricate textiles and fire the black-as-night pots that have made this region famous. Oaxaca truly is a city of the ages: as evocative and intoxicating today as it was some 500 years ago.

Despite the hiccup of the 2006 conflict, large numbers of foreigners, particularly Americans, still visit the state capital every year. Oaxaca takes them in its stride, maintaining its cosmopolitan atmosphere with a relaxed grace. Dry mountain heat, the colonial center's manageable scale, lovely architecture (including some phenomenal churches), broad shady plazas and leisurely cafés help slow the pace of life. The arts are highly valued here, and talented locals are joined by others attracted from around Mexico and other parts of the world to create a cultural crossroads of sorts.

The city has some first-class museums and galleries, arguably the best handicrafts shopping in Mexico, and a vivacious cultural, culinary, bar and music scene. It's a popular venue for taking Spanish-language courses, cooking classes or simply hanging out. It's also ground zero for the *nueva cocina mexicana*

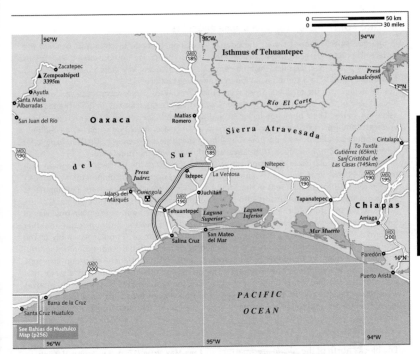

(nouveau Mexican cuisine) movement. See p37 for more on *la nueva cocina mexicana*.

Head first for the *zócalo* (main plaza) and taste the atmosphere. Then ramble and see what markets, crafts, galleries, cafés, bars and festivities you run across.

HISTORY

The Aztec settlement here was called Huaxyácac (meaning 'In the Nose of the Squash'), from which 'Oaxaca' is derived. The Spanish laid out a new town around the existing *zócalo* in 1529. It quickly became the most important place in southern Mexico.

Eighteenth-century Oaxaca grew rich from exports of cochineal, a highly prized red dye made from tiny insects living on the prickly pear cactus in the Mixteca Alta, and from textile weaving. By 1796 it was probably the third biggest city in Nueva España, with about 20,000 people (including 600 clergy) and 800 cotton looms.

In 1854 an earthquake destroyed much of Oaxaca city. It wasn't until decades later, under the presidency of Porfirio Díaz, that Oaxaca began to grow again; in the 1890s

its population exceeded 30,000. Then in 1931 another earthquake left 70% of the city uninhabitable.

Oaxaca's major expansion has come in the past 25 years, with tourism, new industries and rural poverty all encouraging migration from the countryside. The population of the city proper has almost doubled in this time, and together with formerly separate villages and towns it now forms a conurbation of perhaps 450,000 people.

ORIENTATION

Oaxaca centers on the *zócalo* and the adjoining Alameda de León, a tree-lined promenade in front of the cathedral. Calle Alcalá, running north from the cathedral to the Iglesia de Santo Domingo (a universally known landmark), is pedestrian-only for four blocks.

The road from Mexico City and Puebla traverses the northern part of Oaxaca as Calz Niños Héroes de Chapultepec. The 1st-class bus station is on this road, 1.75km northeast of the *zócalo*. The 2nd-class bus station is almost 1km west of the center, near the main market, the Central de Abastos.

OAXACA

BOILING POINT: INSIDE OAXACA'S 2006 PROTESTS

In one of Mexico's poorest states, the tides of revolution continue to churn just beneath the surface. The 2006 Oaxaca protests – when teachers, students, fed-up housewives, electricians and farmers took over Oaxaca's historic center as well as many key state media outlets and institutions – finally saw these revolutionary tendencies boil over.

It all began with the teachers. Small-scale strikes by Oaxaca state's *maestros* have long been a ritual part of their annual pay negotiations with the state government. In 2006 the teachers asked for more. 'Their demands included additional funds for school infrastructure, school breakfasts and free textbooks' in addition to a salary increase, according to Jill Irene Freidberg, who produced and directed a documentary film on the protest movements, *Un Poquito de Tanta Verdad* (A Little Bit of So Much Truth), available through www.corrugate.org.

But the unpopular state governor, Ulises Ruiz of the PRI party, refused to negotiate with the teachers that year, and they went on strike, setting up large encampments in Oaxaca's city center. On June 14 Ruiz sent in thousands of police to smash the teachers' encampments and barricades, but the protestors retook the *zócalo* within hours – and the violence of the police action transformed the protest into a much wider movement whose main goal was to force the resignation of Ruiz. A broad grouping of political and social groups came together to form APPO, the Asamblea Popular del los Pueblos de Oaxaca (Popular Assembly of the Peoples of Oaxaca), which took over the city center with camps, barricades, bonfires, graffiti and frequent marches hundreds of thousands strong. This disenfranchised group also took over several radio stations and even a TV station. It was this 'megaphone of dissent' that really ignited the masses. Throughout the protests, the radio towers or stations themselves were often 'taken back' by the police – and the police even broadcast on a 'pirate signal' in an attempt to undermine the protests – but they often fell back into the hands of the protesters.

The blocks north of the *zócalo* are smarter, cleaner and less traffic-infested than those to the south. The commercial area occupies the blocks southwest of the *zócalo*.

INFORMATION
Bookstores

Amate (☎ 516-69-60; www.amatebooks.com; Plaza Alcalá, Alcalá 307-2; 🕙 10:30am-2:30pm & 3:30-7:30pm Mon-Sat) Probably the best English-language bookstore in all Mexico, stocking almost every Mexico-related title (in print) in English. This is also a good spot to pick up maps – it even distributes a free tourist map.

Emergency
Emergency services (☎ 066) For police, fire and ambulance services.

Internet Access
Internet cafés are everywhere, and cost anywhere from M$6 to M$10 per hour. We've marked a few on the map (pp220–1).

Laundry
Same-day wash-and-dry service is available at several laundries for about M$12 per kilogram. Many hotels offer laundry service as well.

Lava-Max (Bravo 317; 🕙 8am-8:30pm Mon-Sat)
Lavandería Antequera (☎ 516-56-94; Murguía 408; 🕙 9am-8pm Mon-Fri, 9am-6pm Sat) Also does dry cleaning, and offers free delivery to area hotels.

Libraries
Biblioteca Circulante de Oaxaca (Oaxaca Lending Library; ☎ 518-70-77; Pino Suárez 519; 🕙 10am-2pm & 4-7pm Mon-Fri, 10am-1pm Sat) Sizable collection of books and magazines on Oaxaca and Mexico, in English and Spanish; a month-long membership (M$100) allows you to borrow books. Also offers wireless internet access, a café and notice boards to set up homestays and the like.
Instituto de Artes Gráficas de Oaxaca (☎ 516-69-80; Alcalá 507; 🕙 9:30am-8pm) The excellent library here covers art, architecture, literature, botany, ecology and history. There's also a small museum on-site (closed Tuesday) with rotating exhibits. Admission to the museum is free, but donations are welcome.

Media
Go-Oaxaca (www.go-oaxaca.com) A free monthly bilingual (English and Spanish) paper available at various places around town offering useful practical information about the city and state.
Notice boards (Plaza Gonzalo Lucero, Calle 5 de Mayo 412) Check these for ads for rental apartments, classes in

The summer's main touristic event, the Guelaguetza dance festival, was officially canceled. '[The festival] was replaced with a popular, alternative, free version of Guelaguetza, organized by the APPO,' says Freidberg. 'It was a direct response to the Oaxacan peoples' belief that the Guelaguetza has been appropriated and commercialized by the PRI. So they decided to take it back. And the People's Guelaguetza was a huge success.' As the protesters ramped up their nonviolent direct action – blockades, marches and building occupations – the police began to turn up the heat, and frequent outbreaks of violence resulted in 23 deaths (all protesters or bystanders) by late October. With their backs to the wall, the federal government finally sent in heavily armed riot police to retake the city center.

But why didn't President Fox step in? According to many pundits, there are two scenarios: either Fox's refusal to act against Ruiz was part of a deal struck by Fox's PAN party to win the PRI's support for PAN legislation in the national congress, or it was a sort of smokescreen to avoid more protests over the highly contested presidential election that had already kicked off massive protests in Mexico City.

APPO continued to stage protests and marches demanding Ruiz' resignation and the release of those jailed during the protests. There was more violence before the Guelaguetza in 2007, though the festival went ahead. To outward appearances the city had returned to normalcy by late 2007, and the important tourism business, which had ground to a halt for over a year, began to recover, though as of 2008 most businesses said they were only running at about 60% of normal capacity. But political opinion in Oaxaca has been radicalized, and Ulises Ruiz is in office until 2010.

'It was a response to decades of social, economic and cultural injustice,' posits Freidberg. 'Oaxacans have been organizing and mobilizing for decades…and it is one of the poorest states in the country. It is also one of the most indigenous states, and has been on the receiving end of the institutional racism that exists in Mexico towards indigenous peoples.'

everything from Spanish to yoga, and other interesting stuff. You'll also find useful notice boards in the language schools.
Oaxaca Times (www.oaxacatimes.com) Available at various places around town. Similar to Go-Oaxaca but in English only.

Medical Services
Clínica Hospital Carmen (☎ 516-26-12; Abasolo 215; ☽ 24hr) One of the town's best private hospitals, with emergency facilities and English-speaking doctors.

Money
There are plenty of banks and ATMs around the center. Banks with reasonable exchange rates include those listed.
Banamex (☎ 514-57-47; Valdivieso 116; ☽ 11am-6pm Mon-Fri)
Consultoria Internacional (☎ 514-91-92; Armenta y López 203C; ☽ 8:30am-7pm Mon-Fri, 9am-2pm Sat) Changes cash euros, yen, sterling, Canadian dollars and Swiss francs too.
HSBC (☎ 516-19-67; cnr Armenta y López & Guerrero; ☽ 8am-7pm Mon-Sat)

Post
Main post office (Alameda de León; ☽ 8am-7pm Mon-Fri, 9am-1pm Sat)

Telephone & Fax
There are many *casetas telefónicas* (public telephone call stations) scattered about; those on Independencia and Trujano offer fax service too.
ATSI (Calle 20 de Noviembre 402) Cheaper than payphones for national long-distance calls and calls to Europe; offers fax service as well.
dspot (García Vigil 512D; ☽ 9am-10pm) Behind La Biznaga restaurant; offers probably the cheapest foreign calls in town, via the internet.
Interactu@ndo (Pino Suárez 804) Calls to the USA are around M$4 per minute, M$8 to the rest of world.

Toilets
Clean facilities under the bandstand in the middle of the *zócalo* cost M$2.

Tourist Information
Municipal tourist kiosks (cnr García Vigil & Independencia, cnr Gurrión & Alcalá; ☽ 10am-7pm) Offer the standard array of brochures.

Travel Agencies
Turismo Joven (☎ 514-22-20; Alcalá 407, Local 19; ☽ 9am-7pm Mon-Sat) Books tours, issues ISIC cards and sells student air fares and trips to Cuba and elsewhere.

Volunteering

Centro Esperanza (☎ 501-10-69; www.oaxaca streetchildrengrassroots.org; Crespo 308) This nonprofit is always looking for volunteers to work with kids.

DANGERS & ANNOYANCES

It's best not to go up on Cerro del Fortín, the hill with the Auditorio Guelaguetza (Guelaguetza auditorium), except for special events such as the Guelaguetza (p224). It's a well-known haunt of robbers.

Traffic can be horrendously slow during the morning and evening rush hours; the Periférico near the 2nd-class bus terminal is particularly bad.

Those traveling by bus (especially 2nd-class) between Oaxaca city and coastal destinations should keep a close eye on their personal possessions.

While the violence of 2006 seems well in the past, tourists are better off avoiding political protests.

SIGHTS & ACTIVITIES
Zócalo, Alameda & Around

Traffic-free, shaded by trees and surrounded by *portales* (arcades) with many cafés and eateries, the *zócalo* is the perfect place to soak up the Oaxaca atmosphere. The adjacent alameda, also traffic-free but without the cafés, is popular too.

The south side of the *zócalo* is occupied by the former **Palacio de Gobierno** (admission free; ☾ 9:30am-7pm), whose stairway mural by Arturo García Bustos depicts famous Oaxacans and Oaxacan history. There's a small on-site museum that reveals a bit of local history. The city's **cathedral**, begun in 1553 and finished (after several earthquakes) in the 18th century, stands just north of the *zócalo*.

Fine carved facades adorn two nearby colonial churches: **Iglesia de La Compañía**, just off the southwest corner of the *zócalo*, and the popular **Iglesia de San Juan de Dios** (cnr Aldama & Calle 20 de Noviembre), whose first incarnation was finished in 1526, making it the oldest church site in Oaxaca. The 18th-century **Templo de San Felipe Neri** (cnr Independencia & JP García) offers up a fine example of Mexican baroque architecture.

Many colonial-era stone buildings have been cleaned up or restored on **Calle Alcalá**; its four pedestrian-only blocks make it a good route north from the *zócalo* to the Iglesia de Santo Domingo.

IGLESIA DE SANTO DOMINGO

Four blocks north of the cathedral, **Santo Domingo** (cnr Alcalá & Gurrión; ☾ 7am-1pm & 4-8pm) is the most splendid of Oaxaca's churches. It was built mainly between 1570 and 1608 as the city's Dominican monastery. The finest artisans from Puebla and elsewhere helped with its construction. Excluding the transept, nearly every square inch of the church's interior above floor level is decorated in 3-D relief: a base of white stucco bursts into elaborate gilt and colored designs that swirl around a profusion of painted figures. It all takes on a magically warm glow during candlelit evening Masses.

Museums

The excellent **Museo Regional de Oaxaca** (☎ 516-29-91; cnr Alcalá & Gurrión; admission M$48, over 60 & under 13 free; ☾ 10am-6pm Tue-Sun) occupies the beautifully restored ex-Convento de Santo Domingo, adjoining the Iglesia de Santo Domingo. These old monastery buildings were used as military barracks for more than a hundred years until 1994, when they were handed over to the city of Oaxaca. The comprehensive museum takes you through the history and cultures of Oaxaca state up to the present day. One of its big draws is a priceless treasure trove discovered at Monte Albán in 1932, featuring beautifully worked silver, precious stones, pearls, crystal goblets, a skull covered in turquoise, and gold.

Wrapping around the back of the museum is the **Jardín Etnobotánico** (☎ 516-79-15; cnr Constitución & Reforma; ☾ tours in English 11am Tue, Thu & Sat, in Spanish 10am, noon & 5pm Mon-Sat), a fascinating landscaped display of Oaxaca state plants, most of them cacti. You can only see the garden on a tour (M$100 for English, M$50 for Spanish); sign up at the entrance in advance (the day before or earlier).

The **Museo de Arte Contemporáneo de Oaxaca** (☎ 514-22-28; Alcalá 202; admission M$20; ☾ 10:30am-8pm Wed-Mon) occupies a handsome colonial house built around 1700. Its changing exhibits feature recent art from around the world, and work by leading modern Oaxacan artists such as Rufino Tamayo, Francisco Toledo, Rodolfo Morales, Rodolfo Nieto and Francisco Gutiérrez.

Museo Casa de Juárez (Juárez House Museum; ☎ 516-18-60; García Vigil 609; admission M$30; ☾ 10am-6pm Tue-Fri, 10am-5pm Sat & Sun), opposite the Templo del Carmen Alto, is where Benito Juárez found work as a boy, with a bookbinder. The orphaned Zapotec Indian went on to become president of Mexico in 1861. The renovated house shows how the early-19th-century Oaxacan middle class lived.

Museo Rufino Tamayo (☎ 516-47-50; Morelos 503; admission M$30; ☺ 10am-2pm & 4-7pm Mon & Wed-Sat, 10am-3pm Sun), an excellent museum of Mexican pre-Hispanic artifacts, was donated to Oaxaca by its most famous artist, the Zapotec Rufino Tamayo (1899–1991).

Basílica de la Soledad

The image of Oaxaca's patron saint, the Virgen de la Soledad (Virgin of Solitude), resides in this 17th-century **church**, about four blocks west of the alameda along Independencia. The church, with a rich carved-stone baroque facade, stands where the image is said to have miraculously appeared in a donkey pack a few centuries ago.

In the mid-1990s, the Virgin's 2kg gold crown was stolen, along with the huge pearl and many of the 600 diamonds with which she was adorned.

Temascal

The traditional **sweat lodge** at hotel Las Bugambilias (p223) costs M$1500 for two people. It also offers massages.

COURSES

Oaxaca is a terrific place to study, and the following schools have received complimentary reviews from some of our readers. The language schools can arrange accommodation.

Cooking

The following well-received classes are (or can be) held in English, and include market visits to buy ingredients. See p39 for more cooking courses and tours in the area.

La Casa de los Sabores (☎ 516-57-04; www.laolla .com.mx; Libres 205; 4hr class per person M$650) Pilar Cabrera, owner of La Olla restaurant, gives classes from 9:30am to 2pm on Wednesday and Friday at her guesthouse (p223) in central Oaxaca. Participants prepare and eat a five-course meal, usually including some vegetarian dishes. The price is reduced if you attend more than one class, or if more than 10 people attend.

La Casa de Mis Recuerdos (☎ 515-56-45; www .misrecuerdos.net; Pino Suárez 508; classes from M$650) Nora Gutiérrez, from a family of celebrated Oaxacan cooks, conducts classes for groups of up to 10 at her family's charming B&B (p224). You prepare a Oaxacan

lunch (planned a couple of days ahead), then sit down to eat it. The price depends on the number of participants and what they want to cook. Vegetarian classes are available.

Language

Oaxaca International (☎ 514-72-24; www.oaxaca international.com; Libres 207; per week M$800-1750, per hr M$150-300) Includes a wide range of workshops with its lessons, from cooking and crafts to dance. Its offerings are tailored to student interest. Special programs for professionals are also offered.

Soléxico (☎ 516-56-80; www.solexico.com; Abasolo 217; private 1hr class M$210, 15hr instruction M$1370, month-long program M$5390, homestays M$250 per night) This traveler favorite offers homestays, excursions and mixers.

TOURS

A variety of tours foster closer contact with Mexican nature or Mexican communities; most reach destinations that few other visitors get to; see also p231 for bike rental.

Bicicletas Pedro Martínez (☎ 514-59-35; www .bicicletaspedromartinez.com; Aldama 418; ☺ 9am-7pm Mon-Sat) Offers a variety of rides and hikes, including four-hour bike jaunts (M$650) to the northern fringe of the city, and multiday, all-inclusive bike-and-hike trips in outlying areas for M$1100 to M$5000. An increasingly popular hike takes you into the sierra and some of the smaller villages of the valley for M$1100.

Expediciones Sierra Norte (☎ 514-82-71; www .sierranorte.org.mx; Bravo 210; ☺ 9:30am-7pm Mon-Fri, 9am-2pm Sat) This very well-run rural community organization offers walking, mountain biking and accommodations in the beautiful Sierra Norte, northeast of the city.

Tierraventura (☎ 501-13-63; www.tierraventura.com; Abasolo 217; ☺ 10am-3pm Mon-Sat) Run by a multilingual Swiss and German couple who take groups to some fairly remote destinations in Oaxaca state; there's a focus on hiking, nature, crafts, traditional medicine and meeting locals, wherever possible working with local community tourism projects.

Several companies offer less adventurous day trips to outlying attractions. A typical three- or four-hour trip to Monte Albán costs around M$150. An eight-hour tour to Monte Albán, Cuilapan, Coyotepec, Arrazola and Zaachila will set you back around M$180. There are also agencies with a wide choice of itineraries:

Continental-Istmo Tours (☎ 516-96-25; Alcalá 201)

Viajes Turísticos Mitla Hotel Rivera del Ángel (516-61-75; Mina 518); Hostal Santa Rosa (☎ 514-78-00; Trujano 201)

CENTRAL OAXACA CITY

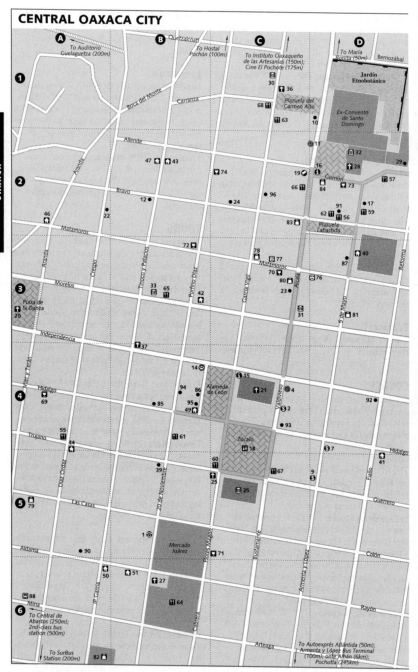

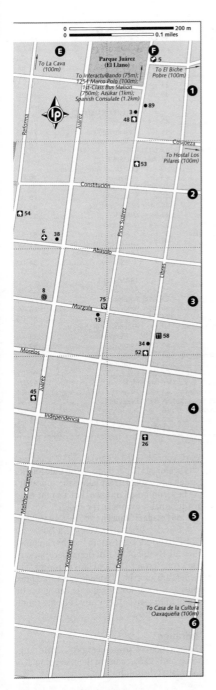

OAXACA

FESTIVALS & EVENTS

All major national festivals are celebrated here, and Oaxaca has some unique fiestas of its own, the biggest and most spectacular being the Guelaguetza (p224).

There are many other festivities throughout the year.

Fiesta de la Virgen del Carmen (a week or more before July 16) The streets around the Templo del Carmen Alto on García Vigil become a fairground and the nights are lit by processions and fireworks.

Blessing of Animals (about 5pm, August 31) Pets are dressed up and taken to the Iglesia de La Merced, on Independencia.

Día de Muertos (November 2) Day of the Dead is a big happening here, with associated events starting several days in advance. These include music and dance at the main cemetery, the Panteón General, on Calz del Panteón about 1.25km east of the *zócalo*.

Posadas (December 16 to 24) Nine night-time neighborhood processions symbolizing Mary and Joseph's journey to Bethlehem.

Día de la Virgen de la Soledad (December 18) Processions and traditional dances, including the Danza de las Plumas (Feather Dance), at the Basílica de la Soledad.

Noche de los Rábanos (Night of the Radishes; December 23) Amazing figures carved from radishes are displayed in the *zócalo*. Sounds silly, but it's really neat.

Calendas (December 24) These Christmas Eve processions from local churches converge on the *zócalo* about 10pm, bringing music, floats and fireworks.

SLEEPING

Prices given here are for Oaxaca's high seasons, generally mid-December to mid-January, a week each side of Easter and Día de Muertos, and from mid-July to mid-August (dates vary from one establishment to another). Outside of these periods many places drop their prices by between 15% and 30%. Those in the hard-core budget bracket tend to hold prices steady throughout the year. Streetside rooms everywhere tend to be noisy.

Budget

Oaxaca has more backpacker hostels than any other city in Mexico, and many budget hotels. Hostels in the following listings all have shared bathrooms.

Hostel Luz de Luna Nuyoo (☎ 516-95-76; emayoral71@ hotmail.com; Juárez 101; dm M$70) Readers continue to praise this friendly, slightly grungy hostel run by a pair of Oaxacan musician brothers. Separate bunk rooms for women, men and couples (eight beds each) open on to a patio, and

OAXACA

you can hang a hammock or stay in the rooftop *cabaña*. It has a shared kitchen and wi-fi.

Hostal Pochón (☎ 516-13-22; www.hostalpochon.com; Callejón del Carmen 102; dm M$105-110, r M$260-350, all incl breakfast; 🖥) While it's a bit away from the main action of the city center, this hostel gets high marks for its small four- to six-bed dorms and laid-back atmosphere. It offers a full kitchen, good common areas and no curfew, as well as bike rental, cooking classes, luggage storage, cheap phone calls and free internet access. The polyglot owners speak English, French and Spanish.

Hostal Paulina (☎ 516-20-05; www.paulinahostel.com; Trujano 321; dm/s/d/tr M$150/280/300/450, all incl breakfast) Impeccably clean and efficiently run, this splendid 92-bed hostel provides bunk dorms for up to 11 people, and rooms with one double bed and a pair of bunks, all with lockers. It offers a

4% discount if you have an HI or ISIC card, and internet for M$10 per hour. A neat little interior garden and a roof terrace add to the appeal. It's the best-run hostel in town, but also the most institutional – you make the choice.

Hotel Posada El Chapulín (☎ 516-16-46; hotelchapulin@hotmail.com; Aldama 317; s/d/tr/q M$220/250/280/360; 🖥) This good, eight-room family-run hotel, perennially full of international backpackers, has a roof terrace, TV and fans in rooms. The owners are amazingly friendly, and are a great source of local knowledge. It can get a bit stinky in the small lobby area, but the rooms are less odiferous.

Midrange

Oaxaca boasts some delightful midrange hotels and B&Bs, many of them in colonial or colonial-style buildings.

our pick **Hotel Las Mariposas** (☎ 515-58-54; www
.lasmariposas.com.mx; Pino Suárez 517; s/d M$450/500,
studio apt s/d M$500/550, all incl breakfast; ☐) Las
Mariposas offers six studio apartments (with
a small kitchen) and seven rooms. All are
large, spotlessly clean and simply but prettily
decorated. It's a tranquil, friendly and very
secure place. Free wireless internet access, a
library, a kitchen for use by all guests, luggage
storage and a good breakfast are among the
many extras that make this a great deal.

Hotel Las Golondrinas (☎ 514-21-26; www.hotel
lasgolandrinas.com.mx; Tinoco y Palacios 411; s/d M$460/520;
☒ ☐) This fine small hotel has about 30
rooms that open out onto three beautiful,
leafy and labyrinthine patios. It's often full,
so book ahead. None of the rooms is huge but
all are tastefully decorated and immaculate.
Good breakfasts (not included in room rates)
are served in one of the patios.

Hotel Monte Albán (☎ 516-23-30; hotelmontealban@
prodigy.net.mx; Alameda de León 1; s M$450-600, d M$550-
700) A 'grande dame' hotel 40 years past its
prime, the Monte Albán is located smack on
the Alameda de León. It's an atmospheric
place all in all, though the fluorescent lighting
and somewhat threadbare rooms diminish the
romance. The cheaper, interior rooms are no
great shakes, but the exterior rooms are large
and have balconies or views of the cathedral.
The hotel restaurant serves three meals and
has nightly Guelaguetza shows.

Hotel Posada Catarina (☎ 516-53-38; www.hoteles
deoaxaca.com, in Spanish; Aldama 325; s/d M$500/750; ☐)
Posada Catarina is on a busy street southwest
of the zócalo, but inside it's spacious and elegant with lush garden patios and a dramatic
rooftop terrace. Rooms are clean and comfortable, if poorly ventilated. Readers love it.

Las Bugambilias (☎ 516-11-65, in the US 866-829-
6778; www.lasbugambilias.com; Reforma 402; s M$500-950,
d M$950-1150, all incl breakfast; ☒ ☒ ☐) This
slightly overpriced B&B has nine rooms
decorated with inspired combinations of folk
and contemporary art. Some have air-con
and/or a balcony; all have tiled bathrooms
and fans. A big treat here is the gourmet two-
course Oaxacan breakfast, as are the rotating
art exhibits in the modern common areas.
There's also an inviting roof terrace with
fantastic views.

Hotel Azucenas (☎ 514-79-18; www.hotelazucenas
.com; Aranda 203; s/d/tr M$550/650/725) Probably a
last-ditch option, this small hotel is in a restored colonial house, with dirt that may,
in fact, go back to colonial times. Breakfast
(not included) is served on the lovely rooftop
terrace.

La Casa de los Sabores (☎ 516-57-04; www.laolla
.com.mx; Libres 205; s/d incl breakfast M$600/650; ☒ ☐)
Sabores offers five individually decorated,
high-ceilinged rooms with ultracomfortable
beds. Four of them are around the quiet patio
in which owner Pilar Cabrera gives her twice-
weekly cooking classes (see p219). The breakfasts are large and gourmet, and the service
attentive. A roof terrace provides a change
of scene.

Hostal Casa del Sótano (☎ 516-24-94; www.hotel
delsotano.net; Tinoco y Palacios 414; s/d with continental
breakfast M$680/980; ☐) This small, quality hotel
has a very interesting history. The sótano
(cellar) was once used as a bunker during
the Mexican Revolution. Today, it is a chapel
done up in colonial style. The good-sized
rooms are arranged along two elegant patios
with fountains, little water gardens and pools.
They have solid wooden furnishings, cable

DAY TRIPPER: THREE GREAT ESCAPES

This book just touches the surface of the adventures to be had in Oaxaca. Here are three great
day trips from Oaxaca to get you started on your own by-the-seat-of-your-pants adventure:

■ **Markets of the Valles Centrales** These resplendent markets offer up a symphony of sights,
sounds and smells. Head out to Tlacolula (Monday), Atzompa (Tuesday), San Pedro y San
Pablo Etla (Wednesday), Zaachila and Ejutla (Thursday), and Ocotlán and San Bartolo
Coyotepec (Saturday).

■ **Pueblos Mancomunados** Expediciones Sierra Norte (p219) can arrange guided tours to these
seven remote Zapotec villages. There's camping and cabañas along the way.

■ **Western Oaxaca** Head out for a day or two to marvel at the beauty of the 16th-century
Dominican monastaries in the Mixteca towns of Yanhuitlán, Coixtlahuaca and San Pedro
Teposcolula.

GUELAGUETZA GALA

In its full-scale form, the Guelaguetza (geh-la-*gets*-ah) is a brilliant feast of Oaxacan folk dance. It's held from 10am to 1pm on the first two Mondays after July 16 in the open-air Auditorio Guelaguetza on Cerro del Fortín. Thousands of people flock to Oaxaca for it and associated events, turning the city into a feast of celebration and regional culture (and a rich hunting ground for visiting pickpockets, so stay alert). On the appointed Mondays, known as Los Lunes del Cerro (Mondays on the Hill), magnificently costumed dancers from the seven regions of Oaxaca state perform a succession of dignified, lively or comical traditional dances, tossing offerings of produce to the crowd as they finish. The excitement climaxes with the incredibly colorful pineapple dance by women of the Papaloapan region, and the stately Zapotec Danza de las Plumas (Feather Dance), which reenacts, symbolically, the Spanish conquest.

Seats in the amphitheater (which holds perhaps 10,000) are divided into four areas called *palcos*. For Palcos A and B, the two nearest the stage, tickets (around M$400) go on sale online about three months beforehand, and are for sale on www.ticketmaster.com.mx. Tickets guarantee a seat, but you should arrive before 8am if you want one of the better ones. The two much bigger rear *palcos*, C and D, are free and fill up early – if you get in by 8am you'll get a seat, but by 10am you'll be lucky to get even standing room. Wherever you sit, you'll be in the open air for hours, with no shelter, so equip yourself accordingly.

Many other events have grown up around the Guelaguetza. Highlights include the **Desfile de Delegaciones** (on Saturday afternoons preceding Guelaguetza Mondays), a parade of the regional delegations through the city center; and the **Bani Stui Gulal** (on Sunday evenings preceding Guelaguetza Mondays), a vibrant show of music, fireworks and dance telling the history of the Guelaguetza, in Plaza de la Danza by the Basílica de la Soledad. There is a mezcal fair and lots of concerts, exhibitions and sports events.

TV, phone and fan; some have balconies. The Sótano also has a restaurant and a high terrace with amazing views.

La Casa de Mis Recuerdos (☎ 515-56-45, in the US 877-234-4706; www.misrecuerdos.net; Pino Suárez 508; s/d incl breakfast M$700/900; ✦) A marvelous decorative aesthetic prevails throughout this guesthouse. Old-style tiles, mirrors, *milagros* (votives), masks, tinwork and all sorts of other Mexican crafts adorn the walls and halls. The best rooms overlook a fragrant central garden; two are air-conditioned and two have a shared bathroom. A large breakfast in the beautiful dining room is included in the price, and there's wi-fi for the laptop set.

Top End

Top-end accommodations range from a converted convent to modern resort hotels.

Hostal Casa Antica (☎ 516-26-73; www.hotelcasantica.com; Morelos 601; s/d from M$990/1040; ✦ 🖥 🖳) The remodeling and furnishings of this 200-year-old former convent sometimes work and sometimes don't. It's comfortable enough, with lots of exposed stone or brick in the rooms, and extras like room service and wi-fi.

Casa de Sierra Azul (☎ 514-71-71; Hidalgo 1002; s/d/ste M$1000/1200/1400) The Sierra Azul is a 200-year-old house converted to a beautiful small hotel, centered on a broad courtyard with a fountain and stone pillars. The 14 good-sized, tasteful rooms have old-fashioned furnishings, high ceilings, and good tiled bathrooms.

Hostal Los Pilares (☎ 518-70-00; www.lospilares hostal.com; Curtidurías 721, Colonia Jalatlaco; d/tr M$1100/1300; 🖥 🖳) Opened in mid-2005, Pilares is a very well-equipped, faux-colonial hotel. Rooms have plasma TVs (with Sky satellite reception), minibars, nice beds and attractive furniture. The hotel has garden-terrace dining, a bar, pool, wi-fi and Jacuzzi.

Camino Real Oaxaca (☎ 501-61-00, in the US & Canada 800-722-6466; www.caminoreal.com/oaxaca; Calle 5 de Mayo 300; d M$3809, ste M$4898-5782; 🅿 ✕ ✦ 🖥 🖳) Built in the 16th century as a convent, the majestic Camino Real served time as a prison, and was converted to a hotel in the 1970s. It has been designated a national treasure by the Mexican government and a historic monument by Unesco. The old chapel is a banquet hall, and one of the five lovely courtyards contains an enticing swimming pool. Beautiful thick stone walls help keep the place cool and add to the considerable atmosphere.

Despite all this grandeur, the hotel remains a bit impersonal, and is certainly overpriced.

EATING

Oaxaca is home to one of Mexico's most varied regional cuisines, and traveling your taste buds in down-home corner eateries and upscale bistros is sure to be a trip highlight.

On & Near the Zócalo

All the cafés and restaurants beneath the *zócalo* arches are great spots for watching Oaxaca life, but quality and service vary.

Mercado 20 de Noviembre (btwn Calle 20 de Noviembre & Cabrera; mains M$17-30) Cheap *oaxaqueño* meals can be had in this market south of the *zócalo*. Most of the many small *comedores* (inexpensive eateries) here serve up local specialties such as chicken in *mole negro* (cooked in a dark sauce of chilies, fruits, nuts, spices and chocolate). Pick one that's busy – they're worth the wait. Many *comedores* stay open until early evening, but their food is freshest earlier in the day.

Terranova Café (☎ 514-05-33; Portal Juárez 116, Bustamante; mains M$45-80) Terranova serves good breakfasts until 1pm, and a variety of mostly Oaxacan and Mexican standards for lunch and dinner. Children's plates are on offer also.

El Asador Vasco (☎ 514-47-55; Portal de Flores 10A; mains M$80-175; 🕙 1-11:30pm) Upstairs at the southwest corner of the *zócalo*, the Asador Vasco serves up good Oaxacan, Spanish and international food. It's strong on meat and seafood. For a table overlooking the plaza on a warm evening, book earlier in the day. Downstairs, Café del Jardín is a good lunch option.

West of the Zócalo

Fidel Pan Integral (Calle 20 de Noviembre 211; baked goods around M$3-5; 🕙 9am-9:30pm Mon-Sat) Fidel is a brown-bread-lover's dream, serving wholewheat cookies, *pandulces* (sweet breads) and even croissants.

Café Alex (☎ 514-07-15; Díaz Ordaz 218; mains M$35-45, set lunch M$50; 🕙 7am-10pm Mon-Sat, 7am-1pm Sun) Airy, full of people, clean and comfortable, Alex is a great place to fill up on good cheap food. Breakfast combinations are only part of the larger menu of traditional Oaxacan dishes.

North of the Zócalo

Café Los Cuiles (☎ 514-82-59; Plaza de las Vírgenes, Plazuela Labastida 115-1; breakfast M$25-35, salad, soup & snacks M$15-30; 🕙 8am-10pm) With a handy central location and spacious lounge-gallery feel, Los Cuiles is an excellent spot for breakfast, outstanding organically grown, fair-traded coffee or light eats at any time of day. Sit inside and make use of the wi-fi internet access, or enjoy the courtyard and its fountain.

Cenaduría Tlayudas Libres (Libres 212; servings around M$30; 🕙 9pm or 10pm-4:30am) Drivers double park along the entire block to eat here. Enormous tortillas *(tlayudas)* are folded over frijoles, *quesillo* (Oaxacan goat's cheese) and your choice of salsa, and crisped directly atop hot coals; you can add tough *tasajo* (strips of marinated beef) or spicy *salchicha* (pork sausage). It's a filling, tasty meal, but half the fun is taking in the great local, late-night scene as the cooks fan the street-side charcoal grills, raising showers of sparks.

El Biche Pobre (☎ 513-46-36; cnr Calz de la República & Hidalgo; mains M$30-70; 🕙 8am-9pm Wed-Mon) El Biche Pobre, 1.5km northeast of the *zócalo*, is an informal place serving a range of Oaxacan food at about a dozen tables, some long enough to stage lunch for a whole extended Mexican family. For an introduction to local cuisine, you can't beat the M$70 *botana surtida*, a dozen assorted little items that add up to a tasty meal.

Gaia (☎ 516-70-79; Plaza de las Vírgenes, Plazuela Labastida 115-3; breakfast M$35-60, panini M$40, salads M$30; **Ⓥ**) Behind Café Los Cuiles, and sharing courtyard space with it, Gaia is a mellow

OAXACA

CHO-CO-*LA*-TE

Oaxacans love their chocolate. A bowl of the steaming hot liquid, served with porous sweet bread to dunk, is the perfect warmer when winter sets in 1500m above sea level. Hot milk or water is added to a blend of cinnamon, almonds, sugar and, of course, ground cacao beans. The area around the south end of Oaxaca's Mercado 20 de Noviembre has several shops specializing in this time-honored treat – and not just chocolate for drinking but also chocolate for moles, hard chocolate for eating, and more. You can sample chocolate with or without cinnamon, light or dark chocolate with varying quantities of sugar, and many other varieties at any of these places. And most of them have vats where you can watch the mixing.

café–juice bar serving many vegetarian dishes. Choose from breakfast combinations, panini, omelets, frittatas, excellent organic salads, pastas, and good cold veggie soups with yogurt. Plus a wide range of healthful and delicious juice blends, *licuados* (fruit blended usually with milk, sometimes just with ice) and smoothies (mostly M$30).

1254 Marco Polo (☎ 513-43-08; Pino Suárez 806; breakfast M$25-35, mains M$50-100; ⏰ 8am-6pm Wed-Mon) Popular Marco Polo has a large garden dining area, attentive waiters and great food. The large breakfasts come with bottomless cups of coffee; from noon until closing, *antojitos* (snacks), *ceviche* and oven-baked seafood are the main draws.

La Olla (☎ 516-66-68; Reforma 402; dishes M$30-90, menú del día M$75; ⏰ 8am-10pm Tue-Sat, 9am-10pm Sun; Ⓥ) This restaurant produces marvelous Oaxacan specialties, good whole-wheat *tortas* (Mexican-style sandwiches made with rolls), juices and salads made with organic lettuce. There are plenty of vegetarian choices, and the *menú del día* (aka lunch special) is a multicourse gourmet treat.

María Bonita (☎ 516-72-33; cnr Alcalá & Humboldt; breakfast M$30-50, mains M$65-120; ⏰ 8:30am-9pm Tue-Sat, 8:30-5pm Sun) Readers love the economical and tasty variety of traditional Oaxacan food here. Precede your mole with one of a good range of appetizers and soups, such as the *sopa xóchitl* (squash, squash blossom and sweet corn). The old building is on a noisy traffic corner, but the tasteful art on the walls and relaxed, unhurried service make it all OK.

Restaurant Flor de Loto (☎ 514-39-44; Morelos 509; mains M$40-70; Ⓥ) Flor de Loto makes a pretty good stab at pleasing a range of palates from vegan to carnivore. The chicken brochette is a large and very tasty choice. Vegetarian options include spinach and soy burgers, and *vegetales al gratín* (vegetables with melted cheese). The M$50 *comida corrida* (set-price menu) is quite a meal.

Zandunga (☎ 044-951-156-27-02; cnr García Vigil & Carranza; mains M$50-65; ⏰ 2-11pm Mon-Sat) Give *istmeño* (isthmian) cooking a preview here before you head off to Tehuantepec. The *cochito horneado* (baked pork) goes down easily, as do the *tamales de cambray* (stuffed with beef and chicken and cooked in a banana leaf) and other dishes. The corner location's warm decor includes grade-A artwork on the walls and low light. Service is friendly and low-key.

La Biznaga (☎ 516-80-00; García Vigil 512; mains M$70-100; ⏰ 1-10pm Mon-Sat, 2-8pm Sun) La Biznaga's cutting-edge ambience is the work of two brothers from the Distrito Federal (Federal District, which includes half of Mexico City). The courtyard is ringed with slick art, an eclectic music mix plays, and someone will take your order, eventually (for best results, sit close to the full bar). People rave about the *cocina mestiza* (mestizo cuisine) dishes here, including great salads made with organic produce, and fish, fowl and meat cleverly prepared and presented.

Casa Oaxaca (☎ 516-88-89; Constitución 104A; mains M$85-199; ⏰ 1-11pm Mon-Sat) This is Oaxacan fusion at its finest. The chef here works magic by combining ingredients and flavors: witness the chayote and banana puree, or the 'cannelloni,' with thinly sliced jicama in place of pasta tube, surrounding a filling of grasshoppers and *huitlacoche* (corn truffle, a fungus that grows on maize). Presentation is outstanding as well, and all is enhanced by the courtyard setting and a good selection of wines. There's also a nice gallery on-site, making this a worthwhile stop for nondiners as well.

our pick Restaurante Los Danzantes (☎ 501-11-84; Alcalá 403; mains M$85-215, set lunch M$75; ⏰ 11am-11:30pm) Innovative Mexican food and a dramatic architect-designed setting make Los Danzantes one of the most exciting places to eat in Oaxaca. A formerly derelict colonial patio now sports high patterned walls of adobe brick, tall wooden columns and cool pools of water in an impeccably contemporary configuration, half open to the sky. Efficient and welcoming young staff serve up a short but first-class selection of food: you might start with a delicious salad or a *sopa de nopales con camarón* (prawn and prickly pear cactus soup) and follow it with pork ribs in plum sauce. Wine selections and desserts are very good, and the restaurant has its own line of mezcal.

DRINKING

Tapas y Pisto (☎ 514-40-93; Alcalá 403; ⏰ 5pm-2am Tue-Sun) Upstairs from Restaurante Los Danzantes and in keeping with its ultrasensual theme, T&P has a black light in the bar, and a rooftop terrace (well removed from the bar) with fabulous views.

Coffee Beans (Calle 5 de Mayo 500C; coffee drinks M$12-20; ⏰ 8am-midnight) This place roasts and brews some of the best coffee in town; it's strong,

---

GO AHEAD, EAT THE WORM

Central Oaxaca state – especially around Santiago Matatlán and the Albarradas group of villages, south and east of Mitla – produces probably the best mezcal in Mexico (and therefore the world). Just like its bellicose cousin tequila, mezcal is made from the maguey plant and is usually better when *reposado* or *añejo* (aged). There are also some delicious *crema* varieties with fruit or other flavors.

Most bottles of mezcal contain a worm – most commonly an agave snout weevil (yum) or the caterpillar of the hypopta agavis moth (double yum) – and a proper shot should be topped off with a bit of salt-chili-and-worm powder. To get that rough taste out of your mouth, chow down on some *chapulines* (grasshoppers) before you head on to the next round or the next bar.

Several Oaxaca shops southwest of the *zócalo* specialize in mezcal. Try **El Rey de los Mezcales** (Las Casas 509) or look along Aldama, JP García or Trujano. Around M$110 will buy you a decent bottle but some M$40 mezcals are also fine. For some export-quality mezcals from Santiago Matatlán (up to M$550), head to **La Cava** (☎ 515-23-35; Gómez Farías 212B; ☾ 10am-3pm & 5-8pm Mon-Sat), north of the center. It has a good selection of wines, too.

---

tasty and available in several forms, including a good variety of espresso drinks. It also serves an assortment of teas and some good desserts, cookies and the like in a relaxed atmosphere.

Café del Borgo (Matamoros 100B; ☾ 10am-1am) A very small but neatly arranged, semisubterranean space, the Borgo offers some unique street views and a jazzy, arty atmosphere.

La Cucaracha (☎ 501-16-36; Porfirio Díaz 301A; ☾ 7pm-2am Mon-Sat) A good place to make the acquaintance of some classic Mexican beverages, this specialist bar pours 40 varieties of mezcal, including fruit-flavored types and shots from jugs holding scorpions awash in the stuff. A six-flavor sampler runs M$100, while shots are M$20 and M$40. Various tequilas are on offer also. Everyone's welcome here, food is available and on Friday and Saturday a small disco operates in one corner, with live Latin music (*trova, rancheras* and boleros) in another.

ENTERTAINMENT
Live Music

Candela (☎ 514-20-10; Murguía 413; admission M$20-30 Tue & Wed, M$50 Thu-Sat; ☾ 1pm-2am Tue-Sat) Candela's writhing salsa band and beautiful colonial-house setting have kept it at the top of Oaxaca nightlife for over a decade. Arrive fairly early (9:30pm to 10:30pm) to get a good table, and either learn to dance or learn to watch. Candela is a restaurant too, with a good lunch-time *menú* (M$40). Tuesday and Wednesday are mellow *trova* (folk music) nights, but salsa, merengue and *cumbia* (a style of music and dance that originated in Colombia) take over Thursday through Saturday.

Other places with regular live music include **La Cucaracha** (☎ 501-16-36; Porfirio Díaz 301A; ☾ 7pm-2am Mon-Sat) and **Azúkar** (☎ 513-11-70; cnr Calz Porfirio Díaz & Escuela Naval Militar; ☾ Thu-Sat), about six blocks north of Calz Niños Héroes de Chapultepec in Colonia Reforma. It alternates between live salsa and other *música tropical* and DJs spinning house, techno and electronica. The *banda* (Mexican big-band music) club next door, La Mata, provides large doses of quintessentially Mexican music.

Free **concerts** in the *zócalo* are given several evenings each week at 7pm, and at 12:30pm on Wednesday and Sunday, by the state *marimba* (wooden xylophone) ensemble or state band.

Bars & Clubs

La Divina (☎ 582-05-08; Gurrión 104; ☾ 5pm-1am Tue-Sun) Loud, busy La Divina has a disco-esque interior – divided into heaven, hell, earth and purgatory – and music from Spanish-language rock and house to English pop. A mixed-nationality crowd generates a warm atmosphere that spills out onto the street if you're lucky.

The bar at **La Biznaga** (☎ 516-80-00; García Vigil 512; ☾ 1-10pm Mon-Sat, 2-8pm Sun) is an utterly cool spot for drinks.

Cinema, Theater & Dance

Cine El Pochote (☎ 514-11-94, 516-69-80; García Vigil 817; admission free, donations accepted; ☾ screenings 6pm & 8pm Tue-Sun) El Pochote shows independent, art-house and classic Mexican and international movies (the latter in their original language with Spanish subtitles). There's usually a different

OAXACA

theme each month. To reach it, duck under the old aqueduct into Parque El Pochote.

Casa de Cantera (☎ 514-75-85; Murguía 102; admission M$140; ☼ 8:30pm) A lively mini-Guelaguetza is staged here nightly in colorful costume with live music. To make a reservation, phone or stop by during the afternoon. Food and drinks are available.

Casa de la Cultura Oaxaqueña (☎ 516-24-83; Ortega 403) This place stages musical, dance, theater and art events several evenings and a few mornings a week. These are largely nontouristic events and many of them are free; drop by to see the programs.

SHOPPING

The state of Oaxaca has the richest, most inventive folk-art scene in Mexico, and the city is its chief marketplace. You'll find the highest-quality crafts mostly in the smart stores on and near Alcalá, Calle 5 de Mayo and García Vigil, but prices are lower in the markets. Some artisans have grouped together to market their own products directly (see right).

Special crafts to look out for include the distinctive black pottery from San Bartolo Coyotepec; blankets, rugs and tapestries from Teotitlán del Valle; *huipiles* (indigenous women's tunics) and other Oaxacan indigenous clothing; pottery figures from Ocotlán; and stamped and colored Oaxacan tin. Jewelry is also made and sold here, and you'll find pieces using gold, silver or precious stones, but prices are a bit higher than in Mexico City or Taxco. Many shops can mail things home for you.

Just as fascinating as the fancy craft stores is Oaxaca's commercial area, which stretches over several blocks southwest of the *zócalo*. Oaxacans flock here, and to the big Central de Abastos market, for all their everyday needs.

Markets

Mercado de Artesanías (Crafts Market; cnr JP García & Zaragoza) This sizable indoor crafts market is strong on pottery, rugs and textiles. As you walk through, you're likely to see many of the vendors passing the time by plying their crafts, such as weaving or embroidering.

Central de Abastos (Supplies Center; Periférico) The enormous main market, on the western edge of the city center, is a hive of activity every day, though Saturday is the biggest day. If you look long enough, you can find almost anything here. Each type of product has a section to itself, and you can easily get lost in the profusion of household goods, CDs, *artesanía* (handicrafts) and overwhelming quantities of every sort of produce grown from the coast to the mountaintops.

Craft Shops

MARO (☎ 516-06-70; Calle 5 de Mayo 204; ☼ 9am-8pm) This is a sprawling store with a big range of good work (such as woven-to-order rugs) at good prices, all made by the hundreds of members of the MARO women artisans' co-operative around Oaxaca state. Head upstairs to see how the women work the loom.

Instituto Oaxaqueño de las Artesanías (☎ 514-40-30; www.oaxaca.gob.mx/ioa; García Vigil 809; ☼ 9am-8pm Mon-Fri, 10am-5pm Sat, 10am-1pm Sun) Government-run IOA offers a large variety of beautiful craft items, including some gorgeous textiles.

La Mano Mágica (☎ 516-42-75; www.lamanomagica .com; Alcalá 203; ☼ 10:30am-3pm & 4-8pm Mon-Sat) They sell some wonderfully original and sophisticated craft products here, including work by master weaver Arnulfo Mendoza.

Casa de las Artesanías de Oaxaca (☎ 516-50-62; Matamoros 105; ☼ 9am-9pm Mon-Sat, 10am-6pm Sun) This store sells the work of 80 family workshops and crafts organizations from around Oaxaca state. Its patio is surrounded by several rooms full of varied crafts.

Oro de Monte Albán (☎ 516-45-28; www.orode montealban.com; Alcalá 307, Plaza Alcalá) This firm's goldsmiths produce high-class jewelry in gold, silver and semiprecious stones, including copies of pre-Hispanic jewelry and pieces inspired by colonial-era designs. It has multiple locations on Calle Alcalá and one at Monte Albán itself. The tour (in Spanish) of the workshop on Gurrión is very interesting and includes a demonstration of lost-wax casting.

GETTING THERE & AWAY
Air
Most international flights to Oaxaca city (airport code OAX) connect through Mexico City. Direct flights to/from Mexico City (one hour) are operated by Mexicana at least four times daily and Aviacsa once, while Azteca flies once a day except Thursday. Continental has daily flights to/from Houston, Texas.

The half-hour hop over the Sierra Madre del Sur to Puerto Escondido and Bahías de Huatulco on the Oaxaca coast is spectacular. Aerotucán (with a 13-seat Cessna) flies daily to/from both destinations, with fares to either around M$1200 one way. Aerovega flies a seven-seater daily to/from Puerto Escondido (M$1000 one way) and to/from Bahías de Huatulco (M$1100).

AIRLINE OFFICES
Aeroméxico (☎ 516-10-66; Hidalgo 513; ⏰ 9am-7pm Mon-Fri, 9am-5:30pm Sat)
Aerotucán (☎ 501-05-30; www.aerotucan.com.mx; Alcalá 201, Interior 204)
Aerovega (☎ 516-49-82; aerovega@prodigy.net.mx; Alameda de León 1; ⏰ 9am-8pm Mon-Fri, 9am-5pm Sat)
Aviacsa Centro (☎ 513-72-14; Pino Suárez 604); Airport (☎ 511-50-39)
Mexicana Centro (☎ 516-73-52; Fiallo 102); Airport (☎ 511-52-29)

Bus
The **1st-class bus station** (Terminal de Autobuses de Primera Clase or Terminal ADO; ☎ 515-12-48; Calz Niños Héroes de Chapultepec 1036) is 2km northeast of the *zócalo*. It's used by, among others, UNO and ADO GL (deluxe lines), and the 1st-class lines ADO and Cristóbal Colón (OCC). The **2nd-class bus station** (Terminal de Autobuses de Segunda Clase; Trujano) is 1km west of the *zócalo*; the main companies serving the coast and Isthmus of Tehuantepec from it are **Estrella del Valle/Oaxaca Pacífico** (EV/OP; ☎ 516-54-29); **Fletes y Pasajes** (Fypsa; ☎ 516-22-70); **Estrella Roja** (ER; ☎ 516-06-94) and **Transportes Oaxaca-Istmo** (TOI; ☎ 516-36-64). Some of EV/OP's services stop at the **Armenta y López terminal** (☎ 501-02-88; Armenta y López 721), 500m south of the *zócalo*, after leaving the 2nd-class terminal. Sur and AU buses use the **Sur bus station** (☎ 514-44-86; Periférico 1014).

DIVING INTO A DREAMSCAPE: CONTEMPORARY ART IN OAXACA

Inspired by diverse influences ranging from the area's contrasting landscapes to indigenous mythology and contemporary globalization, Oaxaca's talented artists continue to produce some of the country's most vibrant and pioneering art.

The Oaxacan artists who laid the basis for today's flowering of art in their homeland were the great muralist, and explorer of color and light, Rufino Tamayo (1899–1991) and Francisco Gutiérrez (1906–44). The next generation was led by three artists. The colorful, dreamlike art of Rodolfo Morales (1925–2001) from Ocotlán, with its trademark childlike angel figures, has deep local mythical roots. Rodolfo Nieto (1936–85) populated his work with vividly colorful fantasy animals and dream figures. Francisco Toledo (b 1940), from Juchitán, still a prominent figure in Oaxacan life and a tireless worker for the arts, works in many media; his always arresting art often has grotesque or imaginary beasts as its subject matter.

A series of annual workshops for young Oaxacan artists organized by Tamayo in the 1970s encouraged such now highly successful talents as Abelardo López, Arnulfo Mendoza, Ariel Mendoza, Alejandro Santiago and Felipe de Jesús Morales – in part by helping them find markets for their art. Their work is highly varied, but fantasy, landscape, imaginary animals, indigenous roots and that persistent dreamlike quality run consistently through much of it. More-or-less contemporary are Sergio Hernández, whose limitless imagination melds the figurative with the abstract and the fantastic with the concrete, and Marco Bustamante with his oddly haunting hyper-realist images.

OAXACA

THE LONG & WINDING ROAD: ROADS TO THE PACIFIC COAST

Three main paved routes connect Oaxaca city and the Pacific coast:

■ **Highway 175** A spectacular, winding road passing through Miahuatlán and ending in Pochutla (about seven hours by 2nd-class bus, 245km), the jumping-off point for Puerto Ángel, Zipolite and other nearby beaches. Mind your wallet and carry-on luggage, as thieves work this route.

■ **Highway 190** First-class buses use this, the longest, smoothest route. They take about five hours to reach Hwy 200 at the coast near Salina Cruz, then head west to Bahías de Huatulco (eight hours total), Pochutla (nine to 10 hours, 450km) and on to Puerto Escondido (10 to 12 hours).

■ **Highway 131** A few decent 2nd-class buses travel directly to Puerto Escondido (six to eight hours, 250km) via this road, which is scenic but poorly maintained in parts, with many potholes.

The most picturesque route is Hwy 175, climbing high into mountainous pine forests then dropping precipitously to the coast. All in all, it's the happy, quick and affordable medium; however, some bus and van drivers take its many curves nauseatingly fast. Many seasoned travelers tell tales of fear and barfing; others report having no problems. When choosing among the routes, consider your destination, budget, schedule and intestinal fortitude (literally and figuratively). Traveling by day is recommended, for general road safety, sightseeing value, and security and to avoid motion sickness. Be aware that Hwys 131 and 175 are particularly susceptible to landslides in periods of heavy rain (most likely from June through October).

It's advisable to buy your ticket a day or two in advance for some of the less-frequent services, especially in high season. **Ticket Bus** Calle 20 de Noviembre (☎ 514-66-55; Calle 20 de Noviembre 103D; ☻ 8am-10pm Mon-Sat, 8am-9pm Sun); Valdivieso (☎ 516-38-20; Valdivieso 2A; ☻ 8am-10pm Mon-Sat, 8am-9pm Sun), in the city center, sells tickets for many 1st-class lines. See the boxed text above for information on bus routes to the coast.

Other daily bus departures from Oaxaca:
Mexico City (M$378, six hours, 47 daily from 1st-class terminal); Fypsa (M$296, six hours, three daily) Most go to Terminal Oriente (TAPO), and a few to Terminal Sur or Terminal Norte.
Pochutla OCC (M$234, nine to 10 hours, five daily, via Hwys 190 & 200); EV/OP (M$76, seven hours, 10 ordinarios; M$91, six hours, three directos at 9:45am, 2:45pm and 10:30pm, all via Hwy 175); AL (M$80, one daily)
Puebla ADO/ADO GL (M$270 to M$304, 4½ hours, 12 daily from 1st-class terminal)
Puerto Ángel ER (M$76, seven hours, 11:15pm)
Puerto Escondido OCC (M$240, 10 hours, five daily, via Hwys 190 & 200); EV/OP (M$110, 8½ hours, 10 ordinario; M$100 to M$110, 7½ hours, three directo at 9:45am, 2:45pm and 10:30pm, all via Hwys 175 & 200); AL (M$88, 6½ to seven hours, five daily, via Hwy 131)
Santa Cruz Huatulco OCC/ADO-GL (M$228, eight hours, six daily, via Hwys 190 & 200); EV/OP (M$111, eight hours, 10pm, via Hwys 175 & 200)
Tehuantepec (M$152, 4½ hours, 16 1st-class daily from 1st-class terminal); Sur (M$95, 4½ hours, seven daily); TOI (M$95, 5½ hours, 13 daily)

Car & Motorcycle

See the boxed text above for information on roads to the coast.

Car tolls from Mexico City to Oaxaca on Hwys 150D and 135D total M$326; the trip takes about six hours. Hwy 135D is signed as 131D for some stretches. The main toll-free alternative, via Huajuapan de León on Hwy 190, takes several hours longer.

There are several rental-car agencies in Oaxaca. Prices can start as low as M$350 a day, including tax and insurance, for an old-style VW Beetle without air-con.
Alamo Centro (☎ 514-56-53; Calle 5 de Mayo 315); Airport (☎ 511-62-20)
Hertz Centro (☎ 516-24-34; Plaza de las Vírgenes, Plazuela Labastida 115); Airport (☎ 511-54-78)

Van

Autoexprés Atlántida (☎ 514-70-77; La Noria 101) runs 14-seat, air-conditioned vans 10 times daily via Hwy 175 to Pochutla (M$120, 6½ hours); try to reserve a seat up front.

GETTING AROUND
To/From the Airport

Oaxaca airport is 6km south of the city, 500m off Hwy 175. Transporte Terrestre *combis* (minibuses) from the airport will take you to anywhere in the city center for M$35. Catching a cab outside the terminal should cost around M$100 to M$130, depending on your destination. A taxi ticket desk at the south end of the terminal charges M$120 if you want to avoid possible hassles.

You can book a *combi* seat from the city to the airport, a day or more ahead, at **Transportes Aeropuerto** (☎ 514-43-50; Alameda de León 1G; ☺ 9am-2pm & 5-8pm Mon-Sat).

Bicycle

Two full-service establishments rent excellent mountain bikes: **Bicicletas Pedro Martínez** (☎ 514-59-35; Aldama 418; per day M$120) and **Zona Bici** (☎ 516-09-53; García Vigil 406; M$120 per day, per hr M$30). Rentals at both incorporate helmet, lock and tools.

Bus & Taxi

Most points of importance in the city are within walking distance of each other, but you might want to use city buses (M$4.50) to/from the bus stations.

From the 1st-class bus station, a westbound 'Juárez' bus will take you down Juárez and Melchor Ocampo, which are three blocks east of the *zócalo*; a 'Tinoco y Palacios' bus will take you down Tinoco y Palacios, which is two blocks west of the *zócalo*. To return to the bus station, take an 'ADO' bus north up Xicoténcatl (which becomes Pino Suárez), four blocks east of the *zócalo*, or up Díaz Ordaz (which becomes Crespo), three blocks west of the *zócalo*.

Buses between the 2nd-class bus station and the center make their way slowly along congested streets. 'Centro' buses head toward the center along Trujano, then turn north up Díaz Ordaz. Going out to the 2nd-class bus station, 'Central' buses head south on Tinoco y Palacios, then west on Las Casas.

A taxi anywhere within the central area, including the bus and train stations, costs about M$30 to M$50. Taxis charge more at night.

OAXACA COAST

As the oft-forgotten Oaxaca coast continues its turn to the east, it becomes more wild, more overgrown, more visceral, and somehow more real. And while this is one of the off-track portions of the coast covered in this book, things are changing, and rapid-fire development is coming to towns like Puerto Escondido, Bahías de Huatulco and even the small villages around Puerto Ángel.

The biggest draw here is the former coffee port of Puerto Escondido. Now a buxom and brawny resort town, PE just feels right. To the west, a couple of bird-choked lagoons – Manialtepec and Chacahua – are perfect for an afternoon nature break.

Next up are the famed backpackers' hangouts around Pochutla. First there's Puerto Ángel. With its fishing derbies and down-at-heel air, this town is worth a stop, but travelers looking to get away from it all will want to continue west toward the sheltered hippie enclaves of Zipolite, San Agustinillo and Mazunte.

From there, it's a long ride east before you hit the last big traveler spot on the coast at Bahías de Huatulco. The biggest attractions at this mainstream resort area are a series of remote lagoons.

The coast is hotter and much more humid than the highlands. Most of the year's rain falls between June and September, turning everything green. From October the landscape starts to dry out, and by March many of the trees – which are mostly deciduous – are leafless. May is the hottest month.

The coast is described from west to east, except for the towns around Pochutla (including Puerto Ángel, Zipolite and Mazunte), which are described in the order you reach them when coming from that transportation hub.

Internet Resources

Pacific Coast of Oaxaca (www.tomzap.com) is a mine of information about the coast.

Sleeping

The peak tourism seasons on this coast are from mid-December to mid-January, Semana Santa (Holy Week), and the months of July and August. At other times hotel prices may come down anywhere between 10% and 50% from the prices we list.

Dangers & Annoyances

Though incidents have decreased greatly in recent years, there have been cases of highway robbery along Hwy 200 from Pochutla north to Acapulco, as well as on Hwy 175 between Oaxaca and the coast. Much of coastal Oaxaca is cattle country, and the numbers of cows (and burros and horses) wandering loose on the highway at all hours give new meaning to the term 'free range.' Both robbery and road-kill occur with greater frequency at night, so try to do your traveling in the daytime.

OAXACA

DETOUR: MONTE ALBÁN

The ancient Zapotec capital of **Monte Albán** (☎ 951-516-12-15; admission M$48; ☯ 8am-5pm) stands on a flattened hilltop 400m above the valley floor, just a few kilometers southwest of Oaxaca city. It's one of the most impressive ancient sites to be found in Mexico. Its name, pronounced 'mohn-teh ahl-*bahn*,' means White Mountain. The site is also open Thursday and Saturday from 5pm to 8pm for '*visitas vespertinas*,' guided night tours (M$160) that include information on astronomy and area archaeology.

At the site's entrance are a very good museum (with artifacts from the site, including several skulls and a recreated burial; explanations in Spanish only), a café, a bookstore and an Oro de Monte Albán (p229) jewelry store. Official guides offer their services, in Spanish, English, French and Italian, outside the ticket office (about M$200 for a small group). Unofficial guides, just locals hanging about, cost significantly less (M$30 to M$45). Parts of the site are wheelchair-accessible. A good scale model of the site, with a handy north point, lies just past the entrance turnstiles.

HISTORY

Monte Albán was first occupied around 500 BC, probably by Zapotecs, though it's likely it had early cultural connections with the Olmecs to the northeast.

Archaeologists divide Monte Albán's history into five phases. The years up to about 200 BC (phase Monte Albán I) saw the leveling of the hilltop, the building of temples and probably palaces, and the growth of a town of 10,000 or more people on the hillsides. Hieroglyphs and dates in a dot-and-bar system carved during this era may well mean that the elite of Monte Albán were the first to use writing and a written calendar in Mexico. Between 200 BC and about AD 300 (Monte Albán II) the city came to dominate more and more of Oaxaca. Buildings of this period were typically made of huge stone blocks and had steep walls.

The city was at its peak from about AD 300 to 700 (Monte Albán III), when the main and surrounding hills terraced for dwellings, and the population reached about 25,000. Most of what we see now dates from this time. Monte Albán was the center of a highly organized, priest-dominated society, controlling the extensively irrigated Valles Centrales, which held at least 200 other settlements and ceremonial centers. Many Monte Albán buildings were plastered and painted red, and *talud-tablero* (a stepped building style with alternating vertical and sloping sections) architecture indicates influence from Teotihuacán. Nearly 170 underground tombs from this period have been found. Skulls with holes drilled, cut or scraped into them have been found in more than 20 burials here – thought to be evidence of medical treatments unique in ancient Mexico. Between about AD 700 and 950 (Monte Albán IV), the place was abandoned and fell into ruin. Monte Albán V (AD 950–1521) saw minimal activity, except that Mixtecs arriving from northwestern Oaxaca reused old tombs here to bury their own dignitaries.

SIGHTS

Gran Plaza

About 300m long and 200m wide, the **Gran Plaza** was the center of Monte Albán. Its visible structures are mostly from the peak Monte Albán III period. Some were temples, others residential. The following description takes you clockwise around the plaza. Many of the structures in and around the plaza are cordoned off to prevent damage by too many visitors' feet.

The stone terraces of the deep, I-shaped **Juego de Pelota** (Ball Court), constructed about 100 BC, were probably part of the playing area, not stands for spectators. The **Pirámide** (Edificio P) was topped by a small pillared temple and was probably an observatory of some sort. At the bottom of its staircase a very low tunnel leads into a tomb. The **Palacio** (Palace) bears atop it a patio surrounded by the remains of typical Monte Albán III residential rooms.

The big **Plataforma Sur** (South Platform), with its wide staircase, is still good for a panorama of the plaza and the surrounding mountains, and has some carvings at the corner of its eastern base. **Edificio J**, an arrowhead-shaped building constructed about 100 BC and riddled with tunnels and staircases (unfortunately you can't go inside), stands at an angle of 45 degrees to the other Gran Plaza structures and was an observatory. Figures and hieroglyphs carved on its walls record Monte Albán's conquest of other towns.

Edificio O, at the front of **Sistema M** (a patio-temple-altar complex from the Monte Albán III phase), was added to an earlier structure in an apparent attempt to conceal the plaza's lack of symmetry. (The rock mounds supporting the Plataforma Sur and Plataforma Norte are not directly opposite each other.)

Edificio L is an amalgam of the Monte Albán I building that contained the famous Danzante carvings and a later structure built over it. The **Danzantes** (Dancers), some of which are seen around the lower part of the building, are thought to depict leaders of conquered neighboring people. Carved between 500 and 100 BC, they generally have open mouths (sometimes downturned in Olmec style) and closed eyes. Some have blood flowing where their genitals have been cut off. Hieroglyphs accompanying them are the earliest known examples of true writing in Mexico.

Sistema IV, the twin to Sistema M, combines typical Monte Albán II construction with overlays from Monte Albán III and IV.

Plataforma Norte

The **North Platform**, over a rock outcrop, is almost as big as the Gran Plaza, and offers the best views overall. It was rebuilt several times over the centuries. Chambers on either side of the main staircase contained tombs, and columns at the top of the stairs supported the roof of a hall. Atop the platform is a ceremonial complex built between AD 500 and 800; points of interest here include the **Patio Hundido** (Sunken Patio), with an altar at its center; **Edificios D**, **VG** and **E** (which were topped with adobe temples); and the **Templo de Dos Columnas**. Stele VGE-2, on the southern side of Edificio E, shows members of Monte Albán's ruling class around AD 800 – four women and a fifth figure represented by a jaguar.

Tombs

Most of Monte Albán's ancient tombs are usually closed to visitors to help their preservation. But if you're lucky you might be able to peer into one of the following. Behind Plataforma Norte, **Tumba 104** dates from AD 500 to 700. Above the tomb's underground entrance is an urn in the form of Pitao Cozobi, the Zapotec maize god, wearing a mask of Cocijo, the rain god whose forked tongue represents lightning. The walls are covered with colorful Teotihuacán-style frescoes. The figure on the left wall is probably the Zapotec flayed god and god of spring, Xipe Tótec; on the right wall, wearing a big snake-and-feather headdress, is Pitao Cozobi again.

Tumba 7, just off the main parking lot, was built around AD 800, beneath a dwelling. In the 14th or 15th century it was reused by Mixtecs to bury a dignitary, two sacrificed servants and one of the richest ancient treasure hoards in the Americas, the famed Mixtec treasure, now in the Museo Regional de Oaxaca (p218).

Behind the Juego de Pelota Chica (Small Ball Court), **Tumba 105** features decaying Teotihuacán-influenced murals showing a procession of figures that may represent nine gods of death or night and their female consorts. It lies beneath one of Monte Albán's biggest palace-residences, built between AD 500 and 800.

GETTING THERE & AWAY

Autobuses Turísticos (☎ 951-117-96-01; lescas_co@hotmail.com) runs buses to the site from Hotel Rivera del Ángel, at Mina 518 in Oaxaca, six blocks (a 10- to 15-minute walk) southwest of the *zócalo*. The buses leave every half-hour from 8:30am to 3:30pm (details of the schedule change from time to time). The ride up takes 20 minutes. The M$38 fare includes a return trip at a designated time, giving you about two hours at the site. If you want to stay longer, you must hope for a spare place on a later return bus and pay a further M$15. The last bus back leaves Monte Albán at 6pm.

A taxi from Oaxaca to Monte Albán costs about M$90, but coming down you may have to pay more. Walking up from the city center takes about 1½ hours.

Getting There & Away

If you're coming from Guerrero state (Acapulco usually), Pinotepa Nacional will be the first major town you'll pass on Hwy 200. From Oaxaca city, you'll either hit Pochutla from Hwy 175, Puerto Escondido from Hwy 131 or Bahías de Huatulco from Hwy 190/200. See p230 for routes from Oaxaca city.

PINOTEPA NACIONAL

☎ 954 / pop 25,800

Pinotepa is the biggest town between Puerto Escondido (145km) and Acapulco (260km). It's an important market town and urban center for indigenous Mixtecs and Amuzgos who live here and in outlying villages. Though there's little to do *in* Pinotepa, there is lots to do *around* the town, and many of the nearby villages, most of them Mixtec, make good day trips.

Pino's bus terminal is about 2km west of the central plaza. Two banks on the main drag, Bancomer and Bancrecer, change traveler's checks and have ATMs.

The following hotels are friendly and clean and have private bathrooms with hot water.

Your best bet is **Hotel San Antonio** (☎ 543-44-84; Carretera a Acapulco, Km 1.5; d/ste M$300/450; **P** 🔀), a roadside business hotel about 700m east of the bus station.

The well-sterilized **Hotel Las Gaviotas** (☎ 543-28-38; Carretera a Acapulco s/n; s/d M$150/200, with air-con M$240/300; **P** 🔀), about 100m toward downtown from the San Antonio, has decent rooms with good bathrooms and OK beds.

All Estrella Blanca buses between Puerto Escondido and Acapulco stop here. It's three hours to Puerto Escondido (1st-class/*colectivo* M$81/70), 1½ hours to Cuajinicuilapa (M$30), and five to 6½ hours to Acapulco (1st-class/2nd-class M$140/123). First-class OCC buses and 2nd-class Fypsa buses go north on Hwy 125 through the Mixteca, some reaching Oaxaca (M$228, 10 hours, 1st-class) that way. Estrella Roja has two buses nightly to Oaxaca via Puerto Escondido and Hwy 131 (M$151, nine to 10 hours).

AROUND PINOTEPA NACIONAL
Playa Corralero

Southwest of Pinotepa, Playa Corralero is a fine beach near the mouth of **Laguna Corralero**. You can stay in *palapas* (thatched-roof shelters) at Corralero village. To get there from Pinotepa by car go about 25km west on Hwy

200, then some 15km southeast. Ten *camionetas* (pickups) run there daily from Pinotepa (M$20, one hour).

East of Pinotepa Nacional

About 20km (a 20-minute drive) east of Pinotepa, the village of **Huazolotitlán** is famous for its colorful wooden Carnaval masks; the village maestro is José Luna López, and anyone can point you to his home. Another longtime carver to ask for is Florencio Gallardo Sánchez. There are many others.

The mainly Mixtec town of **Jamiltepec** (population 9300), 30km east of Pinotepa Nacional on Hwy 200, holds a colorful Sunday market below the *plaza central*. Many Mixtec women here wear their colorful *pozahuancos*: horizontally striped, purple wraparound skirts traditionally dyed with *púrpura* (a purple dye made from the shells of sea snails from near Bahías de Huatulco) and cochineal. Mixtec women traditionally wear nothing above the waist, but now often don a small white cloth over their shoulders as a nod to mestizo culture. Mixteca men dress mostly in white.

Buses to both places leave from a small terminal on Pinotepa's main drag just east of the *zócalo*.

PARQUE NACIONAL LAGUNAS DE CHACAHUA

The area around the coastal lagoons of Chacahua and La Pastoría forms the beautiful Parque Nacional Lagunas de Chacahua. Birds from Alaska and Canada migrate here in winter. Mangrove-fringed islands with stands of mahogany trees harbor cormorants, wood storks, herons, egrets, ibis and roseate spoonbills, as well as crocodiles and turtles. El Corral, a mangrove-lined waterway filled with countless birds, connects the two lagoons. Among the Puerto Escondido agencies offering good day trips is **Hidden Voyages Ecotours** (per person M$500, minimum 4; 🕐 Thu, Dec-Mar). See p245.

Red de los Humedales de la Costa de Oaxaca (☎ 954-582-35-40; www.humedalesoaxaca.org.mx) is a community-based conservation organization helping to protect the local environment here and on the rest of the coast. Volunteer opportunities may be possible.

Zapotalito

About 60km west of Puerto Escondido, a 5km road leads south from Hwy 200 to Zapotalito, a small fishing village with a few simple restaurants on the eastern edge of Laguna La Pastoría. A cooperative here runs three- to four-hour boat tours of the lagoons (M$800 per boat for up to 10 people). The trips visit islands, channels to the ocean, and the fishing village of Chacahua, at the western end of the park.

You can travel straight to Chacahua village by a *colectivo* (shared) boat and truck combination (see below).

Chacahua

Chacahua village straddles the channel that connects the western end of Laguna Chacahua to the ocean. The ocean side of the village, fronting a wonderful beach, is a perfect place to bliss out. The waves here (a right-hand point break) can be excellent for surfers, including beginners, but there are some strong currents: check with locals on where it's safe to swim. The inland half of the village contains a **crocodile-breeding center** (admission free) with a sorry collection of about 320 creatures kept for protection and reproduction. They range from 15cm to 3.5m in length; Chacahua's wild croc population (not human-eating) has been decimated by hunting.

SLEEPING & EATING

Several places along the beach at Chacahua village offer basic *cabañas*. You can sleep in a hammock or camp for free if you eat at a particular establishment. However, this arrangement is not exactly secure, and some readers have complained of theft.

Cabañas Los Almendros (r or cabañas M$80-120) The waters of the lagoon lap against this place, just two minutes' walk from the beach. It's run by a friendly young couple, and although it's not luxury it's fine. There are three *cabañas* and a couple of other rooms – the upstairs *cabaña* is the pick of the bunch. The shared bathroom is acceptable.

Restaurante Siete Mares (mains M$55-90) At the west end of the beach, the Siete Mares prepares phenomenal fish and seafood meals. It has some of Chacahua's better *cabañas* (doubles M$250), 300m away along the beach, with two beds, fans, nets and clean bathrooms. The señora here will lock up your valuables.

GETTING THERE & AWAY

From Puerto Escondido, you first have to get to the town of Río Grande, 50km west on Hwy 200. Río Grande–bound minibuses

(M$15, one hour) leave 2 Norte just east of the Carretera Costera, in the upper part of Puerto Escondido, about every half-hour. Most Estrella Blanca buses between Puerto Escondido and Acapulco stop at Río Grande too. From the minibus stop in Río Grande, cross the dirt road and get a *colectivo* taxi (M$10) to Zapotalito, 14km southwest.

The simplest one-way route from Zapotalito to Chacahua village is by a combination of shared *lancha regular* (fast, open, outboard boat) and *camioneta*, for M$30. You travel half an hour across the lagoon from Zapotalito to meet with a *camioneta* that will make the half-hour trip along the spit to Chacahua. *Lanchas* leave Zapotalito every two hours from 7:20am to 5:20pm (schedule is subject to change); the last return is at 5pm. Their departure point is 300m further along the main road beyond the tours departure point. This route is adventurous but misses out on the delights of the Lagunas de Chacahua.

Shared *directo* boats to Chacahua village (M$50 per person, 45 minutes, 25km), which take you the full length of the lagoons, also leave from 300m beyond the *lancha* tours departure point. They have no schedule, however, and only leave when M$500 worth of fares is aboard, so you may have a long wait. You should be able to return to Zapotalito by direct boat, but you need to allow for waiting time. If this fails, take the last afternoon *camioneta/lancha regular* service. Check its departure time before you settle in for the day!

Chacahua village is linked to San José del Progreso, 29km north on Hwy 200, by a sandy track that is impassable in the wet season. A very few *camionetas* travel this route daily (M$30) when possible.

PUERTO ESCONDIDO

☎ 954 / pop 20,000

Don't be fooled by the few multistory buildings dotting the landscape: Puerto Escondido (Hidden Port) has held on to its relaxed atmosphere, and boasts a lively travelers' scene. The big draw from day one has been Puerto's astounding waves – this is home to Mexico's Pipeline – which attract an amazing number of tanned, buff and good-looking surfer dudes and dudettes. The rest of the twizzler-necked visitors settle for watching the surfers and enjoying any of several beaches, a broad range of accommodations, some excellent

PUERTO ESCONDIDO

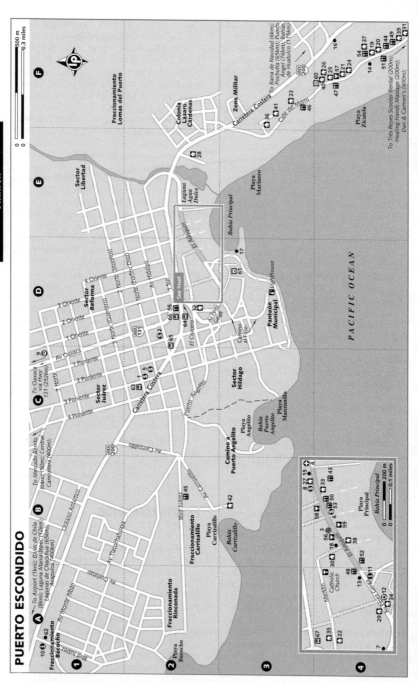

OAXACA

restaurants and cafés and a spot of nightlife. When that gets old, several nearby ecotourist destinations provide a change of pace.

Orientation

The town rises above the small, south-facing Bahía Principal. Hwy 200, here called the Carretera Costera, runs across the hill halfway up, dividing the upper town – where buses arrive and most of the locals live and work – from the lower, tourism-dominated part. The heart of the lower town is referred to by all as El Adoquín (*adoquín* is Spanish for paving stone). This is the pedestrianized section (from 5pm until late) of Pérez Gasga. The west end of Pérez Gasga winds up the slope to meet Hwy 200 at an intersection with traffic signals, known as El Crucero.

Bahía Principal curves around at its east end to the long Playa Zicatela, the hub of the surf scene, with loads more places to stay and eat. About 1km west of El Crucero, the area above Playa Carrizalillo has a few places to stay, restaurants and services. Both Pérez Gasga and Calle del Morro, the main drag in Zicatela, were undergoing massive construction projects at press time. Plans are in place

to add bike baths and pedestrian zones to Calle del Morro.

Information
BOOKSTORES
PJ's Book Bodega (☎ 044-954-100-36-56; Calle del Morro s/n) A large collection of new and used books in English, Spanish and other languages.

EMERGENCY
Tourist police (☎ 582-34-39, 24hr; Pérez Gasga s/n) Assistance in English or Spanish.

INTERNET ACCESS
Cofee Net (Calle del Morro 310; per hr M$15; ☉ 24hr) In Hotel Surf Olas Altas; free coffee.
Copacabana (Pérez Gasga 705; per hr M$10)
Internet Acuario (Calle del Morro s/n; per hr M$15) Located in Hotel Acuario building.

LAUNDRY
Hotel Olas Altas (☎ 582-23-15; www.surfolasaltas .com.mx; Calle del Morro 310) On Playa Zicatela, Olas Altas does laundry for M$13 per kilogram.
Lava-Max (☎ 540-16-17; Pérez Gasga 405A; ☉ 8am-8pm) Self-service. Wash up to 3.5kg of clothes for M$13 (plus M$7 for detergent, M$13 for dryer); complete wash and dry service costs M$10 per kilogram.

MEDIA

The free monthly paper **El Sol de la Costa** (www.el soldelacosta.com), in Spanish and English, is full of information about what's on and what to do.

MEDICAL SERVICES

In a medical emergency, your best bet is to call the tourist police. English-speaking Dr Mario Alba can normally be contacted through **Farmacia San Antonio** (Pérez Gasga s/n).

MONEY

Many hotels give a fair rate for dollars. The town's *casas de cambio* (exchange bureaus) open longer hours than the banks, and most change US-dollar traveler's checks, and cash US dollars and euros. A handy **HSBC ATM** (Calle del Morro s/n) is right next to Beach Hotel Inés in Zicatela, and there's another on El Adoquín. The following banks in the upper part of town all have ATMs and will change US dollar traveler's checks and cash US dollars:

Bancomer (cnr 3 Poniente & 2 Norte; ⊗ 9am-2pm Mon-Sat)
Banorte (Hidalgo 4; ⊗ 9am-4pm Mon-Fri, 10am-4pm Sat)
HSBC (1 Norte btwn 2 & 3 Poniente; ⊗ 8am-7pm Mon-Sat) Changes cash euros.

POST

Post office (cnr Av Oaxaca & 7 Norte; ⊗ 8am-3pm Mon-Fri) A 20- to 30-minute uphill walk from El Adoquín, but you can take a 'Mercado' bus or *colectivo* taxi up Av Oaxaca.

TELEPHONE

You'll find Telmex card phones and a couple of *casetas telefónicas* on El Adoquín, and more card phones along Calle del Morro on Zicatela and in other parts of town.

TOURIST INFORMATION

Sectur (☎ 582-01-75; www.aoaxaca.com; cnr Carretera Costera & Blvd Juárez; ⊗ 9am-2pm & 4-7pm Mon-Fri, 10am-2pm Sat) This state tourist office (the sign probably still reads Sedetur) is about 2.5km northwest of the center on the road to the airport.
Tourist information kiosk (ginainpuerto@yahoo.com; cnr Pérez Gasga & Marina Nacional; ⊗ 9am-2pm & 4-6pm Mon-Fri, 10am-2pm Sat) This very helpful place is at the west end of El Adoquín. Gina Machorro, the energetic, multilingual information officer usually found here, happily answers your every question.

TRAVEL AGENCIES

Viajes Dimar Pérez Gasga 905B (☎ 582-15-51); Calle del Morro s/n (☎ 582-23-05) You can buy air tickets, as well as book excursions and rental cars here.

Dangers & Annoyances

Puerto Escondido's safety record is improving, but to minimize any risks, avoid walking in isolated or empty places, and stick to well-lit areas at night (or use taxis). Some residents say the greatest danger on the beach at night is the local cops: if you are discovered drinking, peeing or even making out beachside, you could end up paying an on-the-spot fine.

Sights
BAHÍA PRINCIPAL

The main town beach, **Playa Principal**, is long enough to accommodate restaurants at its west end, the local fishing fleet in its center and sun-worshippers and young bodyboarders at its eastern end (called Playa Marinero). Occasional flocks of pelicans wing in inches above the waves. Boats bob on the swell, and a few hawkers wander up and down. The smelly water entering the bay at times from the inaptly named Laguna Agua Dulce will put you off dipping away from Playa Marinero.

PLAYA ZICATELA

Long, straight Zicatela is Puerto's happening beach, with enticing cafés, restaurants and accommodations as well as the waves of the legendary 'Mexican Pipeline' just offshore, which test the mettle of experienced surfers from far and wide.

Nonsurfers beware: the Zicatela waters have a lethal undertow and are definitely not safe for the boardless. Lifeguards rescue several careless people most months (their base, the Cuartel Salvavidas, is in front of Restaurante El Jardín).

BAHÍA PUERTO ANGELITO

The sheltered bay of Puerto Angelito, about 1km west of Bahía Principal, has two small beaches separated by a few rocks. **Playa Manzanillo**, the eastern one, is quieter because vehicles can't reach it. Puerto Angelito is a 20- to 30-minute walk or a M$20 taxi ride west of El Adoquín.

PLAYAS CARRIZALILLO & BACOCHO

Just west of Puerto Angelito, small Playa Carrizalillo is in a rockier cove reached by a stairway of about 170 steps. It's OK for swimming, snorkeling, bodyboarding and surfing, and has a bar with a few *palapas*.

Playa Bacocho is a long, straight beach on the open ocean west of Carrizalillo; it has a dangerous undertow.

Activities

More than anything, Puerto is known for surfing. The main break is **Zicatela**, and it's at its biggest from late April to August. When it's big, it's unforgiving, offering serious punishment to all but the most experienced surfers. If you're a beginner, try **La Punta**, a rolling left point at the far end of Playa Zicatela. When swells are really pumping, Carrizalillo shapes up with some soft lefts and fast rights out over the reef. Check out www.tomzap.com for details on area surf spots.

You can rent boards for surfing and bodyboarding in a few places on Playa Zicatela. One is **Central Surf** (☎ 582-22-85; www .centralsurfshop.com; Calle del Morro s/n; boards & boogie boards per day M$100-120) in the Hotel Acuario building. Central Surf also offers two-hour surfing lessons (in English or Spanish) for M$700, including board rental. This is also a good spot to buy a board.

Other places offering rental and lessons, for about the same prices, include **PJ's Book Bodega** (☎ 044-954-100-36-56; Calle del Morro s/n), which also buys and sells boards, and the **Instituto de Lenguajes** (☎ 582-20-55; www.puertoschool.com; Carretera Costera, Zicatela).

Lanchas from the west end of Bahía Principal will take groups of four out for about an hour's **turtle-spotting** for around M$300, with a dropoff at Puerto Angelito or Playa Carrizalillo afterwards. You can sometimes see other marine life, such as loggerhead turtles, manta rays, dolphins and whales. **Omar's Sportfishing** (☎ 044-954-544-57-90) at Puerto Angelito offers a unique twist to this activity

with an underwater microphone that lets you eavesdrop on marine mammals.

Local marlin and sailfish anglers will take two to four people **fishing** with them for three hours for M$850. Ask at the *lancha* kiosk at the west end of Bahía Principal. The price includes cooking some of the catch for you at one of the town's seafood restaurants.

Diving is another possibility. There's no coral, but there are interesting formations and tons of rays. Whales come in November. PADI-certified **Aventura Submarina** (☎ 582-23-53; asubmarina@hotmail.com; Pérez Gasga 601A; 1-/2-tank dive trips per person M$380/570, Discover Scuba Diving M$700, 4-day open-water certification course M$3300) teaches diving courses and leads dive trips for all levels. **Deep Blue Dive School** (☎ 582-07-92; lorenzo@escon dido.com; Calle del Morro s/n; 1-/2-tank dive trips per person M$400/600, minimum 2 people), in Beach Hotel Inés (p242), also offers a variety of trips, as well as PADI courses and certificates. **Puerto Dive Center** (☎ 102-77-67; www.puertodivecenter.com; cnr Andador Libertad & Pérez Gasga; dives M$450-650, snorkeling M$250) is not yet PADI-certified, but it does offer snorkeling.

Horseback riding on Playa Zicatela looks fab. Ask the guys on the beach or arrange your rides through Beach Hotel Inés.

Courses

Instituto de Lenguajes (☎ 582-20-55; www.puerto school.com; Carretera Costera, Zicatela) offers private Spanish classes for M$120 and group lessons for M$80. It also has excursions and can arrange homestays (about M$1500 per week), one of the best ways to learn a language.

Healing Hands Massage (☎ 107-10-56; Bajada de Brisas s/n, Playa Zicatela) has yoga classes Monday, Wednesday and Friday at 6pm for M$40. It also gives killer massages (M$200 to M$350).

EXPLORE MORE: THREE GREAT INLAND JOURNEYS

Grassroots ecotourism is on the rise in Oaxaca. Just slightly inland, there are a number of small villages worth checking out. Visit http://ochovenado.wikispaces.com for more details on these towns. It's easiest to get there by car.

■ **Santa Ana** About 1½ hours from Puerto Escondido, this little town has a pretty darned big waterfall and guided coffee-plantation walks. There are rustic cabins in town.

■ **Santiago Jocotepec** About an hour from town, this village has cabins and you can walk or ride horses to a rather unimpressive waterfall. The real draw of pueblos like these are their relative lack of visitors, which can certainly make for an authentic experience.

■ **Mata de Ajo (El Zanjón)** Around 1½ hours from Puerto, this just-started ecotourism site has some captive iguanas and occasional classes (in Spanish) on organic agriculture.

Festivals & Events

Semana Santa is a big week for local partying; a local surf carnival is held at this time. At least two international **surf contests** are held on Zicatela each year, usually in August or September, and the **national surfing championships** happen on the last weekend of November.

November is a big month in other ways too: the **Festival Costeña de la Danza** (a fiesta of Oaxaca coastal dance), a sailfishing contest and art exhibitions all take place over the second and/or third weekends of the month. Puerto has begun putting on a **Carnaval** celebration – normally February or March – but it's still pretty low-key.

Sleeping

The main accommodation zones are the central Pérez Gasga area and the surf beach Playa Zicatela. In peak seasons the most popular places will probably be full, especially on Zicatela. Your best chance of getting into a place, if you haven't booked ahead, is to ask early in the day, about 9am or 10am. Many places drop prices drastically in low season from those listed here, and some offer discounts for longer stays. Most hotels have wi-fi.

Several apartments and houses are available for short and long stays. Apartments start at M$4000/8000 a month in low/high season; houses overlooking the beach start at around M$15,000. Ask at the tourist information kiosk on Pérez Gasga.

BUDGET

Playa Zicatela is about the only beach with decent budget accommodations, but the supply is limited.

Hotel Mayflower (☎ 582-03-67; minniemay7@hotmail .com; Andador Libertad s/n; dm M$100, r M$620) The attractive, popular Mayflower, beside the steps leading down to El Adoquín from the east end of Merklin, has five fan-cooled dormitories (the best hostel in town) with more than 40 places in all. Rates include filtered water and the use of a kitchen with fridge and microwave. The 16 pleasing private rooms have slightly concaved beds and dingy baths. There are semi-open sitting areas, a billiard table, board games, a safety box and luggage storage facilities. An HI card gets you a 10% discount.

Mandala Hostel (Calle del Morro s/n; r M$180) One of your cheapest – and most beat-down – options in town, the Mandala has a basic *palapa*-covered bungalow and a few hammocks.

Dan & Carmen's (☎ 582-27-60; www.casadanycarmen .com; Jacaranda 14, Colonia Santa María; cabañas M$250-450; P ⓧ) This excellent place offers 13 self-contained units with fully equipped kitchens and lovely Talavera-tiled bathrooms. Units vary in size from small *cabañas* for one or two people to larger family rooms for three to four people, with terrace and views. There's a terrific extra-long lap pool. Reservations are essential, and all the units are available weekly and monthly. It's up the paved road just south of Hotel Papaya Surf, then right across a small bridge.

Cabañas Pepe (☎ 582-20-37; Merklin 101; s/d M$250/450) Close to El Crucero, friendly and funky Pepe's is geared to backpackers and offers 12 simple, well-maintained rooms with two good double beds, concrete floors, fan, nets and hot-water bathroom. Five have superb views and a shared balcony; the others have hammocks slung outside for relaxing in the shade.

Hotel Papaya Surf Beach (☎ 582-11-68; www .papayasurf.com; Calle del Morro s/n; d with fan/air-con M$300/400; ⓧ ⓧ) You're probably better off someplace else, but these simple, cramped rooms will do in a pinch. Upstairs rooms have shared balconies with hammocks. A restaurant-bar, rooftop *palapa* and pool round out the scene.

Hotel Acuario (☎ 582-10-27; www.bytravel.com; Calle del Morro s/n; r with fan/air-con M$350/400, cabañas M$600-800; P ⓧ ⓧ ⓧ) The 30 or so accommodations here range from cramped rooms and wooden *cabañas* to spacious upstairs rooms with terrace and beach view. The more substantial bungalows have kitchens and the most appealing interiors. Acuario's complex includes a surf shop, an internet café and an inviting pool area.

Hotel Rincón del Pacífico (☎ 582-01-01; www .rincondelpacifico.com.mx, in Spanish; Pérez Gasga 900; r M$400) This hotel on El Adoquín has 30 spacious, big-windowed rooms with spongy beds and cramped hot-water bathrooms, but you can hear the waves crashing from your room… nice!

Hotel San Juan (☎ 582-05-18; www.sanjuanhotel.com .mx; Merklin 503; d with fan/air-con M$400/750; P ⓧ ⓧ) The friendly San Juan, just below El Crucero, has bright and comfy rooms. All have hot water, mosquito screens, cable TV and a security box; some have terraces and excellent views. The hotel also boasts a rather junky pool and a rooftop sitting area.

MIDRANGE

There's plenty of choice near the beaches. Zicatela is sublime but it can get hectic in high seasons. There's also a good range of places around Pérez Gasga.

Hotel Casablanca (☎ 582-01-68; www.ptohcasablanca .com; Pérez Gasga 905; s/d/tr M$420/580/680, r with air-con M$1000; 🖳) The efficient and industrial-feeling Casablanca is right at the heart of things on the inland side of El Adoquín, and it fills up with guests quickly. It has a small pool and 21 large, clean, tile-floored rooms with fans. Some have fridges; the best are street-side with balconies.

Bungalows Puerta del Sol (☎ 582-29-22; Calle del Morro s/n; s/d M$450/695; P 🍴 🖳) This place has a small pool, a communal kitchen, a *temascal* (steam bath) and 16 spacious, well-constructed rooms with big TVs. Go for an upstairs *palapa*-roofed room.

Tabachín del Puerto (☎ 582-11-79; www.tabachin .com.mx; r M$550-650; P 🍴) Despite its rather off-putting location at the end of a short lane behind Hotel Santa Fe, Tabachín is still a fairly decent value. There are six *azulejo* (ceramic tile)-covered studio rooms of various sizes (including an enormous one). All the rooms have kitchen, air-con, TV and phone, most have balcony access and some have sea views.

Hotel Buena Vista (☎ 582-14-74; buenavista101@ hotmail.com; Calle del Morro s/n; r with fan/air-con M$600/700) You might just kill yourself on the stairs leading to this cozy hotel set up above Playa Zicatela. But if you're into the cardio workout, this place has good-sized, spotless rooms, mosquito screens or nets, and a hot-water bathroom. Many have breezy balconies, and the views are great.

Hotel Loren (☎ 582-00-57; Pérez Gasga 507; d with fan/air-con M$600/800; P 🍴 🖳) A minute uphill from El Adoquín, this friendly, sky-blue-and-lobster-colored hotel has bare, dimly lit but spacious rooms and a pleasant central pool. All rooms have two or three (somewhat springy) double beds, cable TV and balconies; some catch a sea view.

Casas de Playa Acali (☎ 582-07-54; bungalows_acali@ hotmail.com; Calle del Morro s/n; r with fan/air-con M$600/900; 🍴 🖳) Acali's fenced property holds a fair bit of greenery. The varnished-wood *cabañas* are fairly rustic but ample, each with one double and one single bed. The bungalows have decent bathrooms, screens and beds (two doubles in each), as well as kitchens. While it's a bit spendy in the high season, prices

drop quickly the rest of the year, making this the second-best spot in town, after Dan & Carmen's.

Hotel Flor de María (☎ 582-05-36; www.mexonline .com/flordemaria.htm; 1a Entrada a Playa Marinero; r M$700; 🖳 🖳) A friendly Canadian couple run this good hotel on a lane behind Playa Marinero. While you are not down by the beach, this isn't a bad option, as it has a large central courtyard and an old-time feel. Extras include a rooftop pool and bar with fabulous views, and a good international restaurant.

Hotel Arco Iris (☎ 582-04-32; www.hotel-arcoiris .com.mx; Calle del Morro s/n; d/tr M$730/780; P 🖳) One of the best 'hotel-style' spots in town, the attractive, hacienda-style Arco Iris has 32 big, clean rooms with balconies or terraces, most looking straight out to the surf, plus a large pool and a good upstairs restaurant-bar open to the breeze. All rooms have two double beds and ceiling fans, and some have a kitchen. You can also park a camper in the sizable grounds.

Hotel Rubi (☎ 582-36-84; Pérez Gasga 309; d M$800-900; P 🍴 🖳) Though the rooms are dark and don't have a sea view, they seem to be pretty clean. The funky pool and proximity to the bay make this a possibility for those wanting to stay in town, though it's a bit pricey for what you get.

Bungalows Zicatela (☎ 582-07-98; www.bungalows zicatela.com.mx; Calle del Morro s/n; r/bungalow M$800/1080; 🍴 🖳) The straightforward Zicatela has a sociable pool and restaurant, and all its solidly built 40-odd accommodations are a good size, with mosquito-netted windows. The grounds could use a bit of maintenance, and the beds can be a bit moist, but the baths are clean, making this an OK value.

Hotel Paraíso Escondido (☎ 582-04-44; www.hotel pe.com; Unión 10; d/q/ste M$950/1050/1250; 🍴 🖳 🖳) While it's still not exactly the Ritz, this hilltop hotel is one of your best bets in the town center. It has a pleasant garden and pool area and outstanding views all the way down to the sea. The rooms are super-clean – each has a terrace.

Hotel Villa Roca (☎ 582-35-25; Pérez Gasga 602; d with street/ocean view M$1000/1500; 🍴) This slightly overpriced, gleaming-white hotel is definitely one of the nicer spots in the center of town. There's a handful of tidily appointed rooms. Some even have sea views, which are only slightly obstructed by the ongoing construction in a neighboring building.

TOP END

Hotel Zicatela Dorada (☎ 582-37-27; www.oaxaca-mio .com/zicateladorada.htm; Calle del Morro s/n; r/ste M$1200/1300; **P** **X** **R**) The semi-Mediterranean-style ZD features 60 rooms with hot water and cable TV set around a courtyard with swimming pool, bar and restaurant. Most have two double beds; the upper ones have small balconies and air-con. If you're after modern conveniences, this may be the place, though it still seems overpriced for the area.

Hotel Santa Fe (☎ 582-01-70, in the US 888-649-6407; www.hotelsantafe.com.mx; cnr Blvd Zicatela & Calle del Morro; s/d M$1210/1386, bungalow M$1320-1672; **P** **X** **□** **R**) Your best buy in the top-end on Zicatela, the well-landscaped, hacienda-style Santa Fe has more than 60 rooms attractively set around small terraces and three pools (a fourth, smaller pool is shared by the master suites). Rooms vary in size and view, but all are well designed and decorated, and have air-con and room safes. Also available are eight appealing bungalows with kitchens, and two impressive master suites furnished with colonial antiques and fabulous modern art.

Villas Carrizalillo (☎ 582-17-35; www.villascarri zalillo.com; Carrizalillo 125, Carrizalillo; apt M$1350-1800) Sublimely perched on the cliffs above the small Bahía Carrizalillo, Villas Carrizalillo has apartments for two to six people, with fully equipped kitchens and private terraces. Some have stunning sea views. A path goes directly down to Playa Carrizalillo.

Beach Hotel Inés (☎ 582-07-92; www.hotelines.com; Calle del Morro s/n; r M$1400; **P** **X** **□** **R**) The decidedly unfriendly Inés has a wide range of bright, cheerful *cabañas*, rooms, bungalows and suites. All have safes, good mosquito screens and fans; most have wireless internet access, and some come with kitchens, some with air-con. Tasteful art and *artesanía* abound, and other pluses include a sauna, sundeck and spa, and a relaxed, shaded pool area with a café serving good food. You can arrange horseback riding and scuba here as well.

Hotel Surf Olas Altas (☎ 582-23-15; www.surf olasaltas.com.mx; Calle del Morro 310; d/tr M$1650/1850; **P** **X** **□** **R**) This modern, three-story 61-room hotel is all business. But you didn't come here for a food-additives convention, so you may consider going elsewhere. This said, you do get some nice creature comforts like room safes, air-con and satellite TV. Some rooms catch a sea view, some look over the pool, some do neither.

Eating

Puerto has some excellent eateries, a large proportion of them Italian thanks to the tide of Italian travelers drawn here by the movie *Puerto Escondido*. Most places are at least partly open-air. You'll eat some of the freshest fish and seafood you've ever had. Tofu products and a mind-boggling range of fruit and vegetable juices and milk and yogurt combos make this a vegetarian's paradise.

UPPER TOWN

Mercado Benito Juárez (cnr 8 Norte & 3 Poniente; veg/fish dishes M$30/40) Several clean stalls in the market prepare good fare, and the sights and smells of the produce section make it worth a wander as well, even if you're not hungry.

Súper Che (Carretera Costera s/n) Grab your picnic supplies at this supermarket. The 'Che' stands for Chedraui, not the famous Argentine revolutionary.

PLAYAS ZICATELA & MARINERO

Zicatela also has two or three small convenience stores.

El Cafecito (☎ 582-05-16; Calle del Morro s/n; breakfast M$35-55, lunch & dinner mains M$38-85; ☽ 6am-midnight) The cinnamon rolls alone are worth a visit, but the Cafecito also serves good breakfasts, whole-wheat *tortas*, espresso drinks and excellent pastries, croissants and cakes. A second El Cafecito at Carrizalillo on Blvd Juárez features the same great food and the same sullen service.

Restaurante El Jardín (☎ 582-23-15; Calle del Morro s/n; sandwiches M$35-45, mains M$55-100; ☽ 8am-midnight; **V**) This *palapa* restaurant in front of the Hotel Surf Olas Altas serves very good vegetarian dishes, including good gado gado, tempeh dishes, hummus, many salad varieties and, of course, tofu offerings. The menu also includes some seafood dishes and an extensive beverage and juice list.

Greko's (☎ 103-39-69; Calle del Morro s/n; mains M$40-100; ☽ 7am-11pm) Beachfront Greko's offers the best guacamole and homemade tortilla chips on the beach. You'll also find slamming breakfasts to get started, and a smorgasbord of seafood options.

Restaurant Flor de María (☎ 582-05-36; 1a Entrada a Playa Marinero; mains M$40-100; **V**) In the hotel of the same name, the dinner menu here changes daily depending on what's fresh, and includes fish, grilled meats and Italian dishes. There's always a vegetarian option.

our pick **Esmeralda** (☎ 588-52-27; Calle del Morro s/n; mains M$40-110; ⏱ 10am-midnight) The super-friendly Italian owners recently started this beach-front spot right on Playa Zicatela. Adan's love of cooking and Monica's effortless service make this one of the best spots on the beach. They have *tortas*, steaks, seafood, and of course a bevy of pasta dishes, perfect for carb-loading for your next day of adventure. Adan even makes a passable *amatriciana* sauce.

Restaurante Bar Los Tíos (Calle del Morro s/n; mains M$40-150; ⏱ 9am-10pm Wed-Mon) Right on the beach rather than across from it, 'The Uncles' serves great *licuados* and several fresh fruit juices to go with its tasty egg dishes, *antojitos*, burgers, salads and seafood. It's wonderfully relaxed and very popular with locals.

La Hostería (☎ 582-00-05; Calle del Morro s/n; mains M$68-100; ⏱ 8am-12:30am; **V**) The Hostería is a labor of love, from its gleaming, super-pro kitchen (with computerized, wood-fired pizza oven) down to the excellent Talavera-tiled bath-rooms. A broad selection of delicious Italian, Mexican and international dishes – including many veggie selections – is paired with a great wine list, and the espresso is some of the best in town. There's even wi-fi for you laptoppers.

Hotel Santa Fe (☎ 582-01-70; cnr Zicatela & Calle del Morro; mains M$70-180; **V**) The airy and romanti-cally sited restaurant here looks down on the west end of the Pipeline. Sink into a comfy leather chair and choose from the list of in-spired vegetarian and vegan meals. Seafood choices are average, but service is excellent.

PÉREZ GASGA

Restaurant Alicia (mains M$30-85; set lunch M$35) Economical little Alicia offers multiple spa-ghetti variations, seafood cocktails and good fish dishes. Breakfasts and beer are cheap, too – why not try them together?

Danny's Terrace (☎ 582-02-57; breakfast M$45-65, mains M$80-125) Reader-recommended Danny's is the beachside eatery at the Rincón del Pacífico Hotel. In addition to the usual sea-food, chicken and meat dishes, it serves up… *vichyssoise!* A decent selection of desserts and wines ties up the package.

La Galería (☎ 582-20-39; mains M$49-102, pizza M$56-89) At the west end of El Adoquín, La Galería is one of Puerto's more agreeable Italian spots, with art on the walls and good fare on the tables. The pasta dishes and pizza are original and tasty, and the jumbo mixed green salad is a real treat. You can breakfast here, too.

Restaurant Junto al Mar (☎ 582-12-72; mains M$70-180) On the bay side of El Adoquín, 'The Jam' has an appealing terrace over-looking the beach. Attentive waitstaff serve up excellent fresh seafood here; the squid dishes and the fish fillet *a la veracruzana* (with tomato, onion and pepper sauce) get the thumbs up.

Restaurant Los Crotos (☎ 582-00-25; mains M$90-200; ⏱ 7am-11pm) With romantic night lighting and an attractive setting almost on the sands of Playa Principal, Los Crotos is a good choice for seafood.

Drinking

Casa Babylon (Calle del Morro s/n; ⏱ 10am-late) This cool little travelers' bar has board games and a big selection of secondhand books to sell or exchange. The owner prides herself on her Cuban and Brazilian specialty drinks: *mojitos* and *caipirinhas*.

Blue Station (Pérez Gasga) The 2nd-story bal-cony, music and drink mixes draw a lively crowd most nights.

Rival drinking dens with loud music on El Adoquín include Terraza Bar, Wipeout Bar and Los 3 Diablos. Most of these hold two-for-one happy hours from 9pm to 10pm, but don't expect much action before 11pm.

A few bars and restaurants overlooking the sea, including Danny's Terrace (left) off the Adoquín and the bar at Hotel Arco Iris (p241) on Zicatela, have happy hours from about 5pm to 7pm to help you enjoy Puerto's spectacular sunsets.

Entertainment

Club Tribal (Marina Nacional; admission M$50; ⏱ 10pm-4am Fri off-season, Fri & Sat high season) One of a cluster of discos a block or so southwest of El Adoquín.

La Hostería (Calle del Morro s/n) La Hostería shows the 1993 Italian travel-and-crime film *Puerto Escondido* nightly at 6pm. This film (directed by Gabriele Salvatores, who also did *Mediterraneo*) has attracted thousands of Italians and others to Puerto and is worth seeing, even if it makes the place seem more remote than it really is.

Cinemar (Calle del Morro s/n; admission with popcorn & drink M$50; ⏱ film showings at 5pm, 7pm & 9pm) Air-conditioned Cinemar, sharing the building with PJ's Book Bodega, shows films rang-ing from classics to latest general releases, in Spanish and English.

OAXACA

Shopping

The Adoquín is great for a browse – shops and stalls sell fashions from surf designers and from Bali. You'll also find new age and silver jewelry, souvenirs, and classy crafts that are works of art.

Getting There & Away

AIR

Aerotucán (☎ 582-17-25; Puerto Escondido airport) flies to/from Oaxaca. See p229 for details. **Click Mexicana** (☎ 01-800-122-54-25; Calle del Morro s/n) flies nonstop to/from Mexico City twice daily. Continental Express flies from Houston to Bahías de Huatulco from one to four times a week in winter; from there it's an easy bus ride to Puerto Escondido.

BUS

Puerto Escondido's main bus terminal, the Central Turística de Autobuses (generally known as the *central camionera*), is between 3 and 4 Poniente, north of 10 Norte. All long-distance lines use it except **OCC** (☎ 582-10-73), which has a new facility on the Carretera Costera just west of Av Oaxaca. Bus companies include **Estrella Blanca** (EB; ☎ 582-00-86), Estrella del Valle/Oaxaca Pacífico (EV/OP) and **Estrella Roja** (ER; ☎ 582-38-99). The only true 1st-class bus services are OCC's and a couple of the Estrella Blanca Mexico City runs.

It's advisable to book ahead for all OCC buses and the better services to Oaxaca. You can book tickets on all lines at **Ticket Bus** (Pérez Gasga s/n), right next to Restaurant Junto al Mar. Keep a particularly close eye on your belongings when going to/from Acapulco or Oaxaca, and be sure to get a ticket for any bags placed in the baggage hold.

Oaxaca City

See the boxed text on p230 for an explanation of the three possible routes between Oaxaca and Puerto Escondido. There are various daily departures from Puerto:

Via Highway 131 ER (M$130, six to eight hours, five daily)
Via Highways 200 & 175 EV/OP (M$110, 7½ to 8½ hours, 14 daily)
Via Highways 200 & 190 OCC (M$242, 10 to 11 hours, three daily) Salina Cruz route.

Other Destinations

There are also daily departures to other destinations:

Acapulco EB (M$249 *semi-directo*, eight hours, three daily; M$238 *ordinario*, 9½ hours, nine daily)
Bahías de Huatulco OCC (M$76, 2½ hours, 11 daily); EB (M$82, 2½ hours, eight daily)
Juchitán OCC (M$188, six hours, three daily)
Mexico City EB (M$493, 12 to 13 hours, 870km, two 1st-class); OCC (M$604, 18 hours, via Hwys 200 and 190, one nightly)
Pinotepa Nacional EB (M$81 *semi-directo*, three hours, 151km, three daily; M$70 *colectivo*, 3½ hours, nine daily)
Pochutla OCC (M$46, 1½ hours, seven daily); EB (M$46, 1½ hours, eight daily); Servicio Mixto de Río Grande (M$25, 1½ hours, from El Crucero every 20 minutes from 5am to 7pm)
Tehuantepec OCC (M$144, 5½ hours, three daily)
Zihuatanejo EB (M$350, 12 hours, 640km, one 1st-class at 8pm)

EB 2nd-class *económicos* leave every hour to Acapulco and will drop you anywhere you want to get off along coastal Hwy 200.

CAR

Budget (☎ 582-03-12; Blvd Juárez), opposite the tourist office, charges walk-ins M$900 a day for its cheapest cars, including unlimited kilometers and insurance.

Getting Around

The **airport** (☎ 582-04-92) is 4km west of the center on the north side of Hwy 200. A taxi costs around M$40, if you can find one (look on the main road outside the airport). Otherwise, *colectivo combis* (M$40 per person) will drop you anywhere in town. You should have no problem finding a taxi from town to the airport for about M$40. A taxi from the bus station to most parts of town should cost no more than M$35.

Taxis are the only available transportation between the central Pérez Gasga/Bahía Principal area and the outlying beaches if you don't want to walk. Taxis wait at each end of El Adoquín. The standard fare to Playa Zicatela is M$25.

Trés Reyes (☎ 114-01-57; Bajada de Brisas s/n) rents ATVs (hour/day M$300/800) and scooters (hour/day M$150/450), and is located just down from Dan & Carmen's in Playa Zicatela.

AROUND PUERTO ESCONDIDO
Laguna de Manialtepec

This lagoon, 6km long, begins about 14km west of Puerto Escondido along Hwy 200. It's home to ibis, roseate spoonbills, parrots and several species of hawks, falcons, ospreys, egrets, herons, kingfishers and iguanas. December to March is the best time to observe birds, and they're most often seen in the early morning. The lagoon is mainly surrounded by mangroves, but tropical flowers and palms also accent the oceanside. It makes an excellent day trip from Puerto Escondido.

The best (and practically only) way to see the lagoon is by boat. Several early-morning or sunset tours (from four to five hours, including road time) can be booked from Puerto Escondido. Not all of them include English-speaking guides.

Hidden Voyages Ecotours (☎ 954-582-15-51; www .peleewings.ca; Pérez Gasga 905B, Puerto Escondido; tours for 4-10 people Dec 1-Apr 1 per person M$450-600) offers highly recommended trips – morning tours are led by a knowledgeable Canadian ornithologist – but they are only open during winter months. Hidden Voyages' office is in the Viajes Dimar travel agency.

Lalo's Ecotours (☎ 954-588-91-64; www.lalo-ecotours .com; Las Negras Mixtepec; tours per person M$350) is run by a lagoon local who has worked as a boatman for Hidden Voyages and knows his birds. Tours are year-round. Lalo also rents kayaks, leads nature hikes and offers nighttime visits to the lagoon when it contains phosphorescent plankton, a magnificent sight that only happens every once in a while – check ahead of time.

A handful of restaurants along the lagoon's north shore (just off Hwy 200) run boat trips.

Restaurant Isla del Gallo (2hr trip for up to 6 people M$600), halfway along the lake, offers shaded boat trips, and the boatmen are knowledgeable about birds. Good grilled fish and seafood are available at the restaurant for M$60 to M$100.

Restaurán Puesta del Sol (☎ 954-588-38-67; Km 24; 2½hr trip for up to 5 people M$500), toward the west end of the lake, is another recommended embarkation point. One- or two-person kayaks run M$50 per hour; fish and shrimp dishes cost M$60 to M$80.

GETTING THERE & AWAY
From Puerto Escondido, take a Río Grande–bound minibus from 2 Norte just east of the Carretera Costera, in the upper part of town. They leave every half-hour from 6am to 7pm (M$9). These and westbound 2nd-class EB buses stop along the lagoon.

Bajos de Chila
Pelota mixteca (a Mixtec ball game), a five-a-side team sport descended from the pre-Hispanic ritual ball game, is played at 3pm every Saturday in the village of Bajos de Chila, 10km west of Puerto Escondido along Hwy 200 (5pm if weather is hot). This is a living relic of Mexico's ancient culture, played for the enjoyment of the participants. The field, called the *patio* or *pasador,* is easy to find in the village.

Colectivos leave Puerto Escondido's bus station every 30 minutes, stopping at 2 Norte, just east of the Carretera Costera, on their way to Bajos de Chila (M$5, 15 minutes).

Lagunas Los Naranjos & Palmazola
These coastal lagoons, near the village of Barra de Navidad (p150; 6km southeast of Puerto Escondido and just off Hwy 200), offer another chance to get up close to the abundant birdlife of the Oaxaca coast – and to the less-lovable local crocodile population. Villagers have formed a society to protect the lagoons and offer guided visits (M$150) lasting about 1¼ hours, including a 30-minute boat ride. It's best to go in the early morning or late afternoon. To visit, you'll need to do a tour, as unaccompanied visits are not permitted.

Barra de Navidad is a short walk south from Hwy 200 on the east side of the Río Colotepec bridge; catch a 'La Barra' *colectivo* from the highway west of El Crucero in Puerto Escondido.

POCHUTLA
☎ 958 / pop 12,000
Not worth a stop in and of itself, this bustling, sweaty market town is the starting point for transportation to the nearby beach spots of Puerto Ángel, Zipolite, San Agustinillo and Mazunte. It also has the nearest banks to those places.

Orientation
Hwy 175 from Oaxaca runs through Pochutla as Cárdenas, the narrow north–south (uphill–downhill) main street, and meets coastal Hwy 200 about 1.5km south of town. Everything described in this section is on Cárdenas, with the approximate midpoint for sites being Hotel Izala. The long-distance bus stations cluster 300m to 400m downhill from the Izala.

Information

HSBC (Cárdenas 48; ☺ 8am-7pm Mon-Fri, 8am-3pm Sat) One block uphill from Hotel Izala. Changes traveler's checks and cash US dollars, and has an ATM. There are several other banks on this street with exchange services and ATMs.

Post office (Cárdenas s/n; ☺ 8am-3pm Mon-Fri) About 150m downhill from Hotel Izala.

Telnet (Cárdenas 94; internet access per hr M$10; ☺ 8am-10pm Mon-Sat) Opposite the EV/OP bus terminal, this has fast internet connections plus long-distance telephone service.

Sleeping & Eating

Hotel Santa Cruz (☎ 584-01-16; Cárdenas s/n; s/d with fan M$120/150, s/d with air-con M$250/300; ⌘) About 150m north of the main cluster of bus stations, the Santa Cruz has simple, somewhat dirty rooms, but will keep you safe for the night.

Hotel Izala (☎ 584-01-15; Cárdenas 59; s/d with fan M$150/400, d with air-con M$500; ⓟ ⌘) The Izala offers plain, clean rooms – with good beds, clean showers and cable TV – on two levels around a leafy courtyard.

Hotel Costa del Sol (☎ 584-03-18; Cárdenas 47; s/d with fan M$200/225, s/d with air-con M$250/300; ⓟ ⌘) Pochutla's best central hotel, 1½ blocks uphill from the Izala, this hotel has a few artistic touches and some greenery. Rooms have good bathrooms and cable TV. The super-friendly owner was planning to add a restaurant and an internet café.

Restaurant y Marisquería Los Ángeles (Cárdenas s/n; mains M$40-90; ☺ 10am-9pm Mon-Sat) This breezy little upstairs place, downhill from the OCC bus station, serves a good octopus cocktail.

Getting There & Away

The three main bus stations, in north–south order along Cárdenas, are **EV/OP** (☎ 584-01-38), on the left side of the street; **OCC/Sur** (☎ 584-02-74), on the right side; and **EB** (☎ 584-03-80), also on the right side. See the boxed text (p230) for information on routes to Oaxaca city.

There are daily bus departures to various destinations:

Acapulco EB (M$300 semi-directo, eight to nine hours, seven daily)

Bahías de Huatulco OCC (M$30, one hour, eight daily); EB (M$30, one hour, five daily); Sur (M$15, one hour, every 40 minutes); Transportes Rápidos de Pochutla (M$15, one hour, every 15 minutes 5:30am to 8pm, from terminal just uphill from EV/OP)

Juchitán OCC (M$149, five hours, five daily)

Mexico City OCC (M$600, 15 to 16 hours, one daily 7:20pm); EB (M$600, 14 to 15 hours, two daily)

Oaxaca OCC (M$234, nine to 10 hours, five daily, via Hwys 200 and 190); EV/OP (M$80, seven hours, 10 ordinarios; M$90, six hours, three directos at 9:45am, 2:45pm & 10:30pm; all via Hwy 175)

Pinotepa Nacional EB (M$163, four hours, seven daily); Sur (M$30, 1½ hours, hourly 7:30am to 7:30pm)

Puerto Escondido OCC (M$46, 1½ hours, five daily); EB (M$40 semi-directo, one hour, seven daily); Sur (M$30, 1½ hours, hourly 7:30am to 7:30pm)

Tehuantepec OCC (M$128, 4½ hours, five daily)

PUERTO ÁNGEL

☎ 958 / pop 2440

The small fishing town, naval base and travelers' hangout of Puerto Ángel (pwerr-toh ahn-hel) straggles around a picturesque bay between two rocky headlands, 13km

---

TRANSPORTATION BETWEEN POCHUTLA & BEACH TOWNS

Transportation services to the nearby coast change frequently. When all is in harmony, frequent camionetas (pickups) and taxis colectivos (painted two-tone, either dark-red and white, or cream and blue) run from Pochutla to the coastal towns between 7am and 7pm, usually picking up passengers in Pochutla in front of Mueblería García, a furniture store about five doors uphill from Hotel Santa Cruz, on the same side of Cárdenas.

At the time of writing, plenty of taxis colectivos were running to Puerto Ángel (M$10, 20 minutes, 13km), Zipolite (M$20, 30 minutes, 16km), San Agustinillo (M$25, 40 minutes, 20km) and Mazunte (M$25, 45 minutes, 21km). Camioneta service, though even cheaper (M$5 to Puerto Ángel, M$8 to either Zipolite or Mazunte), was much less frequent.

Be aware that some vehicles reach the coast by heading west on Hwy 200 from Pochutla, stopping first in Mazunte, then San Augustinillo, and so on; this gives quicker service to Mazunte and San Agustinillo, but longer to Zipolite and Puerto Ángel.

Private (servicio especial) cabs during the day should cost around M$60 to Puerto Ángel, M$80 to Zipolite and M$90 to San Agustinillo or Mazunte, but you may have to negotiate hard to even get close to these prices; at night they are the only game in town and charge even more.

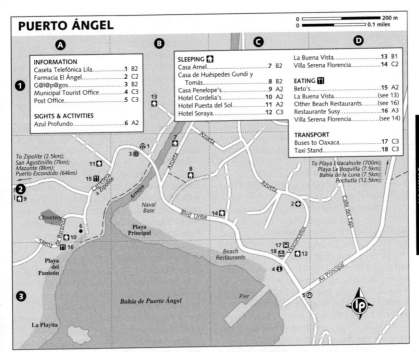

PUERTO ÁNGEL

0	200 m
0	0.1 miles

INFORMATION
Caseta Telefónica Lila.........................**1** B2
Farmacia El Ángel..............................**2** C2
G@l@p@gos..**3** B2
Municipal Tourist Office......................**4** C3
Post Office...**5** C3

SIGHTS & ACTIVITIES
Azul Profundo....................................**6** A2

SLEEPING
Casa Arnel...**7** B2
Casa de Huéspedes Gundi y
Tomás...**8** B2
Casa Penelope's.................................**9** A2
Hotel Cordelia's...............................**10** A2
Hotel Puesta del Sol.........................**11** A2
Hotel Soraya....................................**12** C3

La Buena Vista.................................**13** B1
Villa Serena Florencia.......................**14** C2

EATING
Beto's..**15** A2
La Buena Vista.............................(see 13)
Other Beach Restaurants................(see 16)
Restaurante Susy..............................**16** A3
Villa Serena Florencia....................(see 14)

TRANSPORT
Buses to Oaxaca...............................**17** C3
Taxi Stand.......................................**18** C3

To Zipolite (2.5km);
San Agustinillo (7km);
Mazunte (8km);
Puerto Escondido (64km)

To Playa Estacahuite (700m);
Playa La Boquilla (7.5km);
Bahía de la Luna (7.5km);
Pochutla (12.5km)

Naval Base
Playa Principal
Cemetery
Playa del Panteón
Bahía de Puerto Ángel
Beach Restaurants
Pier
La Playita

OAXACA

south of Pochutla. Many travelers prefer to stay out on the beaches a few kilometers west at towns like Zipolite, San Agustinillo or Mazunte, but the marginally more urban (and odiferous) Puerto Ángel is a good base too. It offers its own little beaches, some good places to stay and eat, and easy transportation to/from Zipolite.

Orientation

The road from Pochutla emerges at the east end of the small Bahía de Puerto Ángel. The road winds around the back of the bay, over an often-dry arroyo and up a hill. It then forks – right to Zipolite and Mazunte, left to Playa del Panteón. It's called Blvd Uribe through most of town, though after it crosses the arroyo it's also referred to as Carretera a Zipolite.

Information

Banks The nearest banks are in Pochutla, but several accommodations and restaurants will change cash or traveler's checks at their own rates.

Caseta Telefónica Lila (Blvd Uribe) Has internet, phone and fax service.

Farmacia El Ángel (☎ 584-30-58; Vasconcelos) Dr Constancio Aparicio's practice is here (9am to 2pm, and 4pm to 8pm Monday to Saturday).

G@l@p@gos (Blvd Uribe s/n; internet access per hr M$15) Does phone calls also.

Post office (Av Principal; ☽ 9am-2pm Mon-Fri) East end of town.

Municipal tourist office (Blvd Uribe; ☽ 9am-4pm & 5:30-8pm Mon-Fri) In a *palapa*-roofed building at the entrance to the pier; useful for transportation details.

Sights & Activities

Snorkeling and **fishing** are popular around Puerto Ángel, and **diving** is also an option. The drops and canyons out to sea from Puerto Ángel are suitable for very deep dives; a nearby shipwreck, dated 1870, is a popular site.

Some of the café-restaurants on Playa del Panteón rent snorkel gear (M$30/70 per hour/day). SSI-certified **Azul Profundo** (☎ 584-30-15; azul_profundomx@hotmail.com; Playa del Panteón; 4½hr snorkeling trips per person M$150, fishing trips per person per hr M$330), run by friendly Chepe, offers snorkeling, fishing and dives at all levels. Dives run M$500 (one tank) and M$800 (two tanks). Ask at Hotel Cordelia's if you can't find Chepe.

Casa Penelope's (☎ 584-30-73; Cerrada de la Luna s/n) offers a 1½-hour yoga course for M$50.

BEACHES

On the west side of Bahía de Puerto Ángel, **Playa del Panteón** is shallow, calm and good for snorkeling, and its waters are cleaner than those near the pier across the bay.

About 500m north from the post office, along the road to Pochutla, a sign points right along a path to **Playa Estacahuite** 700m away. The three tiny, sandy bays here are all great for snorkeling, but watch out for jellyfish. A couple of shack restaurants serve good, reasonably priced seafood or spaghetti, and may rent snorkel gear.

The coast northeast of Estacahuite is dotted with more good beaches, none of them very busy. A good one is **Playa La Boquilla**, on a small bay about 5km (by boat) from town; it's the site of the Bahía de la Luna bungalows and restaurant (right). To get to the beach, take a turnoff 4km out of Puerto Ángel on the road toward Pochutla and then follow the road for 3.5km. A taxi from Puerto Ángel costs around M$50 each way, but it's more fun to go by boat – you can arrange one for a few people from Playa del Panteón, from the pier or through Hotel Soraya (right) for around M$150 per person, including a return trip at an agreed time.

Sleeping

Accommodations with an elevated location are more likely to catch any breeze, and mosquito screens are a big plus too. Some places develop a water shortage now and then.

Hotel Puesta del Sol (☎ 584-33-15; www.puerto angel.net; Blvd Uribe s/n; s/d/tr from M$120/200/240; 🖳) The friendly German/Mexican-owned Puesta del Sol offers sizable, clean rooms with fans and screens. Some sleep up to six people. The more expensive ones have their own terraces and hot-water bathroom. The sitting room has a small library and satellite TV. Hammocks on a breezy terrace invite relaxation.

Casa de Huéspedes Gundi y Tomás (☎ 584-30-68; www.puertoangel-hotel.com; off Blvd Uribe; s/d M$150/350) Your best budget deal in town, the Gundi y Tomás is reached via a serious flight of stairs. Once there, you'll find a funky little place with thick, comfy mattresses, mosquito nets and large, clean, tiled baths. Gundi, the friendly German owner, speaks good English and Spanish and provides a safe for valuables, a book exchange, bus and plane tickets and an exchange service for cash or traveler's checks.

Casa Penelope's (☎ 584-30-73; Cerrada de la Luna s/n; s/d with continental breakfast M$200/250) Penelope's is set in a quiet, leafy neighborhood high above Playa del Panteón. It's just off the Zipolite road, clearly signposted about 200m beyond the fork to Playa del Panteón. The brick rooms are a bit dark and cramped, but there's a kitchen and common area, as well as an amazing yoga studio.

Casa Arnel (☎ 584-30-51; Azueta 666; d/tr M$250/300; 🖳) Casa Arnel, up the lane past the market, has five musty, ample, tile-floored rooms with fans, OK beds and bathrooms. It has an upstairs hammock area as well as a small library. All in all, it feels like staying in someone's house, and the owner even takes travelers out fishing for the day (M$100).

Villa Serena Florencia (☎ 584-30-44; Blvd Uribe s/n; s/d/tr with fan M$270/370/420, air-con extra M$30; 🕏) The well-established Florencia has 13 agreeable, smallish rooms with fans, springy beds, clean baths and screens, all set off a couple of walkways. It also offers a shady sitting area and a good Italian restaurant.

Hotel Cordelia's (☎ 584-31-09; azul_profundomx@ hotmail.com; Playa del Panteón; d with/without ocean view M$450/400, tr M$900; 🅿 🕏) One of the few true beach hotels in town, Cordelia's has clean modern rooms, several of which overlook the sea. While it's not the Ritz, it's a good buy for beach lovers.

Hotel Soraya (☎ 584-30-09; hotelsorayapuertoangel@ hotmail.com; Vasconcelos s/n; s/d with fan M$500/550, with air-con M$600/700; 🅿 🕏) Overlooking the town, this hotel has the best beds in town. And while the rooms are pretty small, it's a good bet for comfort. Ocean-view rooms all have air-con and are worth the extra dinero.

La Buena Vista (☎ 584-31-04; www.labuenavista.com; La Buena Compañía s/n; r M$600-750; 🕏) A great 'high-end' hilltop spot with pleasantly furnished rooms, nice terraces and excellent sea views, this hacienda-styled hotel is a bit out of the way, but is your best midrange buy. All the rooms have private bathrooms with pretty Talavera tiles, fans, mosquito screens and comfortable beds. It has a good restaurant on an expansive terrace, and a truly lovely pool area.

Bahía de la Luna (☎ 589-50-20; www.bahiadelaluna .com; Playa La Boquilla; s/d from M$700/850; 🅿) This tropical hideaway out at gorgeous Playa La Boquilla (left) has attractive adobe bungalows set on a tree-filled hillside overlooking the beach. Two two-bedroom bungalows can each hold up to five people, and a house holds up to eight (M$2450 for six). It also has a good beachside restaurant-café with moderate prices, and offers snorkeling gear, sea kayaks and yoga and meditation instruction.

Eating & Drinking

La Buena Vista (☎ /fax 584-31-04; La Buena Compañía s/n; breakfast M$24-40, dinner mains M$50-90; ☽ 7-11am & 6-10pm Mon-Sat) Be sure to pre-book dinner out of the high seasons or you may find they're not serving food. On an airy terrace overlooking the bay, La Buena Vista's restaurant offers well-prepared Mexican and Italian fare, from hotcakes to *chiles rellenos* (stuffed peppers) with a *quesillo* filling.

Villa Serena Florencia (☎ 584-30-44; Blvd Uribe s/n; dishes M$30-70) A reliable standby, this Italian restaurant turns out good pasta dishes, salads, Mexican fare and pizzas, all at very good prices. Breakfasts (served in high season only) are inexpensive.

Beto's (Blvd Uribe s/n; mains M$40-90; ☽ 4pm-midnight) On the uphill stretch of Blvd Uribe, Beto's is a relaxed, economical, friendly and clean little place with a large terrace.

The restaurants on Playa del Panteón offer fish and seafood for M$50 to M$120, plus cheaper fare such as *entomatadas* (a variation on enchiladas, made with corn tortillas, tomato sauce, spices and various fillings, such as chicken or cheese) and eggs. Be careful about the freshness of seafood in the low season. The setting is very pretty after dark. **Restaurante Susy** (☎ 584-30-19) is one of the better beachside establishments.

You'll also find several economical places to eat on the main town beach, though none is very well frequented.

Getting There & Away

See the boxed text on p246 for details on transportation from Pochutla. An EV/OP bus to Oaxaca (M$76, seven hours) departs at 10pm nightly from near the foot of Vasconcelos. A taxi to/from Zipolite costs M$5 *colectivo,* or M$50 for the whole cab (more after dark). You can find cabs on Blvd Uribe; there's a stand at the foot of Vasconcelos.

A taxi to Bahías de Huatulco airport costs around M$350, to Puerto Escondido airport around M$450.

ZIPOLITE
☎ 958 / pop 931

The beautiful 1.5km stretch of pale sand called Zipolite, beginning about 2.5km west of Puerto Ángel, is fabled as southern Mexico's perfect budget chill-out spot. Inexpensive places to stay and eat line nearly the whole beach, and the combination of thundering sea and sun, open-air sleeping, eating and drinking, unique scenery and a lively travelers' scene makes Zipolite a great place to indulge yourself for a few days. Or overindulge, if you follow the lead of some visitors. While locals generally frown on the practice, girls can go topless at Zipolite and Mazunte (p253), though boys should definitely leave their trunks on.

Orientation

The eastern end of Zipolite (nearest Puerto Ángel) is called Colonia Playa del Amor, the middle part is Centro, and the western end (divided from Centro by a narrow creek or lagoon, often called *el arroyo*) is Colonia Roca Blanca. The few streets behind the beach are mostly nameless; Av Roca Blanca, a block back from the beach in Colonia Roca Blanca, is the most prominent and is more commonly known as the Adoquín, for its paving blocks. It's a pedestrian-only spot from 5pm to 6am.

Information

Azul Profundo (584-34-37; Av Roca Blanca s/n) This dive shop has an office here and in Puerto Ángel, and offers diving and snorkeling trips; see p247 for pricing.

Banks The nearest banks are in Pochutla, but some accommodations may accept US dollars or euros. A combination surf shop and money exchange lies at the west end of the Adoquín.

Caseta Oceana (Av Roca Blanca) Has a long-distance phone service.

Lavandería Paty (Av Roca Blanca; same-day laundry service per kg M$13; ☽ 8am-5pm Mon-Sat)

Telmex card phone Outside the Buon Vento restaurant.

Dangers & Annoyances

By most reports, security in Zipolite has improved, but theft can be a problem, and it's not advisable to walk along the Puerto Ángel–Zipolite road or the beach after dark.

Sleeping

Most accommodation is right on the beach, where nearly every business rents small rooms, *cabañas* or hammocks. Unless otherwise stated, rooms here have shared bathrooms and

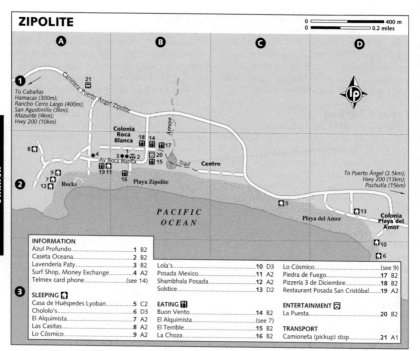

ZIPOLITE

beds have mosquito nets. Rates here are for the high season (roughly mid-November to mid-April, as well as August for many places).

Casa de Huéspedes Lyoban (☎ 584-31-77; www .lyoban.com.mx; Colonia Playa del Amor; hammock/s/d/tr M$70/170/210/260) Relaxed, friendly Lyoban has basic, clean rooms; the beds are comfy, but the walls don't reach the ceiling. Common areas include a sociable bar-restaurant space with board games; ping-pong, foosball and pool tables; a small library; and an upstairs deck for lounging. The hammock price includes a blanket, a sturdy locker and shower usage.

Shambhala Posada (www.shambalavision.tripod.com; dm M$100, r M$250-350, cabaña M$600; P) This ecologically (if somewhat shambhalically) run guesthouse climbs the hill at the west end of Playa Zipolite like a disjointed rooster, and has some great views, making it the best budget spot in town. Some lodgings have private bathrooms; the shared bathrooms are all right. Shambhala also has a restaurant, a meditation area, and a luggage room to keep your stuff safe.

Solstice (www.solstice-mexico.com; Colonia Playa del Amor; dm/cabaña M$150/490) This friendly retreat set back from the beach specializes in yoga

courses, but may be closing its doors, so check ahead of time. Thatched bungalows, studios and dorm accommodations, all fan-cooled, are set around a central space; decor is bright and homey. Bathrooms have a barrel and bucket in lieu of showers. The yoga room is large and inviting, with a full inventory of props.

Chololo's (☎ 584-31-59; Colonia Playa del Amor; r M$200; P) With five simple rooms at the easternmost spot on Playa del Amor, this very friendly place has good mossie nets, and serves good Mexican and Italian food.

Lola's (☎ 584-31-62; Colonia Playa del Amor; s/d M$200/300; P □) Third from the east end of Playa del Amor, Lola's was in mid-construction last time we passed through, but has 25 reasonable rooms on two levels of a brick building. They come with good beds, tiled floors, OK private bathrooms, fans and mosquito screens.

Las Casitas (☎ 585-72-63; www.las-casitas.net; bungalows s/d/tr from M$200/280/360) At the west end of Playa Zipolite and set back from the beach on a hill, Las Casitas has seven tasteful, semi-open-air bungalows (six with private bathrooms and kitchens). Most have good views

---

DEADLY SURF

The Zipolite surf is deadly, literally. It's fraught with riptides, changing currents and a strong undertow. Locals don't swim here, and going in deeper than your knees can mean risking your life. Most years several people drown here. Local voluntary *salvavidas* (lifeguards) have rescued many, but they don't maintain a permanent watch. If you do get swept out to sea, swim calmly parallel to the shore to get clear of the current pulling you outward. *Surfistas* take note: the beach break here – there's a nice spot that breaks left in front of El Alquimista – is one only experienced surfers and boogie boarders should attempt.

---

as well, at least in the dry, leafless season, and some have swinging beds. Meals in the beautifully situated restaurant start at M$200.

Lo Cósmico (www.locosmico.com; r with/without bath M$300/250) Very relaxed Lo Cósmico has conical-roofed *cabañas* dotted around a tall rock outcrop at the west end of Playa Zipolite. Each has a double bed, hammock and fan; the cheaper ones are a bit enclosed, while the pricier ones have two stories and views. The hammock area is on a clifftop overlooking the beach and has lockers. A security box is available to *cabaña* guests, and there's a good on-site restaurant.

Posada México (☎ 584-31-94; www.posadamexico .com; Av Roca Blanca; r with/without bathroom M$500/400) The latest arrival on the Zipolite beachfront injects some welcome freshness. All rooms have safes and good beds, and touches of a pleasing Italian sensibility are everywhere, including in the shared bathrooms.

El Alquimista (☎ 587-89-61; www.el-alquimista .com; bungalow M$600-1000, with air-con M$1200) One of Zipolite's most luxurious accommodations, this place has eight fine bungalows on the beach (at the west end of Playa Zipolite), each with homespun textiles, fan, bathroom and hammocked porch. They're often full. The attached restaurant is one of Zipolite's best.

Eating

Eating and drinking in the open air a few steps from the surf is an inimitable Zipolite experience. Most accommodations have a restaurant of some kind, and some good independent places serve food as well.

Lo Cósmico (dishes M$30-50; ☺ 8pm-4am; **V**) Mellow out on the rocks above the beach, at the west end of Playa Zipolite, at this open-air restaurant with good food from an impeccably clean kitchen. Especially tasty are the crepes (sweet and savory) and salads.

Buon Vento (Colonia Roca Blanca; pastas M$35-50; ☺ 6pm-midnight Thu-Tue) On the street between Av Roca Blanca and the main road, this excellent Italian restaurant has good music and subtle vibes. The huge pasta list includes some delicious baked options, and the wine list is decent for Mexico.

Piedra de Fuego (Colonia Roca Blanca; mains M$35-50; ☺ 3-11pm) At this superbly simple, relaxed and family-run place, you'll get a generous serving of fish fillet or prawns, accompanied by rice, salad and tortillas. It has four rooms for rent also, smelling pleasantly of wood.

Restaurant Posada San Cristóbal (☎ 584-31-91; Colonia Roca Blanca; mains M$35-120) St Chris' wide variety of food runs from several breakfast items to *antojitos*, salads, whole fish, prawns, octopus and chicken.

Pizzería 3 de Diciembre (Colonia Roca Blanca; prices M$37-60; ☺ 7pm-2am Wed-Sun) The 3 de Diciembre serves not only excellent pizzas but also good pastry pies with fillings such as cauliflower and Parmesan or baked spinach. It's the place for late-night munchies.

El Terrible (Colonia Roca Blanca; pizzas M$80-100, crepes M$40-50; ☺ 6am-midnight Fri-Wed) The Francophone couple here make a variety of damn good pizzas large enough to feed two moderate people or one gluttonous travel writer. Fresh anchovies, anyone? It does sweet and savory crepes as well.

ourpick El Alquimista (mains M$40-100; ☺ 8am-11pm) One of Zipolite's classiest joints, the Alchemist is delightfully sited in a sandy cove at the west end of Playa Zipolite. Its wide-ranging fare runs from falafel *tortas* to good meat and chicken dishes, complemented by a full bar and good espresso.

La Choza (☎ 584-31-90; Colonia Roca Blanca; mains M$50-80) La Choza's beachside restaurant has a wide-ranging menu including many Mexican favorites, such as *pescado al mojo de ajo* (grilled fish with garlic sauce), most done well, with generous servings.

Drinking & Entertainment

Zipolite's beachfront restaurant-bars have unbeatable locations for drinks around sunset and after dark. Those toward the west end of the beach are generally the most popular – especially El Alquimista, which plays cool music and serves cocktails as well as the usual beer, mezcal and so forth. The swing seats at the bar can get tricky after a few. The open-air *discoteca* **La Puesta** (Colonia Roca Blanca; ☺ 9pm-late Tue-Sat) provides slightly more active nightlife than the bars, cranking tunes out through the ether into the wee hours. Nothing much happens before midnight.

Getting There & Away

See the boxed text on p246 for details on transportation from Pochutla. The *camionetas* between Pochutla and San Agustinillo, via Mazunte, terminate on the main road at the far west end of Zipolite (about 2km from the east end of the beach). *Colectivo* taxis from Puerto Ángel will go to the same spot too, but pass along the length of Av Roca Blanca, making it easy to ask for a special stop in front of your hotel.

After dark, an *especial* taxi is your only option for getting to Puerto Ángel or San Agustinillo (about M$50 from 6pm until about 10pm, more after that).

SAN AGUSTINILLO

☎ 958 / pop 229

Long, straight and nearly empty Playa Aragón stretches west from the headland at the west end of Zipolite to the growing village of San Agustinillo. This town is still mellow, but a bit less hippie-dippie (or dopey) than Zipolite, and families will find it a bit more welcoming. Footpaths behind Shambhala Posada cross the headland from Zipolite; by the main coast road, it's a 4km drive. Most tourist facilities are right on or just off the main road.

Sights & Activities

San Agustinillo's small curved bay has waves that are perfect for **boogie-boarding** and often good for **bodysurfing**. The **swimming** is very good as well, but don't get near the rocks. Several relaxed little places to stay and a line of open-air beach *comedores* round out the picture. San Agustinillo has much more of a family atmosphere than its sometimes hedonistic neighbors, Zipolite and Mazunte, and generally higher standards of sanitation. You can rent surfboards and boogie boards at México Lindo y qué Rico! for M$50/200 and M$30/100 an hour/day respectively; snorkel gear costs M$20/40 per hour/day. It can also

hook you up with surfing lessons, snorkeling trips, guided hikes, coffee *finca* (farm) tours and other activities, like the 2½-hour *lancha* trips for M$200 per person for turtle-viewing (and occasionally dolphin-viewing). Internet access at Hotel Malex, on the east side of town, is M$15 per hour.

The coast between Zipolite and Puerto Escondido is a major sea-turtle nesting ground. Until hunting and killing sea turtles was banned in Mexico in 1990, San Agustinillo was the site of a slaughterhouse where some 50,000 turtles were killed per year for their meat and shells.

Sleeping & Eating

As with most places along the coast, unscreened rooms (and sometimes screened rooms) come with mosquito nets over the beds. Most of the hotels here have good restaurants.

Palapa Olas Altas (r M$250) At the west end of Playa San Agustinillo, Olas Altas has 16 palatable fan rooms, one with sea views. The beachside restaurant serves decent food (mains M$50 to M$70).

México Lindo y qué Rico! (faustojasso@gmail.com; r M$350; ☺ closed Oct) Fourth along from the western end of Playa San Agustinillo, México Lindo's seven large rooms feature slat windows, fans and some bright touches such as tiled bathrooms. Especially good are the pair of breezy upstairs rooms under the tall *palapa* roof. The young, friendly owners serve good food (mains cost M$40 to M$70), including pizzas cooked in a brick oven.

Paraíso del Pescador (☎ in the US & Canada 705-266-7771; www.paraiso-del-pescador.com; d with fan/air-con M$350/400; P ❄) In the center of town, uphill from the road, Pescador's spacious, modern rooms all have tile floors and good bathrooms, plus delicious views. The Canadian co-owner does sportfishing trips, and you can get decent coffee in the friendly restaurant.

Un Sueño (www.unsueno.com; d M$650; P) At the east end of Playa San Agustinillo, Sueño boasts large, freestanding *cabañas* right on the isolated beach. Each has its own terrace with hammock, table and chairs, and artistic touches throughout, especially in the bathrooms. Fans augment the breeze coming through slatted-shutter windows.

Hotel Punta Placer (www.puntaplacer.com; d/tr M$900/1000; P) Opened in 2007, this clutch of lovely stone-and-concrete *cabañas* has more amenities – like minibars – than others in the area. It follows the rustic-adobe design ethos that we love so much, and is one of the friendliest spots on the beach. It's located just west of El Paraíso del Pescador.

Palapa de Evelia (M$60-80; 8am-5pm) Evelia's, third along from the west end of Playa San Agustinillo, does some of the best food on the beach, with straightforward but well-prepared fish and seafood, and great guacamole. There are also simple rooms (M$250) with pitched ceilings here.

Two places have stunning positions atop the steep slope backing Playa Aragón (between Zipolite and San Agustinillo). Both can be reached by drivable tracks from the road or by paths up from the beach.

Rancho Cerro Largo (ranchocerrolargomx@yahoo.com .mx; Playa Aragón; r M$450-850, all incl breakfast & dinner; P) Offers a variety of excellent accommodation in some half-dozen fan-cooled *cabañas* (both individual and shared, some with private bathrooms and some with tiny fridges). The beds and meals are top-notch, and the views from the shared toilets are superb.

Cabañas Hamacas (589-85-48; hamacasilva@ hotmail.com; Playa Aragón; cabañas M$200; P) Further west on the hilltop from Rancho Cerro Largo, this place has six *cabañas* with double beds. Half have fridges and gas burners.

Getting There & Away

See p246 for information about transportation from Pochutla. *Colectivo* taxis to/from Zipolite or Mazunte cost M$5 to M$7, and *camionetas* between Roca Blanca and Mazunte run M$3.

MAZUNTE
958 / pop 702

A kilometer west of San Agustinillo, Mazunte feels greener and grittier than its neighbors. It boasts a decent chocolate-sand beach, an interesting turtle research center and a variety of places to stay and eat, many of them inexpensive and right on the sand. It's well known as a travelers' hangout and in recent years has seen an increase in foreign residents attracted by either the area's beauty or, as one person put it, the 'old-time hippie vibe.' After 1990, when the turtle industry was banned, several attempts at replacing Mazunte's former mainstay were made. Among those that stuck are the research center, a natural cosmetics factory and, obviously, tourism. The waters

here are generally safe, though the waves can be quite big.

Orientation & Information

Getting around town is a bit confusing, but get out of your car and walk around for a bit and you're sure to get your bearings. The paved road running west from Zipolite to Hwy 200 passes through the middle of Mazunte. Three sandy lanes run from the road to the beach (about 500m). The western one is called Camino al Rinconcito, as the west end of the beach is known as El Rinconcito, while the middle one is Camino a la Barrita. The eastern one shall remain nameless. **Mazunet** (Camino al Rinconcito; per hr M$15), near the main road, offers internet access.

Sights & Activities

The **Centro Méxicano de la Tortuga** (Mexican Turtle Center; 584-30-55; admission M$20.50; 10am-4:30pm Tue-Sat) is a turtle aquarium and research center with specimens of all seven of Mexico's marine turtle species on view in large tanks. It's enthralling to get a close-up view of these creatures, some of which are *big*. Visits are guided (in Spanish) and run every 10 to 15 minutes.

Mazunte's natural cosmetics workshop and store, **Cosméticos Naturales** (9am-4pm Mon-Sat, 9am-2pm Sun), is on the Pacific side of the main road toward the west end of the village. It's a small cooperative making excellent shampoo and cosmetics from natural sources such as maize, coconut, avocado and sesame seeds. It also sells organic coffee, peanut butter and natural mosquito repellents.

Aromatherapy massage is available at **Cabañas Balamjuyuc** (www.balamjuyuc.com; Camino a Punta Cometa), where a full-body massage costs M$200 per half-hour.

PUNTA COMETA

This rocky cape, jutting out from the west end of Playa Mazunte, is the southernmost point in the state of Oaxaca and a fabulous place to be at sunset, with great long-distance views in both directions along the coast. You can walk here in 30 minutes over the rocks from the end of Mazunte beach, or start up the path that leads from the beach to Cabañas Balamjuyuc and make the first left.

PLAYA VENTANILLA

Some 2.5km along the road west from Mazunte, a sign points left to Playa Ventanilla,

1.2km down a dirt track. The settlement here includes a handful of simple homes, a couple of *comedores* and the *palapa* of **Servicios Ecoturísticos La Ventanilla** (☎ 589-92-77; laventa nillamx@yahoo.com.mx; 1½hr lagoon tours adult/child M$50/25, under 6 free; ⏰ 8:30am-5pm). This local cooperative provides interesting 10-passenger canoe trips on a mangrove-fringed lagoon, the Estero de la Ventanilla, 400m along the beach. You'll see river crocodiles (there are about 380 in the lagoon), lots of water birds (most prolific from April to July) and, in an enclosure on an island in the lagoon, a few white-tailed deer. For the best fauna-spotting, make your trip in the early morning. Servicios Ecoturísticos also offers three-hour horseback rides (M$200; by reservation only) to another lagoon further west, as well as nighttime turtle tours. Remember not to use flashlights or camera flashes as you head out to view this natural phenomenon.

Frequent *camionetas* pass the turnoff, leaving you with the 1.2km walk. A taxi from Mazunte costs upwards of M$30.

Sleeping
PLAYA MAZUNTE

Most places along Playa Mazunte (including restaurants) have basic rooms or *cabañas*, hammocks to rent and often tent space. Bathrooms are shared unless otherwise stated. Security can be a problem here.

Palapa Omar (hammock or camping per person M$50, r per person M$100) Omar is beside the end of the middle lane (Camino a La Barrita) to Playa Mazunte. The eight rooms in brick buildings have mosquito nets, fans and one or two double beds.

Palapa El Pescador (camping per person M$50, s/d M$200/250) This popular restaurant in the middle of Playa Mazunte has a small tent/hammock area on the sand and good, clean upstairs rooms with power.

Palapa Yuri (hammock per person M$50; tr with shared bathroom M$150, d with private bathroom M$300) Near the east end of Playa Mazunte, Yuri has adequate rooms that are plain but clean and have fans. Those with shared bathroom have OK views; a thatched roof blocks the view from those with a private bathroom. There's a safety deposit box.

El Agujón (elagujonmazunte@yahoo.com.mx; Camino al Rinconcito; s/d cabaña M$70/120; ℗) Friendly El Agujón has 10 small, very rustic, clean *cabañas* on the hillside just above its restaurant.

La Nueva Luna (Camino a La Barrita; r M$100 per person) Two-hundred meters off the beach, the Luna is an exception among low-end Mazunte lodgings in that it has plenty of good (shared) bathrooms, as well as a shared kitchen. The three rooms are adjacent to a bar, so you may have a noisy night.

Estrella Fugaz (☎ 583-92-97; estrellafugazmazunte@ hotmail.com; Camino al Rinconcito; r per person M$150-250) The nine rooms here tend toward the gloomy and some are a bit malodorous, but all have fans and mosquito nets, and sleep up to four people. Six have private bathrooms, and the restaurant upstairs has a good selection of Mexican and international dishes (mains M$40 to M$80), as well as veggie and fruit drinks and coffees.

Restaurante Tania (☎ 583-95-94; d M$250) Near the end of 2005, Tania completed a few simple rooms above her restaurant on the hill at the western edge of town about 600m from the beach. They're solid if not cheerful, with ceiling fans, private bathrooms and a distant sea view.

Cabañas Ziga (☎ 583-92-95; www.posadaziga.com; d with shared/private bathroom M$300/400; ℗) Friendly Ziga, at the far east end of Playa Mazunte, is near the end of the easternmost access road, on a breezy beachside promontory that gives up some marvelous views after a very short climb. It has a good restaurant, a little flower garden and 17 fan rooms, all with good mosquito nets. The more expensive rooms have tile floors, good bathrooms and beds, as well as hammocks and terraces. Some of the best views are from the shared-bathroom quarters, which are in a wooden section at the front of the hotel.

AROUND PLAYA MAZUNTE

The first two properties here are perched next to each other on a hilltop above the west end of the beach, with some superb views. Their entrances are about 400m along a road that leads uphill from Camino al Rinconcito, and they're also reachable by steps up from the beach (it can be a hot climb).

Cabañas Balamjuyuc (www.balamjuyuc.com; Camino a Punta Cometa; r M$250-300; ℗) This quiet, tree-covered property has about seven *cabaña* rooms, some of which are large and airy with good sea views. The shared showers are prettily tiled, and for true budget travelers there's a *palapa* with hammocks and tents (with mattresses). The restaurant here is pretty good.

Alta Mira (☎ 584-31-04; www.labuenavista.com /alta_mira; Camino a Punta Cometa; d with private bathroom M$250-450; **P**) The Alta Mira is run by the people from La Buena Vista at Puerto Ángel, and its 10 electricity-free rooms are among Mazunte's classiest and comfiest, all with beautiful Talavera-tiled bathrooms, mosquito nets and a terrace with hammock. They're strung beside steps leading down the hillside, and most catch some breeze and excellent views. The restaurant serves breakfast and dinner, and there's also a safety box.

Posada Arigalan (www.arigalan.com; r M$550-850; **P** 🌣 🗙) Up a steep dirt track (above Playa Mazunte) from the main road, between Mazunte and San Agustinillo, Arigalan has commanding views of the Pacific and Punta Cometa, lovely landscaping and nine simple but tastefully furnished air-con rooms with private bathrooms. Its restaurant is open mid-November to mid-January (room rates outside of this time are 30% lower). A trail from the beach provides access as well.

Eating

Most places to stay are also places to eat, or vice versa.

La Empanada (sushi M$15-40; rice dishes M$15-50; 🌣 from 5pm low seasons, 9am-late high seasons) Choose from a Mexican-Asian mix of delectable items including vegetable and sushi, all lovingly prepared. You'll find La Empanada on the main road, at the west edge of town.

Restaurante Tania (comida corrida M$35; mains M$20-50) At the western edge of town, on the main road, Tania's scores high marks for both its good-value food and hospitality.

El Agujón (Camino al Rinconcito; dishes M$25-70) Another good restaurant, with a very wide range from large and excellent French-bread *tortas* to crepes, fish and, in the evening, pizzas.

Palapa El Pescador (mains M$30-70) One of the best and most popular places, El Pescador offers fish, seafood and lighter eats such as quesadillas, tacos, fruit salad, eggs and *tortas*. It's on Playa Mazunte, east of the lagoon.

Restaurante Bar Bella Vista (mains M$35-50) With its elevated position at the east end of Playa Mazunte, this restaurant, which belongs to Posada Ziga, catches a breeze.

La Dolce Vita (mains M$50-80; 🌣 closed Oct) This Italian restaurant, on the main road (east of Cosméticos Naturales), is well known for its excellent food.

Entertainment

La Nueva Luna (Camino a La Barrita; 🌣 6pm-late, closed October) Adjacent to the lodgings of the same name, this bar has a ping-pong table and a pleasantly shady ambience.

Getting There & Away

See p246 for information about transportation from Pochutla. *Camionetas* between Mazunte and San Agustinillo or Zipolite cost M$7.

BAHÍAS DE HUATULCO

☎ 958 / pop 18,000

Mexico's newest big coastal resort is strung along a series of beautiful sandy bays, the Bahías de Huatulco (wah-*tool*-koh), 45km east of Pochutla. This stretch of coast had just one small fishing village until the 1980s. The Mexican government has trod more gently here than at other resorts: pockets of development are separated by tracts of unspoiled shoreline, the maximum building height is six stories, and water-processing plants supposedly ensure no sewage goes into the sea. (Testing by Mexico's environmental agency has shown that there is in fact some water contamination.) Lower than expected occupancy rates have slowed development and, for now at least, Huatulco is still a relatively uncrowded resort with a succession of scenic beaches lapped by beautiful water and backed by forest. You can have an active time here – agencies offer all sorts of energetic pursuits from rafting and horseback riding to diving and kayaking. Huatulco is not a place to stay long on a tight budget, however.

The Parque Nacional Huatulco, declared in 1998, protects 119 sq km of land, sea and shoreline west of Santa Cruz Huatulco. The most common way to visit the park is by booking a seven-bay tour (p259), where you'll get to swim, snorkel and sun on the park's sandy bays. Balancing this, a cruise-ship pier has gone in at Bahía de Santa Cruz, and between October and May an average of two ships a week dock there, discharging thousands of passengers for brief visits to the area.

Orientation

A divided road leads about 4km down from Hwy 200 to **La Crucecita**, the land-locked service town for the resort. La Crucecita has the bus stations, the market, most of the shops, a cute *plaza principal* and virtually

OAXACA

BAHÍAS DE HUATULCO

the only cheap accommodations. One kilometer south, on Bahía de Santa Cruz, is **Santa Cruz Huatulco** (often just called Santa Cruz), with somewhat plush hotels and a harbor. The other main developments so far are at Bahía Chahué, with mainly midrange hotels, 1km east of Santa Cruz; Tangolunda, 4km further east with most of the luxury hotels; and El Faro, near Playa La Entrega, 2.5km south of Santa Cruz.

The Huatulco bays are strung along the coast about 10km in each direction from Santa Cruz. From southwest to northeast, the main ones are San Agustín, Chachacual, Cacaluta, Maguey, El Órgano, Santa Cruz, Chahué, Tangolunda and Conejos.

Bahías de Huatulco airport is 400m north of Hwy 200, 12km west of the turnoff to La Crucecita.

Information

INTERNET ACCESS

Most hotels in the area have wi-fi access, and there are numerous internet cafés in La Crucecita, costing about M$10 per hour.
Surf Conejo (Guamuchil 208, La Crucecita)

LAUNDRY

Lavado Express (☎ 587-27-37; Bugambilia 402, La Crucecita; ☺ 9am-9pm Mon-Sat, 10am-3pm Sun) Washes and dries for M$15 per kilogram. Ask for it *sin suavizante* to avoid the perfumey fabric softener.

MEDICAL SERVICES

The big hotels have English-speaking doctors on call.
Dr Andrés González Ayvar (☎ 587-06-00, 044-958-587-60-65) Provides 24-hour medical assistance.
Hospital IMSS (☎ 587-11-84; Blvd Chahué) Halfway between La Crucecita and Bahía Chahué; some doctors speak English.

MONEY

Banamex (Map p258; Blvd Santa Cruz, Santa Cruz Huatulco) Changes cash and traveler's checks and has an ATM.
Banamex ATM (cnr Carrizal & Guamuchil, La Crucecita) This is one of several ATMs and banks in La Crucecita.
Bancomer (Map p258; Blvd Santa Cruz, Santa Cruz Huatulco)
HSBC (cnr Bugambilia & Sabalí, La Crucecita; ☺ 9am-7pm Mon-Sat) Changes cash and traveler's checks, and has two ATMs, with another in Hotel Plaza Conejo.
HSBC ATM (Blvd Juárez, Tangolunda) In Hotel Gala.

POST

Post office (Blvd Chahué, La Crucecita) About 300m east of Plaza Principal.

TOURIST INFORMATION

Information kiosk (Plaza Principal, La Crucecita; 9am-2pm & 4-7pm Mon-Fri, 9am-1pm Sat, closed in off-season)

Municipal tourist office (581-28-80; cnr Blvd Chahué & Guamuchil, La Crucecita; 9am-5pm Mon-Sat) This office is located on the 2nd floor. Staff may be able to help you, but it's doubtful.

State tourist office (581-01-77; sedetur@oaxaca. gob.mx; Blvd Juárez s/n, Tangolunda; 8am-4pm Mon-Fri, 9am-2pm Sat) In Tangolunda, on the left as you arrive from the west.

TRAVEL AGENCIES

Bahías Plus (587-02-16; upstairs, Carrizal 704, La Crucecita) Can help with air tickets; also books rafting tours, coffee *finca* visits etc.

Sights & Activities

There's some good sportfishing from here. You can go fishing for swordfish, sailfish and dorado year-round, marlin from October to May and roosterfish from April to August. Trips cost anywhere from M$1800 to M$4000, depending on the size of the boat. You can arrange trips through Bahías Plus (above) or at the Santa Cruz Huatulco Harbor.

La Crucecita's modern church, the **Parroquia de Nuestra Señora de Guadalupe** (Plaza Principal, La Crucecita), has an impressively large image of the Virgin painted on its ceiling. The rest of the area's attractions are on the water, at the beaches or in the jungle hinterland. You can sail, snorkel, dive, kayak, surf, fish, raft, canoe, walk in the jungle, watch birds, ride horses, rappel, canyoneer, cycle, visit a coffee plantation and waterfalls and more. Most outings cost M$250 to M$350. **Bahías Plus** (587-09-32; www.bahiasplus.com; Guamuchil 208, La Crucecita) and several hotels will book many of the activities listed here.

BEACHES

Huatulco's beaches are sandy with clear waters (though boats and jet skis leave an oily film here and there). Like the rest of Mexico, all beaches are under federal control and anyone can use them – even when hotels appear to treat them as private property. Some have coral offshore and excellent snorkeling, though visibility can be poor in

rainy season. Some beaches are best reached by boat (p259).

At Santa Cruz Huatulco, the small, accessible **Playa Santa Cruz** is rather pretty, though its looks are somewhat marred by the cruise-ship pier. **Playa La Entrega** lies toward the outer edge of Bahía de Santa Cruz, a five-minute *lancha* trip or 2.5km by paved road from Santa Cruz. The 300m-long beach, backed by a line of seafood *palapas*, can get crowded, but it has calm water and good snorkeling in a large area from which boats are cordoned off. 'La Entrega' means 'the Handover': it was here in 1831 that Mexican independence hero Vicente Guerrero was betrayed to his enemies by a Genoese sea captain. Guerrero was taken to Cuilapan near Oaxaca and shot.

Some of the western bays are accessible by road; at times groups of young men congregate in their parking lots, offering to 'watch your car' and touting for the beach restaurants. A 1.5km paved road diverges to **Bahía Maguey** from the road to La Entrega, about half a kilometer out of Santa Cruz. Maguey's fine 400m beach curves around a calm bay between forested headlands. It has a line of seafood *palapas*. There's good snorkeling around the rocks at the left (east) side of the bay. **Bahía El Órgano**, just east of Maguey, has a 250m beach. You can reach it by a narrow 10-minute footpath that heads into the trees halfway along the Santa Cruz–Maguey road. El Órgano has calm waters good for snorkeling, but it lacks *comedores*.

The beach at **Bahía Cacaluta** is about 1km long and protected by an island, though there can be undertow. Snorkeling is best around the island. Behind the beach is a lagoon with birdlife. The road to Cacaluta (which branches off just above the parking lot for Maguey) is paved except for the last 1.5km, but it can be a long, hot walk, and there are no services at the beach itself. You probably wouldn't want to leave a car at pavement's end, either, as it's quite isolated. Cacaluta has a research station for the study of turtles and sea snails.

Bahía Chachacual, inaccessible by land, has a headland at each end and two beaches. The easterly **Playa La India** is one of Huatulco's most beautiful and is a prime place for snorkeling.

Thirteen kilometers down a dirt road from a crossroads on Hwy 200, 1.7km west of the airport, is **Bahía San Agustín**. After 6km the road fords a river. The beach is long and sandy,

SANTA CRUZ HUATULCO

INFORMATION
Banamex.................................**1** B2
Bancomer..............................**2** B2
HSBC......................................**3** C2

SIGHTS & ACTIVITIES
Hurricane Divers.....................**4** C3

SLEEPING
Hotel Castillo Huatulco.............**5** C1
Hotel Marina Resort................**6** D2
Hotel Sol y Mar......................**7** B3

EATING
Café Huatulco........................**8** C2
Restaurant Ve El Mar..............**9** D3

SHOPPING
Mercado de Artesanías............**10** C2

TRANSPORT
Colectivo Taxi & Microbus Stop...**11** C2
Cooperativo Tangolunda
(boat tickets)......................**12** C2
Lancha Kiosk.........................(see **12**)
Private Taxi Stand...................**13** C2

---

with a long line of *palapa comedores,* some with hammocks for rent overnight. It's popular with Mexicans on Saturdays, Sundays and holidays, but quiet at other times. Usually the waters are calm and the snorkeling is good (some of the *comedores* rent equipment).

A paved road runs to the eastern bays from La Crucecita and Santa Cruz, continuing eventually to Hwy 200. **Bahía Chahué** has a good beach and a new marina at its east end. Further northeast, **Bahía Tangolunda** is the site of the major top-end hotel developments to date. The sea is sometimes rough here, so be wary of currents and be sure to heed the colored-flag safety system. Tangolunda has an 18-hole **golf course** too. Three kilometers further east is the long sweep of **Playa Punta Arena**, on Bahía Conejos. Around a headland at the east end of Bahía Conejos is the more sheltered **Playa Conejos**, unreachable by road.

PARQUE ECOLÓGICO RUFINO TAMAYO

This park on the edge of La Crucecita is composed mainly of natural vegetation, with some paved paths and tile-roofed shelters with benches.

SNORKELING & DIVING

You can rent snorkeling gear beside the *lancha* kiosk at Santa Cruz harbor for about M$60 a day. At Playa Maguey you can rent a snorkel, mask and fins for M$60 a day. Tour guides will take you snorkeling for M$200 to M$450, or you can arrange a trip with one of the dive outfits listed here.

Huatulco has around 13 dive sites, with a wide variety of fish and corals, as well as dolphins and sea turtles. At least two companies will take you diving and offer instruction from beginner's sessions through to full certification courses. There's a good divemap at www.tomzap.com/divemap.html.

Centro de Buceo Sotavento La Crucecita (☎ 581-00-51; Plaza Oaxaca, Local 18 Interior, Flamboyán); Tangolunda (☎ 581-00-51; Plaza Las Conchas, Local 12) offers a range of diving options from a four-hour introduction (M$650) to full certification (five days, M$4000) or specialty night dives (M$700); it also does two-hour fishing trips for one to six people (M$450 to M$800, depending on vessel), as well as snorkeling trips for M$150 per person. Ask to review the equipment before you head out.

The professional international crew at **Hurricane Divers** (Map p258; ☎ 587-11-07; www.hurricanedivers.com; Santa Cruz Huatulco) speaks English, Spanish, Dutch and German, and offer a variety of courses and dives for similar prices to those of Sotavento.

RAFTING
The Copalita and Zimatán Rivers near Bahías de Huatulco have waters ranging from class I to class IV or V in rafting terms. They're at their biggest in the rainy season, between July and November. Bahías Plus (p257) books rafting and kayaking trips for M$300 to M$650 per person, or check out **Agencia Zicaro** (☎ 106-65-21; Guanacastle 309, La Crucecita).

HORSEBACK RIDING
Rancho Caballo de Mar (☎ 587-03-66; Playa Punta Arena, Bahía de Conejos; 3½hr rides M$500) runs a beach and forest tour (reservations necessary); the staff speak English and French.

YOGA & TEMASCAL
Yoga Huatulco (☎ 100-73-39; www.yogahuatulco.com; Guanacastle s/n, La Crucecita) offers yoga classes for M$100. **Agencia Zicaro** (☎ 106-65-21; Guanacastle 309, La Crucecita) can arrange a sweat-lodge experience in a *temascal*, as well as the standard tours listed above.

Sleeping
All midrange and top-end rooms listed here are air-conditioned. Rates quoted in those categories are for the high seasons (roughly December to April and July to mid-August). Peak periods around Christmas and Easter see considerably higher rates. La Crucecita has the majority of budget accommodations, while the beach areas around Santa Cruz

Huatulco offer resort-style midrange and top-end digs.

LA CRUCECITA
With the exception of holiday peak periods such as Christmas, Easter, and July and August (when their rates roughly double), these hotels maintain their prices year-round.

Posada Michelle (☎ 587-05-35; Gardenia 8; s/d M$300/400; ✲) Beds are springy and bathrooms poor, but the dozen or so rooms are brightly decorated and have decent air-con, a modern feel and cable TV. A little sitting area with hammocks adds some appeal.

Hotel Busanvi I (☎ 587-07-39; Carrizal 601; r M$450; ✲) Prices stay low year-round at this La Crucecita hotel. The rooms are depressing and dark with threadbare sheets, but you get antiquated air-con and TV, and the showers are excellent.

Hotel Plaza Conejo (☎ 587-00-54; turismoconejo@hotmail.com; Guamuchil 208; s/d M$500/770; ✲ ▢) This friendly hotel has 10 tidy, clean rooms off an interior patio. The air-con is good, rooms are a bit cramped and bathrooms are just so-so.

Hotel Jaroje (☎ 583-48-01; http://jaroje.tripod.com.mx, in Spanish; Bugambilia 304; s/d incl continental breakfast M$700/800; ✲ ▢) The bright, fresh, three-story Jaroje is a great deal in low season, and has good-sized, pleasantly decorated rooms with air-con, cable TV, a delightful color scheme and fine bathrooms. Prices include beach club access and wi-fi.

Hotel Suites Begonias (☎ 587-03-90; www.hotelbegonias.com; Bugambilia 503; s/d M$700/800; ✲) Rooms are slightly aromatic – and not in a good way – but it's central and somewhat affordable. Most of the lodgings here are comfortable two-room suites with two double beds and attractive bathrooms.

BOAT EXCURSIONS FROM SANTA CRUZ HUATULCO
Lanchas will whisk you out to most of the beaches from Santa Cruz Huatulco harbor any time between 8am and 5pm or 6pm, and they'll return to collect you by dusk. Taxis can get you to most beaches for less money, but a boat ride is more fun. Hire and board the *lanchas* (Map p258) beside the harbor. **Cooperativo Tangolunda** (Map p258; ☎ 587-00-81, Santa Cruz Harbor) sells tickets, or you can arrange a tour through Bahías Plus (p257).

A private round-trip launch for up to 10 people costs around M$1500 per person, and most often visits Playa La Entrega, Bahía Maguey, Bahía Órgano and La India, but you are truly in charge on these ships, and you can tell the captain to take you wherever you wish. Another possibility for a fun day is a 6½-hour, **seven-bay boat cruise** (per person M$250; ◷ 11am-5:30pm) with an open bar. This cruise only stops in San Agustin and Maguey.

Hotel María Mixteca (☎ 587-23-36; www.travel bymexico.com/oaxa/mariamixteca; Guamuchil 204; s/d M$900/1000; ✖ ▣) Small and a good value, the MM has 14 modern, very well-equipped rooms on two upper floors, with super-comfy beds, great bathrooms, and room safes. It's a bit pricey in high season, but a steal the rest of the year.

Misión de los Arcos (☎ 587-01-65; www.misiondelos arcos.com; Gardenia 902; r/ste M$944/1003; P ✖ ▣) This ivory-white, American-owned hotel is embellished by a touch of interior greenery. It has big, bright comfortable rooms (all decorated in simple white and beige), a gym and a good restaurant. The upstairs rooms are more contemporary with flat-screen TVs and a cool boutique feel – room 204 is our fave.

Hotel Arrecife (☎ 587-17-07; www.hotelarrecife .com/mx; Colorín 510; r with fan/air-con M$1100/1200; P ✖ ▣ ☎) In a quiet, leafy neighborhood, the Arrecife has a small pool and a good little restaurant. It's a bit away from the action, and well overpriced in high season, but the rooms are comfortable – some even have balconies.

Hotel Flamboyant (☎ 587-01-13; www.hoteles farrera.com/flamboyant; Plaza Principa; r/ste incl breakfast M$1200/3200; P ✖ ☎) This pink colonial-style hotel has a pleasant courtyard, an attractive pool, its own restaurant and 70 rooms. The rooms, though modern and clean, are a bit stuffy, and leave something to be desired for the price.

SANTA CRUZ HUATULCO & AROUND

Air and lodging packages are your best bet for an affordable holiday in a top-end Huatulco hotel. Another way to save is to look for promotions at hotel websites; you can often find prices well below the rack rates given here.

Hotel Sol y Mar (Map p258; Mitla s/n, Santa Cruz Huatulco; s/d M$500/900; ✖) This small hotel, which has good-sized rooms with air-con and decent bathrooms, has some of the cheapest beds in Santa Cruz.

Hotel Marina Resort (Map p258; ☎ 587-09-63; www .hotelmarinaresort.com; Tehuantepec 112, Santa Cruz Huatulco; r/ste with buffet breakfast M$1600/2100; P ✖ ☎) Three pools highlight the 50-room Marina Resort. Located on the east side of Santa Cruz harbor, this friendly 'resort-ish' hotel has a nearby *temascal* (a traditional-style steam bath where mud is rubbed on you) and beach club, and lots of pastel green. Rooms have balconies, while suites have kitchenettes and private terraces with marina views.

Hotel Castillo Huatulco (Map p258; ☎ 587-01-44; www.hotelcastillohuatulco.com; Blvd Santa Cruz 303, Santa Cruz Huatulco; r M$1610; P ✖ ☎ ✚) Colonial-style Castillo Huatulco has an attractive pool, a restaurant and 113 good-sized, brightly decorated rooms with safes. Transportation to the Castillo's beach club on Bahía Chahué is free. The hotel also offers packages with the third night for free.

Las Brisas (☎ 583-02-00; www.brisas.com.mx; Bahía de Tangolunda Lote 1, Tangolunda; r from M$2000; P ✖ ▣ ☎ ✚) Sprawling across more than 22 hectares, with its own four beaches, this former Club Med boasts 484 rooms, most enjoying ocean views. It also offers 12 tennis courts; volleyball, squash and basketball courts; a children's club (babysitting available); and a full range of aquatic activities.

Camino Real Zaashila (☎ 583-03-00; www.camino real.com/zaashila; Blvd Juárez 5, Tangolunda; r incl breakfast from M$2000; P ✖ ✖ ▣ ☎) Toward the east end of Tangolunda, this tranquil, attractive, Mediterranean-style property has a big pool in lovely gardens. There are 120 rooms; of these, 41 come with their own small pool and, of course, a higher price!

LOCAL LORE: THE CROSS OF HUATULCO

The chapel in Santa Cruz de Huatulco is home to a very famous piece of wood. Legend has it that a man brought a large piece of timber in the shape of a cross here some 2000 years ago. This bearded man was, no doubt, an incarnation of Quetzalcoatl or perhaps St Thomas, depending on who tells the story. Revered since its arrival – Huatulco comes from Quautolco, or 'the place where the timber is adored' in Nahuatl – the cross endured a number of travails over the years, most notably enduring fire, flame, axe and saw during the 1587 attack on the city by English pirate Thomas Cavendish. In 1612 the timber was sent to Oaxaca, where smaller crosses were fashioned from the wood. One of the crosses made it back to the small chapel in Santa Cruz, while the others are now in the Vatican, Puebla (perhaps) and Oaxaca (for sure). The anniversary of the Holy Cross is celebrated in late February.

Quinta Real (☎ 581-04-28; www.quintareal.com; Paseo Juárez 2, Tangolunda; ste from M$3090; P ⊠ ⊠ 🖳 🖳) The utterly gorgeous Quinta Real has a hilltop position at the west end of Tangolunda. Its 27 suites have Jacuzzi and ocean view; some have fountain-fed private pools that threaten to spill down the hillside to the beach and main swimming pool area. In case you were wondering, Tangolunda means 'beautiful-faced woman' in Nahuatl.

Eating
LA CRUCECITA
Paletería Zamora (cnr Flamboyán & Bugambilia) Don't let the name fool you; in addition to a wide variety of popsicles and ice cream, Zamora blends up a full range of fresh fruit drinks, *licuados* and *aguas frescas* (literally, 'cool waters' – fruit blended with water and sweetener).

Terra-Cotta (☎ 587-12-28; cnr Gardenia & Priv Tamarindo; breakfast dishes M$30-78, sandwiches M$65-98, mains M$57-139; ☯ 8am-11:30pm) Soothing air-con and a garden view complement the good food at popular, American-run Terra-Cotta. Egg dishes, waffles, baguettes, fine espresso and ice cream go down easy, as do the several Mexican dishes on the menu.

La Veva (Flamboyán 208; comidas corridas M$45-60, mains M$40-75) Popular with locals, this traditional eatery has an excellent set lunch and regional fare. The horse saddle seats add to the appeal.

Tostado's Grill (☎ 587-02-19; Flamboyán 306; mains M$45-199) Much of the menu is Italian food here, but Tostado's also serves a mean spinach salad with bacon. It's found in front of Hotel Posada del Parque.

Don Wilo (☎ 587-06-23; Guanacastle, Plaza Principal; mains M$48-130; ☯ closed Tue) The Don's Oaxacan dishes, including tamales and *tlayudas*, are very popular. He also does fish, steaks and pizza.

Mercado (cnr Bugambilia & Guanacastle; fish or shrimp platters M$55-65) The market's very clean *comedores* serve up good food, including *enfrijoladas* (corn tortillas smothered in beans, with a sprinkling of cheese) or *entomatadas* for M$35 each.

Restaurant-Bar Oasis (☎ 587-13-00; Flamboyán 211, Plaza Principal; sushi M$59-79, mains M$67-179) The Oasis has good, moderately priced fare, including *tortas*, fish fillets, steaks and Oaxacan specialties, sushi and other Japanese food. It's a popular breakfast spot but the

execrable pop music can be hard to take in the morning.

SANTA CRUZ HUATULCO
Café Huatulco (Map p258; ☎ 587-12-28; Plaza Santa Cruz; breakfast M$45-60, coffee M$15-30, cake M$30; ☯ 8am-10:30pm) Mid-plaza near the harbor, Huatulco serves good Pluma coffee in many different ways – the *capuchino paraíso* (cold cappuccino with a dollop of ice cream) is well worth a try.

Restaurant Ve El Mar (Map p258; ☎ 587-03-64; Playa Santa Cruz; mains M$80-212; ☯ 8am-10pm) Food at the eateries on Playa Santa Cruz is mostly average, but this place at the east end is an exception. The seafood is fine and the margaritas mighty. Try a whole fish, an octopus or shrimp dish or, if you prefer, lobster (M$280).

BAHÍA CHAHUÉ & TANGOLUNDA
Tangolunda's big hotels offer a choice of expensive bars, coffee shops and restaurants.

Casa del Mar (☎ 581-02-03; Balcones de Tangolunda 13, Tangolunda; mains M$70-140) A great view and romantic setting make it worth the trouble to get here. Try the *tamal de pescado* (steamed corn dough stuffed with fish). Flambéed bananas to finish? Why not?

L'échalote (☎ 587-24-80; Calle Zapoteco s/n, Chahué; mains M$75-150; ☯ 2-11pm Tue-Sun) This restaurant is attached to the Hotel Posada Edén Costa in Chahué. The Swiss-French chef here prepares French, Thai, Vietnamese, Oaxacan and other dishes. The Thai salad with prawns and bean sprouts is delicious. The quiche lorraine, *nem* (spring rolls) and chicken-liver salad are also quite good, and the desserts aren't too shabby either.

BEACHES
There are decent seafood *palapas* at Playas La Entrega, Maguey, and San Agustín. A whole grilled *huachinango* (red snapper) will cost M$60 to M$100.

Drinking
Café Dublin (Carrizal s/n, La Crucecita; ☯ 5pm-3am) The best Irish pub this side of Tehuantepec, the Dublin has darts, a super friendly manager and an upstairs 'chill' room.

Tipsy Blowfish (Flamboyán s/n, La Crucecita; ☯ 5pm-3am) Right on Plaza Principal, this open-air street-side joint has sexy waitresses and bartenders, live music and great people-watching ops.

OAXACA

Entertainment

La Peña (Carrizal s/n, La Crucecita; ☉ 7pm-3am) Head across the street from La Crema for a great Latin party vibe, with good live music, Cuban-style, from Tuesday to Saturday.

La Papaya (☎ 583-94-11; Blvd Juárez, Chahué; admission M$120; ☉ 11pm-5am Thu-Sat) This long-standing disco above Plaza del Mezcal appeals to the 18-to-25 age group.

Noches Oaxaqueñas (☎ 581-00-01; Blvd Juárez s/n, Tangolunda; admission M$110; ☉ 8:30pm Tue, Thu & Sat off-season, daily high season) Catch a Guelaguetza regional dance show here, by the Tangolunda traffic circle. Drinks and/or dinner (M$70 to M$180) are extra.

Cinemas Huatulco (Guamuchil s/n, La Crucecita) La Crucecita's cinema is in Plaza Madero, a shopping mall at the corner of Guamuchil and Carrizal.

Shopping

Mercado de Artesanías (Map p258; Plaza Santa Cruz) Santa Cruz' market has a wide range of beach gear and handicrafts, including some good jewelry and textiles, but with the cruise ships arriving constantly you're not likely to find many bargains.

Getting There & Away

AIR

Mexicana and its subsidiary, Click Mexicana, offer three to five flights daily to/from Mexico City. **Aerotucán** (☎ 951-501-05-30) flies daily to/from Oaxaca, as does **Aerovega** (☎ 951-516-49-82), both have offices in Oaxaca city; see Map pp220–1. **Continental Express** (☎ 01-800-900-50-00) flies from Houston up to four times a week in winter, and cheap charters from Canada, the US and the UK are sometimes available.

BUS

Some buses coming to Huatulco are marked 'Santa Cruz Huatulco,' but they still terminate in La Crucecita. Make sure your bus is not headed to Santa María Huatulco, which is a long way inland. See the boxed text on p230 for information on bus routes to Oaxaca city.

First-class **OCC** (☎ 587-02-61; Blvd Chahue s/n, La Crucecita) is eight blocks north of the plaza. Most of its buses are *de paso* (buses that start their journeys elsewhere but stop to drop off and pick up passengers; scheduled times are often very approximate). **Sur** buses pull up here too. **Estrella Blanca** (EB; ☎ 587-06-80; cnr Alfarreros & Carpinteros, La Crucecita) has a station about 2km

inland from the main plaza in La Crucecita by the Pemex station. It offers *primera* services that are quick and fairly comfortable, and typical *ordinario* buses. Daily departures include the following:

Acapulco EB (M$307, 10 hours, seven daily)

Oaxaca OCC (M$228 to M$270, eight hours via Salina Cruz, three daily)

Pochutla OCC (M$30, one hour, six daily); EB (M$26 to 30, one hour, seven daily); Transportes Rápidos de Pochutla (M$16, every 15 minutes 6am to 8pm) From Blvd Chahué, opposite the north end of Bugambilia in La Crucecita.

Puerto Escondido OCC (M$76, 2½ hours, eight daily); EB (M$69 to M$82, 2½ hours, seven daily)

Tehuantepec OCC (M$94 to M$100, 3½ hours, five daily)

For coastal destinations west of Huatulco, take an Acapulco-bound EB bus; the 2nd-class buses will stop just about anywhere along Hwy 200. OCC also runs a few buses to Juchitán (M$118, four hours); OCC and EB go to Mexico City (M$525 to M$730, 15 hours).

CAR

Hertz (☎ 581-90-92; Airport)

Thrifty (587-00-10; cnr Ocotillo & Jazmín, La Crucecita)

Getting Around

TO/FROM THE AIRPORT

Transportación Terrestre (☎ 581-90-14) provides *colectivo combis* for M$87 per person from the airport to La Crucecita, Santa Cruz or Bahía Chahué, and for M$102 to Tangolunda. Get tickets at the company's airport kiosk. For a whole cab at a reasonable price, walk just outside the airport gate, where you can pick one up for about M$120 to La Crucecita, Santa Cruz or Tangolunda, or M$150 to Pochutla. Even cheaper, walk 400m down to Hwy 200 and catch a microbus for M$7 to La Crucecita or M$15 to Pochutla. Those buses heading to La Crucecita may be marked 'Santa Cruz' or 'Bahías Huatulco' or something similar.

BUS & COLECTIVO

Colectivo taxis and a few microbuses provide transportation between La Crucecita, Santa Cruz Huatulco and Tangolunda. In La Crucecita catch them just east of the corner of Guamuchil and Carrizal, one block east of Plaza Principal. In Santa Cruz they stop by the harbor (Map p258), and in Tangolunda at the traffic circle outside

Hotel Gala. Fares are the same in either type of vehicle: from La Crucecita to Santa Cruz M$3, and to Tangolunda M$5.

TAXI

Official taxi rates are posted on the east side of Plaza Principal in La Crucecita, from where you pay around M$15 to Santa Cruz, M$25 to Tangolunda, M$45 to Bahía Maguey and M$95 to the airport. There's a private taxi stand (Map p258) in Santa Cruz Huatulco, on the east side of the main plaza. By the hour, cabs run M$150.

BARRA DE LA CRUZ
☎ 958 / pop 572

This tranquil fishing village is reached via a good 1.5km road that heads coastward from Hwy 200 about 20km east of Santa Cruz. At the mouth of the Río Zimatán, Barra is known for its excellent surfing. At its peak, the right-hand point break gets up to a double overhead. A lack of undertow makes for good swimming as well. Barra's beach has showers and toilets, and a *comedor* offering food, drinks and plenty of hammocks and shade. The municipality charges M$20 per person to pass along the last stretch of road to the beach, and imposes a 7:30pm curfew; after sunset it's off *la playa*, baby.

You can rent surfboards just outside the toll gate for M$100 per day. Villagers will rent rooms in their houses for around M$50 a night, but conditions are very rustic. Go more upscale and stay at **Barradise** (☎ 044-958-585-03-03; pablo_rafting@yahoo.com; r M$80), which consists of two fan-cooled rooms with private bathrooms above the surf shop. It's run by the very able Pablo Nárvaez, who in addition to doing surf guiding can also take you rafting, mountain biking and birding, and has the certificates to prove it.

Taxis from La Crucecita to Barra cost about M$140. Eastbound 2nd-class buses will drop you at the turnoff on Hwy 200; the total distance from there to the beach is just under 4km.

From Barra to the east, Hwy 200 provides almost no views of the Pacific until you begin to approach Salina Cruz, and then it's mostly tantalizing glimpses of sea and beaches with enormous dunes piled against rocks, testament to the force of the winds that blow across the isthmus.

ISTHMUS OF TEHUANTEPEC

Eastern Oaxaca comprises the southern half of the 200km-wide Isthmus of Tehuantepec (teh-wahn-teh-*pek*), Mexico's narrowest point. Though dramatic mountains are seldom out of view, this is sweaty, flat country. Zapotec culture is strong here, and foreign visitors few. Spend some time and you're bound to encounter some lively, friendly people; you may even get an impromptu tour from schoolkids curious to see a foreign face in their midst.

TEHUANTEPEC
☎ 971 / pop 39,500

Tehuantepec is a good introduction to this region. There's not much to do in town but dawdle around the markets and gawk at the 16th-century church. And there's often a fiesta going on in one of its barrios.

Orientation

The Oaxaca–Tuxtla Gutiérrez highway (Hwy 190) meets Hwy 185 from Salina Cruz about 1km west of Tehuantepec. The combined highways then skirt the west edge of the town center and turn east to form the northern edge of town. It's here where Tehuantepec's bus stations – collectively known as La Terminal – cluster just south of the highway (1.5km northeast of the town center via the highway, considerably closer in a straight line on foot). To walk to the plaza from La Terminal, follow Héroes until it ends at a T-junction, then turn right along Guerrero for four blocks to another T-junction. Then go one block left along Hidalgo – the Palacio Municipal (town hall) stands on the south side of the plaza.

Information

There are numerous internet joints in town, charging around M$10 per hour. Bancomer and Banorte banks, both on Calle 5 de Mayo, are a few steps west of the Palacio Municipal. Both have ATMs; Banorte changes US dollars.

Cruz Roja (☎ 55-1084-9000) Call in a medical emergency. National number.

Santander Serfin (Calle 22 de Mayo; ◷ 9am-4pm Mon-Sat) North side of the plaza; will change traveler's checks and cash US dollars.

Sights

EX-CONVENTO REY COSIJOPÍ

This former Dominican monastery, north and west of the plaza on a short street off Guerrero, is Tehuantepec's **Casa de la Cultura** (Callejón Rey Cosijopí; admission free; ☻ 9am-2pm & 5-8pm Mon-Fri, 9am-2pm Sat). It bears traces of old religious frescoes and has modest but interesting exhibits of traditional dress, archaeological finds, historical photos and the like. King Cosijopí, the local Zapotec leader at the time, provided the funds for its construction in the 16th century, at the urging of Cortés.

MARKET

Tehuantepec's dark, almost medieval indoor **market** (☻ daily) is on the west side of the plaza. It spills out into the surrounding streets, where you can often see flowers for sale.

Sleeping

Hotel Oasis (☎ 715-00-08; h.oasis@hotmail.com; Ocampo 8; d with fan/air-con M$200/400; P ✷) A block south of the plaza, the Oasis has 26 basic rooms (some of the best in town), warm showers and friendly service.

Hotel Donají (☎ 715-00-64; hoteldonaji@hotmail .com; Juárez 12; s/d with fan M$205/285, with air-con M$285/390; P ✷ ✷) The bright Donají is two blocks south of the east side of the central plaza, and has clean rooms with TV on two upper floors around a shady, colorful patio. Bonuses include a small gym, a cool chapel and a small pool.

DIFFERENT STROKES: FEMININE TRADITIONS OF THE ZAPOTEC

Coming from a matrilineal society, Zapotec Isthmus women are noticeably open and confident and take a leading role in business and government. Many older women still wear embroidered *huipiles* (sleeveless tunics) and voluminous printed skirts. For the numerous *velas* (fiestas), Tehuantepec and Juchitán women turn out in velvet or sateen *huipiles*, gold and silver jewelry (a sign of wealth), skirts embroidered with fantastically colorful silk flowers and a variety of headgear. An unusual feature of many *velas* is the *tirada de frutas*, in which women climb onto rooftops and throw fruit at the men below!

Eating

The market has the usual eateries, and at night the entire east sidewalk of the plaza is lined with plastic tables and chairs beside carts serving inexpensive tacos and other delights.

Bar Restaurante Scarú (☎ 715-06-46; Callejón Leona Vicario 4; dishes M$40-110) Two short blocks east and 50m north of Hotel Donají, the relaxed, friendly Scarú occupies an 18th-century house with a courtyard and colorful modern murals of Tehuantepec life. Sit beneath a fan, quaff a *limonada* or a mixed drink and sample one of the many fish, seafood, meat and chicken dishes on offer. On Saturday and Sunday old-timers plunk out *marimba* tunes.

Getting There & Away

At La Terminal, OCC and ADO (1st-class) and Sur and AU (2nd-class) share one building. Some 1st-class buses are *de paso* (buses that start their journeys elsewhere but stop to drop off and pick up passengers; scheduled times are often very approximate).

Local buses to Juchitán (M$15, 30 minutes) depart across the street from OCC at least every half-hour during daylight hours. Other services:

Bahías de Huatulco OCC (M$100, 3½ hours, three 1st-class); Sur (M$76, 3½ hours, two 2nd-class)

Mexico City (TAPO) OCC & ADO (M$684, 11½ hours, six 1st-class and deluxe); AU (M$512, 13 hours, three 2nd-class)

Oaxaca OCC & ADO (M$152, 4½ hours, 15 1st-class)

Pochutla OCC (M$128, 4½ hours, three 1st-class)

Puerto Escondido OCC (M$170, 6½ hours, three 1st-class)

Getting Around

Taxis between La Terminal and the plaza charge around M$15. A delightful local variation on the common Mexican theme of three-wheeled transportation is the *motocarro*, whose passengers sit – or stand, to better catch the breeze – on a platform behind the driver. The sight of colorfully garbed women riding tall is one that lingers in the memory. *Motocarros* congregate by the railway track west of the market.

JUCHITÁN

☎ 971 / pop 70,700

Istmeño culture is strong in this friendly town, which is visited by few gringos. There are nearly 30 neighborhood festivals *(velas)* here each year, mostly held between April

---

DETOUR: GUIENGOLA

In 1496 the Isthmus Zapotecs successfully defended the hillside fortress of Guiengola from Aztec invaders, and the isthmus never became part of the Aztec empire. The stronghold's ruins lie north of Hwy 190 and are reached via a turnoff just past the Km 240 marker, about 11km out of Tehuantepec (signed 'Ruinas Guiengola'). A guide (recommended) may be waiting here or nearer the site. The unpaved 7km stretch of road is passable in dry weather, though the last kilometer or so (heading uphill) requires a high-clearance vehicle. The road ends at a signed trailhead, and about an hour's sweaty walk up the trail gets you to the remains of two pyramids, a ball court, a 64-room complex and a thick defensive wall. You'll also see interesting limestone formations and some fine views over the isthmus.

If you lack a vehicle, catch a bus bound for Jalapa del Marqués from La Terminal. From the turnoff on Hwy 190, it's about a 2½-hour walk. Take plenty of water, and start early (6am or before) to take advantage of the morning cool.

---

and September. Hit it right, and you may just create the most memorable experience of your trip.

Orientation & Information

Prolongación 16 de Septiembre leads into Juchitán from a busy intersection with traffic signals on Hwy 190, on the north edge of town. The main bus terminal is about 100m toward town from the intersection. The street curves left, then right, then divides into Calle 5 de Septiembre (the right fork) and Av 16 de Septiembre. These emerge as opposite sides of the central plaza, Jardín Juárez, after seven blocks. The Palacio Municipal, painted yellow with green and white trim, forms the Jardín's eastern boundary.

At least two banks with ATMs are on the Jardín; at its southwest corner, **Scotiabank** (9am-5pm Mon-Fri) changes traveler's checks and US dollars. Internet places abound, particularly on Prolongación 16 de Septiembre. Most charge M$10 an hour. Try **Hospital Fuentes** (☎ 711-14-41; Efraín R Gómez s/n) in a medical emergency.

Sights

Jardín Juárez is a lively central square. A thriving market on its east side spills into the surrounding streets. Here you can find traditional Isthmus women's costumes, and sometimes iguana on the menus of the market *comedores*.

Juchitán's **Lidxi Guendabiaani** (Casa de la Cultura; Belisario Domínguez; admission free; 10am-3pm & 5-8pm Mon-Fri, 10am-2pm Sat), one block south and one block west of Jardín Juárez, has an interesting archaeological collection and an art collection with works by leading 20th-century Mexican

artists, including Rufino Tamayo and the prolific *juchiteco* Francisco Toledo. It's beside the church, and set around a big patio that often buzzes with children.

Sleeping & Eating

Hotel López Lena Palace (☎ 711-13-88; Prolongación 16 de Septiembre 70; s/d M$290/480; P) Look for the mock Arabic exterior about halfway between the bus station and town center. The Lena has reasonable rooms with comfy beds; the best value are the cheerful but windowless 'minis,' with excellent air-con and showers.

Café Santa Fe (☎ 711-15-45; Cruce de Carretera Transístmica; dishes M$40-80; 24hr) For cool air and good food, try this restaurant, handily wedged between the main bus stations and the highway. It does excellent breakfasts and good espresso, served briskly by white-coated waiters.

Restaurant El Califa (mains M$40-130) Attached to Hotel López Lena Palace, this restaurant prepares some excellent dishes, including fresh salads and stuffed fish, though the breakfasts leave something to be desired.

Casagrande Restaurant (☎ 711-34-60; mains M$65-150) This is the flashest eatery in town, in a pleasant covered courtyard with ceiling fans and tall plants. All the goodies, from regional dishes and pasta to seafood, get 15% tax added. It's on the south side of Jardín Juárez; the Casagrande cinema sign makes it easier to find.

Getting There & Away

OCC and ADO (1st-class) and Sur and AU (2nd-class) use the main bus terminal on Prolongación 16 de Septiembre; they're housed in separate structures. Frequent 2nd-class Istmeño buses to Tehuantepec (M$15, 30 minutes) and Salina Cruz (M$25, one hour) stop at the next corner south on Prolongación 16 de Septiembre during daylight hours. Fletes y Pasajes (Fypsa; 2nd-class) has its own terminal, separated from the main one by a Pemex station and Café Santa Fe.

Some buses are *de paso* (buses that start their journeys elsewhere but stop to drop off and pick up passengers; scheduled times are often very approximate) and leave in the middle of the night; many others originate in nearby Salina Cruz and stop at Juchitán not long after.

Bahías de Huatulco (M$91 to M$144, four hours, five 1st-class)

Mexico City (TAPO) OCC/ADO/UNO (M$980, 10 hours, seven 1st-class and deluxe); AU (M$494, 12 hours, three 2nd-class)

Oaxaca OCC & ADO (M$194, five hours, 20 1st-class & deluxe); Sur & Fypsa (M$100, six hours, many 2nd-class)

Pochutla (M$122 to M$149, five hours, five 1st-class)

Getting Around

'Terminal-Centro' buses run between the bus station and Jardín Juárez. A taxi costs M$15.

Directory

CONTENTS

ACCOMMODATIONS

Accommodations on the Pacific coast range from hammocks strung under palm-thatched huts *(palapas)* to world-class luxury resorts. In between you have beachfront campgrounds, hostels, *casas de huéspedes* (guesthouses), budget hotels and *cabañas* (independent cabins that generally come with a kitchen). This book divides accommodations into three price ranges: budget (where a typical room for two people costs under M$400), midrange (M$400 to M$1000) and top end (above M$1000).

The normal tourist high season is November to April, when many North Americans and Europeans travel to Mexico for the winter. Reservations are advisable for popular places during this time. Tourism peaks during the Christmas-New Year holidays, Semana Santa (the week before Easter and up to a week after it) and the July-August summer holidays. During these periods, reservations are a must. The low season lasts from May to October, with the exception of the holiday jolt in July and August.

Prices quoted throughout this book, unless specified, are for the November to April winter high season. Rates for peak season – which usually runs from December 20 through January 2 and also the week of Semana Santa – may rise 10% to 20% above the high-season rate. Low-season rates are often 10% to 40% lower than those we quote. Rates at budget accommodations tend to fluctuate the least, but you can generally negotiate at smaller budget spots.

Accommodation prices are subject to two taxes: IVA (value-added tax; 15%) and ISH (lodging tax; 2% to 3% in most states). Generally IVA and ISH are included in quoted prices. In top-end hotels a price may often be given as, say, 'M$1000 *más impuestos*' (M$1000 plus taxes), in which case you must add 18% to the figure. When in doubt, you can ask '*¿Están incluidos los impuestos?*' ('Are taxes included?'). Prices given in this book include taxes.

Camping Grounds & Trailer Parks

Camping grounds are common on Mexico's Pacific coast. Most organized camping grounds are trailer parks set up for RVs (campervans) and trailers (caravans), but they accept tent campers at lower rates. Expect to pay about M$50 to pitch a tent for two, and M$100 to M$200 for two people with a vehicle, using full facilities. Some restaurants and guesthouses in beach spots or country areas will let you pitch a tent on their patch for a couple of dollars per person.

All Mexican beaches are public property. You can camp for nothing on most of them, but always assess the safety of the beach before spending the night on it.

Hammocks & Cabañas

You'll find hammocks and *cabañas* available mainly in low-key beach spots. A hammock can be a very comfortable place to sleep (but mosquito repellent often comes in handy). You can rent one and a place to hang it – usually under a palm roof outside a small guesthouse or beach restaurant – for M$30 or M$50 in some places.

Cabañas are usually huts with a palm-thatched roof. Some have dirt floors and nothing inside but a bed; others are deluxe, with electric light, mosquito nets, fans, fridge, bar and decor. Prices for simple *cabañas* range from M$100 to M$400; luxury *cabañas* can set you back as much as M$1000.

Hostels, Casas de Huéspedes & Posadas

Inexpensive and congenial accommodations are often to be found at a *casa de huéspedes,* a home converted into simple guest lodgings.

Hostel accommodation is sparse on the coast, but when you find it, it'll run around M$100 for a dorm room. Some posadas (inns) are like *casas de huéspedes;* others are small hotels. A double typically costs M$200 to M$400, though a few places are more comfy and more expensive.

Hotels

Mexico specializes in good midrange hotels where two people can get a comfortable room with private bathroom, TV and often air-conditioning for M$400 to M$800. Often there's a restaurant and a bar.

Every Mexican town also has cheap hotels. There are clean, friendly, secure ones, and there are dark, dirty, smelly ones where you may not feel your belongings are safe. Decent rooms with private hot shower are available for under M$300 a double in most of the country.

Mexico has plenty of large, modern luxury hotels too, particularly in the coastal resorts and largest cities. They offer the expected levels of luxury – with pools, gyms, bars, restaurants and so on – at prices that are sometimes agreeably modest (and sometimes not!).

Fortunately for families and small groups of travelers, many hotels in all price ranges have rooms for three, four or five people that cost not much more than a double.

Rental Accommodations

Prices fluctuate according to amenities, season and proximity to a beach; a simple bungalow may cost as little as M$4000 per month, while a lavish villa will cost many times that.

PRACTICALITIES

- Mexicans use the metric system for weights and measures.

- Most prerecorded videotapes on sale in Mexico (like the rest of the Americas and Japan) use the NTSC image registration system, incompatible with the PAL system common to most of Western Europe and Australia.

- If buying DVDs, look for the numbered globe motif indicating which regions of the world it can be played back in. Region 1 is the US and Canada; Europe and Japan are in region 2; and Australia and New Zealand join Mexico in region 4.

- Electrical current is 110V, 60Hz, and most plugs have two flat prongs, as in the US and Canada.

- The *News* (www.thenews.com.mx) is an English-language daily covering national news. *Vallarta Today* (www.vallartatoday.com) and *Vallarta Tribune* (www.vallartatribune.com) are dailies in Puerto Vallarta. Other print publications include the *Pacific Pearl* (www.pacificpearl .com) in Mazatlán, *Oaxaca Times* (www.oaxacatimes.com) in Oaxaca city and *El Sol de la Costa* (www.elsoldelacosta.com), which covers the Oaxaca coast.

- For the online editions of about 300 Mexican newspapers and magazines, and links to hundreds of Mexican radio and TV stations and other media sites, visit www.zonalatina.com.

- Free-to-air TV is dominated by Televisa, which runs four of the six main national channels; TV Azteca has two (Azteca 7 and Azteca 13).

- As a rule, don't drink the tap water (p295).

BOOK YOUR STAY ONLINE

For more accommodation reviews and recommendations by Lonely Planet authors, check out the online booking service at www.lonelyplanet.com/hotels. You'll find the true, insider low-down on the best places to stay. Reviews are thorough and independent. Best of all, you can book online.

Start your search at sites like **Choice1** (www.choice1.com/mexico), **Vacation Rentals By Owner** (www.vrbo.com) or **Mexico Vacation Rental Network** (www.mexicovacationrentalnetwork.com).

Resorts

These properties offer deluxe amenities, manicured grounds and often private beaches, as well as a full range of activities, excursions, multiple pools and sports facilities. All-inclusive meal, activity and beverage plans are increasingly the norm.

Rates for all-inclusive resorts presented in this book are guidelines based on each resort's unpublicized 'rack' or 'standard' rate. This is to say that you will likely spend considerably less depending on the source of booking, season and current specials. For the best rates, go to an aggregators such as **Expedia** (www.expedia.com) and **Travelocity** (www.travelocity.com).

ACTIVITIES

Mexico's Pacific coast has a panoply of sports and special-interest activities for those to whom bumming out on the beach spells boredom. More details can be found in the regional chapters or by following the cross-references below.

- Diving and snorkeling (p49)
- Deep-sea fishing (p50)
- Surfing (p49)
- Kayaking (p51)
- Wildlife- and bird-watching (p52)
- Hiking (p53)
- Mountain biking (p53)
- Horseback riding (p54)

BUSINESS HOURS

On the coast, shops are generally open from 9am or 10am to around 9pm Monday to Saturday. They often close for siesta between 2pm and 4pm. Inland, shops will generally skip the siesta and close around 7pm. Shops in malls and tourist resorts often open on Sunday.

Banks are open 9am to 5pm Monday to Friday, and 9am to 1pm Saturday; in smaller towns they may close earlier and not open on Saturday. *Casas de cambio* (currency exchange offices) are open 9am to 7pm.

Internet facilities generally open daily from 8am to 10pm.

Offices have similar Monday to Friday hours, often with the 2pm to 4pm lunch break. Those with tourist-related business might open for a few hours on Saturday. Post offices open from 8am to 6pm Monday to Friday, and 9am to 1pm Saturday.

Typical restaurant hours are from 7am to between 10pm and midnight. Cafés typically open from 8am to 10pm daily. Bars, too, are normally open daily, and often stay open till 3am or 4am, but each seems to have its own special pattern of hours.

Museums are usually closed on Monday; on Sunday nearly all museums are free.

In this book we only spell out opening hours where they do not fit these parameters.

CHILDREN

Mexicans love children, and children are welcome at all kinds of hotels and in virtually every café and restaurant. The sights, sounds and colors of Mexico excite and stimulate most children, but few kids like traveling all the time; they're happier if they can settle into a place for a while and make friends. Try to give them time to do what they like doing back home. Children are also more easily affected than adults by heat, disrupted sleeping patterns and strange food. They need time to acclimatize and you should take extra care to avoid sunburn. Ensure you replace fluids if a child gets diarrhea (p294).

Lonely Planet's *Travel with Children* has lots of practical advice on the subject, drawn from firsthand experience. In our regional chapters, we've also included a child-friendly icon 🛈 for establishments that are especially welcoming to children. This means a hotel might have a kids' club or special services (like day care) for the young ones, or an attraction might have child-specific activities. This is really only a starting point, as all of Mexico is quite child-friendly.

Practicalities

Cots for hotel rooms and high chairs for restaurants are available mainly in midrange and top-end establishments. If you want a rental car with a child safety seat, the major international rental firms are the most reliable providers. You will probably have to pay a few dollars extra per day.

It's usually easy to find a cheap babysitter if parents want to go out on their own – start by asking at your hotel. Diapers are widely available, but if you depend on some particular cream, lotion, baby food or medicine, bring it with you. Public breastfeeding is not common and, when done, is done discreetly.

DOCUMENTS FOR UNDER-18 TRAVELERS

To conform with regulations aimed at preventing international child abduction, minors (under 18s) traveling to Mexico without one or both of their parents may need to carry a notarized consent form signed by the absent parent or parents, giving permission for the young traveler to make the international journey. Mexico does not specifically require this documentation, but airlines flying to Mexico may refuse to board passengers without it. In the case of divorced parents, a custody document may be required. If one or both parents are dead, or the traveler has only one legal parent, a death certificate or notarized statement may be required.

These rules are aimed primarily at visitors from the USA and Canada but may also apply to people from elsewhere. Procedures vary from country to country; contact your country's foreign affairs department and/or a Mexican consulate to find out exactly what you need to do. The required forms are usually available from these authorities.

Sights & Activities

In larger resort towns, apart from the obvious beaches and swimming pools, you'll find excellent attractions such as water parks, including Parque Papagayo (p200) in Acapulco, Sea Life Park (p68) in Puerto Vallarta, and MazAgua (p108) in Mazatlán.

Kids don't have to be very old to enjoy activities such as snorkeling, boating, riding bicycles and horses, watching wildlife (p269), and even – for some! – shopping and visiting markets. Archaeological sites (eg Monte Albán, p232) can be fun if the kids are into climbing pyramids and exploring tunnels.

CLIMATE CHARTS

June to October are the hottest and wettest months across most of Mexico. For tips on the best seasons to travel, see p12.

COURSES

Taking classes in Mexico can be a great way to meet people and get an inside angle on local life. The country specializes in short courses in the Spanish language. In addition, Mexican

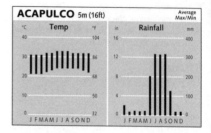

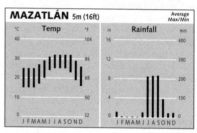

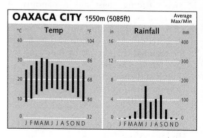

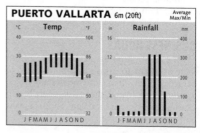

universities and colleges often offer study-abroad courses to complement college courses you may be taking back home. For long-term study in Mexico you'll need a student visa; contact a Mexican consulate.

Hit the internet to learn about study possibilities in Mexico from sites such as the **Council on International Educational Exchange** (CIEE; www.ciee.org), the **National Registration Center for Study Abroad** (www.nrcsa.com) and **AmeriSpan** (www.amerispan.com).

Cooking Courses
See p219 for Oaxaca's excellent cooking schools for foreigners, and p39 for other general information about cooking courses.

Language Courses
Mexico's best, most popular language schools are inland. Oaxaca (p219) is an excellent place to study Spanish. Multi-week courses can also be taken in Puerto Vallarta (p68), Mazatlán (p108) and La Manzanilla (p145), Manzanillo (p155) and Puerto Escondido (p239).

Course lengths range from a few days to a year, and 15 hours instruction per week is pretty standard. In many places you can enroll on the spot and start any Monday. You may be offered accommodations with a local family as part of the deal – one of the best ways to improve your language skills. In a growing number of schools, extra or alternative courses in art, crafts, dance, indigenous languages or in-depth study of Mexico are also available.

Costs per week (15 hours) are around M$800 to M$1370, depending on the city, the school and how intensively you study.

CUSTOMS REGULATIONS
Things that visitors are allowed to bring into Mexico duty-free include items for personal use such as clothing; a camera and video camera; up to 12 rolls of film or videotapes; a cellular phone; a laptop computer; a portable radio or CD player; medicine for personal use, with prescription in the case of psychotropic drugs; 3L of wine, beer or liquor (adults only); 400 cigarettes (adults); and M$3000 worth of other goods (M$500 if arriving by land).

The normal routine when you enter Mexico is to complete a customs declaration form (which lists duty-free allowances), and then place it in a machine. If the machine shows a green light, you pass without inspection. If a red light shows, your baggage will be searched.

On leaving Mexico, you may be subjected to an exit inspection. Certain cultural and religious artifacts require exit permits, and most pre-Hispanic objects cannot legally be removed from the country.

Returnees to the US are allowed a fixed value of duty-free goods, including no more than 1L of alcoholic spirits, 200 cigarettes and 100 cigars. At the time of research, the allowance was US$400 per person.

DANGERS & ANNOYANCES
Official information can make Mexico sound more alarming than it really is, but for a variety of useful information on travel to Mexico consult your country's foreign-affairs department:

Australia (☎ 1300-139-281; www.dfat.gov.au)
Canada (☎ 800-267-6788; www.dfait-maeci.gc.ca)
UK (☎ 0845-850-2829; www.fco.gov.uk)
USA (☎ 888-407-4747; www.travel.state.gov)

If you're already in Mexico, you can contact your embassy (p272). Keep an ear to the ground as you travel.

Theft & Robbery
Tourism on the Pacific coast is a *major* source of income, both locally and nationally, and Mexico has a vested interest in keeping it safe for visitors. Major coastal resorts have a large and visible police presence, so violent crimes are rare. Remote beach spots and dark streets are the places where muggings are most likely to occur.

Purse- or bag-snatching and pickpocketing can occur in crowded buses, bus stops, bus stations, airports, markets, thronged streets and plazas.

HIGHWAY ROBBERY
Bandits occasionally hold up buses, cars and other vehicles on intercity routes, especially at night, taking luggage or valuables. Sometimes buses are robbed by people who board as passengers. The best ways to avoid highway robbery are to travel by day and to travel on toll highways as much as possible. Deluxe and 1st-class buses use toll highways, where they exist; 2nd-class buses do not.

Hwy 200 along the Pacific coast through Michoacán and Guerrero states and as far south as Pochutla in Oaxaca has been the scene of many highway robberies over the years but is now mostly safe for travel. Hwys

134 and 51 between Ixtapa and Iguala and Hwy 175 between Oaxaca city and Pochutla are also known to be robbery-prone.

IN THE CITY

To avoid being robbed in cities, steer clear of lonely places like empty streets or little-used pedestrian underpasses where there are few other people. Use ATMs only in secure locations and not those that open to the street.

Pickpockets often work in teams; the operative principle is to distract you and get you off balance. If your valuables are *underneath* your clothing (in a money belt, a shoulder wallet or a pouch on a string around your neck), the chances of losing them are greatly reduced. Visible round-the-waist money belts are an invitation to thieves. Carry a small amount of ready-money in a pocket, and avoid conspicuous jewelry.

Some city police forces are reputed to be quite corrupt. See p196 for details on how to deal with them.

DISABLED TRAVELERS

Mexico is not yet very disabled-friendly, though some hotels and restaurants (mostly towards the top end of the market) and some public buildings and archaeological sites now provide wheelchair access. Mobility is easiest in the major tourist resorts and the more expensive hotels. Bus transportation can be difficult; flying or taking a taxi is easier.

Mobility International USA (☎ 541-343-1284; www.miusa.org) advises disabled travelers on mobility issues and runs exchange programs (including in Mexico). Its website includes international databases of exchange programs and disability organizations, with several Mexican organizations listed.

In the UK, **Radar** (☎ 020-7250-3222; www.radar.org.uk) is run by and for disabled people. Its excellent website has links to good travel and holiday sites.

DISCOUNT CARDS

The ISIC student card, the IYTC card for travelers under 26 and the ITIC card for teachers can help you obtain reduced-price air tickets to or from Mexico at student- and youth-oriented travel agencies. Reduced prices on Mexican buses and at museums, archaeological sites and so on are usually only for those with Mexican education credentials,

but the ISIC, IYTC and ITIC will sometimes get you a reduction. The ISIC card is the most recognized. Apply at www.isic.org.

EMBASSIES & CONSULATES

Mexico City entries in the following selective list are for embassies or their consular sections; other entries are consulates. Embassy websites are often useful sources of information about Mexico. For details of Mexican embassies or consulates in your home country, check out the listings on www.sre.gob.mx.

Australia (☎ 55-1101-2200; www.mexico.embassy.gov.au; Rubén Darío 55, Polanco, Mexico City)

Canada Acapulco (Map p192; ☎ 744-484-13-05; Centro Comercial Marbella, Local 23); Guadalajara (☎ 33-3671-4740; World Trade Center, Piso 8, Torre Pacífico, Av Otero 1249, Colonia Rinconada del Bosque); Mazatlán (Map p106; ☎ 669-913-73-20; Hotel Playa Mazatlán, Playa Gaviotas 202, Zona Dorada); Mexico City (☎ 55-5724-7900; www.canada.org.mx; Schiller 529, Polanco); Oaxaca (Map pp220-1; ☎ 951-513-37-77; Pino Suárez 700, Local 11B); Puerto Vallarta (Map p59; ☎ 322-293-00-98; Edificio Obelisco, Francisco Medina Ascencio 1951, Local 108, Zona Hotelera Las Glorias)

France Acapulco (Map p192; ☎ 744-484-45-80; La Costera 91, Local 205, Fraccionamiento Club Deportiva); Mexico City (☎ 55-9171-9700; www.francia.org.mx in Spanish & French; Campos Elíseos 339, Polanco); consulate in Mexico City (☎ 55-9171-9840; Lafontaine 32, Polanco)

Germany Acapulco (Map p192; ☎ 669-913-51-00; Alaminos 26, Casa Tres Fuentes, Colonia Costa Azul); Guadalajara (☎ 33-3810-2146; Calle 7 No 319, Colonia Ferrocarril); Mazatlán (Map p106; ☎ 669-914-93-10; Av Playa Gaviotas 212, Zona Dorada); Mexico City (☎ 55-5283-2200; www.mexiko.diplo.de in Spanish & German; Horacio 1506, Los Morales)

Ireland (☎ 55-5520-5803; embajada@irlanda.org.mx; Cerrada Blvd Ávila Camacho 76, Piso 3, Lomas de Chapultepec, Mexico City)

Netherlands Acapulco (Map p192; ☎ 744-486-83-59; Hotel Ritz, La Costera 159); Guadalajara (☎ 33-3673-2211; 2nd fl, Av Vallarta 5500, Colonia Lomas Universidad, Zapopan); Mexico City (☎ 55-5258-9921; www.paisesbajos.com.mx in Spanish & Dutch; Edificio Calakmul, Av Vasco de Quiroga 3000, 7th fl, Santa Fe)

New Zealand (☎ 55-5283-9460; kiwimexico@compuserve.com.mx; Balmes 8, Level 4, Los Morales, Mexico City)

Spain (Map p192; ☎ 435-15-00; La Costera 75, Acapulco)

UK Guadalajara (☎ 33-3343-2296; Jesús de Rojas 20, Colonia Los Pinos, Zapopan); Mexico City (☎ 55-5242-8500; www.britishembassy.gov.uk/mexico; Río Lerma 71, Colonia Cuauhtémoc); consulate in Mexico City (☎ 55-5242-8500; Río Usumacinta 26)

USA Acapulco (Map p192; ☎ 744-469-05-56; Hotel Continental Plaza, La Costera 121, Local 14); Guadalajara (☎ 33-3268-2100; Progreso 175); Mazatlán (Map p106; ☎ 669-916-58-89; Hotel Playa Mazatlán, Playa Gaviotas 202, Zona Dorada); Mexico City (☎ 55-5080-2000; mexico .usembassy.gov; Paseo de la Reforma 305); Oaxaca (Map pp220-1; ☎ 951-514-30-54; Plaza Santo Domingo, Alcalá 407, Interior 20); Puerto Vallarta (Map p59; ☎ 322-222-00-69; Sur Paradise Plaza, Paseo de los Cocoteros 85, Interior Local L7, Nuevo Vallarta)

FESTIVALS & EVENTS

Mexico's many fiestas are full-blooded, highly colorful affairs that often go on for several days. In addition to the major national festivals listed below, each town has many local saint's days, regional fairs, arts festivals and so on (see destination chapters for information on these). There's also a national public holiday just about every month (see p274), often an occasion for further partying.

January

Día de los Reyes Magos (Three Kings' Day or Epiphany; January 6) This is the day when Mexican children traditionally receive gifts, rather than at Christmas.

February/March

Día de la Candelaría (Candlemas; February 2) Commemorates the presentation of Jesus in the temple 40 days after his birth; celebrated with processions, bullfights and dancing in many towns.

Carnaval (late February/early March) A big bash preceding the 40-day penance of Lent, Carnaval takes place during the week or so before Ash Wednesday (which falls 46 days before Easter Sunday). It's celebrated wildly in Mazatlán with parades and masses of music, food, drink, dancing, fireworks and fun.

March/April

Semana Santa Holy Week starts on Palm Sunday (Domingo de Ramos); most of Mexico seems to be on the move at this time.

September

Día de la Independencia (Independence Day; September 16) The anniversary of the 1810 start of Mexico's independence war provokes an upsurge of patriotic feeling every year: on the evening of the 15th, the words of Padre Miguel Hidalgo's famous call to rebellion, El Grito de Dolores, are repeated from the balcony of every town hall in the land, usually followed by fireworks. The biggest celebrations are in Mexico City, where the Grito is issued by the national president from the Palacio Nacional.

November

Día de Todos los Santos (All Saints' Day; November 1) The souls of dead children (*angelitos,* little angels) are celebrated on All Saints' Day.

Día de Muertos (Day of the Dead; November 2) Every cemetery in the country comes alive as families visit graveyards to commune with their dead on the night of November 1 and the day of November 2, when the souls of the dead are believed to return to earth.

December

Día de Nuestra Señora de Guadalupe (December 12) A week or more of celebrations throughout Mexico leads up to the Day of Our Lady of Guadalupe, the Virgin who appeared to an indigenous Mexican, Juan Diego, in 1531, and has since become Mexico's religious patron. The biggest festivities are at the Basílica de Guadalupe in Mexico City.

Día de Navidad (December 25) Christmas is traditionally celebrated with a feast in the early hours of December 25, after midnight mass.

FOOD

Some Eating sections in chapters of this book are divided into budget, midrange and top-end categories. We define a midrange restaurant as one where a main dish at lunch or dinner costs between M$60 and M$140. Budget and top-end places are, respectively, less than M$60 and over M$140. If a restaurant has a closing day, it's usually Sunday, Monday or Tuesday. For a full introduction to Mexico's fabulously piquant cuisine, see the Food & Drink chapter (p35).

GAY & LESBIAN TRAVELERS

Mexico is more broad-minded about sexuality than you might expect. Gays and lesbians don't generally maintain a high profile, but rarely attract open discrimination or violence. There are large, lively gay communities and/or gay tourism scenes in Puerto Vallarta (p81 and p75), Acapulco (p205), Guadalajara and Mexico City. Mazatlán (p113) has a couple of gay clubs. Gay men have a more public profile than lesbians, however. Discrimination based on sexual orientation has been illegal since 1999, and can be punished with up to three years in prison.

The **International Gay and Lesbian Travel Association** (www.iglta.org) provides information on the major travel providers in the gay sector. San Diego–based **Arco Iris Tours** (☎ 800-765-4370; www.arcoiristours.com) specializes in gay travel to Mexico and organizes an annual International Gay Festival in Cancún.

The **Out&About** (www.gay.com/travel/outandabout) website has a detailed Mexico gay-travel guide and articles. Another good source of information is the **Gay Mexico Network** (www.gaymexico.net).

HOLIDAYS

The chief holiday periods are Christmas to New Year, Semana Santa (the week leading up to Easter and a couple of days afterward), and mid-July to mid-August. Transportation and tourist accommodations are heavily booked at these times. At Easter, businesses usually close from Good Friday (Viernes Santo) to Easter Sunday (Domingo de Resurrección). Many offices and businesses close during major national festivals (p273). Banks, post offices, government offices and many shops throughout Mexico are closed on the following national holidays:

Año Nuevo (New Year's Day) January 1
Día de la Constitución (Constitution Day) February 5
Día de la Bandera (Day of the National Flag) February 24
Día de Nacimiento de Benito Juárez (anniversary of Benito Juárez' birth) March 21
Día del Trabajo (Labor Day) May 1
Cinco de Mayo (anniversary of Mexico's victory over the French at Puebla) May 5
Día de la Independencia (Independence Day) September 16
Día de la Raza (commemoration of Columbus' discovery of the New World) October 12
Día de la Revolución (Revolution Day) November 20
Día de Navidad (Christmas Day) December 25

INSURANCE

A travel-insurance policy to cover theft, loss and medical problems is a good idea. Some policies specifically exclude dangerous activities such as scuba diving, motorcycling and even trekking.

You may prefer a policy that pays doctors or hospitals directly rather than you having to pay on the spot and claim later. If you have to claim later, ensure you keep all documentation. Check that the policy covers ambulances or an emergency flight home. For further information on medical insurance, see p291.

Worldwide travel insurance is available at www.lonelyplanet.com/travel_services. You can buy, extend and claim online anytime – even if you're already on the road.

For information on motor insurance, see p284.

INTERNET ACCESS

Most travelers make constant use of internet cafés (which cost M$10 to M$20 per hour). A number of Mexican internet cafés are equipped with CD burners, webcams, headphones (for internet calling) and so on. But a lot don't have card readers, so bring your own or the camera-to-USB cable if you plan on burning photos to CD along the way.

Quite a few accommodations provide internet access of some kind – they receive an 🖳 icon in this book if they provide computers to access the net. Facilities vary from a couple of computers in the lobby, for which you may or may not have to pay, to well-equipped business centers. Many hotels now offer wi-fi access *(internet inalámbrico)* in the rooms or lobby. You may also be able to connect your own laptop or hand-held to the internet through the telephone socket in your room. Be aware that your modem may not work once you leave your home country. The safest option is to buy a reputable 'global' modem before you leave home. A second issue is the plug: Mexico uses 110V plugs with two flat prongs, like those found in the US.

See p14 for some useful websites.

LEGAL MATTERS
Mexican Law

Mexican law is based on the Roman and Napoleonic codes, presuming an accused person is guilty until proven innocent.

The minimum jail sentence for possession of more than a token amount of any narcotic, including marijuana and amphetamines, is 10 months – trafficking gets you a minimum of 10 years. As in most other countries, the purchase of controlled medication requires a doctor's prescription.

Travelers driving around the region should expect occasional police or military checkpoints. They are normally looking for drugs, weapons or illegal migrants. Drivers found with drugs or weapons on board may have their vehicle confiscated and may be detained for months while their cases are investigated.

See p284 for information on road rules and the legal aspects of road accidents.

Useful warnings on Mexican law are found on the website of the **US Department of State** (www.travel.state.gov).

A FEW LEGAL TIPS

▪ Drinking: Must be 18 (rarely enforced)

▪ Sex: The age of consent ranges from 12 to 18, but is trending upward toward the 18-year range. Prostitution is legal in most of the country (prostitutes must be over 18).

Getting Legal Help

If arrested, you have the right to contact your embassy or consulate. Consular officials can tell you your rights, provide lists of local lawyers, monitor your case, make sure you are treated humanely and notify your relatives or friends – but they can't get you out of jail. More Americans are in jail in Mexico than in any other country except the USA – about 800 at any one time. By Mexican law the longest a person can be detained by police without a specific accusation is 72 hours.

Tourist offices in Mexico, especially those run by state governments, can often help you with legal problems such as complaints or reporting crimes or lost articles. The national tourism ministry, **Sectur** (☎ 55-3002-63-00, 800-987-82-24; www.sectur.gov.mx, in Spanish), offers 24-hour telephone advice.

If you are the victim of a crime, your embassy or consulate, or Sectur or state tourist offices, can give advice. In some cases, you may feel there is little to gain by going to the police, unless you need a statement to give to your insurance company. If you go to the police and your Spanish is poor, take a more fluent speaker. Also take your passport and tourist card, if you still have them. If you just want to report a theft for the purposes of an insurance claim, say *'quisiera levantar un acta por robo'* (I wish to make a record of a robbery). This should make it clear that you merely want a piece of paper and you should get it without too much trouble.

If Mexican police wrongfully accuse you of an infraction, you can ask for the officer's identification, ask to speak to a superior or to be shown documentation about the law you have supposedly broken. You can also note the officer's name, badge number, vehicle number and department (federal, state or municipal). Pay any traffic fines at a police station and get a receipt, then make your complaint at Sectur or a state tourist office. See p196 for more on dealing with corrupt cops.

MAPS

GeoCenter, Nelles, ITM and the AAA (American Automobile Association) all produce good country maps of Mexico, available internationally for between US$6 and US$15. The map scales vary between 1:2,500,000 (1cm:25km) and 1:3,700,000 (1cm:37km). ITM also publishes good 1:1 million (1cm:10km) maps of some Mexican regions including the Pacific coast.

City, town and regional maps of varying quality are often available free from local tourist offices in Mexico, or for about M$30 to M$50 at bookstores, newsstands and department stores like Sanborns. **Guía Roji** (www .guiaroji.com.mx, in Spanish) produces some of the best maps.

Inegi (Instituto Nacional de Estadística, Geografía e Informática; ☎ 800-111-46-34; www.inegi.gob.mx, in Spanish) publishes a large-scale map series covering all of Mexico at 1:50,000 (1cm:500m) and 1:250,000 (1cm:2.5km), plus state maps at 1:700,000 (1cm:7km).

US-based **Maplink** (www.maplink.com) is an excellent source for mail-order maps; it stocks nearly all the above maps, including Inegi topo maps. Another good source is **Maps of Mexico** (www.maps-of-mexico.com), which has detailed maps of all the states and of 90 cities.

MONEY

Mexico's currency is the peso, usually denoted by the '$' sign. Any prices quoted in US dollars will be written 'US$x' to avoid misunderstanding. This book lists prices in pesos (M$). The peso is divided into 100 centavos. Coins come in denominations of five, 10, 20 and 50 centavos and one, two, five, 10, 20 and 100 pesos. There are notes of 20, 50, 100, 200, 500 and 1000 pesos.

For exchange rates, see inside the front cover. At press time, the peso had dropped 34% against the US dollar in just three months. In an economy largely based on US dollars, which are used for most major business transactions, this may mean that relative peso prices go up. For information on costs, see p13.

The most convenient form of money in Mexico is a major international credit card or debit card. Visa, MasterCard and American Express cards can be used to obtain cash easily from ATMs in Mexico. Making a purchase by credit card normally gives you a more favorable exchange rate than exchanging money at a bank, and isn't subject to commission, but you'll normally have to pay your card issuer a 'foreign exchange' transaction fee of around 2.5%. Note that Visa, Amex or MasterCard stickers on a door or window in Mexico do *not* necessarily mean that these cards will be accepted for payment there.

US dollars are by far the most easily exchangeable foreign currency in Mexico. In tourist areas you can even pay for some things in US dollars, though the exchange rate used will probably not be in your favor. Euros, British pounds and Canadian dollars, in cash or as traveler's checks, are accepted by most banks and some *casas de cambio* (exchange houses).

For tips on keeping your money safe, see p271.

ATMs

ATMs (*caja permanente* or *cajero automático* in Spanish) are plentiful in Mexico, and are the easiest source of cash. You can use major credit cards and some bank cards, such as those on the Cirrus and Plus systems, to withdraw pesos from ATMs. The exchange rate that banks use for ATM withdrawals is normally more in your favor than the 'tourist rate' for currency exchange.

Banks & Casas de Cambio

You can exchange cash and traveler's checks in banks or at *casas de cambio*. Banks are more time-consuming than *casas de cambio*, and usually have shorter exchange hours (typically 9am to 5pm Monday to Friday and 9am to 1pm Saturday). *Casas de cambio* can be found easily in just about every large or medium-size town and in many smaller ones. These places are quick and often open evenings or weekends, but some don't accept traveler's checks, whereas banks usually do.

Exchange rates vary a little from one bank or *cambio* to another. There is often a better rate for *efectivo* (cash) than for *documento* (traveler's checks).

If you have trouble finding a place to change money, particularly on a weekend, try a hotel, though the exchange rate won't be the best.

International Transfers

Should you need money wired to you in Mexico, an easy and quick method is the 'Dinero en Minutos' (Money in Minutes) service of **Western Union** (☎ in the US 800-325-6000; www.westernunion.com). It's offered by thousands of bank branches and other businesses around Mexico, and is identified by black-and-yellow signs proclaiming 'Western Union Dinero en Minutos.'

US post offices (☎ 888-368-4669; www.usps.com) offer reasonably cheap money transfers to branches of Bancomer bank in Mexico. The service is called Dinero Seguro.

Taxes

Mexico's *impuesto de valor agregado* (IVA, value-added tax) is levied at 15%. By law the tax must be included in virtually any price quoted to you and should not be added afterward. Signs in stores and notices on restaurant menus often state '*IVA incluido.*' Occasionally they state instead that IVA must be added to the quoted prices.

Hotel rooms are also subject to the *impuesto sobre hospedaje* (ISH, lodging tax). Each Mexican state sets its own rate, but in most it's 2%. See p267 for further information on taxes on hotel rooms.

Tipping

In general, workers in small, cheap restaurants don't expect much in the way of tips, while those in expensive resorts expect you to be lavish in your largesse. Workers in the tourism and hospitality industries often depend on tips to supplement miserable basic wages. In resorts frequented by foreigners (such as Acapulco, Puerto Vallarta and Mazatlán) tipping is up to US levels of 15%; elsewhere 10% is usually plenty. If you stay a few days in one place, you should leave up to 10% of your room costs for the people who have kept your room clean (assuming they have). A porter in a midrange hotel will be happy with M$10 a bag. Taxi drivers don't generally expect tips unless they provide some special service. Car-parking attendants expect a tip of M$2 to M$5, and the same is standard for gas-station attendants.

Traveler's Checks

Along with your credit card or bank card, you may also consider taking some traveler's checks (denominated in US dollars) and a little US cash. Traveler's checks should be a major brand such as American Express or Visa. Amex traveler's checks are recognized everywhere, and are a good choice. The **Amex**

24-hour hotline (☎ 001-800-221-72-82 toll free from anywhere in Mexico) can help if you have lost traveler's checks or cards.

POST

Post offices (oficinas de correos) are typically open along the Pacific coast from 8am to 6pm Monday to Friday, and 9am to 1pm Saturday. An airmail letter or postcard weighing up to 20g costs M$10.50 to the US or Canada, M$13 to Europe or South America, and M$14.50 to the rest of the world. Spanish speakers can visit www.correosdemexico.gob.mx for updated prices. Mark airmail items 'Vía Aérea.' Delivery times (outbound and inbound) are elastic. An airmail letter from Mexico to the USA or Canada (or vice versa) should take somewhere between four and 14 days to arrive. Mail to or from Europe may take between one and two weeks; for Australasia, two to three weeks.

If you are sending a package internationally from Mexico, be prepared to open it for customs inspection at the post office. In light of this, it is better to take packing materials with you, or not seal it until you get there. For assured and speedy delivery, you can always use one of the more expensive international courier services, such as **UPS** (☎ 800-902-92-00; www.ups.com), **Federal Express** (☎ 800-900-11-00; www.fedex.com) or Mexico's **Estafeta** (☎ 800-903-35-00; www.estafeta.com). Your best bet for receiving mail in Mexico is to have it sent to your hostel or hotel – but don't have money or valuables sent. You can also have it sent to the local post office, noting Poste Restante below the addressee's name. You can find information on Poste Restante service at www.sepomex.gob.mx (in Spanish).

SHOPPING

Because the Pacific coast is a popular tourist destination, you'll find all sorts of shops and mercados de artesanías (artisans markets) selling handicrafts from all over the country, often at very reasonable prices. In markets bargaining is the rule, and you may pay much more than the going rate if you accept the first price quoted.

THE ARTISAN TREASURES OF MEXICO

From around Mexico, here are just a few of the many items to keep an eye out for:

- **Animalitos & alebrijes** Animalitos are tiny, light-brown and rust-colored ceramic animals from Chiapas. Alebrijes are little multicolored figurines from Oaxaca.

- **Baskets & hats** Colorful, homemade baskets are great for carrying other souvenirs home. The Mexican straw sombrero (literally 'shade maker') is a classic souvenir.

- **Ceramics** The Guadalajara suburbs of Tonalá and Tlaquepaque are renowned pottery centers. Watch for the distinctive black pottery from San Bartolo Coyotepec, Oaxaca.

- **Hammocks** The best are the tightly woven, cotton, thin-string ones from the Yucatán and Oaxaca.

- **Huaraches** Sandals! Can't spend any time on the coast without a pair of these. Guadalajara is known for good huaraches.

- **Huipiles** Sleeveless tunics for women, mostly made in the southern states. They're often embroidered and wonderfully colorful. Coastal Mixtec and Amuzgos of Oaxaca are famous for them.

- **Jewelry** Silverwork from the central Mexican town of Taxco is sold everywhere.

- **Masks** Guerrero is famous for its masks, as are the villages of San Juan Colorado and Huazolotitlán, Oaxaca.

- **Rug weavings** Those from Teotitlán del Valle, Oaxaca, are most famous.

- **Sarapes** An indigenous men's garment worn over the shoulders – essentially a blanket with an opening for the head.

- **Skulls & skeletons** These crafty creations come in all shapes, sizes and materials, and have their origin in the November 2 Día de los Muertos (Day of the Dead) festival.

SOLO TRAVELERS

Lone travelers don't generally need to remain alone when traveling in Mexico, unless they choose to. It's very easy to pair up with others, as there's a steady stream of people following similar routes around the country. In well-touristed places, notice boards advertise for traveling companions, flatmates, volunteer workers and so on. Local tours are a good way to meet people and get more out of a place.

Solo travelers should be especially watchful of their luggage when on the road, and should stay in places with good security for their valuables so that they don't have to be burdened with them when out and about.

Traveling alone can be a very good way of getting into the local culture, and it definitely improves your Spanish skills. You can also get a kick out of doing what you want, when you want. Eating by yourself night after night can get a bit tiresome, but you'll only be left alone if you want it that way, as Mexicans are very sociable.

See p281 for information regarding women traveling solo.

TELEPHONE

Local calls are cheap, while international calls can be expensive. The cheapest way to call internationally is through a Voice Over Internet Protocol (VOIP) service like **Skype** (www.skype.com). Many internet cafés now accommodate VOIP calling, and laptoppers can easily hook into a wi-fi system in most towns. Mexico is well provided with fairly easy-to-use public card phones. *Casetas telefónicas* (call offices where an on-the-spot operator connects the call for you) are quite widespread and can be cheaper than card phones. A third option is to call from your hotel, but hotels charge what they like for this service. It's nearly always cheaper to go elsewhere.

Calling Cards

Some calling cards from other countries can be used for calls from Mexico by dialing special access numbers. Warning: If you get an operator who asks for your credit card instead of your calling-card number, or says the service is unavailable, hang up. There have been scams in which calls are rerouted to super-expensive credit-card phone services.
AT&T (☎ 01-800-288-2872, 01-80-462-4240)

Bell Canada (☎ 01-800-123-0200, 01-800-021-1994)
BT Chargecard (☎ 01-800-123-02-44, 01-800-021-6644)
MCI (☎ 01-800-674-7000)
Sprint (☎ 01-800-877-8000)

Casetas Telefónicas

Costs in *casetas* are often lower than those for Telmex card phones (see opposite), and their advantages are that they eliminate street noise and you don't need a phone card to use them. They often have a telephone symbol outside, or signs saying '*teléfono*,' 'Lada' or 'Larga Distancia.'

Cell Phones

If you want to use a cell phone in Mexico, one option for short visits is to get an international plan for your own phone, which will enable you to call home. You can also buy a Mexican cell phone or chip (make sure it works first) for as little as US$30 to US$60 including some air time. The most widespread cellular phone system in Mexico is **Telcel** (www.telcel.com, in Spanish), which has coverage almost everywhere that has a significant population, and roaming partnerships with systems from many other countries. Amigo cards, for recharging Telcel phones, are widely available from newsstands and minimarts.

Collect Calls

If you need to make a *llamada por cobrar* (collect call), you can do so from card phones without a card. Call an operator on ☎ 020 for domestic calls, or ☎ 090 for international calls, or use a 'home country direct' service, through which you make an international collect call via an operator in the country you're calling. The Mexican term for 'home country direct' is *país directo;* be prepared to provide the access numbers for the country you're trying to call.

Some telephone *casetas* and hotels will make collect calls for you, but they usually charge for the service.

Dialing Codes

If you're calling a number in the town or city you're in, simply dial the local number (eight digits in Mexico City, Guadalajara and Monterrey; seven digits everywhere else).

To call another town or city in Mexico, you need to dial the long-distance prefix ☎ 01, followed by the area code (two digits for Mexico City, Guadalajara and Monterrey;

three digits for everywhere else) and then the local number. You'll find area codes listed under city and town headings through this book.

To make international calls, you need to dial the international prefix ☎ 00, followed by the country code, area code and local number.

To call a number in Mexico from another country, dial your international access code, then the Mexico country code (☎ 52), then the area code and number.

Phone Cards

These are common in towns and cities: you'll usually find some at airports, bus stations and around the main plaza. Easily the most common, and most consistent on costs, are those marked with the name of the country's biggest phone company, Telmex. To use a Telmex card phone you need a phone card known as a *tarjeta Ladatel*. These are sold at kiosks and shops everywhere – look for the blue-and-yellow signs that read *'De venta aquí Ladatel.'* The cards come in denominations of 30 pesos (about US$3), 50 pesos (US$5) and 100 pesos (US$10).

Calls from Telmex card phones cost M$1 per minute for local calls; M$4 per minute long-distance within Mexico; M$5 per minute to the mainland USA or Canada; M$10 per minute to Central America; M$20 per minute to Europe, Alaska or South America; and M$25 per minute to Hawaii, Australia, New Zealand or Asia.

In some parts of Mexico frequented by foreign tourists, you may notice a variety of phones advertising that they accept credit cards, or that you can make easy collect calls to the USA on them. While some of these phones may be of fair value, others charge very high rates.

TIME

Most of the country, including Jalisco, Michoacán, Guerrero and Oaxaca, are on Hora del Centro, the same as US Central Time (GMT minus six hours in winter, and GMT minus five hours during daylight saving). Five western states, including Nayarit and Sinaloa, are on Hora de las Montañas, the same as US Mountain Time (GMT minus seven hours in winter, GMT minus six hours during daylight saving). *Horario de verano* (daylight saving time) runs from

the first Sunday in April to the last Sunday in October.

TOILETS

Public toilets are rare, so take advantage of facilities in places such as hotels, restaurants, bus stations and museums. When out and about, carry some toilet paper with you if you think you're going to need it because it often won't be provided. If there's a bin beside the toilet, put paper in it because the drains can't cope otherwise.

TOURIST INFORMATION

For general information about travel in Mexico consult the **Mexico Tourism Board** USA & Canada (☎ 800-446-3942, 800-44-MEXICO); Europe (☎ 00-800-11-11-22-66; www.visitmexico.com). Alternatively, you can call the Mexico City office of the national tourism ministry **Sectur** (☎ 55-3002-63-00, 800-987-82-24; in the US & Canada 800-446-3942, 800-482-9832; in Europe 00-800-1111-2266) at any time – 24 hours a day, seven days a week – for information or help in English or Spanish.

Just about every town of interest in Mexico has a state or municipal tourist office. They are generally helpful with maps, brochures and questions, and usually some staff members speak English. Here are the contact details for the head tourism offices for the states covered in this book:

Colima (☎ 312-316-20-21; www.visitacolima.com.mx)
Guerrero (www.guerrero.gob.mx, in Spanish)
Jalisco (☎ 33-3668-1600, 800-363-22-00; www.visita .jalisco.gob.mx, in Spanish)
Michoacán (☎ 443-317-78-05; www.turismo michoacan.gob.mx, in Spanish)
Nayarit (☎ 311-214-80-71, www.visitnayarit.com)
Oaxaca (☎ 951-502-12-00; www.aoaxaca.com, in Spanish)
Sinaloa (☎ 669-981-88-83, www.vivesinaloa.com)

TOURS

For travelers seeking an activity-based holiday – and particularly for those who are short on time – organized tours are a good way to get to the most popular places and partake in hassle-free outdoor activities such as mountain biking, diving or horseback riding. More and more providers are adding cultural excursions to hard-to-get-to places to attract travelers who might not otherwise consider an organized tour. The biggest and best-regarded operator in the region is Vallarta Adventures (p69).

VISAS

Every tourist must have an easily obtainable Mexican government tourist card. Some nationalities must also have visas. Because the regulations sometimes change, it's wise to confirm them with a Mexican embassy or consulate before you go (see www.sre.gob.mx for listings).

Citizens of the USA, Canada, EU countries, Australia, New Zealand, Iceland, Israel, Japan, Norway and Switzerland are among those who do not require visas to enter Mexico as tourists. Again, check with your local Mexican embassy or consulate well ahead of travel in case the list has changed. Visa procedures, for those who need them, can take weeks and you may be required to apply in your country of residence or citizenship.

For information on passport requirements, see p282. Non-US citizens passing (even in transit) through the USA on the way to or from Mexico, or visiting Mexico from the USA, should also check the passport and visa requirements for the USA.

Tourist Card & Tourist Fee

The Mexican tourist card – the *forma migratoria para turista* (FMT) – is a document that you must fill out and get stamped by Mexican immigration when you enter Mexico and keep till you leave. It's available at official border crossings, international airports and ports, and often at airlines, travel agencies and Mexican consulates. At the US-Mexico border you won't usually be given one automatically – you have to ask for it.

At many US-Mexico border crossings you don't have to get the card stamped at the border itself, as Mexico's Instituto Nacional de Migración (INM, National Immigration Institute) has control points on the highways into the interior where it's also possible to do it. But it's better to get it done at the border in case there are complications elsewhere.

One section of the card deals with the length of your stay in Mexico, and this section is filled out by the immigration officer. The maximum possible stay is 180 days for most nationalities (90 days for Australians, Austrians, Israelis and Italians, among others), but immigration officers will often put a much lower number (as little as 15 or 30 days) unless you tell them otherwise. It's advisable to ask for more days than you think you'll need in case you are delayed or change your plans.

Though the tourist card is free, it brings with it the obligation to pay the tourist fee of about US$22, called the *derecho para no inmigrante* (DNI, nonimmigrant fee). If you enter Mexico by air, the fee is included in your airfare. If you enter by land, you must pay the fee at a bank in Mexico before you reenter the frontier zone on your way out of Mexico (or before you check in at an airport to fly out of Mexico). The frontier zone is the territory between the border and the INM's control points on the highways leading into the Mexican interior (usually 20km to 30km from the border). Most Mexico border posts have on-the-spot bank offices where you can pay the DNI fee immediately. When you pay at a bank, your tourist card will be stamped to prove that you have paid.

Look after your tourist card because it may be checked when you leave the country. You can be fined M$450 for not having it.

EXTENSIONS & LOST CARDS

If the number of days given on your tourist card is less than the maximum for your nationality (90 or 180 days in most cases), its validity may be extended one or more times, up to the maximum. To get a card extended, apply to the INM, which has offices in many towns and cities; they're listed on the **INM website** (www.inm.gob.mx), under 'Servicios Migratorios.' The procedure costs about M$200 and should take between half an hour and three hours, depending on the office. You'll need your passport, tourist card, photocopies of the important pages of these documents and, at some offices, evidence of 'sufficient funds.' Most INM offices will not extend a card until a few days before it expires.

If you lose your card or need further information, contact a tourist office, the **Sectur tourist office** (☎ 55-3002-63-00, 800-987-82-24) in Mexico City, or your embassy or consulate. Any of these should be able to give you an official note to take to an INM office, which will issue a duplicate for M$450.

See opposite for information on the documentation required to work in Mexico.

VOLUNTEERING

Volunteering is one of the best ways to learn about local culture and create a positive impact. You can volunteer with Oaxaca city street children at Centro Esperanza (p218), help protect the sea turtles of Playa San Francisco with the

Grupo Ecológico de la Costa Verde in Nayarit (p135), or protect the Oaxaca coastal environment through Red de los Humedales de la Costa de Oaxaca (p234). Good resources for volunteering in Mexico include **Pronatura** (www.pronatura.org.mx), **Alliance of European Voluntary Service Organisations** (www.alliance-network.org), **Volunteer Abroad** (www.volunteerabroad.com), **Adelante Abroad** (www.adelanteabroad.com) and **Amerispan** (www.amerispan.com).

WOMEN TRAVELERS

Women can have a great time in Mexico, traveling with companions or solo, but in the land that invented machismo, some concessions have to be made to local custom. Gender equalization has come a long way in a few decades, and Mexicans are generally a very polite people, but they remain, by and large, great believers in the difference (rather than the equality) between the sexes.

Lone women must expect a few catcalls and attempts to chat them up. Often these men only want to talk to you, but you can discourage unwanted attention by avoiding eye contact (wear sunglasses), dressing modestly, moving confidently and speaking coolly but politely if you are addressed and must respond. Wearing a wedding ring can prove helpful. Don't put yourself in peril by doing things that Mexican women would not do, such as challenging a man's masculinity, drinking alone in a cantina, hitchhiking or going alone to remote places.

On local transportation it's best to don long or mid-calf-length trousers and a top that meets the top of your pants, with sleeves of some sort. That way you can keep your valuables out of sight with ease.

Most of all, appear self-assured.

WORK

Mexicans need jobs, so people who enter Mexico as tourists aren't legally allowed to take employment. The many expats working in Mexico have usually been posted there by their companies or organizations with all the necessary papers. Permits are issued to people sponsored by companies in Mexico (or foreign companies with Mexican operations/subsidiaries), or to people with specific skills required in Mexico. English-speakers (and a few German- or French-speakers) may find teaching jobs in language schools, *preparatorias* (high schools) or universities, or can offer personal tutoring. The pay is low, but you can live on it. Press ads, especially in the various local English-language papers and magazines, and the Yellow Pages are sources of job opportunities.

Schools will often pay a foreign teacher in the form of a *beca* (scholarship), and thus circumvent the laws precluding foreigners from working in Mexico without a permit. In some cases, the school's administration will procure the appropriate papers. Apart from teaching, you might find a little bar or restaurant work in tourist areas.

Jobs Abroad (www.jobsabroad.com) posts paid and unpaid job openings in Mexico. The **Lonely Planet** (www.lonelyplanet.com) website has several useful links.

Transportation

CONTENTS

TRANSPORTATION

GETTING THERE & AWAY

ENTERING THE COUNTRY

Immigration officers won't usually keep you waiting any longer than it takes to flick through your passport and enter your length of stay on your tourist card (p280). Anyone traveling to Mexico via the USA should be sure to check the current US visa and passport requirements. Flights, tours and rail tickets can be booked online at www.lonelyplanet.com/travel_services.

Passport

Passport and visa restrictions change constantly, so check with your embassy, consulate or state department to ensure you have all the proper documentation. US citizens are now required to

---

THINGS CHANGE...

The information in this chapter is particularly vulnerable to change. Check directly with the airline or a travel agent to make sure you understand how a fare (and ticket you may buy) works, and be aware of the security requirements for international travel. Shop carefully. The details given in this chapter should be regarded as pointers and are not a substitute for your own careful, up-to-date research.

---

have a passport for air travel to Mexico. By land and sea you'll need a passport or a **US Passport Card** (www.travel.state.gov/passport/ppt_card/ppt_card_3926 .html), a cheaper document that does not work for air travel. Canadians currently get away with just an official ID like a driver's license and a birth certificate if they fly directly to Mexico. In any case it's better to have a passport – you will often need one to change money or when you check into a hotel. For more information on the regulations, visit the **US State Department website** (http://travel.state.gov).

All citizens of countries other than US and Canada should have a passport that's valid for at least six months after they arrive in Mexico.

Travelers under 18 who are not accompanied by both parents may need special documentation (p270).

For information on Mexican visa requirements and the tourist card, see p280.

AIR

Most visitors to Mexico's Pacific coast arrive by air. You can fly direct to Mexico's Pacific coast from at least a dozen US cities and from Toronto. From anywhere else you'll have to either fly first to Mexico City or to the cities with direct connections. Airports in the region are shown in the boxed text, opposite.

Airports & Airlines

The following airlines service Mexico's Pacific coast. The phone numbers are those in Mexico.

Aeroméxico (code AM; ☎ 800-021-40-00; www.aeromexico.com) Hub Mexico City.

Air Canada (code AC; ☎ 800-719-28-27; www.aircanada.com) Hub Toronto.

Alaska Airlines (code AS; ☎ 001-800-252-75-22; www.alaska-air.com) Hub Seattle.

American Airlines (code AA; ☎ 800-904-60-00; www.aa.com) Hub Dallas.

Continental Airlines (code CO; ☎ 800-900-50-00; www.continental.com) Hub Houston.

Delta Air Lines (code DL; ☎ 800-123-47-10; www.delta.com) Hub Atlanta.

Interjet (code IJ; ☎ 800-011-23-45; www.interjet .com.mx) Hub Toluca.

Mexicana (code MX; ☎ 800-801-20-10; www.mexicana .com) Hub Mexico City.

TRANSPORTATION

PACIFIC COAST AIRPORTS

Acapulco (ACA; ☎ 744-466-94-34)
Guadalajara (GDL; ☎ 33-3688-5504)
Huatulco (Bahías de Huatulco) (HUX;
☎ 958-581-90-04; www.asur.com.mx)
Ixtapa-Zihuatanejo (ZIH; ☎ 755-554-20-70)
Manzanillo (Playa de Oro) (ZLO; ☎ 314-333-25-25)
Mazatlán (MZT; ☎ 669-928-04-38)
Oaxaca (OAX; ☎ 951-511-50-88; www.asur
.com.mx)
Puerto Vallarta (PVR; ☎ 322-221-28-48)

US Airways (code US; ☎ 001-800-428-43-22;
www.usairways.com) Hub Phoenix.

Tickets

The cost of flying to Mexico's Pacific coast is usually higher around Christmas and New Year, and during July and August.

Try international online booking agencies such as **CheapTickets** (www.cheaptickets.com) and, for students and travelers under the age of 26, **STA Travel** (www.statravel.com).

A departure tax equivalent to about US$25 is levied on international flights from Mexico. It's usually included in the cost of your ticket, but if it isn't you must pay in cash at check-in. Ask your travel agent in advance.

Asia

You normally have to make a connection in the US or Canada (often Los Angeles, San Francisco or Vancouver), and maybe one in Asia as well. From more westerly Asian points such as Bangkok, routes via Europe are also an option. There are numerous branches in Asia of **STA Travel** Bangkok (☎ 662-236-0262; www .statravel.co.th); Singapore (☎ 6737-7188; www.statravel .com.sg); Hong Kong (☎ 2736-1618; www.statravel.com.hk); Japan (☎ 03-5391-2922; www.statravel.co.jp). Another resource in Japan is **No 1 Travel** (☎ 03-3205-6073; www.no1-travel.com).

Australia & New Zealand

The cheapest routes are usually via the USA (normally Los Angeles). You're normally looking at A$2300 or NZ$2300 or more, round-trip (several hundred dollars extra during high season).

The following agents are well-known for cheap fares and have branches throughout both countries:

Flight Centre Australia (☎ 133-133; www.flightcentre .com.au); New Zealand (☎ 0800-243-544; www.flight centre.co.nz)
STA Travel Australia (☎ 134-782; www.statravel.com.au); New Zealand (☎ 0800-474-400; www.statravel.co.nz)

Canada

Montreal, Toronto and Vancouver all have direct flights to Mexico, though better deals are often available with a change of flight in the USA. Round-trip fares from Toronto start around C$900 to Mexico City, Cancún or Puerto Vallarta. **Travel Cuts** (☎ 866-246-9762; www.travelcuts.com) is Canada's national student-travel agency.

Europe

Flights to Mexico City or Cancún cost €600 to €700 from Frankfurt, Paris or Madrid. Airlines with direct flights to Mexico City include Aeroméxico, Air Europa, Air France, Air Madrid, British Airways, Iberia, Jetair, KLM and Lufthansa. An alternative is to fly with a US or Canadian airline or alliance partner, changing planes in North America.

For online bookings throughout Europe, try **Opodo** (www.opodo.com) or **Ebookers** (www.ebook ers.com).

THE UK

Round-trip fares to Mexico City start around UK£500 to UK£600 from London.

An excellent place to start your inquiries is **Journey Latin America** (☎ 020-8747-3108; www .journeylatinamerica.co.uk), which offers a variety of tours as well as flights. Or try **STA Travel** (☎ 0871-230-0040; www.statravel.co.uk).

FRANCE

Nouvelles Frontières (☎ 01-49-20-65-87; www .nouvelles-frontieres.fr)
OTU Voyages (☎ 01-55-82-32-32; www.otu.fr) A student and youth travel specialist.

GERMANY

Just Travel (☎ 089-747-3330; www.justtravel.de)
STA Travel (☎ 069-743-032-92; www.statravel.de) For travelers aged under 26.

OTHER EUROPEAN COUNTRIES

Airfair (☎ 0900-7-717-717; www.airfair.nl) Dutch company.
Barceo Viajoes (☎ 902-116-226; www.barceloviajes .com) Spanish company.
CTS Viaggi (☎ 06-462-0431; www.cts.it) Italian specialist in student and youth travel.

South America

You can fly direct to Mexico City from at least eight cities in South America. Round-trip fares start around US$800 to US$1000. Recommended ticket agencies include the following:

ASATEJ (☎ 011-4114-7595; www.asatej.com) In Argentina.
IVI Tours (☎ 0212-993-6082; www.ividiomas.com) In Venezuela.
Student Travel Bureau (☎ 3038-1555; www.stb.com.br) In Brazil.

USA

You can fly to Mexico without changing planes from around 30 US cities. There are one-stop connecting flights from many other cities. You can get round-trip fares from the USA to Mexico for US$250 to US$500. Aggregators like www.expedia.com offer great deals, but you may be able to get a better deal on airline sites.

LAND
Border Crossings

There are about 40 crossings on the USA-Mexico border, including the following:
Arizona Douglas–Agua Prieta, Nogales-Nogales, San Luis–San Luis, Río Colorado and Naco-Naco (all open 24 hours); Sasabe–El Sásabe (open 8am to 10pm); Lukeville-Sonoita (open 8am to midnight).

California Calexico-Mexicali (two crossings, one open 24 hours); San Ysidro–Tijuana (open 24 hours); Otay Mesa–Mesa de Otay (near Tijuana airport; open 6am to 10pm); Tecate-Tecate (open 6am to midnight).
New Mexico Columbus–General Rodrigo M Quevedo (also called Palomas; open 24 hours).
Texas Brownsville-Matamoros, McAllen-Reynosa, Laredo–Nuevo Laredo, Del Rio–Ciudad Acuña, Eagle Pass–Piedras Negras, Presidio-Ojinaga and El Paso–Ciudad Juárez (all open 24 hours).

There are also 10 border crossings between Guatemala and Mexico and two crossings between Belize and Mexico.

See below for more information on entering Mexico with a car.

Car & Motorcycle

The regulations for taking a vehicle into Mexico change from time to time. See p286 if you're bringing in a vehicle from the US or Canada. For information on driving and motorcycling once you're inside Mexico, see p288.

INSURANCE

It's foolish to drive in Mexico without Mexican liability insurance. If you are involved in an accident, you can be jailed and have your vehicle impounded while responsibility is assessed. This could take weeks or months to arrange.

CLIMATE CHANGE & TRAVEL

Climate change is a serious threat to the ecosystems that humans rely upon, and air travel is the fastest-growing contributor to the problem. Lonely Planet regards travel, overall, as a global benefit, but believes we all have a responsibility to limit our personal impact on global warming.

Flying & Climate Change

Pretty much every form of motor travel generates CO_2 (the main cause of human-induced climate change) but planes are far and away the worst offenders, not just because of the sheer distances they allow us to travel, but because they release greenhouse gases high into the atmosphere. The statistics are frightening: two people taking a return flight between Europe and the US will contribute as much to climate change as an average household's gas and electricity consumption over a whole year.

Carbon Offset Schemes

Climatecare.org and other websites use 'carbon calculators' that allow jet-setters to offset the greenhouse gases they are responsible for with contributions to energy-saving projects and other climate-friendly initiatives in the developing world – including projects in India, Honduras, Kazakhstan and Uganda.

Lonely Planet, together with Rough Guides and other concerned partners in the travel industry, supports the carbon offset scheme run by climatecare.org. Lonely Planet offsets all of its staff and author travel.

For more information check out our website: lonelyplanet.com.

Mexican law recognizes only Mexican motor *seguro* (insurance), so a US or Canadian policy, even if it provides coverage, is not acceptable to Mexican officialdom. Sanborn's and the AAA are both well worth looking into for motor insurance in Mexico. Mexican insurance is also sold in US border towns; as you approach the border from the USA, you will see billboards advertising offices selling Mexican policies.

Short-term insurance costs about US$15 a day for full coverage on a car worth under US$10,000; for periods longer than two weeks it's often cheaper to get an annual policy. Liability-only insurance costs around half the full coverage cost.

DRIVER'S LICENSE
To drive a motor vehicle in Mexico, you need a valid driver's license from your home country.

VEHICLE PERMIT
You will need a *permiso de importación temporal de vehículos* (temporary vehicle import permit) if you want to take a vehicle to Mexico's Pacific coast. The permits are issued at offices at border crossings or (for some border crossings) at posts a few kilometers into Mexico. Information on their locations and application forms for the vehicle permit are available online at www.banjercito.com.mx (mostly in Spanish). The person importing the vehicle will need the original and one or two photocopies (people at the office may make photocopies for a small fee) of each of the following documents, which as a rule must all be in their own name (except that they can bring in a spouse's, parent's or child's vehicle if they can show a marriage or birth certificate proving a relationship):

- tourist card (FMT): go to *migración* before you get your vehicle permit
- certificate of title or registration certificate for the vehicle (note: you should have both of these if you plan to drive through Mexico into Guatemala or Belize)
- a Visa, MasterCard or American Express credit card issued by a non-Mexican institution; if you don't have one, you must pay a returnable deposit of between US$200 and US$400 (depending on how old the car is) at the border. Your card

details or deposit serve as a guarantee that you'll take the car out of Mexico before your tourist card (FMT) expires.
- proof of citizenship or residency such as a passport
- driver's license
- if the vehicle is not fully paid for, a partial invoice and/or letter of authorization from the financing institution
- for a leased or rented vehicle (though few US rental firms allow their vehicles to be taken into Mexico), the contract, which must be in the name of the person importing the vehicle

At the border there will be a building with a parking area for vehicles awaiting permits. After some signing and stamping of papers, you sign a promise to take the car out of the country, pay a processing fee of about US$29 to the Banco del Ejército (also called Banjército; it's the army bank), and go and wait with your vehicle.

You have the option to take the vehicle in and out of Mexico for the period shown on your tourist card. Ask for a *tarjetón de internación,* a document that you exchange for a *comprobante de retorno* each time you leave Mexico; when you return to Mexico, you swap the *comprobante* for another *tarjetón.* When you leave Mexico the last time, you must have the import permit canceled by the Mexican authorities. An official may do this as you enter the border zone, usually 20km to 30km before the border itself. If you leave Mexico without having the permit canceled, the authorities may assume you've left the vehicle in the country illegally and decide either to keep your deposit, charge a fine to your credit card, or deny you permission to bring a vehicle into the country on your next trip.

Only the owner may take the vehicle out of Mexico. If the vehicle is wrecked completely during your visit, you must contact your consulate or a Mexican customs office to make arrangements to leave without it.

Belize & Guatemala
Buses take you from Belize and Guatemala City into Mexico. Most take you to Chetumal, Quintana Roo, though from Guatemala you can cross into Chiapas. From there, you can hop on a long-distance bus to the Pacific coast.

TRANSPORTATION

USA

BUS

Cross-border bus services, mainly used by Mexicans working in the US, link many US cities with northern Mexican cities. They're not very well publicized: Spanish-language newspapers in the US have the most ads. The major companies include **Autobuses Americanos** (www.autobusesamericanos.com.mx, in Spanish), operating to northeast Mexico, central north Mexico and central Mexico from Los Angeles, Denver, Albuquerque, Chicago, Phoenix and Tucson and several Texan cities; and **Autobuses Crucero USA** (☎ in the US 1-800-531-5322; www.crucero-usa.com), operating from California, Nevada and Arizona to northwest Mexico. **Greyhound** (☎ in the US 800-231-2222; www.greyhound.com) also has some cross-border routes.

You can also, often in little or no extra time, make your way to the border on one bus (or train), cross it on foot or by local bus, and then catch an onward bus on the other side. Greyhound serves many US border cities; to reach others, transfer from Greyhound to a smaller bus line.

For train travel to the border, **Amtrak** (☎ in the US 800-872-72-45; www.amtrak.com) serves four US cities from which access to Mexico is easy: San Diego, El Paso, Del Rio and San Antonio, which is linked by bus to Eagle Pass and Laredo.

CAR & MOTORCYCLE

For information on the procedures for taking a vehicle into Mexico, check with the **American Automobile Association** (AAA; www.aaa.com), **Sanborn's** (☎ 800-222-0158; www.sanbornsinsurance.com), a Mexican consulate or the **Mexican tourist information numbers** (☎ 800-446-3942, 800-482-9832) in the USA and Canada. If you're traveling from Mexico into the USA at a busy time of year, have a look at the website of **US Customs & Border Protection** (www.cbp.gov), which posts waiting times at entry points.

SEA

If you'd like to combine snatches of Mexico with a life of ease on the high seas, take a cruise! On the Pacific route (the Mexican Riviera in cruise parlance), the main ports of call are Ensenada, Cabo San Lucas, Mazatlán, Puerto Vallarta and Acapulco, each with more than 100 cruises a year (over 200 at Puerto Vallarta); some cruises also call at Manzanillo, Zihuatanejo and Bahías de Huatulco, and a new cruise port is opening at Puerto Chiapas, near Tapachula.

Following are some of the cruise lines visiting Mexico, with US phone numbers:

Carnival Cruise Lines (☎ 888-227-6482; www.carnival.com)

Celebrity Cruises (☎ 800-722-5941; www.celebrity.com)

Crystal Cruises (☎ 800-804-1500; www.crystalcruises.com)

Holland America Line (☎ 877-724-5425; www.hollandamerica.com)

Norwegian Cruise Lines (☎ 800-327-7030; www.ncl.com)

P&O Cruises (☎ 415-382-8900; www.pocruises.com)

Princess Cruises (☎ 800-774-6237; www.princess.com)

Royal Caribbean International (☎ 800-398-9813; www.royalcaribbean.com)

GETTING AROUND

AIR

Flying is considerably cheaper between an inland city (Mexico City, Guadalajara or Oaxaca) and a coastal destination, than from one coastal destination to another. This is because nearly all flights head to/from Mexico City and Guadalajara, making it necessary to purchase two fares to get from coastal-point A to coastal-point B (via the inland city). Mazatlán, Tepic, Puerto Vallarta, Manzanillo, Colima, Lázaro Cárdenas, Acapulco, Puerto Escondido, Ixtapa-Zihuatanejo, Oaxaca, and Bahías de Huatulco all passenger airports.

Aeroméxico and Mexicana are the country's two largest airlines. There are also smaller ones, often flying to/from smaller cities on the coast that the big two companies don't bother with (see the boxed text, opposite, for websites and telephone numbers in Mexico). Information on specific flights can be found within the Getting There & Away sections of individual city sections.

AeroMexico Connect, Click Mexicana and Aeromar are low-cost carriers for Aeroméxico and Mexicana, and normally share their ticket offices and booking networks.

Tickets

Fares can depend on whether you fly at a busy or quiet time of day, week or year, and how far ahead you book and pay. High season generally corresponds to the Mexican holiday seasons (p274). Round-trip fares are usually simply twice the price of one-way tickets, though some advance-payment cheaper deals do exist.

MEXICAN DOMESTIC AIRLINES

Airline	Phone	Website	Areas served
Aeromar	☎ 800-237-66-27	www.aeromar.com.mx	Central Mexico, west, northeast, Gulf coast, southeast
Aeroméxico	☎ 800-021-40-00	www.aeromexico.com	Mexico City & more than 50 cities nationwide
AeroMexico Connect	☎ 800-800-23-76	www.aerolitoral.com	Central Mexico, Baja California, north, west, Gulf coast
Aviacsa	☎ 800-284-27-22	www.aviacsa.com	Mexico City & 19 other cities nationwide
Avolar	☎ 800-681-95-91	www.avolar.com.mx	Puebla, Acapulco, Tijuana, Hermosillo, Uruapan
Click Mexicana	☎ 800-122-54-25	www.clickmx.com	Mexico City & 16 other cities nationwide
Interjet	☎ 800-011-23-45	www.interjet.com.mx	Guadalajara, Toluca, Cancún, Monterrey
Magnicharters	☎ 800-201-14-04	www.magnicharters.com.mx	Mexico City, Guadalajara, Toluca, Aguascalientes, Monterrey, Bajío, Torreón, San Luis Potosí, Morelia, Mérida
Mexicana	☎ 800-502-20-00	www.mexicana.com	Mexico City and more than 50 cities nationwide

TRANSPORTATION

Here are examples of one-way fares to/from Mexico City for trips booked two weeks in advance:

To/from	Fare
Acapulco	M$1600
Bahías de Huatulco	M$1300
Guadalajara	M$1600
Ixtapa–Zihuatanejo	M$1800
Manzanillo	M$3000
Mazatlán	M$2500
Oaxaca	M$1500
Puerto Vallarta	M$2200

BICYCLE

Cycling is not a common way to tour Mexico's Pacific coast: reports of highway robbery, poor road surfaces and road hazards are deterrents. However, this method of moving up or down the coast is not impossible if you're prepared for the challenges. You should be very fit, use the best equipment you can muster and be able to handle your own repairs. Take the mountainous topography and hot climate into account when planning your route.

It's possible to rent bikes in many resort towns for short excursions, and the same places often offer guided rides.

BOAT

Vehicle and passenger ferries connecting Baja California with the Mexican mainland travel between La Paz and Mazatlán, and La Paz and Topolobampo, Sinaloa. For more information, see p115.

BUS

Mexico has a good road and bus network, and comfortable, frequent, reasonably priced bus services connect all cities. Most cities and towns have one main bus terminal where all long-distance buses arrive and depart. If there is no main terminal, different bus companies will have separate terminals scattered around town.

Baggage is safe if stowed in the bus's baggage hold, but get a receipt for it when you hand it over. Keep your most valuable documents (passport, money etc) on you, and keep them closely protected.

Classes
DELUXE

De lujo (deluxe) services, sometimes termed *ejecutivo* (executive), run mainly on the busy routes. They are swift, modern and comfortable, with reclining seats, adequate legroom, air-conditioning, few or no stops, toilets on board (but not necessarily toilet paper), and sometimes drinks or snacks.

1ST-CLASS

Primera (1a) clase buses have a comfortable numbered seat for each passenger. All sizable towns have 1st-class bus services. Standards of comfort are adequate at the very least. The buses usually have air-conditioning and a toilet, and they stop infrequently. They always show movies (often bad ones – not to disparage the life's work of a certain Jean-Claude

TRANSPORTATION

Van Damme) for most of the trip: too bad if you don't want to watch, as all seats face a video screen. As with deluxe buses, buy your ticket in the bus station before boarding.

2ND-CLASS

Segunda (2a) clase buses serve small towns and villages, and provide cheaper, slower travel on some intercity routes. Many 2nd-class services have no ticket office; you just pay your fare to the conductor. These buses tend to take slow, nontoll roads in and out of big cities and will stop anywhere to pick up passengers: if you board midroute you might make some of the trip standing. The small amount of money you save by traveling 2nd-class is not usually worth the discomfort or extra journey time entailed.

Second-class buses can also be less safe than 1st-class or deluxe buses, due to lower maintenance or driver standards, or because they are more vulnerable to being boarded by bandits on some roads. Out in the remoter areas, however, you'll often find that 2nd-class buses are the only buses available.

You may also encounter various other types of buses in your travels:
- *directo:* very few stops
- *semi-directo:* a few more stops than a *directo*
- *ordinario:* stops wherever passengers want to get on or off the bus

Costs

First-class buses typically cost roughly M$60 per hour of travel (70km to 80km). Deluxe buses may cost just 10% or 20% more than 1st-class, or about 60% more for super-deluxe services such as ETN, UNO and Turistar Ejecutivo. Second-class buses cost 10% or 20% less than 1st-class.

Reservations

For trips of up to four or five hours on busy routes, you can usually just go to the bus terminal, buy a ticket and head out without much delay. For longer trips, or routes with infrequent services, buy a ticket a day or more in advance.

Deluxe and 1st-class bus companies have computerized ticket systems that allow you to select your seat when you buy your ticket. Try to avoid the back of the bus, which is where the toilets are and the ride tends to be bumpiest.

CAR & MOTORCYCLE

Driving in Mexico is not as easy as it is in North America and Europe (much of Europe anyway), but few experiences can replace dodging donkeys and homemade speed bumps as you buzz along coastal Hwy 200 or chug up mountain roads in a VW Beetle. It's often the only way to reach those isolated beaches and tiny villages.

See p271 for a warning about the risk of highway robbery in some areas, and p285 for information on the paperwork required for bringing a vehicle into Mexico. For information on road maps, see p275.

Automobile Associations

Sectur, the Mexican tourism ministry, maintains a network of *Ángeles Verdes* (Green Angels) – bilingual mechanics in green uniforms and green trucks, who patrol 60,000km of major highways throughout the country daily during daylight hours looking for tourists in trouble. They make minor repairs, change tires, provide fuel and oil, and arrange towing and other assistance if necessary. Service is free; parts, gasoline and oil are provided at cost. If you are near a phone when your car has problems, you can call their **24-hour hotline** (☎ 078). There's a map of the roads they patrol at www.sectur.gob.mx/wb2 /sectur/sect_9454_rutas_carreteras.

Bring Your Own Vehicle

Drivers should know some Spanish and have basic mechanical knowledge, reserves of patience and access to extra cash for emergencies. Good makes of car to take to Mexico are Volkswagen, Nissan, General Motors and Ford, which have plants in Mexico and dealers in most big towns. A sedan with a trunk (boot) provides safer storage than a station wagon or hatchback. For security, have something to immobilize the steering wheel, and consider getting a kill switch installed.

Motorcycling in Mexico is not for the fainthearted. Roads and traffic can be rough, and parts and mechanics hard to come by. The parts you'll most easily find will be for Kawasaki, Honda and Suzuki bikes.

Driver's License

To drive a motor vehicle in Mexico, you need a valid driver's license from your home country.

Fuel & Spare Parts

All *gasolina* (gasoline) and diesel fuel in Mexico is sold by the government's monopoly, Pemex (Petróleos Mexicanos). Most towns, even small ones, have a Pemex station, and the stations are pretty common on most major roads. Nevertheless, in remote areas you should fill up whenever you can.

The gasoline on sale is all *sin plomo* (unleaded). At the time of research, a liter cost about M$7.60 (M$34.50 a US gallon). Gas stations have pump attendants (who appreciate a tip of M$2 to M$5).

Mexican mechanics are resourceful, and most repairs can be done quickly and inexpensively, but it still pays to take as many spare parts as you can manage (spare fuel filters are very useful). Tires (including spare), shock absorbers and suspension should be in good condition.

Hire

Auto rental in Mexico is expensive by US or European standards, but not hard to organize. You can book by internet, phone or in person, and pick up cars at city offices, airports, many big hotels and sometimes bus terminals.

Renters must provide a valid driver's license (your home license is OK), a passport and a major credit card, and are usually required to be aged at least 21 (or sometimes 25; otherwise, if you're aged 21 to 24 you may have to pay a surcharge). Be sure to read the small print of the rental agreement. In addition to the basic rental rate, you pay tax and insurance costs to the rental company, and the full insurance that rental companies encourage can almost double the basic cost. You'll usually have the option of taking liability-only insurance at a lower rate (about M$100 per day). Ask exactly what the insurance options cover: theft and damage insurance may only cover a percentage of costs. It's best to have plenty of liability coverage: Mexican law permits the jailing of drivers after an accident until they have met their obligations to third parties. The complimentary car-rental insurance offered with some US credit cards does not usually cover Mexico.

Local firms may or may not be cheaper than the big international ones. The international firms are far more likely to have decent roadside assistance and multiple offices. In most places the cheapest car available (often a Volkswagen Beetle) costs M$400 to M$600 a day including unlimited kilometers, insurance and tax. If you rent by the week or month or during the low season the per-day cost can come down by 20% to 40%.

Here is contact information (with Mexican phone numbers) for some major firms:

Alamo (☎ 800-849-80-01; www.alamo.com)
Avis (☎ 800-288-88-88; www.avis.com.mx)
Budget (☎ 55-5705-5061; www.budget.com.mx)
Dollar (☎ 998-886-23-00; www.dollar.com)
Hertz (☎ 800-709-50-00; www.hertz.com)
National (☎ 800-716-66-25; www.nationalcar.com.mx)
Thrifty (☎ 55-578-982-68; www.thrifty.com.mx)

Insurance

For information about motor insurance in Mexico, see p284.

Road Conditions

Many Mexican highways, even some toll highways, are not up to the standards of US, Canadian or European ones. Still, the main roads are serviceable and fairly fast when traffic is not heavy. Mexicans on the whole drive cautiously, and traffic density, poor surfaces and frequent hazards (potholes, speed bumps, animals, bicycles, children) all help to keep speeds down.

Road Hazards

Driving on a dark night is best avoided since unlit vehicles, rocks, pedestrians and animals on the roads are common. Hijackings and robberies do occur, most often after dark.

In towns and cities and on rural roads, be especially alert for stop signs, which read *Pare, Alto* or Stop, *topes* and *reductores* (speed bumps) and holes in the road. They are often not where you'd expect, and missing one can cost you a traffic fine or car damage. Speed bumps are also used to slow traffic on highways that pass through built-up areas: they are not always signed, and some of them are severe!

Road Rules

Drive on the right-hand side of the road. Speed limits range between 80km/h and 120km/h on open highways (less when highways pass through built-up areas), and between 30km/h and 50km/h in towns and cities. Seatbelts are obligatory for all occupants of a car, and children under five must be strapped into safety seats in the rear.

One-way streets are the rule in cities. Priority at street intersections is indicated by thin black and red rectangles containing white arrows. A black rectangle facing you means you have priority; a red one means you don't. The white arrows indicate the direction of traffic on the cross street; if the arrow points both ways, it's a two-way street.

HITCHHIKING

Hitchhiking is never entirely safe in any country in the world, and is not recommended. Travelers who decide to hitch should understand that they are taking a small but potentially serious risk. People who do choose to hitch will be safer if they travel in pairs and let someone know where they are planning to go. A woman traveling alone certainly should not hitchhike in Mexico, and even two women together is not advisable.

LOCAL TRANSPORTATION
Bicycle

Most Mexican towns and cities are flat enough to make cycling an option. Seek out the less traffic-infested routes and you should enjoy the experience. Even Acapulco has its biking enthusiasts. You can rent bikes in several towns and cities for M$100 to M$150 a day.

Boat

Here and there you may find yourself traveling by boat to an outlying beach, along a river or across a lake or lagoon. The craft are usually *lanchas* (fast, open, outboard boats). Fares vary widely: on average, costs are about M$10 a minute if you have to charter the whole boat (haggle!), or around M$10 for five to 10 minutes if it's a public service.

Bus

Generally known as *camiones*, local buses are often the cheapest way to get around cities and out to nearby towns and villages. They run everywhere frequently and are cheap. Fares in cities are rarely more than M$5. In many cities, fleets of small, modern microbuses have

replaced the noisy, dirty and crowded older buses.

Buses usually halt only at fixed *paradas* (bus stops), though in some places you can hold your hand out to stop one at any street corner.

Colectivo, Combi, Minibus & Pesero

These are all names for vehicles that function as something between a shared taxi and a bus, running along fixed urban routes usually displayed on the windshield. They're cheaper than taxis and quicker than buses. They will pick you up or drop you off on any corner along their route: to stop one, go to the curb and wave your hand. Tell the driver where you want to go. Usually, you pay at the end of the trip and the fare (a little higher than a bus fare) depends on how far you go. In some northern border towns, *pesero* is used to mean a city bus.

Taxi

Taxis are common in towns and cities, and surprisingly economical. City rides cost around M$10 per kilometer, and in some cities there's a posted fixed rate for journeys within defined central areas. If a taxi has a meter, you can ask the driver if it's working (*'¿Funciona el taxímetro?'*). If it's not, or if the taxi doesn't have a meter, establish the price of the ride before getting in (this may involve a bit of haggling).

Some airports and big bus terminals have a system of authorized ticket-taxis: you buy a fixed-price ticket to your destination from a special *taquilla* (ticket window) and then hand it to the driver instead of paying cash. This saves haggling and major rip-offs, but fares are usually higher than you could get on the street.

In some (usually rural) areas, some taxis operate on a *colectivo* basis, following set routes, often from one town or village to another, and picking up or dropping off passengers anywhere along that route. Fares per person are around one-quarter of the normal cab fare.

Health Dr David Goldberg

CONTENTS

Travelers to Pacific Mexico need to be concerned chiefly about food-borne diseases, though mosquito-borne infections can also be a problem. Most of these illnesses are not life threatening, but they can certainly have an impact on your trip or even ruin it. Besides getting the proper vaccinations, it's important that you bring along a good insect repellent and exercise great care in what you eat and drink – for the most part, you should not drink tap water.

BEFORE YOU GO

INSURANCE

Mexican medical treatment is generally inexpensive for common diseases and minor treatment, but if you suffer from a serious medical problem, you may want to find a private hospital or fly out for treatment. Travel insurance can typically cover the costs. Some US health insurance policies stay in effect (at least for a limited time) if you travel abroad, but it's worth checking exactly what you'll be covered for in Mexico. For people whose medical insurance or national health systems don't extend to Mexico – which includes most non-Americans – a travel policy is advisable. Check the Travel Services section of the **Lonely Planet website** (www.lonelyplanet.com.au/travel_services) for more information.

RECOMMENDED VACCINATIONS

The only required vaccine for entry into Mexico is yellow fever, and that's only if you're arriving from a yellow fever–infected country in Africa or South America. However, a number of vaccines are recommended (see table p292). Note that some of these are not approved for use by children and pregnant women – check with your physician.

MEDICAL CHECKLIST

It is a very good idea to carry a medical and first-aid kit with you, to help yourself in the case of minor illness or injury. Following is a list of items you should consider packing.

- acetaminophen/paracetamol (eg Tylenol) or aspirin
- adhesive or paper tape
- antibacterial ointment (eg Bactroban) for cuts and abrasions
- antibiotics
- antidiarrheal drugs (eg loperamide)
- antihistamines (for hay fever and allergic reactions)
- anti-inflammatory drugs (eg ibuprofen)
- bandages, gauze, gauze rolls
- DEET-containing insect repellent for the skin
- iodine tablets (for water purification)
- oral rehydration salts
- permethrin-containing insect spray for clothing, tents and bed nets
- pocket knife
- scissors, safety pins, tweezers
- steroid cream or cortisone (for poison ivy and other allergic rashes)
- sunblock
- syringes and sterile needles
- thermometer

INTERNET RESOURCES

It's usually a good idea to consult your government's travel health website before departure, if one is available.

Australia www.dfat.gov.au/travel
Canada www.hc-sc.gc.ca/english/index.html
New Zealand www.mfat.govt.nz/travel
UK www.dh.gov.uk/policyandguidance/healthadvicefor travellers/fs/en
USA www.cdc.gov/travel

HEALTH

Vaccine	Recommended for	Dosage	Side effects
hepatitis A	all travelers	1 dose before trip; booster 6-12 months later	soreness at injection site; headaches; body aches
typhoid	all travelers	4 capsules by mouth, 1 taken every other day	abdominal pain; nausea; rash
yellow fever	travelers arriving from a yellow fever–infected area in Africa or the Americas	1 dose lasts 10 years	headaches; body aches; severe reactions are rare
hepatitis B	long-term travelers in close contact with the local population	3 doses over 6-month period	soreness at injection site; low-grade fever
rabies	travelers who may have contact with animals and may not have access to medical care	3 doses over 3-4 week period	soreness at injection site; headaches; body aches
tetanus-diphtheria	all travelers who haven't had booster within 10 years	1 dose lasts 10 years	soreness at injection site
measles	travelers born after 1956 who've had only 1 measles vaccination	1 dose	fever; rash; joint pains; allergic reactions
chickenpox	travelers who've never had chickenpox	2 doses 1 month apart	fever; mild case of chickenpox

HEALTH

IN TRANSIT

DEEP VEIN THROMBOSIS (DVT)

Blood clots may form in the legs (deep vein thrombosis) during plane flights, chiefly because of prolonged immobility. The longer the flight, the greater the risk. Though most blood clots are reabsorbed uneventfully, some may break off and travel through the blood vessels to the lungs, where they could cause life-threatening complications.

The chief symptom of DVT is swelling or pain of the foot, ankle, or calf, usually but not always on just one side. When a blood clot travels to the lungs, it may cause chest pain and breathing difficulties. Travelers with any of these symptoms should immediately seek medical attention.

To prevent the development of DVT on long flights you should walk about the cabin, perform isometric compressions of the leg muscles (ie contract the leg muscles while sitting), drink plenty of fluids, and avoid alcohol and tobacco.

JET LAG & MOTION SICKNESS

Jet lag is common when crossing more than five time zones, resulting in insomnia, fatigue, malaise or nausea. To avoid jet lag try drinking plenty of fluids (nonalcoholic) and eating light meals. Upon arrival, get exposure to natural sunlight and readjust your schedule (for meals, sleep etc) as soon as possible.

Antihistamines such as dimenhydrinate (Dramamine) and meclizine (Antivert, Bonine) are usually the first choice for travelers treating motion sickness. Their main side effect is drowsiness. An herbal alternative is ginger, which works like a charm for some people.

IN MEXICO

AVAILABILITY & COST OF HEALTH CARE

There are a number of first-rate hospitals in Puerto Vallarta, Oaxaca city and Acapulco. In general, private facilities offer better care, though at greater cost, than public hospitals. Many doctors and hospitals expect payment in cash, regardless of whether you have travel health insurance.

Adequate medical care is available in other major cities, but facilities in rural areas may be limited. The **US consulate** (http://guadalajara .usconsulate.gov/puerto_vallarta.html) in Puerto Vallarta provides an online directory of local physicians and hospitals in the Puerto Vallarta area.

Mexican pharmacies are identified by a green cross and a 'Farmacia' sign.

INFECTIOUS DISEASES
Cholera
Only a handful of cases have been reported in Mexico over the last few years. Cholera vaccine is no longer recommended.

Hepatitis A
This illness occurs worldwide, but the incidence is higher in developing nations. Symptoms may include fever, malaise, jaundice, nausea, vomiting and abdominal pain. The vaccine for hepatitis A is extremely safe and highly effective. If you get a booster six to 12 months later, it lasts for at least 10 years. You really should get it before you go to Mexico. Because the safety of hepatitis A vaccine has not been established for pregnant women or children under the age of two, they should instead be given a gammaglobulin injection.

Hepatitis B
The hepatitis B vaccine is recommended only for long-term travelers (on the road more than six months) who expect to live in rural areas or have close physical contact with the local population. Additionally, the vaccine is recommended for anyone who anticipates sexual contact with the local inhabitants or a possible need for medical, dental or other treatments while abroad, especially if a need for transfusions or injections is expected.

The hepatitis B vaccine is safe and highly effective. However, a total of three injections is necessary to establish full immunity.

Malaria
Malaria occurs in every country in Central America, including parts of Mexico. It's transmitted by mosquito bites, usually between dusk and dawn. The main symptom is high spiking fevers, which may be accompanied by chills, sweats, headaches, body aches, weakness, vomiting, or diarrhea. Severe cases may involve the central nervous system and lead to seizures, confusion, coma and death.

Taking malaria pills is recommended when visiting rural areas in the states of Oaxaca, Chiapas, Sinaloa and Nayarit; and when visiting an area between 24° and 28° north latitude, and 106° and 110° west longitude, which includes parts of the states of Sonora, Chihuahua and Durango.

For Mexico, the first-choice malaria pill is chloroquine, taken once weekly in a dosage of 500mg, starting one to two weeks before arrival and continuing through the trip and for four weeks after departure. Protecting yourself against mosquito bites (see p294) is just as important as taking malaria pills, since no pills are 100% effective.

Malaria pills are not recommended for the major resorts along the Pacific coast.

Rabies
Most cases in Mexico are related to dog bites, but bats and other wild species remain important sources of infection.

Rabies vaccine is safe, but a full series requires three injections and is quite expensive. Those at high risk for rabies, such as animal handlers and spelunkers (cave explorers), should certainly get the vaccine. In addition, those at lower risk for animal bites should consider asking for the vaccine if they are traveling to remote areas and might not have access to appropriate medical care if needed. The treatment for a possibly rabid bite consists of rabies vaccine with rabies immune globulin. It's effective, but must be given promptly. Most travelers don't need rabies vaccine.

Typhoid Fever
Typhoid fever is caused by ingestion of food or water contaminated by a species of *Salmonella* known as *Salmonella typhi*.

Unless you expect to take all your meals in major hotels and restaurants, typhoid vaccine is a good idea. It's usually given orally, but is also available as an injection. Neither vaccine is approved for use in children under the age of two.

The drug of choice for typhoid fever is usually a quinolone antibiotic such as ciprofloxacin (Cipro) or levofloxacin (Levaquin), which many travelers carry for treatment of travelers' diarrhea. However, if you self-treat for typhoid fever, you may also need to self-treat for malaria, since the symptoms of the two diseases can be indistinguishable.

Yellow Fever
Yellow fever no longer occurs in Mexico. Even so, authorities still require you to have been vaccinated against yellow fever before entry into Mexico if you're arriving from a country in Africa or South America where yellow fever occurs.

HEALTH

Other Infections

Brucellosis, Chagas disease, gnathostomiasis, histoplasmosis, HIV/AIDS, leishmaniasis, tularemia and typhus are all reported in the area. The best way to prevent these is to watch what you eat, protect yourself from bug bites and wear condoms.

TRAVELERS' DIARRHEA

To prevent diarrhea, avoid tap water unless it has been boiled, filtered or chemically disinfected (iodine tablets); only eat fresh fruits or vegetables if cooked or peeled; be wary of dairy products that might contain unpasteurized milk; and be highly selective when eating food from street vendors.

If you develop diarrhea, be sure to drink plenty of fluids, preferably an oral rehydration solution containing lots of salt and sugar. A few loose stools don't require treatment, but if you start having more than four or five stools a day you should start taking an antibiotic (usually a quinolone drug) and an antidiarrheal agent (such as Loperamide). If diarrhea is bloody or persists for more than 72 hours or is accompanied by fever, shaking chills or severe abdominal pain you should seek medical attention.

ENVIRONMENTAL HAZARDS
Air Pollution

Air pollution may be a significant problem. Pollution is typically most severe from December to May. Minimize the risk by staying indoors, avoiding outdoor exercise and drinking plenty of fluids.

Animal Bites

Do not attempt to pet, handle or feed any animal, with the exception of domestic animals known to be free of any infectious disease. Most animal injuries are directly related to a person's attempt to touch or feed the animal.

Any bite or scratch by a mammal, including bats, should be promptly and thoroughly cleansed with large amounts of soap and water, followed by application of an antiseptic such as iodine or alcohol. It may also be advisable to start an antibiotic, since wounds caused by animal bites and scratches frequently become infected. One of the newer quinolones, such as levofloxacin (Levaquin), which many travelers carry in case of diarrhea, would be an appropriate choice.

Mosquito Bites

To prevent mosquito bites, wear long sleeves, long pants, hats and shoes (rather than sandals). Bring along a good insect repellent, preferably one containing DEET, which should be applied to exposed skin and clothing, but not to eyes, mouth, cuts, wounds or irritated skin. Products containing lower concentrations of DEET are as effective, but for shorter periods of time. In general, adults and children over 12 should use preparations containing 25% to 35% DEET, which usually lasts about six hours. Children between two and 12 years of age should use preparations containing no more than 10% DEET, applied sparingly, which will usually last about three hours. Neurological toxicity has been reported from DEET, especially in children, but appears to be extremely uncommon and generally related to overuse. Don't use DEET-containing compounds on children under the age of two.

Insect repellents containing certain botanical products, including oil of eucalyptus and soybean oil, are effective but last only 1½ to two hours. Where there is a high risk of malaria or yellow fever, use DEET-containing repellents. Products based on citronella are not effective.

For additional protection, apply permethrin to clothing, shoes, tents and bed nets. Permethrin treatments are safe and remain effective for at least two weeks, even when items are laundered. Permethrin should not be applied directly to the skin.

Don't sleep with the window open unless there is a screen. If sleeping outdoors or in accommodation that allows entry of mosquitoes, use a bed net treated with permethrin, with edges tucked in under the mattress. The mesh size should be less than 1.5mm. Alternatively, use a mosquito coil, which will fill the room with insecticide through the night. Repellent-impregnated wristbands are not effective.

Snake & Scorpion Bites

Venomous snakes in the region include the bushmaster, the fer-de-lance, the coral snake and various species of rattlesnakes. In the event of a venomous snake bite, place the victim at rest, keep the bitten area immobilized, and move them immediately to the nearest medical facility. Avoid tourniquets, which are no longer recommended.

Scorpions are a problem in much of Mexico. If stung, you should immediately apply ice or cold packs, immobilize the affected body part and go to the nearest emergency room. To prevent scorpion stings, be sure to inspect and shake out clothing, shoes and sleeping bags before use, and wear gloves and protective clothing when working around piles of wood or leaves.

Sun

To protect yourself from excessive sun exposure or heatstroke, you should stay out of the midday sun, wear sunglasses and a wide-brimmed hat, and apply sunscreen with SPF 15 or higher, providing both UVA and UVB protection. Sunscreen should be generously applied to all exposed parts of the body approximately 30 minutes before sun exposure and be reapplied after swimming or vigorous activity. Drink plenty of fluids and avoid strenuous exercise when the temperature is high.

Tick Bites

To protect yourself from tick bites, follow the same precautions as for mosquitoes, except that boots are preferable to shoes, with pants tucked in. Be sure to perform a thorough tick check at the end of each day.

Water

Tap water in Mexico is generally not safe to drink. Vigorous boiling for one minute is the most effective means of water purification. At altitudes greater than 2000m, boil for three minutes.

Another option is to disinfect water with iodine pills. Instructions are usually enclosed and should be carefully followed. Or you can add 2% tincture of iodine to one quart or liter of water (five drops to clear water, 10 drops to cloudy water) and let stand for 30 minutes. If the water is cold, a longer time may be required. The taste of iodinated water can be improved by adding vitamin C (ascorbic acid). Don't consume iodinated water for more than a few weeks. Pregnant women, those with a history of thyroid disease and those allergic to iodine should not drink iodinated water.

A number of water filters are on the market. Those with smaller pores (reverse osmosis filters) provide the broadest protection, but they are relatively large and are readily plugged by debris. Those with somewhat larger pores (microstrainer filters) are ineffective against viruses, although they remove other organisms. The small 'Steripen' filter is also effective.

TRAVELING WITH CHILDREN & WOMEN'S HEALTH

In general, it's safe for children and pregnant women to go to Mexico. However, because some of the vaccines listed previously are not approved for use by children or during pregnancy, these travelers should be particularly careful not to drink tap water or consume any questionable food or beverage. Also, when traveling with children, make sure they're up to date on all routine immunizations. It's sometimes appropriate to give children some of their vaccines a little early before visiting a developing nation. You should discuss this with your pediatrician. If pregnant, bear in mind that should a complication such as premature labor develop while abroad, the quality of medical care may not be comparable to that in your home country.

Since yellow fever vaccine is not recommended for pregnant women or children less than nine months old, if you are arriving from a country with yellow fever, obtain a waiver letter, preferably written on letterhead stationery and bearing the stamp used by official immunization centers to validate the International Certificate of Vaccination.

HEALTH

Language

CONTENTS

The predominant language of Mexico is Spanish. Mexican Spanish is unlike Castilian Spanish (the language of much of Spain) in two main respects: in Mexico the Castilian lisp has more or less disappeared and numerous indigenous words have been adopted. About 50 indigenous languages are spoken as a first language by more than seven million people, and about 15% of these don't speak Spanish.

Travelers in cities, towns and larger villages can almost always find someone who speaks at least some English. All the same, it is advantageous and courteous to know at least a few words and phrases in Spanish. Mexicans will generally respond much more positively if you attempt to speak to them in their own language.

It's easy enough to pick up some basic Spanish, and for those who want to learn the language in greater depth, courses are available in several cities in Mexico (see Language Courses, p271). You can also study using books, records and tapes before you leave home. These resources are often available for loan from public libraries. Evening or college courses are also an excellent way to get started.

For a more comprehensive guide to the Spanish of Mexico, get a copy of Lonely Planet's *Mexican Spanish* phrasebook. For

words and phrases that will come in handy when dining, see p39.

Language is an ever-evolving monster, and Mexicans have come up with some fabulous slang terms over the years. There's a Mexican slang dictionary at www.mexico guru.com.

PRONUNCIATION

Spanish spelling is phonetically consistent, meaning that there's a clear and consistent relationship between what you see in writing and how it's pronounced. In addition, most Spanish sounds have English equivalents, so English speakers shouldn't have too much trouble being understood.

Vowels

a	as in 'father'
e	as in 'met'
i	as in 'marine'
o	as in 'or' (without the 'r' sound)
u	as in 'rule'; the 'u' is not pronounced after **q** and in the letter combinations **gue** and **gui**, unless it's marked with a diaeresis (eg *argüir*), in which case it's pronounced as English 'w'
y	at the end of a word or when it stands alone, it's pronounced as the Spanish **i** (eg *ley*); between vowels within a word it's as the 'y' in 'yonder'

Consonants

As a rule, Spanish consonants resemble their English counterparts. The exceptions are listed below.

While the consonants **ch**, **ll** and **ñ** are generally considered distinct letters, **ch** and **ll** are now often listed alphabetically under **c** and **l** respectively. The letter **ñ** is still treated as a separate letter and comes after **n** in dictionaries.

b	similar to English 'b,' but softer; referred to as 'b larga'
c	as in 'celery' before **e** and **i**; otherwise as English 'k'
ch	as in 'church'
d	as in 'dog,' but between vowels and after **l** or **n**, the sound is closer to the 'th' in 'this'

g	as the 'ch' in the Scottish *loch* before **e** and **i** ('kh' in our guides to pronunciation); elsewhere, as in 'go'
h	invariably silent. If your name begins with this letter, listen carefully if you're waiting to be called.
j	as the 'ch' in Scottish *loch* (written as 'kh' in our guides to pronunciation)
ll	varies between the 'y' in 'yes' and the 'lli' in 'million'
ñ	as the 'ni' in 'onion'
r	a short **r** except at the beginning of a word, and after **l**, **n** or **s**, when it's often rolled
rr	very strongly rolled (not reflected in the pronunciation guides)
v	similar to English 'b,' but softer; referred to as 'b corta'
x	usually pronounced as **j** above; in some indigenous place names it's pronounced as an 's'; as in 'taxi' in other instances
z	as the 's' in 'sun'

Word Stress

In general, words ending in vowels or the letters **n** or **s** have stress on the next-to-last syllable, while those with other endings have stress on the last syllable. Thus *vaca* (cow) and *caballos* (horses) both carry stress on the next-to-last syllable, while *ciudad* (city) and *infeliz* (unhappy) are both stressed on the last syllable.

Written accents will almost always appear in words that don't follow the rules above, eg *sótano* (basement), *porción* (portion), *América*.

GENDER & PLURALS

In Spanish, nouns are either masculine or feminine, and there are rules to help determine gender (there are of course some exceptions). Feminine nouns generally end with -**a** or with the groups -**ción**, -**sión** or -**dad**. Other endings typically signify a masculine noun. Endings for adjectives also change to agree with the gender of the noun they modify (masculine/feminine -**o**/-**a**). Where both masculine and feminine forms are included in this language guide, they are separated by a slash, with the masculine form first, eg *perdido/a*.

If a noun or adjective ends in a vowel, the plural is formed by adding **s** to the end. If it ends in a consonant, the plural is formed by adding **es** to the end.

MAKING A RESERVATION
(for phone or written requests)

To ...	*A ...*
From ...	*De ...*
Date	*Fecha*
I'd like to book ...	*Quisiera reservar ...* (see under 'Accommodations' for bed and room options)
in the name of ...	*en nombre de ...*
for the nights of ...	*para las noches del ...*
credit card ...	*tarjeta de crédito ...*
number	*número*
expiration date	*fecha de vencimiento*
Please confirm ...	*Puede confirmar ...*
availability	*la disponibilidad*
price	*el precio*

ACCOMMODATIONS

I'm looking	*Estoy*	e·stoy
for ...	*buscando ...*	boos·kan·do ...
Where is ...?	*¿Dónde hay ...?*	don·de ai ...
a cabin/cabaña	*una cabaña*	oo·na ca·ba·nya
a camping	*un área para*	oon a·re·a pa·ra
ground	*acampar*	a·kam·par
a guesthouse	*una pensión*	oo·na pen·syon
a hotel	*un hotel*	oon o·tel
a lodging	*una casa de*	oo·na ka·sa de
house	*huéspedes*	wes·pe·des
a posada	*una posada*	oo·na po·sa·da
a youth hostel	*un albergue*	oon al·ber·ge
	juvenil	khoo·ve·neel

Are there any rooms available?

¿Hay habitaciones	ay a·bee·ta·syon·es
disponibles?	dees·po·nee·bles

I'd like a ...	*Quisiera una*	kee·sye·ra oo·na
room.	*habitación ...*	a·bee·ta·syon ...
double	*doble*	do·ble
single	*individual*	een·dee·vee·dwal
twin	*con dos camas*	kon dos ka·mas

How much is it	*¿Cuánto cuesta*	kwan·to kwes·ta
per ...?	*por ...?*	por ...
night	*noche*	no·che
person	*persona*	per·so·na
week	*semana*	se·ma·na

full board	*pensión*	pen·syon
	completa	kom·ple·ta
private/shared	*baño privado/*	ba·nyo pree·va·do/
bathroom	*compartido*	kom·par·tee·do
too expensive	*demasiado caro*	de·ma·sya·do ka·ro
cheaper	*más económico*	mas e·ko·no·mee·ko
discount	*descuento*	des·kwen·to

Does it include breakfast?
  ¿Incluye el desayuno?   een-*kloo*-ye el de-sa-*yoo*-no
May I see the room?
  ¿Puedo ver la   *pwe*-do ver la
    habitación?   a-bee-ta-*syon*
I don't like it.
  No me gusta.   no me *goos*-ta
It's fine. I'll take it.
  Está bien. La tomo.   es-ta byen la *to*-mo
I'm leaving now.
  Me voy ahora.   me *voy* a-*o*-ra

CONVERSATION & ESSENTIALS

When approaching a stranger for information you should always extend a greeting, and use only the polite form of address, especially with the police and public officials. Young people may be less likely to expect this, but it's best to stick to the polite form unless you're quite sure you won't offend by using the informal mode. The polite form is used in all cases in this guide; where options are given, the form is indicated by the abbreviations 'pol' and 'inf.'

Saying *por favor* (please) and *gracias* (thank you) are second nature to most Mexicans and a recommended tool in your travel kit.

Hi.	*Hola.*	o-la (inf)
Hello.	*Buen día.*	bwe-n *dee*-a
Good morning.	*Buenos días.*	bwe-nos *dee*-as
Good afternoon.	*Buenas tardes.*	bwe-nas *tar*-des
Good evening/	*Buenas noches.*	bwe-nas *no*-ches
night.		
Goodbye.	*Adiós.*	a-*dyos*
See you soon.	*Hasta luego.*	as-ta *lwe*-go
Yes.	*Sí.*	see
No.	*No.*	no
Please.	*Por favor.*	por fa-*vor*
Thank you.	*Gracias.*	*gra*-syas
Many thanks.	*Muchas gracias.*	moo-chas *gra*-syas
You're welcome.	*De nada.*	de *na*-da
Apologies.	*Perdón.*	per-*don*
May I?	*Permiso.*	per-*mee*-so
Excuse me.	*Disculpe.*	dees-*kool*-pe

  (used before a request or when apologizing)

How are things?
  ¿Qué tal?   ke tal
What's your name?
  ¿Cómo se llama usted?   ko-mo se *ya*-ma oo-*sted* (pol)
  ¿Cómo te llamas?   ko-mo te *ya*-mas (inf)

SIGNS

Entrada	Entrance
Salida	Exit
Información	Information
Abierto	Open
Cerrado	Closed
Prohibido	Prohibited
Comisaria	Police Station
Servicios/Baños	Toilets
Hombres/Varones	Men
Mujeres/Damas	Women

My name is ...
  Me llamo ...   me *ya*-mo ...
It's a pleasure to meet you.
  Mucho gusto.   moo-cho *goos*-to
The pleasure is mine.
  El gusto es mío.   el *goos*-to es *mee*-o
Where are you from?
  ¿De dónde es/eres?   de don-de es/*er*-es (pol/inf)
I'm from ...
  Soy de ...   soy de ...
Where are you staying?
  ¿Dónde está alojado?   don-de es-ta a-lo-*kha*-do (pol)
  ¿Dónde estás alojado?   don-de es-tas a-lo-*kha*-do (inf)
May I take a photo?
  ¿Puedo sacar una foto?   pwe-do sa-*kar* oo-na *fo*-to

DIRECTIONS

How do I get to ...?
  ¿Cómo llego a ...?   ko-mo ye-go a ...
Is it far?
  ¿Está lejos?   es-ta *le*-khos
Go straight ahead.
  Siga/Vaya derecho/   see-ga/va-ya de-*re*-cho/
    directo.   dee-*rek*-to
Turn left.
  Doble a la izquierda.   do-ble a la ees-*kyer*-da
Turn right.
  Doble a la derecha.   do-ble a la de-*re*-cha
Can you show me (on the map)?
  ¿Me lo podría señalar   me lo po-*dree*-a se-nya-*lar*
    (en el mapa)?   (en el *ma*-pa)

north	*norte*	*nor*-te
south	*sur*	soor
east	*este*	*es*-te
west	*oeste*	o-*es*-te
here	*aquí*	a-*kee*
there	*ahí*	a-*ee*
avenue	*avenida*	a-ve-*nee*-da
block	*cuadra*	*kwa*-dra
street	*calle/paseo*	*ka*-lye/pa-*se*-o

HEALTH

I'm sick.
  Estoy enfermo/a.   es·toy en·*fer*·mo/a
I need a doctor.
  Necesito un doctor.   ne·se·*see*·to oon dok·*tor*
Where's the hospital?
  ¿Dónde está el hospital?   don·de es·*ta* el os·pee·*tal*
I'm pregnant.
  Estoy embarazada.   es·toy em·ba·ra·*sa*·da
I've been vaccinated.
  Estoy vacunado/a.   es·toy va·koo·*na*·do/a

I have ...	*Tengo ...*	*ten*·go ...
diarrhea	*diarrea*	dya·*re*·a
nausea	*náusea*	*now*·se·a
a headache	*un dolor de cabeza*	oon do·*lor* de ka·*be*·sa
a cough	*tos*	tos

I'm allergic to ...	*Soy alérgico/a a ...*	soy a·*ler*·khee·ko/a a ...
antibiotics	*los antibióticos*	los an·tee·*byo*·tee·kos
penicillin	*la penicilina*	la pe·nee·see·*lee*·na
peanuts	*los cacahuates*	los ka·ka·*wa*·tes

I'm ...	*Soy ...*	soy ...
asthmatic	*asmático/a*	as·*ma*·tee·ko/a
diabetic	*diabético/a*	dya·be·*tee*·ko/a
epileptic	*epiléptico/a*	e·pee·*lep*·tee·ko/a

LANGUAGE DIFFICULTIES

Do you speak (English)?
  ¿Habla/Hablas (inglés)?   a·bla/a·blas (een·*gles*) (pol/inf)
Does anyone here speak English?
  ¿Hay alguien que hable inglés?   ai al·*gyen* ke a·ble een·*gles*
I (don't) understand.
  (No) Entiendo.   (no) en·*tyen*·do
How do you say ...?
  ¿Cómo se dice ...?   *ko*·mo se *dee*·se ...
What does ...mean?
  ¿Qué significa ...?   ke seeg·nee·*fee*·ka ...

Could you please ...?	*¿Puede ..., por favor?*	*pwe*·de ... por fa·*vor*
repeat that	*repetirlo*	re·pe·*teer*·lo
speak more slowly	*hablar más despacio*	a·*blar* mas des·*pa*·syo
write it down	*escribirlo*	es·kree·*beer*·lo

NUMBERS

1	*uno*	*oo*·no
2	*dos*	dos
3	*tres*	tres
4	*cuatro*	*kwa*·tro

5	*cinco*	*seen*·ko
6	*seis*	says
7	*siete*	*sye*·te
8	*ocho*	*o*·cho
9	*nueve*	*nwe*·ve
10	*diez*	dyes
11	*once*	*on*·se
12	*doce*	*do*·se
13	*trece*	*tre*·se
14	*catorce*	ka·*tor*·se
15	*quince*	*keen*·se
16	*dieciséis*	dye·see·*says*
17	*diecisiete*	dye·see·*sye*·te
18	*dieciocho*	dye·see·*o*·cho
19	*diecinueve*	dye·see·*nwe*·ve
20	*veinte*	*vayn*·te
21	*veintiuno*	vayn·tee·*oo*·no
30	*treinta*	*trayn*·ta
31	*treinta y uno*	trayn·ta ee *oo*·no
40	*cuarenta*	kwa·*ren*·ta
50	*cincuenta*	seen·*kwen*·ta
60	*sesenta*	se·*sen*·ta
70	*setenta*	se·*ten*·ta
80	*ochenta*	o·*chen*·ta
90	*noventa*	no·*ven*·ta
100	*cien*	syen
101	*ciento uno*	syen·to *oo*·no
200	*doscientos*	do·*syen*·tos
1000	*mil*	meel
5000	*cinco mil*	*seen*·ko meel

PAPERWORK

birth certificate	certificado de nacimiento
border (frontier)	la frontera
car-owner's title	título de propiedad
car registration	registro
customs	aduana
driver's license	licencia de manejar
identification	identificación
immigration	migración
insurance	seguro
passport	pasaporte
temporary vehicle import permit	permiso de importación temporal de vehículo
tourist card	tarjeta de turista
visa	visado

SHOPPING & SERVICES

I'd like to buy ...
Quisiera comprar ...   kee·sye·ra kom·prar ...
I'm just looking.
Sólo estoy mirando.   so·lo es·toy mee·ran·do
May I look at it?
¿Puedo verlo/la?   pwe·do ver·lo/la
How much is it?
¿Cuánto cuesta?   kwan·to kwes·ta
That's too expensive for me.
Es demasiado caro   es de·ma·sya·do ka·ro
para mí.   pa·ra mee
Could you lower the price?
¿Podría bajar un poco   po·dree·a ba·khar oon po·ko
el precio?   el pre·syo
I don't like it.
No me gusta.   no me goos·ta
I'll take it.
Lo llevo.   lo ye·vo

I'm looking for (the) ...	Estoy buscando ...	es·toy boos·kan·do
ATM	el cajero automático	el ka·khe·ro ow·to·ma·tee·ko
bank	el banco	el ban·ko
bookstore	la librería	la lee·bre·ree·a
exchange house	la casa de cambio	la ka·sa de kam·byo
general store	la tienda	la tyen·da
laundry	la lavandería	la la·van·de·ree·a
market	el mercado	el mer·ka·do
pharmacy/ chemist	la farmacia	la far·ma·sya
post office	la oficina de correos	la o·fee·see·na de ko·re·os
supermarket	el supermercado	el soo·per·mer·ka·do
tourist office	la oficina de turismo	la o·fee·see·na de too·rees·mo

Do you accept ...? ¿Aceptan ...?   a·sep·tan ...

American dollars	dólares americanos	do·la·res a·me·ree·ka·nos
credit cards	tarjetas de crédito	tar·khe·tas de kre·dee·to
traveler's checks	cheques de viajero	che·kes de vya·khe·ro

less	menos	me·nos
more	más	mas
large	grande	gran·de
small	pequeño/a	pe·ke·nyo/a

What time does it open/close?
¿A qué hora abre/   a ke o·ra a·bre/
cierra?   sye·ra
I want to change some money/traveler's checks.
Quisiera cambiar dinero/   kee·sye·ra kam·byar dee·ne·ro/
cheques de viajero.   che·kes de vya·khe·ro
What is the exchange rate?
¿Cuál es el tipo de   kwal es el tee·po de
cambio?   kam·byo
I want to call ...
Quisiera llamar a ...   kee·sye·ra lya·mar a ...

airmail	correo aéreo	ko·re·o a·e·re·o
letter	carta	kar·ta
registered (mail)	certificado	ser·tee·fee·ka·do
stamps	timbres/ estampillas	teem·bres/ es·tam·pee·yas

TIME & DATES

What time is it?
¿Qué hora es?   ke o·ra es
It's one o'clock.
Es la una.   es la oo·na
It's seven o'clock.
Son las siete.   son las sye·te
Half past two.
Dos y media.   dos ee me·dya

midnight	medianoche	me·dya·no·che
noon	mediodía	me·dyo·dee·a
now	ahora	a·o·ra
today	hoy	oy
tonight	esta noche	es·ta no·che
tomorrow	mañana	ma·nya·na
yesterday	ayer	a·yer

Monday	lunes	loo·nes
Tuesday	martes	mar·tes
Wednesday	miércoles	myer·ko·les
Thursday	jueves	khwe·ves
Friday	viernes	vyer·nes
Saturday	sábado	sa·ba·do
Sunday	domingo	do·meen·go

January	*enero*	e·*ne*·ro
February	*febrero*	fe·*bre*·ro
March	*marzo*	*mar*·so
April	*abril*	a·*breel*
May	*mayo*	*ma*·yo
June	*junio*	*khoo*·nyo
July	*julio*	*khoo*·lyo
August	*agosto*	a·*gos*·to
September	*septiembre*	sep·*tyem*·bre
October	*octubre*	ok·*too*·bre
November	*noviembre*	no·*vyem*·bre
December	*diciembre*	dee·*syem*·bre

TRANSPORT
Public Transport

What time does	¿*A qué hora ...*	a ke *o*·ra ...
... leave/arrive?	*sale/llega?*	*sa*·le/ye·ga
the boat	*el barco*	el *bar*·ko
the bus (city)	*el camión*	el ka·*myon*
the bus (intercity)	*el autobús*	el ow·to·*boos*
the minibus	*el pesero*	el pe·*se*·ro
the plane	*el avión*	el a·*vyon*

the airport	*el aeropuerto*	el a·e·ro·*pwer*·to
the bus station	*la estación de*	la es·ta·*syon* de
	autobuses	ow·to·*boo*·ses
the bus stop	*la parada de*	la pa·*ra*·da de
	autobuses	ow·to·*boo*·ses
a luggage locker	*un casillero*	oon ka·see·*ye*·ro
the ticket office	*la boletería*	la bo·le·te·*ree*·a

A ticket to ..., please.
Un boleto a ..., por favor.   oon bo·*le*·to a ... por fa·*vor*
What's the fare to ...?
¿Cuánto cuesta hasta ...?   kwan·to *kwes*·ta *a*·sta ...

student's	*de estudiante*	de es·too·*dyan*·te
1st class	*primera clase*	pree·*me*·ra *kla*·se
2nd class	*segunda clase*	se·*goon*·da *kla*·se
single/one way	*viaje sencillo*	vee·*a*·khe sen·*see*·yo
round-trip	*redondo*	re·*don*·do
taxi	*taxi*	*tak*·see

Private Transport

I'd like to	*Quisiera*	kee·*sye*·ra
hire a/an ...	*rentar ...*	ren·*tar* ...
4WD	*un cuatro por*	oon *kwa*·tro por
	cuatro	*kwa*·tro
car	*un coche*	oon *ko*·che
motorbike	*una moto*	*oo*·na *mo*·to

bicycle	*bicicleta*	bee·see·*kle*·ta
hitchhike	*pedir aventón*	pe·*deer* a·ven·*ton*
pickup (ute)	*pickup*	*pee*·kop
truck	*camión/*	ka·*myon*/
	camioneta	ka·myo·*ne*·ta

ROAD SIGNS
Though Mexico mostly uses the familiar international road signs, you should be prepared to encounter these other signs as well:

Acceso	Entrance
Estacionamiento	Parking
Camino en Reparación	Road Repairs
Ceda el Paso	Give way
Conserve Su Derecha	Keep to the Right
Curva Peligrosa	Dangerous Curve
Derrumbes	Landslides
Despacio	Slow
Desviación	Detour
Dirección Única	One way
Escuela (Zona Escolar)	School (zone)
Hombres Trabajando	Men at Work
Mantenga Su Derecha	Keep to the Right
No Adelantar	No Overtaking
No Hay Paso	Road Closed
Pare/Stop/Alto	Stop
Peaje	Toll
Peligro	Danger
Prepare Su Cuota	Have Toll Ready
Prohibido Aparcar/	No Parking
** No Estacionar**	
Prohibido el Paso	No Entry
Puente Angosto	Narrow Bridge
Salida de Autopista	Freeway/Highway Exit
Topes/Vibradores	Speed Bumps
Tramo en Reparación	Road Under Repair
Vía Corta	Short Route (often
	a toll road)
Vía Cuota	Toll Highway

Where's a petrol station?
¿Dónde hay una   *don*·de ai oo·na
gasolinera?   ga·so·lee·*ne*·ra
How much is a liter of gasoline?
¿Cuánto cuesta el litro   kwan·to *kwes*·ta el *lee*·tro
de gasolina?   de ga·so·*lee*·na
Please fill it up.
Lleno, por favor.   *ye*·no por fa·*vor*
I'd like (100) pesos worth.
Quiero (cien) pesos.   *kye*·ro (syen) *pe*·sos

diesel	*diesel*	*dee*·sel
gas (petrol)	*gasolina*	ga·so·*lee*·na
unleaded	*gasolina sin*	ga·so·*lee*·na seen
	plomo	*plo*·mo
oil	*aceite*	a·*say*·te
tire	*llanta*	*yan*·ta
puncture	*agujero*	a·goo·*khe*·ro

Is this the road to (...)?
¿Por aquí se va a (...)?
por a·*kee* se va a (...)

(How long) Can I park here?
¿(Por cuánto tiempo) Puedo estacionarme aquí?
(por *kwan*·to *tyem*·po) pwe·do ess·ta·syo·*nar*·me a·*kee*

Where do I pay?
¿Dónde se paga?
don·de se *pa*·ga

I need a mechanic/tow truck.
Necesito un mecánico/remolque.
ne·se·*see*·to oon me·*ka*·nee·ko/re·*mol*·ke

Is there a garage near here?
¿Hay un taller mecánico cerca de aquí?
ai oon ta·*yer* me·*ka*·nee·ko ser·ka de a·*kee*

The car has broken down (in ...).
El coche se descompuso (en ...).
el *ko*·che se des·kom·*poo*·so (en ...)

The motorbike won't start.
La moto no arranca.
la *mo*·to no a·*ran*·ka

I have a flat tire.
Tengo una llanta ponchada.
ten·go oo·na yan·ta pon·*cha*·da

I've run out of petrol.
Me quedé sin gasolina.
me ke·*de* seen ga·so·*lee*·na

I've had an accident.
Tuve un accidente.
too·ve oon ak·see·*den*·te

TRAVEL WITH CHILDREN

I need ...
Necesito ...
ne·se·*see*·to ...

Do you have ...?
¿Hay ...?
ai ...

a car baby seat
un asiento de seguridad para bebés
oon a·*syen*·to de se·goo·ree·*dad* pa·ra be·bes

a child-minding service
un club para niños
oon kloob pa·*ra* nee·nyos

a children's menu
un menú infantil
oon me·*noo* een·fan·*teel*

a day care
una guardería
oo·na gwar·de·*ree*·a

(disposable) diapers/nappies
pañales (de usar y tirar)
pa·*nya*·les de oo·*sar* ee tee·*rar*

an (English-speaking) babysitter
una niñera (que hable inglés)
oo·na nee·*nye*·ra (ke a·bla een·*gles*)

formula (milk)
leche en polvo para bebés
le·che en *pol*·vo pa·ra be·*bes*

a high chair
una silla para bebé
oo·na *see*·ya pa·ra be·*be*

a potty
una bacinica
oo·na ba·see·*nee*·ka

a stroller
una carreola
oona ka·re·*o*·la

Do you mind if I breast-feed here?
¿Le molesta que dé el pecho aquí?
le mo·*les*·ta ke de el *pe*·cho a·*kee*

Are children allowed?
¿Se admiten niños?
se ad·*mee*·ten *nee*·nyos

Also available from Lonely Planet:
Mexican Spanish phrasebook

Glossary

For general information on Spanish, see p296. For food and drink terms, see p39; for transportation terms, see p301.

abarrotería – small grocery
Afro-mestizos – people of mixed African, European and indigenous descent
agave – family of plants, including *maguey*
alebrijes – colorful wood sculptures from the state of Oaxaca
alfarería – potter's workshop
amate – paper made from tree bark
antojitos – appetizers; literally 'little whims'
Apdo – abbreviation for Apartado (Box) in addresses; hence Apdo Postal means Post Office Box
arroyo – brook, stream
artesanías – handicrafts, folk arts
auriga – transport pickup

bahía – bay
balneario – bathing place, often a natural hot spring
banda – Mexican brass-based big-band music
barrio – district, neighborhood, often a poor neighborhood
béisbol – baseball
billete – bank note
boleto – ticket
brujo, -a – witch doctor, shaman; similar to *curandero, -a*

caballeros – literally 'horsemen,' but corresponds to 'gentlemen' in English; look for it on toilet doors
cabaña – cabin, simple shelter
cabrón – a strong slang word meaning asshole or bastard; can also be used in a friendly manner
calle – street
callejón – alley
camión – truck or bus
camioneta – pickup truck
campesino, -a – country or rural person, peasant
casa de cambio – exchange bureau; place where currency is exchanged
casa de huéspedes – guesthouse
caseta de larga distancia, caseta de teléfono, caseta telefónica – public telephone call station
cazuela – clay cooking pot; usually sold in a nested set
cerro – hill
chapulines – grasshoppers; a delicacy in many parts of Mexico
charreada – Mexican rodeo
charro – Mexican cowboy

HERE, FISHY FISHY – TRANSLATIONS FOR YOUR FAVORITE CATCHES

Keep in mind that some terms are regional. Sea bass, for instance, might be called *robalo, cabrilla* or *corvina*, depending on whom you talk to.

atún – tuna
atún de aleta – yellowfin tuna
cabrilla – sea bass
corvina – sea bass
dorado – dolphin fish (mahimahi)
garropa – grouper
guahu – wahoo
huachinango – red snapper
jurel – yellowtail
lenguado – halibut
lisa – mullet
marlín azul – blue marlin
marlín negro – black marlin
marlín rayado – striped marlin
mero – grouper
pargo – red snapper
peto – wahoo
pez espada – swordfish
pez gallo – roosterfish
pez vela – sailfish
picuda – barracuda
robalo – sea bass
sierra – Spanish mackerel
tiburón – shark

---

chido – cool; especially used in Mexico City
chilago, -a – a resident of Mexico City
chingar – literally 'to fornicate'; has numerous colloquial usages in Mexican Spanish equivalent to 'fuck' in English
Churrigueresque – Spanish late-baroque architectural style; found on many Mexican churches
cigarro – cigarette
clavadistas – the cliff divers of Acapulco and Mazatlán
colectivo – minibus or car that picks up and drops off passengers along a predetermined route; can also refer to other types of transport, such as boats
colonia – neighborhood of a city, often a wealthy residential area
combi – minibus
comedor – simple, inexpensive eatery

comida corrida – set-price lunch or dinner menu

completo – no vacancy, literally 'full up'; a sign you may see at hotel desks

conquistador – early Spanish explorer-conqueror

cordillera – mountain range

correos – post office

criollo – Mexican-born person of Spanish parentage; in colonial times considered inferior by peninsular Spaniards

crucero – crossroads or turnoff

crudo – hangover

cuota – toll; a vía cuota is a toll road

curandero, -a – literally 'curer'; a medicine man or woman who uses herbal and/or magical methods and often emphasizes spiritual aspects of disease

damas – ladies; the sign on toilet doors

dársena – pier, dock

Día de los Muertos – a celebration of the memory of the deceased, observed on November 1

Distrito Federal – the official name for Mexico City; often shortened to DF

edificio – building

ejido – communal landholding

embarcadero – jetty, boat landing

encomienda – a grant made to a *conquistador* of labor by or tribute from a group of indigenous people; the conquistador was supposed to protect and convert them, but usually treated them as little more than slaves

enramada – literally a bower or shelter, but it generally refers to a palm frond–covered, open-air restaurant

enredo – wraparound skirt

escuela – school

esq – abbreviation of esquina (corner) in addresses

ex-convento – former convent or monastery

faja – waist sash used in traditional indigenous costume

feria – fair or carnival; typically occurs during a religious holiday

ficha – locker token available at bus terminals

fútbol – football (soccer)

gringo, -a – US visitor to Latin America; can be used derogatorily or in a friendly manner; correctly used, gringo only applies to people from the US, but it is sometimes used for other people of European descent

gruta – cave, grotto

guarache – also *huarache;* woven leather sandal, often with tire tread as the sole

guardería de equipaje – room for storing luggage, eg in a bus station

güero, -a – fair-haired, fair-complexioned person; a more polite alternative to *gringo*

güey – colloquial salutation, meaning dude, friend or a clumsy, ignorant person; also spelled *wey*

hacienda – estate; Hacienda (capitalized) is the Treasury Department

hombres – men; sign on toilet doors

huarache – see *guarache*

huipil, -es – indigenous woman's sleeveless tunic, usually highly decorated; can be thigh-length or reach the ankles

huitlacoche – a black fungus that grows on young corn; considered a delicacy

iglesia – church

INAH – Instituto Nacional de Antropología e Historia; the body in charge of most ancient sites and some museums

indígeno, -a – indigenous; pertains to the original inhabitants of Latin America; can also refer to the people themselves

INI – Instituto Nacional Indigenista; set up in 1948 to improve the lot of indigenous Mexicans and to integrate them into society

ISH – *impuesto sobre hospedaje;* lodging tax on the price of hotel rooms

isla – island

IVA – *impuesto de valor agregado,* or 'ee-bah'; a 15% sales tax added to the price of many items

jai alai – the Basque game *pelota,* brought to Mexico by the Spanish; a bit like squash, played on a long court with curved baskets attached to the arm

jefe – boss or leader, especially political

lancha – fast, open, outboard boat

latifundio – large landholding; these sprang up after Mexico's independence from Spain

latifundista – powerful landowner who usurped communally owned land to form a *latifundio*

lleno – full; as in a car's fuel tank

machismo – Mexican masculine bravura

maguey – a type of agave; tequila and *mezcal* are made from its sap

malecón – waterfront street, boulevard or promenade

mariachi – ensemble of street musicians playing traditional ballads on guitars and trumpets

marimba – wooden xylophone-type instrument; popular in the south

menú del día – lunch special; also called *comida corrida*

mercado – market

Mesoamerica – the region inhabited by the ancient Mexican and Mayan cultures

mestizo – person of mixed (usually indigenous and Spanish) ancestry, ie most Mexicans

metate – shallow stone bowl with legs; for grinding maize and other foods

mezcal – an alcoholic drink made from the sap of the *maguey* plant

mirador, -es – lookout point(s)

Montezuma's revenge – Mexican version of Delhi-belly or travelers' diarrhea

mordida – literally 'little bite'; a small bribe to keep the wheels of bureaucracy turning

mota – marijuana

mujeres – women; seen on toilet doors

municipio – small local-government area; Mexico is divided into 2394 of them

NAFTA – North American Free Trade Agreement; see *TLC*

Nahuatl – language of the Nahua people, descendants of the Aztecs

nievería – frozen-dessert shop

Nte – abbreviation for *norte* (north); used in street names

ola – wave; as in 'as olas están grandes, güey' (dude, the waves are big)

Ote – abbreviation for *oriente* (east); used in street names

pachanga – party

palacio municipal – town or city hall; headquarters of the municipal corporation

palapa – thatched-roof shelter

paleta – frozen fruit on a stick

pandulces – sweet breads

panga – motorized skiff for fishing, excursions and transport

para llevar – (to go) in reference to food

parada – bus stop; usually for city buses

paranda – the act of partying; as in 'vamos de paranda' (let's go party)

parque nacional – national park

paseo – boulevard, walkway or pedestrian street; also the tradition of strolling in a circle around the plaza in the evening

Pemex – government-owned petroleum extraction, refining and retailing monopoly

periférico – ring road

petate – mat, usually made of palm or reed

peyote – a hallucinogenic cactus

piñata – clay pot or papier-mâché mold decorated to resemble an animal, pineapple, star etc; filled with sweets and gifts and smashed open at fiestas

playa – beach

plaza de toros – bullring

plazuela – small plaza

Porfiriato – Porfirio Díaz's reign as president-dictator of Mexico for 30 years, until the 1910 revolution

portales – arcades

posada – inn

presidio – fort or fort's garrison

PRI – Partido Revolucionario Institucional (Institutional Revolutionary Party); the political party that ruled Mexico for most of the 20th century

propina – tip; different from a *mordida*, which is closer to a bribe

Pte – abbreviation for *poniente* (west); used in street names

puerto – port

pulmonía – special type of open-air taxi similar to a golf cart

Quetzalcóatl – plumed serpent god of pre-Hispanic Mexico

raicilla – rare agave distillage that may or may not have slightly psychedelic properties

ramada – thatched shelter

rebozo – long woolen or linen shawl covering the head or shoulders

reserva de la biósfera – biosphere reserve; an environmentally protected area where human exploitation is steered towards ecologically unharmful activities

retablo – altarpiece; or painting in a church to give thanks for miracles, answered prayers etc

río – river

s/n – sin número (without number); used in street addresses

sanitario – toilet; literally 'sanitary place'

sarape – blanket with opening for the head, worn as a cloak

Semana Santa – Holy Week, the week from Palm Sunday to Easter Sunday; Mexico's major holiday period, when accommodations and transportation get very busy

servicios – toilets

sierra – mountain range

sitio – taxi stand; place

supermercado – supermarket

sur – south; often seen in street names

taller – shop or workshop; a taller mecánico is a mechanic's shop, usually for cars; a taller de llantas is a tire-repair shop

tapatío, -a – person born in Jalisco state

taquilla – ticket window

telar de cintura – backstrap loom
temascal – steam bath
templo – church; anything from a wayside chapel to a cathedral
tianguis – indigenous people's market
tienda – store
típico, -a – characteristic of a region; particularly used to describe food
TLC – Tratado de Libre Comercio; the North American Free Trade Agreement *(NAFTA)*
topes – speed bumps; found on the outskirts of many towns and villages
torta – Mexican-style sandwich made with a roll
trova – folk music, ballad

UNAM – Universidad Nacional Autónoma de México (National Autonomous University of Mexico)

viajero, -a – traveler

wey – see *güey*

zócalo – main plaza or square; a term used in some (but not all) Mexican towns
Zona Dorada – literally 'Golden Zone'; an area of expensive shops, hotels and restaurants in Mazatlán and Acapulco frequented most by the wealthy and tourists; by extension, a similar area in another city

The Authors

GREG BENCHWICK
Coordinating Author

Greg first came to Pacific Mexico in the 1990s when his Dad brought him and his sister down to Manzanillo for a family Christmas vacation. He has returned regularly since, traveling up and down the coast in search of the perfect sunset and the perfect margarita. Greg specializes in Latin America, new media and sustainable travel, and has written more than a dozen guidebooks over the years. Greg now lives in Colorado with his fiancée and their three-legged Turkish street dog, spending his days studying Mexican history, writing and speaking about travel in Latin America, and heading into the high-country for skiing and backpacking adventures.

Greg wrote the introductory chapters, as well as Directory and Transportation. He updated the following chapters: Jalisco, Colima & Michoacán Coasts; Ixtapa, Zihuatanejo & the Costa Grande; Acapulco & the Costa Chica; and Oaxaca.

JOHN HECHT

John's love affair with Mexico began more than a decade ago when he headed south of the border to study Spanish in Guadalajara. Three years later, and still speaking with a thick gringo accent, he said adios to the mariachi heartland to try his luck in the big city, Mexico City that is. As a native of Los Angeles, the smog and traffic in the sprawling Mexican capital made him feel right at home. Currently, he is a Mexico-based travel writer. Mom constantly tries to convince him to return to the good ol' USA, but she doesn't seem to understand that you just can't get a good taco there.

John updated the Puerto Vallarta, Mazatlán and Nayarit chapters.

CONTRIBUTING AUTHORS

Jürgen Buchenau A professor of history and director of Latin American Studies at UNC Charlotte, Jürgen is a native of Germany who has lived and traveled extensively in Mexico. He received his PhD from the University of North Carolina at Chapel Hill in 1993. He is the author of several books, including *In the Shadow of the Giant: The Making of Mexico's Central America Policy, 1876–1930* (Tuscaloosa, 1996); *Tools of Progress: A German Merchant Family in Mexico City, 1865–Present* (Albuquerque, 2004); *Mexico OtherWise: Modern Mexico in the Eyes of Foreign Observers* (Albuquerque, 2005); and *Plutarco Elías Calles and the Mexican Revolution* (Lanham, MD: Rowman and Littlefield, 2007). Jürgen fact-checked the History chapter.

David Goldberg, MD David completed his training in internal medicine and infectious diseases at Colombia-Presbyterian Medical Center in New York City, where he has also served as voluntary faculty. He is an infectious diseases specialist in Scarsdale, New York, and the editor-in-chief of the website MDTravelHealth.com. David wrote the Health chapter.

LONELY PLANET AUTHORS

Why is our travel information the best in the world? It's simple: our authors are passionate, dedicated travelers. They don't take freebies in exchange for positive coverage so you can be sure the advice you're given is impartial. They travel widely to all the popular spots, and off the beaten track. They don't research using just the internet or phone. They discover new places not included in any other guidebook. They personally visit thousands of hotels, restaurants, palaces, trails, galleries, temples and more. They speak with dozens of locals every day to make sure you get the kind of insider knowledge only a local could tell you. They take pride in getting all the details right, and in telling it how it is. Think you can do it? Find out how at **lonelyplanet.com**.

Carolina A Miranda Though she is South American, Carolina has spent countless vacations wandering through Mexico listening to *rancheras* (classical Mexican country music), reading Octavio Paz and learning the secret to a killer mole. She contributed to the 5th edition of Lonely Planet's *Central America on a Shoestring*. She has also written for numerous travel publications, and blogs on the arts and culture website C-Monster.net. Carolina wrote The Culture chapter.

James Peyton James has written three books and countless magazine articles on Mexican cooking. He appears on TV, conducts cooking classes, and lectures on Mexican cuisine. He also maintains a website (www.lomexicano.com) providing information about Mexico and Mexican cooking, and consults on recipe development for the Mexican food industry. His latest book is *Jim Peyton's New Cooking from Old Mexico*. James wrote the Food & Drink chapter.

Behind the Scenes

THIS BOOK

Puerto Vallarta & Pacific Mexico 3 was researched and written by Greg Benchwick and John Hecht. Carolina A Miranda wrote The Culture chapter, James Peyton wrote the Food & Drink chapter, and the Health chapter was adapted from text by Dr David Goldberg. Jürgen Buchenau fact-checked the History chapter.

Michael Read and Ben Greensfelder wrote the 2nd edition and Danny Palmerlee and Sandra Bao wrote the 1st edition.

This guidebook was commissioned in Lonely Planet's Oakland office, and produced by the following:

Commissioning Editor Catherine Craddock
Coordinating Editors Simon Williamson, Carolyn Bain
Coordinating Cartographer Julie Dodkins
Coordinating Layout Designer Frank Deim
Senior Editors Helen Christinis, Katie Lynch
Managing Cartographer Alison Lyall, Shahara Ahmed
Managing Layout Designer Laura Jane
Cover Designer Marika Mercer
Project Manager Rachel Imeson

Thanks to Lucy Birchley, Daniel Corbett, Diana Duggan, Carol Jackson, Robyn Loughnane, Trent Paton, Branislava Vladisavljevic

THANKS
GREG BENCHWICK

Un abrazo fuerte to Gautham and Lara Iyer, who let me stay with them in their lovely Oaxaca home. You are tremendous friends. A big shout out has to go to the mystery man with the green hands that got our car started after a breakdown near Mazunte. And thanks, as always, to my dear soon-to-be-bride Alejandra. *Te quiero verde y para siempre.*

Thanks to those who helped with our 'Ask a Local' features, and to the folks at the Acapulco and Puerto Escondido visitor centers. Jürgen Buchenau did a great job fact-checking our History section, as did Alejandra Castañeda for language content. Jill Friedberg offered tremendous insight into the Oaxaca protests. Gracias to Danny Palmerlee, who paved the way with the 1st edition, my ever-patient editor Catherine Craddock, co-author John Hecht, and the always-innovative editors, designers and cartographers out of Melbourne.

Beyond the people that made this book are the people who made me. Thanks to my family most of all. Dad, who took us kids to Manzanillo when we were just tikes; Mom and George, whose affirmations lift me up every time; and to my sister and brother-in-law, a constant source of support and inspiration.

THE LONELY PLANET STORY

Fresh from an epic journey across Europe, Asia and Australia in 1972, Tony and Maureen Wheeler sat at their kitchen table stapling together notes. The first Lonely Planet guidebook, *Across Asia on the Cheap,* was born.

Travelers snapped up the guides. Inspired by their success, the Wheelers began publishing books to Southeast Asia, India and beyond. Demand was prodigious, and the Wheelers expanded the business rapidly to keep up. Over the years, Lonely Planet extended its coverage to every country and into the virtual world via lonelyplanet.com and the Thorn Tree message board.

As Lonely Planet became a globally loved brand, Tony and Maureen received several offers for the company. But it wasn't until 2007 that they found a partner whom they trusted to remain true to the company's principles of traveling widely, treading lightly and giving sustainably. In October of that year, BBC Worldwide acquired a 75% share in the company, pledging to uphold Lonely Planet's commitment to independent travel, trustworthy advice and editorial independence.

Today, Lonely Planet has offices in Melbourne, London and Oakland, with over 500 staff members and 300 authors. Tony and Maureen are still actively involved with Lonely Planet. They're traveling more often than ever, and they're devoting their spare time to charitable projects. And the company is still driven by the philosophy of *Across Asia on the Cheap*: 'All you've got to do is decide to go and the hardest part is over. So go!'

BEHIND THE SCENES

JOHN HECHT

My heartfelt gratitude goes out to all the kind people who shared their interesting lives with me and to the long list of folks who steered me in the right direction. I'm especially indebted to commissioning editor Catherine Craddock for believing in me on this project, coordinating author Greg Benchwick for laboring through my manuscript and his unflagging support, and managing cartographer Alison Lyall for answering all of my silly mapping questions. I'm very grateful as well to the previous authors of this book, whose thoughtful and humorous insights provided a constant source of inspiration. In addition, I want to thank Professor Juan Manuel Gomez, Raul Sanchez and Miguel Ruiz Contreras for all their good-natured advice. Finally, I can't thank my sweetheart Laura Condado enough, who cleaned up my messy maps, looked after the cat and put up with me every step of the way. Cheers to all, it's been a wonderful ride.

OUR READERS

Many thanks to the travelers who used the last edition and wrote to us with helpful hints, useful advice and interesting anecdotes:

Wendy Benbrook, Flavia Bertini, Gustavo Buhacoff, Guillaume Cazaumayou, Jennifer Craig, Kent Derdivanis, Kerry Hennigan, Robin Krause, John Milliken, Karen Nelson, Patrick Newman, Isadora O'Boto, Alex Padalka, Michele Pearce, M Petersen, Christopher Petitpas, Jean-Claude Picard, Michael Pohl, Robert Price, Sylvia R, Elin Sætersdal, Helenna Santos, Cindi T, George Tacik, Mark Terry, Martine Twigge, Mark Wilson

ACKNOWLEDGMENTS

Many thanks to the following for the use of their content:

Globe on title page ©Mountain High Maps 1993 Digital Wisdom, Inc.

Index

000 Map pages
000 Photograph pages

000 Map pages
000 Photograph pages

GreenDex

The following activities, tour operators, attractions, cafés, stores and accommodation choices have all been selected by Lonely Planet authors because they meet our criteria for sustainable tourism. We've selected these places for a variety of reasons: because they are run locally, have a committed environmental program or, most importantly, because they give back to the community, helping to protect and preserve the culture, environment and historic patrimony that make this part of Mexico great.

We want to keep developing our sustainable-travel content. If you think we've left something out, please contact us at www.lonelyplanet.com/contact. For more on sustainable travel, check out www.lonelyplanet.com/responsibletravel.

320

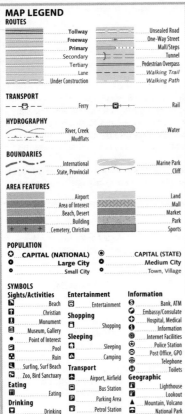

LONELY PLANET OFFICES

Australia
Head Office
Locked Bag 1, Footscray, Victoria 3011
☎ 03 8379 8000, fax 03 8379 8111
talk2us@lonelyplanet.com.au

USA
150 Linden St, Oakland, CA 94607
☎ 510 250 6400, toll free 800 275 8555
fax 510 893 8572
info@lonelyplanet.com

UK
2nd fl, 186 City Rd,
London EC1V 2NT
☎ 020 7106 2100, fax 020 7106 2101
go@lonelyplanet.co.uk

Published by Lonely Planet Publications Pty Ltd
ABN 36 005 607 983

© Lonely Planet Publications Pty Ltd 2009

© photographers as indicated 2009

Cover photograph: La Quebrada cliff divers, Acapulco, Mexico; Superstock/Photolibrary. Many of the images in this guide are available for licensing from Lonely Planet Images: www.lonelyplanetimages.com.

All rights reserved. No part of this publication may be copied, stored in a retrieval system, or transmitted in any form by any means, electronic, mechanical, recording or otherwise, except brief extracts for the purpose of review, and no part of this publication may be sold or hired, without the written permission of the publisher.

Printed through Colorcraft Ltd, Hong Kong.
Printed in China.

Lonely Planet and the Lonely Planet logo are trademarks of Lonely Planet and are registered in the US Patent and Trademark Office and in other countries.

Lonely Planet does not allow its name or logo to be appropriated by commercial establishments, such as retailers, restaurants or hotels. Please let us know of any misuses: www.lonelyplanet.com/ip.

Although the authors and Lonely Planet have taken all reasonable care in preparing this book, we make no warranty about the accuracy or completeness of its content and, to the maximum extent permitted, disclaim all liability arising from its use.